THE COLONIAL ORIGINS OF
MODERN SOCIAL THOUGHT

Princeton Modern Knowledge

MICHAEL D. GORDIN,
PRINCETON UNIVERSITY, SERIES EDITOR

For a list of titles in the series, go to https://press.princeton.edu/series/princeton-modern-knowledge.

The Colonial Origins of Modern Social Thought

FRENCH SOCIOLOGY AND THE OVERSEAS EMPIRE

George Steinmetz

PRINCETON UNIVERSITY PRESS
PRINCETON & OXFORD

Copyright © 2023 by Princeton University Press

Princeton University Press is committed to the protection of copyright and the intellectual property our authors entrust to us. Copyright promotes the progress and integrity of knowledge created by humans. Thank you for supporting free speech and the global exchange of ideas by purchasing an authorized edition of this book. If you wish to reproduce or distribute any part of it in any form, please obtain permission.

Requests for permission to reproduce material from this work should be sent to permissions@press.princeton.edu

Published by Princeton University Press
41 William Street, Princeton, New Jersey 08540
99 Banbury Road, Oxford OX2 6JX

press.princeton.edu

All Rights Reserved

First paperback printing, 2025
Paperback ISBN 9780691237442

The Library of Congress has cataloged the cloth edition as follows:

Names: Steinmetz, George, 1957– author.
Title: The colonial origins of modern social thought : French sociology and the overseas empire / George Steinmetz.
Description: Princeton, New Jersey : Princeton University Press, [2023] | Series: Princeton modern knowledge | Includes bibliographical references and index.
Identifiers: LCCN 2022042601 (print) | LCCN 2022042602 (ebook) | ISBN 9780691237428 (hardback) | ISBN 9780691237435 (ebook)
Subjects: LCSH: Sociology—France—History—20th century. | France—Colonies.
Classification: LCC HM477.F8 S74 2023 (print) | LCC HM477.F8 (ebook) | DDC 301.0944—dc23/eng/20221018
LC record available at https://lccn.loc.gov/2022042601
LC ebook record available at https://lccn.loc.gov/2022042602

British Library Cataloging-in-Publication Data is available

Editorial: Eric Crahan and Barbara Shi
Production Editorial: Nathan Carr
Jacket/Cover Design: Hunter Finch
Production: Danielle Amatucci
Publicity: William Pagdatoon
Copyeditor: Karen Verde

This book has been composed in Miller

To Julia, and to the memory of my father

CONTENTS

Acknowledgments · xi
Abbreviations · xv

PART I   THE SOCIOLOGY OF COLONIES AND
          EMPIRES IN THE HISTORY OF SCIENCE   1

CHAPTER 1 Writing the Historical Sociology of Colonial
           Sociology in a Postcolonial Situation   3

CHAPTER 2 Constructing the Object, Confronting
           Disciplinary Amnesia   29

PART II   THE POLITICAL CONTEXTS
          OF COLONIAL SOCIAL THOUGHT
          IN POSTWAR FRANCE   51

CHAPTER 3 Colonial Reconquest, Scientification,
           and Popular Culture   53

CHAPTER 4 Colonial Developmentalism, Welfare,
           and Sociology   63

CHAPTER 5 Colonialism, Higher Education, and Social
           Research   74

PART III THE INTELLECTUAL CONTEXTS
          OF POSTWAR FRENCH SOCIOLOGY   101

CHAPTER 6 The Earliest Colonial Social Sciences and Their
           Engagement with Sociology: Geography, Law,
           Economics, and the Sciences of the Psyche   103

CHAPTER 7 Other Neighboring Social Sciences and Their
           Engagement with Sociology and Colonialism:
           History, Statistics, Demography, and Anthropology   126

CHAPTER 8	Theoretical Developments in Interwar Sociology as a Context for Postwar Colonial Sociology	147
PART FOUR	**THE SOCIOLOGY OF FRENCH COLONIAL SOCIOLOGY, 1918–1960s**	169
CHAPTER 9	The Sociology of Sociology and Its Colonial Subfield (France and Belgium, 1918–1965)	171
CHAPTER 10	Outline of a Theory of Colonial Sociological Practice	195
PART FIVE	**FOUR SOCIOLOGISTS**	229
CHAPTER 11	Raymond Aron as a Critical Theorist of Empires and Colonialism	231
CHAPTER 12	Jacques Berque: A Historical Sociologist of Colonialism and "the Decolonial Situation"	247
CHAPTER 13	Georges Balandier: A Dynamic Sociology of Colonialism and Anticolonialism	271
CHAPTER 14	Pierre Bourdieu: The Creation of Social Theory in the Cauldron of Colonial War	315
CHAPTER 15	Conclusion: The History of Sociology, Reflexivity, and Decolonization	347
	APPENDIXES	361
APPENDIX 1	Sociologists Whose Academic Careers Started before 1965 in France or the French Overseas Empire and Were Active in Colonial Research between the Late 1930s and the 1960s	363
APPENDIX 2	Greater French Sociology Field in 1946	367
APPENDIX 3	Greater French Sociology Field in 1949	369
APPENDIX 4	Greater French Sociology Field in 1955	371

APPENDIX 5   Greater French Sociology Field in 1960   373

APPENDIX 6   Belgian Colonial Sociologists   375

Notes · 377
Sources · 499
Index · 541

ACKNOWLEDGMENTS

HAVING WRITTEN ABOUT EMPIRES and states, and the history of sociology, I decided more recently to combine these themes. This led me back to some of the places where I was first initiated into archival research while writing my master's thesis on social movements of unemployed workers in Paris during the 1860s and 1870s, and to some of the historians whose work I first read at that time. Among other things, this led me back to Pierre Bourdieu, who had sent me a copy of his book *Algeria 1960* and a kind note in response to my sending him a paper based on my master's thesis. I abandoned French history (though not Bourdieu) for a long time, before returning to it in this book.

I have worked for so many years on the present book that I have accumulated many debts. For critique and stimulation, I am enduringly thankful to colleagues in North America, especially Julia Adams, Margaret Buckner, Craig Calhoun, Chas Camic, Joshua Cole, Alice Conklin, Frederick Cooper, Mathieu Desan, Geoff Eley, Didier Fassin, Marcel Fournier, Julian Go, Phil Gorski, Zine Magubane, Michael Mann, Suzanne Marchand, Ann Orloff, Orlando Patterson, William Sewell, Jr., the late Tyler Stovall, Helen Tilley, Xiaohong Xu, Loïc Wacquant, Jonathan Wyrtzen, the late Immanuel Wallerstein, all of the contributors to the volume *Sociology and Empire*, and the many participants in our "Empire dinners" at the annual meetings of the American Sociological Association. In France, I received invaluable advice from the late Georges Balandier and from Remy Bazenguissa-Ganga, Christophe Bonneuil, Jérôme Bourdieu, Christophe Charle, Alain Chenu, Jean Copans, Yves Dezalay, Julien Duval, Jean-Louis Fabiani, Olivier Godechot, Johan Heilbron, Choukri Hmed, Paul Lagneau-Ymonet, Christine Laurière, Jacques Lautman, Thomas Le Bianic, Brigitte Mazon, Françine Muel-Dreyfus, Amín Pérez, Catherine Perlès, Ioana Popa, Franck Poupeau, Anne Rocha Perazzo, Gisèle Sapiro, Christian Topalov, Béatrice Touchelay, Roland Waast, and Tassadit Yacine. In Germany and Austria, I am grateful to Manuela Boatcă (Freiburg), Sebastian Conrad (Berlin), Andreas Eckert (Berlin), Wolfgang Knöbl (Hamburg), Anne Kwaschik (Konstanz), Klaus Lichtblau (Frankfurt am Main), Klaus Schlichte (Bremen), and Steffan Stetter (Munich), and to Christian Dayé, Christian Fleck, and Stephan Moebius of the Karl-Franzens-Universität Graz. During my lecture visit to Australia, I received generous hospitality and intellectual stimulation from Robert Aldrich and Raewyn Connell in Sydney, and Peter Beilharz, Ghassan Hage, Trevor Hogan, and Sian Supski in Melbourne. During my research trips to Britain, I have greatly appreciated visits with George Lawson, Monika Krause, and Tarak Barkawi at the London School of Economics, and the late Michael Banton. Other interlocutors for me during this project include Kristoffer

Kropp (Roskilde, Denmark), Alexander M. Semyonov (St. Petersburg), and Miguel Bandeira Jerónimo (Lisbon).

I received feedback on my book-in-progress from audiences at a number of institutions: Bielefeld University (Germany); University of California–Berkeley; University of Chicago; Central European University (Budapest, now Vienna); Centre Marc Bloch (Berlin); Deutsches Literaturarchiv (Marbach); École des hautes études en sciences sociales (Paris); Göttingen University (Germany); Harvard University; University of Illinois Urbana-Champaign; the Institute for Advanced Study (Princeton); LaTrobe University (Melbourne); University of Lisbon, Institute of Social Sciences; National Research University Higher School of Economics (St. Petersburg); New School for Social Research; Northwestern University; University of Paris–Dauphine; Princeton University; University of Minnesota; University of Sydney; University of Toronto; University of Wisconsin–Madison; and Yale University. I presented material from this book at the meetings of the American, British, and German Sociological Associations, the American Historical Association, and the Social Science History Association, and at the Hamburg Institute for Social Research during my lectures in January 2020 for the Siegfried Landshut Prize. I wish to thank my hosts and audiences at all of these events.

I received generous financial support for researching and writing this book. I was able to develop the idea for the book during three visiting professorships at the *École des hautes études en sciences sociales* in Paris in 2007, 2012, and 2014. I received funding from the Letters, Arts, and Sciences Division of the University of Michigan and the American Sociological Association/National Science Foundation Fund for the Advancement of the Discipline, Fellowships from the National Endowment for the Humanities, and the Deutsches Literaturarchiv in Marbach. A visiting professorship at the Institute for Advanced Studies provided an ideal setting to begin writing the book, in 2017–2018, during which time I enjoyed the hospitality of Didier Fassin, Joan Scott, and Michael Walzer and the comradeship of all of the Members. My research leave at the American Academy in Berlin in 2020 allowed me to complete the first draft of the book. I am grateful to the staff of the American Academy for making our stay there so productive and enjoyable, and for being so accommodating when the global pandemic forced us to interrupt our visit and return precipitously to the United States.

Every historical scholar is utterly dependent upon archivists and librarians. I want to thank the archivists at the *Archives nationales de France*, the *Archives nationales d'outre-mer* in Aix-en-Provence, the *Bibliothèque nationale de France*, UNESCO (Paris), the Rockefeller Archives Center in Sleepy Hollow, New York, and the *Académie de Mâcon*. I also wish to thank Brigitte Mazon at the *École des hautes études en sciences sociales*, Isabelle Dujonc at the archives of the *Centre national de la recherche scientifique* (Gif-sur-Yvette), Marie-Dominique Mouton at the *Bibliothèque Éric-de-Dampierre* (Nanterre),

Michel Prat at the *Bibliothèque du Musée social*, and Emmanuelle Aldebert at the *Centre de Documentation IRD France-Nord* (Bondy). I could never have written this book without the contributions of librarians at the *Bibliothèque nationale de France*, the Institute for Advanced Study, and the University of Michigan, particularly Hailey Mooney. I am grateful, finally, for the extraordinary research assistance of Andrew Covert, Selin Levi, and Todd Maslyk.

Several people have been particularly important for me in conceptualizing, researching, and completing this book. Historians Fred Cooper and Andreas Eckert have been my main guides in recent years into French colonial history and African history. Chas Camic's exemplary research on the history of social science was a beacon to me all along. I am especially grateful to Johan Heilbron for introducing me into this specialized field of scholarship, and for his lasting friendship and advice.

I am indebted to Eric Crahan and Nathan Carr at Princeton University Press for agreeing and helping me guide this book to completion. Michael D. Gordin, the series editor, expressed early interest in the book and convinced me that historians of science could be interested in it. Kim Greenwell did a spectacular job helping me sculpt this book into its final form, displaying once again her legendary precision in matters of writing, editing, and logic. Karen Verde's copyediting was superb.

My father and I talked about this book numerous times, and I am aggrieved that he was unable to have a chance to see it in print before he died. His rational, scientific spirit is a lasting inspiration for me, as is my mother's keen interest in history and literature. While finishing the book, I was finally able to visit the site of the American Expeditionary Forces University in Beaune, where my grandfather studied after serving with the American Expeditionary Forces in Château-Thierry and elsewhere on the Western Front in World War I. This Franco-American educational experiment marked the beginning of my grandfather's lifelong involvement with the useful application of science. *Most* of all, I wish to thank Julia Hell, my lifetime companion, my lodestar on my restless journeys between the shores of science and culture, America and Europe, past and present.

This book relies partly on previously published articles. My first stab at the materials presented here appeared as "The Imperial Entanglements of Sociology in the United States, Britain, and France since the 19th Century," published in the journal *Ab Imperio* in 2009. Chapter 11 draws on my contribution to Janne Lahti's edited volume, *German and United States Colonialism in a Connected World* (Palgrave Macmillan, 2012), "Between France, Germany, and the United States: Raymond Aron as a Critical Theorist of Colonialism and Empire." Chapters 12–14 draw on "Soziologie und Kolonialismus: Die Beziehung zwischen Wissen und–Politik," in *Mittelweg 36*, volume 29, no. 3 (June–July 2020), pp. 17–36, and on "Sociology and Colonialism in the British and French Empires, 1940s–1960s," *Journal of Modern History*, vol. 89, no. 3 (September 2017), pp. 601–648.

ABBREVIATIONS

ANOM Archives nationales d'outre-mer
BN Bibliothèque nationale (National Library, Paris)
CHEAM *Centre des hautes études d'administration musulmane* (Center for Advanced Studies in Muslim Administration)
CNRS *Centre national de la recherche scientifique* (National Center of Scientific Research)
EHESS *École des hautes études en sciences sociales*
ENFOM *École nationale de la France d'outre-mer* (National School of Overseas France), previously *École coloniale*.
FERDES *Fonds d'équipement rural et de développement économique et social* (Fund for Rural Equipment and Economic and Social Development)
FIDES *Fonds d'investissements pour le développement économique et social des territoires d'outre-mer* (Fund for the Economic and Social Development of the Overseas Territories)
IEC *Institut d'études centrafricaines* (Institute of Central African Studies)
IEDES *Institut d'étude du développement économique et social,* Paris
IFAN *Institut français d'Afrique noire* (French Institute of Black Africa)
IFS *Institut français de sociologie*
INED *Institut national d'études démographiques* (National Institute of Demographic Studies)
INSEE *Institut national de la statistique et des études économiques (pour le métropole et la France d'outre-mer)* (National Institute of Statistics and Economic Studies [for the Metropole and Overseas France])
ISA International Sociological Association
ORSC *Office de la recherche scientifique coloniale* (Office of Colonial Scientific Research)
ORSOM *Office de la recherche scientifique outre-mer* (Office of Overseas Scientific Research)

ORSTOM *Office de la recherche scientifique et technique outre-mer* (Office of Overseas Scientific and Technical Research)

UNESCO United Nations Educational, Scientific and Cultural Organization

THE COLONIAL ORIGINS OF
MODERN SOCIAL THOUGHT

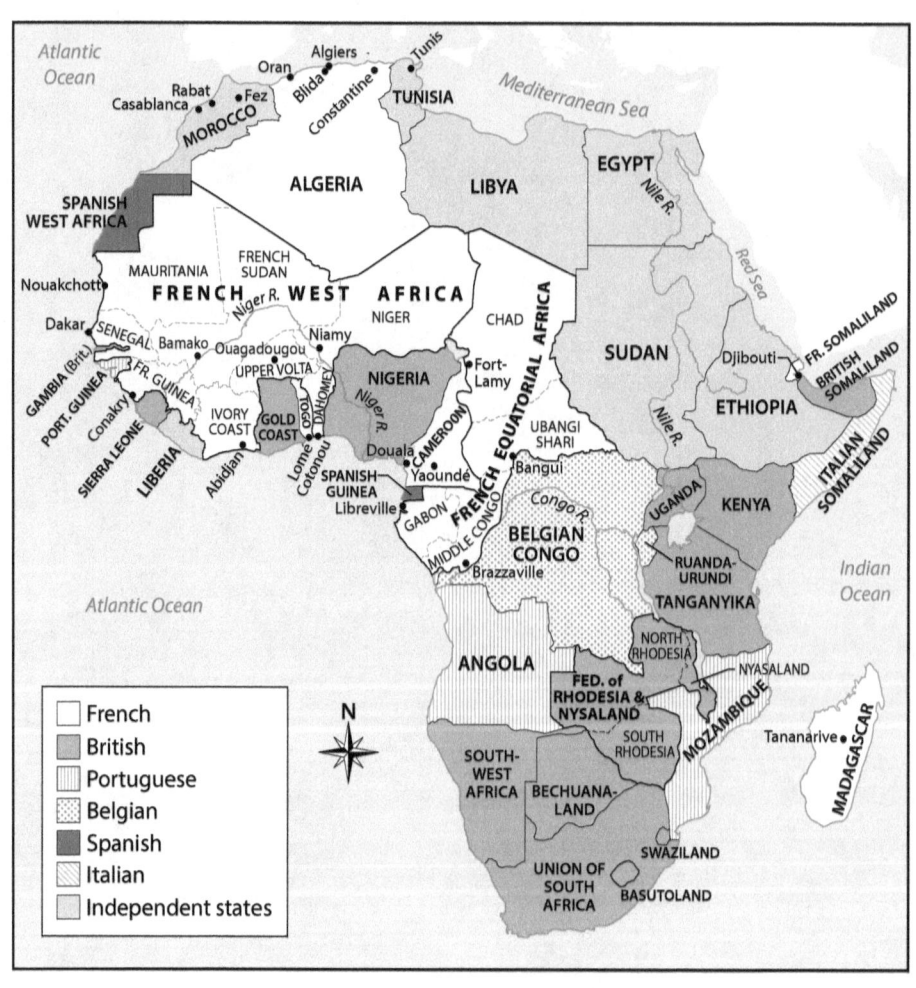

FIGURE 0.1. Map of Africa, showing location of French colonies, 1957.

PART I

The Sociology of Colonies and Empires in the History of Science

CHAPTER ONE

Writing the Historical Sociology of Colonial Sociology in a Postcolonial Situation

Europe is literally the creation of the Third World.
—FANON, THE WRETCHED OF THE EARTH[1]

The Penumbra of Colonialism

Shadows of empire are draped across the lands of erstwhile conquistadors and their erstwhile victims. More precisely, there is an imperial penumbra that allows only part of the light source to be seen. This hidden source of energy is the imperial past. The Roman Empire, one of the deepest sources of imperial energy, is both omnipresent and absent. Words like *colonia*, *imperium*, *emperor*, *dictator*, *proconsul*, and *praetorianism* are still used to describe the imperial textures of our political realities. From Augustus to Hitler, through to the present, western rulers have been haunted by scenarios of decline and ruination, and by the appearance of former "barbarians" at the heart of the metropole.[2]

The world in which we live is also engraved with the markers of modern colonial empires. From 1492 through the mid-twentieth century, populations in Africa, America, Oceania, and Asia were annexed by a global system dominated by empire-states. Most of the existing states in Africa, Oceania, America, and the Middle East were created as colonies, or emerged from the breakup of former colonies and the collapse of the Soviet Union.[3] The boundaries between and within states, the internal lines of ethnic rivalry, the unequal internal distributions of resources, and the administrative structures and institutional practices of governance—in other words, the entire *state culture* of postcolonial polities—can only be understood against the backdrop of colonialism.[4] A vast ocean of trauma, among individuals and groups, from Botswana to Algeria, Cambodia to the Pine Ridge Indian Reservation, indexes colonial violence.[5]

European states also bear the stamp of empire. Eric Williams and Immanuel Wallerstein argued that the rise of the capitalist world system was triggered by the conquest of America, the pillaging of its wealth, and the slave-based plantation economies that emerged there.[6] For W. E. B. Du Bois, the colonial-era slave system was an essential element in the rise of industrial capitalism, and European cities like Liverpool were "virtually built on the bodies of black slaves."[7] According to critical theorists of geopolitics, the entire system of international relations can only be understood against the backdrop of empire, from the Concert of Europe to the League of Nations and the postwar hegemonic US order.[8]

Empires have yielded a vast reservoir of knowledge, concepts, and images.[9] European languages bear the marks of the *Lingua Imperii* (to paraphrase Victor Klemperer).[10] The very category of *race* illustrates imperialism's seemingly inexpungable presence.[11] Many of the racial structures and ideologies that undergird contemporary racist practices were forged in colonial settings.[12] The last colonial exhibition took place in 1950 in Bordeaux,[13] yet museums of ethnography and non-western art continue to reanimate the spirit of earlier colonial exhibitions. Just as "African youth . . . are unaware of not only the richness and creativity" of the "cultural and artistic resources inherited from Africa's past itself, held and stored in museums and countries completely out of reach" to them, European youth for generations, even after decolonization, have been given to understand that these collections of African culture are part of their own heritage.[14] Museums are only beginning to revise their narratives and restitute objects that were expropriated from the colonies. The former colonial or "tropical" museums in Brussels and Amsterdam have tried to decolonize their collections.[15] While the new Humboldt Forum in Berlin has also started to move in this direction, that entire museum takes the form of an asynchronous project teleported from the era of European high imperialism.[16]

The colonial past continues to shape popular politics in Europe and the postcolonies. On the one hand, European nations face the return of the colonial-repressed, in the form of immigration and recharged forms of neocolonial racism directed against immigrants. On the other hand, various social movements have been forcing the imperial unconscious and colonial ideologemes into the public realm of open contestation.[17] Debates over "decolonizing" the curriculum and the public sphere are as intense in South Africa as in Britain and the United States.[18]

Colonialism also insinuated itself into organized social science disciplines and broader formations of social thought. Historians of colonial science have examined economics, anthropology, Orientalism, psychology, geopolitics, law, architecture, comparative religion, historiography, political theory, and the natural sciences.[19] The present book examines the main French social science disciplines in their entanglements with colonialism, while focusing on sociology.

Sociology might not seem like the most obvious candidate for a study of the entwinement of empire and social thought.[20] US sociology today is rather relentlessly focused on the immediate present in the American *Heimat*. The US invasions of Iraq provoked barely a whisper among US sociologists. Such silence stems from several sources. First, "foreign" policy is felt to be off limits in a discipline relentlessly focused on the continental United States and modestly tending to its national turf.[21] The blowback effects of empire or "colonial boomerangs" are also left unstudied by sociology, even though they are presumably "domestic" phenomena and were first discussed by the British proto-sociologist John Hobson.[22] One might assume that Native Americans are "American" enough to escape US sociology's *ukase* against studying foreign cultures. There was, in fact, a non-exoticizing sociology of Native Americans between the 1930s and the 1960s.[23] However, Native Americans have conventionally been claimed by anthropology in the US academy's absurd division of topics, or ontological spheres. With the exception of a small number of indigenous sociologists, US sociology ignores the internally colonized native other.[24]

Avoidance of empire cannot, therefore, be attributed entirely to sociology's parochial focus on the "homeland." It is the result of a more elaborate set of assumptions, sanctions, and cues. American sociology avoids global imperial phenomena due to a pervasive positivist epistemology that sees singular events as lying outside the realm of possible scientific objects.[25] Sociologists tend to embrace a rather "spontaneous" belief in axiomatic neutrality, even if this contradicts the equally widespread endorsement of mainstream liberal political values and the calls for "public" versions of sociology. The words "empire" and "colonialism" seem too politically charged, too rebarbative, for the value-free sociologist.

Despite these impediments, sociology has repeatedly intersected with questions of empire and colonialism. In a foundational article, Raewyn Connell called attention to the ways in which early European and American sociology was permeated by the colonial context of high imperialism (1880s–1918).[26] This includes many proto-sociologists and disciplinary founders, such as Auguste Comte, Karl Marx, John Stuart Mill, Aléxis Tocqueville, Herbert Spencer, Ludwig Gumplowicz, Émile Durkheim, and Max Weber. Connell argued that sociologists turned inward toward the domestic homeland after World War I. Closer investigation reveals that this account of turning inward applies mainly to the United States, and only if we disregard American sociologists' involvement with modernization theory during the Cold War.[27] Moreover, African American sociologists diverged from the disciplinary mainstream and continued to thematize colonialism during the interwar and postwar eras.[28] At the forefront was W. E. B. Du Bois, who analyzed colonialism extensively and linked it to the oppression of Blacks in the United States.[29] Other African American sociologists (St. Clair Drake, E. Franklin Frazier) taught in the British Gold Coast and postcolonial Ghana. Finally, even if Talcott Parsons temporarily became a "canonical" figure in American sociology, as Connell argues, large swathes of European sociology went down entirely different paths, becoming immersed in colonial research and largely ignoring American sociology. This era of mid-twentieth-century colonial sociological research has been almost entirely overlooked and in some cases actively repressed by historians of sociology, as I will show in the next chapter.

One might find it self-evident that European sociology would have been involved in colonial topics and problems. After all, imperialism was omnipresent in European everyday life, even after 1945 (chapter 3). Schoolchildren were still taught about "their" empires; images of colonies appeared in magazines and films; "primitive art" was sold in art galleries and displayed in museums. Gear for colonial tours was sold in Parisian shops. National airlines offered direct flights to colonial capitals. Colonial wars were front-page news throughout the postwar era in France and Britain.

Future sociologists could hardly have been immune to all of this, one might assume. Colonies still offered employment and, for some, the allure of adventure. Medical advances now protected against many tropical diseases, and allowed colonial officials and researchers to bring their families along with them on their overseas postings. There were as many opportunities for jobs and research funding for sociologists in the colonies as in the metropoles. As we will see in chapter 13, the Africanist sociologist Georges Balandier was fascinated as a child by tales of exotic colonial adventures and stories told by his relatives. Balandier leapt at the chance for a colonial career in 1946. Others had less choice in the matter and were drawn into imperial social science by the force of circumstance. Raymond Aron was driven into exile by the Nazi Occupation and felt compelled to try to make sense of Nazi imperialism. Returning to France, Aron applied some his theories of Nazi imperialism to understanding the French, American, and Soviet empires (chapter 11). Jacques Berque was recruited into colonial research by his father, a colonial official in Algeria, which led him to become an Arabist and sociologist of colonialism (chapter 12). Pierre Bourdieu was drafted unwillingly and sent to Algeria, where he underwent a conversion to sociology and developed the lineaments of his theoretical system, which he continued to revise during the next four decades (chapter 14). Albert Memmi, Abdelmalek Sayad, Anouar Abdel-Malak, Paul Sebag, and other sociologists were born as French subjects and driven to understand these colonial conditions (chapter 10). Put differently, if colonies and decolonization had failed to register in French sociology, this very absence would be a conundrum calling for explanation. Yet all of this only seems obvious now, in light of the research that has led to the present book. The puzzle discussed in the next chapter is the failure of most historians of mid-twentieth-century French sociology even to have registered the "colonial fact."

Why Focus on Mid-Twentieth-Century France?

A reader might wonder why this book concentrates on mid-twentieth-century France, rather than, say, the late-nineteenth-century era of "high imperialism," or the 1920s, when European empires reached their greatest dimensions. This decision is a function of my interest in sociology and social science more generally. The natural sciences were more central to colonialism in the earlier periods. Before 1914, colonial rulers drew mainly on medicine, engineering, and the like. In the 1920s, ethnology became the colonial social science par excellence. Sociology remained a small and uncertain discipline between the wars in all of the colonizing countries. Only in Germany and the United States were there coherent and sizable academic interwar sociology fields. However, most US sociologists had retreated back into their domestic shell. Germany lost its colonial empire in World War I, and the Nazi takeover in 1933 resulted in the loss of most of the leading German sociologists to exile. Between 1933 and 1942, the Nazis dangled the possibility of a reconquered African empire before the eyes of the colonial revanchists. A few sociologists, such as Berlin University professor Richard Thurnwald, resurrected the moribund subfield of colonial sociology. Some German sociologists contributed to the interdisciplinary imperial field of *Ostforschung* (research on the East) or offered applied research to the Nazi colonization of occupied Poland. Like American modernization theory, this Nazi imperial sociology differed from western European colonial sociology in fundamental ways. After 1945, colonialism and empire disappeared almost completely from German sociology, although a few of the previously Nazified sociologists promoted the social study of development (Karl-Heinz Pfeffer, Gunther Ipsen) or "international" sociology (Wilhelm Mühlmann).[30]

I am interested here in the version of colonial sociology that was carried out by professional social scientists, distinguished itself from anthropology, and involved a critical mass of practitioners. This constellation began to emerge at the end of the 1930s and crystallized in the late 1940s and 1950s. French sociology was carried out in a variety of colonies, which gained their independence at different moments. Tunisia and Morocco became independent in 1956; Guinea in 1958, and most of the remaining French colonies in 1960. Algeria, one of the key locales for colonial sociology, became independent in 1962. Rather than ending this study on a specific date, therefore, the book continues until the end of each of the colonies. I will also linger for a few years after decolonization, in order to make sense of the ambiguous transition period between formal independence and scientific decolonization.

Several other factors are involved in defining the book's time frame. First, colonies existed within geographically and politically defined federations and regions. Some countries that gained independence relatively early, like Tunisia and Morocco, were located in the close vicinity of countries that were still under colonial domination. Second, colonialism lived on in the hearts, minds, and publications of sociologists who had worked in the colonies or started their doctoral research overseas before independence. Several Africanist sociologists who began their research during the final years of the colonial period or the first years of independence agreed with comments made by French sociologist Roland Waast. Speaking specifically about scientific and educational matters, Waast called attention to "an acute period between decolonization and independence which [was] sometimes almost colonial."[31] Third, the overseas universities and research institutes where colonial sociology had established a foothold remained in European hands in most cases for several years after independence.[32] The sociology program in Dakar, which began delivering advanced degrees in 1962–1963, was directed by the French sociologist Louis Vincent Thomas.[33] Tunisia gained its independence in 1956, and Tunisian students could work toward a *licence* degree in sociology starting in 1959. The founder of the sociology laboratory there was the Frenchman Georges Granai, and one of the instructors of sociology students in 1959 and 1960 was Frantz Fanon.[34] Most French instructors abandoned the University of Algiers in 1962, but the university's rector from 1962 to 1965 was the anticolonial French historian, André Mandouze, and several French-born social scientists continued to teach there. Bourdieu left the University of Algiers in 1960 and was replaced by the ethno-sociologist Jeanne Favret-Saada. Three French sociologists taught at Algiers after independence: Andrée Michel (née Vielle), a feminist, anticolonial sociologist whose earliest publications include a study of Algerian labor migrants in France and who actively supported the Algerian war of independence; Claudine Chaulet, discussed below; and Émile Sicard, a specialist in the sociology of Slavic cultures who relocated to North African sociology and development studies in the 1960s.[35]

In short, professional colonial sociology reached its apex between the late 1930s and the mid-1960s. This means that I am focusing here on several different political regimes: the late Third Republic, Vichy France, Nazi-occupied France, and the territories controlled by Free France during World War II, the Fourth Republic (1944–1958), the early Fifth Republic, and the various semi-autonomous "regimes" in the various colonies and colonial federations.

Another reason for concentrating on the period between the late 1930s and the end of decolonization is the greater relevance of this work to current concerns and debates. Much of the present-day writing on "decolonizing" sociology focuses on figures who are completely irrelevant to present-day social research, such as Lester Ward, W. I. Thomas, Franklin H. Giddings, William Graham Sumner, Albert Keller, Leopold von Wiese, and the like. In the French case, by contrast, some of the leading sociologists of colonialism remain extremely relevant to contemporary work. The most obvious case is Bourdieu, still the most cited sociologist in the world. To Balandier, we owe the framework of analyzing colonized societies *as colonies*. Balandier is also the inventor of the historical sociology of Africa, including its precolonial states, twentieth-century religions, and colonial-era cities. Jacques Berque was the original theorist of decolonizing social science. Aron's acute comparisons between Nazi, French, American, and Soviet imperialism allow us to understand the ongoing decline of the American empire.

One might ask whether organizing the analysis of colonial sociology around a nation-state and its empire risks a sort of methodological "empire-ism," along the lines of "methodological nationalism."[36] Considered as a form of politics, colonialism is centered primarily on a particular nation-state.[37] Of course, groups of core powers have sometimes exercised joint control over a single colony or zone of imperial domination.[38] In general, however, the colonial form was inherently national, in the sense that each colony was ruled by a particular metropolitan state. The colonies that made up the overseas empire of any given colonial power were linked to one another via the circulation of officials, military, professionals, expert advisors, laws, and policies. The borders of different empires were clearly demarcated in treaties and on maps, and were visible on the ground in the form of signs, marker stones, and armed guards.

The nation-state level might seem like a less appropriate analytic unit, however, if we are interested in the cultural aspects of empire. After all, precolonial narratives of travel, exploration, and conquest were often written by citizens of nations other than those who eventually did the colonizing.[39] These accounts were quickly translated into major European languages, especially during the early modern period. The Haitian revolution (1791–1804) reverberated across Europe and was discussed in the newspapers Hegel was reading in Jena.[40] Missionary workers tended to ignore the boundaries set by European colonial powers. African tribes were divided between different colonies.[41]

Sociology, however, has been one of the most nationally specific of the academic disciplines. Historians have detailed national traditions and peculiarities even in the natural sciences, contradicting the description of science as an international enterprise.[42] Sociology emerged in a period of extreme nationalism and was originally connected to projects of national self-fashioning.[43] Sociology existed mainly in universities, and each European country had a nationally distinct system of higher education. Each country also had distinctive intellectual heritages that shaped sociology. Sociology varied cross-nationally in terms of the overall size of the discipline, the timing of its emergence, expansion, and contraction, its relations to government, industry, and social movements, and the mix of disciplinary backgrounds represented among its founders. German sociology was created by historical economists and historians and French sociology by philosophers, while American sociology was originally located mainly in economics departments. Yet sociologists' intellectual exchanges were never limited to their compatriots. Sociologists from the various European empires interacted regularly at conferences and international organizations and in joint publications. Organizations such as the United Nations Educational, Scientific and Cultural Organization (UNESCO) promoted colonial science; American foundations and universities became deeply involved in the social sciences of the European colonies and their metropoles (chapter 5). We might expect national differences to have been undercut by the homogenizing processes linked to Americanization. Yet there was no simple convergence along an American model, even in places like postwar West Germany, much less in France. This does not mean that American foundations did not seek to "reinforce conceptual and technical standardization and to thereby eliminate national differences in the production of social science."[44] Foundation projects were explicitly oriented toward establishing "beachheads" for creating social science disciplines "as we in the US know them," in the words of one Rockefeller Foundation report.[45] Yet European social science remained relatively autonomous from these American pressures.

French sociology may be the most dramatic example of a social scientific discipline that was stamped by colonialism. As I will show in this book, around half of the French sociologists during the postwar era worked on colonial themes or in colonial sites. British sociology was similar—around half of the sociologists were engaged in colonial research after 1945.[46] Sociology in the Dutch and Portuguese colonial empires also resembled the French in this respect. What is especially noteworthy is the emergence of specific methods for studying Dutch and Portuguese colonial social processes that adopted Balandier's approach, which urged researchers to focus on the degeneration of older forms of social solidarity and their reconstitution along new lines, attending to "reactions to the administrative structures imposed by European nations," i.e., to the "colonial situation."

Dutch sociologists lost most of their colonial field sites when Indonesia became independent in 1949, but a new subfield called "non-western" sociology was created to provide jobs for the suddenly unemployed researchers. Like the French and British colonial sociologists, Dutch "non-western" sociologists differentiated their approach from anthropology, which they understood as focusing on the supposedly "homogeneous social relationships of tribal cultures" and ignoring "problems attending modernization, the sociology of the colonial situation or other macro-sociological conceptions."[47]

Sociology was also tied to colonialism in Portugal, although it was much more weakly developed as a discipline. The Centro de Estudos Políticos e Sociais at the *Junta das Missões Geográficas e de Investigações Coloniais* (Board of Geographical Missions and Colonial Studies) embarked on hundreds of research projects starting in 1956, and social scientists, including sociologists, played a central role in these research teams. The first Portuguese sociology and anthropology chairs were introduced at the Colonial School in Lisbon (*Escola Superior Colonial*) in the mid-1950s, and the country's first social sciences degrees were delivered there starting in 1972. The *Centro de Estudos da Guiné Portuguesa* explicitly adopted Balandier's approach.[48]

There was very little sociology in the residual Spanish colonies of Equatorial Guinea and the Spanish Sahara. Carmelo Viñas Mey, a Spanish sociologist of the "third generation" and a specialist in colonial history, tried without success to interest his colleagues in carrying out empirical studies in the overseas colonies.[49]

Italy lost its colonies in World War II, but recovered quasi-colonial control of Somalia as a trusteeship between 1950 and 1960. During this decade, Corrado Gini continued to teach colonial sociology and included a hundred-page discussion of "elements of colonial sociology" in his 1957 *Corsi di Sociologia*. Gini did not acknowledge the newer sociological literature on colonialism.[50]

My focus in this book is on sociology in Greater France, or France plus "exterior France," as it was sometimes called.[51] This was an empire-wide disciplinary field that encompassed universities, research organizations and institutes, conferences, and journals in the colonies and metropoles. Sociologists from France and its colonies moved through an imperial sociological field centered on Paris to outposts in French cities such as Lille, Aix-en-Provence, and Bordeaux, to colonial cities such as Algiers, Tunis, Rabat, Dakar, and Brazzaville, and to field sites throughout the empire, from Gabon to Tahiti. These locales were part of an increasingly integrated set of scientific fields defined by French institutions, use of the French language, and reference to a common core of texts, concepts, and debates. Sociologists born in the metropole or as French settler-citizens moved with relative ease through this global imperial space. Belgian Francophone sociologists also moved with relative ease between French and Belgian metropolitan and imperial scientific sites. The international movement of sociologists born as colonial subjects was much more constrained, even after decolonization, and their movements were usually bilateral ones, between their home countries and France, rather than ranging across the entire empire (chapter 10). This was a dense network of intellectual and scientific fields and subfields.

Defining Colonial Sociology

The phrase *sociologie coloniale* (colonial sociology) was an "emic" category, used by sociologists themselves. The *Congrès international de sociologie coloniale* (international colonial sociology conference) was held in 1900 in conjunction with the Paris Universal Exposition. *Sociologie coloniale* was the title of a three-volume work by the Sorbonne professor René Maunier, a lifelong supporter of French colonialism.⁵² However, the label *sociologie coloniale* fell out of favor after 1945, around the same time that the words "colony" and "colonial" in the names of colonial offices, organizations, and publications were being replaced with euphemisms. Some argued for replacing the label *colonial sociology* with *sociology of colonialism*.⁵³ Jacques Berque noted that "the optic of colonial sociology was generally one of colonization," and was "focused above all on legitimating usurpation by illustrating the archaism" of foreign cultures.⁵⁴ This is the reason sociologists whose careers began in the colonies during the period discussed here sometimes bristled at the phrase *sociologie coloniale* when I interviewed them for this book.⁵⁵ I will discuss the various relabeling efforts, paying close attention to the ways these labels correlated with stable and changing scientific approaches to the colonial subject matter. I will use the phrases *colonial sociology* and *sociology of colonialism* throughout this book as interchangeable analytic categories. Both terms refer to all forms of sociological writing and research focused on overseas colonies and colonial phenomena and empires and imperial phenomena. I remain conscious of the fact that the phrase *colonial sociology* retains the sting of the phenomenon it originally designated: a largely *colonialist* sociology. This is useful in reminding us that this work was being produced within structures predicated on foreign sovereignty and the rule of difference—even when its producers were explicitly critical of colonialism.⁵⁶

The politics of colonial sociologists working after 1945 ranged from militant anticolonialism to fervent support of colonial rule, with most located closer to the former pole. This was also true of the other sciences. At one extreme was the French colonial botanist Pierre Boiteau, who commented in 1948 that "A researcher who does not opt for the national emancipation of the people he is studying cannot fully accomplish his [scientific] mission."⁵⁷ At the opposite extreme was the sociologist Jean Servier, a researcher in Algeria between 1949 and 1955, funded by the *Centre national de la recherche scientifique* (CNRS). Servier tried to contribute directly to the French counterinsurgency campaign by creating an ill-fated "free village" (*djema'a libre*) in the Zakkar region.⁵⁸ Eric de Dampierre allegedly supported the preservation of European rule, at least in equatorial Africa.⁵⁹ Bourdieu and Sayad sharply criticized French Algerian policy and supported the Algerian revolution from a liberal perspective. Andreé Michel became a *porteuse de valises* during the Algerian War and a professor at the University of Algiers after independence.⁶⁰ Claudine Chaulet, a sociologist in Algeria, joined the National Liberation Front (FLN) in the 1950s. Her husband, Dr. Pierre Chaulet, introduced Fanon to the FLN. Claudine Chaulet took Algerian citizenship after independence and remained there as a professor.⁶¹

European sociologists also varied in terms of their professional and personal relations with indigenous sociologists. Some reproduced the hierarchical relationship between colonizer and colonized, while others worked closely with Arab and African researchers.[62] The first French colonial subject trained and employed as a sociologist was Nguyễn Văn Huyên. He studied with Marcel Mauss, wrote his doctoral thesis at the Sorbonne in 1935 with Lucien Lévy-Bruhl, and was hired as a researcher at the French *École française d'extrême-orient* in Hanoi in 1940.[63] Georges Balandier worked with a number of African social scientists, intellectuals, and political leaders, both within the framework of the *Institut français d'Afrique noire* and in his contributions to creating the pan-Africanist journal *Présence africaine* (see chapter 13). Bourdieu was the first French sociologist who co-authored an important study with a colleague born as a colonized subject, Abdelmalek Sayad.[64]

Three final clarifications are in order. First, not all of the sociologists posted to the colonies focused on colonial phenomena in their research and teaching. The standard metropolitan curriculum was extended to the universities in Algeria, Indochina, and Senegal. I will *not* refer to these overseas teachers of metropolitan curricula as colonial sociologists. Second, a sociologist did not necessarily have to work in colonies to count as a colonial sociologist. The entire subfield of colonial sociology began as "armchair" research that synthesized existing ethnographies and travel reports.[65] This synthetic genre did not disappear entirely after 1945.[66] When Bourdieu criticized "theoretical theory" and "materialists without material," he was echoing a wider rejection at this time of "pure theory" divorced from research and fieldwork. This critique is completely at odds with the stereotype of "French Theory" as highly abstract. Third, colonies or empires were rarely the sole focus for any sociologist throughout their career. Although colonial specialists were among the first French sociologists to conduct archival research and ethnographic fieldwork, most of them moved away from the colonial *topos* after decolonization. Some became Africanists or area specialists; others became specialists in "Third World" development; a small number broadened their perspective to empires and imperialism. The majority, however, simply pulled back into the metropole, like the French population as a whole.[67]

Identifying Sociologists and Disciplinary Fields

Although the history of modern science cannot be limited to disciplinary history, it is just as misleading to ignore disciplines.[68] This is particularly true for the postwar period, when the human and social sciences began to be more clearly distinguished. There were powerful pressures at the national and international levels toward disciplinary differentiation and self-definition. The French CNRS was divided from the start into distinct sections, each organized around a discipline or group of disciplines. At the international level, UNESCO spurred the creation of international and national disciplinary organizations. American foundations supported the crystallization of disciplines. It is just as misleading to assume that social science disciplines did not yet exist in postwar France as to assume that they were hermetically sealed silos of self-contained activity.

How can we determine who belonged to a given academic field in the past? Who, in other words, were the sociologists? The most fundamental rule of thumb is that membership in a specialized universe like academic sociology encompasses anyone who was recognized *at the time* as a member of that field by other contemporary participants in it. This approach only seems circular if we ignore the inherent consubstantiality between social structure and agency, persons and their social *Umwelt*. Any intellectual history has to rely on an explicit approach to delimiting the universe in question or risk falling into arbitrary and ad hoc approaches.

Historians sometimes rely on expedient operational definitions, such as counting as a sociologist anyone who referred to themselves as such, published in sociology journals, appeared at sociology conferences, or used the language of sociology in their publications.[69] This approach begs the question of determining which journals are sociological, how different contributors to them were viewed at the time by sociologists, and how such journals were hierarchically arranged—all questions that are stakes of struggle within the sociology field. The most arbitrary approach would count as sociologists only those who look like sociologists to the present-day observer. Yet struggles over the boundaries of fields and the field-specific "dominant principle of domination" are one of the most important features of the history of science. It is a methodological error to adopt the structuring principles of intra-scientific struggle as one's own classificatory principles. Many of the sociologists discussed in this book would be spontaneously classified as anthropologists today because they worked on non-western societies.

Bourdieu's field theory offers a methodological solution.[70] A scientific or academic discipline can best be understood through a historical reconstruction of its genesis, starting with its *nomothets*—the founders of the scientific *nomos*—and then following the field forward in time, tracking the evolution of structural positions and axes of polarization. The historian also needs to reconstruct the field's genesis in order to determine which *founders* had the most power in the past.[71] There is often a continuous process of genealogical reconstruction through which new figures are recognized and included while others are forgotten or expunged from the field's history. Scientific canons are constantly being revised. The only secure way to determine the population of a disciplinary field at a given moment is to reconstruct the judgments of acknowledged members of that field at that moment.

Bourdieu's theory is not just concerned with practice, inequality, and domination *within* fields. It is also a theory of the demarcation of the *borders* among different fields and between fields, and a theory of *non-fielded* activities. Bourdieu observed that the boundaries of fields are often more like the edges of clouds or the selvage at the fringe of a forest, and less like the frontiers separating nation-states.[72] That said, the edges of sociology were becoming more sharply demarcated from adjoining disciplines during the postwar period. One example of this hardening of frontiers can be seen in the postwar CNRS, which located sociology in a different section from ethnology, despite the tendency among many practitioners to equate the two fields or to move between them.[73]

It is sometimes possible to identify a field's members using information other than judgments by direct participants. As Bourdieu noted, "one of the most characteristic properties of a field is the degree to which its dynamic limits . . . are converted into a juridical frontier, protected by a right of entry which is explicitly codified, such as the possession of scholarly titles, success in a competition, etc., or by measures of exclusion and discrimination, such as laws intended to assure a *numerus clausus*."[74] Once a specific degree is required for entrée, it may become a necessary condition, though usually not a sufficient one, for field membership.[75] However, scientific and academic fields vary greatly in their degree of specialization and codification. A strict definition based on "juridical frontiers" would imply that, before the 1960s, sociology existed only in the United States, Germany, Britain, South Africa, and a handful of other countries. In France, sociology already existed as an intellectual and academic discipline, but its only recognition in the universities was a *certificate* in *morale et sociologie* (ethics and sociology) that could be earned as part of the philosophy *licence* degree.[76] Separate *licence* and *doctorat* degrees in sociology were created only in 1958. Most of the great French sociologists of the twentieth century had earned an *agrégation* in philosophy but had no sociology degree at all. There were still no "juridical" rules governing inclusion and exclusion. The closest thing to a sociological membership badge in France was a *chaire* in sociology at a university or one of the *grandes écoles*, or employment as a sociologist by a legitimate research institution such as the CNRS.[77] Another criterion in the postwar period was membership in the *Centre d'études sociologiques*.[78] Membership on the editorial board of one of the key sociology journals—*Année sociologique*, *Cahiers internationaux de sociologie*, and *Revue française de sociologie* (after 1960), or in the reconstituted French Institute of Sociology, was significant, but not always decisive, since these organizations' members continued to be drawn from a range of disciplines.

Where this type of information is lacking, we have to fall back on a case-by-case reconstruction of individual scholars' careers and perceptions of them by others in the field. We can try to determine whether established members of a given discipline, in a given place and time, regarded a particular individual as one of their own.[79] In some cases it is impossible to identify an academic discipline. This is especially true of people who moved between academia and the intellectual, cultural, and political fields, or who were associated with interdisciplinary institutions such as the *Collège de France*, where it was possible to invent one's own title and specialization. Some scholars deliberately resisted disciplinary identification.

A more common pattern in our scientific universe was the combination of sociology and ethnology/anthropology. A number of the sociologists examined here moved in and out of metropolitan employment and published in journals dedicated to the study of a particular culture, region, or country, rather than in generic sociology outlets. Many worked on objects that had traditionally belonged to anthropology and that have been largely recaptured by anthropology in the intervening period. This pattern obscures the very different constellation of the mid-twentieth century. In some cases, individuals were categorized as sociologists where there was no "ethnology" position available, but were recategorized as ethnologists as soon as they moved to a different institution. The *Office de la recherche scientifique et technique outre-mer* (Office of Overseas Scientific and Technical Research), for example, subsumed ethnology under sociology in its publications, and had sociologists but no ethnologists on staff during the postwar period.[80] European anthropologists who moved from metropolitan universities to universities in the colonies or postcolonies were often relabeled as sociologists there, due to hostility to anthropology for its complicity with colonialism.[81] This turn against anthropology foreshadowed a reverse trend today in which non-western sociologists specialized in their own (postcolonial) societies are rechristened as anthropologists when they arrive in European or North American universities. This is a straightforward application of the usually unspoken rule according to which anthropology occupies the "savage slot" in the disciplinary division of labor.[82]

Recognition as a member of a given field often goes hand in hand with other disciplinary markers, such as a specific intellectual *habitus* and reliance on discipline-specific jargon and references. Immersion in a discipline's *illusio* (Bourdieu) brings with it commitments to its seemingly esoteric ideas and investment in its stakes, which appear meaningless and arbitrary from the outside. We can often track the gradual immersion of an individual in a discipline by attending to vocabulary and turns of phrase and references to particular authorities.

Who, then, should *not* be included in the academic field of sociology? Are there also methodological rules of exclusion? Which criteria are associated with being located on the extreme margins of the sociology field? Here, I again follow several methodological rules of thumb. First, anyone who worked as a sociology teacher or researcher but did not publish and was not active in the national or international sociological associations, should at least be considered extremely marginal to the field. These people lacked visibility beyond the local scene and were usually unrecognized by the wider field; at best, they might be understood as participants in a local sociological field. The same is generally true of administrators, research assistants, and students. Of course, everything depends on whether someone is recognized as belonging to the field, or not.[83] One of the aims of chapter 10 is to ask about some of the sociological reasons people were excluded from or on the margins of the disciplinary field.

A Neo-Bourdieusian Historical Sociology of Science

The present book pursues an historical version of Bourdieu's approach, which I call a *neo-Bourdieusian historical sociology of science*. The historical sociology of social science has received a huge impetus from the practice-theoretical perspective of Bourdieu and his school. Bourdieu argued that social practice is defined by the interaction between (1) an author's habitus, which has to be reconstructed sociogenetically over biographical time, (2) an author's positions in specific, relevant fields, and the history of those fields, which explains the space of positions in a field at a given moment in time, and (3) an author's practical and strategic "position-taking" (*prises de position*) within those fields.[84] Bourdieu's paradigm takes seriously the idea that fields, including scientific ones, may be relatively autonomous, that is, partially bounded and demarcated from their outside, even while being subjected to and imbedded within environing social fields and spaces.[85] Unlike the American sociology of science in the 1950s and 1960s, with its ideal of the scientific "community," this approach focuses on *divisions* and *conflicts* as well as partial and temporary *consensus* within scientific arenas. Scientific disciplines are typically characterized by unequal distributions of field-specific power and resources and riven by internal conflicts.

My premise is that the sociology of social science needs to examine thinkers and their works both individually and in relation to a series of more proximate scientific contexts and more distanced sociohistorical contexts. This procedure can be compared and contrasted with the original version of the sociology of knowledge, or *Wissenssoziologie*, which was defined by Karl Mannheim as being located between the extremes of, on the one hand, a generalizing account that ignores differences between individuals and works, and, on the other hand, accounts in which the "unique qualities of each individual's thought are overemphasized, and the significance of his social *milieu* for the nature of his thought is ignored."[86] Mannheim provided examples of this approach in his case study of German conservativism. He also discussed this in his self-reflexive explanation of the conditions of possibility for his own theoretical perspective.[87] The Nazi seizure of power forced Mannheim into exile, brutally interrupting ongoing discussions of the sociology of knowledge.[88] Mannheim never developed a systematic theory of societal contexts, cultural works, or the scientific subject. Those who picked up the sociology of knowledge in the United States, such as Robert K. Merton, Edward Shils, and Alvin Gouldner, were located within a discipline that discouraged these questions, since these questions seemed closer to Marxism, psychoanalysis, and literary criticism.

Mannheim was embedded within German philosophical discussions based in Kant and Hegel, whereas American sociology was innocent of most philosophy other than neopositivism.[89] The disappearance of *Wissenssoziologie* in Germany and Austria was a result of the intense hostility to Mannheim on the anti-Semitic Right.[90] After a promising start in the United States between the wars in Merton's early work, the sociology of science narrowed its focus to the intermediate level of the scientific community.[91] Merton's project, especially after World War II, was to convert *Wissenssoziologie* into "an Americanized 'sociology of knowledge,'" and then to "turn against" it, "and in so doing, to spoil the potential reception of Mannheim's ideas in the United States."[92] Merton warned in 1952 that any investigation of "the connections between sciences and society constitute[d] a subject matter which ha[d] become tarnished for academic sociologists who know that it is close to the heart of Marxist sociology."[93] The new sociology of science focused not so much on science as *scientists*—"their career patterns, work organization, patrons, and professed values." With the rise of the "strong program" in the sociology of science and Science and Technology Studies, researchers lowered their gaze even further to the laboratory while bracketing wider contexts and striking a "studiously descriptive stance" to the sciences, sending the message that "science normally is as it ought to be."[94]

This book will demonstrate that the sociology of knowledge came to fruition in the completely different set of conditions of the late French colonial empire. The surprising migration and maturation of the sociology of knowledge in mid-twentieth-century France was also a result of French sociology's greater openness to questions of scientific reflexivity than the American sociology or post-1933 German sociology. Another key factor was that French sociology was closer to philosophy, due to the training of many of the discipline's central figures at the *École normale supérieure*. French sociology was also opened to the sociology of knowledge due to its permeable disciplinary boundaries, which sensitized it to ongoing discussions in philosophy, anthropology, linguistics, psychoanalysis, history, and (neo)Marxism. Bourdieu was singularly equipped to integrate these diverse intellectual resources and to generate a sociological theory that bridged the social sciences and humanities. This is akin in its ambition to Karl Marx's merger of young Hegelian philosophy with British political economics and French socialist doctrine. It recalls Gustave Flaubert's invention of an unprecedented position in a newly created French literary field, discussed by Bourdieu in *The Rules of Art*.[95] It also resembles the creation by philosophers Jacques Derrida and Michel Foucault of new theories and structural positions located between philosophy and adjoining fields. At the same time, Bourdieu's innovation was made possible by the intellectual, political, and colonial contexts discussed in this book.[96] What is unique about Bourdieu's theory is that it is a social theory of fields and objects other than science, and that the discussion of every social object is simultaneously a discussion of the sociology of the knowledge of these objects.

I have argued here and in earlier publications that Bourdieu's overarching framework can best be reconstructed as a practice of *historical socioanalysis*. This is a *neo-Bourdieusian* rather than an orthodox Bourdieusian or a post-Bourdieusian perspective, since it builds on his main ideas while revising them to differing degrees. Bourdieu's approach pays attention to four key components in analyzing intellectual production: field, context, author, and text. Each of these four components needs to be theorized explicitly. Bourdieu has provided a great deal of guidance for the first two components, while limiting his discussion of the third element, the author, to the theory of habitus. As for textual analysis, we need to turn to resources other than Bourdieu.

More specifically, there are six areas of Bourdieu's theory that require rethinking or reconstruction: (1) the relations between fields and more encompassing social or historical contexts; (2) the spatial coordinates of field theory; (3) the theory of the subject, which Bourdieu limits to the concepts of habitus and practice; (4) the need for more explicit methods for analyzing textual and visual works; (5) a restatement of the underlying philosophy of science, in ways that make it compatible with critical realism and postcolonial epistemology; (6) the theory of reflexivity.

With respect to the first point, I have tried to demonstrate here and in other publications that social fields and social spaces should be situated within wider environing contexts, which may be patterned by modes of societal regulation, dominant cultural discourses, "styles of thought" (*Denkstile*; Karl Mannheim), or the political, economic, and social forces that sometimes stamp an entire epoch or geospace, providing a frame for all fields.[97] These wider contexts are not *supervenient*, in the sense of imposing an asymmetrical relation of dependence upon fields, but they may still shape activity within fields, whose autonomy from their environments is always relative, not absolute. This first point is crucial for defining the range of relevant contexts in the history of science. Bourdieu theorizes social space, which surrounds all fields, and whose basic dimensions are the same as the structural dimensions of fields—different species of capital, forms of habitus, relations of autonomy and heteronomy, etc. However, Bourdieu does not have a theory of the relations among fields, beyond the basic architecture of social space, field of power, and the state, in relation to other fields in general. This is not to say that we should seek a general social theory of epochal contexts. What we need instead is concepts linked to particular historical periods and spaces and defining the widest social contexts—concepts such as developmental colonialism, late colonialism, Fordism, post-Fordism, fascism, totalitarianism, and so on. These concepts help the historian identify the overarching contexts of intellectual production—contexts that are always heterogeneous and changing, but that may still have one or more identifiable emphases.

Closely related is the second point: field theory needs to be grounded in geopolitical space, and not only in (metaphorical) social space. Fields can never be assumed to be spatially identical to the nation-state but often have a smaller or larger geopolitical footprint. The social researcher needs to determine any field's geo-coordinates first, in order to understand the circulation of ideas, objects, and actors within social space. Such a material, spatial grounding is crucial for mapping fields at the scale of studies of empires and colonies, which cannot be equated with fields at the national or global scale.[98] This approach allows us to conceive of fields that link a metropole with specific colonies.[99] Geospatializing field theory can also be crucial for understanding practices at subnational and international levels of analysis, within regions smaller than the national territory or zones that link regions in two or more national territories.

What about the theory of the subject? Bourdieu's theory of habitus and practice provides a starting point that rejects models of rationalism, voluntarism, and psychic unity, on the one hand, and models of the subject as a mere bearer (*Träger*) of social structures, on the other hand. Although Bourdieu argues that practice cannot be understood without reference to a whole array of social contexts, he also understands individuals as being endowed with embodied dispositions (habitus) that may persist beyond their original conditions of genesis, and that exceed conscious thought. Bourdieu's sketchy theory of the subject needs to be reconstructed into a full theory of the psyche and subject. The habitus construct can be retheorized using the Lacanian concept of the imaginary and located at an intermediate level between conscious and unconscious thought.[100] We need to treat individuals—including scientists—as beings endowed with an unconscious. It is this third point that leads me to call my approach *socioanalytic*—following a suggestion by Bourdieu and other French sociologists, but interpreting that term as blending the *sociological* with the *psychoanalytic*.[101]

Any discussion of Bourdieu's theory of subjectivity also needs to encompass his theory of practice. Practice is indeed the central concept in his social theory. Studies of science inspired by Bourdieu therefore necessarily focus on changes in scientific practice over time.[102] Bourdieu's social ontology of practice prevents him from entertaining the idea that social systems are normally reproduced over time, even if he often thematizes social reproduction as a possible, paradoxical state of affairs.[103] Social fields, like social structures in general, are inherently unstable and dynamic; their stabilization or reproduction can therefore only be temporary. Dynamic processualism is thus inherent in Bourdieu's theory at all levels, including his theory of fields. This applies with special force to scientific fields, which rise and fall, intersect and resonate with other fields, and are constantly changing due to perpetual struggles, new generations of scientists, and "specific revolutions."[104] Bourdieu formulated social reproduction as an analytic problem in the 1960s, at a time when the prominence of structuralist theory was reinforced by an unusual situation of relative societal stability, rendering theories of "social reproductionism" more plausible. Social theory was beguiled by the ideal-type of social reproduction, from Parsonsian structural functionalism, to Lévi-Straussian anthropology, to Althusserian Marxism.[105] Thinkers such as Bourdieu, who were exposed to colonial theaters before the 1960s, were immunized against conflating social reproduction with the normal state of affairs. Since the central concept of Bourdieu's social theory is *practice*, studies of science inspired by Bourdieu necessarily focus on changes in scientific practice over time.[106] This point is not so much a reconstruction of Bourdieu as a point of emphasis.

In terms of the fourth revision, Bourdieu recognized that social scientific work is mainly textual and visual, despite efforts to translate social practice into statistics and mathematics. He recognized that social science, like other fields of cultural production, is not only a field of actors and institutions but also a field of *works* that exist in relation to other works. The historical sociology of sociology (or any other primarily textual practice) should analyze texts as being situated within a relational "space of works." Bourdieu was critical of pure formalist approaches to cultural criticism in which works are analyzed *only* internally and in relation to other works, yet he did not shy away from stylistic questions, for example in his lectures on Manet.[107] However, Bourdieu did not develop an interpretive methodology suited to the analysis of textual and visual works. He did not consider the usefulness of theories of narrative or concepts of transtextuality that I rely upon here in order to make sense of the sociology of colonialism.[108] What is called for is an approach to social scientific texts that takes advantage of formal methods and concepts such as those developed in literary criticism and art history, which lead us to pay attention to the structural and formal aspects of texts and the ways in which texts relate to one another, refer to one another, explain one another, or comment upon one another (intertextuality, paratextuality, etc.). It urges us to attend to narrative form, use of perspective, tense, and authorial voice. These relations exist both among works in the immediate discipline or subfield, and in relation to works in other fields.[109] An adequate approach to interpreting cultural products is key to understanding sociological texts.

The fifth point concerns the philosophy of science. Bourdieu argued that "the sociology of sociology is a fundamental dimension of sociological epistemology."[110] Bourdieu's philosophy of science is largely compatible with the critical realist philosophy of science and neohistoricist epistemology.[111] Making this connection has the advantage of linking Bourdieu to a more elaborate and explicit critique of positivism. This is not so much a revision of Bourdieu as an effort to put his epistemology in contact with Anglo-American and German traditions that are positioned similarly vis-à-vis positivism and propose broadly compatible alternatives, even if their terms of discussion are sometimes radically different.[112] Bourdieu's approach is strongly anti-positivist, if we define positivism as belief in the existence of universal, general laws of human behavior. Bourdieu rejects epistemologies of *regularity determinism* and is highly sensitive to questions of contingency and complex causal conjunctures. Bourdieu rejects scientism—the idea that social science should model itself upon imagined norms of natural science. Bourdieu's epistemology of breaking with spontaneous pre-notions is premised on the difference between the level of spontaneous, empirical appearances and "ready-made objects," on the one hand, and a level of underlying real structures and processes, on the other hand. Bourdieu quotes Bachelard to the effect that "there is no science but of that which is hidden."[113] This picture of reality as layered corresponds to critical realism's stratified ontology. Like critical realists, Bourdieu believes that explanatory social science can lead organically to social critique, by identifying "true sites of freedom" as well as sites of fatal constraint, and by peeling away layers of symbolic domination and obfuscation.[114] Sociology is always political. But the "ethical usage of reflexive sociology" is combined with a rigorous rejection of subordinating sociology to politics or anything else that would limit its autonomy.[115] Bourdieu's explanatory accounts of the rise of new artistic or literary styles or events such as May 1968 are grounded in an epistemology of contingent conjunctures of different historical "series." This approach is highly compatible with critical realism's contingentist epistemology and with twentieth-century sociological neohistoricism.[116]

The final point concerns Bourdieu's argument that social science requires a specific form of reflexivity in order to make sense of the underlying social logics of practice. Here, I see less need for revising Bourdieu's thinking than for clarifying it and relating it to the history of social science. One of Bourdieu's arguments is that the historical sociology of science is the centerpiece of scientific reflexivity. As Bourdieu defines it, reflexivity is almost the opposite of what it usually means in popular and pop-sociological discourse. Rather than an embrace of one's existing social, political, and epistemic positions, reflexivity involves a rupture with such preexisting cognitive categories. The first break is with the sociologist's spontaneous theories and concepts about their object. Such scientific "pre-notions" may reflect the doxa of the particular discipline; conversely, they may be rooted in heterodox positions that are adopted unconsciously due to the hierarchical and antagonistic character of social relations within scientific fields. The second break is directed at the categories of the people one is studying, with their understandings of their practice. In the case of the sociology of science, this second move entails a break with scientists' spontaneous interpretations of their practice. Bourdieu's theory thus supersedes the older distinction between "etic" and "emic" ones, between scientific *Fremdbeschreibung* (description of others) and spontaneous forms of *Selbstbeschreibung* (self-description).[117]

Social scientists need to avoid blindly adopting the instruments, theories, and concepts they find readily at hand. They need to reflect on what they are doing when they do science, which assumptions they enact, and which implicit understandings they may unwittingly reproduce. More positively, they might consider how a reflexive approach to scientific practice could contribute to the flourishing of social science and to the creation of a rational framework for social and civic interventions by social scientists. In order to understand their own positions, the researcher needs to *objectify* the scientific fields and the field of power they find themselves in, at the moment of research.[118] This leads them to carry out a historical sociology of their own scientific field, its categories, positions, and polarizations leading up to the present. The researcher reconstructs the field's evolution and its internal structure in order to understand the moves, arguments, and texts within the field, past and present. In some cases (including the present study), a researcher may be so closely linked to the analytic object that their own categories are derived quite directly from the historical categories they are studying. The methodological approach in these cases is the same: one reconstructs one's field and the history of the field one is studying.[119]

The researcher may then situate themself within those historical spaces. While this may take the form of an auto-analysis, such reflexive practice is not the same thing as confessional approaches taking the form "I am writing as an X or speaking as a Y." Although scientists' social backgrounds matter, participation in educational and scientific fields can dramatically transform scientists' habitus, interests, and conscious and unconscious thought. That is why it is much more important to analyze the history of the field of knowledge and its intersection with the individual, rather than focusing on scientists' demographic properties.

This is where we can identify the key differences between standpoint epistemologies, structural anthropology, and Bourdieusian theory. Strict structuralism à la Lévi-Strauss assumes that the spontaneous perceptions of those being studied reveal little about the underlying structures shaping culture and practice. Bourdieu presented his disagreement with structuralism in *Outline of Theory of Practice*.[120] There and in all of his later writings, Bourdieu argues that actors do not simply execute codes or scripts, although they are not free from social structural constraint. Practice always takes place within the structural constraints of individual habitus, the inherited weight of ideas and ways of being, and the relational, conflictual, and cooperative configurations of social fields and social spaces. Yet practice always also involves improvisation in the face of ever-changing situations. Moreover, practice may become more conscious and deliberate through the study of sociohistorical and incorporated structures.

Bourdieu's theory is similarly at odds with versions of standpoint epistemology that argue that insiders have immediate or privileged access to knowledge about their own condition. In the history and sociology of science, this thesis might mean that "only French scholars can understand French society," and by extension, only French sociologists could understand French sociology and only colonial sociologists could understand colonial sociology.[121] The failure of almost all French historians of French sociology even to mention the existence of French colonial sociology (chapter 2) casts immediate doubt on this form of insider epistemology. One's own disciplinary history usually comes packaged in texts, categories, and filters that emphasize certain research objects, theories, founders, and bits of reality, while eliding others. Participants in a given field may indeed have greater access to certain experiences and information, but they may also be subject to systematic forms of blindness and bias, and to the lasting effects of current and past repressions of memory.

The ubiquitous dualism of colonial settings makes it particularly important to avoid naively accepting the self-interpretations of the people one is studying. Colonies are inherently dualistic insofar as the *differentia specifica* of the modern colony is the lack of sovereignty and citizenship on the part of the colonized, the construction of the colonized as inherently inferior (the "rule of colonial difference"), and the caste-like segregation this entails.[122] Colonial scientific fields are dualistic in a different way: they are related to metropolitan ones, without being mere extensions of them. Such dualism distorts perceptions and social relations, making epistemic vigilance especially important. It is far from coincidental that Bourdieu first adumbrated his concept of the split or cleft habitus (*habitus clivé*) in his research in colonial Algeria, and that he discussed the need to execute an epistemological Gestalt switch in making sense of doubled colonial realities (chapter 14).

A conscious *epistemic break* with received pre-notions and disciplinary common sense—one's own and those of the people one is studying—is thus a necessary precondition for social research in general, and for writing the history of science in particular.[123] Reflexivity takes an especially complex form in the study of knowledge produced in colonial settings. In addition to the pervasive dualism of colonial situations, another epistemic difficulty stems from the fact that anticolonialism has become commonsensical among the majority of social researchers. Already in the 1950s and 1960s, social scientists frequently compared colonialism to totalitarianism and Nazism. However, as I have discovered through years of archival research and discussions with participants in late colonial situations, these comparisons are too simple. The differences between colonialism and totalitarianism became especially marked during the last decades of European rule, when the colonial powers, including France, had democratic political systems. Scientific freedom was expanding, even in the colonies—with important exceptions such as Algeria during the revolutionary war. French intellectuals showed increasing readiness, compared to earlier eras, to cross the "global color line" in search of interlocutors, collaborators, and friends. Of course, it was true with respect to wartime Algeria, as Fanon argued, that "science depoliticized, science in the service of man, is often non-existent in the colonies."[124] Just as often, however, colonial researchers demonstrated that they were open to rational argument, to evidence and counter-evidence, to reevaluation of some of their spontaneous pre-notions and prejudices, and to alternative voices and epistemologies.[125] If we do not bracket our own political-epistemic assumptions when studying colonial knowledge, we risk confirming our biases, and we risk historical anachronism.

Overview of the Book and Individual Chapters

Chapter 2 presents postwar colonial sociology in more detail and analyzes its erasure from the history of French social science. The chapter's first section describes the objects, methods, concepts, theories, and epistemologies of colonial sociology. The second section analyzes the repression of this sociological formation in historical writing and disciplinary memory.

The following chapters reconstruct the conditions leading to the rise of this social scientific formation. To answer the questions of how and why colonies became a privileged object and terrain of investigation and a crucial employment site for sociologists between 1945 and 1960, I examine a combination of causal factors located outside the sociological field proper as well as determinants located within sociology. The distinction between internal and external determinants of science is a continuum, and many phenomena are located at the borderline. Yet even if the distinction is a heuristic device, it is a crucial one insofar as it wards off the methodological errors of *methodological scholasticism* and *methodological sociologism*. The former refers to an approach to the history of ideas in which ideas are explained exclusively by other ideas. The latter explains ideas exclusively in terms of social contexts, social structures, epochal social formations, and forces far removed from texts and their immediate conditions of production.[126]

The structure of the present book avoids both of these one-sided approaches by contextualizing at ever more proximate levels, until we arrive at postwar sociology's colonial subfield and individual sociologists and their texts in parts 4 and 5. The contexts discussed in the earlier sections should not be considered as "background material" but as a necessary part of a full account of colonial sociology. The intellectual contexts discussed in the middle sections (chapters 6–8) are equally important. As Bourdieu notes, many of the properties of any particular discipline "derive from the relations between this field and other fields."[127]

Part 2 discusses the more "external" determinants, those most distant in time and social space from the immediate context of the scientific production of colonial sociology. Chapter 3 covers three aspects of postwar France: the re-occupation of the French colonies, the permeation of colonialism by science, including social science, and the continuing enthusiasm for empire among the metropolitan French population. Chapter 4 argues that colonial developmentalist policies contributed to the rising demand for new forms of colonial social scientific expertise. Sociologists became favored partners of colonial governments, especially as development policies took a turn to social welfare. Developmental colonialism provided social scientists with resources, employment opportunities, and conceptual frameworks, while social scientists tried to influence development policies. Chapter 5 reconstructs the *dispositif* of research organizations in France and the overseas colonies in which colonial sociological research was carried out. This chapter also surveys the American and international organizations that provided support to French colonial sociologists, including UNESCO, the International Sociological Association, and the Rockefeller Foundation.

Part 3 discusses the key *intellectual* contexts for postwar French sociology. Continuing to track from more remote contexts toward more proximate ones, chapters 6 and 7 examine the treatment of colonialism in the disciplines that had some overlap with sociology: psychology, law, economics, geography, history, and ethnology.[128] Chapter 8 turns to the most immediate intellectual context for postwar sociology, namely, interwar French sociology. Here, I focus on a series of theoretical and methodological discussions. Especially important for postwar colonial sociology were the interwar sociological debates on theory versus empirics; interpretivism and psychology; historical sociology; morality and ethics; states and empires; and the status of "primitivism" in studying non-western societies. I then examine interwar studies of colonized cultures by a set of ethno-sociologists: Roger Bastide, Charles Le Coeur, Maurice Leenhardt, René Maunier, Alfred Métraux, and Jacques Soustelle.

Part 4 analyzes French sociology and its colonial specialists in structural field-theoretic terms. Chapter 9 examines the sociology discipline and its colonial subfield in morphological terms during the interwar and postwar periods. With regard to the interwar period, the key point is simply to establish that sociology continued to exist as a university and research field. I then show that sociology quickly reemerged after 1945. After determining the overall size of the disciplinary field, my first aim is to establish the size and composition of the colonial grouping. I find that around half of the scholars in the French sociology field between 1945 and 1960 engaged in colonial or imperial research. The chapter then examines the relative status of the colonial specialists. I find that colonial sociologists as a whole were roughly equivalent to their metrocentric colleagues in terms of their professional standing. Most of the key positions in sociology, at the Sorbonne, the Sixth Section of the *École pratique des hautes études*, and the *Collège de France*, were held by scholars with colonial interests.

At the same time, many colonial specialists faced barriers to professional success, and some of them languished in obscurity. Chapter 10 begins by examining some of the specific obstacles faced by colonial scholars. Sociologists were mobilized to contribute to programs of uprooting and resettling

Africans. These displacement programs were beloved by colonial rulers but were increasingly unpopular among French intellectuals and leftists, casting doubt on researchers who contributed to them. Colonial sociologists with administrative or military backgrounds were regarded with increasing distrust, as anticolonialism became more commonsensical. Many colonial sociologists worked in remote overseas locations, which made them invisible to their metropolitan colleagues and kept them out of touch with ongoing discussions in the discipline. One group discussed here that faced an especially steep uphill battle, due to the pervasive racism of the colonies and metropolitan France, were indigenous sociologists. The second part of chapter 10 examines some of the strategies used by colonial sociologists to overcome these barriers. Some of them tried to move into more prestigious fields such as anthropology, philosophy, and literature, or to embed their work within aesthetic and literary forms; others tried to increase their scientific autonomy.

The book's final section, part 5, centers on the work of Raymond Aron, Jacques Berque, Georges Balandier, and Pierre Bourdieu. The foregoing analysis of their intellectual contexts puts us in a better position to understand some of the sources of their ideas, and to discern what is inventive and original in their work.

Aron, discussed in chapter 11, was the most innovative French theorist of the causes and varieties of colonialism and of the specificity of "empire" as a political formation. Aron compares, without equating, Nazi imperialism, French colonialism, and the informal postwar American empire. Aron distinguished among different types of empire.[129] He analyzed empires as inherently fragile, unstable formations, riven by internal contradictions and crises. Aron represented one of the only bridges between postwar European discussions and the neohistoricist epistemology of Weimar sociology, and this gives his work on empire a distinctive historical dimension.

Berque, the subject of chapter 12, was an "Orientalist" sociologist who de-Orientalized the sociology of North African, Arab, and Islamic societies. A reforming colonial official who carried out an intellectual "mutiny" inside the colonial state, Berque's work represents the most historical version of historical sociology that emerged in twentieth-century France. He was the first French sociologist to combine archival and ethnographic methods with social theory in analyzing colonized societies. He effectively invented historical ethno-sociology. Some of Berque's greatest contributions examine the combined effects of colonialism on rural and urban Arab cultures in the Maghreb. Berque's *Dépossession du monde* is a pathbreaking study of decolonization, and *The Arabs* is a unique comparative study of the entire Arab world in the immediate wake of decolonization. Berque coined the critical concept "decolonial" and advocated a form of knowledge he called "transcolonial," defined as a phase of "reciprocal knowledge."[130] Berque is a founder of postcolonial sociology.

Balandier's work, examined in chapter 13, represents a sustained interaction between sociology, ethnology, historiography, and literature. Balandier examined the entire range of destructive effects of colonialism on African societies, and a panoply of African cultural and political responses to the "colonial situation" in urban and rural settings. He is best known for his research on African messianic religions, resistance, and anticolonial nationalist movements, and for his historical research on the formation of African states.

The penultimate chapter turns to Bourdieu, whose extraordinarily generative theoretical concepts can be traced in part to his time in Algeria (1956–1960) and to the repeated reworking of his Algerian research at every stage of his theoretical evolution. The original aspects of his thinking can now be better understood against the backdrop of the intellectual terrain that had already been created by the thinkers examined in the rest of this book. It is crucial here to weigh the relative importance of (1) the intellectual inheritance—both the colonial researchers and the other, noncolonial thinkers Bourdieu brings to bear on the colonial object (Husserl, Merleau-Ponty, Bachelard); and (2) the specific colonial situation in which Bourdieu found himself, including the impact of the war and his friendship with Algerians such as Abdelmalek Sayad. I will argue that Bourdieu's theory of habitus, symbolic capital, and fields, and his specific approach to reflexivity and writing the history of culture, including science, emerged from his wartime experiences and writing in Algeria. Chapter 14 therefore completes the hermeneutic circle traced in this book. We will be able to discern and understand an intellectual formation partly with the help of the theoretical methodology encompassed within that formation and reaching its apotheosis at the end of the colonial era in Bourdieu's thinking.

The book's conclusion turns to the question of the relation of this colonial sociology to the present. Is sociology's colonial moment relevant only as an incubus weighing on the present? Should decolonization work by luring this demon out of hiding to be slain? Autonomy is crucial for overcoming academic dependency and for the production of science in general.[131] Since autonomous work of lasting value was created in this period, I will argue, we should not simply erase it, especially since it has already been erased once before (chapter 2). Moreover, the present historical moment is, still, an imperial moment. The questions raised in the research discussed in this book are alive and well.

The next chapter begins the process of reconstructing the existing doxa of the field in order to pierce the veil of spontaneous knowledge, by addressing the extant history of French sociology. As we will see, colonial sociology has been actively repressed. My first goal is to wrest the history of colonial sociology from the dark waters of the Lethe.[132]

CHAPTER TWO

Constructing the Object, Confronting Disciplinary Amnesia

It is not true that in my schooldays I ever doubted the real existence of Athens. I only doubted whether I should ever see Athens.
—SIGMUND FREUD, "A DISTURBANCE OF MEMORY"[1]

It is in France that a sociology explicitly dedicated to Africa appeared.
—JEAN COPANS, *CRITIQUES ET POLITIQUES DE L'ANTHROPOLOGIE*[2]

COLONIALISM, LIKE FASCISM, goes almost unmentioned as an historical context in writing on the history of sociology, including French sociology.[3] Colonialism is also missing from accounts of particular subfields of sociology, including surveys, urban sociology, the sociology of religion, war, nationalism, racism and race relations, labor, and migration. Yet all of these specializations were present in the colonies, and some even originated there. Even esoteric subfields, such as the sociology of knowledge, emerged in postwar French sociology among networks of colonial specialists.[4]

In order to understand the breadth and depth of the collective amnesia around colonialism in French sociology, we need to have some sense of what exactly is being repressed. The first part of this chapter briefly surveys the sociology of colonialism that emerged in Greater France between the late 1930s and the mid-1960s. I will examine the objects, methods, concepts, theories, and epistemologies of this intellectual formation. The second section looks at the ways in which colonial research has been banished from the history of French sociology in general and from the history of the main sociological subfields. The last part of the chapter asks about the reasons for the erasure of colonial sociology from disciplinary memory.

Colonial Sociology's Objects, Methods, and Theories

One of the unexpected findings of the present investigation is the intellectual generativity of empires. Empires are turbulent, crisis-ridden, and culturally hybrid and complex. In the era of late colonialism, racism and colonialism came under attack by the colonized and by some of the colonizers, and new forms of intellectual contact and interaction became possible. The conditions of social scientific production became less encumbered. This was perhaps especially true in the spaces organized around the still new and poorly understood signifier "sociology," which remained open and interdisciplinary, especially in the colonial outskirts of Greater France.

Sociologists working in colonial settings made a number of theoretical, methodological, and empirical discoveries. Their work foreshadowed transnational and global history, ethno-historical sociology, and postcolonial theory. Sociologists constructed a panoply of new analytic objects, including detribalization, urban-rural circulation, shantytownification, and cultural mixing.[5] Colonial sociology took several basic forms: (1) ethnographies and social surveys conducted in colonies; (2) theoretical analyses of colonies; (3) historical studies of colonies; (4) comparative studies based on information generated in colonies; (5) theories of empires and imperialism. Some of this research was carried out independently; some was conducted at the behest of governments, firms, international agencies, or research organizations. In some cases, sociological research was integrated into ongoing colonial governance. Some of this colonial sociology also shaped the subsequent discipline, although in unacknowledged ways.

Colonial sociologists made a number of *methodological* contributions. One of the simplest but most fundamental features of sociological work on colonies was that it emphasized and explicitly analyzed the role of colonialism, rather than bracketing European domination, as had been the case in most anthropological research on colonized populations. Colonial sociologists tended to reject the static approaches that typified interwar social anthropology and postwar Parsonsian sociology. They emphasized domination, racism, conflict, and change. In a famous 1951 article, Georges Balandier coined the term "colonial situation" to characterize the distinctiveness of the colony as "a society whose function it is to achieve political, economic, and spiritual domination" and to signal that colonialism had to be analyzed relationally, conflictually, and processually, and had to be constructed historically.[6] Balandier's entire approach came to be known as "dynamic sociology," or a "sociology of mutations," in deliberate contrast to static structuralism, and it had a sweeping influence on colonial sociology in France and elsewhere.[7] Jean Duvignaud, who, like Balandier, combined literary writing with sociological research on the effects of colonialism (in Tunisia), argued that colonies and postcolonies were caught in a "movement of destructuration and structuration."[8] Sociologists began analyzing European colonizers within the same analytic frame as the colonized,[9] whereas anthropologists had shied away from studying White settlers and from applying theories of "developed" societies to "primitive" ones.

Colonial specialists were the pioneers of *historical approaches* in French sociology. Historical sociology had previously only existed in Weimar Germany, with a handful of offshoots in Britain and the United States due to the scientific exile from Nazi Germany.[10] Raymond Aron was the sole representative of German-style historical sociology in France before 1945. Aron's studies of historical epistemology from the 1930s directly informed his studies of Nazi, French, and American imperialism. Balandier's 1955 doctoral thesis was also historical and comparative, contrasting the responses to colonialism among the Gabonese Fang and the Bakongo in the French Congo.[11] Balandier's study of the Kongo kingdom was a pioneering work of African history during the "first decade of the modern study of African history."[12] A historical approach seemed to come naturally to sociologists as soon as they accepted Balandier's idea of the historical dynamism, ambiguity, and contradictoriness of colonial situations. Many sociologists continued to publish monographs on specific colonies, ethnic groups, or tribes, but these books now typically started not with an overview of landscape, flora, and fauna, as in the typical Le Playsian monograph (see chapter 8), but with a historical discussion of the precolonial era and the impacts of French colonialism.

The work of Jacques Berque, Eric de Dampierre, Georges Balandier, Paul Mercier, Pierre-Philippe Rey, and Fanny Colonna illustrates the emergence of a full-fledged historical sociology of colonialism. Berque, discussed in chapter 12, carried out intensive research in hitherto unexplored Moroccan archives and wrote a series of historical books on various aspects of Moroccan, Arab, and Muslim history. Balandier, discussed in chapter 13, founded a sociology of Africa he called "dynamic," in opposition to "static" structuralism, and carried out the first sociological history of precolonial African state formation.

Mercier's sociological approach was above all a historical one. He criticized the application of "common sense" concepts of social class to Africa, including "simplifying and rigid" Marxist concepts, which threatened to "completely distort the perspective in the majority of cases."[13] Colonies differed from other societies in terms of the radical opposition between the dominant European group and the rest.[14] The "binary division of colonial society along racial lines" and the "opposition to the colonizers . . . prevented African society from dividing itself against itself."[15] Especially in periods of "extreme crisis," colonial society was likely to split into two internally homogeneous racial camps.[16] The "relations of domination characteristic of colonialism" thus constituted "a brake on the appearance of a diversified system of classes."[17] Breaking with sociological approaches that posited linear models of social development and rejecting ahistorical forms of cultural anthropology, Mercier emphasized "multiple determinants, sometimes in contradiction with one another" and "considerable discontinuities in the development of colonial societies."[18] Cultural practices "that seem to be 'traditional' in these societies in fact represent 'responses' to relatively recent 'challenges'."[19] Mercier approvingly cited African intellectuals and anticolonial leaders on the "non-existence of social class" in contemporary Africa.[20] He also criticized the use of European notions of nationalism to Africa. The difference between "tribal" and "territorial" nationalisms resulted from the ways in which colonial powers had "contributed to a crystallization of ethnic units and to a rigidification of moving boundaries as a matter of policy."[21]

De Dampierre, an early associate of Aron, combined observational fieldwork carried out for many years in French Equatorial Africa with archival research on the history of the colony.[22] In his doctoral thesis, de Dampierre analyzed the transformations that precolonial conquests and French colonialism had brought to three Bandia kingdoms in what is now the Central African Republic. He showed that the Nzakara tried to defend their traditions but ultimately experienced the destruction of their culture, while the culturally similar Vungara dynasties in central and eastern Zandeland succeeded in adapting to the modern colonial world. This study created a precedent for the integration of history, sociology, and ethnography.

Rey, who wrote his doctoral thesis with Balandier, carried out fieldwork and archival research concerning the French Congo. Rey developed what at the time was an innovative neo-Marxist theory of the articulation of modes of production and of the colonial mode of production. This theoretical breakthrough was based on his discovery that the administration of the French Congo had been unable to crush the traditional tribal system, and then sought to find a way to combine this indigenous system with the superimposed colonial one.[23]

Colonna's career began after the end of the colonial period, but it illustrates the influence of Bourdieu on this evolving genre of historical sociology. Colonna was born in Algeria in 1934 as the descendent of French settlers. She joined a group of left-wing opponents of colonialism and opted for dual nationality after Algerian independence.[24] Most important in the present context was her doctoral thesis on colonial teachers in Algeria between 1883 and 1939. Colonna was able to demonstrate the limits on the officially proclaimed policy of assimilation, by showing that teachers defined "excellent" performances by Algerian students as performances that were neither too close to their culture of origin nor too similar to the culture of the French colonizer.[25]

In short, sociologists of colonialism introduced historical approaches to French sociology. These contributions have been completely ignored in discussions of the emergence of that disciplinary subfield.[26]

Another important intervention by colonial specialists was that they turned ethnography into a recognized methodology in French sociology. Of course, the Le Playsians had already carried out a peculiar form of ethnographic research in France and the colonies. After 1945, the ethnographic methods that had already been elaborated by ethnologists started to be picked up by self-described sociologists. André Leroi-Gourhan created a major training program for ethnography, the *Centre de formation aux recherches ethnologiques*, in 1946, with funding from the *Centre national de la recherche scientifique* (CNRS). The *Centre*'s first two managing directors, Paul-Henri Chombart de Lauwe and Georges Granai, were both sociologists, and the third director, Jean Poirier, was associated with ethnology and sociology. By 1953, there were more "sociologists" than "anthropologists" among the 164 people doing full-time ethnographic research in France, according to Leroi-Gourhan. Sociologists were especially predominant among the ranks of younger ethnographers in the CNRS training program.[27] The fact that the sociologist Marcel Maget called his approach *"metropolitan* ethnography" in the 1940s and 1950s indicates that overseas colonies were the default site for ethnography at the time.[28] Community studies that combined surveys with ethnography represented an originally colonial method applied to metropolitan sites. Some of the first major community studies in France were carried out by sociologists and ethnologists whose main research was in overseas colonies (Éric de Dampierre, Lucien Bernot, Pierre Clément, Suzanne Frère, Nelly Xydias).[29]

Applied colonial sociologists were also at the cutting edge of the technical "modernization" of French sociology, embracing the most up-to-date scientific machinery. The "marriage of technology and development" was central to colonial policy in general at the time. This modern veneer enhanced sociology's perceived utility.[30] Colonial sociology's technicist turn was promoted by scientists' relations to private, governmental, and colonial clients and to American foundations and research organizations. Sociology claimed disciplinary expertise in statistics, measuring devices, standardized questionnaires, mathematization, quantitative methods, and modeling. Colonial sociologists worked closely together with statistical offices, and the two roles sometimes merged (chapter 7). *Matériel* played a key role here: jeeps, trucks, boats, and airplanes; computers and microfilm readers; still and film cameras, film editing equipment; and sound recorders. Social scientists were involved in creating archives, libraries, collections, laboratories, research stations, and museums in the colonies. The interwar Dakar-Djibouti expedition, led by Marcel Griaule, pioneered this high-tech approach. The expedition was equipped with a collapsible boat that could carry cameras, recorders, and "materials for developing film and conserving collections."[31] After World War II, the CNRS paid for the construction for Griaule of a larger "Ethnographic Launch Laboratory," called the Mannogo, with a built-in photo lab and recording equipment.[32] Bourdieu used cameras and computers (see fig. 14.1). Researchers at the *Institut d'études centrafricaines* in Brazzaville used projectors, speakers, and portable sound recording equipment (fig. 2.1). Sociologists and psychologists collaborated on the administration of psycho-technical tests (see chapter 6, figs. 6.1.–6.5). The

FIGURES 2.1. Marcel Soret (sitting), with unnamed collaborator, with sound equipment in Shari-Ubangi, 1950s. *Source:* Photograph collection. Marcel Soret Papers, with the kind authorization of the Academy of Mâcon (France).

sociologist Paul Henry Chombart de Lauwe, together with Griaule, pioneered the use of airplanes in social research. They discussed their aerial approach in the popular science journal *Atomes*, the year after the atom bomb was dropped on Japan (figs. 2.2–2.3).[33] Chombart de Lauwe used photographs to contrast the more "organic" and "natural" spatial organization "of rural villages in northern Cameroon with the 'artificial' organization of urban space in France," arguing that French cities were "diseased" in comparison.[34]

This emphasis on modern technology resonated with the economic chasm that still separated colonies and metropoles. The colonies were "essentially rural" and industry remained "quasi non-existent." The result was that the colonies depended "on the Metropole for their supply of products of consumption and equipment."[35] By displaying advanced technology, the research sites strewn throughout the African bush advertised the metropole's domination of the colonies (fig. 2.4).

Colonial sociologists also generated a number of *conceptual* and *theoretical* insights. Bourdieu's main theoretical categories—*habitus, symbolic capital, reflexivity*, and *field*—emerged in their basic outlines from his Algerian experiences and his fieldwork and writing at the time (chapter 14). Berque initiated the genre of criticism of colonial knowledge that would move to the heart of postcolonial theory in Edward Said's *Orientalism*.[36] Berque was the first writer to use the neologism "*decolonial*" as an adjective, speaking of "the *decolonial* situation."[37] Colonial sociologists discussed cultural hybridity, the blowback effects of empire, "traditionalist tradition" and "colonial tradition" (Bourdieu), and the lasting effects of coloniality on the postcolonial world. Aron, Balandier, Berque, and Bourdieu all articulated the "postcolonial" thesis of the racist rule of colonial difference (chapters 10-13). This should not be surprising, since two thinkers who are usually considered precursors of postcolonial theory, Albert Memmi and Abdelmalek Sayad, were sociologists, and since Frantz Fanon, another precursor, was seen at the time as having strong connections to sociology.[38]

Colonial sociologists *started* from the assumption of mixed cultures and the selective appropriation of external ideas, rather than assuming that colonized cultures could or should maintain any semblance of integral tradition. Sociologists also tried to identify the conditions in which the colonized might successfully defend cultural "archaisms" or invented traditions. Balandier and Mercier's study of the Lébou villagers in Senegal (1952) argued that this apparently unchanging culture was fully enmeshed in global history and webs of outside influence, and that the Lébou were able to negotiate repeated invasions by playing "a game of conservation and innovation," filtering outside influences without being "closed to them."[39] Bourdieu discussed similar strategies among the Algerian Mozabites.[40] Bastide's work in Brazil focused on what he called the "interpenetration of cultures" and the ability of Afro-Brazilians to practice the *principe de coupure*, which allowed them to participate in "two different civilizations"—one "occidental," the other part of a "minority."[41]

Psychiatrists, psychoanalysts, and social psychologists analyzed divisions within the identities of the colonized and disjunctures between individual subjectivities and changing social environments. Some tried to develop novel theories and therapeutic methods for dealing with the unique problems they encountered in the colonies. Their concepts included "African Oedipus" (Marie-Cécile Ortigues), "Prospero Complex" (Octave Mannoni), "colonized madness" (Danielle Storper-Perez), and Fanon's "depersonalization" and "epidermalization." Mannoni was also the first social scientist to publish an article in which he proposed to "decolonize" himself in response to Fanon's criticism of his psychoanalytic account of colonialism in *Psychologie de la colonisation*.[42]

A final set of contributions by colonial sociologists were properly *epistemological*. On the one hand, antiracists and anticolonialists argued against the ontological division of labor between sciences allegedly suited to the global North, such as economics, and sciences suited to the colonized, developing, or "primitive" world, such as ethnology. On the other hand, universal

FIGURE 2.2. A military P 51 airplane over French Sudan on a photographic mission. *Source:* Paul Henry Chombart de Lauwe, *La découverte aérienne du monde* (Paris: Horizon de France, 1948), 377.

social theories were also criticized as intellectually imperialist. Both of these responses, which structure much of the current debate on decolonizing the social sciences, were already fully present in discussions among the sociologists of colonialism discussed in this book.[43] But there was an additional counter-colonial gesture in this period that is largely missing from current discussions. European society was described as "primitive" using concepts such as ritual, fetishism, and sacrifice.[44] In other cases, concepts generated in

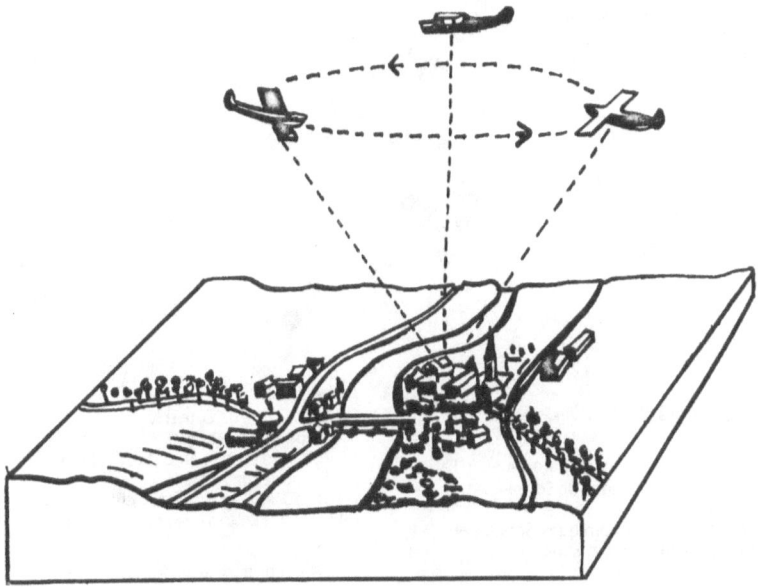

FIGURE 2.3. Chombart de Lauwe's method of shooting landscape via airplane circling overhead. *Source:* Paul Henry Chombart de Lauwe, *La découverte aérienne du monde* (Paris: Horizon de France, 1948), 377.

the colonies were recirculated back to make sense of metropolitan societies. A prime example of the latter is Bourdieu's theory of habitus, which he first articulated in a discussion of *"niya,"* a Kabyle word meaning "a certain manner of being and acting, a permanent, general and transposable disposition in the face of the world and other men" (see chapter 14).[45]

African sociologists at the time began to articulate a standpoint-theoretical critique of European research on their societies. François N'Sougan Agblémagnon, a student of Balandier's, introduced a version of standpoint epistemology in the late 1950s that explored the epistemic advantages of African scholars in the study of African cultures.[46] In Fanon's extreme formulation of this approach, the "fellah, the unemployed and the starving ... are the truth in their very being."[47] Bourdieu's epistemology, including his theory of reflexivity, has to be included here, even though Bourdieu rejected simple versions of standpoint theory (chapter 14). Bourdieu advocated a socioanalysis of the ways in which intellectuals' social situations shape their spontaneous perceptions and concepts.

Postwar colonial social science was the first intellectual formation that led professional social scientists to reflect upon the entanglements of their own thinking with structures of power and exploitation.[48] Berque and Bourdieu called for a "decolonization" of sociology. African sociology departments

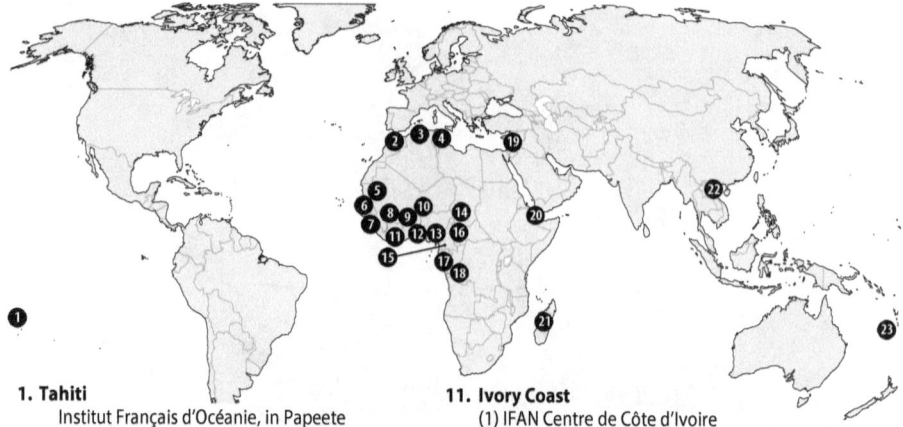

1. **Tahiti**
   Institut Français d'Océanie, in Papeete
2. **Morocco**
   (1) Institut des Hautes Études Marocaines, in Rabat
   (2) Institut de Psychologie et de Sociologie Appliqueés
   (3) Société d'Études Économiques, Sociales et Statistiques du Maroc, in Rabat
3. **Algeria**
   (1) University of Alger, Institut d'Ethnologie; Institut d'Études Orientales; Institut d'Études Supérieures Islamiques; Institut de Recherches Sahariennes
   (2) Institut de Recherches Économiques et Sociale d'Alger
   (3) Service de Statistique, in Alger
   (4) Association pour la Recherche Démographique, Économiques et Sociales, in Alger
   (5) Secrétariat Social d'Alger
4. **Tunisia**
   (1) Centre d'Études de Sciences Humaines
   (2) Institut des Hautes Études Tunisennes, Letters Section
   (3) Secrétariat Social de Tunisie
5. **Mauritania**
   Centrifan, in Saint Louis
6. **Sénégal**
   (1) IFAN Headquarters
   (2) IFAN at Saint-Louis (joined with Mauritania Center in 1958)
   (3) École Française d'Afrique
7. **Guinea**
   IFAN Centre de Guinée, in Conakry
8. **French Sudan**
   IFAN Centre du Soudan Français (Centrifan), in Bamako
9. **Upper Volta**
   (1) Centrifan Haute-Volta: IFAN Centre de Haute Volta, in Ouagadougou
   (2) Centre IFAN-ORSTOM
10. **Niger**
    Centrifan Niger, in Niamey
11. **Ivory Coast**
    (1) IFAN Centre de Côte d'Ivoire (Centrifan) in Abidjan
    (2) Institue d'Enseignement et de Recherches Tropicales, in Abidjan
    (3) ORSTOM Social Sciences Center, in Petit Bassam
    (4) École des Lettres d'Abidjan, in Abidjan
12. **Togo**
    (1) IFAN Centre Local du Togo, in Lomé
    (2) IRTO – Institut de Recherches Togo/Togolaises
13. **Dahomey**
    IFAN Centre du Dahomey (Centrifan), in Porto Novo
14. **Chad**
    Centre de Recherches Tchadiennes, in Fort Lamy
15. **Cameroon**
    (1) IFAN Centre de Douala (Centrifan associé), in Douala
    (2) Institut de Recherches du Cameroun/Camerounaises (IRCAM), in Yaoundé
16. **Oubangui-Chari**
    Institut d'Études Centrafricaines (IEC), in Bangui
17. **Gabon**
    ORSTOM Center
18. **French Congo**
    Institut d'Études Centrafricaines (IEC), in Brazzaville
19. **Syria**
    Institut Français d'Études Arabes, in Damascus
20. **Côte Française des Somalis (Djibouti)**
    IFAN
21. **Madagascar**
    (1) Institut de Recherches Scientifiques de Madagascar (IRSM), in Tananarive
    (2) Académie Malagache
    (3) Institut des Hautes Études de Tananarive
    (4) Institut de Recherches Scientifiques de Madagascar
22. **Indochine (Vietnam)**
    École Francaise d'Extreme Orient, in Hanoi
23. **New Caledonia (Nouvelle Caledonie)**
    Institut Français d'Océanie, in Nouméa

FIGURE 2.4. Institutions supporting French colonial sociological research and teaching, mid-1950s.

engaged in the decolonization of sociology and anthropology after the French exodus.

A Disturbance of Memory

This entire formation of colonial sociology has been actively repressed from historical writing on the history of sociology. *Repression* is the correct word for this. It captures the combination of individual and collective processes involved in burying memory. Colonial sociology has been subject to *amnesia*—another excellent term, when used in its psychoanalytic sense.[51] Intellectual history is a necessary step in a process of *anamnesia*, of unearthing this object.

Let's start with sociological survey research, the *pièce de résistance* of postwar French sociology in some accounts.[52] Philippe Masson's history of *"les grandes enquêtes"* (large social surveys) in postwar French sociology fails to note a single large social survey carried out in the colonies.[53] Yet this exact term—*grande enquête*—was used to describe sociological studies carried out in Algeria in 1846–1847 by Saint-Simonian research teams, who regarded the colony as a gigantic experimental laboratory or test site (*lieu d'essai*) for social experimentation.[54] Frédéric Le Play's school of empirical sociology began with a massive research project, *Les ouvriers européens*, which was carried out by teams of researchers in 12 different countries starting in 1833.[55] This work included four case studies in Algeria, two in Cambodia, and one each in Ivory Coast, La Réunion, Syria, and Tunisia.[56] Social researchers in Algeria and Morocco carried out surveys in teams (*travail en équipe*) between 1890 and 1914.[57] Louis Massignon, who held a chair in Muslim Sociology and Sociography at the *Collège de France* from 1926 to 1954, carried out an extensive questionnaire survey of artisans and merchants in Morocco in 1923–1924.[58] Another Collège de France sociologist, Robert Montagne, conducted a survey of the Moroccan proletariat in the 1940s that mobilized more than 82 researchers.[59] The *Mission démographique de Guinée* (discussed in chapter 7) used teams of indigenous assistants to survey villagers in that colony. Chombart de Lauwe advocated survey teams after returning from his 1935 research trip to Africa.[60] Pierre Bourdieu's Algerian research involved "entire teams of researchers, Algerian students, men and women."[61] A colonial geographer pointed out in 1941 that teamwork research had been tried out "many times" in both "French and English colonies"—forgetting to mention the Belgians (see chapter 9).[62] Survey research and *grandes enquêtes*, like many other scientific, industrial, and cultural techniques, were invented, tested, or perfected in colonies and in the trans-imperial spaces connecting metropoles with colonies.

Historical studies of French *urban sociology* also ignore research on colonial cities and urbanism, even for the period before 1960.[63] One author credits Maurice Halbwachs with the "invention of urban sociology," even though Halbwachs's urban publications were published after a number of colonial urban sociologies that drew on the same Durkheimian theoretical matrix. These included an 1898 study of Tunis by Durkheimian sociologist Robert Lapie, and a 1902 study, *Cities and Tribes of Morocco*, by Alfred Le Chatelier, who first held the chair in the "Sociology and Sociography of Islam" at the *Collège de France*.[64] Le Chatelier created the Moroccan Scientific Mission, which became the "Sociological Section" of the French Native Affairs Office in Morocco in 1919.[65] A series of city studies were issued by this office. It is therefore not suprising that students in the French Protectorate's European *lycées* and colleges in Morocco were required to take introductory lessons in urban sociology. One text used in the primary class in 1954 began by stating that "cities are the domain *par excellence* of Arab-Muslim civilization," and went on to discuss different types of urban settlement in the colony.[66] Jacques Berque analyzed the relations between the urbanisms of the traditional Islamic medina, colonial urbanism, and the new shantytowns in North African cities (chapter 12). The French socio-ethnologist Jean Guiart even found enough material in the French Pacific islands to write a report in 1958 on urban sociology there.[67] Paul Mercier's *thèse complémentaire* (second doctoral thesis) was on the city of Dakar.[68] Georges Granai, a North African specialist who founded the sociology program at the University of Tunis, also specialized in urban sociology and organized urban sociological research at the University of Aix-en-Provence after moving back to France in 1963. This was another clear example of a colonial, "southern" perspective on cities making its way back to the metropole.

The themes of urbanization, "shantytownification," and circulatory migration between villages and cities as well as colony and metropole can be found in sociological writing on nearly every colony. One sociologist-technician, Michel Marie, who was involved in projects of colonial "social engineering" (*ingénierie sociale*) in the context of a "bureau d'études" in Algeria, discussed his own return from the colony to the metropole under the heading "*du bidonville au bétonville.*"[69] The *bidonville* was the colonial shantytown; the *bétonville* or concrete city alluded to the peri-urban high-rise public housing projects built in postwar metropolitan France.

Georges Balandier created an approach that linked urban and rural sociology to the sociology of religion, nationalism, and politics. Balandier noted that the French "Modernization and Equipment" program had first targeted African urban centers, but that by 1950 it was shifting its focus to rural areas.[70] Social scientists needed to consider the rural and the urban as a connected whole, a total system, rather than specializing in one or the other.[71] The modern colonial city tended to create a cosmopolitan civilization that subsumed rural traditions. Yet Balandier found that immigrants from more intact rural cultures such as the Bakongo held on to their traditions longer after migrating to the colonial capital of Brazzaville.[72] Balandier also pioneered an urban historical sociology in his study of the Kongo kingdom, which he framed as a precolonial African "urban civilization." The topography of the early modern Kongo kingdom's capital city, with its separate district for Europeans, "revealed a racial division" that "anticipated the colonial cities of the twentieth century."[73] Balandier was sensitive to the role of urbanization in destroying many aspects of indigenous life in Equatorial and West Africa, including traditional African art. The exquisite aesthetic forms of African art so prized by European collectors and artists were part of a traditional *rural* context that had been torn asunder by colonial administrators, missionaries, and capitalists. In short, colonial urbanism was at the heart of French urban sociology—until it was forgotten.

Historians of the *sociology of labor and industrial relations*, one of the most active subfields in postwar French sociology, have also ignored research in the colonies, with the partial exception of Bourdieu's research on Algerian workers.[74] One study of French labor sociologists between 1950 and 1990 goes so far as to criticize them for focusing on "contemporary societies, not distant ones."[75] Yet, studies of African workers in French colonies were sponsored by the main colonial research organizations, and by UNESCO, the International African Institute, and the Inter-African Labour Institute, with French sociologists as contributors.[76] Balandier's 1955 book *Sociologie des Brazzavilles noires* detailed workers' migrations, salaries, budgets, and consumption patterns.[77] Bourdieu's contributions to the sociology of labor began with an article in the journal *Sociologie du travail (Sociology of Work)*, where he reconstructed the patterns of racial discrimination that structured Algerian labor markets. Colonial researchers were more prone to thematizing unemployment, which was a bigger problem at the time than in France.[78] Bourdieu wrote about the hopeless condition of unemployed Algerians, who were "poorly adapted to the urban world where they wander as if lost, cut off from the rural world and its reassuring traditions . . . without a past or a future."[79]

Histories of *economic sociology* also typically overlook pioneering work done in this area by colonial specialists. However, the entire French field of development economics grew out of colonial research. Balandier taught the sociology of economic development at *Sciences Po* in the 1950s. The Institute for the Study of Economic and Social Development at the Sorbonne was founded in 1957 by François Perroux, a specialist in colonial and postcolonial economies, and many of its sociological members worked in African and non-western settings, including René Dumont. Perroux, discussed in chapter 6, argued that the same economic policies produce different effects in underdeveloped and advanced capitalist economies.[80]

The sociological study of *migration* received an impetus not seen since the publication of *The Polish Peasant in Europe and America* (1918–1920) by William I. Thomas and Florian Znaniecki. Sociologists examined networks and flows of people between the countryside and the colonial city, between colonies and metropoles, and across tribal boundaries.[81] Robert Montagne studied the movement of migrants from the Moroccan interior into the coastal cities, and between Northern Africa and France.[82] Labor migration between village and city was the topic of Balandier's *Brazzavilles noires* and his research in Gabon (see chapter 13). Labor migration was also a central theme in the Marxist-inspired Africanist sociology of the "articulation of modes of production" that emerged in the early 1960s.[83] Abdelmalek Sayad transformed the sociology of migration into a sociology of the migrant exile experience as a "double absence."[84] A transnational framing of social research emerged within colonial theaters long before transnationalism became an explicit desideratum within social science. These approaches to studying migration "migrated" from the colonies to metropolitan France.

French studies of *racism* also grew out of colonial social science. All four of the *dramatis personae* discussed in detail in the last section of this book foregrounded racism as the core ideological structure of colonialism. The volume "Racism and the French" that was sponsored by the *Centre d'études sociologiques* in 1965 was co-authored by two sociologists with colonial backgrounds, Paul H. Maucorps and Albert Memmi. The book was based on a national questionnaire survey of French attitudes about racism. The authors discussed French beliefs about the causes of racism, which included colonialism, responses to "the emancipation of the colonial peoples," and "the Algerian War." This discussion of results was combined with a meta-commentary in which the authors attempted to correct the views of the people interviewed. They argued that "the articulation of racism with colonialism is so obvious that many subjects tend to turn it into a universal cause [of racism], whereas it is only a partial determinant."[85] The methodology of this survey "raises questions," as it was "based on 200 questionnaires returned by members of the 'Mouvement contre le racisme, l'antisemitisme et pour la paix'"—the "very group that commissioned the work."[86] What this does show, however, at the very least, is that the colonial origins of racism were obvious to social researchers at the time.[87]

The French *sociology of religion* is another subfield in which colonial research has been effaced in historical treatments. Religion was the focus of the pioneering French sociologists of the Maghreb, from Doutté, Massignon, Maunier, and Bousquet, through to Rodinson and Berque. Bastide discussed religious syncretism, black Islam, and other religious phenomena in several colonial settings.[88] The Fifth Section of the Paris *École pratique des hautes études* was devoted to the science of religions, and this was where Marcel Mauss held a chair between the wars in the "History of religions of non-civilized peoples" (*histoire des religions des peuples non civilisés*). Maurice Leenhardt, a specialist in New Caledonia (see chapter 8), took over Mauss's chair between 1942 and 1950. In other words, non-western religions, including those located in French colonies, were located at the heart of French religious studies, and were studied by sociologists. Some of the leading colonial sociologists published in the journal *Histoire des religions*, created in 1953, and in *Archives de la sociologie des religions*, founded in 1956.[89] Two editors of *Archives de la sociologie des religions*, Le Bras and Poulat, concentrated in their own work on European Christianity, but they were both oriented toward the "classical" French sociology tradition of Durkheim, which entailed a comparative interest in the non-west and "primitive" religions. The third editor, Henri Desroche, worked in Africa.[90] Even in 1969, fewer than 40 percent of the journal's articles focused on metropolitan France.[91] Desroche helped to create the CNRS "Groupe de sociologie des religions," which initiated a vast study of world religions.[92] Berque, Bastide, and Balandier worked extensively on religious phenomena in colonial and postcolonial contexts, focusing on missionaries, messianic movements, and religious nationalisms. Bastide studied Afro-Brazilian religions in what he called the "slave situation" (*la situation esclavagiste*), in analogy to Balandier's "colonial situation."[93] Bastide rejected earlier analyses of Afro-Brazilian religions as "museum specimens" and described the *candomblé* as "a coherent, functional whole" that enabled its members "to coexist, join forces, or cooperate in a communal task."[94] Berque commented on ancient and contemporary Islamic texts, translated the Qur'an, and analyzed the effects of French colonialism on religious movements in Morocco. Balandier's doctoral dissertation examined twentieth-century African religious movements, among whom "opposition to colonialism ... came to be seen as a religious duty."[95]

Overviews of the sociology of religion written during the colonial era did not collapse religion into metropolitan religions or Christianity.[96] Yet more recent overviews and histories of the sociology of religion tend to ignore this foundational research on African religions, Islam, and other religions in colonial contexts.[97] It is particularly regrettable that the sociology of religion became so centered on Christian France just as the metropole was becoming even more religiously diverse due to immigration from the global South.

Related to the sociology of religion was research on *magic, dance*, rites of *possession*, and related cultural practices. Anthropologists had long analyzed these phenomena, but they tended to bracket the role of colonialism. Fanon discussed the "leopard men, snake men, six-legged dogs, zombies, a whole never-ending gamut of animalcules or giants that encircle the colonized with a realm of taboos, barriers, and inhibitions." His thesis was that "the magical structure that permeates the indigenous society has a very precise function." Specifically, magic was "ego boosting" because the "colonist's powers are infinitely shrunk" in comparison, yet it also played a "key regulating role in ensuring the stability of the colonized world."[98] Magical beliefs, Fanon predicted, would disappear after decolonization.

A final subfield with deep roots in colonial and imperial settings is the sociology of *war*. The French empire was riven by warfare throughout the twentieth century, and this became a sociological topos. Robert Montagne trained dozens of colonial officers in social science at his Center for Advanced Studies in Muslim Administration (*Centre des hautes études d'administration musulmane*; see chapter 4), and many of them wrote their memoirs on topics of war, insurrection, and military strategy.[99] Pierre Rondot was an officer-cum-sociologist like Montagne who was introduced to sociology by Montagne. Rondot directed the French Institute of Arab Studies in Damascus after Montagne stepped down and took over Montagne's Center for Advanced Studies in Muslim Administration in 1954. Rondot's writing includes sociological studies of the French African Army and other military themes.[100] Raymond Aron is the most important founder of the modern sociology of war. As the leading Weber specialist in interwar and postwar France, Aron drew on the German tradition of bellicist theory. What is often overlooked is that Aron's work was also grounded in studies of imperialism, empires, and colonies, beginning with his studies of Nazi imperialism, continuing in his analyses of French colonial wars during the 1950s, and culminating in his book on the militarized American "empire" (see chapter 10). Julien Freund, a protégé of Aron, played a central role in introducing postwar French scholars to the work of Carl Schmitt, including Schmitt's theories of war and empire. Gaston Bouthol, who studied in Tunis and Rabat and wrote his *thèse complémentaire* in 1930 on the "social philosophy" of Ibn Khaldun, became the founder after 1945 of a phenomenological sociology of warfare.[101] Some of Pierre Bourdieu's most original early publications, finally, dealt with the forms and effects of the war in Algeria.

French sociology was so strongly oriented toward the overseas colonies and protectorates that the default definition of an "international" orientation was an imperial one. This continued for several years after decolonization. A collection on the international sociology of women edited by Paul-Henry and Marie-José Chombart de Lauwe in 1964, for example, included essays on women in France, Morocco, Ivory Coast, Togo, and Québec; the only other international case studies were from Yugoslavia and Austria.[102] This "imperial" orientation began to fade away in the second half of the 1960s, however, and was soon forgotten.

The Etiology of Erasure

There are at least five factors that explain the obliteration of colonial sociology from disciplinary memory. The first and simplest reason is the underdevelopment of serious research on the history of sociology. Historians of science turned their attention only recently to the social sciences.[103] Intellectual historians have usually discussed sociology as part of larger intellectual movements such as the "revolt against positivism" of the late nineteenth century.[104] Professional historians who have spent a sustained amount of time on sociology have focused on a handful of luminaries: Max Weber, Émile Durkheim, C. Wright Mills, W. E. B. Du Bois.

Nearly all of the full-time workers on the history of sociology are sociologists. There is, of course, nothing wrong in principle with sociologists writing the history of their own discipline. Insiders may be more sensitive to nuances of language and meaning and may have access to informal and hidden historical sources. At the same time, social science disciplines do not provide their students with training in the methods and epistemologies of historiography. American sociologists who write the history of their own discipline, like historical sociologists in general, rarely have sustained intellectual contact with professional historians, including historians of science.[105] In a study of all English language articles on the history of sociology published between 1945 and 2012, Camic found only a handful that relied or commented on archival materials. As Camic argues, this writing is dominated by a "fundamentally ahistorical" genre of disciplinary history that makes "use of the past to legitimize new theoretical projects" by singling out the antecedents of contemporary trends or to serve other presentist concerns.[106] The French literature on Pierre Bourdieu, for example, is so closely linked to efforts to legitimize current positions in French sociology that it could be used to map that entire field. The US-based literature on sociology's history tends toward the celebratory genre, describing the discipline as an ascending arc of progress, or recovering forgotten figures who can serve present political or theoretical needs. Such histories rarely contextualize their object in terms of a full range of intertextual and social influences. Histories of sociology are often completely unsociological in their approach to understanding the effects on science of non-intellectual contexts. Historical elements that do not correspond to the progressive narrative of disciplinary development are excluded; deviant paths are ironed out. This isolation lends an amateurish cast to much disciplinary history, separating it once again from professional historiography.[107] There is a resulting gulf between the work of historians and social scientists even when they are discussing the same author or analytic object.

However, the situation in French sociology is somewhat unique in this regard. One writer noticed already in 1997 that French sociologists "now seem to be infatuated" with the history of sociology.[108] French and Francophone scholars have produced a historiography of sociology of astonishing richness since the 1970s. Currently, there are dozens of specialists in the history of French sociology working in France, Québec, and elsewhere. Seminars are taught in French universities on the history of the social sciences, and the subfield attracts young scholars rather than being mainly the domain of senior scholars. It is also significant that this work is carried out by both sociologists and historians and often involves sustained interaction between the two disciplines.[109] It is a tribute to the genre that it is often impossible to determine whether the authors of these books are sociologists or historians, or from some other discipline. What this means is that the underdevelopment of the history of sociology cannot fully account for the erasure of colonial sociology in the French case.

The second reason for the "amnesia effect" concerning colonial sociology pertains to efforts to impose a particular vision of the discipline as presentist and neo-positivist. Self-reflexivity and historicization are anathema to a science that is committed to presenting itself as forward-looking, productive, and useful. Camic concludes that "scholarship dealing with the history of sociology—and therefore, frequently... with the *ideas* of sociologists in the past—runs sharply against the disciplinary grain."[110] The *spontaneous philosophy of the social sciences* understands its own history as converging on a universal, neopositivist model.[111] If sociology's ideal is an imagined natural science, then there is no need for history or cross-national comparison. As Whitehead wrote, a "science which hesitates to *forget* its founders is lost." According to Pasteur, "science has no country."[112] Past theories are best forgotten; national differences, according to this account, are like the much-mocked Nazi-era "German approach to physics," the *Welteislehre* (World-Ice Theory) or *Glazial-Kosmogonie* (Glacial Cosmogony), promoted as a German antithesis to the "Jewish" theory of relativity.[113] According to the positivist narrative, European sociology was standardized by being aligned with the approach dominant in the United States between the late 1930s and the mid-1960s—the exact period examined in the present book.

Even those who reject spontaneous philosophies of the social sciences often accept the claim that sociology converged on this neopositivist model during the middle decades of the twentieth century. Critics explain the triumph of this approach in terms of resources, power, or "academic imperialism."[114] A more accurate history acknowledges continuing divisions even within American sociology, and sees the "Americanization" of global sociology after 1945 as an uneven process in which *certain* strands of the dominant US formation were embraced by *specific* sociologists who were trying to impose a vision of the discipline as mathematical, technocratic, and policy-oriented, and who saw their own national sociological traditions as outmoded. French colonial sociology was itself divided between a modernist, technological, and applied wing whose work corresponded to the emerging neopositivist definition of social science, and a more humanistic tendency rooted in philosophy, literature, and non-positivist epistemologies.

Defenders of a neopositivist philosophy of the social sciences have other reasons for ignoring the colonial moment. Colonies and empires are rebarbative to this scientific epistemology for some of the same reasons that sociologists long resisted analyzing Nazism and the Holocaust. Colonies and empires are singular and complex, and are incompatible with a version of social science committed to finding uniform and universal laws. Sociologists avoid studying unique, non-repeated events, such as the Scramble for Africa, the Herero genocide, or the forced transfer during the Algerian revolution of a quarter of the colony's Muslim population to resettlement camps. Such singular processes are avoided not only because they are abhorrent, or because they lie too far in the past, but also because they resist being subsumed under general covering laws. Yet again, neopositivist epistemology has been less pervasive in postwar French sociology than in the United States or Germany. So again, we need to look for a different explanation of the suppression of colonial sociology.

A third reason for the lack of attention to colonial sociology is the *repression of colonialism* in European collective memory at large. In 1964, Jacques Berque already diagnosed an ongoing *"therapeutic* forgetting" of prior colonial assumptions in France.[115] Balandier observed that the Algerian War had led to a "turning in upon the Hexagon" (*repli sur l'Hexagone*) among French youth.[116] This was also true of French sociologists, who largely avoided discussing the colonial past after the mid-1960s. The erasure of sociology's colonial moment from collective memory allowed the discipline to evade the wave of criticism directed against anthropology as complicit with colonialism.

It may seem surprising to speak of the repression of colonialism, since critics (including myself) have been writing about European colonial and imperial *nostalgia* for a number of years.[117] Here, we need to distinguish carefully among different historical periods and social locations. The period following World War I and the German loss of the colonies, for example, was one in which European anticolonialism and antiracism were still weak, and far-right ideologies were building toward a new crescendo. It is not surprising, therefore, that colonial melancholia and *revanchisme* gained a sizable following in Weimar Germany and fueled a movement focused on demands to retake the lost colonies. A plethora of colonial exhibitions attracted large crowds in a country with no colonies; monuments to colonial heroes were installed throughout Germany, just as monuments to Confederate heroes were erected across the US South after the Confederacy lost the Civil War.[118] The politics of this period differ markedly from the 1960s in the wake of decolonization. To understand the precipitous collapse of the legitimacy of empire among Europeans, it is important to recall that official circles considered the European empires to be durable through the 1950s, and that wide swathes of the European public still saw empires as desirable (chapter 3). Empires continued to be located at the heart of national self-understandings, social structures, and everyday practices, until the late 1950s. Colonialism then became morally repugnant almost overnight, at least among middle-class and educated circles.[119] Of course, nostalgia for empire and colonial revanchism also remained present in some sectors of the French public after 1960. For most French social scientists, however, the colonial research of the 1930s–1950s came to be tainted with opprobrium, just as colonialism became morally repugnant. Anti-colonialism turned into anti-imperialism and was redirected against the United States and the American Vietnam war.[120] The most likely explanation of French sociology's colonial amnesia thus involves active repression rather than a simple loss of memory.[121]

The fourth reason for colonial sociology's repression is that the stigma attached to disgraced social objects sometimes attaches itself to scientists studying those objects. Research on objects that are considered ugly, dominated, or distasteful can be afflicted with low levels of symbolic capital, through a kind of *epistemic contagion*.[122] Such contagion affected colonial sociology both before and after decolonization. Although Europeans in general were proud of their overseas empires, they were less keen about specific colonies, which were often described disdainfully. This distaste was nurtured by racism. Colonial settlers were scorned by anticolonial Europeans. Sociologists were not immune to these swirling prejudices, and colonial sociologists tended to become contaminated in the eyes of their metropolitan contemporaries. In chapter 10, I will discuss some of the strategies used by colonial specialists to try to vault over these walls of emotional contempt.

The fifth reason for the repression of colonial sociology from disciplinary memory is scientific *metrocentrism*, which requires a focus on Europe or the global North.[123] This stance is related to a division of social-scientific labor in which the global North is assigned to sociology, the global South, and its indigenous peoples and cultures, to anthropology. Such a distribution of ontological turf has always prevailed within modern American academia, but it was disrupted in Europe during the period analyzed here and it continues to be rejected by many scholars in the former colonies. Its result was that after the mid-1960s, sociology's object domain, even in the former colonizing nations, once again became the global North. Due to this redrawing of disciplinary demarcations, colonial researchers or specialists in Africa, Asia, or indigenous America who were defined as sociologists during the colonial era were now reclassified as anthropologists. Thus, for example, a recent study of colonial fieldwork by Berque, Bourdieu, and Servier classifies them as "ethnologists," even though they were all identified as sociologists at the time.[124] Masson and Schrecker's *Sociology in France after 1945* ignores ethnology in its discussion of sociology's relations with other disciplines between 1945 and 1980. The authors register a *rapprochement* between sociology and "anthropological methods" only after 1980, and only in studies of metropolitan France.[125] In fact, such a rapprochement was widespread among colonial social scientists during the postwar era. Figures such as Balandier and Bastide are not mentioned in Masson and Schrecker's book, even though they were the most sought after advisors for postgraduate students at the Sixth Section of the *École pratique des hautes études* between 1960 and 1965.[126] Authors Masson and Schrecker briefly mention Eric de Dampierre for his editorial contributions to sociology, but not for his pathbreaking work in French Equatorial Africa and his decades-long "sociological mission to the Upper Ubangi"—the research that led to his election to a chair in sociology at Nanterre University.

The next three chapters will discuss some of the key "external" contexts for the production of postwar colonial sociology—keeping in mind that external and internal determinants are best construed as interwoven and as existing along a continuum. I will begin in the next chapter with the postwar French context of reestablishing control over the colonies, and then discuss the popularity of the empire after World War II and the spread of colonial instruction into French higher education.

PART II

The Political Contexts of Colonial Social Thought in Postwar France

CHAPTER THREE

Colonial Reconquest, Scientification, and Popular Culture

We knew that decolonization would come sooner or later but we did not think about it any more than about our own death.

—ROBERT DELAVIGNETTE[1]

In 1945 France possessed one of the greatest colonial empires in the history of the world, second only to that of the United Kingdom.

—TYLER STOVALL[2]

THE POSTWAR ERA WAS MARKED by the refortification of the French, British, and Belgian colonial empires. French officials rejected arguments by the likes of Raymond Aron (chapter 11) about the country's obsolescence as a Great Power. They countered that the empire was still viable, at least in the medium term, especially if it could be reformed to become more acceptable to world opinion and perhaps to the colonized. Colonialism remained legitimate and popular among wide swathes of the French public until the end of the 1950s. Colonial governance began to rely more heavily on science and expertise. These are some of the important "external" factors that indirectly stimulated French sociologists' interest in colonialism.

The Simultaneity of Decolonization and Reconquest

The period between 1945 and the early 1960s is often depicted as little more than a prelude to decolonization. Imperial history is read selectively to make the telos of independence appear inevitable at the time. This gesture does not seem to be perturbed by the unassailable work of historians detailing the postwar *reoccupation* of the British and French empires, nor by the fact that Portuguese colonialism lasted until the mid-1970s, the former British settler colonies in Southern Rhodesia and South Africa until 1980 and the 1990s, respectively, and French New Caledonia up to the present. Formal colonialism did, of course, experience dramatic defeats after 1945. Italy lost all of its colonies in the Paris Peace Treaties. Britain signed the Indian Independence Act in 1947. The Netherlands recognized Indonesia's independence in 1949. The French lost Indochina, which was in many ways the crown jewel of its colonial empire, during a nine-year war lasting from 1946 to 1954. Signs of anticolonial pressure were everywhere, starting with the 1947–1949 Malagasy Uprising and the French West African railway workers' strike of 1947–1948.[3] Arguments for ending colonialism arose throughout Africa and were echoed by African American activists and the 1945 Pan-African Congress in Manchester. The Charter of the United Nations declared that the "main task of a colonial power in its colonies was to develop them and to prepare their inhabitants for greater participation in the administration of their own affairs."[4] The United States and the USSR tried to outdo each other with their anticolonial rhetoric, even as the United States underwrote the reconstruction of the European colonial empires and the USSR only began engaging seriously in Africa in 1957, and only in decolonized countries such as Ghana.[5]

Movements toward independence were counterbalanced by *katechontic* efforts to shore up European imperial control.[6] The rising tide of decolonization occurred simultaneously with countervailing actions that historians have dubbed the "second colonial occupation."[7] W. E. B. Du Bois summarized the discussions leading to the United Nations in 1945 as follows: "[t]here emerged a tentative plan for world government designed especially to curb aggression, but also to preserve imperial power and even extend and fortify it."[8] The postwar period marked the final great revival of European colonialism. The French leaders gathered at Brazzaville in January 1944 "wanted above all else to preserve the empire," although they also recognized that "in order to do so, they had to identify colonial rule with progress."[9] By the same token, Britain's decision to quit India "was not intended to mark the end of empire" but "has to be seen in the light of the simultaneous decision to push British penetration deeper into tropical Africa and the Middle East."[10] American opposition to the continuation of European empires had already wavered during the war. The Marshall Plan contributed heavily to development plans in French and British colonies.[11] America did as much to shore up European empires as to dismantle them, through the Suez Crisis and even afterwards.

The decade after 1945 saw large increases in manpower and metropolitan spending on the colonies and a proliferation of branches of colonial government and new forms of expertise being applied in the colonies. Indeed, according to historian John Gallagher, "[n]ot until the nineteen-forties was there a serious version of imperialism in tropical Africa."[12] The number of employees working for colonial regimes rose steadily. The French administration in sub-Saharan Africa was transformed by the "dispatching of young civil servants"—administrators and technicians—including three hundred workers transferred from posts in the collapsing colony in Indochina.[13] Seen from this angle, the 1940s and 1950s marked not so much colonialism's winding down as its reconstruction and its crescendo, in terms of the mobilization of people, machinery, knowledge, and money.

Rising anticolonial sentiment across the world did not lead European colonial officials to view the remaining colonies as being on the verge of independence after the war. The French colonial administrator, historian, novelist, and educator Robert Delavignette wrote that he and his colleagues knew at the time "that decolonisation would come sooner or later but we did not think about it any more than about our own death."[14] At the same time, even while they were working to preserve their empires as long as possible, European elites were also laying the groundwork for maintaining privileged relations with their former territories and ensuring that some troops, civil servants, and scientists could remain in place after independence.[15] In France, the European Development Fund, created after decolonization, was staffed by former French colonial officers and was directly modeled on the Fund for the Economic and Social Development of the Overseas Territories (FIDES), which invested 8 percent of the French national revenue annually in the colonies between 1948 and 1958 (chapter 4).[16] Dozens of bilateral conventions permitted France to keep troops stationed in its former colonies.[17] Many colonial research institutes remained under at least partial French control after independence.[18] French academics, including sociologists, continued to play a leading role in postcolonial universities for years.[19] The thinking was, if independence had to occur, it could at least be guided in directions beneficial to the former colonizers.

Most specialists after 1945 recognized that the colonial world was in crisis. Indeed, crisis was a common theme in sociologists' discussion of postwar colonies.[20] Yet this did not necessarily signal to French leaders that their empire was terminally ill. Instead, they clung ferociously to their colonies. Minister Pleven declared at the end of 1944 that "at this moment, France is doubtlessly more conscious than it has ever been of the value of its colonies." This was no longer simply an economic question, but concerned France's freedom and global standing. Without the empire, one deputy stated in May 1944, France would only be a "liberated" country, but "thanks to its Empire, it is a vanquishing country."[21]

Soon after liberation, France began simultaneously to *euphemize* its empire, invest large amounts of money in the colonies' social and economic development, and reform colonial governance in modest ways.[22] Postwar Senegal illustrates the difference between the interwar and postwar periods:

> Not only did the French government willingly invest in the city's growth because colonial rule in Black Africa was assumed to have a reasonable

future, but also French capitalists invested heavily there. The ingress of private capital into Senegal and Dakar in particular occurred in two waves: first between 1946 and 1949, when there was fear that France might get a Communist government; second, between 1951 and 1954, when capital was withdrawn from Indochina and relocated in Senegal. In a curious way Dakar was perceived as a solid bastion of colonialism, even when its independence from France was but a dozen years away.[23]

Government institutions began to manipulate official terminology in order to obfuscate the colonial character of the empire. This stood in contrast to the emphatic celebration of the language of colonialism between the wars. Yet already in the late 1930s, the word "colonial" started to be replaced with "overseas" (*outre-mer*) in the names of institutions. Such euphemistic parlance became universal after 1945. The French empire itself was rechristened as the "French Union." African subjects gained the right to participate in elections to colony-level assemblies and to a powerless empire-wide parliament—the Assembly of the French Union—that met in Versailles. Plans for a wholesale integration of the empire into France began to be discussed immediately after Liberation. Although French voters rejected the extension of full citizenship to France's sixty million colonized subjects, the discussion kept alive the idea of an "empire of citizens" or a federation that would closely connect France and its overseas territories.[24] The enormous public investments in the colonies, territories, protectorates, and overseas departments after 1945 can only be understood in light of the belief among large segments of the ruling elite that the empire's life could be prolonged for many more years, and perhaps indefinitely, in one form or another.

The Permeation of Colonialism by Experts and Science

During the twentieth century, science and academic expertise came to dominate an imperial cosmos that had first been permeated by explorers and adventurers, then by conquistadors, then by capitalists and settlers. The new colonial empires of the 1880s were forged at the same time as the so-called second scientific revolution.[25] Colonial governments, associations, and businesses already began investing in scientific research at the time. Overseas administrators were spurred to make the colonies economically self-sustaining and governable, eliminate tropical diseases, resolve demographic crises, and create the conditions for European settlement. All of this pointed them toward an *expertification* and *scientification* of colonialism.[26] The pressure to govern colonies scientifically also stemmed from the pressures of the international imperial system. The German threat to French scientific prestige, which led to French educational reforms in the last third of the nineteenth century, penetrated the colonial realm as well. Germans also gained a reputation for colonial scientificity that was not entirely unwarranted.[27] Counterpressures against colonial scientification emanated from the perennial shortage of funds and the old guard of administrators, who stood to lose power vis-à-vis scientific experts. By the late 1930s, however, the balance of power in imperial and colonial affairs had shifted toward scientists and technicians and away from adventurers and conquerors.

The climax of colonial science, including social science, occurred between the late 1930s and the mid-1960s. Engineers, technicians, and scientists became the characteristic cadres of the postwar empires, even if the traditional military, missionary, and capitalist groups also were still present.[28] Technical services rose to 30 percent of the total personnel of colonial states during the 1950s.[29] In many cases, experts "considerably outnumbered the Administration in the field."[30] Colonial experts were trained in both standard universities and specialized schools and worked in colonial research institutes, universities, and governments.[31] The experts contributing to the conduct of colonial affairs ranged from humanistic Arabists and psychiatrists to agronomists and entomologists.[32]

One of the distinctive features of colonial science, including social science, in contrast to traditional science, was its close connections to applied policymaking. As Pierre Singaravélou has shown for the period before 1940, and as I detail here for the post-1940 era, many colonial scientists moved back and forth between the roles of basic scientist, Cameralistic counselor, and government administrator. Scientists' involvement in colonial policymaking sparked intense discussions of the notion of "disinterested" or autonomous scholarship, especially after 1944. This idea had enormous prestige within the French academic field, including among colonial specialists.[33] Pure research was sometimes argued to be especially important with respect to the education of indigenous scholars. As the French colonial minister wrote in a letter to the Governor General of Indochina in 1936, "we have a political interest in steering the indigenous elite toward disinterested studies."[34] Along with the threats of Soviet and McCarthyite politicization of science, postwar French interest in scientific freedom was a response to the repressiveness of the Vichy regime and Nazi Occupation. Colonial scientists, who had the same educational and political backgrounds as their noncolonial colleagues, faced an even more constrained situation around these issues (see chapter 10), but this only served to intensify their interest in academic freedom.

It is nearly impossible to generate a comprehensive list of *all* colonial researchers in France and its overseas empire after 1945. The largest French agency engaged in colonial science in 1945 was the *Office de la recherche scientifique coloniale* (Office of Colonial Scientific Research), soon renamed *Office de la recherche scientifique outre-mer* (Office of Overseas Scientific Research). This organization admitted in 1945 that it was unable to locate the precise boundaries of "colonial" research. Nonetheless, it kept a file on all French researchers with an interest in the colonies. In 1945, this list contained 1,700 names.[35] Employment of colonial specialists by the *Office de la recherche scientifique coloniale* and other organizations (discussed in chapter 5) increased over the next two decades, growing to more than 2,000. In 1900, by contrast, there were only 150 French specialists in colonial questions, according to Singaravélou.[36]

The zenith of scientific engagement in the colonies after the war included the social sciences. Moreover, sociology suddenly emerged as a privileged partner of the empire. Colonial officials and scientific institutions converged around the idea that sociologists could contribute to understanding and managing the colonial crisis and could perhaps help to ward off independence. In 1954, the French Overseas Minister explained to the incoming class at the Paris *École coloniale* that "we are still in the period of . . . social and intellectual crisis" characterized by "the detribalized, urbanized, proletarianized masses, and the rural collectivities, turned upside down by the migrations of workers, the imitation of Whites, the independence of young people, and the new ideas that are destroying the old social conformism and the ancestral understanding of the universe."[37] This total crisis was presented as the reason for the school's decision to include a new six-week course on "practical sociology" in the curriculum. The adjective "practical" signaled an emphasis on ideas that could be directly applied to colonial social problems. Sociology was considered essential for understanding and managing the colonial crisis. Sociology was once again, as in Weimar Germany, a "crisis science," or *Krisenwissenschaft*,[38] and it was also a *Hilfswissenschaft*, an applied science in the American style. The Minister's statement that "we are still" in crisis also signaled a belief in the durability of colonialism, at least in the medium term. The emphasis was still on reform rather than abandonment. This lasted until the late 1950s.

The Legitimacy and Visibility of Empire after 1945

There had been ubiquitous colonial propaganda by official and commercial agencies during the 1920s and 1930s, aimed at persuading the public to buy French colonial products, to think and act in "colonial" ways, and to support the empire.[39] Jacques Berque, who studied in Paris during the 1930s, recalled that "the word spread out everywhere" about the colonial empire as a result of the 1931 Paris colonial exhibition.[40] According to Georges Balandier, the 1931 exhibition, which he visited at the age of 11, led him to connect the memory of several of his ancestors and relatives who had colonial careers to his personal aspirations.[41] Indeed, Balandier traced his eventual decision to embark on a career as a "sociologist of Black Africans" to these youthful experiences.[42]

Because Vichy France lacked control over more than half of the national territory, it attempted to become "an imperial rather than a continental power."[43] The colonies became a "prize with which to entice—and perhaps extract concessions from—Nazi Germany," as well as a "source of French pride after the successive humiliations of 1940."⁴⁴ The Vichy government produced propaganda, press releases, documentary newsreels, leaflets, and textbooks on the colonies.⁴⁵ Colonial exhibits circulated through the country on trains between 1941 and 1944. "Colonial euphoria" and the "fascination with all things imperial" seemed especially strong in the spa town of Vichy, the capital of collaborating France.⁴⁶

The colonies also played a central role in official and popular patriotic discourse during the war and following Liberation. The first Allied strategic victories in the war occurred in North Africa, starting with the British victories over Italian forces in western Egypt and Cyrenaica and subsequent developments in the Western Desert War. British campaigns in East Africa, Syria-Lebanon, and Iran in 1941 were also successful. Operation "Torch" in November 1942 was the "first great Allied enterprise," and the North African campaign that followed was also the first opportunity for the Free French to participate fully in the liberation of their country.⁴⁷ De Gaulle argued that "[i]n the vast spaces of Africa, France could in fact re-create for herself an army and a sovereignty, while waiting for the entry of fresh allies." Africa offered "an excellent base for the return to Europe, and it would be French."⁴⁸ The colonies provided the Free French with bases, soldiers, and sources of legitimacy.⁴⁹ Although most of the colonies fell into Vichy hands in 1940, French Equatorial Africa rallied to the Free French.⁵⁰ Brazzaville therefore became the "capital of the Resistance" and the "imperial centre of French affairs" after rallying to De Gaulle.⁵¹ De Gaulle organized the Brazzaville conference (January–February 1944) to plan political reforms in postwar France. This included promises to end "forced labor and special native legal codes" in the colonies, establish elected territorial assemblies, and represent the colonized in a federal assembly for the entire empire. Independence for the colonies was explicitly rejected, however.⁵² Between 1940 and 1942, most of the French colonies shifted their allegiance to the Free French, either via *ralliement* or as a result of military compulsion.⁵³ The Committee of National Liberation, which eventually became France's provisional government after liberation, was first established in Algeria in 1943.

As a result, the overseas empire was located at the very center of French national self-consciousness in 1945. Proponents of the "minimal impact thesis" point to evidence of widespread ignorance among British and French citizens regarding even the locations and names of their overseas colonies, while others argue that colonialism continued to resonate widely.⁵⁴ Historian Martin Thomas writes that it is "at best doubtful that empire had seized the popular imagination in France."⁵⁵ The semi-official *Revue des troupes coloniales* suggested in 1946 that it was "not certain" that "the French people" possessed "an imperial consciousness."⁵⁶ We might ask, however, what it means, exactly, to seize the popular imagination or to possess an imperial consciousness. French citizens did not have to have extensive or precise information about the colonies in order to possess an "imperial consciousness." In fact, detailed information could have turned the public *against* colonialism. This seems to be partly what happened over the course of the Algerian War, or for that matter, during the American war in Vietnam. However, historian Charles-Robert Ageron has shown that all political parties, the entire metropolitan press, and a majority of public opinion embraced the empire after World War II.[57] Imperial ideology may be most effective when it can draw from a reservoir of emotionally charged phrases and words, images, sounds, and fantasies, rather than basing itself on accurate information.

The French empire was omnipresent in public culture after the war, and it had strongly patriotic connotations. Even the French occupation of southwestern Germany in 1945 featured a symbolic presence of the colonial empire. Although French African troops "were quickly pulled out of Germany after the end of combat" in 1945, France displayed its colonies in Bastille Day parades in cities such as Konstanz. The commander of the French Rhine Danube Army, General Jean de Lattre de Tassigny, received the Moroccan Sultan and the Tunisian Bey in summer 1945 in his villa in Lindau, Germany.[58]

The years immediately following World War II saw the revival of the myth of empire. In a poll conducted in 1949 by the national statistical office, 81 percent agreed that France had "an interest in having overseas territories."[59] Most of the French public had well-formulated opinions about questions such as the wars in Indochina and Algeria. Sixty-two percent of those polled in 1949 "thought France had basically done good work in its colonial mission." At this point, 7.7 percent of the population reported having spent some time overseas, often in the military. In a 1950 survey, 67 percent of French boys said they would be ready to move to North Africa. Even in 1954, after the loss of Indochina, "forty-five per cent still affirmed that it was 'very important' for the other colonies to remain associated with France." In 1957, 22 percent of those surveyed in a national poll still anticipated that they or their children would move to one of the territories of the French Union.[60] The attempted coup d'état of the generals on May 13, 1958, which caused the collapse of the Fourth Republic, was precipitated by the threat of Algerian independence.[61] As with the dissolution of the German Reichstag after its failure to vote credits for continuing war in Germany's Southwest African colony in 1907, one result of metropolitan anticolonialism was a surge of imperialist patriotism on the right.

There was a slow but steady increase in support for granting independence to the colonies, however, reaching 73 percent by February 1959. While only the French Communist Party had "remained loyal to its doctrine of the liberation of the colonized people" after World War II, the Socialists moved closer to supporting independence at the end of the 1950s; centrist parties began to accept a federalist solution.[62] These changes were connected to an increasingly open discussion of the possibility of giving up the empire. In 1957, the cover of the mass circulation magazine *L'Express* asked "Should we keep Black Africa?"[63]

FIGURE 3.1. Image from advertisement for the colonial outfitter DAC, Blvd. Saint-Martin, Paris, in 1953, with accompanying text: "The clothing specialist for colonials." Advertisement from journal *Colo*, published by the *École coloniale* (various dates).

Another problem with the argument that empires were invisible is that increasing numbers of people circulated between France and the colonies. After the Liberation, "4,000 overseas students were present in metropolitan universities," and these "colonial students were the spearhead of anticolonial contestation in the student milieu."[64] Before 1962, 54 percent of those belonging to "higher social-professional" classes had "direct contacts" with the empire or had visited one or more of its territories.[65] Algeria alone had almost a million *colons*, drawn from all social classes. It does not make sense to disregard the views of the French settlers when assessing the visibility of the empire. Nor should we ignore those who visited or worked occasionally in the colonies. And while some settlers and officials became critical of colonialism, they still tended to believe that the empire would last forever—another "thousand years," in the recollections of sociologist Alain Accardo, a critic of colonialism even at the time who was born and educated in Algeria before independence.[66]

Colonial images and ideas remained pervasive after 1945. The city of Bordeaux reintroduced its *Foire coloniale* (Colonial Fair) in 1947 under the name *Foire colonial et internationale*.[67] Advertisements and packaging for colonial products communicated a general sense of exotic coloniality and France's global reach.[68] It was possible to purchase "colonial" automobiles from car dealers, while colonial outfitters sold uniforms, mosquito netting, tuxedos, sirwals (harem pants), and women's hosiery for use in the colonies (figure 3.1). Colonial accoutrements were a normal part of the urban landscape.

Late Colonialism as a Distinct Epoch

This chapter has detailed several generalized determinants of sociologists' interest in imperial and colonial questions between the 1940s and 1960s. Sociology's increased focus on the colonial realm was a function of the general prominence of the empire in the public sphere, among political parties and leaders, and among the "higher social-professional" classes. Many French officials believed that they could prolong the empire's life, perhaps indefinitely. They turned to experts and science to shore up colonialism's stability and legitimacy. This scientific turn resonated strongly with generalized public enthusiasm for science after 1945.[69] Colonial decision-makers also turned to legal experts, who worked on reforming the empire's constitution, and economists, who offered tools for economic development. They also turned to sociologists.

A particularly important part of this causal nexus channeling sociology toward the colonies was the rise of colonial development policies—the topic of the next chapter.

CHAPTER FOUR

Colonial Developmentalism, Welfare, and Sociology

Je suis devenu sociologue avec et par la décolonisation (I became a sociologist because of and as part of decolonization).[1]

—MICHEL MARIÉ

THE YEARS AFTER World War II were marked by a combination of "large-scale, state-directed reform" in France and developmentalist policies in the overseas colonies.[2] The "diffusion of the ideals of the Resistance and Free France had created an environment that was receptive to social reform."[3] The political consensus in 1945 was that laissez-faire liberalism was in disrepute, and that the "French state should serve as pilot and engine for the postwar reconstruction."[4] Postwar social policies, built upon foundations that reached back to the late nineteenth century and the Popular Front, were now "significantly expanded" and became "available to 20 million employees by the late 1940s, up from 7 million in 1944."[5] Spending on the main branches of metropolitan social insurance (sickness, retirement, family, accident, and occupational disease) increased nearly tenfold between 1946 and 1966, adjusted for inflation.[6]

The close connections between colonial developmentalism and the burgeoning welfare state became evident in the Constantine Plan, "a five-year design to create 100,000 new jobs in the metropole for Algerians and a staggering 400,000 new jobs in Algeria itself." Alongside the industrialization plans, the agrarian plans "were no less ambitious: the redistribution of 250,000 hectares of land and a revolution in agricultural methods nurtured by an army of experts, one for every 200 farmers, combined with big irrigation and electrification projects, marsh drainage, and road building." The plan also included "new housing for a million people and schooling for two-thirds of Algeria's boys and girls," as well as "the setting aside of 10 percent of the posts in the civil service in metropolitan France and Algeria for Muslim Algerians."[7]

Sociologist Michel Marié, a member of the sociology section of the *Centre national de la recherche scientifique* between 1953 and 1955, went to Algeria to work on the Constantine Plan. Marié wrote that he "became a sociologist because of and as part of decolonization".[8] In fact, Michel Marié was involved in colonial developmentalism, which was meant to consolidate colonial control rather than to provide a transition to Algerian independence. The Constantine Plan was one of a vast array of colonial development initiatives undertaken by France after 1944, and Marié represents the dozens of French sociologists who were involved in these projects.

This chapter will first reconstruct the history of colonial developmentalism in broad strokes. I will then examine the two aspects of these development programs that strengthened their affinities with sociology: planning and social policy. This cluster of practices around development, planning, and welfare defines a more immediate social context shaping postwar colonial sociology.

Developmental Colonialism

The first three centuries of European overseas colonialism were characterized mainly by predatory practices—genocide, land expropriation, slavery, settlement, plantation agriculture, and resource extraction. The nineteenth century saw a shift in the main geographic focus of European imperialism from the New World to Africa and Asia.[9] The decline of early modern forms of imperialism did not mean, however, that empire suddenly became "developmentalist." Instead, nineteenth-century colonies were viewed as opportunities for the extraction of raw materials, the super-exploitation of labor, and the expansion of markets for European consumer goods. No official action was taken to promote manufacturing in the colonies, which were intended to support and supply European industry rather than competing with it. Although slavery had been largely abolished, forced labor was ubiquitous across European colonies until the mid-twentieth century.[10] There was a bare minimum of public spending for infrastructure, social services, and education. European powers sought improvements only up to the point at which colonies could finance their own operations. And because European colonial holdings in Africa and Asia were too vast and underfunded to be ruled directly by Europeans, the ongoing administration of local societies was carried out primarily by indigenous chiefs and other native intermediaries, under the supervision of European officials.[11] All nineteenth-century colonizers happened upon this system of rule, although it was most famously codified by the British colonizer Lord Lugard as *indirect rule*.[12] The Governor General of French Indochina, Jean Marie de Lanessan, made a similar argument in favor of governing "with the mandarin and not against the mandarin." French administrators referred to this approach as *Lugardisme* or *Associationisme*.[13] Such policies sought to strengthen traditional customs (or, more precisely, invented traditions) in the pursuit of order and stability. Indirect rule therefore made it even more difficult to introduce developmental improvements.¹⁴ Modern colonial empires between 1800 and the 1930s were not so much developmental as extractive and exploitative in economic terms. In the French case, this was captured by the policy slogan of the interwar period, *mise en valeur*, which meant putting the colonies to profitable use.

Nevertheless, there was rising concern among officials during the interwar years about the colonies' economic stagnation. The first response was to try to stimulate private investment. As the prolonged global depression led to growing unrest in the colonies, however, metropolitan officials began to rethink their parsimonious approach and to question the premise that colonial governments should be self-financing.¹⁵

The main policy that emerged from these interwar discussions was *developmentalism*. The doctrine of indirect rule was partly replaced, starting around 1940, by metropolitan funding of infrastructure, industrialization, and social policy, combined with enhanced participation by the colonized in elected political bodies at the local, regional, national, and eventually the empire-wide scale. Colonial development echoed the ongoing "process of European reconstruction" after the war, and was understood "as an alternative to decolonization."¹⁶ This turn to colonial developmentalism nurtured the expansion of sociology in and of the colonies.

The next section provides a brief overview of the discursive and political history of development, before turning to these postwar programs.

The Development of "Development" Until the End of the Colonial Era

Nowadays, social development is connected to interventions by states, nongovernmental organizations, and other actors, guided by the aim of producing "improvement in the conditions and quality of life of the population."¹⁷ This is a relatively recent set of meanings. Development (*développement, Entwicklung, desarrollo*, etc.) remained a synonym for change, improvement, progress, betterment, *Bildung*, and *civilisation* until the eighteenth century.¹⁸ That does not mean that European states did not engage in policies that would later be called developmentalist during the early modern era. Whereas Machiavellian policy sciences focused on the defense of princely sovereignty and traditional hierarchies, and mercantilism emphasized trade, cameralism or *Polizeiwissenschaft* (police or policy science) pursued proto-developmentalist policies, emphasizing promotion of the common weal as key to the welfare of the king and the state's coffers. Cameralistically trained state personnel had the "explicit duty to function predominantly as a dynamic and formative element" in promoting economic growth. Cameralists advocated early versions of social policy, including health care, education, and poor relief.[19] Cameralism, an early modern formation, is the main precursor of twentieth-century developmentalism, even if historians of the two historical formations have largely ignored these connections.[20]

The development concept acquired new accents as part of the political-intellectual resistance to the Napoleonic invasion of Central Europe. Romanticism and conservative political philosophy, German historicism, and national economics defined development as a gradual process with no absolute beginning or endpoint, and without any connection to a generalized definition of progress.[21] Development thus began to refer to processes of immanent or intransitive social change, in explicit contrast to the intentional incitement of change represented by revolution.[22] Realms such as law, language, and culture should be left to develop according to their organic inner logics, unhindered by external interventions, it was argued. This is an important alternative intellectual tradition that is directly relevant to current discussions of postcolonial theory. It was suppressed by colonial-era developmentalism, which was based on deliberate political interventions. Postcolonial theorists have been understandably hesitant to trace their own anti-universalist thinking to German traditions, which are often incorrectly understood as uniformly right wing, or even as precursors of Nazism.[23]

Theories of the possibility of stimulating development prevailed in the more positivist corners of early French and British social science. Saint-Simon suggested that it should be possible to "know with precision the real laws" of social development,[24] defining *développement* as the level of social progress or "civilisation." Saint-Simon also believed it was possible to "impose constructive order upon [the] industrial disorder of the present."[25] This understanding of development was taken up by Auguste Comte, who argued that political interventions could "advance or retard the course of necessary change" by acting "upon the intensity and secondary operation of phenomena" without altering the underlying social laws.[26] John Stuart Mill praised Comte for rejecting the "error of those who ... imagine that neither ... governments by their acts, nor individuals of genius by their thoughts, materially accelerate or retard human progress."[27] Marx combined arguments for the immanence of socioeconomic development and revolutionary change with arguments in favor of deliberate revolutionary or reformist interventions to accelerate the necessary course of events. Overcoming the division between intransitive and transitive definitions of development had important implications for developmental policies.

The idea of development remained antithetical to overseas colonies, however, until the end of the nineteenth century. The idea of "constructive exploitation" began to replace ideas of conquest and plunder, "becoming official policy in 1895."[28] The emerging French colonial "civilizing mission," according to Alice Conklin, encompassed everything from education to the elimination of noxious practices such as slavery.[29] French spending on large colonial public works peaked between the 1890s and 1914, collapsed during the war, and slowly revived in a limited way during the 1920s. In 1921, Colonial Minister Albert Sarraut proposed a program of government loans for colonial infrastructure plans.[30] Although Sarraut's proposal was turned down by the National Assembly, he succeeded in his call for France to embark on a major developmental project, the Office du Niger. This program was ostensibly oriented toward African welfare through the production of rice, but it also served French capitalist interests, focused on cotton production.[31] Christophe Bonneuil writes that "one can locate the birth of the developmentalist state in tropical Africa in the 1930s, when colonial governments confronted the disorders and the threats of the Great Depression, adopted a more *dirigiste* agenda, intervened more directly in the economy, and took steps toward planning and state regulation.[32] Laws were passed in 1932 authorizing loans to colonies to help pay for large public works projects. An "economic conference on metropolitan and overseas France" in 1935 called for "great investments" in order to outfit the colonies with a "complex and costly imperial infrastructure."[33]

This means that there was not one decisive and "first great materialization of the development idea" for colonies during the 1940s, as one writer claims,[34] but rather, a drawn-out series of moves in which new elements were added incrementally. By the early 1930s, a definition of development had crystallized as state policies directed at improving economic performance. What was added over the course of that decade was a melding of the languages of economic development and social welfare, i.e., improvement of "living standards of poor colonies and poor nations through state administration."[35]

Wartime Colonial Development

The movement toward more encompassing understandings of development was not halted by World War II. The colonies' fiscal resources were devastated by the wartime collapse of exports and imports. Colonial policy also became more repressive compared to the interwar years. Forced labor returned even in the colonies aligned with the Free French.[36] The ideological tenor of the French version of fascism led Vichyist colonial governors, who were in the majority at the beginning of the Vichy period, to favor traditional, associationist native policies and to oppose urbanization and industrialization, at least publicly.[37] Yet developmentalism continued to advance. Vichy France and its colonies had a number of "technocrats in power" who developed vast plans for industrializing the colonies, especially in North Africa, even if only a small portion of these plans were realized. Vichy's Colonial Minister, the rabid anti-Semite Admiral Charles Platon, argued in 1941 that "infrastructural works of imperial interest should be financed, if not in their entirety at least primarily, by resources that do not come from the colonies."[38] The Vichy government reinvested in the Office du Niger, which had lost funding during the Popular Front.[39] The 1942 Vichy *Plan d'équipement* led to the creation of colonial public works by forced labor.[40] The Vichyist administration in Algeria built the first section of the trans-Saharan railway, completed dams and irrigation projects, and made "precise plans for educational provision" and "public health improvements."[41] In Indochina, the Vichyist governor "extended his public works programme, increasing road-building and irrigation projects."[42]

At the start of the German occupation of France, only a small number of the colonial governors rallied to the Free French—in Equatorial Africa, New Caledonia, and Tahiti. De Gaulle did not have resources to pursue developmental projects in these colonies. But the fact that De Gaulle's main power base was located in the French colonies (chapter 3) increased the salience of the Empire in the Gaullists' postwar planning. The idea of metropolitan investment in colonial development was discussed at the Brazzaville Conference, which called for industrialization, a weekly day off work, an eight-hour workday, and "public investments to support economic, social, and educational development" as well as health care in the colonies.[43] The working committees at the Brazzaville conference included "family and social customs and labor," "education," and "hygiene and public health."[44] The French were also eager to seem to be making "a new departure" in the "promises of wider citizenship offered to French colonial subjects."[45] According to Frederick Cooper, the "issue of extending the category of citizen across the empire.... was on the table as early as 1943," and "most participants in the discussion were aware that one could not go back to colonial business as usual."[46] Once the French Committee of National Liberation gained control over the administration of Algeria in 1943, it quickly produced a social reform plan containing "educational provision, public health improvements and support for industrial diversification."[47] In neighboring Morocco and Tunisia, the Residents-General promised infrastructural improvements "to improve rural living standards" and as an alternative to political and constitutional reform.[48] One of the sociologists directly caught up in this movement at the end of the war was Jacques Berque, whose program for combining collectivized agriculture with social welfare is discussed in chapter 12.

The Postwar Takeoff in Colonial Developmentalism

The war marked a more decisive turning point toward to a series of unprecedented practical interventions—a veritable "development crusade," as the journal *Empire* of the British Labour Party's Fabian Colonial Bureau called it in 1947.[49] The French *Fonds d'investissements pour le developpement économique et social des territoires d'outre-mer* (Fund for the Economic and

Social Development of the Overseas Territories), or FIDES, was created in 1946. Between 1948 and 1958, FIDES invested one trillion francs, or 8 percent of the national revenue, in the overseas territories.[50] Algeria, Morocco, and Tunisia were covered by the separate plans for the French metropole.[51] Another fund specifically for agricultural development (*Fonds d'équipement rural et de développement économique et social*, FERDES) was added in 1949. Specific four-year development plans were created for French West Africa and other colonies.[52]

Several factors underpinned the postwar emphasis on colonial developmentalism. Metropolitan populations had become more aware of the colonies, while political rulers believed their empires were indispensable for maintaining national prestige (chapter 3). After 1945, France needed its empire as a source of raw materials and dollar earnings.[53] The new colonial policies marked a repudiation of "the old system of budgetary autonomy" and self-financing.[54] Traditional colonial commercial circuits had been disorganized by the war. Other factors contributing to the developmentalist push included the debt France owed to its colonial subjects who had participated heavily in wartime fighting; the rise of African branches of metropolitan political parties and labor unions, coupled with early independence struggles; and pressure from the United States and the United Nations to decolonize or at least democratize the overseas dependencies.

Another factor undergirding postwar colonial developmentalism was the unprecedented developmental push within the metropolitan economies.[55] In France, the authoritarian *dirigisme* of the Vichy state was transformed into postwar policies of planning and nationalization, framed as economic development.[56] The metropolitan French plans provided the immediate framework for the colonial modernization funds. The intense focus on modernizing French industrial and agricultural *équipement* (infrastructure) in the first French Plan (the "Monnet Plan") in 1946 was echoed in the FIDES legislation, which also focused on "équipement."[57] The logic of the Monnet Plan recalled earlier colonial developmentalism insofar as it was intended to "modernize the economy to the point where it could correct its payments deficit [to the United States] and generate its own investments" and to "walk alone" without the help of the United States, as Monnet put it.[58]

Social science, including sociology, was present in the postwar French Plans from the start. And the colonies were fully encompassed within this nexus of social science and planning. This refutes arguments that French sociology's breakthrough to resources came with the Fifth Republic (1958) or the Fourth Plan (1962–1965).[59] French sociologists were involved in promoting collective agriculture, resettling Africans in modernized villages, and in building vast urban housing projects such as those associated with the Constantine Plan.[60]

Colonial Welfare and Social Policy in the Context of Developmentalism

The aspect of developmentalism perhaps most closely connected to sociology was its emphasis on social policy. Medicine, social hygiene, labor regulation, and welfare policies were some of the most contradictory realms of colonial intervention. Some of these policies reached back to the late nineteenth century. Although the first colonial medical stations were set up to treat settlers, officials, and soldiers, Europeans soon recognized the need for hygienic interventions among the colonized, if only to protect themselves from contagious diseases and to prevent epidemics among the labor force. French Equatorial Africa, which had high rates of labor recruitment in the mining, forestry, and plantation sectors, established regulations for apprenticeships in 1926 and fixed legal minimum wages as early as 1920—although these latter were "automatically understood by employers" also "as a maximum wage."[61] The French colonial welfare state in Indochina began in 1904 with the creation of a Health Directorate, whose programs eventually "domesticated the most serious manifestations of tropical pathology." The French went on to create a "solid infrastructural network" of hospitals, research centers, and medical education in Indochina.[62] In the first decades of the French protectorate in Morocco, the French Resident, General Lyautey, "had indigenous affairs posts built on the borders of dissident zones" and "these military posts included a free health clinic and a weekly market (*suq*) where the French would pay inflated prices for the livestock or other wares nearby tribes wanted to sell."[63] In Algeria, French colonial physicians and surgeons "eradicated endemic disease and improved sanitary conditions."[64]

The French empire had already seen a gradual turning "from liberalism to welfarism" during the interwar years.[65] The "French social week" (*semaine sociale de la France*), an annual conference sponsored by the Catholic Church, dedicated its 1930 meeting to "the social crisis" incited by colonization. When the Popular Front government took power in 1936, it advocated reforming rather than abolishing the empire. The Socialist Party Congress in 1936 called for the "application of French social legislation overseas," among other reforms.[66] Socialist Colonial Minister Marius Moutet tried with limited success "to extend parts of the Front's social legislation to the colonies and to wind down forced labor" and encouraged a shift to more direct metropolitan spending, although the Assembly blocked his proposal for a Colonial Economic Development fund.[67] In Gabon, the colonial administration "enacted a number of regulations concerning the treatment of labor in the camps" for the timber industry, and "began to conduct inspection tours."[68] In Morocco, the French created a network of public job placement offices patterned on the metropolitan *bourses du travail*, beginning operations in 1921.[69] The French Residency deployed an entire "médico-social welfare state" that was "intended to preserve the health of the Moroccan population and prevent anticolonial rebellion."[70] Hospitals and medical research centers were concentrated in the colony's more urbanized centers but were also strewn across the hinterlands. As in the metropole, private charities complemented the public welfare apparatus.[71]

There were advances in colonial social policy immediately following the Liberation. In 1946, the Colonial Minister demanded that all colonial governors create social service organizations dedicated to social work and social surveys.[72] A delegate at the Provisional Consultative Assembly in 1945 argued that France's social laws would have to be extended to its overseas colonies.[73] The FIDES and FERDES programs included spending on social policies and services.[74] Around 18 percent of total FIDES spending and loans were directed at social programs between 1946 and 1956, and around 21 percent between 1956 and 1960.[75] By the mid-1950s, French social legislation had been partially extended to the colonies, including laws on health care, retirement pensions, and family allocations. By 1956, there were "more than 20 *secrétariats sociaux*" (Social Service Offices) in various French colonies, and the number of social workers was increasing.[76] Unemployment relief, which was the most politically contested program in the metropole, was sometimes provided in French colonies.[77] The relative balance between coercion and assistance in colonial governance was shifting.

International organizations reinforced this emphasis on social policy. In 1944, the International Labor Organization formed a committee on social policy in the "non-metropolitan territories," and in 1947 it "demanded higher commitment from member nations" to "social policy" in colonies.[78] In 1949, the United Nations sponsored a series of studies of social problems in the colonies.[79] The Commission for Technical Co-operation in Africa, an international organization created in 1947, held conferences on "rural welfare in Africa."[80]

What is important in the present context is the reliance of colonial governments and other organizations on sociologists. This was based on sociology's long-standing association with questions of poverty, labor, and "social problems," and with expertise in reform measures, from social insurance and labor legislation to charity. Sociologists were active in colonial development measures directed at consumption, poverty, housing, family structure, and migration. The Le Playsian sociologist Joseph Wilbois (see chapter 8) discussed social work in the colonies in the 1930s and 1940s.[81] The *Service des affaires sociales d'outre-mer*, which hired people with diplomas in nursing and social work, also sponsored social research and pilot studies in the colonies.[82] Some French social workers were educated as nurses in France and received additional training in social work and sociological research in the colonies.[83] Simonne Crapuchet, a French social worker in the Ivory Coast during the 1950s, conducted studies, described as sociological, on African women's personal budgets and their aspirations relative to spending, marriage, and electoral participation. There was also movement between medicine and social research at more advanced levels. Colonial officials received some training in tropical medicine. Medical doctors were included in colonial research institutes and social survey projects. The boundaries between social science and medicine were particularly fluid in colonial psychology and psychiatry (chapter 6).

Three examples from the 1950s illustrate the interaction between social scientists and medical specialists in the French colonies. The first involves the *Centre d'études et d'informations des problèmes humains dans les zones arides* (Center for Studies of Human Problems in Arid Zones). This research organization, based in Algeria, studied medical welfare, job selection, work productivity, and cultural adaptation to capitalist industrialization among inhabitants of the French regions of the Sahara. Its director, Francis Borrey, was a former colonial army surgeon who created mobile care units in Niger to fight tuberculosis, founded a hospital, and was elected as a representative of Niger in the Assembly of the French Union (1947–1953).[84] The projects and conferences organized by the *Centre d'études et d'informations des problèmes humains dans les zones arides* brought together medical specialists, demographers, anthropologists, and psychologists. Its conference in Algiers in 1960 included lectures by (1) a doctor from the colony's Pasteur Institute; (2) the Centre's full-time ethno-sociologist, Joseph Petit; and (3) the leading French quantitative sociologist, Jean Stoetzel.[85] The same year, this organization carried out a "medical-social study" among the semi-sedentarized Mekhadma "tribe," located near Ouragla in the Algerian Sahara. This involved investigation of social structures, "anthropology" (physical measurements), public hygiene, employment aspirations and work, emigration patterns, and education. The study also included a detailed series of "psycho-technical" (i.e., intelligence) tests, which were correlated with sociological factors said to influence performance on the tests (see chapter 6, figures 6.2–6.5).[86]

The second example of interdisciplinary interaction between social scientists and medical personnel is the *Mission démographique de Guinée*, carried out in 1954–1955. This survey of the Guinean population was sponsored by the French Statistical Service, INSEE, but its participants also included sociologists, statisticians, administrators, and most important here, members of the Medical Service of French West Africa (see chapter 7).

The third example is an individual scholar, Anne Retel-Laurentin.[87] She was a doctor specializing in tropical medicine whose colonial career began with studies of demography and family budgets in French Soudan in 1956–1957. In 1958, Retel-Laurentin moved to the French colony of Ubangi-Chari, where she collaborated with Eric de Dampierre on the "Sociological Mission to the Upper Ubangi." The funding for this project was originally directed toward solving the perceived problem of falling birthrates among Nzakara women, creating a sedentary peasantry in the colony, and investigating family budgets.

De Dampierre told the funding agency that it would be imperative to include a medical doctor in the "mission to study the depopulation of the country."[88] Retel-Laurentin participated in three of De Dampierre's annual "sociological missions to the Upper Ubangi" between 1957 and 1961, focusing her attention on questions of kinship, fecundity, birth rates, infancy, sexual relations, and marital stability. By partially alleviating local women's health problems in Upper Ubangi, Retel-Laurentin generated African support for De Dampierre's larger research project. In this instance, the social service orientation of late French colonialism contributed materially to the development of colonial sociology and to its generalized interdisciplinarity. Retel-Laurentin's doctoral thesis, an "ethno-medico-sociological" study of the Nzarka, established her reputation as a medical anthropologist.[89]

Sociology as a Colonial Welfare Science

The embrace of sociology by colonial administrators and funding agencies was closely tied to colonial developmentalism, particularly to programs concerned with "welfare." The next chapter will turn to a somewhat more immediate context for the production and distribution of colonial sociology: institutions of higher education and social research.

CHAPTER FIVE

Colonialism, Higher Education, and Social Research

The colonial phenomenon appears to us today as the central phenomenon in the history of the world.

—S. CHARLÉTY, RECTOR OF THE ACADEMY OF PARIS (1931)[1]

France's role is no longer military and cultural imperialism. France's role is to promote the barely known cultures that make Black Africa one of the most amazing ensembles of humanity. And, to fulfill this role, it is advisable that the many trained sociologists and ethnographers study this part of the world and illuminate its institutions, customs, languages.

—MARCEL GRIAULE, "L'ACTION SOCIOLOGIQUE EN AFRIQUE NOIRE" (1948)[2]

THE PRECEDING CHAPTERS DISCUSSED some of the factors that shaped colonial sociology from a greater social distance, including colonial re-occupation, scientification, popular approval, and developmentalism. In order to understand the place of colonialism in sociology, we also need to situate the social sciences within the development of higher education and research institutions in France and its colonies. As Wagner and Wittrock observe,

> One of the characteristics of modern science is its organized form in separate knowledge-producing institutions. These institutions, their internal structure and their relations to society at large, cannot be taken for granted in a sociology of the sciences but are one of its key problematiques. Even if the day-to-day activities of scientists at work were hardly distinguishable from other social activities—a claim some scholars have raised based on ethnomethodological and interactionist research—still the location of these activities in particular institutions makes for sociologically relevant differences.[3]

This chapter examines the role of educational and research institutions in the efflorescence of colonial sociology between the late 1930s and the mid-1960s. Specifically, I will discuss the expansion of colonial courses of study in higher education, the emergence of an archipelago of research organizations dedicated to research on and in the French colonies, and the support given by American and global organizations to French scholars of colonial phenomena. These factors provided material and symbolic resources, clients, audiences, and general encouragement to sociologists who chose to focus on colonialism and empire.

Colonialism and Sociology in Higher Education, 1930s–1960s

In order to understand the consolidation of a sociology of colonialism, we need to situate the social sciences within higher education and understand the institutional contexts in which colonial instruction was delivered. After briefly presenting the development of the universities and *grandes écoles*, I will examine colonial studies in various schools, the training of colonial administrators, and the creation of universities in the colonies.

There is a vast literature on the rise of the modern French university, its transformations after World War II, and the place of research, including social research, in these institutions.[4] The story of the social sciences takes place primarily in the Letters faculties. By 1854, there were 15 Letters faculties in France. Each was "accorded five identical chairs—philosophy, history, ancient literature, French literature and foreign literature."[5] The idea of "science" began gaining support in the first decades of the Third Republic. The traditional focus on style and rhetoric in literary studies gave way to the more rational literary procedure known as "explication de textes."[6] These preconditions allowed the social sciences to "invade" the Letters faculties at the end of the nineteenth century.[7] Starting in 1880, students could earn part of the *licence* (bachelor) degree in Letters in a specialized field. By 1894, one of the two written examinations for the *licence* was allowed to treat an individual research topic. In 1907, the written Latin thesis was abolished.[8] A new system was created in 1920 wherein the *licence* degree required four specialized certificates.[9] Chapter 9 will reconstruct trends in the numbers of sociology certificates, which were part of philosophy *licence* degrees, as well as doctorates in philosophy with a sociology focus.

What we are interested in here is specifically colonial studies. Instruction in colonial social sciences began during the 1880s and 1890s. Since "colonization was considered from the beginning as a cultural phenomenon," scholars in the human sciences "were located at the heart of the Third Republic's colonial project."[10] A number of institutions of higher education offered courses, public lectures, degrees, and certificates in colonial social science. Historian

Pierre Singaravélou tallies around 700 doctorates written on colonial questions in the juridical, economic, and political fields during the entire Third Republic and estimates that there were 148 French university professors oriented toward these colonial social sciences between 1871 and 1940.[11] Bordeaux University offered the first certificates in colonial studies, starting in 1902, and delivered *licence* degrees in colonial studies from 1936. In 1945, the University of Paris began offering a *licence* in colonial studies. Several human science disciplines, discussed in the next two chapters, developed distinct colonial specializations, with dedicated journals and professorial chairs.

The universities in the colonies were, for obvious reasons, even more oriented toward colonial studies. The literature on metropolitan science, social science, and the scholarly explosion after 1945 has largely ignored parallel developments in European overseas empires. The Brazzaville Conference called for increasing the number of Africans earning advanced education and degrees so they could assume leading positions in their countries. A report on the modernization of the colonies in 1949 recommended that "the number of African students sent to France be increased" and also that "institutions of higher education in Africa be developed rapidly."[12] France already had universities in Algeria and Indochina, and planning began immediately after the war for a university in Dakar, which opened on the eve of decolonization. A new university was created in Madagascar, beginning operations just after independence. In Morocco and Tunisia, there were Institutes of Advanced Study (*Instituts des hautes études*) that played the role of universities, delivering French upper-level diplomas under the supervision of the University of Paris.[13] Both of these North African institutions formed the core of the universities that emerged shortly after independence (1957 in Morocco, 1960 in Tunisia).[14] All of these colonial institutions of higher education offered instruction in sociology and other social sciences.[15]

With the exception of the University of Algiers, these colonial institutions were subordinated to metropolitan universities, which controlled their administration, curriculum, and examination grading. Colonial universities were therefore participants—dominated participants—in the same academic and scientific fields as their metropolitan counterparts. Teaching staff, students, and researchers circulated between metropolitan institutions and colonial outposts. Metropolitan scholars were sent to colonies for examination committees and lectures and to write policy reports on educational and scientific reforms.

The University of Algiers, created in 1909, had the same official status as metropolitan universities, and was ranked third among French universities in the 1950s.[16] There were 2,258 students at Algiers in 1937, 429 of them in Letters.[17] Almost all of the students at Algiers before the war were Europeans, but the number of Algerian students grew steadily after 1945. The University of Algiers "defined itself from the start as being specialized in teaching colonial science."[18] The Law School taught Algerian legislation, Muslim law, and indigenous customs, in addition to the standard curriculum of the metropolitan law faculties.[19] Other courses of study included colonial geography, living oriental languages, colonial history, colonial geography, and ethnography.[20] Most interestingly in the present context, the University of Algiers was one of the first universities in the world (alongside Berlin University, London School of Economics, and Yale) to offer specialized courses in the *sociology* of colonies. The Letters faculty was founded by Emile Masqueray, a proto-sociologist and pioneer of Kabyle studies, and a creator of the so-called Kabyle myth.[21] Masqueray taught a lecture course on comparative colonization starting in 1886, at the instigation of the colony's Governor General. Masqueray's replacement in the Letters faculty, the historian Edouard Cat, lectured on the colonization of Madagascar and Algeria during the 1890s.[22] The sociologist René Maunier took over instruction in colonial and Algerian sociology between 1919 and 1924, before moving to a chair at the University of Paris Law faculty that was relabeled as a chair in "general and colonial sociology" in the 1930s.[23] Georges-Henri Bousquet, at the University of Algiers Law School, taught North African economics and sociology after Maunier's departure. Pierre Bourdieu taught the course in *morale et sociologie* (ethics and sociology) that counted as one of the certificates for the philosophy degree in 1957–1960 at the University of Algiers. Bourdieu was replaced by the ethno-sociologist Jeanne Favret-Saada, who arrived in Algeria in 1959.[24]

In addition to the regular academic departments, other institutions at the University of Algiers offered courses in colonial social science. The *Institut des sciences administratives, sociales et coloniales* (Institute of Administrative, Social, and Colonial Science) offered courses in "sociology, colonial law, and colonial economics" and "North African sociology."[25] This institution operated between 1947 and 1949, when it closed due to overlap with the Algiers branch of *Sciences Po* (the *Institut d'études politiques*).[26]

The French university in Hanoi opened in 1902 as a medical school, but schools of education and business were soon added, along with sections in literature, sciences, and law, in 1917. Nearly all of the students were Vietnamese. In 1945, the Letters faculty had nine different departments, including one in "sociology and anthropology."[27] The other key institution for the human sciences in French Indochina was the *École française d'extrême-orient* (French School of the Far East), created in 1900 as a "pluridisciplinary" advanced studies institute with an emphasis on Orientalism, philology, and archaeology.[28] Unlike other colonial research institutions at the time, the *École française d'extrême-orient* had several indigenous (i.e., Vietnamese) members, including the literary scholars Lê D' and Nguyễn Văn Tố and the ethno-sociologist Nguyễn Văn Huyên, who was hired as a full-time researcher in 1940.[29]

The Tunis *Institut des hautes études* (Institute of Advanced Studies) was founded in October 1945. Like the Institutes of Advanced Studies in Dakar and Morocco, this school was placed under the supervision of the University of Paris.[30] It was the core of the future university in Tunis, which opened in 1960. The Institute had 1,092 students in October 1950, 1,595 in 1951, 1,934 in 1952, 1,473 in 1953, and 1,542 in 1954.[31] Two-thirds of the students in 1948 were Muslim Tunisians; the other third were labeled in official statistics as French, Jewish (i.e., Tunisian Jews), Italian, etc.[32] According to the Tunisian career counseling center in 1953, most Tunisian students were interested in teaching careers, particularly in Letters. Enrollments in the Letters faculty increased at a faster rate than in the other faculties through the 1950s.[33] Following the metropolitan model, social science emerged within the Letters faculty, which was initially directed by geographer Jean Despois and then by the historian-cum-sociologist Pierre Marthelot. Starting in 1953, the Letters faculty published *Cahiers de Tunisie* (*Tunisian Journal*), whose subtitle was "revue des sciences humaines" (*Journal of the Human Sciences*). In 1957, the Letters section began offering instruction in sociology and sociology *licence* degrees. Sociologist Jean Cuisenier, whose research focused on underdevelopment in Tunisia, taught at the Tunis Institut starting in 1956. Georges Granai, a sociological ethnographer specialized in cities, directed the Tunis sociology program from 1958 to 1965. The Durkheimian sociologist Jean Duvignaud was a *chargé de cours* at the Tunis Institut; Claudine Chaulet was *attaché de recherche* (research associate).[34] The most famous instructor in Tunis was Frantz Fanon, who taught the first cohort of sociology students in 1959–1960.[35]

SCHOOLS TRAINING COLONIAL ADMINISTRATORS AND COLONIAL SOCIAL SCIENTISTS

Five other Parisian institutions of higher education offered instruction in colonial social science, including sociology: *Sciences Po*, the *École coloniale*, the *Centre des hautes études d'administration musulmane*, the *École nationale d'administration*, and the Sixth Section of the *École pratique des hautes études*. The first four schools also trained administrators for the colonies.

Institute of Political Studies (Sciences Po)

The Paris institution known as *Sciences Po* illustrates the impact of the postwar reorientation toward new forms of colonial policy.[36] *Sciences Po* was created as *l'École libre des sciences politiques* (The Liberal School of Political Science) in 1871. It was a private institution whose main mission was preparing candidates for the examinations for upper state administrative positions. The school was designed "to keep the *grande bourgeoisie* from losing its primacy and its social prestige by insuring that it remained a functional elite."[37] As a result, *Sciences Po* became "entirely dependent on the bureaucracies that it served."[38] Its governing body was dominated by leaders of the economic and political fields, and its teaching staff consisted mainly of practitioners— "active economists, journalists, financiers, and diplomats."[39] *Sciences Po* was the first French institution of higher learning "to officially welcome instruction in the 'colonial sciences,'" starting with chairs in colonial geography and comparative colonial systems, in 1886.[40] The school's annual guidebooks listed the "careers for which the *École* prepares students" in order of importance and prestige, starting with the State Council and Inspection of Finances and descending to overseas careers, including the General Government of Algeria, the Tunisian and Morocco Protectorates, and civil service in French West Africa and Indochina. Between 10 and 20 percent of the school's course offerings and 13 percent of the articles published in the school's journal, *Annales*, concerned colonial topics.[41] Most of the courses on Morocco, Algeria, and Tunisia and "administrative life in France and the colonies" were taught by former colonial administrators or members of the French Council of State, the most powerful sector of the French administration.

Sciences Po was criticized in the wake of the Liberation in 1944 as "a caste school" linked to monopoly "trusts" that had been a "hotbed of collaboration" during the Occupation. This led to its nationalization in 1945.[42] However, there was notable continuity in the school's emphasis on colonial instruction. In his remarks at the reopening ceremony, the new director of *Sciences Po* listed colonial politics as one of four key areas that would be taught at the reconfigured institution. Whereas lecturers before 1945 had emphasized the empire's economic and political aspects, more attention was now paid to social and cultural issues and colonial development. This was partly a function of the inclusion among the school's instructors of academic specialists in sociology and ethnology. Among the new teachers were René Dumont, a specialist in African cooperatives, Henri Brunschwig, a professional colonial historian, and Jean Dresch, a colonial geographer and anticolonialist member of the French Communist Party.[43] Georges Balandier lectured at *Sciences Po* starting in 1952 on social research applied to colonies and "underdeveloped countries." Ironically, Balandier lectured in an amphitheater named after Leroy-Beaulieu, who "had exalted the virtues of colonialism."[44] This fact encapsulated the mix of colonial politics among the instructors at postwar *Sciences Po*, which ranged from conventional, to liberalizing, to fiercely anticolonial.

L'École coloniale

The Paris *École coloniale* (Colonial School), established in 1889, had evolved from a simple training school for colonial administrators and magistrates into an institution that aspired to be recognized as a *grande école*. The *École coloniale* trained 15 percent of colonial administrators in 1907 and 21 percent in 1921, competing mainly with *Sciences Po*. During its seven decades of existence, the *École coloniale* educated 4,500 colonial civil servants.[45] It was officially renamed *École nationale de la France d'outre-mer* (National School of Overseas France) in 1934, in one of the first official efforts to euphemize the empire. I will refer to it as the *École coloniale* throughout, following the practice of its students and faculty.

The *École coloniale* was initially "less an educational institution . . . than a training center for one Ministry—the Ministry of Overseas France." The training was focused on inculcating "moral" values and orientations into future administrators, such as the ability to command.[46] The school's other roles were training colonial police, prison wardens, magistrates, businessmen, and after 1945, labor inspectors. Initially, all of the students at the *École coloniale* were required to earn a *licence* in law before applying. The school's entrance examinations were reformed in 1927 by the new director, historian Georges Hardy, who began referring to the institution as "the colonial university of France."[47] Preparatory classes for the school's entrance exams were now taught in several French *lycées*, as was done for the other *grandes écoles*.[48] The move toward higher scholarly standards was part of a general transition from the "legal era" of the *École coloniale* to its "university era," in the words of the director after 1937, Robert Delavignette.[49] The *École coloniale* began to invite students enrolled at other *grandes écoles* and universities to attend its public lectures.[50] Although the *École coloniale* never had more than six permanent professorial chairs, an increasing number of its courses were taught by visiting university professors, in contrast to the earlier years, when retired colonial administrators had done most of the teaching.

These improvements went hand in hand with raising the profile of the human sciences in the school's curriculum and ending the domination of the law professors.[51] The *École coloniale* was associated from the beginning with the ideal of "scientific colonization." A plan for a French *licence* degree in colonial studies emerged from discussions between *École coloniale* officials and members of the Colonial Ministry. This project came to fruition in 1945.[52] It now became routine for students to be admitted to the Colonial School after two years of *lycée* study toward the Colonial Studies degree.[53] Those who were admitted to the *École coloniale* were required to perform a yearlong internship (*stage*) in a colony, under the authority of the colony's governor, during their second year of studies. The third year of studies was devoted to practical training in colonial research and administration. The ultimate goal of the entire curriculum was to train colonial functionaries who were "cultivated" and "curious about research," in the words of the Colonial Office in 1945.[54]

The *École coloniale* also placed an increasing emphasis on sociology. In 1937, the school began offering courses on "sociology applied to colonization" and "the sociology and ethnology of Black Africa."[55] In 1951, the French Overseas Ministry recommended that the *École coloniale* introduce several new disciplines, particularly in the social sciences.[56] The culmination of the move toward social scientific expertise was the appointment of Paul Mus as director in 1946. Mus was a brilliant specialist in Vietnam and De Gaulle's main advisor on Indochina and East Asia during the Second World War.[57] Mus insisted that colonized populations now expected "social and political forms . . . inspired by those existing in France." This convergence between metropole and colonies

FIGURE 5.1. Building façade of *École coloniale* (2, avenue de l'Observatoire, Paris) from Bibliothèque nationale de France, Agence Meurisse (BNF website).

meant that students at the *École coloniale* should also undertake internships in France or other advanced countries, and not just in the overseas colonies.[58] The overseas internship was lengthened to eight months in 1950, and there was a second, shorter internship in the metropole.[59] In 1956, a number of *École coloniale* students signed a petition denouncing the school's curriculum as obsolete and "imperialist" and demanding more "serious economic and sociological training."[60] An entire group of *École coloniale* graduates went on to "distinguish themselves in the human sciences."[61]

Enrollments at the *École coloniale* began to decline after the closing of the school's Indochina section in 1954 following Vietnamese independence. A further decline resulted from the 1956 Framing Law (*loi-cadre*), which called for the Africanization of administration in the overseas territories. The *École coloniale* began accepting indigenous students for training as colonial administrators in 1957. Two years later, on the eve of independence for most of the

FIGURE 5.2. Grand Hall in the *École coloniale*, from *École Nationale de la France d'Outre-Mer* (Paris: Librairie Vuibert, 1955), 4.

French African colonies, the school stopped accepting new students. A new institution, the *Institut des hautes études outre-mer* (Institute of Advanced Overseas Studies) opened in the *École coloniale* building on the avenue de l'Observatoire and began training Africans to run their own countries. The number of African students increased rapidly at the outset. The Institute of Advanced Overseas Studies was transformed again in 1966, becoming a school for training all foreign students in public administration. This institution was fused with the *École nationale d'administration* (National School of Administration) in 2002, marking the final demise of the *École coloniale*.

École nationale d'administration

The *École nationale d'administration* (ENA) was created in 1945 as part of the "revolutionary situation of the Liberation" and in response to a long-standing project of creating a national training school for state administrators.[62] The school's original goal was to democratize the French elite by wresting the monopoly over their training and recruitment away from *Sciences Po*. This plan was soon scaled back.[63] Those responsible for colonial instruction at ENA included Pierre Rondot (see below); the progressive historian of North Africa, Charles-André Julien; and the ethno-sociologist, Jean Poirier, who co-authored the widely read *Ethnologie de l'Union française* with André Leroi-Gourhan. The most important aspect of ENA in the present context is its involvement in colonial training between 1945 and 1962. In 1945, ENA obtained the right, previously monopolized by the Colonial School, to train the Algerian Civil Service and the Corps of Civil Controllers for Tunisia and Morocco.[64] Between 1947 and 1955, 170 of its students carried out internships in the North African colonies. Dozens of its graduates went on to careers in the Tunisian, Moroccan, and Algerian administrations.[65] As part of their degree, ENA students were required to carry out so-called *stages de dépaysement* (internships of *denationalization* or *deprovincialization*). Half of these interns went to North Africa, mainly to Algeria, after 1955.

Centre des hautes études d'administration musulmane and Robert Montagne

The *Centre des hautes études d'administration musulmane* (CHEAM), or Center for Advanced Studies in Muslim Administration, was involved in training colonial administrators and officers and producing social knowledge about an array of practical colonial problems, ranging from insurgency to social welfare. It was created in 1936 by the Popular Front's Foreign Affairs Ministry, and was directed by Robert Montagne.[66] Montagne's education began in 1911 when he entered the French Naval School. Montagne then participated in the Rif War (1920–1927), and together with his brother, conducted the negotiations that led to the surrender of Abd el-Krim in 1926, leading to the end of that war. His military service lasted from 1919 to 1921, at which time he was swept up into Lyautey's governing cabinet in Morocco and appointed to the position of Counselor to the French Residency and director of the "Ethnological and Sociological Section" in the colony's Indigenous Affairs Office. Montagne was charged with carrying out ethnographic surveys among the tribes of the Rif Mountains. In addition to his research projects, some of which pertained to French military campaigns, Montagne taught at the *Institut des hautes études marocaines* in Rabat between 1924 and 1930 and published in that school's journal, *Hésperis*.

Montagne's scientific career took off after he published his doctoral thesis on relations between Berber tribes and the *Makhzen*, the Moroccan central state, in the Durkheimian series *Travaux de l'Année sociologique*, in 1930.[67] He was then asked to direct the *Institut français des études arabes* in Damascus (1930–1938). During this time, Montagne was charged by the Rector of the University of Paris with coordinating a large "sociological study" on the "modern evolution of the Arab countries."[68] For several years he also taught courses at the University of Algiers (1934–1937).[69] During the Nazi Occupation, Montagne moved CHEAM from Paris to Algeria, where it continued operating at a reduced level. After teaching during the 1941 session, the 1942 session was interrupted by the Allied landing in North Africa and the 1943 and 1944 sessions were cancelled.[70] In 1943, Montagne was appointed to direct the North African Affairs Office of the French National Liberation Committee in Algiers. There, he gathered information on the attitudes of North African Muslims and began advocating policies of economic and social development.[71] In 1948, Montagne was named to a chair in the history of the "expansion of the Occident" at the *Collège de France*.[72] He continued to direct CHEAM until his death in 1954, when it was taken over by Pierre Rondot. Montagne's admirers included two very different groups: colonial "deciders" like Rondot and academic "connoisseurs" such as Ernest Gellner, François Pouillon, Daniel Rivet, and Marcel Mauss.[73] Entering the social sciences before World War II, Montagne was able to avoid the reputational disadvantages attached to colonial military and administrative careers after the war (see chapter 10).

CHEAM's mandate overlapped considerably with the *École coloniale*, the National School of Administration, and *Sciences Po*, but it differed in several ways.[74] All of its students were in the military or civil service. All students had at least six years of active service, four of which had to have been spent overseas. Most of CHEAM's students were between 30 and 40 years old. CHEAM offered three-month internships, during which interns took 200 hours of lectures and participated in group discussions, visits, and courses in Arabic language and dialects.[75] All of the courses were jointly taught by a professor and a colonial administrator, in order to maintain the desired balance between academic theory and practice.[76] Applicants were required to submit a "little thesis," as Montagne called it, on some aspect of "the political, economic, or social life of the natives," and to defend their thesis in an oral examination.[77] Interns could earn a "Certificate in Higher Studies of Muslim Administration" from the Sorbonne by writing the final thesis after completion of their internship.[78] This certificate was created in 1936 by a joint action of the Ministries of Foreign Affairs, Colonies, War, Interior, and Public Instruction.

CHEAM's disciplinary center of gravity was sociology, broadly defined. By the time he created CHEAM, Montagne was an established practitioner of a type of "sociology closely aligned with the concerns of the administration."[79] The work of Montagne and his institute was located in the "synthetic spirit of the Algerian *Bureaux Arabes*,"[80] created in Algeria in the 1830s, which combined information-gathering with policy, taxation, surveillance, control of tribunals and Qur'anic schools, markets, public works, and health.[81] This was an early sign of the shift toward social science in colonial administration. The focus on unifying the fields of knowledge concerning the Muslim countries under French domination was also motivated by the "particularities" of these colonies' administrations and the absence of any analytic synthesis of the French North African experience.[82] CHEAM supported research on all Islamic colonies and countries, although its core activity was training civil servants, officers, and magistrates for the North African territories. After 1945, CHEAM expanded its purview to encompass the rest of the French empire.[83] CHEAM was renamed *Centre des hautes études sur l'Afrique et l'Asie modernes* in 1958, signaling its transformation into a general area studies institute. It was closed by the French government in 2000.

Sixième section de l'école pratique des hautes études

Another school of higher education that was centrally involved in studying the colonial empire was the *Sixième section de l'école pratique des hautes études* (Sixth Section of the Practical School of Advanced Studies), which became the

École des hautes études en sciences sociales (School for Advanced Studies in the Social Sciences) in 1975.[84] The Sixth Section was centered around an interdisciplinary approach to the human and social sciences dominated by history and strongly oriented toward area studies.[85] Between the mid-1950s and the mid-1960s, a group of scholars connected to colonial and postcolonial research played a key role in the Sixth Section. This colonial/postcolonial network accounted for around 15 percent of the professors (*Directeurs d'études*) at the Sixth Section in 1965.[86] Several generations of Africanist social researchers took seminars at the *Centre d'études africaines* (Center for African Studies), which was originally associated with the Sixth Section. Africanist sociology was located at the center of French postgraduate student interest until 1965, and the Sixth Section was at the center of colonial sociology. The director of African studies, Georges Balandier, was the most sought after thesis advisor and committee member at the Sixth Section overall between 1960 and 1964.[87] The modal thesis committee between 1960 and 1965 consisted of the sociologists Balandier, Paul Mercier, and Roger Bastide, and the ethnologist Denise Paulme, all of whom advocated an approach to African societies that emphasized the impact of colonialism, crisis, and historical change.

These were not the only institutions of tertiary education that engaged in colonial instruction after 1945. The *École normale supérieure* trained educators for the colonies. Dozens of that school's graduates, including Pierre Bourdieu, became involved in colonial social science. The *École polytechnique* had an enormous impact on colonial administration and practice in North Africa, training military and civil engineers, including colonial officers, bound for Algeria and Morocco. Military Arabists trained at the *École polytechnique* were involved in the colonization of Algeria between 1830 and 1870, staffing the *Bureaux arabes* and directing the first "grandes enquêtes" (large surveys) of Arab society.[88] A number of professors at the *Collège de France* were specialized in colonial aspects of the natural, social, and human sciences.[89] Although the *Collège de France* is not a degree-granting institution, it received 10,000 francs in 1897 to introduce "higher colonial education."[90] Its professors also have access to large research budgets. This brings us to the organizations that promoted colonial research, including sociological research.

Scientific Research and Colonialism from the Nineteenth Century to the 1960s

A wide array of research institutions promoted colonial research.[91] The *Muséum national d'histoire naturelle*, created in 1793, was the first French scientific institution with a specifically colonial vocation. The *Musée d'Ethnographie du Trocadéro* was created in 1880 by Jules Ferry, a fierce advocate of colonial expansion. In 1883, the French Colonial Office created the *Conseil supérieur des colonies*, an advisory council on colonial legislation that included university professors.[92] The School of Colonial Agronomy at

Nogent-sur-Seine outside Paris began operations in 1902, training natural scientists for technical posts in the colonies and offering courses on colonial administration and hygiene.[93] Colonial institutes emerged in several provincial cities, focusing mainly on applied natural science and business. In Bordeaux, a training school for colonial doctors and pharmacists was created in 1890.[94] By the 1930s, there were around 30 scholarly societies nationwide with a colonial orientation.[95]

Scientific research was also conducted at universities and free-standing institutes in Algeria, Indochina, Morocco, Tunisia, Senegal, and Madagascar. Pasteur Institutes for medical science were created in Indochina, Madagascar, Tunis, Casablanca, Algiers, and various parts of French Africa.[96] A medical school was created in 1863 in Pondicherry, the French enclave colony on India's southeastern coast. A colonial agricultural school was opened in Tunisia in 1898.[97] A Scientific Mission (*Mission scientifique du Maroc*) was inaugurated in Morocco in 1904, eight years before most of that country was even subjected to French "protection." In 1920, the entire Scientific Mission in Morocco was transformed into a "Sociological Section" inside the colony's Directorate of Native Affairs.[98] The *Comité d'études historiques et scientifiques de l'Afrique Occidentale Française* was created in 1915 in Dakar, in order to coordinate research in the sciences and humanities under the supervision of the Governor General of French West Africa.[99]

The First World War created a new sense of urgency around the need for increased production of raw materials in the colonies. Pressures for a more "systematic use of science" in the empire were expressed in an interwar campaign promoting the colonies' *mise en valeur*—a widespread phrase that suggested profitable exploitation. A Paris-based learned society, the *Académie des sciences coloniales*, was inaugurated in 1926. This was a setting in which colonial specialists of all sorts congregated. It was also a lobby for the creation of a national fund to finance colonial scientific research.[100] In 1937, the Popular Front government established a "Council of Overseas France" within the Superior Council of Scientific Research. The *Office de la recherche scientifique coloniale* (Office of Colonial Scientific Research), discussed below, emerged out of this organization and was inaugurated by the Vichy government in 1943.

A number of new scientific institutes and technical positions were created in the overseas colonies.[101] In 1921, the Colonial Ministry centralized the professions of colonial agrarian engineers and laboratory scientists, making it easier to pursue a colonial career by allowing such experts to move freely among colonies.[102] In 1918, the *École africaine de médecine* (African Medical School) was created in Dakar. General scientific institutes were created in Saigon and Morocco in 1919. A network of technical assistance stations for agriculture was set up in the French West African colonies in 1924.[103] The *Institut français d'Afrique noire* (Institute of Black Africa), a scientific research organization based in Dakar, was created in 1936 (see below).

FIGURE 5.3. *The Empire calls on elite men, scholars, and technicians.* Vichy-era poster from the State Secretary of Colonies.

Colonial science continued to expand even during World War II in occupied and Vichy France and in the colonies. The Vichy government gave a new impetus to colonial science and propaganda, calling on "elite men, scholars, and technicians" to contribute to the empire's success (figure 5.3). The *Institut français d'Afrique noire* remained open while the colony was controlled by Vichy governor Pierre François Boisson (June 1940–July 1943). Boisson signed an order in 1942 creating a framework for hiring Africans as professional researchers, whereas the personnel had previously been entirely French.[104] The Governor General of French Equatorial Africa, Félix Éboué, who was aligned with the Free French, created the *Centre de recherches ethnologiques* (Center for Ethnographic Research) at Brazzaville in 1943. This was the precursor of the research center directed by Georges Balandier after the war, the *Institut d'études centrafricaines* (see below).

The stage was now set in institutional terms for the postwar boom in colonial science. Numerous representatives of the *Centre national de la recherche scientifique* (CNRS) were recruited in 1944–1945 to join a "Commission of Colonial Programs and Research" coordinated by France's Minister of Colonies.[105] A *Conseil supérieur de la recherche scientifique coloniale* (Superior Council of Colonial Scientific Research), presided over by the Colonial Minister and attached to the national planning agency, was created in May 1945.[106] The most important decision from the standpoint of colonial science was the government's choice to maintain the Office of Colonial Scientific Research rather than scrapping it or folding it into the CNRS.

Just as colonial developmental funding preceded metropolitan developmental spending after the war, colonial science received a powerful impulse even before metropolitan science. The first three national "plans" did not focus on science, but research and education were important components of colonial planning starting with the 1944 Brazzaville Conference.[107] The Fund for the Economic and Social Development of the Overseas Territories (FIDES), together with the special development fund for the Overseas Departments, sponsored scientific research centers and projects, including the large-scale demographic survey of Guinea in 1954–1955.[108] Individual colonies contributed additional funds to research institutes from their territorial budgets.[109]

RESEARCH ORGANIZATIONS PROMOTING COLONIAL SOCIAL SCIENCE

The most significant aspect of these organizations in the present context is that many of them were involved in social scientific research. This was particularly the case after the late 1930s. The key organizations for colonial sociology were the CNRS, the Office of Colonial Scientific Research, the Superior Council of Overseas Colonial Research, and *Institut français d'Afrique noire*.[110]

The CNRS

Scientific research became a serious national priority during the 1930s, and the Front Populaire government created the *Caisse des recherches*, a national research fund, in 1937.[111] In 1939, this fund became the CNRS, which was intended to provide France "with an infrastructure of research institutes similar to that created in Germany after 1911 by the Kaiser Wilhelm Society."[112] The overarching purpose of the CNRS was to "ensure social and economic progress."[113] CNRS soon became the leading French promoter of basic scientific research, the largest employer of scientific researchers, and the overseer of "all state organizations connected with basic or applied research." The Vichy government did not eliminate the CNRS, though it strongly favored applied research.[114]

The CNRS budget doubled during the first four years of its existence and increased by 130 percent between 1950 and 1957, in constant, inflation-controlled francs.[115] The number of full-time CNRS researchers also increased steadily, from 600 in 1945 to 4,500 in 1964.[116] In 1958, research personnel at CNRS included 2,328 in the "exact sciences" and 663 in the "sciences humaines" (social sciences and humanities).[117] The creation of the Office of Colonial Scientific Research, widely viewed at the time as the "colonial CNRS," explains why there was no colonial section inside the CNRS, but this did not prevent the latter from funding research projects and scientific centers in the colonies.[118] Most important for our current purposes is the fact that the CNRS provided long-term employment to sociological researchers specialized in colonial and postcolonial themes, including Anouar Abdel-Malek, François N'Sougan Agblémagnon, Manga Bekombo, Suzanne Frère, René Gouellain, Haroun Jamous, Paul-Henri Maucorps, Andrée Michel, Pierre Naville, and Abdelmalek Sayad, as well as shorter stints of employment to many others.[119]

ORSTOM: The Office of Colonial Scientific Research

The Office of Colonial Scientific Research was located at the center of postwar French colonial science. In 1953, it became the Office of Overseas Scientific and Technical Research (ORSTOM).[120] During its first year of operation, its finances were controlled by CNRS, but they were moved to the Colonial Ministry in November 1943.[121] The Office survived the transition to the Fourth Republic, defying the CNRS, whose leaders opposed its creation.[122] It was controlled by the Colonial Ministry, whereas the CNRS was located under the Education Ministry. The Vichy Law of 1943 stipulated that the colonies would finance the Office, and this pattern continued until the creation of FIDES, which assumed financial responsibility for it.[123]

The organization's original logo (figure 5.4) atavistically recalled the era of buccaneering imperialism, despite the fact that colonial administration was becoming an ever more bureaucratic and expert-dominated enterprise at the time. A new logo in 1949 registered this change by depicting a scientific expert in a tropical setting, with "native" figures hovering in the background (figure 5.5). As in the Vichy-era image (figure 5.3), the colonial scientist is shown here hunched over a microscope, but he is no longer wearing a pith helmet or sitting in the shadow of an officer. In other words, the colonial scientist has gained autonomy here. After 1954, ORSTOM's logo changed again, emphasizing the agency's pedagogical efforts vis-à-vis the colonized. Here, Black and White scientists are depicted sitting side by side, bent over their microscopes (figure 5.6). The implication is that the colonized may lack political citizenship, but they are budding scientific citizens.

The original mission of the Office of Colonial Scientific Research included the development of natural resources and "assuring the health and wellbeing of men." In 1945, the mission was redefined as follows: "to create the scientific

FIGURES 5.4–5.5. Logos of *Office de la recherche scientifique coloniale* (Fig. 5.4, left) in 1943 and *Office de la recherche scientifique outre-mer* in 1949 (Fig. 5.5, right). *Sources:* (Fig. 5.4) Marie-Lise Sabrié, *Sciences au Sud. Dictionnaire de 50 années de recherche pour le développement* (Paris: ORSTOM, 1994), 98; (Fig. 5.5) *Courrier des chercheurs* (ORSTOM).

FIGURE 5.6. Letterhead logo of the *Office de la Recherche Scientifique et Technique Outre-mer*, mid-1950s.

infrastructure (*l'équipement scientifique*) necessary for the industrial and economic development of Overseas France." In addition to emphasizing development, the statement contains the keyword *équipement*, which referred to supplies, machinery, and infrastructure and was ubiquitous in postwar French metropolitan and colonial planning. In 1954, the word "technological" was added to the organization's name, further underscoring this emphasis on *équipement*.[124]

The 1945 report of the Office of Colonial Scientific Research emphasized that it was focused on teaching as well as research, and that it would finance research not just in the colonies but also in the metropole, if the latter had a colonial focus (e.g., tropical medicine).[125] The organization immediately began offering instruction in the "human sciences" as well as applied natural sciences. Teaching initially took place in Paris, but was soon moved to overseas centers such as the one at Adiopodoumé in the Ivory Coast. In 1952, a new center was inaugurated in Bondy, outside Paris. In order to be admitted to the two-year training programs, students had to have obtained a diploma from a university or *grande école*. Courses in the first year were taught at Bondy, and had a theoretical focus. Students spent the second year either at Adiopodoumé or one of the other overseas ORSTOM centers. By 1951, there were already several hundred workers at Adiopodoumé.[126] In 1953, ORSTOM began admitting indigenous students from the colonies and postcolonies.[127] Around 1,500 students participated in the two-year diploma program between 1944 and 1986, when the program ended.

In the summer of 1945, the Office of Colonial Scientific Research developed a plan to create a "network of educational and research centers" across the entire empire. New institutes were opened in 1946 in New Caledonia, Madagascar, the French Congo, and the Ivory Coast, followed by Senegal, Cameroon, Togo, French Guyana, and Niger.[128] By 1953, ORSTOM boasted a network of 14 overseas institutes (figure 5.7). Several years later, there were 19 institutes in Africa alone, along with new centers in New Caledonia, Guyana, and Tahiti. The number of full-time ORSTOM researchers rose from 200 in 1944–1955, to 588 (plus 120 administrators, 616 technicians, and 790 personnel) in 1965, reaching 800 in 1970.[129]

The key feature of ORSTOM in the present context was its inclusion of the social sciences. ORSTOM's director in 1942 specified that the organization would not try to replace the highly successful colonial Pasteur Institutes, but would supplement them by pursuing "ethnography in the broad sense," meaning "not just the study of customs and languages but also demography, sociology, the study of law, indigenous arts, and religion."[130] By the mid-1950s, there were more than one hundred ORSTOM researchers in the human sciences.[131]

One exemplary ORSTOM center was the *Institut d'études centrafricaines* (IEC), created in 1946 in Brazzaville by the High Commissioner of French Equatorial Africa. Two outlying research stations of the IEC were created in Bangui (in French Ubangi-Chari) and Pointe-Noire (in the French Middle Congo).[132] Social science was introduced into this institute by Georges Balandier, who created and directed the IEC's Sociology section starting in 1948.[133] By 1952, the IEC had 18 full-time researchers—12 in the natural sciences and six in the social sciences. The Institute's staff also included seven administrative employees (three Europeans and four Africans), ten full-time

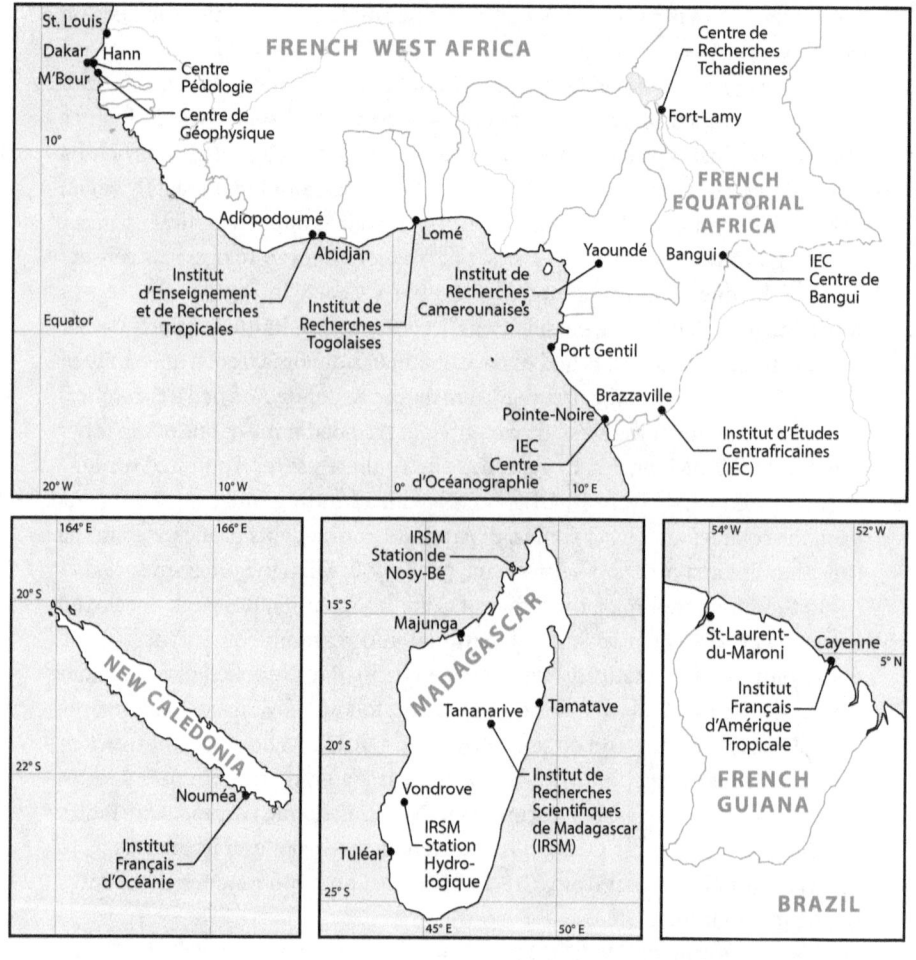

FIGURE 5.7. ORSTOM's overseas centers in 1953. *Source: Office de la Recherche Scientifique et Technique Outre-mer. Organisation—Activités 1944–1955* (Paris: ORSTOM, 1955), 15.

technical workers, numerous manual laborers, and at least 16 African research assistants, all of whom were trained on the spot as interpreters, draughtsman-cartographers, etc. The IEC had lodging for married and unmarried researchers (figure 5.8). The other social sciences encompassed within the Institute, besides sociology, were demography, geography, and ethno-musicology.

The IEC illustrates the aspirational ORSTOM model of total coverage of a colony by a full array of natural and social sciences. Figure 5.9 shows how ORSTOM mapped colonies scientifically. Here, we can see which parts of the former French colony of Middle Congo (referred to here as "Republic of the Congo") had been analyzed by 1962 by research projects based in

FIGURE 5.8. Institut d'études centrafricaines, villa for married researcher with family, "1948 type." *Source:* "Case de l'Institut d'études centrafricaines, 14 July 1951," Marcel Soret Fund, with the kind authorization of the Academy of Mâcon (France).

sociology, economics, and natural sciences. ORSTOM's continued growth and expansion after independence points to another important feature of French colonial science—its persistence into the postcolonial era, under the guise of developmentalism.

The Superior Council of Overseas Sociological Research
The *Conseil supérieur des recherches sociologiques outre-mer* (Superior Council of Overseas Sociological Research) was initiated and directed by the colonial administrator-cum-historian Hubert Deschamps, who also headed ORSTOM's Human Sciences Division. Dissatisfied with what he saw as ORSTOM's meager resources for social science research, Deschamps obtained separate funds from FIDES to launch the Superior Council.[134] The Council's "optic was above all sociological," even though it encompassed all of the social sciences.[135] Its vice president and the director of its "Sociological Committee" was Georges Davy, Sorbonne sociology professor, Dean of the Letters Faculty of the University of Paris (1950–1955), and last surviving member of Durkheim's original circle.[136] Davy was a ubiquitous presence during the immediate postwar period in university programs relevant to the social sciences, including colonial sociology. He was one of two instructors in the program for the *licence coloniale* (discussed above) at the Sorbonne.[137] The Africanist sociologist Paul Mercier held the

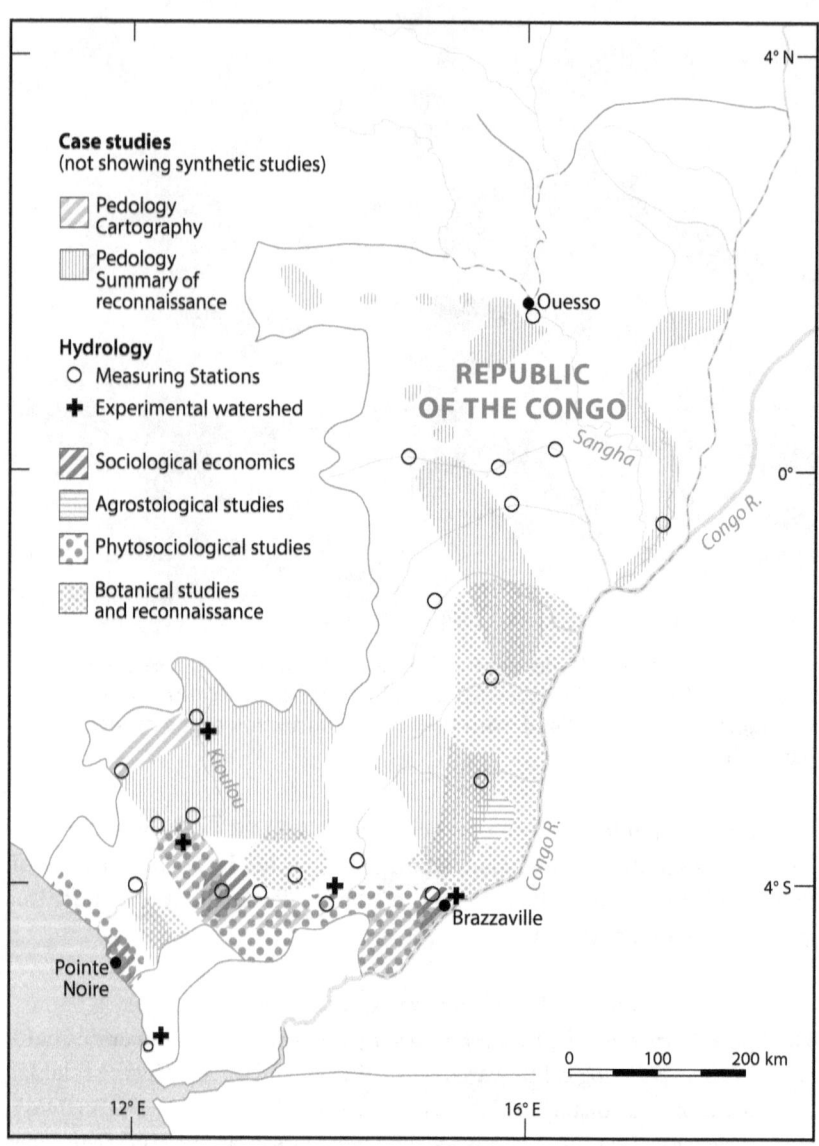

FIGURE 5.9. Map showing territorial coverage of Congo Republic (former colony of French Congo) by ORSTOM projects in economics and sociology and natural sciences, in 1962. ORSTOM, *L'ORSTOM et les recherches scientifiques et techniques en vue du développement économique et social en Afrique et en Madagascar* (Paris: Orstom, 1962). Map located between pages 18 and 19.

post of Assistant (*adjoint*) in the Superior Council of Overseas Sociological Research.

One example of a sociologist whose research was sponsored by this Council was Suzanne Frère. Frère was one of the early participants in the CNRS-funded *Centre d'études sociologiques*. She collaborated with Charles Bettelheim on a CES-sponsored community project on the city of Auxerre, published in 1950, which was considered the "French equivalent of Robert and Helen Lynd's well-known study of Middletown."[138] After 1950, Frère conducted the research for her doctoral dissertation in Madagascar.[139] While in Madagascar, she also carried out a survey initiated by the Superior Council of Overseas Sociological Research. The Council also offered financial support for Eric de Dampierre's "sociological mission" in Ubangi Shari.

IFAN: French Institute of Black Africa

The other major colonial research organization that encompassed sociology and connected it to other social science disciplines was the *Institut français d'Afrique noire* (IFAN). Like its forerunner, the *Comité d'études historiques et scientifiques de l'Afrique Orientale Française*, IFAN was created by the colony's Inspector General of Education.[140] IFAN was originally financed entirely out of French West Africa's budget, but after 1945 it obtained additional funding from the French Education Ministry and FIDES. IFAN extended its purview beyond French West Africa to the rest of French Africa, initiating and publishing research and creating museums, libraries, archives, and scientific collections. Because French West Africa did not have a university until the late 1950s, IFAN began offering courses at its *École française d'Afrique* in Dakar. It distributed three annual research fellowships, "one each in ethnology or linguistics, the natural sciences, and geography."[141]

After 1945, IFAN became embroiled in competition with ORSTOM, which was richer and more powerful and which laid claim to existing IFAN centers in Cameroon and Togo and installed its own office in Dakar (figure 5.10). Despite this challenge, IFAN survived and eventually merged into the University of Dakar in 1957. IFAN also moved into a modern new building on the Dakar campus. It changed its name to *Institut fondamental d'Afrique noire* in 1966, six years after independence, allowing it to retain the IFAN acronym.[142]

IFAN's emphasis was initially on the natural sciences, but it soon embraced the social sciences. It was important in this context that the *Comité d'études historiques et scientifiques de l'Afrique Orientale Français* had placed equal emphasis on scientific and humanistic research. The journal of the *Comité d'études*, which existed between 1917 and 1939, carried articles by colonial administrators on indigenous customs. One of the corresponding members of the *Comité d'études* in 1917 was Émile Durkheim, and Lucien Lévy-Bruhl and Marcel Griaule both contributed to its journal. IFAN's director, Théodore Monod, was a natural scientist who strongly supported the human sciences.[143]

FIGURE 5.10. Original IFAN building at Place Tascher, Dakar (now Place Soweto). Photo courtesy of Alex Nadège Ouedraogo.

By 1948, IFAN had sections in geography, ethnography, anthropology, linguistics, archaeology-prehistory, history, botany, and zoology.[144] A separate sociology section, directed by Paul Mercier, was added in 1952.[145] The continuing separation of sociology and ethnology made sense, insofar as the effort to differentiate the two disciplines in African studies was initiated by Balandier, Mercier, and others while they were in Dakar. After 1960, the University of Dakar offered *licence* degrees and *diplômes d'études supérieures* in sociology but not anthropology.[146] This pattern continued into the 1970s, at which time doctorates were still being written at the University of Dakar in sociology but not in ethnology.[147] This was part of a general pattern among postcolonial African universities of resisting the institutionalization of anthropology and giving precedence to sociology.[148]

The Paris Institute of Ethnology and the Museum of Man
The organization most directly linked to colonial sociology without being exclusively centered on it was the Paris *Institut d'ethnologie* (Institute of Ethnology). Created in 1925 and dedicated to the legacy of Durkheim, it was the first French institution to offer detailed instruction and university certificates in ethnology.[149] The Institute sponsored 104 research "missions" between 1928 and 1940, the most famous of which was the Dakar-Djibouti Mission of 1931–1933.[150]

The Institute's express mandate was to study the French colonies, and it received its principal funding from the colonies and the colonial ministry.[151] Marcel Mauss, one of the Institute's founders, together with Lucien Lévy-Bruhl and Paul Rivet, tried to convince government officials that "sociological studies could be the best guides for administrators of the colonies." According to Mauss, "colonial policy may be the area in which the adage 'knowledge is power' is best confirmed."¹⁵² In a letter to the French Resident General of Morocco in 1925, Mauss stated that the Institute of Ethnology "was at the disposal of colonial governments and protectorates for any information concerning expeditions (French or foreign), the study of indigenous races, the conservation and study of monuments and collections, or the study of social facts."¹⁵³ Half of the Ethnological Institute's advisory council consisted of "representatives from either the Ministry of Colonies or the colonies themselves."¹⁵⁴ Paul Lapie, *Recteur* of the Paris Academy, characterized the Institute of Ethnology in terms of an "alliance of practice and theory." Its research would "find its applications in our colonial empire."¹⁵⁵ Nonetheless, the Institute's teachers "remained resolutely detached from the actual work of colonizing" and did not generally seek to place their students in colonial service, in contrast to the *École coloniale* or *Sciences Po*.¹⁵⁶ In 1938, the Ethnological Institute moved into the newly built *Musée de l'homme* (Museum of Man), which grew out of the Ethnographic Museum at Trocadéro, created in 1878.¹⁵⁷ The *Musée de l'homme* received about half of its budget from the colonies. Its director described it as a colonial museum, and it was decorated with imperial motifs.¹⁵⁸

The Institute for Ethnology sponsored, funded, and published ethnographic studies and trained students, who could earn a *diplôme d'études supérieures* or a certificate toward a *licence libre* in Letters or Sciences.¹⁵⁹ Although the Ethnological Institute is nowadays usually connected to the history of anthropology, it was actually an interdisciplinary research institute like ORSTOM and IFAN.¹⁶⁰ Its pluridisciplinary character is demonstrated by the wide array of specialties taught there at the end of the 1920s, which included archaeology, biology, zoology, and geology, in addition to ethnology, sociology, and linguistics.¹⁶¹ The Institute's three founders also came from different disciplines. Paul Rivet was an Americanist ethnologist active in the emerging sociology discipline, participating in the interwar meetings of the *Institut français de sociologie* and the postwar *Centre d'études sociologiques*.¹⁶² Lucien Lévy-Bruhl was a philosopher but was also seen at the time as close to sociology, and was eulogized by Mauss in 1938 as "Lévy-Bruhl, sociologist."¹⁶³ Like Durkheim, Mauss, and other founders of sociology, Lévy-Bruhl engaged in armchair theorizing about colonized cultures based on ethnographic raw material gathered by others. He is best known, and most notorious, for his book *How Natives Think* (*Les fonctions mentales dans les sociétés inférieures*), although he published on many other philosophical themes.¹⁶⁴

Mauss, the Ethnology Institute's long-time director and its most famous and active teacher, belonged to at least four different disciplines: sociology, anthropology, philosophy, and religious studies. Mauss thus embodied the multidisciplinary orientation he encouraged at the Institute for Ethnology. The disciplinary trajectories of the Institute's graduates in the human sciences underscore his success in this respect.¹⁶⁵ A number of these graduates oscillated between ethnology and sociology: Jean-Louis Boutillier, Louis Dumont, Jacques Faublée, Jean-Paul Lebeuf, Alfred Métraux, Paul Mus, and Jean Poirier. Some were more consistently identified as ethnologists, including Marcel Griaule, Michel Leiris, André Leroi-Gourhan, Claude Lévi-Strauss, Denise Paulme, and André Shaeffner. Others identified primarily with sociology—Jean Cazeneuve, René Gouellain, Charles Le Coeur, Maurice Leenhardt, René Maunier, Jean-Claude Pauvert, and Maxime Rodinson.

Support for French Colonial Research by American and International Organizations, 1930s–mid-1960s

What about applying American techniques? We Europeans, and especially French sociologists, remain skeptical about this approach.

—BERQUE (1956)

The rise of colonial developmentalism and colonial social science was not just part of an *inter-imperial* conjuncture but of a new global economic, political, and cultural system hegemonized by the United States. The United States played a discordant role in postwar European colonialism, pushing publicly for decolonization while propping up colonial rule behind the scenes.

There was also a scientific side to this contradictory American colonial engagement. The British Africanist Meyer Fortes spoke of an "American invasion" at the start of the 1950s, in response to the "growing influx of US-American researchers into" the European colonial territories.[166] While Americans were more active in the British colonies, for obvious linguistic reasons, US foundations were present in the French empire. The Rockefeller Foundation supported French professors and doctoral students in ethnology and sociology on an individual basis beginning in 1929 and through grants to the University of Paris between 1934 and 1939.[167]

The United Nations Educational, Scientific and Cultural Organization (UNESCO), which was not based in the United States but was strongly influenced by it, played a role in the consolidation of colonial sociology. Three of the sociologists who directed UNESCO's Social Sciences division were supporters of colonial sociology: Robert Angell, T. H. Marshall, and E. Franklin Frazier.[168] French social scientists had a strong influence on UNESCO during its earlier years.[169] French delegates to UNESCO between 1946 and 1949 included Paul Rivet and Alfred Métraux, while Raymond Aron was a "technical adviser." Roger Bastide was entrusted with compiling UNESCO's French dictionary of social science. Jacques Berque was delegated to report on UNESCO's plans to develop social science teaching and research in Tunisia, Morocco, and Lebanon.[170]

UNESCO helped to create sociology in postwar Europe and in the colonial and postcolonial world. At one point, there were 50 UNESCO social science posts—most of them teaching assignments—"scattered around Africa, Asia, Latin America, and even Southern Europe."[171] Although UNESCO's full-fledged "shift to serving decolonized nations" occurred after 1965, the ideological effects of this shift were felt during the 1950s and early 1960s, when UNESCO's social science spending was at its peak.[172] UNESCO financed most of the budget of the International Sociological Association (ISA) in the 1950s, and US foundation grants paid for "travel to World Congresses and for the [ISA] research programme."[173] The first six World Congresses of the ISA allowed European colonial sociologists and sociologists from the colonized world to interact with one another across nation-state and imperial boundaries. Some of the conferences organized by UNESCO were trans-imperial, encompassing French, Belgian, and British colonial sociologists. For example, the conference on the "Social Impact of Technological Change in Africa," held in the Ivory Coast in 1954, conjured up an inter-imperial space of colonial social science, in which sociology played a key role.[174]

UNESCO's Social Sciences division financed research projects in colonies and subsidized the creation of social science and sociology departments in postcolonial universities. A UNESCO-sponsored study of Stanleyville (Kisangani) in the Belgian Congo in the mid-1950s was carried out by British anthropologist Daryll Forde, Dutch-born sociologist Valdo Pons, and French colonial psychologist Nelly Xydias.[175] UNESCO's postwar project on race and racism brought together sociologists, ethnologists, and social psychologists, and situated race in the context of the history of colonialism and slavery.[176] The original 1950 UNESCO Statement on Race was authored by eight experts, including sociologists Franklin Frazier and Morris Ginsberg and anthropologist Claude Lévi-Strauss, who also published *Race and History* in 1952.[177] In 1962, UNESCO undertook a comparative sociological study of the social preconditions of industrialization in Tunisia that employed two Tunisian sociologists (Abdelwahab Bouhdiba and Paul Sebag) and one Tunisian psychologist (Carmel Camilleri).[178] UNESCO's 1967 Statement on Race, one of whose authors was Balandier, focused on colonialism, arguing that "many forms of racism have arisen out of the conditions of conquest, out of the justification of Negro slavery and its aftermath of racial inequality in the West, and out of the colonial relationship," and that "the anti-colonial revolution of the twentieth century has opened up new possibilities for eliminating the scourge of racism."[179]

Another inter-imperial scientific agency that supported sociology during the 1950s was the Scientific Council for Africa South of the Sahara. It was set up in 1952 through an intergovernmental agreement between Britain, France, and other states with the aim of "keeping the whole system under review from the scientific viewpoint, and emphasizing those questions in which one subject or discipline impinges on another." The Council's Inter-African Labour Conference organized meetings of researchers from different countries, including the French colonial sociologists Georges Balandier and Rémi Clignet.[180] Social anthropology and sociology were both included, and the head of the Council's Division of Social Sciences, Jacques Maquet (chapter 9), had doctorates in both disciplines.[181]

From Social to Intellectual Contexts

This chapter has mapped the presence of the empire among French university students, scholars, and departments, in French research institutes, and in international and inter-imperial organizations, with a focus on the postwar era and sociology. In the next two chapters, I will explore the wider intellectual and intertextual contexts for postwar French sociology's colonial emphasis. More specifically, the next two chapters explore theoretical and methodological developments relevant to colonialism in the disciplines that were closest to French sociology at the time. Chapter 8 will then examine discussions of colonialism within the French sociology field itself, during the interwar years.

PART III

The Intellectual Contexts of Postwar French Sociology

CHAPTER SIX

The Earliest Colonial Social Sciences and Their Engagement with Sociology

GEOGRAPHY, LAW, ECONOMICS, AND
THE SCIENCES OF THE PSYCHE

THE BOUNDARIES BETWEEN sociology and the disciplines surrounding it remained quite permeable through the end of the 1960s. Within the research institutions, there was an enhanced tendency toward multi- and interdisciplinarity, stemming from the focus of much colonial research on solving immediate problems. Colonial administration, like other bureaucracies, was less concerned with scientific boundaries than were disciplinary founders like Durkheim. Colonial sociology was therefore continuously exposed to ongoing developments in adjacent fields.[1] The social sciences that had the greatest degree of overlap with sociology were psychology, law, economics, history, geography, statistics and demography, and anthropology. By focusing on these disciplines' involvement in colonial research, this chapter and the next provide additional evidence for the argument that twentieth-century French intellectual life in general was profoundly shaped by the empire.[2]

Cultural currents ran in both directions between colony and metropole. On the one hand, ideas were generated in the colonies and transferred back to the metropole. Legal scholars suggested that certain aspects of colonial law should be reimported to France, for example, arguing that "in the realm of property law, our colonies in Africa and Indochina already possess a very superior system."[3] Entire sociological subfields, including community ethnographies and the study of economic reciprocity or gift-giving, moved in the same counterimperial direction. The economic sociology of underdevelopment, originally focused on the "Third World," called attention to the existence of "peripheries" within the metropoles. The entire conceptual foundation of Bourdieu's sociology originated in the Algerian colony (chapter 14).

On the other hand, and more predictably, ideas and practices were exported to the colonies. This is obviously the case for models of economic production, legal codes and administrative structures, political organizations (parties, labor unions), religious institutions (missionaries), and general education, not to mention language itself. It was also true of the sciences, including social science. Yet while many aspects of science were exported to the colonies without revision or translation, science was also adapted to the colonial context. Tropical medicine shifted from studying "diseases in the tropics" to the study of "tropical diseases."[4] Urban planners and architects used local materials and aesthetics and relied on indigenous builders, resulting in styles that were by turns neo-traditionalist, modernist, and mixtures of both.[5] Practitioners of some social sciences "emancipat[ed] themselves from disciplinary traditions and elaborat[ed] new methods and categories of analysis" they deemed appropriate to the settings.[6] Statisticians and demographers, for example, developed "particular methods adapted to [the] diverse milieus" of African colonies, as discussed in the next chapter.[7] Legal scholars concluded that "there is no branch of law that is not subjected to more or less profound transformations by being transplanted to the colonies."[8] Social scientists also began to pay conscious attention to the importance of the colonial context as an explanatory factor. Some began to build the colonial context directly into their narratives, theories, and interpretations, developing concepts such as "colonial mode of production," "the colonial situation," "colonial system," "colonial society," and "colonial traditionalism."[9]

The academic fields examined in this chapter and the following one were all involved in colonial studies, albeit in different ways and to varying degrees. They entered the imperial stage at different historical moments. Law was present from the beginning of European empires in the ancient world, through to modern European colonialism. Law became ever more specialized and intricate as the colonial state expanded. Geography was an integral part of the exploration that preceded formal conquest, and of the construction of the colonial state and the *mise en valeur* of the territory. Economics generated some of the most influential arguments for and against colonization, starting in the mid-nineteenth century. Economists were involved in all stages of the twentieth-century colonial developmentalist agenda. Psychology and psychiatry were also older disciplines, but they did not begin to permeate the colonial realm until the nineteenth century. As new forms of psychological testing and psychiatric treatment emerged, including the latecomer, psychoanalysis, they were transferred to overseas colonies. The present chapter will discuss this earlier set of neighboring disciplines—geography, law, economics, and psychology—and their entanglements with colonialism and sociology. Chapter 7 will discuss three disciplines whose involvement with colonialism began slightly later but became at least as extensive: history, statistics, demography, and ethnology.

Colonial Legal Studies and Sociology

Law and geography were the first humanistic disciplines to become fully enmeshed in colonial rule, beginning with the Roman empire. Everyday governance in the Spanish empire in the Americas was dominated by "university graduates trained in the law."[10] Modern colonized populations were subject to a mix of codes imported by the conqueror, native codes written by the ruling power, and genuine indigenous legal cultures that preexisted conquest. Colonies were always sites of "double legislation, double government, double administration," and "double status: status for the natives, status for the French."[11] There coexisted (1) native law; (2) national laws and decrees, extended to colonial territory; (3) imperial laws, valid for the entire empire; (4) general colonial laws, valid for all of the colonies but not the metropole; (5) federal colonial laws; (6) local colonial laws and decrees; (7) directions and instructions on the application of colonial law.[12] Unequal legal treatment was a defining feature of the rule of colonial difference, and it was strengthened by the ubiquitous reliance on indirect rule.[13] Europeans tried to convince themselves of the legitimacy of their rule by insisting on the incapacity of indigenous populations to govern themselves. This premise made it impossible to apply metropolitan legal systems equally to indigenous populations without falling into a performative contradiction that would undermine the legitimacy of conquest.[14] More pragmatically, all colonizing powers were forced to develop legal frameworks in order to regulate criminal cases involving their own foreign citizens, civil and criminal disputes among the colonized, and legal affairs pitting colonizing individuals against colonized individuals. Colonizers' determination to control indigenous society drew them into the intricacies of non-European law and into the incompatibilities among differing non-European legal systems.[15]

In every modern colony, there was at least a rudimentary European administration, and in many there was a full-fledged modern state, with a continuously operating bureaucracy, army and police, and judicial apparatus.[16] Like all modern states, colonial states were erected around legal codes. In the Portuguese empire, metropolitan law was simply extended to the colonies. In other empires, distinct legal codes were elaborated for overseas dominions.[17] French colonies saw the creation of intricate judicial structures, with criminal and civil courts, native courts, appellate courts, attorney generals (*procureurs généraux*), judges, defense attorneys, and clerks, and a complex mosaic of legal codes.[18] Legal specialists were confronted with the "contradictions and ambiguities of the colonial presence" and were forced to weigh the importance of "the essentially economic interests of colonization" against "respect for the indigenous customs" of the colonized.[19] Colonial rule often took the form of a permanent state of exception, which meant that legally a "regime of decrees" or ordinances prevailed.[20] Yet even the emergency character of colonies generated a demand for lawyers. Colonial law became a vast "experimental laboratory" characterized by improvisation and "trial and error" processes.[21] One historian has described the system as a "juridical monstrosity."[22]

Legal experts were present from the beginning to the end of the French overseas empire. Some of the first colonial courses in French universities were located in law faculties. Starting in 1895, the *agrégation* degree in law included an optional track in colonial legislation.[23] By the end of the nineteenth century, all of the French law faculties were offering courses in "colonial legislation and economics." The law faculty at Algiers began teaching "Algerian legislation, Muslim law, and indigenous customs."[24] After 1945, colonial developmentalism created new demands for legal experts to draft legislation on issues such as work safety and hours, overtime pay, collective bargaining, and social insurance.[25] Legal scholars drafted the transitional "framing law" of 1956 and the law creating the French imperial "Communauté" in 1958.[26]

Colonial law was tied to sociology in the work of René Maunier, Marcel Mauss, and Henri Lévy-Bruhl, son of the philosopher. Lévy-Bruhl compared colonial customary law to archaic law.[27] Maunier (discussed in greater detail in chapter 8) held a chair at the Sorbonne Law Faculty from 1927 to 1944. He wrote extensively on the law of colonies and empires and comparative law, including customary and Muslim law. During World War II, Maunier began advocating a federalized approach to the overseas territories and a more expansive form of "imperial citizenship" within a framework he called "Eurafrica" (*Eurafrique*).[28] Maunier's conception was modeled on the US Monroe Doctrine, which codified its hegemony over the western hemisphere, and on Friedrich Naumann's image of Germany as *führender Oberstaat* without direct colonization of Eastern Europe.[29] Although this less colonialist approach to geopolitical domination was central to postwar French discussions of the empire, Maunier's wartime adhesion to the Vichy regime led to his ostracism after 1944 and the elision of his work from the secondary literature on the Eurafrica idea and sociological history.[30]

During the Fourth Republic, many younger legal scholars turned against colonialism and began developing frameworks for a "devolution of power." Here again, there were connections between law and sociology.[31] One of the most critical colonial legal scholars was P. F. Gonidec, who wrote on colonial labor law and analyzed the "French Union" as a crypto-colonial system aimed at preserving French dominance.[32] After independence, Gonidec specialized in questions of law and political sociology in postcolonial societies.[33] Another law professor, François Luchaire, based his analysis of the legal issues involved in decolonization and underdevelopment on economics and sociology, including what he called "colonial sociology."[34]

Colonial Geography and Sociology

Geography and history formed a single course of study in the French university, but they were separate scientific fields and I will treat them separately here. Both disciplines had connections to sociology, but geography was much more strongly oriented toward colonial and imperial questions.[35] Indeed, geography was the discipline whose supporters could rally behind the slogan "knowledge is power, geographical knowledge is world power."[36] French geography emerged as a proto-discipline after the Napoleonic era. The geographers who had mapped the Napoleonic empire constituted "a central constituency in the clientele of the *Société de Géographie*, "the world's first geographic society," created in 1821.[37] During the Third Republic, the *Société de Géographie* was "one of the most important organizations in the *Parti Colonial*," and its members chaired "twenty-six of the forty-five largest colonial societies."[38] The geographical societies were among the rare academic supporters of the government's resumption of colonial expansion starting in 1879.[39] Colonial specialists also constituted a "high proportion" of the university chairs in geography, which increased from 20 in 1914 to 180 by 1963.[40] There were forty-two teachers of colonial geography and numerous other "university geographers who published works on colonial questions" between 1880 and 1940. One-fifth of the geography theses defended in France between 1872 and 1961 "were concerned with the colonies." An older approach focused on geographic accounts of explorations.[41] The newer journal *Annales de géographie*, created in 1891, sought to promote a more "scientific geographical study of the colonies." Its founders were Marcel Dubois, who held a chair in colonial geography at the Sorbonne, and Paul Vidal de la Blache, geographer at *l'École normale supériere*. According to Singaravélou, "in its first year, half of the review's 32 articles were dedicated to the colonies."[42] Geography was the only humanities field in which students could earn a *certificate d'études supérieur* with a specifically colonial focus during the interwar period.[43]

Colonial geography continued to thrive after World War II, although its leading representatives now became sharp critics of colonialism. According to the left-wing geopolitical theorist Yves Lacoste, these postwar geographers tackled local and regional political problems "that today would be called geopolitical," and many of them "supported independence movements."[44] Moreover, some of these colonial geographers had connections to sociology.[45] The most interesting figure in this respect is Gilles Sautter, who cofounded the Paris *Laboratoire de sociologie et géographie africaines* and worked with Balandier in French Equatorial Africa.[46] Sautter's geographical method resembled Balandier's sociological approach insofar as it focused on the crises induced by colonialism. Sautter's study of the Congo River region examined the ways in which "negative events" produced by colonialism—"the destruction of populations, mass emigration, failed agricultural experiments, economic failures"—led to a "geography of . . . void and absence," ruins, and decay.[47]

Colonial Economics and Sociology

Until the mid-nineteenth century, most liberal French economists followed Adam Smith in rejecting colonization, emphasizing arguments about infringements on free trade and the opportunity costs of lost investments in the metropole. During the 1860s, however, there was "a softening of anticolonial stances" among French economists.[48] New doctrines insisted that imperialism was compatible with free trade and voluntary overseas settlement.[49] In his 1857 *Nouveau traité d'économie politique*, Nicolas Villiaumé defended public investments in the colonies and the awarding of "land to French citizens who agreed to emigrate."[50] Economist Paul Leroy-Beaulieu's influential book *La colonisation chez les peuples modernes* supported colonialism and free trade.[51] Leroy-Beaulieu began advocating for the French to focus on overseas colonization rather than continental conquest in 1880 as a means of redirecting the Republican government away from the possibility of involving France in another war against the more powerful Germans.[52] Most of the French economists in the Third Republic followed Leroy-Beaulieu into positions favorable to colonialization. Colonial themes had also featured prominently in the discussions at the *Société d'économie politique de Paris*, launched by disciples of the anticolonial liberal Jean-Baptiste Say in 1842. Singaravélou calculates that 35 of the 402 discussions held at the meetings of that association between 1850 and 1940 concerned colonial topics.[53] Liberal economic arguments against colonialism were dealt an even more severe blow by the economic crisis of the 1930s, which saw the rise of statist approaches and doctrines of planning. These ideas became even more pervasive after 1945, and as discussed in chapter 4, they went hand in hand with efforts to hold on to the colonies.[54]

French sociology had a troubled relationship with economics during the Durkheimian period. Durkheim pursued a maximalist strategy of disciplinary "replacement" vis-à-vis economics. He rejected political economy's indifference to "moral and social perspectives" and its reduction of society to interactions among individuals construed according to the *homo economicus* model. Durkheim's approach to morality and values called the entire standard version of economics into question.[55] Durkheim's subsequent "revelation" about the central importance of religion in social life widened the gap between his version of sociology and economics.[56]

Other sociologists recognized, however, that economics was not going to be impressed, much less replaced, by an upstart discipline with few followers and only a handful of professorships. Mauss, Halbwachs, and Simiand went on to produce an important body of literature in economic sociology, introducing social and historical contexts to the study of economic processes and developing theories of economic reciprocity.[57] Between the wars, scholars associated with Célestin Bouglé's *Centre de documentation sociale* (chapter 9) became interested in topics such as economic planning (Charles Bettelheim), mechanization (Georges Friedmann), monetary policy (Robert Marjolin), and industrial relations (Philippe Schwob). After 1945, economic topics moved to the center of French sociology because of the increasing influence of Marxism and labor studies and the rise of theories of development and underdevelopment.[58]

The final phase of colonialism saw the rise of economic schools that rejected orthodox economics and the global inequalities of power that undergirded colonialism and the post-independence economic world order. Samir Amin was a leading figure in this transformation of French economics. Amin worked in the planning agencies in Egypt (1957–1960) and Mali (1960–1963) and taught economics in Dakar (1964–1968) and Vincennes-St. Dénis.[59] His French doctoral thesis in 1957 analyzed "the mechanism that engendered the so-called underdeveloped economies."[60] Amin criticized orthodox economics for basing their models on putatively autonomous national economies and for arguing that postcolonies could simply "copy the recipes of western economic history."[61] For Amin, an "imperial world system" continued to exist following decolonization. Global power inequities remained constant; the only difference was that relations between cores and peripheries now replaced relations between metropoles and colonies. The underdevelopment of both colonies and peripheries, Amin argued, was due to the lower price of labor, which stemmed from the monopoly power of capitalists in the core and conditions of unequal exchange, not from differences in labor's productivity. Amin also tried to determine the specificities of class and social structure in each individual colony and postcolony.[62] Amin argued that the peripheries would have to delink themselves as much as possible from the global system in order to accumulate capital and progress socially and politically.

The critiques of underdevelopment placed social structure and political power at the heart of the economics of the Third World, and introduced economics into sociological studies of colonized societies.[63] The "sociology of development" was created and taught in French universities in the 1960s and 1970s by some of the same people who previously had worked on colonial development.[64] The economist François Perroux directed the Institute of Applied Economics at the University of Algiers from 1945 to 1955. During his time in Algiers, Perroux introduced his theory of "domination effects" in the economy. While this partially resembled Schumpeterian theories of monopoly, Perroux argued that the domination effects in colonial economics were distinctive and more extreme.[65] Perroux's approach deviated from orthodox Keynesianism in its orientation toward a processual approach whose central concepts are "asymmetry, domination, equilibration, irreversibility, struggles/competitions, regulation, polarization and human cost."[66] In 1957,

Perroux created the *Institut d'étude du développement économique et social* (Institute for the Study of Economic and Social Development, IEDES). This institution continues to focus on economic development in Africa, Asia, Latin America, and Europe; its journal is *Revue Tiers Monde* (Third World Journal).

Three elements of French development studies and Perroux's IEDES are important in the present discussion. First, IEDES brought together economists, geographers, historians, and sociologists. This integration of non-economists helped IEDES and its journal resist orthodox trends in economics, from the neoclassicism of the 1970s to the "Washington Consensus" of the 1980s through to the microeconomic approaches since the mid-1990s.[67] Second, this scholarly field is unusual in foregrounding *continuities* between the colonial and postcolonial periods, rather than repressing the colonial past. Third, this is an intellectual arena in which theories and concepts generated in (post) colonial peripheries have "returned via a boomerang effect for analyzing the North"—ideas such as "informality, exclusion, poverty, etc." French development studies was further radicalized after 1968, emphasizing questions of "debt, adjustment, and hegemony of orthodox thought" and engaging with Marxist theories of imperialism and underdevelopment.[68]

A different array of connections between economics and sociology stemmed from the reception of Althusserian Marxism by some Africanist ethnographers. The doctoral theses by Emmanuel Terray, Maurice Godelier, Claude Meillasoux, and Pierre Philippe Rey combined a neo-Marxist framework grounded in Althusser's theory of "the articulation of modes of production" with archival research and ethnographic fieldwork. By reconstituting and preserving precapitalist modes of production, the colonial system lowered the cost of labor power, generating extra profits for investors. Rey and Terray both taught for a certain period of time in the sociology department at the University of Vincennes.[69]

Three conclusions can be drawn from this discussion of the relations between colonial economics and sociology. First, theories of underdevelopment emerged among social scientists whose early experiences were framed by colonialism—specifically by the developmentalist program of the postwar empire. Second, movements of heterodox, anti-imperialist economics opposed to models of *homo economicus* forged close connections between economics and sociology for the first time in France. Third, French economic sociology, like so many other subfields, was partly a product of colonialism.

The Colonial Sciences of the Psyche and Their Connections to Sociology

Psychology overlapped with psychiatry and psychoanalysis in twentieth-century France, while retaining a distinct disciplinary identity. All three of these disciplines flourished in French colonial settings.[70]

PSYCHOLOGY, SOCIOLOGY, AND COLONIALISM

The relationship between Durkheimian sociology and psychology in pre-1914 France, like sociology's interaction with economics, was highly fraught. Durkheim rejected the introspective and individualist methods of the leading French psychological school in the late nineteenth century, which was known as Spiritualism (see below). Durkheim argued that ideas, representations, beliefs, and morals could be studied only by observing empirical social facts. Durkheim criticized Le Bon's crowd psychology and Tarde's theory of social imitation as being ultimately rooted in individual psychology rather than social facts. Durkheim also criticized them for assuming that group psychology was internally homogeneous. Durkheim rejected any reduction of "the mental life of the individual" to "underlying cerebral processes," that is, to biology or neurology.[71] Each of these arguments exemplified Durkheim's general aim of differentiating sociology from neighboring disciplines and insisting that social facts were emergent from physical and biological ones.

Psychology was not rejected out of hand by most of the other Durkheimian sociologists, however, but was seen as a "legitimate interlocutor."[72] Durkheim's followers Paul Fauconnet and Marcel Mauss suggested that sociology was itself a form of collective psychology, arguing that nearly all "social facts" were also "psychic facts," albeit not individual ones.[73] Sociologists and psychologists "encountered one another regularly at the meetings of the *Société de psychologie de Paris* starting in 1920 and those of the *Institute français de sociologie* since 1924."[74] An explicitly Durkheimian psychology emerged between the wars, led by Charles Blondel, who was trained in medicine and philosophy.[75] According to Blondel, sociology could explain all *normal* psychological processes, since, as Durkheim argued, "all of mental life is profoundly socialized."[76] Psychology's domain was then reduced to psychopathology. Mental illness, for Blondel, was the result not of social determinations but of their *absence*, that is, of the "*desocialization* of the conscience."[77] Thus, psychology's very object domain was defined sociologically using Durkheim's theory of anomie.

Such gestures of "sociological imperialism" were called into question even by some Durkheimians after 1918. Mauss was elected president of the *Société de psychologie de Paris* in 1924. In his inaugural lecture, Mauss abandoned Durkheim's polemical tone and "invited representatives of the two disciplines into a close dialogue."[78] In 1927, Daniel Essertier's doctoral thesis called for "collaboration" between sociology and psychology.[79] Blondel now revised his earlier, sociologically "imperialist," approach in his 1928 *Introduction to Collective Psychology*. He distinguished between a sociological domain, which he called "collective psychology," and "differential psychology," which was "dedicated to the study of everything that exceeds the social in the individual."[80] This meant that much of normal mental life was now allocated to psychology.

As the hostility of Durkheimian sociology to psychology subsided, Durkheim's methodological "banishment of *Verstehen* from sociology"[81] was also rescinded. This opened the door to sociological discussions of hermeneutics, psychoanalysis, existentialism, cultural structuralism, and other methodologies concerned with the interpretation of meaning.

One explanation for the fact that arguments about colonialism were not generated organically from within sociology until somewhat later, in the 1930s, was the central role in the classical Durkheimian framework of the notion of the *primitive* or the *elementary*, as in the "elementary forms of the religious life." Durkheim insisted that "the identity of the 'human mind' ... is always exactly the same at all times and in all places," and his *Elementary Forms of the Religious Life* derived the key epistemological categories of modern cognition from "primitive" religious classifications.[82] This methodology meant that the data gathered in overseas colonies had to be conceptualized as elementary and pure, untouched by modern culture.

Lucien Lévy-Bruhl, by contrast, argued that "primitive" mentality was prelogical, mystical, and fundamentally different from modern mentality. Durkheim criticized Lévy-Bruhl for "exaggerating differentiation or discontinuity" rather than highlighting "resemblance and continuity" between primitive and modern culture.[83] Adorno argued, by contrast, that it was "not external" to Durkheim's conception that Lévy-Bruhl, "one of his most famous students, ... undertook to construct *irrationality*, i.e., the prelogical thinking of the primitives, according to his thesis, as a form of thought in its own right."[84] However objectionable Lévy-Bruhl's argument, the key point at this moment in the genesis of a properly sociological approach to colonialism was that colonized populations were now sharply distinguished from colonizing populations.

In his courses at the Institute of Ethnology, Lévy-Bruhl communicated this theory to his students, some of whom were bound for colonial service. Lévy-Bruhl's ideas were discussed in every edition of René Hubert's influential sociology manual, including the last edition in 1949.[85] Lévy-Bruhl's self-criticism at the end of his life is usually linked to his discussions with ethnosociologist Maurice Leenhardt (see below), who pointed to empirical errors in Lévy-Bruhl's thinking. In 1938, Lévy-Bruhl conceded that "there is not a single primitive mentality that distinguishes itself from the other mentality by ... characteristics which are peculiar to it (mysticism and prelogicality)." Instead, he now argued, "there is a mystical mentality that is more marked and more easily observable among 'primitive peoples' than in our societies, but it is present in every human mind."[86] Lévy-Bruhl had thus returned to a version of Durkheim's original position, due to the intervention of a Durkheimian sociologist, Leenhardt, who had started to thematize colonialism explicitly.

Before turning to the forms of psychology that were directly concerned with colonialism, we should briefly consider the main variants of nineteenth-century

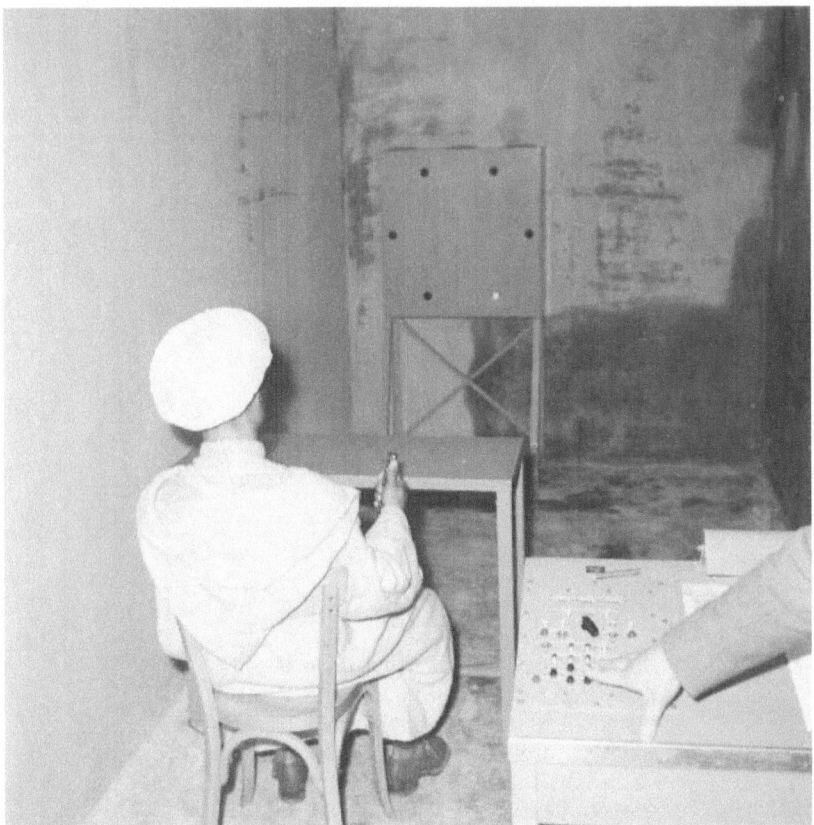

FIGURE 6.1. Psychotechnical tests given to candidates for position as skilled workers at Zellidja mines, Sidi Boubeker, Morocco. Laboratory created by Jean-Paul Trystram, director of the *Institut de psychologie et de sociologie appliquées*, a research organization for industrial enterprises in Morocco. Photograph by Jean Paul Trystram, director of Institut de psychologie et de sociologie appliquées, Casablanca. *Source:* Odile Trystram. Courtesy of Rachid Lamrani, Secrétaire Général, Porte Parole du Collectif pour le développement de l'Oriental, and the Trystram family.

French psychology. Spiritualism was the leading branch of psychology in the nineteenth-century French university.[87] As Jan Goldstein explains, Spiritualism was adamantly opposed to any "conversion of psychology into a branch of biology" and defended "the linkage between metaphysics and any serious investigation of the human mind."[88]

So-called *scientific psychology*, which emerged in the first half of the twentieth century, represented a complete repudiation of Spiritualism. This approach was based on quantitative and experimental methods and a naturalistic, individual-based ontology.[89] Scientific psychology abandoned psychology's roots in philosophy and severed its links with French psychoanalysis, moving

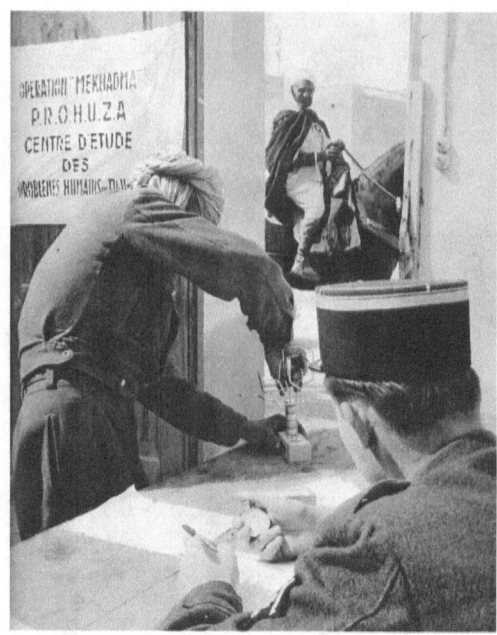

FIGURE 6.2 (*above*) and FIGURES 6.3–6.5 (*overleaf, clockwise from top left*). French psychologists carrying out psychological tests on Algerian subjects from the Mekhadma tribe in the 1950s. *Source:* Prohuza, Comité de coordination scientifique de Sahara, *Les Mekhadma. Étude sur l'évolution d'un groupe humain dans le Sahara moderne, effectuée par le Centre d'études et d'informations des problèmes humains dans les zones arides* (Paris: Arts et métiers graphiques, 1959), 91, 141.

toward the natural sciences, for example by being located (since 1967) within the Biology section of the CNRS rather than the Human Sciences.[90]

This does not mean that scientific psychology was unconnected to sociology, but that it interacted with the more "scientific" sectors of sociology. This axis of interdisciplinarity was widespread in the colonies. The Office of Overseas Scientific Research organized intelligence testing of young people in French West Africa.[91] Paul-Henri Maucorps, a specialist in psychotechnical methods who led the social psychology group in the *Centre d'études sociologiques*, developed a program for intelligence testing and sociometric measurements in French Oceania.[92] In Morocco, the sociologist Jean-Paul Trystram carried out psychotechnical studies in the early 1950s, and created the *Institut de psychologie et de sociologie appliquées* (Institute for Applied Psychology and Sociology) in Casablanca in 1955.[93] Trystram's organization carried out psychometric testing at the behest of private employers such as

FIGURES 6.3–6.5.

the Moroccan *Société des Mines de Zellidja* (figure 6.1).[94] The *Centre d'études et d'informations des problèmes humains dans les zones arides* (Center for Studies and Information on Human Problems in the Arid Zones) carried out intelligence testing in Algeria (figures 6.2–6.5; see chapter 4).

One distinctive feature of these projects is their methodological adaptation to colonial and non-western settings. Psychological testing was not uncontroversial. Pierre Fougeyrollas, the future head of the sociology department at Dakar, criticized psychotechnical sociology in 1951 as a form of "police sociology" aligned with American imperialism.[95] As Jacques Berque noted, the studies by the *Centre d'études et d'informations des problèmes humains dans les zones arides* "employ the most modern methods for determining, among the various groups, the different reactions to a variety of conditionings, and to certain stimuli, such as the presence of foreigners"—i.e., Europeans and colonizers.[96]

Figure 6.2 makes it clear what "the presence of foreigners" in the research setting might mean in a colonial situation, and how this could be complicated by the presence of the delegated intermediaries of the colonial state. The figure on horseback in the center of the photo in Figure 6.2 is "Caïd Keddour," who is "keeping a good eye on the proper execution of the tests." In Algeria, the *caïd* was a functionary installed by the French at the head of the *douar* or rural administrative district. In other words, the testing being carried out by French researchers among the Mekhadma was also being observed by the indirect ruler of the colonized. While the *caïd* was conventionally seen as a collaborator, his presence in this photograph also suggests a form of counterpressure against the unchallenged dominion of colonial science. The caïd is located at the top and center of the photograph. He is the only figure facing the camera. And he does not look intimidated.

COLONIAL PSYCHIATRY AND SOCIOLOGY

Psychiatry was distinct from psychology, as a directly applied discipline. By the end of the nineteenth century both of these disciplines also began to be differentiated from the newest science of the psyche, psychoanalysis. Psychiatric professionals were trained in medicine and had little contact with the human sciences. Psychiatry was grounded in the assumption of a "biological origin of madness" in contrast to psychoanalysis, which "considers the patient as a subject ... who participates in the curing process."[97] Psychiatry had strong elective affinities with colonialism, which is similarly premised on the inherent rather than socially constructed inferiority of the colonized, and the latter's lack of agency.

Throughout the nineteenth century, the sole form of treatment for the insane in the colonies was the dungeon-like asylum; the only alternative to this was transfer to a metropolitan hospital. Thousands of indigenous patients were transported to French asylums during the nineteenth and early twentieth centuries.[98] A movement to treat the insane on the spot in the colonies began in the years before World War I. This led to the creation of psychiatric hospitals in Tunis and Madagascar in 1912, Indochina in 1919, and Algeria, at the famous Blida clinic, in 1938.[99] Psychiatrists controlled the treatment of the seriously mentally ill in the asylums and hospitals. However, there was nothing like the "great confinement" in the colonies that Michel Foucault identified in his discussion of the metropoles, due to paucity of funding. Jock McCulloch argues that even "with the new legislation enacted in the 1930s and 1940s, the majority of the African mentally ill never came to the attention of district commissioners or mental health authorities."[100]

The colonial situation created additional barriers to treating, understanding, and perceiving the mentally ill, above and beyond the lack of material resources. One strand of European psychiatry classified the colonized per se as mentally ill. Some psychiatrists characterized the brains of the colonized as inherently inferior and derived explanations of indigenous madness from biological sources.[101] Others conceived of "native mentality" as degenerate, criminal, and primitive.[102] The mid-nineteenth-century psychiatrist Jacques-Joseph Moreau (Moreau de Tours) argued that Muslim group prayer itself "was eminently suitable to causing insanity."[103] British psychiatrist J. C. Carothers, author of a widely read book on ethno-psychiatry published by the World Health Organization in 1947, argued that "*all* primitive Africans are psychopathic, in that their personalities are by European standards immature."[104] A colonial psychiatrist in Northern Rhodesia argued that the entire Bebme tribe was "suffering from a permanent Obsessional Neurosis."[105] Early French psychiatrists described possession by *djinne* or *rabb* (ancestral spirits) in Senegal and other Islamic colonies as forms of mental illness, and characterized local methods of dealing with the mentally ill as deviant. Other psychiatrists suggested that certain forms of possession were not necessarily delirious, but that the "sacred and venerated Arab insane" had to be classified as "mental patients" and "treated with psychiatric medicine."[106] Henri Aubin, who directed the Algerian psychiatric hospital in Oran, argued that while sorcery was normal among "primitive" people, recourse to magic was intensified among primitive psychopaths.[107]

In stark contrast to these theories of non-European psychopathology, other European psychiatrists argued that insanity did not even exist "among primitive peoples," or blamed the latter's insanity on the "excessiveness" of "civilization."[108] After 1945, psychiatrists pointed to detribalization, exposure to western concepts, and even "the strains inherent in literacy" for precipitating African mental illness.[109] One French psychiatrist working at a neuropsychiatric hospital in Morocco recommended "the greatest prudence" in exposing Muslims to French culture, in order to forestall the kind of "psychosis of civilization" he had diagnosed in one of his patients.[110] Other psychiatrists argued that traditional therapy, while "most often beyond the physician's grasp," should continue to be applied alongside "western" psychiatry.[111] The group around Henri Collomb at Dakar, discussed below, was strongly associated with this sort of intercultural or ethno-psychiatric approach. Just as Frantz Fanon was beginning to trace the origins of mental illness in colonialism (see below), another French psychiatrist argued that some Tunisian students who abandoned their traditional culture were developing a "complex" of cultural "treason."[112]

Colonial psychiatrists thus faced an enormously complex situation. Already in 1912, French psychiatrists concluded that in order even to perceive "psychiatric" abnormality among the colonized, it was necessary to construct a base model of their version of psychological "normalcy."[113] Antoine Porot, the leading figure in the psychiatric *École d'Alger*, argued that Algerians should not be judged using "our European twentieth-century mentality."[114] Practices that were normal in African cultures seemed abnormal from a European perspective, and vice versa. Psychiatrists had to decide whether to analyze the colonized using universal diagnostic criteria, indigenous standards, or some combination of the two. The desire for ethnographic specificity therefore led ineluctably to the creation of ethno-psychiatry. Psychiatry, like law and other fields, confronted a much more difficult task in the colonies than in the metropole.

The middle decades of the twentieth century saw reforms and experiments with new types of psychiatric diagnosis and treatment in the colonies. An "open service" for early and preventative treatment of mental illness in general hospitals was introduced in Tunis.[115] Therapies developed in the metropole were applied in colonial hospitals, including electroencephalograms, hormonal studies, Thematic Apperception Tests (TAT), and narcoanalysis (putting the patient to sleep under the influence of a "truth serum").[116] French psychiatrists in North Africa used electroconvulsive therapy and lobotomy, "insulin therapy, sleeping cures," and "work and occupational therapy."[117]

After 1945, some psychiatrists began to question their earlier dismissal of indigenous understandings and treatments of mental illness and to integrate non-psychiatric ideas and collaborators into their work. Two especially important figures in this regard were Frantz Fanon, who was a psychiatrist at the Blida hospital in Algeria before becoming a full-time anticolonial militant, and Henri Collomb, director of the Fann clinic in Dakar. Both psychiatrists are also relevant in the present context due to their openness to sociology.

Frantz Fanon and Henri Collomb

Most psychiatrists had little exposure to the social sciences, but Fanon and Collomb were important exceptions. These two psychiatrists also ushered the "new psychiatry past the collaborationist agenda" and aligned it with decolonization.[118] Fanon "regarded himself essentially as a psychiatrist," but he was also a theorist of colonialism whose work connected with sociology in various ways.[119] Fanon's biography is too familiar to need rehearsing here, other than recalling several key points that relate to connections in his work between psychiatry, colonialism, and sociology.

At the University of Lyon, where Fanon earned his medical degree with a specialization in psychiatry, he was also exposed to philosophy and anthropology, attending lectures by philosopher Maurice Merleau-Ponty and ethnologist André Leroi-Gourhan. He went to the theater in Lyon and wrote two unpublished plays, one of them closely aligned with surrealism.[120] After his psychiatric residency at the St. Albans hospital with François Tosquelles, the pioneer of "institutional therapy," and a year of practice in France, Fanon moved in 1953 to Algeria to become head of the department at the Blida-Joinville Psychiatric Hospital, which at that point was "the largest psychiatric institution in North Africa."[121] Fanon worked at Blida until his deportation from the colony for political reasons in January 1957. During his time in Algeria, Fanon experimented with approaches to psychotherapy that connected with his patients' cultural backgrounds, rather than simply applying the same methods to Algerians and Europeans. He criticized the unmodified use on Algerians of TAT tests.[122] Fanon and his colleague Jacques Azoulay created a "Moorish café in the hospital" and introduced "the regular celebration of traditional Muslim feasts [and] of periodical meetings around a professional 'storyteller'."[123] Fanon continued to argue that many psychopathologies among the colonized were the product of racist colonialism.

Fanon was not a sociologist, and he is not included in my prosopography of French postwar sociologists in this book. He rarely used the word sociology, and when he did, he seemed to be referring to Octave Mannoni, who was not a sociologist but a trained psychoanalyst, or to the reactionary sociologists of Islam at the École d'Alger.[124] Nonetheless, Fanon's thinking became increasingly sociological over time. In the above-mentioned study of "social therapy in a ward of Muslim men," Fanon and Azoulay refer to the need to "try to grasp the North African *social fact*." They then refer to the "totality which Mauss saw as the guarantee of an authentic sociological study."[125] The notion of the "social fact" in a French context gestured unambiguously toward the Durkheimian notion of "le fait social" from *Les Règles de la méthode sociologique* (1895). Every French social scientist at the time would have recognized this reference. Fanon and Azoulay's reference to Mauss's notion of totality represents an even more direct connection to the contemporary sociologists of colonialism, who referred to the same concept when arguing for conceptualizing colonialism as a complex, overdetermined phenomenon in which each element influences every other element. Fanon had a copy of Mauss's *Sociologie et anthropologie* in his personal library.[126] Elsewhere, Fanon refers to the need for a "sociological" definition of crime, meaning a culturally specific definition, in order to understand practices of confession in the Maghreb.[127]

Concerning his relation to sociology, we should also consider Fanon's association with the *Institut des hautes études de Tunis*. In 1959–1960, Fanon taught a course there on social psychopathology that was part of the social psychology certificate for students working toward the sociology *licence*. This experience would have allowed Fanon to come into contact with a number of sociologists teaching there at the time. Sociologist Jean Cuisenier, who worked on underdevelopment in Tunisia, taught at the Tunis *Institut des hautes études* starting in 1956. Georges Granai, an urban sociological ethnographer, directed the sociology program in Tunis from 1958 to 1965. Sociologist Claudine Chaulet, discussed in chapter 1, was an *attaché de recherche* at Tunis in 1958–1959. Sociologist Jean Duvignaud began working as a *chargé de cours* in the Tunis sociology program in 1960. Jacques Berque carried out a mission for the United Nations Educational, Scientific and Cultural Organization in December 1959 aimed at developing sociological teaching and research in Tunisia. Some of the students in Fanon's course in Tunis described him later as the founder of Tunisian sociology. These students included: Lilia Ben Salem, who wrote a doctorate with Balandier, and Duvignaud and Berque as committee members; and Abdelbaki Hermassi, Abdelkébir Khatiba, Abbès Lahlou, Monique Laks, Frej Stambouli, Claude Tapia, and Khalil Zamiti, all of whom became sociologists.[128] For at least one year, when he was writing *L'an V de la révolution algérienne* and *Les damnés de la terre,* Fanon was close to a milieu of French and Tunisian sociologists, most of whom were working on problems of colonialism and decolonization.

Fanon first became known in 1952 as the author of *Peau noire, masques blancs (Black Skin, White Masks)*.[129] This text was grounded in Hegelian philosophy, phenomenology, existentialism, and Freudian and Lacanian psychoanalytic theory—in other words, everything other than sociology. His analysis is Hegelian and Sartrian, insofar as it argues that Whiteness and Blackness are not essences but are generated through dialectical interactions (29). The Black is overdetermined from without, by the gaze of the other, and by racist ideology. Whereas in Hegel, "the White Master, *without conflict*, one day recognized the Negro slave" (217), Fanon argues that Whites refuse to recognize Blacks as human. The Black subject is fragmented and reconstructed "with a thousand details, anecdotes," according to a "racial epidermal schema" (112). In a concluding chapter, "The Negro and Recognition," Fanon begins by quoting Hegel: "man is human only to the extent to which he tries to impose his existence on another man in order to be recognized by him"; "self-consciousness exists . . . only by being acknowledged or recognized" (216). He continues, still following Hegel, arguing that self-consciousness has to undergo "the experience of *desire*," as the "first milestone on the road that leads to the dignity of the spirit" (218). This "human reality in-itself-for-itself," Fanon argues, "can be achieved only through conflict and through the risk that conflict implies" (218). The problem is that "historically, the Negro . . . was set free by his master" (219). Fanon seems to be referring here to contexts such as his native Martinique. Fanon's example of a situation where the "Negro battles and is battled" in 1952 is the United States (221).

This connects Fanon's reading of Hegel's phenomenology to his commitment to violence as "absolute praxis" in *Les damnés de la terre*, eight years later. In 1952 he did not yet have a concrete idea of how to undo the damage resulting from having been "set free" without risking death. Additional factors played a role in Fanon's embrace of violence, including his personal experiences of racism, his experiences on the battlefield during World War II, and the unrestrained brutality of the French army in Algeria.[130]

Black Skin, White Masks also raises the question of the specificity of colonialism. Many of Fanon's examples here are not specific to colonialism. Yet the first chapter deals with the "problem of language" and argues that the Black in the Antilles is "proportionately whiter in ratio to mastery of the French language," and that this is the same for every colonized person (18). Fanon concludes this chapter by defining the colonized as those "in whose soul an inferiority complex has been created by the death of its cultural originality" (18). Chapter 4 is an extended critique of Mannoni's *Psychologie de la colonisation* (discussed below). Mannoni argued that the colonizer and the colonized were both afflicted by neuroses that preexisted the colonial situation and that needed to be understood before one could make sense of their transfiguration by colonialism. Fanon rejected Mannoni's thesis of a Malagasy "dependency complex" or "inferiority complex ... that antedates colonization," insisting that it was produced by colonialism.[131] Of course, Mannoni was more knowledgeable than Fanon about Malagasy culture, and was also more immersed in psychoanalysis (see below). It is also important that Fanon accepts Mannoni's analysis of the colonizer's "infantile urge to dominate" as setting the stage for colonial domination. Fanon may have adopted his concept of the colonial *mask* from Mannoni.[132] If Fanon's critique of Mannoni is ultimately unconvincing, his chapter is still important, because it inaugurates the project of teasing out what is specific about the colonial situation compared to precolonial and postcolonial situations and what is specifically colonial about texts written in colonial situations.

Fanon's texts from 1959 through 1961 represent his more "sociological" portraits of colonialism and the revolutionary process of anticolonial warfare. In *L'an V de la révolution algérienne* (1959), Fanon analyzes Algerian gender relations, family structure, veiling, radio, and medicine. This is certainly not a work of psychiatry. Indeed, this book was reissued in 1966 under the title *Sociologie d'une révolution* by François Maspero, who understood very well the contemporary connotations of the word sociology in discussions of colonialism.[133] Fanon was at least obliquely connected to the emerging formation of "sociologie de la colonisation," and his texts from 1959–1961 can best be understood by reading them against this context.

Les damnés de la terre is Fanon's most sustained analysis of colonialism, which is described here as a dualistic, brutal, Manichaean world. The colonial world is not hegemonized, but rather governed by sheer violence; there is no political legitimacy, in contrast to the metropolitan state. As in *Peau noire, masques blancs*, Fanon argues here that the colony's central structuring principle is racism. Race determines class position. The ruling class is defined first by its foreignness, and only secondarily by ownership of the means of production, which stems from the first factor. In the colony, Fanon argues, there is no national cultural innovation, no creativity. Instead, the culture of the colonized degenerates into "an inventory of behavioral patterns, traditional costumes, and miscellaneous customs." Magic, dance, and rites of possession play the role of safety valves, "ensuring the stability of the colonized world": these outbursts are followed by peace. Yet the colonized are not petrified "on the inside," Fanon continues; instead, they are constantly ready to boil over. Colonial society is therefore both protean and unbalanced, on the one hand, and "rigid in the extreme, congealed, and petrified," a "world of statues."[134] This shearing tension within society is reproduced within each colonized individual. Mental illness is thus caused by colonialism, and it cannot be resolved without collective struggle, risking death, and national liberation. All of the different strands of sociological, ethnological, and psychological writing on colonies that had accumulated since the late 1930s reach a kind of climax in *Les damnés de la terre*.

Henri Collomb was the most innovative French psychiatrist whose career began in the colonial situation and continued into the postcolony. Collomb was a neuropsychiatrist in the French military who joined the Free French during the war and served as the principal doctor for Haile Selassie and his court in Ethiopia. After a decade in Africa, Collomb was posted to Indochina during the French war there. He moved to Senegal in 1958, where he directed the neuropsychiatric clinic at Fann Hospital in Dakar from 1959 to 1978. Collomb's clinic consisted of French and African workers, and it included psychiatrists, psychologists, ethnologists, sociologists, and philosophers. In other words, it was intercultural and interdisciplinary from the start.[135] Collomb argued that the African lunatic "was recognized as the bearer of a greater truth, a truth which was revealed to him through madness," and that traditional African "healers have even more strength and knowledge because they have had a serious initiatory mental illness" themselves. This suggested a definition of ethno-psychiatry as "the way in which societies and cultures defend themselves against madness, reducing or widening the gap between the mad and the sane." Ethno-psychiatry was "both a mode of understanding mental illness and a practice for curing the sick, an understanding and practice specific to each culture or society." It was a form of "cultural *métissage*" that "allowed the lost or rejected communication between the mentally ill person and their group to be restored."[136] Given Collomb's emphasis on traditional understandings of mental illness and modes of treatment, it is not surprising that he was eulogized by Léopold Senghor.[137]

Collomb's colleagues carried out extensive work on rites of possession, delusional fits (*bouffés délirantes*), other forms of mental illness, and traditional mental health practices. Collomb's collaborator Andras Zempleni was an ethnologically oriented psychiatrist who performed a two-year study of a Senegalese priestess-therapist.[138] The psychoanalyst Marie-Cécile Ortigues explicitly discussed the complications that emerged from the fact that the psychoanalytic situation was also a colonial situation. In her book *African Oedipus (Œdipe africain)*, Ortigues discussed the difficulties of identification and transference across the colonized-colonizer divide, and the need to modify the theory of the Oedipus conflict to take into account the specificities of African cultures and family structures.[139] A postgraduate student in sociology working at the Fann clinic, Danielle Storper-Perez, wrote her doctoral thesis on the psychiatric hospitalization of Wolof patients in Senegal. In her book *Colonized Madness (La folie colonisée)*, Storper-Perez analyzed connections between mental illness, social and family structures, and colonialism, and discussed the inability of traditional European psychiatric methods to deal with mentally ill Africans.[140] It is clear that this intense interrogation of psychiatry could only have been generated in the late colonial situation, even if its development continued afterward.

Colonial Psychoanalysis and Sociology

Psychoanalysis was the third branch of research into psychic processes that was involved in colonialism and that also interacted with colonial sociology. It is impossible to retrace the entire history of French psychoanalysis here, but several points are especially relevant. First, psychoanalysis is a powerful theory of affect and the embodiment of social structures, making it well suited for understanding the unconscious sources and logics of racism and imperial psychopathologies. It is a sharp knife for dissecting the unconscious adoption, hidden storage, and secret reproduction of colonial ideas within metropolitan culture.[141] Second, psychoanalysis has been less encumbered than psychiatry with simplistic divisions between western and "other" cultures. Freud already argued that European subjectivity was not a unified or universal form of rationalism, but was instead "constituted by fractures, repressions and conflicts and by the constant struggle to cover over these conflicts in order to present a coherent and unified subject."[142] Freud reverses the conventional roles, turning the modern European into the psychological "primitive," in a move that was repugnant to colonial racists.[143] Third, colonialism and empire were important background conditions for Freud's own ideas. Freud admired Hannibal even more than Moses, as Edward Said suggests in his lecture that compares Freud's *late style* to Beethoven's.[144] Julia Hell argues that Freud was deeply influenced by the "neo-Roman mimesis" of the Habsburg empire, where he was born, and whose demise he mourned.[145] Fourth, the early French reception of psychoanalysis, as Freud noted, took place among "men of letters," notably Surrealists, some of whom belonged to the *Collège de Sociologie*, a school that linked Surrealism with colonialism and sociology.[146] Georges Bataille, André Breton, Roger Caillois, and Michel Leiris, members of the *Collège de Sociologie*, were fascinated by the colonies; Caillois and Leiris experienced colonialized societies firsthand. Caillous and Leiris's postwar protégé Georges Balandier both became sociologists.[147]

Psychoanalysis did not stand still after Freud, and some of the most interesting revisions that are relevant to colonialism occurred in Francophone contexts. Octave Mannoni (1899–1989) studied with the Durkheimian psychologist Charles Blondel (see above), worked as a philosophy teacher in colonial Martinique and Madagascar, and then became an administrator in charge of Madagascar's Information Service. Later, he taught at the Paris *École coloniale*. Mannoni was psychoanalyzed by Lacan and married to a renowned Lacanian psychoanalyst, Maude Mannoni. In his classic *Psychologie de la colonisation* (1950), Mannoni introduced for the first time the concept of the "colonial situation" by combining Hegel's master-slave dialectic, the Sartrian notion of the *situation*, and psychoanalytic concepts such as transference and countertransference, staging, scenes, theatricality, masks, and veils.[148] Mannoni's notion of the colonial situation was adopted and elaborated by Balandier (chapter 13).

Georges Devereux and Roger Bastide represent different combinations of psychoanalysis, psychiatry, sociology, and ethnology. Bastide, discussed in more detail in chapter 8, published the first French book connecting sociology to psychoanalysis in the interwar period (*Sociologie et psychanalyse*, 1950–1951).[149] He continued to combine psychoanalysis and sociology in his studies of colonized and postslavery populations in Brazil, including his research on religious practices among descendants of African slaves. Devereux was a student of Mauss who linked social science to *clinical* psychoanalysis and worked among Mohave and Navajo Indians. After completing a PhD in anthropology at the University of California in 1935 and training as a psychoanalyst at the Menninger Clinic, Devereux worked with Native American veterans suffering from traumatic neuroses between 1946 and 1953. After Devereux's return to France in 1963, he taught at the Sixth Section of the *École pratique des hautes études* and developed a distinctive school of *ethno-psychoanalysis*.[150]

Contrary to certain "postcolonial" critiques—though in agreement with Edward Said—psychoanalysis represented a crucial resource in making sense of normal and pathological psychic phenomena among the colonized. Fanon insisted in his polemic against Mannoni that the colonized did not have an unconscious. The traumas of the colonized, Fanon asserted, were rooted in obvious empirical experiences that were consciously perceived. In this respect Fanon seemed to agree with J. C. Carothers, the British colonial psychiatrist whom Fanon rejected as an "old-fashioned" racist, who argued in his widely read book that "the rather clear distinction that exists in Europeans between the 'conscious' and the 'unconscious' elements of mind does not exist in rural Africans."[151] However, Fanon's writings and psychiatric practices suggest that he did not actually believe that Africans, or the colonized, did not have an unconscious. Indeed, it was a radical move, in light of theories of "primitive mentality," to argue that the psychic life of the colonized was at least as complex, internally divided, and multilayered as that of the colonizers.

CHAPTER SEVEN

Other Neighboring Social Sciences and Their Engagement with Sociology and Colonialism

HISTORY, STATISTICS, DEMOGRAPHY, AND ANTHROPOLOGY

THIS CHAPTER EXAMINES A group of disciplines whose involvement with colonialism began slightly later than those in the preceding chapter: history, statistics and demography, and ethnology. Colonial specialists were slow to be accepted by professional historians. Intensive interactions between history and sociology began between the wars, but they involved only a small number of people. With rare exceptions, there was little interaction between colonial historians and colonial sociologists. This only started to change toward the end of the colonial era. Statistics and demography, by contrast, were involved in the French overseas empire from early on, and both became closely entwined with sociology in the twentieth century. Anthropology represents the discipline with the deepest roots in colonialism, and also with the closest links to sociology, at least in the French (and British) context. As we will see, however, this does not mean that cross-disciplinary relations between sociology and anthropology have been unchanging or entirely peaceful.

Colonial Historiography and Colonial Sociology

Colonial historians were marginal to their discipline during the nineteenth century and remained so well into the twentieth century. This was partly due to the heavy representation of amateurs, officials, and politicians among their ranks. French professional historians' struggles for legitimacy during the Third Republic were directed against hobbyists and notables.[1] Colonial historians' heteronomy also clashed with the the emerging norm of scientific objectivity. The frequent emphasis in colonial history on heroic conquerors and military battles, and its use of colonialist tropes and ideologies put it directly at odds with the leading journal *Annales d'histoire économique et sociale*, created by Marc Bloch and Lucien Febvre in 1929. Febvre criticized the candidates for a chair in colonial history at the *Collège de France* in 1937 as being steeped in an approach he called "*l'histoire bataille*"—the history of battles. This phrase resonated with the famous *Annales* epithet, "*histoire événementielle*"—the history of mere events.[2]

A more scientific variant of colonial history emerged over the course of the twentieth century. In 1913, Henri Froidevaux described a move away from older approaches based on dogmas and "intangible axioms," toward a method based on "precise and rigorously determined facts" and "absolutely authentic and carefully edited" textual sources. Froidevaux compared this new French colonial historiography to the *Linchoten Vereeniging* in Den Haag and the Canadian *Société Champlain*, which were respected by professional historians.[3] Research standards were also improved by the creation of professionally staffed historical archives at the Colonial and Navy Ministries and in colonies such as Senegal, Morocco, Algeria, and the French Congo.[4] A professional ethos permeated the *Société française d'histoire d'outremer*, created in 1912, the *Revue de l'histoire des colonies françaises*, and new methodological treatises on colonial history. The first university chair in colonial history was created at the Sorbonne in 1921 for Alfred Martineau; this was followed by six additional chairs at provincial universities and the University of Algiers.[5] Other strongholds of colonial history were *Sciences Po*, *l'École coloniale*, and *l'École navale*.[6] According to Singaravélou, 20 doctoral theses in colonial history were defended during the Third Republic.[7] The early 1930s marked a first apogee of the French colonial history movement, which held its first congress in 1931.[8]

Such improvements in scholarly standards did not automatically make colonial history more acceptable to leaders of the discipline. Georges Hardy and Robert Delavignette, two leading colonial historians before World War II, never published in the *Annales* and never overcame their marginalization.[9] Hardy had a doctorate in colonial history, yet his career took place entirely within colonial and academic administration, first as inspector of the school system in French West Africa and Morocco, then as director of *École coloniale*, then as rector at Lille and Algiers. His activities in Vichyist Algeria as university rector led to his being fired and forbidden to teach after the war.[10] Hardy's writing was an uneasy mixture, partly corresponding to the standards of the *Annales* school and partly resonating with colonialist tropes and concerns. For example, in his 1921 text *Les éléments de l'histoire coloniale* (*Elements of*

Colonial History), Hardy began by arguing that colonial history follows the same "methodological principles" as European history. The book concludes with a chapter calling for the creation in the colonies of autonomous historical research institutes, modern archives, public offices to oversee museums and public monuments, and last but not least, a professorship in colonial history at the Sorbonne. However, much of the book is organized around colonialist stereotypes, with entire chapters on "mixed-bloods," the psychology of "the crowd," "the miracle of French tenderness," and French "colonizing virtues."[11] Singaravélou suggests that Hardy and Delavignette (discussed in chapter 10) "paved the way for the movement of 'provincialization of Europe' by postcolonial historians," and this is correct insofar as they both challenged assimilationist ideologies and thematized the impact of colonialism on the colonized. Yet they remained "provincial" within the French history discipline, especially vis-à-vis the dominant *Annales* school.[12]

How was the *Annales* project articulated with French colonialism? Febvre made a few efforts to reform colonial history by including it in the *Annales* program.[13] Bloch strongly supported the work of Jacques Berque, which focused on the social and economic history of rural Morocco and relied on untapped indigenous archival sources (see chapter 12). Bloch was particularly interested in the possibility of comparing Moroccan and French agricultural history. Yet the editors of *Annales* showed little interest in other colonial historians, whom they perceived as heteronomous and amateurish. Another disjuncture resulted from the fact that French colonial history tended to begin in the nineteenth century, with the onset of African colonization.[14] The international Commission on Colonial History, created in 1931, defined its object as *modern* colonialism, and defined colonies as "establishments actually occupied in the name of a State and attached to it by official administrative links." This explicitly excluded the study of "simple trading posts."[15] Such a definition put the subfield directly at odds with the *Annales*, whose central focus was the medieval and early modern periods, as well as the ancient world, and whose leader after 1945, Fernand Braudel, was specifically interested in early modern colonial "trading posts." *Annales* published just three articles on colonialism between 1929 and 1948, and only one of them dealt with a contemporary theme.[16]

One might expect Braudel to have shown more interest in modern colonial history. After all, Braudel taught history in an Algerian *lycée* between 1922 and 1932 and wrote his doctoral thesis on Spain in North Africa and the Mediterranean.[17] His first major article appeared in the very colonial Algerian journal, *Revue africaine*.[18] Braudel's first publication in the *Annales*, in 1938, was a review of recent publications on North Africa, in which he praised the interdisciplinarity of the annual conferences of the *Fédération des sociétés savantes de l'Afrique du Nord* (Federation of Learned Societies of the Maghreb) and likened them to the *Annales* program. In 1938, Braudel called for more studies of the colonial "European present," which encompassed "settlers, functionaries, agrarian and urban workers."[19]

Yet Braudel did not import this program into *Annales* when he became its editor and leader of the school's "second generation." The colonial present was now kept at arm's length, covered mainly in book reviews and articles written by sociologists, geographers, and ethnologists.[20] The rare exceptions were historians from Algiers University, such as Marcel Emerit, who studied nineteenth-century Ottoman and French colonialism.[21] Otherwise, historical studies of colonialism published in *Annales* until the 1960s focused on the ancient world and the early modern era. Braudel's agenda-setting masterpiece, *The Mediterranean*, published in 1949, discusses empires, trading colonies, and settler colonization in great detail, but it ends with the death of Philip II of Spain, seven years before the founding of France's first formal colonial empire and more than two centuries before the French invasion of North Africa. The third volume of Braudel's *Civilisation matérielle, économie et capitalisme, XVe-XVIIIe siècles*, published in 1979, deals with early modern colonialism and empires, but only discusses the nineteenth century in a short section on the Industrial Revolution that does not even mention the second wave of colonialism.

The "refusal of eventful history" and the "focus on almost immobile inclines and remote pasts" diverted the attention of the *Annales* historians away from "the dynamics of a [colonial] world being turned upside down."[22] The journal only started to publish historical articles on modern colonialism in 1960, i.e., just as colonialism was being transformed from *contemporary history* into *modern history*.[23] One of the young colonial historians at the time, Catherine Coquery-Vidrovitch, who published in *Annales* in the 1960s, describes her cohort as being "concerned to tell the story of a colonial past that was about to end."[24]

A younger and more critical group of colonial historians emerged outside of the *Annales* circle after 1945. These historians were "counter-colonial" in their politics.[25] They addressed new historical themes such as the slave trade, economic exploitation, colonial administrative strategies, anticolonial nationalism, and the role of educated elites among the colonized. They began to transform colonial history into African history and "the history of independent states."[26] The figure who best exemplifies these changes is Charles-André Julien. Long active in socialist and communist politics, Julien was rejected for the colonial history chair at the *Collège de France* in 1937 due to his anticolonial politics. He was elected to the colonial history chair at the Sorbonne in 1948, in a completely different colonial-political situation. Julien was now celebrated as "the Zola of decolonization" and a "grand anticolonial academic."[27] Several of the colonial historians trained during the 1950s were Julien's students. André Nouschi, whose doctoral thesis was supervised by Julien, wrote about living standards among rural populations in Constantine Province in

Algeria between 1830 and 1919.[28] Nouschi was one of the only colonial historians who developed close relations with sociology, specifically with the young Pierre Bourdieu.[29] Abdoulaye Ly, who earned his doctorate at Bordeaux in 1955, was the first African historian of colonialism, the first professional historian hired by the *Institut français d'Afrique noire* (IFAN) in 1952, and the only researcher in IFAN's human sciences division at the time with a doctorate degree.[30]

The key point in the present context, however, is that the *Annales* school did not forge new connections between history and sociology in the arena of colonial research, with the exception of Jacques Berque (chapter 12). The same is true of the Sixth Section of the *École pratique des hautes études*, where many of the colonial social scientists congregated. Braudel directed the Sixth Section and was officially committed to interdisciplinarity, particularly with sociology. Many seminars at the Sixth Section were labeled the "'Histoire et sociologie' of this or that area."[31] However, a network analysis of the composition of thesis committees at the Sixth Section reveals that, even after 1960, there was little interaction between the core cluster of colonial social scientists and the school's historians.[32] In sum, the interdisciplinarity of the *Annales* school contributed to the historicization of social science, including colonial social science. Somewhat paradoxically, however, the Annales school did not promote connections between colonial sociologists and colonial historians and avoided modern colonial history until the end of the colonial era.

Colonial Statistics, Demography, and Sociology

In order to understand the relationship between statistics, demography, and sociology in the colonial empire, we need to begin with a brief overview of the history of statistics and demography. Statistics was the centerpiece of the forms of expertise offered to early modern states by cameralism (chapter 4). Statistics in its "oldest, eighteenth-century sense" was "a description of the state, by and for itself," according to Alain Desrosières.[33] In the eighteenth century, "a sort of statistical fever seems to seize the administration," leading to the collection of data on population, land, and property.[34] A national statistical office was created in 1833, becoming the *Statistique générale de la France* in 1840.[35] Under the Vichy regime, the statistical office was transformed from an "artisanal" establishment into a veritable "factory of enumeration," with 8,042 employees by 1944.[36] After Liberation, a new statistical office was created, the *Institut national de la statistique et des études économiques* (National Institute of Statistics and Economic Studies, or INSEE). INSEE gained "independence towards politics" and was charged with developing statistics into "a vast domain covering the demographic, economic, and social fields."[37] Its professional staff came from a prestigious *grande école*, the *École nationale de la statistique et de l'administration économique*, where they received training in advanced "statistics and probability as well as in economics, econometrics and some sociology."[38] INSEE's full name included the phrase *"pour le Métropole et la France d'outre-mer"* (for the Metropole and Overseas France), and its logo explicitly symbolized the colonies by including maritime images.[39]

The collection of statistics was introduced in the first French empire due to concerns with taxation and military recruitment. In 1635, the directors of the *Compagnie des isles de l'Amérique* instructed its employees to count the conquered islands' inhabitants as soon as the cross had been planted in the ground and the "savages had submitted to His Majesty."[40] Censuses were taken in Martinique starting in 1660 and in Canada starting in 1667.[41] Procedures for regular colonial censuses were established during the reign of Louis XIV.[42] The French statistical office was charged with "establishing the inventory of available administrative facts" both in "the national territory and the colonies."[43] The colonial navy administration published brochures on population, agriculture, and commerce in the empire.[44]

The second French empire, which sprang into existence in the 1880s, saw a standardization of statistics. In 1909, the Colonial Office instructed overseas administrators to provide detailed statistics in their annual reports. Professional statisticians were hired by the Colonial Office during the 1930s, and a full-fledged colonial statistical service (*Service coloniale des statistiques*) was created in 1943.[45] Statistical offices were created in Indochina (1923), Tunisia (1942), Cameroon (1945), and Bamako in French Sudan.[46] Researchers were brought in from the metropole to train indigenous statistical personnel.[47] In Morocco, the French statistical service was responsible for updating the "repertoire of tribes and agglomerations."[48] One of the most active colonial statistical offices was created in 1937 in Algeria, which "had a greater degree of autonomy from the Governor General, compared to its homologues in Tunisia and Morocco."[49] After 1945, a robust program of gathering data was seen as essential for guiding colonial development plans.[50] The Algerian statistical office encompassed a freestanding research division, while the *Association pour la recherche démographique, économique et sociale* provided an official stamp of approval for Bourdieu's research projects, "his first articles, and two additional books," and supplied him with resources.[51] INSEE sent a number of statisticians from the metropole during the Algerian revolutionary war.[52]

Demography is largely a subfield of statistics, the statistical study of human populations. In France, the *Institut national d'études démographiques* (National Institute for Demographic Research, INED) was closely aligned with the Statistical Office. Like statistics in general, demography was also deeply involved in the colonial empire and with sociologists. INED grew directly out of a Vichyist institution, the *Fondation française pour l'étude des problèmes humains*, or Fondation Carrel. This foundation was created by Alexis Carrel, a French Nobel Prize–winning surgeon and biologist who became a defender of ideas about civilizational degeneracy and eugenics after his forced retirement from the Rockefeller Institute for Medical Research in 1939. Carrel enthusiastically endorsed the 1933 Nazi sterilization law. In 1939, he praised Hitler, Mussolini, and Nazi annexations in the east, characterizing critiques of Nazi Germany as "Bolshevik and Jewish propaganda."[53] Carrel returned to France in 1941 and "offered his services to Vichy," setting up his institute in the Paris offices of the Rockefeller Foundation.[54] At its peak, the Carrel Foundation had more than 400 permanent members from a variety of natural and social science disciplines, located in 16 main teams and other specialized units.[55] The entire organization was oriented toward Carrel's goal of improving the French population through eugenics and sociobiology. The foundation granted a great deal of autonomy to its researchers due to Carrel's understanding of the American model of foundations and research institutes. At the same time, all of the research teams "set up links and partnerships with every ministry" of the Vichy government, including the Colonial Office.[56] Similar to the statistical offices described above, the Carrel Foundation promoted a rapprochement between statistics and other disciplines by employing professional social scientists. INED was created in October 1945 as the direct legal successor of the Fondation Carrel, whose employees provided half of INED's original staff. INED also replaced the Vichy *Service de démographie*.[57]

Demography was closely tied to the empire due to administrators' concerns with disease, rising birthrates in North Africa, falling birthrates in Equatorial Africa, and related questions.[58] INED researchers were involved in studies of the colonies and North African immigration to the metropole.[59] INED's first director, Alfred Sauvy, was a polytechnician and student of Halbwachs. Sauvy endowed the institute with a broad focus that reached far beyond demography proper, recruiting economists, survey researchers, a historian, geographer, ethnologist, and several psychologists.[60] Sauvy argued that cultural and historical factors were often more relevant to the problem of underdevelopment than demography.[61] Balandier praised Sauvy's "global approach" for giving "almost equal importance" to the "demographic, economic, and sociological aspects of the problem."[62] Sauvy coined the phrase *tiers monde* ("third world") in analogy to the Third Estate in the French Revolution.[63]

Colonial demography overlapped with a number of different disciplines, including sociology. Robert Gessain, who participated in transpolar expeditions to Greenland before World War II, developed a research focus on Senegal while working as an ethnologist for INED.[64] Historian Louis Chevalier, best known for his book *Classes laborieuses et classes dangereuses* (1958), carried out two colonial projects. In *Le problème démographique nord-africain* (1947), Chevalier discussed population together with economic, social, anthropological, psychological, and religious topics. Chevalier's 1952 study of Madagascar resembled contemporary trends in sociology, focusing on the impact of French colonialism on demographic and economic trends in different regions of the island.[65]

What about sociology's relation to demography and statistics? In contrast to the early polarization between French sociology and economics and psychology, discussed in the previous chapter, the relations here were close. Durkheim's admonition to treat social facts as things was widely understood at the time as a call to quantify social reality. Maurice Halbwachs, who wrote extensively on social statistics and probability theory, was considered to be the "most Durkheimian of the interwar Durkheimians."[66] Two other scholars close to Durkheim, historian Lucien Herr and economist François Simiand, advocated data collection in order to better understand the conditions of wage labor.[67]

The most influential demographer and statistician who merged these fields with French sociology during the middle decades of the twentieth century was Jean Stoetzel. And as it turns out, Stoetzel was also involved in colonial social research.

JEAN STOETZEL AND ROBERT BLANC: DIVERGENT APPROACHES TO COLONIAL DEMOGRAPHY

We must always add that social scientists are increasingly convinced of the usefulness of introducing numbers and measurements into their research whenever possible. . . . the more our sociological knowledge becomes quantitative, the more solid and scientific our knowledge will become.

—JEAN STOETZEL (1946)[68]

Jean Stoetzel graduated from the *École normale supérieure* in the mid-1930s with a degree in philosophy. His thesis, however, was on the seemingly unphilosophical topic of the psychology of advertising. Stoetzel visited Columbia University in 1937–1939 and "got in touch with the Gallup organization and soon learned how polling worked."[69] Stoetzel then returned to France and created the private *Institut français d'opinion publique* in 1938, where he carried out "doxometric" research, i.e., surveys.[70] During the Nazi Occupation, Stoetzel headed a survey department in the French Statistical Services office, directed a Social Psychology team at the Fondation Carrel, and carried out opinion polling for an employers' research organization.[71] After 1944, Stoetzel co-directed the Social Psychology Section of INED and was professor of "Psycho-Sociology" at Bordeaux (1945–1955), before being named to a chair in "Social Psychology" at the Sorbonne (1955–1978). Stoetzel also directed the main postwar organization for sociological research, the *Centre d'études sociologiques*, from 1956 to 1968, and founded and served as editor-in-chief of the *Revue française de sociologie* from 1960 to 1987.

Stoetzel was the leading voice in France advocating an "American-inspired" approach to sociology that rejected theory and promoted quantitative methods, empirical research, a teamwork model organized around a division of social scientific labor, and an orientation toward standardized, commercialized, and applicable results.[72] Stoetzel explicitly rejected Durkheim's legacy in French sociology and advocated Le Play as an alternative founder—despite Durkheim's openness to quantification.[73] Stoetzel epitomizes the postwar merger of demography and statistics into French sociology.

Stoetzel was also involved in research on colonial settings and immigrants from the French colonies. This underscores the fact that colonial settings had become completely normalized as research sites for sociologists of all methodological stripes.[74] Indeed, as director of the *Centre d'études sociologiques*, Stoetzel supported the existence of its "overseas"—i.e., colonial—research group. In 1953–1954, Stoetzel and another demographer-cum-sociologist, Alain Girard, carried out a survey of 500 Algerian immigrants in France.[75] While this study called attention to differences between Algerian and European immigrants, it did not even mention the fact that most Algerian immigrants were also colonized subjects at the time, and that it was still extremely difficult for them to acquire French citizenship.[76] The authors suggest, implausibly, that the problems of the metropolitan French in adjusting to Algerian immigrants were of the same character as the difficulties of the Algerian immigrants themselves. Compared to the work of Balandier and other sociologists at the time, or to Abdelmalek Sayad's future research on the immigrant's suffering and double consciousness, this research is analytically impoverished.[77] In 1958–1959, Stoetzel directed a team of ten researchers studying working-class Algerian families who were resettled in the Sahara. In a summary of this research entitled "what an ideal Saharan city would look like," Stoetzel overlooked the fact that the Algerians he was discussing were French colonial subjects rather than citizens. He went on to compare their "attitudes" to those of French citizens in the metropole.[78] Here again, Stoetzel ignored the colonial context and appeared to be almost willfully ignorant of the sociological research being carried out by members of his adopted discipline and even his own laboratory at the time. Stoetzel's approach to colonial problems demonstrates that colonialist sociology was alive and well after 1945 at the heart of the discipline.

The work of the French demographer Robert Blanc exemplifies a more fruitful collaboration between colonial statisticians and sociology. Blanc wrote extensively on the "special methods of investigation" required for demographic research in sub-Saharan African colonies. He rejected the use of the *tournée* (tour) system, traditionally used by colonial officials. Applied to censuses, this involved "herding people into certain spots which may be a long way from their homes" in order to be counted.[79] Africans regarded these censuses with suspicion because they had been used to "afford a basis for taxation." Blanc replaced the *tournée* approach with a "*hut to hut system*" in which individuals were surveyed at home. He also argued that records should be organized on cards for extended families in order to avoid breaking up "the fundamental cell of the African community." Villagers should be prepared for an upcoming census through "oral propaganda" directed toward "chiefs" and "notables." Most important, the focus should be on "births and deaths as opposed to the administrative censuses where the main purpose is to discover persons liable to tax."[80]

Blanc refined his "methodological doctrines" for "underdeveloped" settings in an ambitious survey of the Guinean population in 1954–1955, the *Mission démographique de Guinée*.[81] This was the first census in French Africa to use sampling techniques. A total of 300,000 individual responses were collected in a colony with around 2,570,000 inhabitants.[82] One of the survey's goals was to train African researchers.[83] The survey team consisted entirely of Guineans, and the number of surveyors from each ethnic group was proportionate to that group's representation in the population.[84]

A noteworthy feature of the *Mission démographique de Guinée* was that it brought colonial statisticians together with sociologists. The survey's supervisors included two members of IFAN's sociology section, Gérard Brasseur and Louis Massé.[85] Blanc explained that it was crucial to include sociology in order to make sure the survey was asking "the right questions . . . in the right form" and that interviews would be "correctly interpreted."[86] Sociology, for Blanc, seemed to offer expertise both in methods and the theoretical interpretation of data.

Anthropology/Ethnology in Greater France and Its Connections to Sociology

Anthropology's borders with sociology were even more porous than the latter's borders with statistics and demography. The intense interaction between anthropology and sociology lasted throughout the modern colonial era, and then declined after the mid-1960s. Indeed, many outsiders, even after 1945, continued to use the word "sociology" to refer to the field that scholars since Griaule had sought to have recognized as distinct. Sociologists' presence at colonial research sites magnified the overlap between the two disciplines. The empire and its indigenous populations had always been the focus for most subfields of ethnology/anthropology, with the exception of folklore, which studied traditional culture in the metropole.[87] Similarly, the idea of "decolonizing" anthropology was already on the agenda in the 1930s, long before its emergence in sociology.[88] Like the other disciplines discussed here, anthropologists varied greatly in their views of the legitimacy of colonial rule, but those entering the discipline after 1945 were generally favorable to independence.

What I am calling "anthropology" actually had three different labels in French, each with a slightly differing relationship to sociology and colonialism: *anthropologie*, *ethnographie*, and *ethnologie*. A fixed meaning began to accrue to *anthropologie* with the establishment of the *Société d'anthropologie* in 1859. This organization was founded by the anatomist, surgeon, and racial scientist Paul Broca, and was "dominated by medical doctors."[89] Anthropology was thus a kind of natural science. Charles Letourneau, who succeeded Broca as secretary general of the *Société d'anthropologie*, furnished the first French example of the scientific genre in which information on contemporaneous colonized or "primitive" societies is assembled to suggest a linear trajectory of social evolution.[90] Durkheim respected Letourneau's socialist politics and agreed with his distinction between ethnography as fact-gathering and sociology as theoretical synthesis, but Durkheim still characterized Letourneau's work as pseudo-scientific.[91] The most extreme version of a raciological anthropology in nineteenth-century France was the "*anthroposociologie*" of Georges Vacher de Lapouge, who reintroduced the ideas of Gobineau, the "inventor of racism."[92] The Durkheimians attacked Lapouge.[93]

Naturalist forms of "anthropology" were the first ones to be represented in the French university system. The only anthropology chair during the nineteenth century was held by Jean-Louis Armand de Quatrefages de Bréau at the *Muséum national d'histoire naturelle* from 1855 to 1892. Quatrefages defined his field as encompassing cultural and physical studies, and he rejected polygenist theories of the origin of races. He was open to "questions regarding the historical development of cultures" and was not a biologically reductionist racist.[94] Quatrefages argued that Polynesian cultures were doomed and urgently needed paternalistic colonial protection.[95] Quatrefages's successor in 1892 was the medically trained Ernest-Théodore Hamy, who promoted ethnographic expeditions and curated the Trocadéro Museum of Ethnography.[96] Hamy founded two journals that combined physical anthropology and ethnography (a less naturalistic term, discussed below).[97] The naturalist connotations of the word *anthropologie* remained intact until the 1950s, when Lévi-Strauss began his energetic and eventually successful campaign to redefine the French word by associating it with British social anthropology and American cultural anthropology.[98]

The word *ethnographie* came into use in French in the 1820s. The term remained "notoriously vague" throughout the nineteenth century, yet it is clear that its connotations were completely different from contemporary understandings of *anthropologie* and from our own present-day understandings of the word "ethnography."[99] In the discussions of the *Société d'ethnographie*, created in 1859, the word *ethnographie* was associated with anti-materialist, humanistic, politically conservative studies of historical peoples understood as unique and incommensurable. This approach stood in stark contrast to the generalizing, scientific approaches associated with *anthropologie*.[100] French *ethnographie* was aligned with the epistemologies of nineteenth-century German historicism, which emphasized the singularity of historical events, individuals, and human societies, and the radical difference between the human and natural sciences.[101] Prior to the creation of the Fifth Section of the *École pratique des hautes études* in 1886, ethnography was taught only at the *École nationale des langues orientales*, although it "necessarily remained peripheral to the school's main purpose," instruction in Oriental languages. Culturally oriented African and American studies were also taught at the Fifth Section of the *École pratique des hautes études*, and professional societies of Americanists and Africanists were founded in 1895 and 1930, respectively.[102] These fields were also often described as forms of *ethnographie*. Durkheim and Mauss argued that ethnography was an entirely *descriptive* endeavor, whereas sociology, which was comparative, theoretical, and generalizing. The *Société d'ethnographie* was thus "reduced gradually to a dilettantish marginality" and "remained distinct" from Durkheimian sociology.[103]

A third keyword, *ethnologie*, surfaced briefly in the nineteenth century and was then "revived in the 1920s by the Durkheimians under the leadership of Marcel Mauss" to describe a new academic specialty.[104] The founding of the *Institut d'ethnologie* in 1925 (chapter 5) shifted French anthropology's center of gravity away from the physical and naturalistic approaches that had been dominant throughout the nineteenth century, even if they retained a place in the Institute's program of instruction. As Paul Rivet explained, the decision to name the broader orientation "ethnology" stemmed from the fact that *anthropologie* "had become associated with physical anthropology alone," while "ethnographie" *excluded* naturalist approaches.[105] *Ethnologie* was thus a compromise term that avoided the extremes of naturalistic scientism and Germanic historicism. Marcel Griaule occupied the first French university chair in ethnology at the Sorbonne, starting in 1942. This was followed by the creation of ethnology chairs in Lyon in 1944, for André Leroi-Gourhan, and Bordeaux in 1953, for Pierre Métais.[106]

RELATIONS BETWEEN ANTHROPOLOGY, SOCIOLOGY, AND COLONIALISM BEFORE 1945

The first step toward a systematic integration of anthropology with the needs of colonial administrators was marked by the creation of the *Institut français d'anthropologie* (IFA) in 1911. This was a result of efforts by Durkheim, Mauss, and Hamy's successor at the Natural Museum's anthropology chair, René Verneau. The IFA became a venue where natural-scientific anthropologists and Durkheimian sociologists interacted with each other and with colonial administrators.[107] Durkheim, Mauss, and Lévy-Bruhl all served as officials in the IFA, and the Durkheimians Henri Hubert and Robert Hertz were active before 1914. Two colonial ethnographers-cum-sociologists were elected as IFA Councilors following the war: Maurice Leenhardt and René Maunier.[108] After 1945, the sociologists Chombart de Lauwe and René Dumont joined the IFA, as did many of the leading ethnologists.[109]

The boundaries between anthropology and sociology were very permeable during the first half of the twentieth century. The cross-disciplinary traffic was unencumbered partially because both disciplines were institutionally weak, with limited resources and public recognition, and a tiny number of full-time teaching or research positions. A relative balance in terms of the institutional and social power of sciences often increases their openness to interdisciplinary exchange.[110] Yet sociology had greater intellectual cachet at the time, due to the Durkheimian school, which was seen as foundational in both disciplines. Durkheim and Mauss defined anthropology and ethnography as "subdisciplines" of sociology and descriptive endeavors whose function was to provide "the kind of information useful to a comparative sociology."[111] Mauss was the key figure bridging the two disciplines after Durkheim's death. Mauss lectured to many emerging scholars in both disciplines at the *Institut d'ethnologie*, the Fifth Section of the *École pratique des hautes études*, and the *Collège de France*.[112] Less imperious than Durkheim, Mauss still continued to locate sociology on a higher intellectual plane than anthropology.[113]

Relations between the two fields were increasingly troubled. Both claimed jurisdiction over the same vast ontological terrain: all of humanity. Marcel Griaule, the leading ethnologist of the interwar years, defined his discipline as "the science of man in his entirety (*homo sapiens et faber*)."[114] This stood in contrast to the situation in the United States, where anthropology tended from the beginning to be assigned explicitly to the study of indigenous and colonized Others, while sociology took as its object the modern, metropolitan Self, or else defined itself abjectly as a science of ontological leftovers, "bits and pieces that the other social sciences do not cover," as one sociologist put it.[115] Tension between the two fields in France also stemmed from the fact that sociology had been more successful in integrating itself into the French educational system. Sociology was introduced into "optional programs in the *baccalauréat* and the philosophy class in the French *lycées*" and even into the training of primary school teachers, whereas "no part of ethnology was ever taught to schoolchildren in France."[116] Sociology and ethnology both gained the right to train students for a certificate that could be used as part of a *licence* degree in the 1920s, but sociology outpaced ethnology in terms of the number of certificates earned (chapter 9). Conversely, anthropology had better success in attracting research funding. Between the wars, the Institute of Ethnology attracted Rockefeller funding before the more sociological *Centre de documentation sociale* (chapter 9).

There was also an undercurrent of political division between the disciplines, at least before the 1930s. The Durkheimians had converged politically as a movement around the Dreyfus case. Several Durkheimians became active in antiracist campaigns between the wars, contributing articles on colonial and fascist racism to the journal *Races et racisme* (1937–1939), for example.[117] Durkheimians published attacks on sociobiology, anthropo-sociology, polygenetic theory, and Social Darwinism, all of which were associated with anthropology.[118] Whereas anthropology in the United States was associated with the liberal antiracism of Frantz Boas, Robert Lowie, Margaret Mead, Edward Sapir, and others, French anthropologists were quite openly connected to colonialism during the exploitative era of *mise en valeur* policies between the wars. This made it more difficult for French anthropologists to avoid questions of colonial complicity, especially once Michel Leiris published his exposé *Phantom Africa* (see below).

By 1937, according to one contemporary, French ethnologists were showing "an ever increasing tendency to reassert the autonomy of their discipline" from sociology and "to reject ... sociological hypotheses."[119] These divisions became sharper after 1945, as we will see in the following section.

PRIMITIVISM AND THE SOCIOLOGY-ANTHROPOLOGY RELATION

One of the main differences between sociology and ethnology revolved around *primitivism*. In the next chapter, I will examine the critique of primitivism by several interwar ethno-sociologists. In order to understand this critique, however, we must first reconstruct the primitivist position.

A cluster of political, social-theoretical, aesthetic, moral, and personal factors came together in overdetermining anthropologists' fondness for supposedly primitive cultures. Politically, the alleged backwardness of colonized societies helped to explain to colonizers why they should feel justified in claiming sovereignty over conquered territories. In an era of dawning awareness of human rights and international law, the only plausible justification for foreign overrule was the incapacity of local inhabitants to govern themselves. This was the colonial-era equivalent of the present-day doctrine of "failed states." This legitimation strategy primarily sought the approval of the inhabitants of imperial European countries themselves, particularly those who were sensitive to ethical arguments and international objections to colonialism coming from the United States or the USSR.[120]

The primitivizing ideology was reinforced by the colonial policies known as indirect rule or associationism (chapter 4). This approach necessitated the preservation of indigenous traditions or invented traditions. Anthropologists were called upon to identify native leaders, reconstruct their customs, and contribute to the codification of customary law. This context strengthened anthropologists' predilections for seeking out the most foreign, exotic, or traditional populations for study. Delegating power to native chiefs, who were charged with governing their own tribes according to customary doctrine, reinforced primitivism. As French sociologist Charles Le Coeur observed in 1939, based on his ethnographic research among the Téda of Chad, European colonialism *caused* primitivization. Le Coeur rejected what he called the "inanity" of Lévy-Bruhl's theory of "primitive mentality," writing that "the Téda are not 'primitives' in European scholars' sense; but they are becoming so, as European rule pushes them from science and rationality into ritual and magic."[121] Fanon made an identical argument 22 years later, writing that religion, magic, dance, "vampirism, possession by djinns, by zombies, and by Legba, the illustrious god of voodoo," all play "a key regulating role in ensuring the stability of the colonized world."[122] Colonial overrule was preserved by slowing the advance of the modernizing forces unleashed by European penetration. Modern colonialism was a contradictory formation whose policies pushed simultaneously toward cultural mummification and turbulent change. Social scientists may have endorsed primitivism mainly for other reasons, but their preferences resonated with these colonial policies, and were correspondingly reinforced, at least until the 1940s. The intellectual movement away from primitivism at midcentury was thus also a function of ongoing trends in colonial policy toward deliberate development.[123]

In addition to its usefulness in legitimating colonialism and its resonance with indirect rule, primitivism also served European psychological and aesthetic needs. Cultural movements of longing for a primitive alternative to European civilization existed throughout the modern era, varying by period and geography.[124] The memoirs of many colonial officials, travelers, traders, and social scientists reveal a fascination with worlds that differed as strongly as possible from their European homelands.[125] Contemporary "archaic" cultures were appropriated by modern art in its turn toward primitivism and by the surrealists of the *Collège de sociologie* in their critique of Europe.[126]

The leading advocate of a version of primitivism in French anthropology was Marcel Griaule, a student of Mauss best known for his work on the Dogon and Bambara in the French Sudan. Griaule led the two-year Dakar to Djibouti expedition for the Institute of Ethnology, financed by the French government and the Rockefeller Foundation. Its aim was "to study certain Black populations and their various activities" along a route stretching from Senegal to Ethiopia. They were also to collect records and objects for French museums.[127] Griaule directed other expeditions before and after World War II, wrote pathbreaking studies of Dogon culture, and mentored many ethnologists.[128] He inspired the ethnographic filmmaking of Jean Rouch, which took a distinctly anticolonial turn.[129] Griaule's own relationship to French colonialism, however, was basically supportive. He wrote that "knowledge of mentalities is useful in the current practice of [colonial] government."[130] In his African fieldwork, Griaule "played colonial roles with gusto."[131]

Griaule's political position began to shift in the late 1930s. He was highly critical of the Italian invasion of Ethiopia in 1936, and was involved in ill-fated plans to foment revolts in Abyssinia and Morocco.[132] After Liberation, Griaule joined the liberal French political party, *Mouvement républicaine populaire*, which contained some of the most "diehard colonialists in the French political establishment."[133] However, Griaule now argued that France's role was "no longer cultural and military imperialism," but that it should send "numerous and well-equipped sociologists and ethnologists" to study African cultures and contribute to the autonomous development of newly independent postcolonies.[134]

According to Benoît de l'Estoile, the expeditions sponsored by the Institute of Ethnology were "blind to everything that did not correspond to the image of a preserved Africa."[135] Paul Rivet argued that ethnography should completely exclude "the European aspects of overseas civilizations" in their "presentation of other cultures."[136] Griaule tried to prevent the colonial context from intruding into his depiction of African customs—even though his large research teams, with their airplanes, boats, and recording equipment in remote locations, "drastically changed life in [whatever] village" they were studying.[137] Griaule deliberately sought out the most "archaic" African cultures and individuals and prioritized uncolonized countries like Ethiopia. The Dakar-Djibouti expedition prepared a detailed study of the Kirdi in northern Cameroon, who had not been assimilated to Islam, while ignoring the Islamic neighboring tribes. As Leiris noted ironically, the latter tribes seemed "artificial" and "corrupt" alongside the Kirdi, these "extremely sympathetic people who walk around stark naked and present exactly what we mean when we talk about 'savages.'"[138] Griaule excoriated Balandier for studying the new, messianic, syncretic African churches rather than traditional religions.[139] In his posthumously published *Méthode de l'ethnographie*, Griaule warned students against using informants who represent "the type of liar ... who has been subjected to European influence," that is, the *indigène évolué* (evolved native).[140] This vision of the colonized subject as endangering the colonizer by nimbly switching between native and European codes was a widespread colonial trope and, indeed, a central determinant of colonial policymaking, since "lying" and code-switching threatened to undercut efforts to stabilize colonized cultures around controlled versions of their own tradition.[141]

Griaule was not the only ethnologist who preferred his natives "pure."[142] The Africanist Denise Paulme, a student of Griaule, expressed this preference half-jokingly. Paulme recalled pitying Alfred Métraux, who had done research in Argentina, Easter Island, and Hawaii, for encountering only "displaced and sick people and anemic societies where the observer, arriving too late, can only collect faded memories that interest no one." "Nothing could be more depressing," she concluded.[143] However, Paulme broke with primitivism in her 1940 doctoral thesis, which detailed the degradation of social conditions among the Dogon, previously described by Griaule as idyllic. Paulme also rejected Griaule's model of the large expeditionary research team.[144]

After 1945, many French ethnologists moved away from the reflexive preference for rural, isolated, supposedly motionless cultures. A few already made this move in the 1930s, and Leiris was one of the first. A founding member of French surrealism who combined ethnography and psychoanalysis, Leiris was renowned as a writer, art critic and collector, and public intellectual.[145]

Leiris earned *certificats* in sociology and ethnology and a *licence* diploma in Letters. He was invited by Griaule to participate in the Dakar-Djibouti mission in 1931–1933 as archivist and notetaker. Leiris published his first report on the mission in the Marxist journal *Masses* in March 1933, immediately after his return from Africa. Here Leiris "did not repeat the leitmotif of the utility of ethnography for the governance of the colonies," nor the theme of the urgency of salvaging customs and artefacts in "doomed cultures." Instead, Leiris called for the study of material culture and "insisted on the dynamism of the populations too often assimilated to historical relics." He even suggested, "in total contradiction with the practices of the period, that the field of ethnographic studies should encompass the oppressed worker and the boss, movements of national liberation, and the capitalist world."[146]

Whereas "the majority of ethnologists working in Black Africa . . . almost never referred to the colonial context," Leiris described the Dakar-Djibouti expedition as a form of "colonial plunder" in his 1934 book *L'Afrique fantôme* (*Phantom Africa*). This publication ruined Leiris's relationship with Griaule, who feared it would "endanger the future of field studies."[147] In a revised preface to *L'Afrique fantôme* written in 1950, Leiris argued that any genuine contact across the colonizer-colonized divide would be possible only on the basis of shared participation in anticolonial struggle.[148] The same year, Leiris argued in *Les temps modernes* that even supposedly autonomous forms of ethnology were inseparably linked to the colonial context.[149] Leiris was the first French social scientist to criticize his colleagues for working with colonial governments. Unlike Lévy-Bruhl and Mauss, who offered sociology's services to the Colonial Office, or Maunier, who tried to analyze colonialism in a value-neutral manner, Leiris forged a role for the ethnologist as anticolonial critic.

More important in the present context, and setting the stage for postwar colonial sociology, Leiris "warned against definitions of authenticity that excluded *evolués* and the impurities of cultural syncretism."[150] Leiris insisted that "ethnographic objectivity consisted in describing the real state of colonized societies," rather than their idealized condition before or outside of colonialism.[151] According to Leiris, "just as what I liked about jazz music was the *mélange*, the aspect '*métis*'—which was forged from African roots and the contribution of Occidental civilization—I also liked the Antilles due to the cultural 'clash' that was produced there."[152] The most "authentic" Africans, in Leiris' words, "the most interesting, humanly," were those whom anthropologists dismissed as "mere imitators" of Western culture.[153] Leiris also introduced a reflection on the *history* of these societies, a dimension neglected by Griaule's Africanist school, but one that would become central to the work of colonial sociologists such as Berque and Balandier after the war.

Those who rejected the primitivist preference often described themselves as sociologists, especially after 1944. Indeed, the very label *sociology* came to signal this move at that moment. I will discuss some of the scholars located at the fluid border between sociology and ethnology in the next chapter.

RELATIONS BETWEEN ANTHROPOLOGY AND SOCIOLOGY, 1945–1965

Sociology and anthropology began to crystallize as more bounded fields between 1945 and the mid-1960s. Sociology chairs were entirely distinct from ethnology chairs. The two disciplines were never combined into a joint section of the CNRS.[154] The French Institute for Black Africa established separate sections and employment lines for sociology and ethnology starting in 1952. ORSTOM had a sociology section but no separate anthropology or ethnology section, at least during the period examined here.

Disciplinary boundaries also became more fraught as sociology became more powerful. Sociology continued to exceed anthropology in terms of the number of certificates earned after 1945 (chapter 9). Sociology began offering specialized *licence* degrees in 1958, a decade before anthropology. The *cursus* for the sociology university degree developed out of the certificate in Morals and Sociology that was part of the philosophy *licence*, whereas the first ethnology *cursus* did not emerge until the early 1970s.[155] Sociology had more professors (*directeurs d'études*) than ethnology at the Sixth Section of the *École pratique des hautes études*. Indeed, Claude Lévi-Strauss was located in the sociology division at the Sixth Section until 1968.

Another reason for increased tension was the encroachment by sociologists on field sites and methods previously understood as belonging to anthropology. Whereas a social scientist observing a colonized culture before the late 1930s would have been assumed to be an ethnologist, this was no longer the case after 1945. A survey of 164 people learning how to conduct "ethnological" research in France in 1953 found that more identified with sociology than anthropology as their main discipline (*discipline de base*). Indeed, there were more "*socio-technologues*" (social science technologists or methodologists)—a different category than *sociologues*—than there were *anthropologues* among these students. The disproportion was largest among the younger researchers, that is, those who had not reached at least the rank of Lecturer (*maître de conférences*), suggesting that the trend would continue into the future.[156]

Sociology also benefitted from its reputation as a more "progressive social science" opposed to clericalism, fascism, anti-Semitism, and racism. Sociology's reputation was less tarnished by fascism than anthropology's at the moment of Liberation, although in reality, both groups had mixed records. Anthropologists at the *Musée de l'homme* had created the first resistance cell in occupied Paris, and some were imprisoned or killed by the Nazis. Sociologists and ethnologists were both driven into exile for "racial" and political reasons.[157] Both disciplines also included fascist collaborators. Sociologist George

Montandon, France's answer to the Nazi eugenicist Eugen Fischer, delivered 3,800 certificates aimed at resolving cases of "membership in the 'Jewish race'" during the Occupation and earned "several million francs for conducting" these examinations.[158] Several scholars close to sociology were active in the above-mentioned Carrel Foundation during the Occupation.[159] Griaule maneuvered to obtain the first Sorbonne chair in ethnology and other advantages during the Occupation, although he was cleared of charges of collaboration.[160] The differing political reputations of sociology and anthropology after Liberation had less to do with differences in their wartime activities than their perceived complicity with colonial racism, which quickly came under attack in progressive circles. Anthropology therefore became suspect.

The French Communist Party played a complex role in all of this. The Comintern came out against colonialism in 1925.[161] Although the Communists' stance on colonialism wavered, the Party constituted a pole of attraction for indigenous and French students and scholars in the colonies. Yet the Communists had a fraught relationship with sociology, which they attacked as a "camouflaged tool of capitalist propaganda" and an "ideological superstructure of the present capitalist mode of production."[162] The rise of a Marxist sociology in the 1930s (Georges Friedmann) and especially in the 1950s (Henri Lefebvre) eroded this line of attack. There was a Communist Party cell named after the surrealist poet Paul Eluard in the *Centre d'études sociologiques*.[163]

Sociology came to be seen after the war as a kind of avant-garde, "a new word," even a "militant position," according to some participants in that moment.[164] Sociology embraced modern methods and techniques, including in the overseas empires, and it insisted on the modernity and equality of the colonized. Although some sociologists also became entangled with colonial administrations after 1945, this did little damage to the discipline's reputation overall. Sociology's presence in colonial regions was a fairly novel phenomenon that lasted for only a few decades, in contrast to anthropology, which had always already been there. More important, sociology pivoted to the metropole after decolonization and purged the colonial episode from its collective memory (chapter 2).

It was also crucial that many African and Arab intellectuals, social scientists, and politicians favored sociology over anthropology. Jacques Berque argued that the "interested parties" in "underdeveloped countries" rejected ethnology because it "humiliated" them by accepting "the colonial stereotype" of race relations and seeing the colonized only as "primitives." He urged these "interested parties" to speak "increasingly in terms of sociology."[165] The Cameroonian Francophone writer Mongo Beti described ethnology as serving the dominant order with a "characteristic violence," which Beti called "ethnologism." Beti developed the African novel using a perspective that he insisted was "resolutely *sociological*," which for him meant that it was "eminently *political*" and focused on internal "differentiations, tensions, crises" rather than frozen cultural essences.[166] In universities across the colonized and postcolonial world, anthropology was "demoted to a subdiscipline of sociology" or eliminated.[167] The *Congrès des hommes de culture noirs*, sponsored by *Présence africaine* in Rome in 1959, included a subcommittee on sociology but not anthropology.[168]

The Algerian revolution accentuated the political animus against ethnology. This was partly in response to the *École d'Alger* and to the fact that the colony had been governed in 1955 by the prominent anthropologist Jacques Soustelle, who militantly opposed Algerian independence (chapter 8). Ethnologist Paul Rivet came out against the Algerian uprising in 1955.[169] The ethnologist and resistance heroine Germaine Tillion supported sweeping social reforms in Algeria, but rejected independence.[170] In response, the Algerian Minister of Higher Education and Research stated in 1971 that ethnology was "contaminated by colonialism." The 24th Conference of the International Institute of Sociology, held in Algiers in 1974, resolved to abolish anthropology outright.[171]

A contrary movement in favor of ethnology began with decolonization. Anthropology quickly regained prestige within the French intellectual and cultural spheres. The Parisian art world remained strongly attracted to primitivism and exoticism, bolstering anthropology's allure. With the publication of *Tristes tropiques* (1955), Lévi-Strauss bridged the literary and anthropological modes, recalling the interwar *Collège de sociologie* and contemporary efforts by Leiris and Balandier.[172] Lévi-Strauss avoided carrying out research in French colonies. His structuralism gave primitivism a new, intellectualized luster, combining it with the most classical of French social scientific traditions—Durkheimianism—and engaging with cutting-edge linguistic and literary theories (structuralism, semiotics), with their scientific allure and universalizing claims. Structuralism à la Lévi-Strauss moved to the heart of the humanities and social sciences, setting the national agenda for a decade.[173] Balandier observed that structuralism was "a liquid in which everything was swimming" until 1968.[174] Bourdieu described himself as having been temporarily seduced by "blissful structuralism" before breaking with it in his *Outline of a Theory of Practice*. Bourdieu also credited Lévi-Strauss with "ennobling" anthropology and thereby easing Bourdieu's own transition from philosophy to the less "noble" social sciences, which had been considered pariah disciplines among French philosophy students at the *École normale supérieure*.[175]

A Meta-Field of Colonial Social Science

This chapter and the preceding one have shown that empire permeated the French social sciences adjacent to sociology throughout the modern colonial era, from the late nineteenth century until the 1960s. Rather than applying metropolitan social scientific models to the colonies, some members of these disciplines developed methods and theories tailored to the peculiarities of colonial life. They constructed colonies and colonialism as distinct analytic objects. New themes emerged in this work: the modernity of colonial societies; the colonies' pervasive racism; the splitting and dualism of social structures and individual consciousness; the overall destructiveness of European rule, in all spheres of life; the impact of empire on the metropole, and the emerging responses by the colonized to their oppression.

Colonial social thought was the most closely contiguous context shaping French sociology. Having mapped this formation, we can now turn to sociology proper. The next chapter will consider French sociology before 1945, including the small number of prewar colonial sociologists, as the most immediate intellectual context for postwar sociological thinking about colonial matters.

CHAPTER EIGHT

Theoretical Developments in Interwar Sociology as a Context for Postwar Colonial Sociology

> *The problems implied by the category of "constellation" require us not only to achieve a synoptical view of all the theoretical problems at a certain moment, but also to take the practical life problems into account.*
>
> —KARL MANNHEIM, "THE PROBLEM OF A SOCIOLOGY OF KNOWLEDGE" (1925)[1]

POSTWAR COLONIAL SOCIOLOGY was shaped both by general discussions in interwar sociology as a whole, and by the sociological literature specifically on colonialism that emerged in this period. These two interwar formations are the topic of this chapter. In chapter 9 I will argue that sociology did not disappear organizationally or institutionally between the wars, as some have suggested. Here, I am interested in interwar sociology's intellectual inventiveness. In the first part, I will discuss four unresolved problems that lingered in French sociology after Durkheim's death, relating to fieldwork, history, morals, and macro-level political forms. Sociological discussion of these topics between the wars provided some of the springboards for postwar colonial sociology. The second part of this chapter examines a small group of French ethno-sociologists who already began working in colonial settings between the wars. Each of them conducted original fieldwork, rejected primitivism, and explored the ways colonized cultures were responding to and being remade by colonialism. Several also discussed the ways colonialism was remaking Europe.

Theoretical and Methodological Discussions in Interwar Sociology

French sociology faced at least four unresolved analytic problems after Durkheim's death. The manner in which these questions were treated between the wars continued to resonate after 1945, with implications for colonial sociology. These problems concerned (1) sociology's turn to fieldwork and empirical research more generally; (2) sociology's opening to history and historicity; (3) sociology's move away from doctrines of axiological neutrality and toward a moral sociology; and (4) the sociology of states, empires, and colonial states as political formations. These themes emerged separately from colonial ethnosociology, but the two formations intersected, as we will see.

THE TURN TO EMPIRICAL FIELDWORK

Before World War I, French sociology was polarized between two general definitions. On the one hand, Durkheim suggested that the label *sociologist* should be restricted to those who redeployed information collected by others in order to reach theoretical generalizations. On the other hand, sociology was defined by Le Play and his followers as a science based on fieldwork and direct observation. Between the wars, Durkheimians became more open to the Le Playsian tradition. This was key for colonial sociology.

Mauss continued to repeat Durkheim's dictum about the hierarchical relation between theory and empirics. As late as 1935, Mauss still spoke of the "young ethnographers who are not quite capable of deep sociological research."[2] However, Mauss also encouraged all of his students to carry out their own first-hand fieldwork, and this applied even to certain self-described sociologists. The older distinction between ethnographer and sociologist was eroded at both ends of the Durkheimian sociological space. At the more ethnographic pole, figures such as Bastide, Leiris, Maunier, and Soustelle embedded their fieldwork in meta-level discussions of theory. At the more sociological pole, Halbwachs—never abandoned theory, but he also conducted surveys, analyzed statistics, and collected other types of empirical data.[3] Although many sociologists continued to work on conventionally philosophical topics such as ethics, some of the same people also carried out empirical research. This was even true of some of the Durkheimian philosophers teaching in secondary schools.[4]

Another aspect of this interwar metamorphosis of sociology was the Durkheimians' increasing acknowledgment of the Le Playsians' contributions. Mauss called Le Play "one of the founders of French Sociology," whose "great contribution was ... to the development of the technique of observation."[5] Le Play's own work continued to be somewhat disparaged, but there was positive affirmation of his method of "direct observation" and his international orientation.[6] Halbwachs adopted Le Play's methodology of studying workers' budgets in his 1913 *La classe ouvrière et les niveaux de vie*.[7] Georges Davy, a member of Durkheim's original circle, situated contemporary Le Playsians near the center of the French sociological field in 1926.[8] The Le Playsian sociologist Paul Bureau reciprocated this gesture with a largely appreciative discussion of Durkheim in his *Introduction to the Sociological Method*.[9] Another interwar Le Playsian, Joseph Wilbois (discussed below), developed an epistemological position that combined Le Play's dedication to detailed empirical research with a "Durkheimian" focus on causation and social laws, and a "Bergsonian" emphasis on the need to reconstruct subjectivity through "intuition."[10] Célestin Bouglé wrote in 1936 that "the moment might have arrived to marry the traditions of the Le Play school and the Durkheim school" in order "to better orient the efforts of those who have to teach sociology in France."[11] This rapprochement between theory and empirics was reflected in the work of colonial sociologists in both the Durkheimian and Le Playsian schools, as we will see.

The penetration of Durkheimian ideas into colonial social science resulted in a closer articulation between theory and empirical research. Although Bouglé is rarely recognized as a contributor to the sociology of colonialism, in his book *Essais sur le régime des castes*, he examines whether British colonial administration changed the traditional caste system. Bouglé concludes that the system persisted despite British policies that forced members of different Indian social groups into closer contact with one another. Other sociologists close to the Durkheimian tradition conducted colonial fieldwork between the wars. Ethnographers associated with the *École d'Alger* and the *Mission scientifique* in Morocco "self-consciously presented themselves as *sociologists*, and asserted their intellectual connections to the Durkheim school."[12] The Moroccan *Mission scientifique* was transformed into a "Sociological Section" within the colony's Directorate of Native Affairs in 1919.[13] The *Institut des hautes études marocaines*, created in Rabat in 1920, included a "sociological" section.[14] Robert Montagne and Charles Le Coeur both published their doctoral theses, based on Moroccan research, in the *Année sociologique* series. René Maunier's Algerian fieldwork relied on a mainly Durkheimian framework.[15] Mauss largely ignored colonialism in his scholarly work, while simultaneously criticizing it in his political activities and courting the Colonial Ministry and colonial circles in his role as co-founder of the Ethnological Institute. Nonetheless, Mauss began to understand that colonialism needed to be explicitly integrated into social analysis. In his essay "Fragment of a Plan for a General Descriptive Sociology (1934)," he acknowledged that "colonialism gives birth to new societies," and recommended that researchers focus on the "composite societies" created by colonization and the "immense field of changes in which they were engulfed." Such attention to the colonial field, Mauss noted, "as in the case of *métissage* ... opens up an immense field of observations."[16] Mauss was probably the first French social scientist to explicitly advocate a focus on modernizing and mixed native societies rather than putatively "untouched" ones. This was an avant-garde position at the time.

Le Playsian Sociology and Colonialism

The Le Playsian school was strongly associated with colonialism.[17] Like Durkheim, Le Play relied on the European colonial presence in Northern Africa to procure "family monographs of Arabs, Kabyles, and the fellahs, rural and urban, of Egypt." The difference was that Le Play and his followers generated their own data.[18] The second edition of Le Play's *Les Ouvriers européens* included monographs from Syria and Morocco. An even larger survey by Le Play and his successors, *Les ouvriers des deux mondes* (1857–1928) contained over a hundred case studies of individual families, 14 of them in colonial and imperial sites.[19] These monographs differed from other colonial ethnographies in their standardized format and because the subjects were not always selected to represent the most traditional indigenous cultures. Informants included a French settler in Algeria, an indigenous civil servant and a "coolie" in Cambodia, and a freed "mulatto" slave in Réunion.[20]

Le Play was unenthusiastic about colonialism, criticizing Napoleon I for his forceful annexations "against the natural inclination of our race," and arguing in 1872 that France favored "the practice and doctrine of self-determination (*droit des gens*)."[21] At the same time, Le Play bemoaned the decline in the French propensity to emigrate and colonize new lands.[22] Le Play's ideal "stem-family" system—according to which only one son was allowed to inherit—"depended crucially on the possibility of settlement and cultivation, by the remaining sons, of new lands"—that is, of territories seen as "subject to abandonment and barbarism."[23] Several of Le Play's followers were deeply involved in French colonialism.[24]

Two Le Playsian colonial monographs reveal the ways in which the tradition of close attention to empirical detail sometimes revealed facts that contradicted colonial ideologies or Le Play's political doctrines. Pierre Escard's study of a family in *Côte d'Ivoire* in 1910 set out to celebrate French colonialism, described by the author as possessing an "ideal beauty" and pursuing "man's march toward progress." French administration in *Côte d'Ivoire*, Escard wrote, had instituted education, hygiene, security, and tranquility. Yet Escard also described the erosion of the authority of the traditional "group leader" or chief, who had been degraded into an "auxiliary of the administration and the voice of the commandant." This aspect of colonial administration was directly at odds with Le Plays's commitment to strengthening families and local communities.[25]

The contradictions between colonial practice and Le Playsian politics became even more pronounced in a study of the Mandate colony of Cameroon by Joseph Wilbois. Wilbois was a researcher in the private sector working for Christian employers' associations, and a teacher at the *École d'administration et d'affaires*. His early work focused on management psychology and business administration, but during the 1930s he began writing critiques of capitalism and colonialism from a social Catholic perspective. After publishing *Le Cameroun*, he turned his attention to the provision of social services "in the French colonies of Black Africa."

Written at a different moment in the development of the Le Playsian school's methodology and by a more independent thinker, *Le Cameroun* does not focus on a single family, but surveys the entire colony. A dedicated Le Playsian, Wilbois was not satisfied with secondary literature, but travelled to Cameroon himself, where he consulted unpublished documents and "convers[ed] at length with Whites and Blacks."[26] In the book's introduction, Wilbois thanks colonial administrators, missionaries, and businessmen for their assistance. He concludes with the phrase "*magis amica veritas*," from "*Amicus Plato, sed magis amica veritas*" (Plato is my friend but truth is a better friend).

Wilbois's book combines moments of critical insight with the sort of racist stereotypes that were already becoming rare in professional colonial social science. The book's first part, focused on "the natives," hews closely to the traditional Le Playsian format. It begins with an overview of "material life" and then turns to "family life." Wilbois asserts that he is trying to provide a realistic picture of Cameroonian culture *before* European intervention, while acknowledging the impossibility of doing so. This section therefore has a semi-fictional quality that stands in tension with Le Playsian empiricism and seems to draw on nineteenth-century colonial novels and explorers' narratives and on the "primitivist" ethnographies that bracketed colonialism's presence (chapter 7). Wilbois describes African culture here as a Le Playsian patriarchal family utopia. The unity of the village, he asserts, is "not at all territorial" but "exclusively familial," a "fraternity." The difference between *chef de famille* and *chef de village* is a quantitative, not a qualitative one. At the same time, Wilbois observes that traditional family mores are being destroyed by European intrusion. Marriage by dowry has become more common with the rise of the money economy. Polygamy and paternal authority have been eroded. Religion itself is "almost a thing of the past in many parts of Cameroon." The Cameroonian forest, "previously impenetrable," will "soon no longer have any lairs or secrets" that can withstand the "invasion of the Whites." Whereas Escard celebrated the colony's "march toward progress," Wilbois speaks of "*that which we call progress*." But Wilbois then presents a "sketch of a portrait of the Black" that descends into crude stereotypes. This section is antithetical to both the fiction of the intact African family and to the vision of indigenous culture as being transformed by colonialism. Wilbois concludes the first section by admitting that the entire portrait has been fictional, claiming that "we have no other choice" than to "accept this truth, *or this legend*" about precolonial Africans.[27]

In its lurching between incompatible frames, models, and theories, Wilbois's text is closer to the amateur "travelers' tales" discussed by Edward Said in *Orientalism* than to the emerging professional sociology of colonialism.[28]

In the second half of the book, Wilbois addresses a different problem, which he calls "The Action of the Whites." This section is more rigorously empirical than the first, and thus better suited to contradicting stereotypes. Wilbois discusses in some detail the destructive impact of European officials, missionaries, and capitalists. Wilbois's *Le Cameroun* thus seems at first glance to be one of those texts that are "inertly of their time."[29] Yet it is also one of the first sociological studies, along with Maunier's *Sociologie coloniale*, to place colonizers and colonized within a single frame. The book's argument that colonization was more destructive than progressive is especially significant because it is based on empirical observation. In this respect, *Le Cameroun* anticipates certain aspects of the sociology of colonialism that emerged in greater force a decade later.

FRENCH SOCIOLOGY'S OPENING TO HISTORY

Durkheimian sociology's relationship with professional history started out on a tense footing, like its relations to economics and psychology, discussed in chapter 6. Durkheim argued in the first issue of *Année sociologique* that "history cannot be a science except if it is explanatory, and it cannot explain other than through comparison," concluding that "as soon as it compares, history becomes indistinguishable from sociology."[30] Durkheim declared that individuals and contingent events were an irrational residue, adding that he was astonished by "the historians who can live comfortably amid this pile of disordered events," this "indefinite mountain of facts."[31] Rickert's "historical individuals" were not appropriate objects for social scientific investigation. For Durkheim, all genuine social scientific knowledge involved the study of repeated and collective events, with an emphasis on discovering their causal connections rather than merely "interpreting" them.

After this rough start, the interwar period saw a gradual *rapprochement* between the two disciplines.[32] A key contributor to this *détente* was the group of historians around the *Annales*, who were more open to comparison and theory than were traditional historians.[33] Indeed, the journal was patterned on Durkheim's *Année sociologique*. *Annales* historians shifted their attention away from individuals, singular events, and "great" politics and toward social, cultural, and economic structures. As discussed in the previous chapter, the *Annales* journal was relatively indifferent to modern colonial history itself. But by welcoming interdisciplinary relations with sociology, the *Annales* school indirectly supported the rise of a French version of historical sociology that, in turn, was conducive to a sociology of empires and colonies. The thinking of at least four leading French sociologists evolved in a historicist direction between the wars: Maurice Halbwachs, Célestin Bouglé, Charles Le Coeur, and Raymond Aron. All but Halbwachs were involved in colonial research.

Halbwachs's work expressed a "Bergsonian preoccupation" with temporality, although Halbwachs concluded that it "was not inner time or duration that was of the essence but rather time as a social construction."[34] Halbwachs developed his distinctive approach to collective memory in dialogue with *Annales* historian Marc Bloch.[35]

Bouglé hewed to Durkheimian strictures against history early on, but he became more historicist over time, especially after working through Heinrich Rickert's arguments about explaining "unique events" with "the use of general concepts."[36] Bouglé contributed a series of articles entitled "History and Sociology" to *Annales sociologiques* between 1934 and 1936. Here, he argued that sociologists could study individuals who were "historical personalities," and that unique events could be sociologically interesting if they involved the "exercise of force—a conquest, for example," or if they took "the character of a transfer, an extension, or a deepening of civilization."[37] A year later, Bouglé suggested that sociologists could explain unique events by seeking either their "general conditions" (Durkheim) or the plurality of causally relevant "institutional facts" (Weber).[38] Bouglé was clearly trying to combine Durkheimian and Weberian sociology, perhaps as a result of Bouglé's ongoing relationship to his protégé, Aron.

Le Coeur, discussed in detail below, endorsed the idea of focusing on that which is "particular to every society," as opposed to looking for universal laws as in the theories of Comte, Marx, or Spencer. Le Coeur credited Weber with "demonstrating the legitimacy" of this historicist approach.[39]

Aron made the most explicit move in a historicist direction by endorsing German historicist sociology after his studies in Germany in 1930–1933, during which time he immersed himself in the writing of Simmel, Dilthey, Rickert, Freyer, Schütz, Lukács, Mannheim, and "above all Weber."[40] Aron defended a sociology that "tries to distinguish itself from history without excluding the uniqueness of development, the reality of accidents, or the specific character of different ages," and that "does not claim to establish laws, or a system, or a unilinear development of mankind."[41] He was the only prominent French sociologist to defend a genre he called "historical sociology" (chapter 11).[42]

The movement from Halbwachs to Aron represents increasing openness to historicist epistemologies in French sociology. This shift from the definition of sociology as a science of general laws to a sociology of singular events was also relevant for understandings of colonialism. Universal models of social evolution were becoming less plausible to sociologists. A more historicist sociology could attend to variations between colonial and noncolonial societies as well as differences among colonies, groups within a single colony, and historical periods. Sociologists began to treat colonies and their populations as developing along distinct historical trajectories. After 1945, sociologists such as Balandier and Berque began to treat Africa and Asia as fully historical, and to reject the idea of Europe and North America as a universal model of societal progress. An adequate sociology of colonialism and of Africa and Asia had to be historicist.

THE SOCIOLOGY OF MORALITY AND THE MORALITY OF SOCIOLOGY

Interwar sociologists wrestled with the implications of Durkheim's writings on morality.[43] Durkheim rejected transcendental reasoning and universal ethics and recommended an immanent critique of morals. Durkheim's version of immanent critique did not point beyond existing social relations, in contrast to critical theorists of the postwar Frankfurt School.[44] Yet it did provide a strong counterweight to doctrines of value freedom in sociology, and a basis for criticizing existing society according to its own standards. Sociologists could now openly discuss questions such as the morality of colonialism and empire, comparing France's proclaimed universal values with its actual policies and practices.

Durkheim never fully developed his views on the sociology of morality, but he presented two arguments that continued to resonate between the wars and that were relevant for discussions of colonialism. The first was the idea that each society had a moral system corresponding to its social structure. Durkheim's sociology of morality did not afford any basis "for judging *between* societies, no general 'formula for the universal moral ideal.'"[45] This introduced a note of moral relativism into discussions of morality that could contradict certain justifications for colonialism. Second was Durkheim's explicit argument against axiological neutrality and his defense of a "rational critique" of existing social mores.[46]

Durkheim defined morality as "a distinct sphere" of social life, an emergent "sui generis" reality, irreducible to other phenomena. Morality exists independently of individuals, although individuals have moral ideas.[47] Morality consists of a "system of rules of conduct [that are] invested with a special authority by which they are obeyed simply because they command." In addition to this Kantian emphasis on morality's compulsory character, Durkheim argued that a "certain degree of desirability" is "no less important" in morality.[48] Seeking to discern the common features of morality, Durkheim's method was to determine its contents through empirical investigation of legal formulas as well as "proverbs, popular maxims and non-codified customs."[49] This approach led him to conclude that morality cannot have as its object oneself or another individual, but only society or "a group formed by the associated individuals."[50] Societies, he argued, "cannot be constituted without creating ideals" which consist of society's longer-term goals and the "ideas in terms of which a society sees itself" in the present.[51]

Durkheim argued further that "the morality of each people is directly related to the social structure of the people practicing it."[52] The morality "of Greek or Roman cities is not ours, just as that of primitive tribes is not the morality of the city." The Romans, Durkheim argues, "should not have had any other" morality than their own, even if some of their morals seem barbaric to moderns. Lucien Lévy-Bruhl, whose views on morality corresponded in this respect with Durkheim's, wrote that "the ethics of Australian communities are as natural as those of China, Chinese ethics are as natural as those of Europe and America: each is exactly what it was able to become according to the whole of the given conditions."[53] Such relativism echoes that in Durkheim's *Elementary Forms of the Religious Life*, which argues that "moral and legal rules" have been "indistinguishable from ritual prescriptions" until very recently.[54] Bouglé reached similar conclusions in his *Evolution of Values* (1922).[55] We cannot explain intersocietal and historical variations in morality in terms of "imperfect understanding" or underdevelopment. Instead, Durkheim concludes, "each social type has the morality necessary to it."[56]

Durkheim's moral sociology is relevant to discussions of colonialism, even if he did not make those connections directly himself. In his article "Sociologie morale et juridique," Durkheim insists that "it cannot be a question of assigning to a given society ends for which it . . . could not feel any need."[57] How, then, could France justify imposing its own moral project on colonized societies? Durkheim tried to combine the relativist approach to morals with a narrative of moral progress, according to which science improves and individual autonomy increases over time.[58] Yet Durkheim's arguments could also be used to support anticolonial conclusions. For example, his moral sociology could have been used to reject the imposition of legal codes punishing actions judged abhorrent to European sensibilities. These potentials of Durkheim's thought were not explicitly articulated during his lifetime. Yet Durkheim's thought remained familiar to French social thinkers between the wars. This explains why they did not abandon Durkheim when they turned against colonialism, but brought him along. In the hands of Georges Bataille or Jean Duvignaud, Durkheim became an anticolonial thinker.

It was important in this regard that Durkheim rejected Max Weber's doctrine of axiological neutrality. Against Weber's argument that the "the choice of ends" is "beyond the reach of science," Durkheim countered that it is possible to "move from a physics of mores to the moral arts."[59] The science of morality, he argued, allows us to make value judgments, to take positions opposing obsolete and emerging morals, to "enlighten society about the value, the true significance of the needs it experiences."[60] "Assuredly," Durkheim wrote, "the explanation of a moral maxim is not *ipso facto* its justification, but explanation opens the way to justification, far from making it superfluous or impossible."[61] In this way, Durkheim avoided driving a wedge between science and politics, explanation, and justification. Durkheimians thus felt authorized to integrate value judgments into their work. This stance helps explain the unencumbered critique of colonialism that emerged in French sociology starting in the 1930s, which contrasted sharply with the carefully neutral discussions of "imperialism" by Weber in *Economy and Society*.[62]

FRENCH SOCIOLOGY'S OPENING TO THE STUDY OF STATES AND EMPIRES

Classical Durkheimian sociology lacked a stable location in its classificatory system for the state and politics.[63] Between the wars, scholars began to fill this lacuna, developing a sociology of states and empires.[64] Durkheim's writings on the state were published posthumously.[65] The opening to political sociology helped French sociologists to perceive modern colonies as sites of conquest and domination with peculiar governing structures, and eventually to begin studying precolonial African political forms as states and empires.

Durkheim argues that morality consists of attachments to a social group, that the group that enjoys priority over all others is the nation, and that the nation takes the form of a state. The nation-state, however, "can enjoy moral primacy only on the condition that it is not conceived of as an unscrupulously self-centered being, solely preoccupied with expansion and self-aggrandizement to the detriment of similar entities."[66] The state is "the most highly organized form of human organization in existence" and is therefore enjoined to "commit itself as its main goal not to expanding, in a material sense, to the detriment of its neighbors, ... but to the goal of realizing among its own people the general interests of humanity." This seems more like a political philosophy than a political sociology, since Durkheim does not try to explain the moral orientations of different states.[67] Durkheim's comments did, however, introduce the idea of conquest as a political form.

Georges Davy was the only member of the original Durkheimian milieu who developed a sociology of politics and the state.[68] Davy's *From Tribe to Empire* (1923), co-authored with the Egyptologist Alexandre Moret, foregrounded the role of symbolic power in empire formation. The authors relied on Durkheim's theory of totemism to make sense of the centralization and monopolization of power in ancient Egypt. Moret and Davy argued that the "same mystic conception that animated the clan still gave spiritual life" to the vast Asian empires, in which "the divine dominates everything." According to the authors, the pharaoh Shemsu-Hor (the falcon god Horus) succeeded in monopolizing the power of all of the ancient totems and unifying Egyptian political power. His followers "retained the royal insignia already borne by their predecessors" in the totemic age.[69] Henri Berr, a historian close to the Durkheimians, wrote the forward to the book and summarized their argument as follows: "the enlargement of societies is accomplished by violence." Berr framed the book specifically as a study of "imperialism"—a phenomenon "inspired by the will to growth," a "brutal will."[70] Davy's *Éléments de sociologie*, published in 1924, focused on theories of sovereignty and the evolution of the state and nation from "totemistic" societies to "national" ones.[71]

After Davy, however, there was little further development in this area. It is instructive to examine René Hubert's *Manuel élémentaire de sociologie*, which appeared in five different editions from 1925 to 1949 and was a rather orthodox Durkheimian treatment intended for philosophy students earning a certificate in "Morals and Sociology." One of the sections of this text was titled "political evolution." Its discussion of theories of the state included Davy, Granet, and Mauss. In the fifth edition of the textbook, Hubert introduced a new discussion of empires and the "colonial problem."[72] In the "bibliographical analysis" section of the Durkheimian *Année Sociologique*, however, a section on political sociology only appeared in 1967, 70 years after the journal's start. Most French sociological writing on the state took the form of political and legal philosophy, rather than what the Durkheimians called "positive" (i.e., empirically grounded) sociology. French liberalism seems to have been so hegemonic that most sociologists could not bring themselves to study states and empires the way Durkheim studied morality, i.e., by describing them as "social facts." The colonial state itself was absent, or unnamed, in most French sociological studies of colonialism. The lack of an explicit conceptualization of states and empires made it more difficult for colonial sociology to do justice to its object. The first real breakthrough in the sociological study of states, empires, and colonies as political forms and processes began with a series of publications starting at the end of the 1930s by Raymond Aron, discussed in chapter 11.

The Colonial Turn in French Sociology before 1945

In his Sorbonne lectures on moral education, Durkheim discussed the tendency of the European colonizer to be seized by a "veritable intoxication, an excessive exaltation of self, a sort of megalomania," due to the "absence of moral forces which he respects" and "the inferiority he imputes" to the colonized. "Consequently," Durkheim continued, "nothing restrains him; he overflows in violence."[73] This was one of Durkheim's only explicit discussions of colonialism, however. Durkheim bracketed the colonial context in the 17 reviews on African topics he wrote for *Année sociologique*.[74] In *The Division of Labor*, Durkheim ignored the fact that modernization was often imposed, or delayed, by colonialism in non-western societies. In *Suicide*, Durkheim had nothing to say about the ways in which "the uprooting of 'primitive' societies by 'higher' types of civilization made the 'primitive' man ... prone ... to anomic suicide," even though the anthropologist Armand de Quatrefages had discussed this exact effect of European imperialism in the 1860s.[75]

This lack of attention to colonialism changed with the creation of the Institute of Ethnology, discussed in chapter 5. Some of the ethnographers associated with Mauss abandoned the primitivist preference discussed in the previous chapter. Mauss's promotion of colonial studies made it difficult for ethnographers such as Bastide, Berque, Le Coeur, Leenhardt, Maunier, and Montagne to continue ignoring the imperial context of their research. I discussed Montagne in chapter 5, and will defer discussion of Berque until chapter 11. My focus here is Le Coeur, Leenhardt, Maunier, and Bastide, who were defined primarily as sociologists and who represent the emancipation of colonial sociology from ethnology and atheoretical forms of ethnography. I will also discuss two ethnologists, Alfred Métraux and Jacques Soustelle, since their work foreshadowed many of the themes of postwar colonial sociology: breaking decisively with the primitivist preference, focusing attention on the crises and destruction of social structures and cultural practices caused by colonialism, and exploring the ways subjected populations resisted and selectively appropriated foreign influence. These figures are also important in bridging the interwar and postwar periods.

REVERSING THE COLONIAL LENS: CHARLES LE COEUR

Téda society is neither a theorem nor a machine. It is a creation, a free creation of sensibility, which no geographical fatality, no philosophy of history, can explain. Without question, it is the child of many inventions, many unpredictable events.

—CHARLES LE COEUR, *LE RITE ET L'OUTIL* (1939)

Charles Le Coeur described himself as a sociologist at a moment when embracing that label was still an unusual move among French ethnographers. He was strongly supported in that choice by his mentor, Marcel Mauss. Le Coeur differs from Griaule and earlier sociologists in explicitly thematizing the impact of colonialism on the African cultures he studies. Le Coeur's work was also pathbreaking in reversing the colonial lens and examining the metropole as an "exotic" zone, while analyzing the colony as a dynamic historical space of asymmetric domination.[76] His 1939 book *Le rite et l'outil* is a masterpiece of ethnography, sociology, literature, theory, epistemology, and politics, and is clearly inspired by the *Collège de sociologie*. He places himself firmly in the wake of Durkheim, beginning this book with a chapter on "the object and method of sociology" and a subheading referring to "the social fact"—the Durkheimian *fait social* (9).[77] He then launches into a critique of Adam Smith, Marx, Lévy-Bruhl, and other theories that posit a stark dichotomy between primitive and modern mentalities, and that interpret modernity in terms of the absolute dominance of utilitarian rationality and universal laws of behavior, refusing to take seriously the continuing importance of "ritual creations" (16, 33, 147–48). Le Coeur argues that there are two ways to approach sociology: by looking for common traits and general laws, or, in an approach he associates explicitly with Max Weber, by studying the particularities of each culture (9). The book's subtitle is *"Essai sur le rationalisme social et la pluralité des civilisations"*—"Essay on social rationality and the plurality of civilizations."

In all societies, Le Coeur argues, there is a combination of expressive practices, or ritual, and functional practice. Indeed, every act reveals a mix of utilitarian and ritual aspects. Le Coeur lived with and studied the Téda of northern Chad. Téda society, he argued, cannot be explained using general theory or universal laws, but must instead be understood as "a creation, a gratuitous creation of sensibility, one that . . . is the result of many inventions and unforeseeable events" (48). The careful observer will perceive that rites are not some mere "epiphenomenon" of Téda political economy (46). Instead, rites provide the very form of economic practices. Le Coeur identifies a paradoxical effect of European colonialism, which primitivizes rather than civilizes. The visibly irrational features that he identifies in Téda society are the result of colonialism, which led the Téda to shift from science to magic. They did not begin as primitives, but were becoming so under the impact of the civilizing mission (51).

Le Coeur argues that human action is essentially ritualist, but that it misunderstands itself as utilitarian. This is just as true of the educated Moroccans as of the Europeans. The educated Moroccans adopt a stance Le Coeur calls "scientism," meaning that they act as if human action is utilitarian (28). Westernized man appears to himself as a technician, but to the socioanalyst he appears as a creator of rites. Le Coeur's epistemological conclusion is that one should reject all forms of "spontaneous sociology" (*"la sociologie spontanée"*) in favor of what he calls a "reflexive sociology" (33). These phrases are repeated verbatim by Pierre Bourdieu, although Bourdieu never cites Le Coeur. Instead, the two sociologists were participating in a shared intellectual culture, shaped by Durkheim, Bachelard, Aron, and others.

Occidental society itself should be construed as a "historical formation" and not as a "rational" one, Le Coeur insists (201). He describes modern capitalism as a *"Kulturkreis,"* or cultural circle, alluding to the historicist ethnology that arose in Central Europe and harkening back to Herder, Theodor Mommsen, and Oswald Spengler.[78] European society is not a *telos* toward which the entire earth is hurtling, but is just another singular historical formation, a distinct *Kulturkreis* (124), with values that are relative rather than universal. Picking up a central theme of Georges Bataille and the *Collège de sociologie*, Le Coeur argues that the ritual instinct persists even in "modern" societies and is the source of revolt against rationalist capitalism (139).

For Le Coeur, sociology is both science and art. It is a form of art, or art history, "because it has to appreciate the unique nuance of every fact," and because societies themselves are unique configurations and thus "essentially artworks" (221). Sociology is also a science, but in a specifically historicist sense: to understand a culture like the Téda in the present, the ethnographer must also be its historian and psychologist.

Like Durkheim, but in contrast to Weber, Le Coeur rejects a sharp division between sociology and ethics (5). He attributes his own critique of axiological neutrality to the rise of fascism, which was threatening the French with the same "devastating torrent" that Morocco faced with "the establishment of the Protectorate" (3). Le Coeur's comparison of colonialism with fascism is also precocious.

Le Coeur worked as a teacher for Muslim students at the Collège Moulay Youssef and for future Moroccan schoolteachers (most of whom were French) at the *Institut des Hautes Études Marocaines*. Le Coeur argued that he could not bring himself to communicate to his students the "infinite prejudices that constitute western civilization," and instead had to "change himself from professor into student," and indeed, to identify with "the native" (6).

Le Coeur joined the Free French Forces in 1943 and was killed in combat in Italy in 1944. Jacques Berque recognized Le Coeur's brilliance, and Georges Balandier republished *Le rite et l'outil* in his series "Bibliothèque de sociologie contemporaine" in 1969.[79] Le Coeur's texts retain their relevance to the present, brushing up "unstintingly against historical constraints."[80]

RENÉ MAUNIER AND THE SOCIOLOGY OF COLONIALISM

French colonialism has always inspired research in comparative sociology.

—RENÉ MAUNIER, "LEÇON D'OUVERTURE D'UN COURS DE SOCIOLOGIE 'ALGÉRIENNE'" (1922)[81]

René Maunier was a key contributor to colonial studies during the interwar period. In his earliest publications, he already presented himself as a sociologist conducting sociological research.[82] In the second, interwar series of the *Année sociologique*, Maunier was jointly responsible, with Maurice Halbwachs and Albert Demangeon, for the rubric "social morphology."[83] Along with Mauss and Davy, Maunier was a founder of French legal sociology and his main teaching field was colonial law.[84] He taught criminal law and political economy at the Khedivial law school in Cairo starting in 1911, lectured on "Algerian sociology" at the University of Algiers from 1920 through 1926, and then moved to a chair in Colonial Law at the University of Paris. Maunier's approach, especially his analysis of North African gift exchange, is clearly situated in the Durkheimian lineage.[85] His writing on the Kabyle house was cited by Bourdieu (chapter 14).

Maunier is especially interesting in the present context due to his invention of a field he called *colonistics (la colonistique)*. His longest book, *Sociologie coloniale* (3 volumes, published between 1932 and 1949), set out to focus on the "human" rather than the economic aspects of colonization.[86] Maunier conceptualized colonization as a Durkheimian "social fact" (*fait social*) involving "contact" between two "hitherto separated" societies. This act of singling out colonialism as a social object was an important intervention.[87] Maunier defined colonization in terms of *occupation* and *government* by a foreign conqueror.[88] Although this definition did not emphasize the centrality of racism or the "rule of difference," Maunier recognized that every form of colonialism was also a form of *imperialism*, which he defined as "the doctrine of domination."[89] His theory of colonialism was not historically specific; for example, he called attention to the fact that "the colonies of one period become colonizers in the next, and so on."[90] Maunier theorized empire as well as colonialism. Although he did not embed empire within a theory of geopolitical relations, Maunier attributed his theory of *imperial overstretch* to Ibn Khaldun, the fourteenth-century theorist of Arab empires.[91] Maunier was one of the first social scientists to observe that "colonization itself organized the space of Algerian nationalism and gave it its main idea."[92]

European colonizers had long been tormented by the perceived ability of the non-European Other to switch between the codes of the colonizer and colonized.[93] Durkheimian sociologists had tried to ignore colonial syncretism and acculturation, given their effort to develop models of "elementary" social forms. Maunier broke decisively with Durkheimianism in this regard and made cultural "*mixité*" the centerpiece of his approach. Maunier also transformed the age-old colonial trope of "going native" into a theory of the "conversion of the conqueror by the conquered." Cultural mixing involved not just the "fusion" or "racial and social blending of the two groups," he insisted. There "has been action and reaction between the natives and the Europeans: 'race contact' has left its mark, and institutions have been borrowed in both directions."[94] This theme of the colonial boomerang, already present in Hobson's *Imperialism* (1902), was repeated by Le Coeur, Sartre, Fanon, and many others. Maunier also noticed that imitation did not consist of "pure and simple diffusion" or "transmission," arguing that "it is always at the same time alteration and adulteration."[95] This was an advanced notion at the time, although it became a mainstay of colonial sociology after World War II. The most generative anthropologists in the United States between the wars, such as Melville Herskovits, were proposing theories of "acculturation" under conditions of colonialism and slavery.[96] Herskovits's early concepts of syncretism and acculturation were "eventually superseded" in his writing "by the concept of *reinterpretation*," creative processes permitting "a people to retain the inner meanings of traditionally sanctioned modes of behavior while adopting new outer institutional forms," and to carry out such borrowing selectively rather than taking place "evenly over the total range of a culture."[97] Balandier and Mercier reworked these ideas in their study of the Senegalese Lébou in 1952 (chapter 13), and Bastide theorized reinterpretation as semiotic recoding in his studies of Afro-Brazilian religion (see below).

As a Sorbonne professor, Maunier was located close to the center of French sociological discussions of colonialism between the wars. However, his status collapsed almost immediately after Liberation.[98] Maunier had organized the meeting of the International Institute of Sociology in 1939 that was cancelled due to the outbreak of war, but the partially fascist contributions to this study were published in 1940. The proceedings included an annihilationist anti-Semitic treatise by the future founder of social history in West Germany, Werner Conze.[99] Maunier was rejected as a wartime collaborator and lambasted for his views of colonialism, which suddenly appeared completely outmoded.[100] When the third volume of Maunier's *Sociologie coloniale* appeared in 1949, it was attacked in the pages of *Année sociologique* by Maxime Rodinson as ahistorical, typologizing, overly psychological, and not Marxist enough. Perhaps worst of all, Rodinson described Maunier as being "out of touch" with contemporary developments, such as anticolonialism, decolonization, and "the 'revenge' of the colonized" in all of its guises.[101] Rodinson disdainfully singled out Maunier's passing comment in a 1941 publication that the natives of colonies like Tasmania "had the tact to disappear and to fade away entirely." Statements such as that one now seemed outrageously racist and genocidal.[102]

NATIVE AMERICANS AND COLONIAL MÉTISSAGE: ALFRED MÉTRAUX AND JACQUES SOUSTELLE

While many of Mauss's students challenged the preference for primitivism and cultural purity, specialists in indigenous American and African American cultures seem to have found it particularly difficult to ignore the effects of colonial transculturation.[103] Two students of Mauss stand out in this regard: Alfred Métraux and Jacques Soustelle. Both identified as ethnologists, but their approaches are indistinguishable from colonial ethno-sociology.

Métraux carried out research among the Cipaya Indians of Bolivia during the 1930s. This isolated tribe had been exposed to European influence for centuries but had preserved many traces of pre-Columbian culture. They had also been transformed through contact with the Aymara, a more Europeanized indigenous group, and with Bolivians of mixed race.[104] Cipaya elites lived in houses built in a westernized, rectangular style, while Cipaya commoners lived in traditional round huts. The Cipaya tribe was divided into two "moieties," but by the time Métraux arrived, there were no longer restrictions on marriage between the two sides. Marriages took place in church. Although the Cipaya had ostensibly converted to Christianity centuries earlier, their religious ceremonies were a mix of "Christian elements" with "ancient rites" that recalled "the idolatrous practices whose survival had been denounced by the Spanish Inquisitors in Peru during the seventeenth century." Christian saints had simply been "added to the list" of the pagan "gods, demons, and genies protecting the Cipaya," which included mountains, rivers, caves, and other features of the natural environment. Every unusual object in the natural environment was assumed to contain a divinity, and stuffed animals guarded each Cipaya house. The Virgin Mary was equated with the principal Cipaya divinity, the *Pača-mama* (mother earth).[105]

After World War II, while employed as a UNESCO official, Métraux carried out research in Haiti. He described Haitian peasant culture as "eminently flexible and permeable," and noted that he had always been interested in "syncretic cults." He opposed the repression of one such cult, voodoo, by priests and the Haitian government.[106] Yet, at other times, Métraux reverted to the more conventional ethnological preference for unspoiled, unmixed cultures. He argued, for example, that a study of the Huallaga valley in the Amazon was "not an ideal choice" for UNESCO by noting: "[n]ot only has the Indian population almost entirely disappeared from the region, but from the earliest days the whole area has been subjected to cultural influences of Andean origin which have profoundly modified its Amazonian characteristics."[107] Métraux himself was a hybrid thinker in this respect, vacillating between more "ethnological" and more "sociological" positions.

Jacques Soustelle is mainly known today for his political activities as a leading member of the Free French Forces and the French Constituent Assembly (1945–1946), Minister for the Colonies in 1945, and Governor General of French Algeria in 1955, at which point he became a strong advocate of Algeria's political integration with France. Soustelle's fierce polemic against Algerian independence culminated in his joining the paramilitary OAS (*Organisation de l'armée secrète*) in 1960, followed by his exile from France between 1961 and 1968.[108] Before World War II, however, Soustelle was regarded as one of Mauss's most brilliant students and as both a sociologist and ethnologist. When he passed his *agrégation* exam in philosophy in 1932, the "inspector general of higher education and chairman of the jury" received Soustelle with the words, "Ah, so you're the sociologist."[109] This was presumably an allusion to Soustelle's preference for teaching Durkheim rather than Kant. It may also be suggestive of another feature of Soustelle's thinking: his interest in mixed cultures. Soustelle completed two doctoral theses in 1937 on the Lacandon and Otomi Indians of Mexico. He designed his thesis deliberately as a comparison, since the Lacandon were thought to be the only group of Maya that had remained "untouched and uninfluenced by the Europeans," subjected only to "pseudo-colonization."[110] Soustelle hoped to contrast the Lacandon with the Otomi, who had been more thoroughly Europeanized. It is also worth recalling that the comparative method itself was associated with Durkheimian sociology.

The Lacandon were discussed by Soustelle in a series of articles in the 1930s as being almost "completely isolated." They had fiercely resisted colonialism and had "never been incorporated, even imperfectly, into the Mexican nation." Even their relations with nearby ranchos resembled a "sort of modus vivendi between foreign powers." Lacandon cultural borrowings from the outside world were "negligible," limited to trade for machetes, salt, and alcohol; money was unknown to them.[111] In contrast to other Mexican natives, the Lacandon had "never been evangelized," and their religion "had been preserved, entirely intact, lacking even that superficial varnish of Christianity that characterizes their linguistic and racial parents, the Yucatan Maya." Soustelle acknowledged the existence of non-indigenous cultural elements and mixed practices among the Lacandons. Spanish-speaking prospectors and earlier ethnographers had left their mark on the culture.[112] Soustelle identified a zither-like stringed musical instrument of non-indigenous origin, but noted that it did not resemble any instrument imported by the Spaniards and must have been introduced by "black slaves," perhaps "fugitives from the plantations who took refuge in the impenetrable forest."[113]

Soustelle's second thesis represented Otomi culture as a veritable "clash of civilizations." He discussed Spanish colonial policy vis-à-vis the Otomi and "foreign elements" introduced "by the conquest." The Otomi were so "extremely hispanicized" in some regions that their clothing did "not present any indigenous character at all." The Spanish conquest had transformed their language into the site of a "surreptitious war being fought beneath the apparently calm surface, in which the more prestigious language gnaws away on its adversary, penetrating it little by little."[114] Some of the Otomi's woven objects were decorated with "the two-headed eagle of the House of Austria, taken from coins used at the time of Spanish rule."[115] Soustelle analyzed the performance of a dance called *le torito*, in which Otomi dancers imitated the life of the distant *vaqueros* and *charros* and more generally evoked the ancient Mediterranean theme of the struggle between man and bull. The dancers sang in Spanish, the language of the *métis*, even though they barely understood it.[116]

Soustelle proposed a theory of strategic cultural adoption and adaptation based on his Mexican research. In the case of the *torito* dance, he argued, outside observers generally perceived little more than "a group of natives taking over a set of themes and images borrowed from nonnatives." In fact, Soustelle countered, Otomi culture represented "an original synthesis," and was neither "the religion of their ancestors" nor "the Christianity of Latin Europe." The *torito* dance was, ultimately, an homage to Our Lady of Guadalupe, the "Indian Virgin."[117] With the exception of the Lacandon, Soustelle concluded, the "religion of the natives of Mexico" had become a "Hispano-Indian and Christiano-pagan syncretism." Indian converts "were not so much renouncing their old beliefs as incorporating them into a new body of faith and ritual." In subsequent historical studies of pre-Columbian cultures, Soustelle provided examples of syncretism going back to the sixteenth century, when Mayan human sacrifices mingled "Christian crucifixion . . . with the rite of ripping out the heart," an act performed by "two baptized Indians." Soustelle insisted that Mexico should allow Indians to be integrated into the polity "without requiring them to commit cultural suicide."[118]

MAURICE LEENHARDT: MISSIONARY, ETHNOGRAPHER, COLONIAL SOCIOLOGIST

Maurice Leenhardt was the first sociologist who studied the symbolic aspects of anticolonial struggle. Already in his 1902 bachelor's thesis, Leenhardt interpreted the messianic "Ethiopian" church in Southern Africa as enacting resistance through the selective appropriation of colonial culture.[119] Leenhardt then began a long career in the French colony of New Caledonia, where he worked as a Protestant missionary until 1926, when he returned to France. Leenhardt continued to write for the missionary society while deepening his ties to Mauss and Lévy-Bruhl in Paris. During the 1930s, Mauss began sharing with Leenhardt his Chair in "the religions of uncivilized peoples" at the Fifth Section of the *École pratique des hautes études*.[120] Leenhardt returned to New Caledonia in 1938 for another round of research.[121] When Mauss was forced to resign in 1940 under the Vichy government's anti-Semitic laws, he asked Leenhardt to take over his Chair. Michel Leiris was Leenhardt's first student while he served in this function. After 1945, Leenhardt taught the course in general ethnography at the *Institut d'ethnologie*.[122]

Leenhardt was described by contemporaries as both a sociologist and an ethnologist.[123] The first component of his identity stemmed from his membership in the core of Mauss's circle, his use of Durkheimian concepts, and his participation in the *Année sociologique*. After World War II, Leenhardt was also a founding member of the *Centre d'études sociologiques*, where he carried out research on "the social structure of colonies."[124] He continued to study the dynamic responses by colonized cultures to foreign domination during the postwar period.[125] Leenhardt encouraged New Caledonians to craft a "civilization adequate to their mentality," rather than abandoning their culture.[126] A new conclusion to the 1953 edition of his 1937 book *Gens de la Grande Terre* situated New Caledonian indigenous life within a critical narrative of the French "invasion" that brought expropriation, cultural decimation, and racism. Leenhardt suggested the colony might become a kind of syncretic society, with acculturation moving in both directions in a *"jeu de transferts"* (a play of cultural transfers). He supported the framework of the French Union, which he saw as offering New Caledonians "the grand idea of citizenship."[127] Leenhardt's writings and his ideas seem as relevant as ever today, especially after voters in New Caledonia overwhelmingly rejected independence in a third referendum held on December 12, 2021.

ROGER BASTIDE AND THE TRANSITION TO POSTWAR COLONIAL SOCIOLOGY

Roger Bastide's writing, like that of Métraux, Soustelle, and Leenhardt, spans the interwar and postwar epochs. Unlike the other scholars discussed thus far, Bastide was more strongly identified with sociology and psychoanalysis than with ethnology. In this respect, Bastide personifies sociology's emancipation from ethnology in (post)colonial fieldsites. His trajectory also underscores the generative importance of the interdisciplinary interwar matrix of Maussian social science for the fabrication of a non-exoticizing sociology of colonialism.

Like most of the classical Durkheimians, Bastide earned a philosophy *agrégation*. His path differed from most of the other interwar ethno-sociologists, however, who were more squarely located within the Durkheimian heritage. Bastide was initiated into sociology at Bordeaux by Gaston Richard, who had distanced himself from Durkheim starting in 1907.[128] Richard helped Bastide to prepare for the state examination in philosophy, and as a result, Bastide "did not declare himself to be heir to Durkheim."[129] Instead, his main loyalty between the wars was to the *International Institute of Sociology* and its journal, edited by Gaston Richard at the time.[130] Like Richard himself and Richard's student Daniel Essertier, Bastide sought to integrate psychology and sociology.

However, Bastide eventually embraced the neo- or post-Durkheimian tradition. Gaston Richard warned Bastide in 1924 against the "influential school ... that had led us to Australia, to the Redskins, the Polynesians," and counseled his student to study "rural France and its small towns."[131] Fourteen years later, however, after publishing books on *Problèmes de la vie mystique* and *Éléments de sociologie religieuse*, Bastide left for Brazil. He spent the years 1938–1954 at the University of São Paulo, where he took over the sociology chair previously held by Claude Lévi-Strauss. In 1946, Bastide explained in a lecture to the *Centre d'études sociologiques* that his research among "creole" populations in Brazil would be considered the ontological property of anthropologists in the United States, but that French sociology could make distinctive contributions to this area by following up on suggestions made by Durkheim, thereby "perhaps going farther than the North Americans."[132] Bastide continued to mend fences with the latter-day Durkheimians by contributing to the revived *Année sociologique* and even becoming the journal's general editor (*Secrétaire Générale*) in 1962. Bastide's *thèse d'état* in 1960 was received with congratulations by a "star-studded" jury that included sociologists Raymond Aron and Georges Gurvitch, psychologist Jean Piaget, and anthropologist André Leroi-Gourhan.[133] Bastide was a Professor at the Sixth Section of the *École des hautes études en sciences sociales* from 1951 to 1974, teaching "Ethnic Sociology," and in 1959 he became Professor of Ethnology and Religious Sociology at the Sorbonne.

Bastide's main research area was the African societies of Brazil, with a focus on folklore, suicide, dreamwork, and especially religion. He also carried out studies in Dahomey and on African migrants in France.[134] This resembled the careers of other colonial sociologists who first worked in overseas colonies before returning to the metropole and redeploying their concepts, reversing the usual direction of the circulation of ideas. Bastide broke explicitly with ethnology's "primitivist preference," arguing that "the old fondness for the exotic and the barbaric" had to be "expelled from serious ethnographic studies." In the "distant cults" he studied in Brazil, Bastide argued, "we do not meet 'original man' but other civilized human beings."[135] Bastide's sociology of religion linked Europe, Africa, and the New World in a web of flows and transfers, foreshadowing postwar research by scholars like Michael Banton and later work on the Black Atlantic by Paul Gilroy.[136] Bastide was completely immune to evolutionary theories of civilization and American modernization theories, always drawing "attention to persistent singularities."[137]

Bastide's main contributions lay in his theorization of the "interpenetration of cultures," which he called "cultural interfecundation."[138] Where some observers perceived only incoherent, irrational, or pathological behavior, Bastide perceived "another coherence and rationality." Whereas the term "syncretism" was sometimes used pejoratively to suggest a *disharmonious mélange*—a "sickness" and "decadence" of "cultures in contact"—Bastide rejected all notions of degeneracy.[139] Bastide's most original concept was culture splitting or "cutting"—his *principe de coupure*. This was connected to his argument that Afro-Brazilian thought was not characterized by *associating* or *binding* concepts, but was *"coupante,"* meaning involved in separating and dividing categories.[140] Marginalized or dominated individuals in such societies were not, Bastide clarified, "cut in two," as suggested by American sociology's theory of the "marginal man."[141] Rather, the ability to split concepts apart allowed the dominated to participate in "two different civilizations"—one "occidental," the other "minority."[142] Afro-Brazilians moved easily between cultures. The *candomblé* was thus a coherent Afro-American religious system.[143] In this sense, Bastide's *principe de coupure* is similar to the ideas of the *Gestalt* switch, used by Bourdieu (chapter 14), or *code-switching*.

Bastide deepened his account of the distinctiveness of a sociological account of colonization in 1946. The "sociological terrain," he suggested, was distinct from the ethnographic. Sociologists are interested in "counter-acculturation"—the moment when a civilization senses that it is threatened by death ... and thus responds by struggle." The American anthropologist Herskovits had begun discussing "counter-acculturation" just two years earlier, and Bastide credits Herskovits for this. Second, Bastide argues, ethnography is only interested in "outcomes" (*au résultat*), while the process (*le processus*) is the "domain of the sociologist."[144] This position resonated with Bastide's rejection of definitions of syncretic cultures as stabilized hybrids. Bastide accused

Durkheim of a bias toward systems of order, which he countered with the idea that cultures are in constant, dynamic flux and processual emergence. This underscores the fact that all of the leading colonial sociologists, from Bastide to Bourdieu, pursued a dynamic and processual approach.

Bastide was also one of the first sociologists to systematically integrate psychoanalysis into his thinking. He worked on a social psychoanalysis of Afro-Brazilians' dreams, picking up where Halbwachs had left off in his sociological research on his own dreamwork.[145] Bastide's immersion in psychoanalysis was also expressed in his argument that the "gaps" in collective memory resulted from collective traumas, such as the uprooting of African slaves from their homelands. These gaps were selectively filled by "homologous" or structurally similar materials from the new culture. This approach linked psychoanalysis to structuralist linguistics. Bastide applied his revised methodology to the analysis of counter-acculturation, which he now described not as "a return to African civilization, but to a myth of it that the slaves have developed for themselves," a "collective memory" that could fill in these "unbearable lacunae."[146]

Intellectual Flourishing Amidst Institutional Stagnation

Interwar sociology was institutionally weak but intellectually vibrant. The field thus presented scholars after the war with certain ideal conditions of possibility. French sociology represented a splendorous past and a set of intriguing but unanswered questions. It combined openness to interdisciplinary and post-disciplinary interaction with an absence of constraining professionalization, in an institutional configuration in which material resources had been gradually increasing since the late 1930s.[147] Without rejecting the Durkheimian foundation, some of the most inventive sociologists embraced fieldwork, history, and ethics, and began to explicitly thematize states and empires. A movement that broadened sociologists' interest in the overseas empire was already taking form before 1944. This paved the way to an ethno-sociology of colonized cultures that began to make sense of practices of cultural mixing, reinvention, and resistance. Sociologists of colonialism thematized the axes of epistemic and cultural blowback.

The next chapter will examine French sociology before and after 1945 from a more structural point of view, considering the discipline as a scientific field-in-formation and the emergence of colonial sociology as a specialized subfield therein.

PART IV

The Sociology of French Colonial Sociology, 1918–1960s

CHAPTER NINE

The Sociology of Sociology and Its Colonial Subfield (France and Belgium, 1918–1965)

> *Does the student have more chances of earning a decent livelihood outside the university? Public or private subsidies sometimes enable him to devote his time to demography, industrial relations, or colonial problems.*
> —JEAN-RENÉ TRÉANTON, AT THE SECOND WORLD CONGRESS OF SOCIOLOGY, LIÈGE, 1953

THIS CHAPTER EXPLORES THE social structure of the French sociology field as a whole and the relative symbolic power of the colonial specialists, compared to their metrocentric counterparts. I begin by estimating the overall size of the discipline and its colonial subfield.[1] After determining that colonial specialists constituted around half of the discipline throughout the 1944–1965 period, I then ask about their academic qualifications, where they were employed, where they published, and which conferences they attended. My conclusion is that the field-specific symbolic capital of the colonial subgroup was similar to that of the metrocentric group until the mid-1960s. Like the metrocentric sociologists, the colonial network was internally heterogeneous and stratified in terms of symbolic capital.

The time frame of this chapter covers the interwar, wartime, and postwar eras (1918 until the mid-1960s). It is important to return to the interwar period in order to address the objection that sociology disappeared institutionally during this time. Vichy and the wartime occupation marked a caesura in terms of the loss of key figures (Halbwachs, Mauss); reputational transformations due to activity in the Resistance (Aron, Balandier) or as collaborators (Maunier); and the creation of new research capacities in the colonial realm (chapter 5). Sociology declined but did not disappear. Postwar sociology, including colonial sociology, arose on these foundations. At the end of this chapter, I will also briefly examine Belgian Francophone sociology and its relation to Belgian colonialism, given its geographic and intellectual proximity to French colonial sociology.

Finis sociologiae? *Revising the Standard Narrative*

One of the most important changes in writing the history of science, intellectuals, and, indeed, culture in general involves a shift in the geographical unit of analysis to the imperial scale.[2] As we saw in the preceding chapters, once we shift our attention from the metropole to the empire, new disciplinary fields and interdisciplines come into focus. Participants in these knowledge circuits and sites directly confronted the imperial lineaments of geopolitics and the colonial nature of social structures and practices.

Historians of interwar French sociology have spoken of its "quasi-disappearance" and "semi-failure," some suggesting that it was "a lost cause."[3] It is uncontested that the decimation of the ranks of Durkheimians in World War I and Durkheim's death in 1917 had a dramatic effect on the discipline. There was also a "stagnation in the number of teaching positions" in all of the human sciences between the wars that hindered the reemergence of the fledgling discipline. In Heilbron's less dire account, Durkheimian sociology had a "dispersed diffusion" after 1918, meaning that while sociology was not an established discipline, Durkheimian ideas were present and influential in a variety of adjoining disciplines. Indeed, the previous three chapters have shown that Durkheimian ideas were abundant among colonial specialists in various disciplines, such as psychiatry, law, and ethnology.[4]

Historians also suggest that French sociology went into abeyance during the Nazi Occupation and Vichy regime. Sociology during the postwar era is then usually seen as narrowly empirical, atheoretical, presentist, and applied. In 1946, Raymond Polin suggested that many scholars who had previously identified with sociology had "stopped giving themselves the title of sociologist," while "keeping the name of economist, historian, geographer, or linguist."[5]

Dismissing or skipping over the sociology of the middle third of the twentieth century is sometimes linked to strategies favoring specific positions in contemporary scientific struggles. A recent survey insists that French sociology was moribund in the middle of the twentieth century and did not begin to reemerge until the 1970s. The authors structure their account around a mapping of French sociology that aligns it as closely as possible with an imagined American sociological configuration. The book is titled *Les sociologies françaises (French Sociologies)*, but its first section is "French Sociology Seen from America."[6] If one agrees that "American" sociology is a universal *telos*, then French sociology in the interwar years can only appear barren, and the 1950s can at best be described as a period of catching up. After all, metrocentric

French sociology at the time featured very little rational choice theory, multivariate regressions, path analysis models, structural functionalism, or modernization theory.

Skipping over the middle third of the century also elides an intellectual formation in which field boundaries were weak but connections between sociology and other disciplines, especially ethnology, were strong (chapter 8). This kind of intensive interdisciplinarity is also contrary to the imagined "American" model, in which disciplinary boundaries are carefully tended. The powerful background role played by philosophy, psychoanalysis, and the arts in French sociology is antithetical to the more scientistic American model. Most important, leapfrogging over the middle decades suppresses nearly all of the sociological research in and on the colonies and obliterates awareness of the first generation of Francophone sociologists from Africa, North Africa, and the Caribbean.

Systematic research has already challenged the claim that French sociology in the 1945–1960 era was entirely negligible.[7] In his superb book, *French Sociology*, Johan Heilbron argues that this period was less one of disciplinary stagnation than of "a near-total separation" between "empirical research" and "university sociology," the latter defined as a "purely reflective and professorial activity." Expanding research opportunities provided empirical social researchers with some "material advantages" and some measure of "social recognition." Heilbron argues that the *Centre d'études sociologiques* was not just located at the center of the empirical research pole but that it dominated the entire discipline, since "virtually all members of the postwar generation of sociologists started their career" there. Heilbron goes on to analyze postwar sociology's "double exclusion" from the French intellectual and political fields. On the one hand, among Marxists and other intellectuals, sociology was seen as a "suspicious enterprise, mostly associated with American-style empiricism in the service of the ruling classes." Empirical sociology was isolated from key theoretical developments in French intellectual life such as existentialism and structuralism. On the other hand, sociology did not have "an established position in policy research" and was of marginal importance to the French state.[8] According to this account, French sociology only broke out of its intellectual torpor in the wake of the expansion of the universities during the 1960s and the cultural revolution of 1968.

A different story comes to light once we direct our attention to the imperial scale. This procedure revises Heilbron's meticulous analysis in several ways. First, some of these colonial sociologists *combined* theory and empirics. Second, some colonial sociologists influenced policymaking directly in the colonies. Third, some of these colonial sociologists were connected to the intellectual field, publishing in *Les temps modernes* and *Esprit*, engaging with existentialism and structuralism, and combining social research with literary publications or genres. Before delving more deeply into these discussions, however, we should first establish the morphology of the sociology field between the wars, and its overall developmental trajectory. Specifically, we need to ask how many students studied sociology, and how many full-time teachers and researchers were dedicated to sociology.

SOCIOLOGY STUDENTS

Sociology entered the French university for the first time in a systematic way in 1920. In that system, one of the certificates that students working toward the *licence de philosophie* could earn was *morale et sociologie* (morality and sociology).[9] French students could also earn a certificate in sociology proper as part of a *licence libre* or self-designed degree. Many of the students who enrolled in this sequence came from the Law faculty or *Sciences Po*.[10] University instruction in sociology was carried out almost entirely by philosophers. Victor Karady's prosopographic study of French sociology before 1940 demonstrates that the Durkheimians were concentrated in the Letters faculties.[11] Most of the scholars who gravitated toward Durkheim were educated in Letters at the *École normale supérieure*. They were "trained as philosophers, or less often, as historians."[12] Philosophy was "by far the most prestigious disciplinary association accessible to the new sociology."[13]

By the late 1930s, more than a quarter of all French university students were enrolled in Letters. The existence of a job market for *lycée* teachers in humanities disciplines made this a relatively attractive career choice. Indeed, there were more teaching jobs in Letters than Sciences between the wars.[14] As figure 9.1 shows, the percentage of students in Letters rose from 10 percent in 1890 to 30 percent by the late 1950s.[15] Peak enrollment corresponded with the renaming of the division as "Letters and Social Sciences" in the mid-1950s.

Sociology was far from the leading discipline within the Letters divisions. More students tried to obtain certificates in Greek, Latin, French, English, and History than in *morale et sociologie* or *sociologie* proper. A more relevant comparative statistic is the difference between the numbers studying sociology and those enrolled in the disciplines that were sociology's closest social scientific competitors. The numbers earning certificates in *morale et sociologie* or *sociologie* outstripped psychology, geography, linguistics, and, perhaps most significantly, ethnology. During the two university examination seasons in 1925, for example, 114 people earned a certificate in *morale et sociologie* and 22 in *sociologie*; 100 certificates were obtained in psychology and 42 in geography. Only a handful of students graduated in all of the other relevant fields, including linguistics. No certificates were granted in ethnology until 1927, following the establishment of the *Institut d'ethnologie*. In 1938, 145 certificates were granted in *morale et sociologie* and 32 in *sociologie* proper, 141 in psychology, 123 in geography, and 22 in ethnology.[16] For students earning a *licence* in one of the social sciences, sociology was the most popular field.

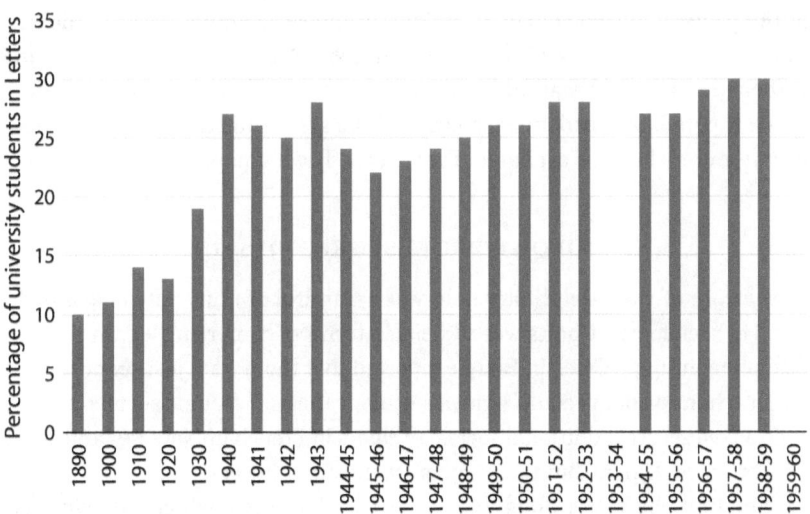

FIGURE 9.1. Percentage of students in French and colonial French universities studying Letters, 1890–1959. *Sources:* Statistique générale de la France, *Annuaire statistique* (Paris: Statistique générale, 1940–45, 1946, 1954–61); Institut national de la statistique et des études économiques, *Annuaire statistique de l'Union française 1949-1954* (Paris: Impr. Nationale, 1956), 48; Antoine Prost, *Histoire de l'enseignement en France, 1800–1967* (Paris: Colin, 1968), 234; Fritz Ringer, *Education and Society in Modern Europe* (Bloomington: Indiana University Press, 1979), 148; Pierre Bourdieu and Jean-Claude Passeron, *The Inheritors. French Students and their Relation to Culture* (Chicago: University of Chicago Press, 1979), 103; Theodore Zeldin, "Higher Education in France, 1848–1940." *Journal of Contemporary History* 2, pp. 53–80; OECD, *Reviews of National Science Policy: France* (Paris: OECD, 1966).

What about advanced theses? Sociology was listed as a separate subcategory among philosophy theses, which were summarized in the annual reports by the Paris Letters faculty.[17] In 1938, for example, 16 titles were listed under the heading *sociologie*, including Jean Stoetzel's doctoral thesis on "Public Opinion and Propaganda."[18] By contrast, just ten theses were defended in psychology and three in geography that year. Ethnology topics were subsumed under sociology, which therefore included theses such as "The Cult of Communal Gods in Annam."[19] Several doctoral theses in colonial sociology were supervised by René Maunier in the Law faculty.[20]

Sociology thus attracted an increasing number of students, despite the fact that the number of university positions for sociology professors was close to zero. Sociology's value in terms of a career was limited to *lycée* teachers of philosophy. Yet student interest is not the only sign of the existence of a discipline, or even the most important one. A disciplinary field consists, above all, of full-time researchers. The next section will try to identify all of the professional sociologists working in interwar France and its colonies. The conclusion is that sociology had a limited representation in research and higher education and that the ranks of sociologists were aging. Sociology was a sparsely populated academic terrain awaiting systematic reconstruction, once new resources became available. That is exactly what happened after 1945.

SOCIOLOGY PROFESSORS, 1918–1945

At the core of the disciplinary field was a handful of university chairs dedicated to sociology.[21] Chairs were crucial in terms of conferring legitimacy on a discipline. In 1934, Célestin Bouglé reported that there were just six professors under whom students could write a sociology thesis.[22] Bouglé seemed to have overlooked several additional sociology chairs in French universities and at the University of Algiers, but the numbers were still miniscule.

The first chair was Bouglé's own, at the Sorbonne, which he held until 1938.[23] A second sociology chair was created at the Sorbonne in 1932 for Paul Fauconnet, who had been a lecturer in education and sociology since 1921.[24] Following Fauconnet's death in 1938, this chair was given to Albert Bayet, who delivered the opening speech at the first meeting of *Centre d'études sociologiques* in 1946.[25] The third sociology chair, and the first labeled "sociology" *tout court*, was held by Gaston Richard at Bordeaux from 1905 to 1930, after which it was conferred on Max Bonnafous, who held the chair until 1940.[26] A fourth chair in philosophy and sociology was created at Clermont Ferrand in 1925 for Émile Lasbax, a student of Gaston Richard.[27] There was a fifth sociology chair at Strasbourg, occupied by Maurice Halbwachs from 1919 to 1935, and then by Georges Gurvitch. In 1935, Halbwachs moved to the Sorbonne for a newly created sixth sociology chair, and in 1944, he relocated to a chair at the *Collège de France* in social psychology.[28] Georges Davy taught philosophy at the *lycée* level before becoming a sociology professor at the Sorbonne in 1945. The existence of these chairs relativizes the claim that French sociology disappeared between the wars.

Four other university chairs were directly connected to sociology and colonial studies. The first was the chair in "Muslim sociology and sociography" at the *Collège de France*, held by Louis Massignon starting in 1919.[29] A chair in "social philosophy" was created at the *Collège de France* in 1897 and occupied by Jean Izoulet until 1929; in 1931, it was bestowed upon Mauss and was renamed as the chair in sociology. Georges-Henri Bousquet held a chair in comparative Muslim law and North African sociology at the University of Algiers starting in 1932.[30] It is ironic that Bouglé, and later historians of French sociology, do not include the sociologists at the University of Algiers in their overviews, given how ardently the French state insisted that Algeria was part of France proper.

Several French sociologists working in the Le Playsian tradition held teaching positions in other institutions of higher education.[31] Joseph Wilbois, discussed in the previous chapter, taught at the *École d'administration et d'affaires*. Paul Bureau (1865–1923) was a professor at the Catholic *Faculté libre de droit* in Paris, and Pierre du Maroussem was appointed there in 1912.[32]

French sociologists taught in several other overseas settings in university chairs or state research institutes. Paul Arbousse-Bastide and Claude Lévi-Strauss occupied sociology chairs at the University of São Paulo during the mid-1930s.[33] Lévi-Strauss's chair was transferred to Roger Bastide (chapter 8) in 1938. Another French sociologist, Émile Sicard, taught at the *Institut d'études françaises* at the University of Belgrade from 1935 to 1941.[34] Robert Montagne taught in Rabat and Algiers between the wars.

Another important interdiscipline for sociology was law, as discussed in chapter 6. Although the efforts in the 1930s by law professors to situate sociology in the law faculty ultimately failed, "the best indication of the intellectual credit of Durkheimian sociology is probably the extent to which it had penetrated the Faculty of Law," according to Heilbron.[35] René Worms, Durkheim's competitor along with Gabriel Tarde for leadership of French sociology in the decade before World War I, taught in the law faculties at Caen and Paris until his death in 1926.[36] René Maunier (chapter 8) moved to the Sorbonne's law faculty in 1925 and was appointed to a chair in colonial law, economics, and sociology in 1936.[37] Gabriel Le Bras, who played a central role in reestablishing the sociology of religion, held a Sorbonne chair in the history of canonical law starting in 1931.

Between 1918 and 1945, then, sociologists occupied around 20 chairs in universities, *grandes écoles*, and other institutions of higher education funded by the French state. This does not include scholars in other disciplines who were closely identified with sociology. Daniel Essertier, René Hubert, Raymond Lenoir, and Lucien Lévy-Bruhl all held philosophy chairs, taught courses for the certificate in *morale et sociologie*, wrote on sociological topics, and were considered to be at least "half-sociologists."[38] A number of Orientalists also had strong connections to Durkheimian sociology.[39] These chairs were located on the borders of the sociological field-in-formation.

THE *CENTRE DE DOCUMENTATION SOCIALE*

Sociological research was not entirely devoid of resources between the wars, though there were fewer employment opportunities and much less funding than after 1945. International sources such as the Rockefeller Foundation sustained French sociology.[40] Sociologists Paul-Henry Chombart de Lauwe and Jean-Paul Lebeuf conducted fieldwork in Cameroon in 1936 with the support of the French Ministries of Air, National Education, and the Colonies, the High Commissioner for Cameroon, and the Institute of Ethnology.[41] Younger sociological researchers had a key patron, alongside Mauss: Célestin Bouglé, founder and director of the *Centre de documentation sociale*, which was located at the École normale supérieure between 1920 and 1940.

Bouglé's research organization nurtured sociology and other social sciences between the wars. Bouglé had passed the state *agrégation* examination in philosophy. He emulated Durkheim's approach of generating sociological questions by reframing philosophical concepts and problems, including ethics and natural law. Bouglé's empirical research addressed egalitarianism, caste, Marxism, and the emergence of the social sciences in Germany. In 1926, Bouglé was part of a group of Sorbonne philosophers sent by the French Philosophical Society to Harvard, where he lectured on the "influence of the sociological movement on French philosophy."[42] As one of just three sociology professors at the Sorbonne, Bouglé supervised between 70 and 120 doctoral theses and *mémoires* for the *Diplôme d'études supérieures*.[43]

Reflecting the interdisciplinary spirit of French social science and the philosophical grounding of Durkheimian sociology, the *Centre de documentation sociale* (CDS) encompassed sociology, history, economics, and philosophy. The first steering committee of the CDS included a specialist in "social economics," a law professor, three Letters professors, and the philosopher Henri Bergson.[44] Funding for the CDS during the first 12 years came from a French philanthropist, Albert Kahn, but following Kahn's bankruptcy, Bouglé approached the Rockefeller Foundation, which agreed to continue financing the center.[45] This led to a stronger emphasis on contemporary social problems and a preference for "the development of an 'inductive sociology' based on fieldwork," signaling a slight distancing from the more "deductive" Durkheimian approach.[46] This was the first significant move against the dominance of the Durkheimian legacy in French sociology from the side of the Americans and their French scientific allies.

The CDS underwrote research trips, sponsored lectures and visiting scholars, and supported a handful of postgraduate students.[47] The statutes of the CDS specified that its "secretary-archivist" would be selected from the ranks of young *normaliens* (graduates of the École normale supérieure) who had recently achieved their *agrégation*. The secretary-archivist's job was to assist Bouglé with his research, supervise the Center's Reading Room, and "master the methods of research and critique of social facts." The first secretary-archivist was the budding sociologist and future fascist politician Marcel Déat.[48] Other secretary-archivists included the philosophers René Maublanc and Jean Cavaillès, who both participated in the French Resistance, and the historian Jean Meuvret. The CDS also provided fellowships to two young philosophy *agrégés* to support their research: Raymond Aron (who became "general secretary" of the CDS) and Raymond Polin.[49] Georges Friedmann,

Robert Marjolin, and Philippe Schwob pursued empirical research in political economy with assistance from the CDS.[50]

SOCIOLOGICAL SCHOLARLY ASSOCIATIONS

There were two scholarly associations focused on sociology with a French presence before 1945, the *Institut français de sociologie* and the *Institut international de sociologie*. A third organization, the *Association internationale des sociologues de langue française*, was created in 1958, and played an important role for sociologists from the independent postcolonies.

The Institut français de sociologie

The *Institut français de sociologie* (IFS) existed between 1924 and 1964, and was the only national sociological organization during most of the period examined in this book. Its main publishing activity until 1930 was editing the second series of Durkheim's *Année sociologique*. After 1930, the IFS began sponsoring lectures and issued a new journal with a slightly different title, *Annales sociologiques*. The IFS was headed by Mauss. Its members came from multiple disciplines and were all part of the "university establishment." They included the leading occupants of sociology chairs, "professors from the Faculty of Law," and several ethnologists.[51] Members of a few other disciplines were present, including history (Marc Bloch, Georges and Hubert Bourgin, Henri Hubert, André Piganiol), linguistics (Antoine Meillet), classics (Louis Gernet), and economics (François Simiand). Paul Lapie, a member of Durkheim's original circle, participated in the IFS even though he had moved into educational administration.[52] The ranks of colonial researchers in the IFS expanded after 1945 to include Bousquet, Griaule, Leenhardt, Leroi-Gourhan, Massignon, Montagne, Rivet, Rodinson, Sauvy, Sicard, and Soustelle.[53] Membership in the IFS between the wars provides a map of the wider Durkheimian milieu; after the war, it reveals the close connections between this group and colonial social science.

The International Institute of Sociology

The main international sociology organization with a French presence before 1945 was the International Institute of Sociology (*Institut international de sociologie*). The Institute had a preponderance of non-French members,[54] but its original leadership and headquarters were French. It was founded by René Worms in 1893, who directed it until 1925, after which Bordeaux sociology professor Gaston Richard assumed control. Its main journal, *Revue internationale de sociologie*, was edited by Worms until 1925 and subsequently by Émile Lasbax. Before the 1950s, the journal was written entirely in French.[55]

The Durkheimians shunned the International Institute of Sociology. Its French contingent drew heavily from the Le Play school and from younger sociologists who were still unestablished. Conforming to a nineteenth-century organizational model rather than that of modern scholarly associations, many of the Institute's members were political notables and non-academics. These included the French Prime Minister Georges Clemenceau, the French President and Prime Minister Alexandre Millerand, and the progenitor of crowd sociology Gustave Le Bon. The non-French membership, by contrast, tended to come from scholarly backgrounds, and it included some of the most prominent figures in British, American, German, Italian, and Austrian sociology. Patrick Geddes, Corrado Gini, Leonard Hobhouse, J. A. Hobson, Ludwig Gumplowicz, William F. Ogburn, Gustav Schmoller, Georg Simmel, Werner Sorokin, Ferdinand Toennies, Thorstein Veblen, and Max Weber were all members. Max Horkheimer participated in the Institute's 11th congress in Geneva in 1933.

French sociologists further distanced themselves from the International Institute of Sociology after World War II due to its wartime association with fascism. UNESCO created a new, uncompromised alternative, the International Sociological Association, in 1948, to which most French sociologists gravitated. The International Institute of Sociology was "seen (correctly) by anti-fascists and liberals from all corners of Europe as the meeting place for former Nazis and their friends," at least until the 1960s.[56] Participants in the Institute's first postwar meeting in 1950 included former Nazis and Italian fascists, and just a handful of French sociologists.[57] The new president of the Institute and editor of the *Revue* in 1954 was Italian demographer Corrado Gini, who had played the role of colonial policy expert and advisor during the fascist era.[58]

The International Institute of Sociology is noteworthy in the present context due to its emphasis on colonialism and empire. Worms taught "colonial economics" at Caen between 1897 and 1902, presided over the Sociology and Ethnography section of the annual French Colonial Congresses starting in 1907, and edited various volumes on colonial studies, including *Études de sociologie coloniale (Studies in Colonial Sociology)*.[59] Entire sections of the *Revue internationale de sociologie* were devoted to colonial themes, often based on lectures at the *Société de sociologie de Paris*, Worms's Paris-based organization.[60] There was nothing particularly sociological about most of these articles, but Worms managed to make the phrase *"sociologie coloniale"* familiar even before Maunier. In 1939, Maunier was elected president of the International Institute of Sociology, assuring the place of colonial studies at its very core. The *Revue internationale de sociologie* published an article that year entitled "René Maunier, sociologist of colonization."[61] This was its final issue until 1954, when it resumed publishing. One of the articles in the first issue of the new, postwar series was by the disgraced German political theorist Carl Schmitt, who had been removed from teaching in postwar West Germany due to his rabidly anti-Semitic and anti-democratic activities during the Nazi era.[62] The *Revue internationale de sociologie* thus continued to represent a colonialist sociology, in contrast to the critical *sociology of colonialism* represented by the postwar sociology journals *Année sociologique* and *Cahiers internationaux de sociologie*.[63]

From Wartime to Postwar Sociology and the Colonial Moment

Even though sociology had been a tiny field between 1918 and 1945, it had maintained a certain allure. Bouglé described sociology as a "science à la mode" in his *Notes of a French Student in Germany* in 1895, and he repeated this formula in each edition of his book *Qu'est-ce que la sociologie (What Is Sociology?)*, including the last edition in 1939.[64] Sociology was not eliminated by the Vichy government and the German occupation, though it was transformed in substance and reduced in size. The directors of the *Institut français de sociologie* suspended all activities in March 1940, on the eve of the German invasion. Many of the leading figures in interwar French sociology were lost during the four years of fascism and war, in a tragic repetition of the destruction of the Durkheimians in World War I. Bouglé and Granet died of natural causes in 1940; Halbwachs was deported and died at Buchenwald; Le Coeur fell in battle; Mauss was excluded from the university and did not resume teaching after the war (and died in 1950). Bonnafous was disgraced by his Vichyism, Déat by his Nazism, Maunier by his collaborationism; none of them reentered academic life after the war.

By 1945, then, the Durkheimian legacy finally seemed to be on the verge of disappearance.[65] The pollster Jean Stoetzel and the demographer Alain Girard moved into central positions in the French sociological field. As discussed in chapter 7, Stoetzel attacked Durkheim's legacy and advocated Le Play as an alternative founder. The only Durkheimian sociologists who were still holding university chairs were Georges Davy and Maurice Leenhardt. Yet the connections to the Durkheimian legacy were not entirely lost. As discussed in the previous chapter, theoretical and methodological developments between the wars had left intellectual resources and unresolved problems. The *Année sociologique* was revived after 1945, and its editors remained loyal to the Durkheimian/Maussian lineage.[66] The journal's classic Durkheimian format was revived, according to which each issue opened with a small number of articles, followed by a longer section consisting of book reviews organized according to a modified version of Durkheim's original schema. Familiar headings such as "*sociologie générale*," "*morphologie sociale*," "*sociologie juridique et morale*" appeared alongside new headings such as "*sociologie et psychologie*," "*sociologie du travail*," "*systèmes sociaux et civilisations*," and "*linguistique*." There were articles on classic Durkheimian topics such as suicide, religion, law, education, custom, and myth. Sociologists of different generations published in the postwar *Année sociologique*. It was clearly considered to be a leading journal at the time. Indeed, it was one of just two generalist French sociology journals, alongside Gurvitch's *Cahiers internationaux de sociologie*, until 1960.

After 1945, French sociology was open for campaigns of annexation and redefinition. As government policies began to increase the number of teaching and research positions, sociology became a more viable career option. The rest of this chapter will sketch the outlines of postwar sociology as a social field and then turn to the structure of the subfield of colonial specialists.

THE SIZE OF THE SOCIOLOGY FIELD AND ITS COLONIAL SUBFIELD IN GREATER FRANCE, 1945–1965

What did the sociology field look like at the moment of Liberation? Here, it is worth recalling the methodological issues discussed in the first chapter. In order to delimit the sociological subfield focused on colonialism, we need to first establish the contours of the sociology field and its members. The key criterion for determining membership in any specialized social universe is reciprocal recognition by its participants. We can also use certain objective criteria. Here, we include anyone who held a full-time academic position labeled "sociology" or located in a sociology division or department. The number of sociologists employed by the *Centre national de la recherche scientifique* (CNRS) rose from 18 in 1949, to 20 in 1950, 37 in 1955, 50 in 1958, and 75 in 1965.[67] The number of researchers at the *Centre d'études sociologiques* increased from 29 in 1953 to 52 in 1956, and reached around 100 by the end of the decade.[68] In addition, there were approximately 20 sociologists teaching at universities and *grandes écoles* in 1958, and around 50 in 1965.[69] The French Institute of Black Africa added a sociology section in 1952, which had four full-time sociologists along with assistants and auxiliaries.[70] At least 26 researchers worked as sociologists in 15 different research centers of the *Office de la recherche scientifique et technique outre-mer* (ORSTOM) before 1960.[71]

How many of these sociologists worked on colonies and empires? Appendix 1 lists 88 French sociologists who worked on colonies and empires between the 1930s and 1965. Appendixes 2–5 list the names of all sociologists in Greater France at specific moments, allowing us to track the relative size of the colonial subfield over time. The first year presented is 1946—the year in which Gurvitch inaugurated the *Centre d'études sociologiques* and the *Cahiers internationaux de sociologie*. This was also the year in which the two main colonial research organizations (*Institut français d'Afrique noire* and ORSTOM) hired their first full-time sociological researchers, and in which sociology gained a "privileged position" (*place de choix*) within the CNRS.[72]

Using these criteria, we can estimate the number of full-time researchers and professors in the sociology discipline in France and the wider French Empire (appendix 5). In 1946, there were 31 sociologists, of whom 15 were specialized in colonial or imperial themes. In 1949, the total number of sociologists was 36,

Table 9.1. Total number of full-time sociologists in Greater France and those working on or in colonies, 1949–1960

Year	Total number of sociologists	Total number of sociologists working on or in colonies	Percentage of discipline working on colonial topics
1946	31	15	48
1949	36	20	55
1955	94	43	46
1960	127	64	50

20 of whom (55%) were working on colonial topics. By 1955, the sociological field had grown to 94 members, with 43 colonial specialists. In 1960, near the very end of the colonial era, there were 127 French sociologists. Sixty-four of them, slightly more than half, were oriented toward colonial studies.[73]

WHERE DID COLONIAL SOCIOLOGISTS WORK?

These figures strongly support the argument that colonialism was a central preoccupation for postwar French sociologists. This argument gains further evidence when we look at research employment sites for colonial sociologists, as discussed in chapter 5. The French sociologist Jean-René Tréanton singled out "colonial problems" as one of three promising employment areas for sociologists outside of the university in a paper given in Liège in 1953 at the second congress of the International Sociological Association.[74] Heilbron shows that teaching positions began to outweigh research positions in metropolitan French sociology only after the 1970s. This was also true in the colonial arena. The French Institute of Black Africa and the *Office de la Recherche Scientifique Coloniale* employed around 27 researchers as sociologists between 1945 and 1965.[75] CNRS employed at least 28 sociologists who were involved in colonial research during the same period.[76] In 1959, the "Sociology and Demography" section of the CNRS was presided over by Gurvitch and had twenty members, ten of whom were involved at some point in research on colonies.[77]

The *Centre d'études sociologiques* is usually described as the spearhead of atheoretical, empirical, applied, American-style sociology in postwar France. This suggests, at least implicitly, that the *Centre* was dedicated to metrocentric research, since American sociology was itself overwhelmingly metrocentric. In fact, the organization's original mandate was to study France sociologically, and this explicitly included "overseas France." One of its permanent research groups was "specialized in overseas France."[78] The Center's first meeting in 1946 was presided over by none other than the French Colonial Minister, Marius Moutet. Georges Gurvitch, the "major force behind the creation" of the

Center and its first Director (1945–1949), was a strong supporter of colonial research and an active anticolonialist, as discussed below, even if this did not figure centrally in Gurvitch's writing.[79] The Center's original directing committee included three key representatives of interwar colonial social science: Leenhardt, Rivet, and Mauss. During the 1946–1947 academic year, Leenhardt and Massignon conducted research under the aegis of the Centre on "different aspects of social life in overseas France."[80] Roger Bastide lectured at the Centre on "the interpenetration of civilizations." André Leroi-Gourhan lectured on the Japanese colonization of the Ainu people of Hokkaido and on processes of colonial cultural "symbiosis."[81] The inclusion of the colonies in the Center's purview makes sense once we stop equating France with metropolitan France and break through the repression of memory.

The most important site of advanced social science research and education in postwar France was the Sixth Section of the *École pratique des hautes études*. There were 36 professors (*directeurs d'études*) and one associate professor in the "Sociology and Ethnology" division of the Sixth Section by 1961–1962. Half of these professors were associated with research on colonial topics.[82] A quarter of all the colonial sociologists in the postwar French empire taught at the Sixth Section at some point before 1965.[83]

A further source of employment and support for sociologists was the *Centre de sociologie européenne* (Center of European Sociology), created in 1958 by Raymond Aron. The *Centre de sociologie européenne* differed from the *Centre d'études sociologiques* in several important respects. Aron chose the center's name in order to signal an emphasis on European sociological traditions rather than American ones. Since the center was initiated near the end of the colonial period, one might expect it to have had a metrocentric focus. Yet Aron was one of the leading sociological theorists of imperialism, and was acutely aware that empire was not synonymous with colonialism and would not end with decolonization (chapter 11). Aron's interest in imperial questions was reflected in the people he invited to join the Center. One of the first was Pierre Bourdieu, who was completing his Algerian fieldwork at the time; another was Eric de Dampierre, who had been doing fieldwork in French Ubangi-Chari since the mid-1950s. A report on the Center's planned activities in 1959 noted that Bourdieu and de Dampierre were studying "the transfer of European institutions to underdeveloped countries, especially in Africa and South Asia."[84] Aron also brought in Jean Cuisenier, who had directed a survey of economic underdevelopment in Tunisia, and François Bourricaud, who had supervised a social survey in Upper Volta.[85] Two other colonial specialists joined the *Centre de sociologie européenne* before 1965: Salah Bouhedja, who had participated in Bourdieu's research on the resettlement of Algerians as a guide and interpreter, and Françine Muel, a student of Balandier's who started her social research career in Rwanda.[86] Bourdieu's Algerian collaborator Abdelmalek Sayad did not have a statutory position at the Center during the first half of the 1960s, but later in the decade he organized the Center's exchanges with Algerian institutions. Sayad organized lectures in Algeria by Bourdieu, Cuisenier, Robert Castel, Jean-Claude Passeron, Sayad himself, and other members of the Center.[87]

Colonial specialists obtained advanced lectureships and professorships in French universities during the two decades before 1965, as shown in table 9.2.

COLONIAL SOCIOLOGISTS' PERTINENT SOCIAL PROPERTIES: DIPLOMAS AND DEGREES

Academic degrees influence the distribution of power in disciplinary fields, even if they are not the sole factor or even the most important one. It is worth recalling that Pierre Bourdieu never finished his doctoral thesis and never studied sociology. Yet it was crucial for Bourdieu's success that he completed his state *agrégration* in philosophy with such distinction. Without this, Bourdieu's early career would have been completely different. He would not have been singled out to write official reports on Algeria during his military service, an experience that reoriented his interests toward the study of social science and colonialism. He would not have been invited to teach at the University of Algiers in 1957. He would not have been invited to publish on Algeria in leading journals such as *Esprit*, *L'homme*, and *Les temps modernes* at the start of his academic career, and his first books on Algeria would not have been published by Beacon Press, Mouton, and Les éditions de minuit. He would not have been sought out by Aron and recruited to the most promising new sociological "laboratory" in France in 1960.

There were several academic degrees that helped individuals to gain status in sociology. Heilbron reconstructs the percentage of sociologists who were *normaliens* or who had passed the highly competitive annual national *agrégation* exams. These continued to be important markers of scholarly prestige during the postwar years. Heilbron calculates that the pre–World War I Durkheimian network had a high percentage of *normaliens* (more than 50%) and *agrégés* (more than 80%), while the postwar *Centre d'études sociologiques* had only one or two *normaliens* among its ranks during the 1950s, and tended to have just two *agrégés* at any given moment.[88] Turning to our group of 88 colonial sociologists, we find 17 *agrégés*, almost 20 percent. This is a higher percentage than among the members of the *Centre d'études sociologiques*. In this respect, and several others, colonial sociologists more closely resembled the Durkheimian/ Maussian formation than the profile of the *Centre d'études sociologiques*.

A doctorate was not a necessary condition for qualification as a sociologist until *after* the period examined here, but it was certainly important. The most prestigious doctorate was the traditional *thèse d'état*, which required two separate theses. In 1958, it became possible to write a shorter doctorate, the *thése de troisième cycle*. More than half (46) of the colonial sociologists

Table 9.2. Colonial sociologists with lectureships or professorships in universities in Greater France, 1945–1965

Name	University and dates of early employment
André Adam	University of Aix-en-Provence (professor, 1962–)
Raymond Aron	Sorbonne (professor, 1955–); Sixth Section, EPHE (professor, 1960–)
Georges Balandier	Sixth Section, EPHE (professor, 1954–); Sorbonne (professor, 1962–)
Roger Bastide	University of São Paulo (professor, 1938–1954); Sixth Section, EPHE (1951–, Sorbonne (1959–)
François Bourricaud	Sorbonne (assistant, 1947–1950); Bordeaux (maître de conférences, 1955–1966); Paris V (professor, 1969–)
Pierre Bourdieu	University of Algiers (1958–1960); Sorbonne (assistant, 1960); Lille (chargé de cours, 1961–1964); Sixth Section, EPHE (professor 1964–)
Georges-Henri Bousquet	University of Algiers (professor 1927–1947); Bordeaux (professor 1962–)
Jean Cazeneueve	Sorbonne (chargé de cours, 1960–1961); Louvain (lecturer, 1963–1964); Sorbonne (professor 1966–)
Jean Cuisenier	Tunis Institut des hautes études (1955–1959)
Eric de Dampierre	Sixth Section, EPHE (assistant professor, 1959–1969); Nanterre (professor, 1967–1995)
Jean Duvignaud	Tunis Institut des hautes études (professor, 1960–1965); University Orléans–Tours (professor, 1965–1979); University of Paris VII (professor, 1980)
Pierre Fougeyrollas	Dakar (professor, 1961–1968); University of Paris VII (professor, 1970–)
Georges Granai	Lyon (assistant professor, 1955–1958); Tunis (professor, 1958–1965)
Jean-William Lapierre	University of Aix-en-Provence (assistant professor, 1962); Tananarive (lecturer 1962–1966)
Marcel Lesne	University of Algiers (assistant professor, 1961); Nancy (professor, 1963–)
Pierre Marthelot	Tunis, Institut des hautes études (1950–1956), Sixth Section, EPHE (professor, 1959–1979), Paris V (professor)
Paul Mercier	Sixth Section, EPHE (1956–1976), Paris V (assistant professor, 1970–1976)
Paul Pascon	Rabat (professor, 1961–)
Paul Sebag	University of Tunis (assistant professor, 1959–1977); University of Lille (maître-assistant, 1977–1979)
Jean Henri Servier	University of Montpellier (professor, 1957–)
Emile Sicard	University of Algiers (professor, 1963–1967); University of Bordeaux (professor, 1967–)
Louis-Vincent Thomas	University of Dakar (professor, 1958–1968); Sorbonne (professor, 1968–1988)
Jean-Paul Trystram	University of Aix-en-Provence (professor, 1955–1961); University of Lille (professor, 1966–); University of Paris (professor, 1969–)

in our census completed the prestigious *thèse d'état*. Seventeen wrote a *thèse de troisième cycle*, and three earned both types of doctorate, writing three different theses. Five colonial sociologists (including Bourdieu) obtained a *diplôme d'études supérieures* but no doctorate, and a dozen earned only a *licence* degree. Many also earned diplomas and certificates for specialized languages. In short, the formal qualifications of colonial sociologists were varied, but as a whole they had extremely elite levels of "institutionalized" or scholarly symbolic capital.[89]

Another social property influencing sociologists' relative standing relates to the specific discipline in which they earned their *agrégation, licence,* or doctorate degrees. Most of the doctorates earned by colonial sociologists were in Letters. Of the 53 colonial sociologists who earned *licence* degrees, 38 had a concentration in philosophy or an undefined concentration in Letters.[90] The majority of the colonial sociologists who earned the *agrégation* specialized in philosophy.

WHERE DID COLONIAL SOCIOLOGISTS PUBLISH?

Colonial specialists were well represented in the two generalist French sociology journals that existed before 1960, *Année sociologique* and *Cahiers internationaux de sociologie*. In *Année sociologique* a large amount of space was dedicated to ethnographic studies of indigenous, colonized, and postcolonial societies, especially in a new book review section called "Social Systems and Civilizations" (*Systèmes sociaux et civilisations*). The first editor of this section was Maurice Leenhardt. Between 1952 and 1964, it was edited by Roger Bastide (chapter 8), and then by Pierre Métais, a student of Mauss and Leenhardt and a specialist in New Caledonia.[91] There was clear continuity with the focus on "ethnological and exotic" topics in the first series of *Année sociologique* and with the Durkheimian vision of ethnography as a "branch of sociology."[92] Within the section on "Social Systems and Civilizations," there was a subsection labeled "Contacts of civilizations; Colonialism" (*Contacts de civilizations; Colonialisme*), which reviewed books on medieval, early modern, modern, and contemporary colonialism worldwide.[93] Contributors to the *Année sociologique* no longer exhibited any primitivist preference for unmixed cultures, but tended instead to emphasize cultural "interpenetration" and the historicity of colonized societies.[94] Louis Gernet's review of Paul Mercier's book *The Tasks of Sociology* (1951) agreed with its author that sociologists should focus on the ways "dependent" societies had been "affected and more or less shaken by the colonial phenomenon."[95] Jean Chesneaux, a historian of China and Vietnam, argued that analysts of colonialism should examine the social backgrounds and interests of different groups of colonial officials, pointing to the need for a sociology of the colonial state.[96] Maxime Rodinson's review of René Maunier's *Sociologie coloniale* called for more attention to the "revenge of the colonized."[97]

Cahiers internationaux de sociologie was the first new French sociology journal created after the war, and was the first to begin publishing after Liberation. The "internationalism" in the journal's title initially reflected the Anglo-American contributors brought on board by Gurvitch as a result of contacts he made during his period of exile in New York. The journal's "Directing Committee" included American social scientists such as Robert Lowie, Pitirim Sorokin, and Florian Znaniecki, and contributors from the United States, UK, and Germany. The connotations of the word *international* soon began to shift, however, as an increasing number of articles looked at colonial phenomena or were based on overseas fieldwork. The journal's colonial turn was crystallized in 1951 with the publication of Balandier's essay on the "colonial situation." A second milestone was the publication of Albert Memmi's "Sociology of the relations between the colonizer and the colonized" in 1957.[98] Gurvitch made Balandier Editorial Secretary in 1954 and soon gave Balandier complete control over the journal. Balandier's influence was felt immediately; colonial topics constituted more than half of the articles in the 1961 volume. *Cahiers internationaux de sociologie* also continued to publish the leading noncolonial sociologists, however, which kept the journal from becoming peripheral to French sociology until long after decolonization.

The other new professional sociology journal, *Revue française de sociologie*, began publication in 1960, just as most of the colonies were achieving independence. Its first six volumes though 1965 blotted out the colonial problematic almost entirely. There was just one issue, in 1963, on "Black problems" (*problèmes noirs*), in which colonialism and postcolonialism made an isolated appearance, with articles by Roger Bastide and the Dakar-based sociologists Pierre Fougeyrollas and Louis V. Thomas. In the 25 other issues between 1960 and 1965, the colonial world disappeared without a trace. Just 16 of the 540 book reviews published between 1960 and 1965 dealt with the colonial or postcolonial world. Bourdieu, who was still publishing on Algeria at this time, appeared in *Revue francaise de sociologie*, but only with metrocentric topics. The sociological mainstream was clearly leaving the already infamous colonial era behind. A new division of intellectual labor was being proposed in which professionalized French sociology would look more like its American analogue. Values were to be separated from research, the present was neatly severed from even the very recent past, and the colonial and postcolonial worlds were ignored. Yet at the same time, the most ambitious and interesting postgraduate students in the Sixth Section of the *École pratique des hautes études* were still flocking to courses on the sociology of Africa, North Africa, Asia, Latin America, and the postcolonial world. The fate of the decolonizing world hung in the balance, and for several years, leading sociologists remained captivated by it, yet none of this registered in the pages of the *Revue francaise de sociologie*.

COLONIAL SOCIOLOGY'S PATRONS

Several leading figures in French sociology supported colonial research in one way or another during the 1945-1965 period. Gurvitch, who was "the unquestioned leader of French sociology until the mid-50's," co-founded the *Association internationale des sociologues de langue française*, whose first conference in 1958 was organized around the theme "La sociologie des pays d'outremer" (Sociology of overseas countries).[99] Thirteen of the 48 chapters in the first edition of Gurvitch's influential *Traité de sociologie* (1958) were written by colonial specialists, including Bastide, Balandier, Mercier, and Memmi.[100] Gurvitch was a strong supporter of the sociology of colonialism and of decolonization. He "headed an academic activist group at the University of Paris that viewed the brutal and bloody Algerian war as unjust."[101] At the 1965 meeting of the *Association internationale des sociologues de langue française*, dedicted to the theme of the "sociology of nation-building in the new states," Gurvich demonstrated how closely he had followed the sociological research on colonialism. He identified "four tendencies" that had "clearly emerged" in this research and he aligned himself with Fanon:

> a) that of my colleague Berque and his followers, who idealize decolonization and, as far as the Maghreb is concerned, expect social benefits to result from the return to the pure Islamic cultural tradition; b) that of my colleagues Balandier and Duvignaud, who glimpse the extreme complexity of the problem, but seek internal balances in the decolonized countries by insisting on research into the creative force of the 'new nations'; c) those who, like my colleague Rodinson, emphasize the inadequacy of returning to ancient religious and national entities to solve the current problems; d) finally, those who, like the followers of Fanon and my own disciples, consider that the only way out of decolonization is a social revolution, both in the decolonized countries and in the colonizing countries.[102]

The Sorbonne sociology professor Georges Davy continued to wield a great deal of institutional power and represented one of the last living links to the original Durkheimian circle. When the Francophone Turkish sociologist Hüseyin Nail brought out Durkheim's writings on morals, law, and the state in 1950, Davy was selected to write the book's preface, given his earlier work on the state (chapter 8).[103] Davy was involved in crafting the advanced studies certificate in ethnology and sociology as part of the French "Colonial Studies" bachelor's degree that was implemented in 1945. Along with Marcel Griaule, Davy co-taught the required course for the colonial studies diploma at the Sorbonne.[104] Davy was also the vice president of the Superior Council of Overseas Sociological Research and the head of its Sociological Committee (chapter 5).

The prominence of colonial themes in postwar French sociology is also suggested by the fact that established colonial researchers from other disciplines gravitated toward sociology. Paul Mus, who carried out Orientalist studies in Southeast Asia during the interwar years, adopted a "sociological" vocabulary in his writing on the contemporary colonial situation in Indochina starting in 1937, for example, in his book *Viêt-Nam, sociologie d'une guerre* (1952).[105] Mus made this connection due to sociology's emerging emphasis on anticolonial resistance and on the changes colonialism was inflicting on the nonwest.

Sociology at the (Belgian) Heart of Darkness

I remembered the old doctor,—"It would be interesting for science to watch the mental changes of individuals, on the spot."

—JOSEPH CONRAD, HEART OF DARKNESS

Indigenous societies, with their slow evolution, have to be studied in this fashion, recommended by the Belgian Sociological Society ... [using] a questionnaire concerned with all classes of social phenomena. ... In this way, the legislator and administrator can guide the people of inferior culture toward "improvement."

—E. DELADRIER (1907)[106]

French colonial sociology was connected to a number of international contexts, ranging from the American philanthropists, universities, and social scientists discussed in chapter 5, to the Arab and African sociologists discussed in chapter 10, to European sociologists in neighboring colonies. Belgian sociology was one of the most important international interlocutors. Most Belgian colonial sociology was written in French. Indeed, Belgium was the second most important Francophone sociology field. Belgium was also the site of a subfield of colonial sociology that was smaller than its French counterpart but remarkable in terms of its importance within the national discipline.

Most Belgian colonial social research was carried out at the universities in Brussels, Louvain, and Liège, or in the Congo and Rwanda-Urundi colonies with their universities and research institutes. Belgian universities produced approximately 25 colonial sociologists between 1900 and 1960. This number includes several doctoral candidates who were still carrying out their African research at the moment of decolonization. Most of these colonial sociologists were involved in applied research on labor and social policies. Empirical sociology had become closely integrated with the operations of Belgian colonial administration. This was part of a broader scientific mobilization during the middle decades of the twentieth century. On the eve of decolonization, more than 500 scientific researchers were active in the Belgian Congo and Rwanda-Urundi.[107]

As in other European countries, sociology in Belgium before 1914 was taken up with models of comparative social evolution. Colonial observations figured here as illustrations, as in the work of Durkheim, Hobhouse, Sumner, and others. What is more distinctive about Belgium is the fact that the first generation of professional sociologists provided colonial administrators with expert advice, based on empirical research, even while the Belgian Congo was still ostensibly an international "free state." In 1905, the *Société belge de sociologie* (Belgian Sociology Society) initiated an enormous survey, the *Enquête sociologique sur peuples de civilisation inferieure*.[108] This was based on questionnaires sent to agents of the Independent Congo State, missionaries, settlers, and "anyone else who could furnish precise information in a serious manner." In addition to written responses, the Sociological Society also requested "drawings, paintings, photographs, instruments, maps, etc."[109] More than half of the pages in the journal of the *Société belge de sociologie* for the years 1907–1910 are devoted to the results of the Congo survey. Separate publications from the Congo survey contain a total of 5,608 total published pages.[110] Belgian sociology was thus closely linked to colonialism from the start.

The *Société belge de sociologie* disappeared between the wars, but the private Solvay Institute for Sociological Research, created in 1902, picked up the slack.[111] The Solvay Institute was dominated by university professors and researchers, and it quickly became associated with Brussels University. The Solvay Institute also involved itself in colonial studies.[112] The Institute's second director was a sociologist, Émile Waxweiler, who "attacked the colonial question with a very special ardor at the core of the institute," and assured that the "colonial program" would become "almost identical" with the institute after World War I.[113] The largest of the nine study groups at the Solvay Institute was dedicated to "colonial studies."[114] The expressed aim of this study group was to unite theory and ethnography in order to create rational colonial policy.[115] The colonial study group published the journal *Congo: Revue générale de la colonie belge* (1920–1940). The Solvay Institute sponsored conferences on the Congo (1932), "colonial studies" (1952), and the "promotion of the indigenous economy" (1956).[116] It also published a book series, *Études coloniales*.[117] After the war, when the Belgians abandoned policies of indirect rule and shifted toward programs of social welfare and development like the French and British, sociologists moved to the front lines.[118] The Solvay Institute immediately positioned itself as an expert in this domain, creating a new "Africa" division dedicated to social service.[119]

The Belgian universities were deeply involved in the nation's colonial empire. Waxweiler taught a course on "Primitive institutions and customs" in the colonial section of the School of Political and Social Sciences at Brussels. This section delivered specialized colonial *licence* and doctorate degrees as early as 1920.[120] The Brussels School of Political and Social Studies was directed by H. Speyer, a law professor who was a member of the Brussels-based *Institut colonial international* and a top-ranked colonial counselor.[121] Louvain University offered a *licence* degree in colonial science. There was also a Colonial University at Antwerp starting in 1923, which was renamed the *Institut universitaire des territoires d'outre-mer* in 1949. The University of Louvain had a separate *École coloniale*. Both the Antwerp and Louvain schools trained colonial officials, and they occasionally sponsored lectures and courses by sociologists.

The first university in the Belgian Congo and the first Francophone university in sub-Saharan Africa was the University of Lovanium, founded by Louvain University in Leopoldville (Kinshasa) in 1954.[122] An *Institut de recherche économique et sociale*, encompassing sociology, anthropology, and economics, was created there.[123] At least a dozen Belgian professors and assistants from Louvain University spent time at Lovanium between 1957 and 1960, including the applied colonial sociologist Guy Malengreau (figure 9.2).[124] By 1956–1957, the faculty of social and administrative sciences at Lovanium had more students than any of the other departments.[125] A second Belgian colonial university, the *Université officielle du Congo belge et du Ruanda-Urundi*, was created in Elisabethville (Lubumbashi) in the mining district of Katanga Province in the Belgian Congo in 1955–1956. Its leading sociologist was René Clémens from the University of Liège.[126] The University of Elisabethville had mainly European students; instruction there was in French and Dutch.

The Belgians also created research institutes in their overseas colonies. The *Centre d'études des problèmes sociaux indigènes* (Center for Studies of Indigenous Social Problems) was inaugurated in 1946 at Elisabethville. This was the most important Belgian institute for colonial sociology. It defined its mission in terms of a focus on "sociological studies capable of guiding action in favor of indigenous welfare rather than basic research in ethnology."[127] Here again, as in the postwar French and British empires, sociology was promoted in preference to anthropology.

The *Institut pour la recherche scientifique en Afrique centrale* (Institute for Scientific Research in Central Africa) was founded in 1947 and mobilized several dozen researchers based in the Belgian Congo and Rwanda-Urundi. Jacques Maquet, who was the most successful sociologist in Belgian Africa, was associated with the *Institut pour la recherche scientifique en Afrique centrale*. Maquet had written a doctoral thesis on the sociology of knowledge at Louvain University, followed by an anthropology doctorate at London School of Economics. Maquet then directed the Rwanda Center of the *Institut pour la recherche scientifique en Afrique centrale* from 1952 to 1957. He then wrote a third doctoral thesis under Balandier and joined the Sixth Section of the Paris *École pratiques des hautes études* in 1962 as a professor for the Sociology of

FIGURE 9.2. The *Centre universitaire Lovanium* in Leopoldville (Kinshasa), 1952; Guy Malengreau, sociologist, second from left in front row. *Source:* Myriam Malengreau, *La naissance de la faculté de médecine de Kinshasa* (2004). At: http://www.md.ucl.ac.be/histoire/malengreau/sld028.htm. Image courtesy of Myriam Malengreau.

Black Africa.[128] Maquet finished his career as a Professor of Anthropology at Case Western Reserve, (1968–1970) and UCLA (1970–1990).

A Disciplinary Field in Formation and Its Colonial Subfield

We have now assembled most of the pieces necessary to explain the postwar emergence of the sociology of colonialism and to account for its intellectual contents and social structure. The key determinants were: (1) policies of colonial development; (2) the creation of an archipelago of research and educational institutions promoting sociology in France and the colonies; (3) the existence of an array of adjacent human sciences that were becoming increasingly focused on colonial problems between the wars and after 1945; (4) the continuing existence of sociology as a disciplinary field-in-formation between the wars, intellectually alive and continuing to raise key questions; and (5) the postwar expansion of sociology as a disciplinary field, with gatekeepers, dominant figures, leading paradigms, field-specific criteria of symbolic distinction, and divisions between autonomous and heteronomous poles. Once we consider these factors together, we can understand why the sociology of colonialism emerged after 1945 as a coherent disciplinary subfield. More precisely, we need to consider these factors as causes that combined in an unpredictable, contingent, conjunctural manner, producing an unusually vibrant sociology of colonialism.[129]

Postwar French sociology was configured as a field, crisscrossed by polarized differences. Sociologists of colonialism were situated astride these polarizations, rather than being concentrated in a single region of the field. They were distributed all along the axis of generic sociological capital, ranging from high to low accumulations; they were also arrayed along the axis running from autonomy to heteronomy. Sociologists of colonialism were neither uniformly dominant nor uniformly dominated within the disciplinary field.[130] Sociologists of colonialism had their own sites of knowledge production and dissemination, their own categories, theories, and methodological perspectives, their own emerging bibliography of key works and keywords. This was a subfield-in-formation, located within a disciplinary field-in-formation. The subfield was therefore far from stabilized. There was no agreed-upon pantheon of key authorities, for example. Balandier's approach was emerging as the most pervasive model, as revealed by his centrality as a thesis supervisor and the frequent references to his concepts. Aron, Bastide, and Berque were less frequently cited by other colonial sociologists, but were still central figures in the subfield and in the scholarly universe. Bourdieu was a newcomer entering this arena at the end of our period, but his adroit moves vis-à-vis the colonial subfield, the discipline as a whole, and the academic and intellectual worlds, explain his rapid rise to prominence (chapter fourteen). Bourdieu combined many of the most valuable concepts and insights from several decades of sociological research in the colonies with the French and international philosophical traditions. By embedding these ideas within original empirical fieldwork, Bourdieu generated a novel oeuvre of colonial sociology and, eventually, a pathbreaking social theory. Given the importance of Bourdieu's work today, it is reasonable to argue that sociology worldwide owes an unexpected debt to the French sociologists of colonialism.

The next chapter continues this chapter's sociological investigation of the colonial subfield by examining structural divisions and inequalities within it. I will also explore the strategies used by colonial specialists to resist marginalization and to ascend within this social space. This mainly involved strategies directed at expanding their margins of scientific autonomy. My goal is to shed light on the dialectical relations among field structure, habitus, and strategic practice, and to illuminate the preconditions for the production of profoundly imaginative social science.

CHAPTER TEN

Outline of a Theory of Colonial Sociological Practice

THE PREVIOUS CHAPTER DEMONSTRATED that as many as half of the full-time sociologists in postwar France engaged in colonial or imperial research at some point before the mid-1960s. Colonial specialists began to constitute something like a subfield within French sociology, with its own institutions, logic, dynamics, polarizations, debates, keywords and concepts, and status hierarchies. The preceding chapter reconstructed the subfield of colonial sociologists as a whole; chapters 11 through 14 will examine four of the most innovative colonial sociologists. This chapter explores some of the asymmetries and inequalities within the colonial subfield, and some of the strategies used by colonial specialists to resist scientific domination within the discipline and subfield.

The first part of the chapter examines a set of specific disadvantages faced by colonial sociologists, in contrast to their metrocentric counterparts. Four groups encountered particular difficulties breaking into and succeeding in the discipline. First were those whose careers began in the colonial administration or military. These colonial careers lost most of their heroic patina after 1945 and were viewed with increasing skepticism. This made transfers into academic life more difficult. A second encumbrance stemmed from the invisibility of many colonial sociologists, captured by the ambiguous phrase discussed below, "*chercheur de brousse*" (bush researcher). The third marginal group, *resettlement sociologists*, worked on one of the most typical forms of applied colonial social science: the uprooting and resettlement of indigenous populations. These policies were ubiquitous in the French African colonies, but they had few admirers among intellectuals and academics.[1] Resettlement became particularly repugnant to most sociologists once the French army began to displace 2.5 million Muslims during the Algerian civil war.

Sociologists who were born as colonized subjects faced the most daunting barriers to academic success. A few overcame some of these disadvantages and gained a certain degree of recognition. Tunisian sociologist and writer Albert Memmi stands out in this regard. Others, such as the Algerian sociologist Abdelmalek Sayad, faced long delays in becoming established. Still others languished on the field's margins or were driven out altogether, such as the Togolese sociologist N'Sougan François Agblémagnon. Some of these "colonized" sociologists reflected on their own marginalization.

It might seem puzzling that colonial specialists and indigenous sociologists were able to succeed at all, in light of these barriers. After examining the social processes by which some actors were relegated to dominated positions, the second part of this chapter explores some of their strategies for countering marginalization. Colonial sociologists tried to improve their positions, to generate new alliances or polarizations, or to create entirely new structural positions within the disciplinary field.[2] Colonial specialists could benefit from their metrocentric colleagues' respect for empirical fieldwork and from the public's taste for descriptions of "exotic" cultures. Colonial sociologists could exploit their relationship to anthropology by describing sociology as more progressive in scientific and political terms, while sharing some of the intellectual cachet of a discipline connected to structuralism and the arts. Some, like Balandier, Duvignaud, Memmi, Morin, and Rouch, were active in the cultural fields. Colonial specialists engaged with philosophy, the most respected academic discipline. Finally, while many fieldworkers were subjected to colonial authorities, this relationship was no longer as constraining as it had been before 1945.

Obstacles

One set of hindrances to colonial researchers stemmed directly from the gradual increase in anticolonial sentiment. As we saw in chapter 3, the majority of the French public continued to support the overseas empire until the end of the 1950s, and anticolonialism remained politically marginal. Intellectuals and scholars were more divided. One scholar concludes that "[w]hile some intellectuals clearly took anticolonial stances and others defended France's claim to Algeria, many occupied the spectrum between these two poles, critical of the one without fully endorsing the other."[3] Nonetheless, on the intellectual left, a great deal of political vehemence was transferred from the antifascism of the Resistance to anticolonialism after 1945.[4] This was particularly true of French sociology, which was predominantly left wing. Nonetheless, many of the sociologists most critical of colonialism were the same ones conducting research in overseas colonies.

A less visible form of disapproval of colonial sociology stemmed from a kind of *epistemic contagion* that caused colonial researchers to be conflated with their objects of research. Early on, the negative views of the colonized that were built into the sinews of the modern colonial state seeped into perceptions of European settlers, and this tainted the image of overseas researchers as well.[5] Older tropes of cultural-racial contagion and "going native" continued to circulate, along with views of colonists as dropouts and failures.[6] Tropical climes were perceived as unsuitable for European habitation, despite medical advances, adding to the perception of degeneracy and contamination. As anticolonial resistance and revolution became more widespread, these regions started to appear even more dangerous and unappealing to Europeans. Tropes of cannibalism, perversion, irrationality, insanity, and disease were still found in discussions of colonies even after 1945.[7] Although Senegalese soldiers, Algerian *harkis*, and Vietnamese Foreign Legionnaires had contributed to French military victories, most French citizens did not register these contributions at the time.[8]

A pervasive problem for all colonial researchers stemmed from their scientific heteronomy, and perhaps even more from their *perceived* subordination to military and administrative authorities. Many interventions in postwar French sociology and social theory revolved around critiques of bureaucracy, technocracy, and the state. Critiques of heteronomy emerged on both the anti-Stalinist, humanist left and the liberal political right. Existentialism, the dominant philosophical force in France between 1945 and 1960, was in part a theory of freedom as autonomy. Poststructuralist critiques of discipline, biopower, and structure after 1968 emerged organically from this postwar intellectual conjuncture. Georges Balandier compared colonialism to the Nazi occupation in 1948; Fanon, Morin, and others followed suit. Colonial researchers were in danger of appearing as the absolute antithesis of these ideals of freedom. As the wartime epithet "collaborator" began to be applied to Africans who contributed to colonial administration, it required just another small step to apply the term to colonial experts as well.[9]

COLONIAL OFFICERS AND OFFICIALS AS SOCIOLOGISTS

Administrators and military officers carried out social research in all modern empires. Colonial social scientists interacted frequently with government agents, and sometimes with the military and police. The power balance between the colonial state and social scientists varied among colonies and shifted over time in favor of the latter. One factor shaping this balance was the degree to which scientists and officials became embedded within semiautonomous fields, shielding them from external influences. The transformation of the colonial state itself into a field with institutional permanency, power, and relative autonomy from the metropole proved useful in contests of force with other fields, such as the metropolitan government. By the same token, the transformation of sociology into a field with resources and a certain autonomy protected it in struggles with the colonial state and its officials, colonial settlers, and other scientific disciplines. Before World War I, colonial policymakers drew on suggestions from the writing of travelers, missionaries, officers, and soldiers, and occasionally university-trained ethnographers. Edward Said's generalization about colonies being the progeny of "travelers' tales" is only accurate, however, for the eighteenth and nineteenth centuries.[10] At that time, colonial policymakers did not rely on professional social expertise, which barely existed then.[11] This situation changed in the twentieth century, once the social sciences began to erect internal standards of evaluation, selection, and quality control. Colonial rulers no longer relied on information from a motley crew of amateur travelers and self-styled experts but could now take their cues from scholarly professionals.

We can observe these changes over a longer time period in the French Protectorate in Morocco.[12] The "Scientific Mission in Morocco" (*Mission scientifique du Maroc*) was created in 1904 and transformed into the "Sociological Section" of the French Native Affairs Bureau in 1920.[13] This office carried out research "in a scientific spirit marked more by Durkheimian sociology than by the 'lettered paradigm' of classical Orientalism."[14] A school of "Muslim sociology" (i.e., sociology of colonized Muslims) produced work that could be directly deployed by colonial rulers. In the early part of the century, this applied Orientalist sociology was produced mainly by full-time officials and officers such as Henry de Castries and Georges Spillmann, and by writers, like Robert Montagne, who left the military or colonial administration for scholarly careers.

In early twentieth-century colonies, the balance of power between "connoisseurs and deciders"[15] was still skewed in favor of the modern conquistadors. After World War II, control over colonial knowledge production began to tip toward the "connoisseurs," as illustrated by Jacques Berque's transition from "decider" to sociologist. Of course, colonial officials were still in charge of policymaking and could choose to ignore their own experts. But the increased self-governance of social science made it more difficult for colonial rulers to shift into academia.

Three careers illustrate these barriers to converting military or administrative capital into scientific capital. Georges Spillmann was a "conqueror of the interior of Morocco" who played a political role in the Fourth Republic and published books on North Africa with leading French publishers. Yet Spillmann was unable to penetrate the academic field.[16] The title of his 1968 autobiography, *Memories of a Colonialist*, was a self-imposed and only partly ironic version of a political scarlet letter.[17]

The second example is Robert Delavignette, who earned a medical degree in 1931, served in various colonial administrative roles between 1920 and 1951, published several novels set in Africa, directed and taught at the École coloniale (1937–1946, 1951–1962), and defended colonial humanism.[18]

Delavignette's 1931 novel *Les paysans noirs* is remarkable for its treatment of Africans as "peasants" rather than "natives," elevating them to the same status as rural Frenchmen.[19] Delavignette was never invited into any of the more prestigious academic institutions. He framed his memoirs as the "life of a colonial functionary" and described his career in terms of "marginalization and exclusion."[20]

The third example, Jean-Claude Froelich, earned a *licence* in Law and degrees from the *École coloniale* and from Montagne's *Centre des hautes études d'administration musulmane* (CHEAM), before becoming a colonial administrator in Togo. Froelich obtained a research post at the office of the *Institut français d'Afrique noire* in Cameroon, directed that Institute's center in Ivory Coast, and then became an instructor at CHEAM and then its director. Froelich continued until the end of his life to be referred to as a "colonial administrator" who "acquired ... profound and direct knowledge of African men and objects by listening to the bush" (*l'écoute de la brousse*).[21] I will discuss this trope of "the bush" below; suffice it to say that this sort of reputation became a handicap outside colonialist circles. Froelich published extensively and lectured at *Sciences Po*, the Paris Catholic Institute, and the University of Montréal, but he never succeeded in crossing over into the core institutions of the French academic world. By contrast, the cases of Montagne (chapter 5) and Berque (chapter 12) demonstrate that it *was* possible to move from colonial service into the core of the metropolitan scholarly field through a combination of luck, timing, effort, intellectual excellence, and in Berque's case, political anticolonialism.

LE CHERCHEUR DE BROUSSE: AN INVISIBLE SOCIOLOGIST

The category of the colonial *broussard* (backwoodsman) was well established. The conference report of a meeting of Africanists in Dakar in 1945 discussed the problems of "the researcher in the 'bush'" ("*le chercheur de 'brousse'*"), described as someone who "works at a great distance from his colleagues" and therefore "has a real intellectual and moral need to periodically refresh his scientific knowledge and to reinvigorate his spirit through contact with ... colleagues."[22] René Maunier described the entire French empire in 1941 as the "*oeuvre de blédards, oeuvre de broussards*" (product of frontiersmen and rednecks), although these terms had more positive connotations in the context of Vichy's celebration of rural virtues.[23] The French colonial ethnologist Maurice Delafosse entitled his memoirs *Broussard, ou les états d'âme d'un colonial* (*Man of the Bush, or the Moods of a Colonizer*). The historian and former colonial administrator Hubert Deschamps called his memoirs *Roi de la brousse* (*King of the Bush*).[24] The phrase *chercheur de brousse* thus referred to the French researcher in the bush, someone with the privileges associated with white skin and connections to the colonial government, but living and working in obscurity, largely left to their own devices, while still being subordinated to the will of higher authorities. These sociologists' work was mainly visible to local colonial officials and other "bush" researchers.

The *sociologues de brousse* worked mainly for IFAN or the *Office de la recherche scientifique et technique outre-mer* (ORSTOM).[25] Many of these researchers remained overseas for a large portion of their careers. They did not become members of high-profile scientific institutions such as *Centre national de la recherche scientifique*, the Sixth Section, or the *Collège de France*. If they had any institutional affiliation in metropolitan France other than ORSTOM, it was typically with the *Académie des sciences coloniales in Paris*, where they mingled with retired colonial officers and civil servants.

The other defining characteristic of "bush sociologists," alongside their rusticity, was their scientific heteronomy—or, at least, their heteronomy as perceived from the metropole. Of course, heteronomous sociologists also existed in metropolitan France, carrying out research for government or industry. And, in reality, sociologists in remote sites in overseas colonies were often able to select their own research topics, questions, theories, and methods. What mattered was the widespread belief that the research questions, goals, and even language of bush sociologists were determined by the colonial context and by political authorities. One widespread symbol of involvement with the colonial regime was the *casque colonial* or pith helmet, which overseas scientists continued to wear during the early postwar years (figure 10.1).[26]

Most of these "bush" sociologists actually *were* more heteronomous, in comparison to the larger group of colonial sociologists. More precisely, bush sociologists tended to produce a bifurcated *oeuvre*. When carrying out research at official behest, their work was narrowly focused, rigorously empiricist, and oriented toward policy. The written results of this work were typically circulated as internal reports within colonial administrations or organizations like ORSTOM. Their scholarly writing also appeared in obscure colony-specific journals, such as *Études dahoméennes (Dahomey Studies)*, published by the IFAN Center at Porto Novo in Dahomey (Benin). Their scientific methodology was distinctive. Many of their studies resembled traditional La Playsian monographs. A portrait of a single tribe or ethnic group would begin with a description of the natural terrain, flora, and fauna; this was followed by "racial anthropology" and demographic tables; the author then moved to topics such as kinship, religion, and economic practice. There was little or no attention given to the impact of colonialism, capitalism, or other outside influences, to cultural mixing, or to resistance, all themes that figured centrally in studies of the same societies by writers such as Bastide, Berque, Balandier, Bourdieu, Duvignaud, Le Coeur, Leenhardt, or Mercier.

It is perhaps paradoxical that the more *dependent* social scientists produced ethnological portraits that made the colonized seem *independent* of

FIGURE 10.1. Marcel Soret wearing a *casque colonial* (pith helmet) ca. 1950. *Source:* Marcel Soret Papers, with the kind authorization of the Academy of Mâcon (France), series E, Photos, no. 4 E 6.

imperial domination. One of the fictions of the colonial state was that the colonized were learning to govern themselves and groping their way toward independence.[27] The Le Playsian-style monograph, like the Griaule-style ethnology, resonated with this narrative. The fictional autonomy of the colonized society in these accounts was an inverted image of the colonial researcher's scientific heteronomy. By masking or euphemizing the colonial situation, the researcher's own embeddedness in colonial governance was obscured. This idealized picture can also be understood as a projection of these writers' own yearnings for autonomy.

One figure who corresponds to the category of the "bush sociologist" is Marcel Soret (figure 10.2). Soret published almost exclusively with ORSTOM and did not obtain a doctorate until the age of 50. As Soret himself pointed out, he was the only researcher in the human sciences at the *Institut d'études centrafricaines* in Brazzaville between 1953 and 1958. The conferences he attended were mainly sponsored by the Scientific Council for Africa South of the Sahara, which was dominated by the natural sciences. The only social scientists he interacted with on a regular basis, other than those he occasionally encountered in Brazzaville, were in the Belgian Congo, particularly at Lovanium University (see chapter 9).[28] Soret was frequently asked to carry out the "most diverse jobs," and he had little control over the publication of much of his work.[29] Balandier, who was Soret's director for several years in Brazzaville,

FIGURE 10.2. Marcet Soret, "chercheur de brousse" in the French Congo. Soret in jeep owned by IEC, Human Sciences Department, Brazzaville (Sept. 3, 1951). *Source:* Marcel Soret Papers, with the kind authorization of the Academy of Mâcon (France), series E, Photos, no. 4 E 3–14.

rarely cited him, and he referred to Soret as a demographer, not a sociologist or ethnologist.

Soret published one book with a major publisher, *Les Kongo Nord-Occidentaux* (figure 10.3).[30] This book was organized along the lines of the Le Playsian monograph, or a conventional interwar ethnological monograph. It began with discussions of tribal and sub-tribal groups, then moved through demography, migrations, history, linguistics, and the physical environment. The book continued with sections on economic, social, political, and cultural themes, such as religion and the arts. Only in the book's conclusion was there a discussion of the "interaction of the 'colonial situation' with traditional elements," and this took up less than a single page.[31] Soret refers to Balandier in this cursory discussion, but he does not rely on Balandier's ideas or refer to any other contemporary theorist of colonialism. The book's cover recalls the cover of Balandier's 1955 *Ambiguous Africa* (figure 13.4). However, Soret's text suggests that he either rejected or failed to grasp Balandier's intervention. It is remarkable, for example, that Soret's discussion of demography does not mention the disruptions of village population structure stemming from resettlement and industrial recruitment, which figured centrally in Balandier's studies of Gabon in the early 1950s (see chapter 13).[32]

The disjuncture between Soret's thinking and the leading sociological approaches to colonialism is revealed even more starkly in his 1970 doctoral

FIGURE 10.3. Cover of Marcel Soret, *Les Kongo nord-occidentaux* (1959).

thesis on the Teke people of the French Congo.[33] By this time, Soret had spent two decades in Brazzaville.[34] His thesis prioritizes the natural world over the social and focuses on topics of practical importance for local colonial and postcolonial administrators, such as roads, crop production, and imports and exports. He devotes the first 100 pages of his thesis to water, flora, and fauna, before even arriving at the "human milieu." This section begins with the prehistory, health, and anthropometry of the Teke, and only then addresses their social and political organization. The next section discusses "cultural contacts." Here, the reader anticipates a discussion of the adoption and mixing of new cultural forms and cultural resistance. Instead, Soret reduces cultural contacts to roads, trucks, canoes, airplanes, etc. The end of this section is titled "tradition and modernity," but it begins with a discussion of dams and the water supply. These emphases point to the concerns of a civil servant charged with the daily operations of a colony, rather than an Africanist social scientist keeping up with the latest developments in the field. Soret spent the last seven years of his employment by ORSTOM as an archivist at the *Académie des sciences d'outre-mer*—the former *Académie des sciences coloniales*—from 1976 to 1983.[35]

Other sociologists whose careers were entwined with colonial administration adopted a similar approach, neglecting or minimizing the importance of resistance and outside influences on colonized societies. In J. C. Froelich's 350-page monograph on the Konkomba people of northern Togo, for example, not a single page is dedicated to discussing the impact of colonialism.[36] Ironically, researchers such as Soret and Froelich are remembered as ethnologists or ethnographers, if they are remembered at all, despite their sociological job titles and identifications at the time.

Adopting this "heteronomous" methodological-epistemic position was not a function of age, intellectual generation, or a "bush" location per se, however, as is demonstrated by Balandier's case. In its bare outlines, Balandier's early biography resembles that of Soret. Both were born in 1920. Both started their scientific careers in 1946 with a fellowship from the Organization for Scientific Colonial Research.[37] Both were initially posted to IFAN in Dakar and, after visiting various other parts of French West Africa, both were posted to the *Institut d'études centrafricaines* in Brazzaville. Like Soret, Balandier was officially part of the colonial administration. Three of Balandier's early research projects were instigated by colonial authorities—his book on the regrouping of Gabonese villages and his dual doctoral theses. Balandier's initial reports circulated within the colonial administration as grey literature. At this stage, Balandier was still barely distinguishable from other *chercheurs de brousse*, and described himself as an "official ethnographer."[38]

But the two careers quickly diverged. Balandier created and directed the "Sociology and Demography" section of the Institute in Brazzaville between 1948 and 1951; Soret arrived in Brazzaville in 1950. Over the next two years, Balandier often asked Soret to carry out particular projects. In 1950, Soret studied the social structure of a neighborhood in the Poto-Poto district of Brazzaville as part of Balandier's study of that city. According to Balandier, Soret carried out this research between his "missions in the bush." This suggested that Balandier was using the contrast with the more *buissonière* Soret to define himself.[39] Soret took over the "Sociology and Demography" section following Balandier's departure. Their paths diverged even more radically starting in 1952, when Balandier began lecturing at *Sciences Po* and began to be hailed as "the founder of sociological research in Africa."[40] Balandier sought to keep his activities as an "applied" researcher separate from his roles as creative researcher and intellectual; Soret's writing became even more narrowly policy oriented.[41]

Three other examples illustrate different ways that colonial sociologists could avoid becoming defined as applied researchers. Louis-Vincent Thomas taught at the *lycée* Van Vollenhoven in Dakar from 1948 to 1958 and was a researcher with the sociology section of IFAN and ORSTOM before becoming a sociology professor at the University of Dakar in 1958. Thomas moved to the Sorbonne in 1968 and shifted from ethnology into sociology. His 1959 paper "From Ethnology to Sociology: Essay on a Research Program in Black Africa" began by quoting Balandier to the effect that "African society cannot be seen as a 'fixed embryo'," but must be seen as "evolving."[42] This was a leitmotif in Thomas's pioneering work on the role of death in African societies.[43]

René Gouellain also identified fully with Balandier's historical approach to colonial Africa. He worked for ORSTOM and IFAN (1955–1965) before entering the CNRS (1970–1981). Like many of the sociologists whose careers began during the colonial era, Gouellain's early research was carried out at the behest of government officials—in his case, the French High Commissioner of Cameroon.[44] Gouellain wrote a doctoral thesis under Balandier's supervision based on extensive archival research and titled *Douala, Sociologie d'une ville coloniale*. The thesis covered the effects of the slave trade and German and French colonial rule on the Duala people and the city of Douala. This was effectively a work of historical sociology, and Gouellain explained that he had been inspired by the "socio-historical optic" of "the works of M. Weber, of R. Aron." He also mentioned the importance of "works of general sociology, notably those of E. Durkheim, Mauss, G. Gurvitch," and "the important works of G. Balandier, P. Mercier, M. Gluckman, specialized in Negro-African problems."[45]

Alfred B. Schwartz, a lifelong ORSTOM researcher (1963–2002), represents a third approach to overcoming the heteronomous colonial-era researcher persona. Schwartz's distinctive biography was partly a function of being born slightly later than the others, in 1937. His career therefore began just after the end of French colonial rule. This changed the stakes completely for researchers who remained overseas in former colonies. They were no longer working for a French administration, although some of them continued to work for ORSTOM centers, which remained largely under French control. This political change actually widened the aperture of structural autonomy for researchers who chose to remain in the tropics and to take advantage of it.

Schwartz was also unique in having been born in Lorraine, which was annexed to Nazi Germany in 1940. He was the son of a coalminer who spoke the *françique lorrain* (*Lothrínger Platt*) dialect. Schwartz benefited from the educational reforms of postwar France and was able to attend *Sciences Po* in Strasbourg on a fellowship. Near the end of the colonial period, Schwartz traveled to Algeria and the Ivory Coast on short research trips. A visit to Tchad in 1961 convinced him to join ORSTOM.[46] Schwartz was supervised by Balandier for both his third-cycle thesis and his traditional doctoral thesis. He adopted a thoroughly historical approach, arguing that researchers should pay attention to the colonial past, to colonizers' destruction of village structures, and to the overall "social atomization" resulting from European rule.[47] This was the language of Berque's description of the peasants of the Moroccan

Gharb in the 1930s (chapter 12), Balandier's discussion of Equatorial Africa in the mid-1950s (chapter 13), and Bourdieu's description of Algerians in 1958 (chapter 14). Schwartz's third-cycle thesis on the village of Ziombli in the Toulépleu Sub-Prefecture of Ivory Coast was based on research in Ivoirian archives and his own ethnography. Ziombli had been created by the regrouping of three communities between 1960 and 1965, after decolonization, in a continuation of earlier French resettlements. Schwartz thus provided a postcolonial coda to the study of the colonial practice of population resettlement, to which I now turn.[48]

RESETTLEMENT SOCIOLOGY

Uprooting and resettling was one of the most ubiquitous practices of modern colonial rule. Colonial conquerors are driven to *territorialize* the conquered landscape, to reorganize and rename the land, and to assert control over space. Territorialization is "the attempt by an individual or group to affect, influence, or control people, phenomena, and relationships, by delimiting and asserting control over a geographic area."[49] The largest displacement project at the start of the modern colonial era was the *Reducción General de Indios* or General Resettlement of Indians in 1569, in which the Spanish government uprooted more than a million people in the Central Andes, destroyed their villages, and relocated them in new towns, the *reducciones*.[50] The Indian Removal Act of 1830 in the United States led to the compulsory relocation of the "Five Civilized Tribes" into Indian Territory.[51] Between 1850 and the 1880s, the U.S. government assigned most Native Americans to reservations, in another round of forcible relocation and racialized spatialization.[52] European colonial governments typically sorted out their subjects geographically according to ethnic, racial, and economic status. In Southwest Africa (Namibia), for example, the German colonial state defined native reserves and territories for each supposed tribe, most of which were assigned distinctive roles in the colonial system. In colonial Qingdao in the Chinese Shandong Province, the Germans laid out segregated districts for Chinese and European inhabitants, destroying, scattering, and relocating entire neighborhoods and towns in the process.[53]

Colonial resettlement projects during the twentieth century served an array of goals, including infrastructural plans, military campaigns, health and sanitation programs, and providing land to settlers. In scope, these projects sometimes approached the ambitions of the sixteenth-century Spanish rulers of Peru.[54] French colonial administrative policy came to be "based on the notion that colonized peoples normally inhabited stable villages which were 'natural', tradition-based units of political organization that could be used as the building blocks of the French colonial administrative system."[55]

After World War II, officials engaging in resettlement programs began to solicit input from sociologists and other experts. Sociology's specialization in "'attitudes,' 'trends,' and 'statistics'"[56] seemed to make it ideally suited for the relocation of populations and the organization of new villages and social structures. This is why David Brokensha, who worked on the Volta River Dam project in Ghana after Norbert Elias, called his own work a "sociology of resettlement."[57]

Sociologists continued to be mobilized into resettlement and regrouping projects during the late colonial era and the years following decolonization, when newly independent governments continued earlier policies. A few examples illustrate the range of French sociologists' involvement in resettlement policies.

The French *Office du Niger*, an agency engaged in large irrigation and agricultural projects utilizing tens of thousands of forced laborers during the 1930s and 1940s, was involved in coercive resettlement of Africans from Upper Volta and Sudan into territories irrigated by the dam. Begun in the early 1930s, the plan was not fully implemented until the 1970s.[58] A related resettlement program in the 1950s in the Sourou River valley in Upper Volta was accompanied by a sociological study of the factors affecting "the mechanisms of migration" among different ethnic groups. Each research team in Sourou observed the reactions to resettlement in a single village over the course of a year. The survey in 1957–1958 was carried out under the auspices of Bordeaux University's *Institut des sciences humaines appliquées* and was overseen by the 36-year-old sociologist François Bourricaud.[59]

In 1956, Balandier and Paul Mercier conducted an "applied sociological study" in French Guinée relating to the social problems posed by the proposed construction of a hydroelectric dam in the Konkouré river, along with a new town and an industrial complex for aluminum production. They were specifically interested in "the problems of displacement of the population caused by the realization of that project."[60] In an unpublished report, Mercier referred to Balandier's Gabonese experiment, writing that "sociologists' role should not be limited" to a study of the conditions before the displacement. Rather, they should also be involved in rehousing the populations, just as sociologists had participated in the "installation of new villages during the operation '*regroupement des villages*'" in Gabon.
The Konkouré project was never completed during the colonial period or after.[61]

In the mid-1950s, sociologists at the Tunisian *Institut des hautes études* carried out a study of a semi-nomadic group in the colony's south that was being sedentarized by the French government. One of the investigators was sociologist Pierre Marthelot, founder and director of the Letters section of the *Institut des hautes études* in Tunis.[62]

In Togo during the Mandate period, the French "forced large numbers of Kabye to settle in the center and south, officially to reduce overcrowding, but really to provide cheap labor reserves for plantations and industrialization."[63] After 1945, a group of sociologists were involved in a survey of this project of "directed emigration and organization of the peasantry."[64]

The Uprooting: Algeria and the Sociologists, 1954–1962

The largest colonial resettlement program in the postwar period took place in wartime Algeria, where more than two million people—around a quarter of the Muslim population—were displaced, partly into so-called New Villages. This was part of a program of "psychological warfare and pacification."[65] As in many other colonies, the goal was to resettle the colonized in rationally planned, stabilized villages as a means to impose control. The resettlement camps represented an extreme caricature of the rational, linear villages the French sought to create in other colonies and in the public housing projects in metropolitan France at the time (see figures 14.2–14.5).

Social science was involved in this project but was subordinated to a military logic. The entire process was overseen by the Specialized Administrative Sections (SAS) of the French army. Some of the SAS officers were enrolled in a year-long traineeship sponsored by the *Service des affaires algériennes*, where they were exposed to "a bit of Muslim sociology."[66] Other SAS officers enrolled in Montagne's *Centre des hautes études d'administration musulmane* in Paris. The SAS officers were charged with studying indigenous villagers before and after resettlement and making the settlements viable.[67] Sociologist-engineers were also involved in planning and executing resettlements in the context of the so-called *bureaux d'études*.[68]

At least four sociologists studied the forced resettlement of Algerians without participating in the uprooting: Marcel Lesne, Marcel Cornaton, Pierre Bourdieu, and Abdelmalek Sayad. Lesne was an educator in Morocco who had been selected to run the Algerian *Centres sociaux* in 1959.[69] In 1961, Lesne became a professor of sociology and ethnology at the University of Algiers, and in 1962 he was repatriated to France and took up a sociology chair at Nancy.[70] According to Lesne's article on the Algerian displacement camps, published in 1962, the streets in the "New Villages" were laid out in a rectilinear grid and surrounded by barbed wire. All "correspondences between land, history, and social structures" that had existed in the evacuated villages were destroyed.[71] The French army and its Algerian allies exercised strict surveillance over all activities in the settlements. Certain contemporaries used the word "genocide," and Bourdieu and Sayad described the New Villages as *"quasi-concentrationnaire"* (quasi-concentration camps).[72]

Michel Cornaton wrote a doctoral thesis under Germaine Tillion in 1967 on the Algerian camps, and returned to the topic several times over the next four decades.[73] Cornaton's doctoral thesis first introduced the term "sociologie événementielle" (eventful sociology), along the model of the *Annales*'s school's "histoire événementielle." He drew heavily on Bourdieu and Sayad for his conceptual framework in his comprehensive history of the regrouping policies.[74]

Bourdieu and Sayad painted such a devastating picture of the consequences of resettlement that their book, *Le déracinement (The Uprooting)* was barred from publication until after the war (chapter 14). The regrouping policy, they argued, was "a *pathological* response to the mortal crisis of the colonial system, laying bare the *pathological* aims at the core of the colonial system," and leading to a *"pathological* acceleration" of cultural change. The authors compared the French officers "charged with organizing the new collectivities"—the SAS—to "Roman colonizers," who "begin by disciplining space" in order to "discipline people."[75]

It tells us little about the precise activities of resettlement sociologists to apply labels such as "biopolitics," "governmentality," or "seeing like a state." Resettlement projects and their effects were as varied as the views of social scientists charged with studying and executing these projects. The regrouping of the Gabonese Fang into new villages after 1945 was initiated by Fang leaders interested in recovering their cultural unity. When Balandier carried out his studies of this Fang regrouping project, he did so at the urging of certain Fang leaders as well as the Colonial High Commissioner. Even during the Algerian war, according to Lesne, "each of the parties involved" in the regrouping "saw things from a different angle and wanted to treat the problems in radically opposing ways."[76] Bourdieu suggested, despite his searing criticism of the regrouping, that the post-independence Algerian government might perceive resettlements as offering "an opportunity for a revolution in agrarian structures."[77] Indeed, many of the resettlements continued to exist as villages after independence.

Balandier, Berque, Bourdieu, and Sayad were operating in the midst of totalizing political, social, and military crises. Yet all of them made intellectual breakthroughs despite, and partly because of, this chaotic context. When Bourdieu wrote that the Algerian war had revealed the "true basis for the colonial order," he was speaking not just about Algerians' insights into the colonial system but also his own.[78] This raises important questions about scientific autonomy and the paradoxical intellectual generativity of empire. Before turning to this question I will first turn to the indigenous or "colonized" sociologists, a group that experienced the greatest obstacles and harshest contradictions in their careers as sociologists.

Indigenous Sociologists: Colonized, Decolonized, and Postcolonial

I was born a native in a region where history had been written by our colonizers.

—MOHAMED TALBI, TUNISIAN HISTORIAN[79]

The knowledge of our African empire can expect much from the collaboration of the natives.

—JULES BRÉVIÉ, GENERAL GOVERNOR OF FRENCH WEST AFRICA (1931)[80]

Being a colonized intellectual was the most severe form of professional disadvantage in the greater French field of sociology.[81] If French sociologists working in Africa were *invisible* to their scientific colleagues, African intellectuals were even more so.[82] Until the moment of independence, all indigenous people were still treated legally as subjects rather than citizens, in most respects. African and Asian intellectuals were subject to structural and individual forms of racism, even if French sociologists and ethnologists had been involved in the critical study of racism since the 1930s.[83] Indigenous sociologists faced linguistic disadvantages. Albert Memmi pointed out in 1957 that a key characteristic of being colonized was a particular kind of *bilingualism* in which "the colonizer's language is the more *efficacious* one; the language of the colonized is *humiliated* and *refused*."[84] Indigenous scholars also tended to face educational disadvantages. As the French socio-ethnographer Georges Condominas pointed out in 1966, French colonial regimes had been "mainly preoccupied with training subaltern cadres." As a result, the newly independent nations "immediately had to face the very serious problem of lack of personnel" across all professional sectors. In addition, the "multiple problems of underdevelopment" facing these countries meant that "it was necessary to prioritize the most pressing tasks." In this context, "scientific research and especially basic research seemed a luxury." Basic research, including in the social sciences, was thus "left to researchers from Western countries, for the most part," during the period following independence.[85]

Indigenous sociologists also faced a specific paradox that is alluded to in the epigram above. The Governor General of French West Africa Jules Brévié made these comments in the context of creating an annual prize for "scientific and documentary" work carried out by "natives" in the fields of history, ethnology, and linguistics. African expertise would thereby contribute at least indirectly to the governance of a colony in which they were subjects rather than citizens (with the exception of a small group of Senegalese in the "Four Communes"). This forces us to raise the question of working wittingly or unwittingly for a political order by providing it with social data and scientific analysis. French sociologists faced this conundrum as well, and indeed, it is a problem for all scientists and intellectuals. For centuries, scientists have criticized expert collaboration with political and imperial powers. C. Wright Mills and Raymond Aron argued, from the 1950s through the 1970s, that academic policy experts had come to play a defining role in US imperialism.[86] Studies of the causes of insurgency by supporters of insurgency can easily be turned into counterinsurgency policies, unless researchers take epistemological precautions.[87] Such questions assume a particularly vexed form for colonized social scientists.

The comments in this section are only the beginning of a fuller investigation of the situation of the indigenous sociologist or intellectual under colonial rule.[88] Here, I will ask about colonized sociologists' educational experiences and career trajectories. I will examine indirect resonances and explicit discussions of their dominated status in their writing. Above all, I am interested in texual and political strategies they used to try to overcome or compensate for scientific and intellectual domination.

I have identified a dozen sociologists who were born as colonized subjects in the French empire and who began writing on colonial topics before decolonization.[89] My focus here is on three individuals. The first two were born in Mandate colonies of the League of Nations in interwar Africa: François N'Sougan Agblémagnon, from Togo, and Manga Bekombo, from Cameroon. Both sociologists were employed by the CNRS. The third case study is the Jewish Tunisian sociologist Albert Memmi. I will also briefly discuss another Jewish Tunisian sociologist, Paul Sebag.

Agblémagnon was the first sociologist from sub-Saharan Africa hired by the CNRS. This was in 1956, four years before Togo's independence. The following year, Agblémagnon published theoretically ambitious articles in *Présence africaine* and *Cahiers internationaux de sociologie*, which I will discuss below. He published in several other journals in the following years, including the leading professional journal *Revue française de sociologie* in 1963. Agblémagnon defended a "third-cycle" doctoral thesis in 1964, under the supervision of Roger Bastide; the thesis was published five years later by Mouton. In 1964, Agblémagnon became Togo's permanent ambassador to UNESCO, a position he held until 1982. Agblémagnon continued to publish through the end of the 1960s on the sociology of temporality, culture, and the African family, with an empirical focus on Togo. During the 1970s, his productivity tapered off, and in 1984, at the age of 55, he resigned from the CNRS. Agblémagnon explained this decision in his final report to the CNRS:

> It is our situation as first-generation African researchers that we have to participate in the birth of an African anthropology and sociology, in the constitution of African networks and associations of researchers, in crafting policies to define and institute research infrastructures, and

in the initiation of interdisciplinary dialogue and international cooperation in the realm of the large international non-governmental scientific associations.

Agblémagnon went on to describe his marginalization by the CNRS. He had "sometimes asked" himself, Agblémagnon wrote, why his activities had never provided the "opportunity to associate myself with the work of this organization," and why the CNRS had never offered him "a few more resources, or asked [him] to participate in this or that project, or this or that discussion, definition, execution, or evaluation" of projects, "much less to participate in the *conceptualization*" of new research programs. Agblémagnon was thus subject to various forms of disadvantage as an African working in predominantly white settings in France and in a newly decolonized country.

Agblémagnon's marginality expressed itself in scientific settings. One of his most contentious public interventions was at a conference sponsored by the *Association des universités partiellement ou entièrement de langue française* (Association of Francophone or partially Francophone Universities) in Beirut in 1966. The ethno-sociologist Georges Condominas presented a paper on the development of French social research on the colonies and the emergence of autochthonous participation in these studies. The only social scientists mentioned by Condominas whose work began prior to independence were from Indochina. This may have insulted Agblémagnon, whose first publications appeared before Togo's independence. We should also note that, while Condominas was best known for his work in Vietnam, the title of his intervention included African as well as Asian scholars, and he had published on Togo in 1954 and carried out fieldwork in Madagascar as well.[90] According to Condominas,

> when a highly qualified native researcher returns to his country and is not absorbed either by political activity or diplomatic service, the first task entrusted to him is an academic post, but the lack of personnel imposes on him such heavy teaching and administrative duties that he has only his meager vacation time available to devote himself to the research for which he had specialized during long years of study abroad.... The research which it would be urgent to carry out in countries in the midst of rapid transformation either are not conducted or are entirely left to foreign researchers.[91]

This may have struck too close to home for Agblémagnon, who spent much of his time building up the *Laboratoire africain de coordination de recherche et d'études interdisciplinaires* (African Laboratory for Coordination of Research and Interdisciplinary Studies) in Lomé and representing Togo in UNESCO. Agblémagnon's intervention in Beirut in 1966 proposed a version of standpoint epistemology and criticized the ability of "Occidental" sociologists to make sense of "certain sociological problems in the Black world."[92] Balandier told me in 2015 that several of his African students in addition to Agblémagnon were developing similar ideas during this period. It is revealing that Agblémagnon sometimes described himself as a "sociologist of knowledge," aligning himself with a notion resonant with the most philosophically sophisticated forms of sociology from the interwar period. The sociology of knowledge had a tiny presence within French sociology in the 1960s and was associated with the circles around Gurvitch, Balandier, and Bastide, including colonial specialists such as Berque, Duvignaud, Maucorps, Memmi, Jean Cazeneuve, Pierre Métais, and the Africanist ethnographer Jacqueline Roumeguère-Eberhardt.[93] Neither Agblémagnon nor his African standpoint epistemology show up here.

Agblémagnon's first important sociological publication in 1957 was "The Concept of Crisis Applied to an African Society." Hewing closely to Balandier's line, Agblémagnon argued that African society had always been dynamic, not static, and that Africa's continuous restructuration was "a sign of health" and a means of reestablishing social equilibrium. Societies could "die" in a healthy, normal way, but "violent" societal death was characteristic of colonialism. Agblémagnon then sketched a model of combined external and internal factors that were giving rise to a "crisis of structure and conjuncture." As a result of this crisis situation, Africa had become

> an immense, absolutely novel and heterogeneous assemblage, a complex whole made up of transfers, sublimations, inhibitions and exhibitions, refusals and contradictory acceptances, a totality that requires the researcher to create completely new techniques and types of explanation.[94]

Agblémagnon then adumbrated a trans-imperial epistemology of transfers as an alternative to both the comparative method and Bastide's concept of interpenetration, arguing that both had "become completely inadequate for explaining the dynamics of the encounter between European and African societies," which create not only social "mixtures" (*métis*) but also "social monsters."[95] Some of these "monsters" consisted of entirely new social elements whose origins could not be found in either occidental or African culture. Agblémagnon then went on to discuss another type of social "monster," which he called "the marginal personality." This phrase was reminiscent of the "marginal man" figure, famous in American sociology.[96] Yet "the marginal personality" also marked a jarring contrast to the more familiar cultural character of the *métis*. While the *métis* was a category associated with colonial settings, and the "marginal man" characteristic of modern, urban, metropolitan settings, Agblémagnon seemed to be gesturing toward a third social type.

As we have seen, some of these ideas were already familiar in the French sociology of colonialism. Balandier's work emphasized the interweaving of "dialectics that operate between a traditional (degraded) system and a modern system, imposed from the outside."[97] If African culture was in this sense *métis*, what could justify the additional category of "marginality"? While Agblémagnon is not entirely clear on this, he seems to be arguing that some colonial social categories were even more peripheral, more dominated than others, even in these intensely and violently mixed societies. Figures like Agblémagnon himself, who made the quantum leap from the crisis-ridden, rural colonial world to the heart of the colonial metropole, faced qualitatively unique forms of insecurity, instability, and peripheralization. In some respects, Agblémagnon was catapulted out of structured social space into a sociological *non-place*. The colonial ethno-sociologist Marc Augé coined the term *non-lieux* (non-places) to describe social sites where humans do not share a common universe of signification and recognition with one another. Augé began his research career in Ivory Coast at the dawn of independence. This sheds a different light on his concept, which is usually associated with the anonymous urban spaces of late capitalism.[98] Non-place also characterizes the situation of the postcolonial migrant sociologist who is not acknowledged within the fields to which he ostensibly belongs.

The emerging conceptual misalignment between Agblémagnon and the milieu of Africanist and (post)colonial sociologists is evident in his doctoral dissertation on the sociology of an oral culture, the Togolese Ewe. Agblémagnon's thesis appeared in print in 1969. None of the reviewers remarked on the fact that the book was written in the "anthropological present tense," or that its approach contradicted Agblémagnon's previous writing. Ewe culture had been subjected to European merchants and slave traders since the early eighteenth century, and the Basel and Bremen missionary societies arrived in the mid-nineteenth century. The Ewe were then divided between German and British colonies in the 1880s. This division became a major theme in anticolonial and postcolonial political struggles. Yet none of this context appears in Agblémagnon's account. Instead, he describes Ewe oral culture as an elaborate, internally coherent totality that is constituted by and constitutive of Ewe social structures. Agblémagnon does not even mention mixed or *métis* elements in Ewe culture. This may explain some of the perplexity of his reviewers, who were unconvinced that his analysis could be called "sociological," despite the authror's insistence. Agblémagnon seems to have abandoned the "dynamic" approach associated with Balandier and realigned himself with some older version of anthropology.

One might understand the attraction of anthropology, including Lévi-Strauss's version, in terms of the privileged status it accords to oral cultures. Agblémagnon may have been trying to convert an apparent disadvantage into a marker of intellectual cachet. Yet this focus on oral culture by a writer who was not trained in linguistics or anthropology, and who continued to identify as a sociologist, makes more sense as a symptom of scientific marginality.

It also recalls the intense interest in questions of language among colonized intellectuals and immigrant writers. Fanon chose to open *Black Skin, White Masks* with a chapter on "The Negro and Language," detailing the racialized discrimination against non-native speakers of French. Memmi, in *The Pillar of Salt*, describes his Tunisian protagonist and fictional alter ego, Alexandre Mordechai Benouillouche, as engaging in "hand to hand struggle" with the French language in an effort to transcend his status as "a native in a colonial country, a Jew in an anti-Semitic universe, an African in a world dominated by Europe."[99] Sayad hoped to write his doctoral thesis on bilingualism and analyzed the condition between languages as part of the "double absence" of the immigrant.[100] Agblémagnon's focus on a pure oral culture, uncontaminated by imperialism and European admixtures, barely even gestures to the linguistic dimensions of colonial racism. This seems like a step backward from his earlier work, and from the analyses of Fanon, Memmi, Sayad, and even Bourdieu, who wrote extensively on linguistic domination.

Manga Bekombo (or Bekombo-Priso) was born in Cameroon in 1932, when it was a League of Nations Mandate colony. Bekombo's university education was at Strasbourg and Nanterre universities, in psychology, sociology, and ethnology.[101] He entered the sociology section of CNRS in 1961 and, for the next three decades, his work was written from the self-declared standpoint of an "Africanist sociologist." Only in 1992, four years before his retirement, did Bekombo move into the ethnology section of CNRS.

Bekombo had a superficially less troubled career as a CNRS researcher, with a steady stream of publications. Yet his colleague Alfred Adler wrote that Bekombo experienced a "double fracture, as an African and an intellectual, with the greatest intensity."[102] This fracture is expressed in Bekombo's uneasy relationship to sociology and ethnology, an ambivalence that recalls François Agblémagnon.

Bekombo's earliest articles focus on the effects on Africans of "agricultural modernization" and "political evolution," including radio and television consumption. Another "sociological" aspect of his early publications is his comparative perspective: Bekombo did not limit himself to one African tribe or country but carried out studies in Madagascar, Congo-Brazzaville, and his native Cameroon, and sometimes discussed Africa in general. His doctoral thesis (1969) and much of his subsequent research focused on the African family, specifically among the Duala.[103] This is already an interesting move, as the study of the family is one of the most "feminized" sectors of French sociology.[104]

One of Bekombo's first articles, which appeared in *Présence africaine* in 1965, provides a window into his identification with sociology. Bekombo describes all of "the so-called underdeveloped countries" as "societies in crisis," rather than focusing on a specific nation. He refers to "the growing importance that the sociologist attributes to social change," and emphasizes that these societies are riven by internal conflicts and the "difficult play of extremely diverse elements," such as Christianity, money, the state, and private property. He then argues that "traditional" societies are also characterized by "cultural dynamism" and "self-transfiguration."[105] Agricultural modernization or westernization transforms these societies in even more thoroughgoing ways. Lineage groups are reinforced in urban settings, while conversely, the new religions meld together members of different lineage groups. Chiefly authority and other traditional authority relations are eroded. Dowries are monetized; marriage is contracted between individuals rather than entire lineage groups. The motivation for work is no longer "social prestige" but money.[106]

Bekombo signed this 1965 article "Manga Bekombo: Sociologue." Indeed, this article is unambiguously situated in the context of the sorts of sociological analyses of colonialism discussed so far. Bekombo was personally close to Balandier at this time.[107] The sociology subcommission of the *Congrès des hommes de culture noirs*, sponsored by *Présence africaine* in Rome in 1959, called for studies of traditional Africa *and* social change in Africa.[108] What Bekombo contributed was a more explicit model of the intersection between indigenous society's internal dynamism and transformations linked to colonialism, capitalism, technological change, and state formation.

A subsequent article by Bekombo discusses the introduction of radio and television broadcasting in the French Congo. He briefly surveys the introduction of radio in 1946 and then presents the results of interviews concerning African attitudes toward television. Interestingly, most of his informants believed that television would exacerbate the gap between the country's poor majority and the tiny elite of Whites and rich Africans. According to one interviewee, television was just "another microbe that will make our lives even more complicated." Bekombo's study appeared in the *Revue française de sociologie*, and is clearly situated within that discipline in terms of its survey methods, its mode of presentation, and its concentration on the contradictory dynamics of interaction between European and African culture.[109]

Like other African and Africanist sociologists, Bekombo was pushed and pulled toward ethnology starting around the middle of the 1960s. Like Balandier, Bekombo's "sociological" origins continued to shape his subsequent "ethnological" work. Yet his 1969 doctoral thesis, supervised by ethnologist Denise Paulme, is written in an explicitly ethnological style. Recalling Agblémagnon's thesis discussed above, the first 200 pages of Bekombo's thesis present an ahistorical, static portrait of the Duala "familial society," the *mboà*. His account completely excludes discussion of any "external" factors. Bekombo describes kinship structures, matrimonial exchanges, initiation rites, and other "traditional" practices of the *mboà*. His sources include historical ethnographies and interviews with a handful of contemporary Duala, who are presented as native "historians," "sociologists," and "poets." The final chapter, however, is a recognizably sociological genre. The title of this chapter is "Le mboà et les temps modernes" (The *Mboà* in Modern Times). Here, Bekombo concedes that the culture he has been describing in the previous chapters "no longer exists." Indeed, it had already started to "dissolve" under the impact of German colonial policy 90 years earlier.[110] In summary:

> The Duala group is losing its tribal homogeneity; the soil it occupies has in some sense become state property due to the fact that the foreigner can now seize it, based on nothing other than authorization by public authorities. The equilibrium that formerly was sought between various clans or lineages is now established as a function of 'national unity'; by virtue of this argument, the Duala woman today marries the man from the same neighboring tribe from which [her *mboà*] used to draw its slaves. Yet at the same time, the clans still exist. Each clan has a chief; the traditional councils meet occasionally and still discuss topics such as the exchange of women.[111]

The fracture running through Bekombo's written work is expressed most vividly in the juxtaposition between an imaginative reconstruction of Duala culture prior to colonial contact and accounts in his other publications of the devastation of that culture and its replacement by a degraded world of money, technology, private property, individualism, and European racism that endured long after decolonization.[112] The careers of Bekombo and Agblémagnon seem relatively successful on the surface, but reveal sharp critiques of European society and colonization and of their own condition as dominated intellectuals. The authors' instability and marginality are expressed in ambiguous combinations of static ethnology and dynamic sociology.

Most African sociologists in this period were unable to break into the French system. Laurent Marie Biffot worked for ORSTOM in Gabon before decolonization and at the University of Gabon afterward. Ousmane Poreko Diallo was an assistant at IFAN's sociology section (1956–1960) and head of the department of Ethnology-Sociology at the *Institut national de la recherche et de la documentation* in the Republic of Guinea.[113] Abdoulaye Bara Diop worked at IFAN beginning in 1954 and earned his PhD at Dakar in 1974, writing with Louis-Vincent Thomas. Diop completed his *Thèse de doctorat* at the University of Paris in 1980, supervised by Balandier. His career took place entirely at the University of Dakar, and his first publications appeared after Senegal became an independent country.

Most of the sociologists who were born as colonial subjects and whose careers began *after* independence did not have careers in France. This was as true in the Maghreb as in sub-Saharan Africa. In Tunis, for example, a group of French and Tunisian students studied sociology together in the late 1950s. Only the French nationals in this group went on to careers in metropolitan France (Monique Laks and Claude Tapia), while the Tunisian students stayed in Tunisia or returned there after their studies.[114] Here again, decolonization resulted in a scientific *unmixing* of French and (North) African sociologists and sociologies. Lilia Ben Salem, for example, studied in Tunis before writing a third-cycle doctoral thesis with Balandier as director and Jean Duvignaud and Jacques Berque as members of the jury, but she taught in Tunisia. Abdelkader Zgahl became a sociology professor at the *Centre d'etudes et de recherches economiques et sociales* in Tunis. Abdelwahab Bouhdibah directed the sociology department at the *Université de Tunis* following Jean Duvignaud's departure in 1965.

Two partial exceptions to this rule were the Jewish Tunisian sociologists Albert Memmi and Paul Sebag. Unlike Algerian Jews, who were granted French citizenship under the Crémieux Decree of 1870 (rescinded under the Vichy regime and then reestablished), many Tunisian Jews remained colonial subjects. Sebag was arrested, tortured, and condemned to forced labor by the Vichy regime. He published extensively on the history of urbanization, politics, industrialization, and Jewish life in Tunisia, and taught sociology at the University of Tunis from 1959 to 1977. In 1977 he became a *maître-assistant* at the Université de Lille. As Bourdieu noted, the *maître-assistant* was a subordinate position "destined for a subaltern career."[115]

Memmi was the most successful of these former colonial subjects, but his achievements as an intellectual and writer vastly overshadowed his renown in sociology. He was born just outside the gates of the Jewish ghetto of Tunis and spoke only Arabic in the Judeo-Tunisian dialect until the age of seven.[116] Because his parents were indigenous Tunisian Jews without French naturalization, Memmi "was considered a colonial subject" in the French protectorate. However, "as a Jew," certain "opportunities for French education and the possibility of an easier path to French citizenship set him apart from his Muslim compatriots." As Memmi himself suggested in *Portrait du colonisé, précédé du Portrait du colonisateur* (*The Colonizer and the Colonized*), published in 1957, he was located "between colonized and colonizer."[117] During the Vichy period, however, Memmi's fate was worse than that of most of the colony's Muslim inhabitants. Like Sebag, he was "interned by the German army and sent to a work camp for Tunisian Jews."[118]

The success of Memmi's six novels guaranteed that he would not fall into obscurity. Indeed, Memmi is "Tunisia's most decorated francophone author and its first writer and contemporary thinker of international renown."[119] His *Portrait du colonisé* has been read throughout the world alongside Fanon's *Wretched of the Earth*. What has remained obscure, however, is Memmi's identity as a sociologist. Literary critics sometimes complain that Memmi's texts are read as straightforwardly autobiographical, and some associate this exegetical shortcut with an overly "sociological" interpretive approach. In fact, the secondary literature is overwhelmingly focused on Memmi as a fiction writer. Only a single volume considers him also as a sociologist, and in a cursory way.[120] The postcolonial writer has a more established niche than the indigenous sociologist of colonialism.[121]

Memmi was hired as a research assistant at CNRS in 1957, and became a member of the *Centre d'études sociologiques* in 1956, where he stayed until 1960.[122] He taught sociology as an assistant professor (*chargé de conferences*) at the Sixth Section of the *École pratiques des hautes études* during the 1960s and at the *École des hautes études commerciales* (1958–1964), and then became a sociology professor and director of Nanterre University's Social Sciences Division (1970–1987). Given the centrality of the Sixth Section in sociological discussions of colonialism at the time, the limited number of sociology teaching posts in higher education, and the importance of Nanterre University in the Parisian events of 1968, Memmi's career could be considered a relatively successful one. At the very least, it places Memmi squarely within the scientific formation discussed in this book—the sociology of colonialism. Yet Memmi's identity as a sociologist is difficult to discern for those unaccustomed to the distinctive French configuration of the discipline at the time, with its colonial preoccupations and its openness to stylistic, methodological, and interdisciplinary experimentation.

Memmi suggested in an interview that he defined himself as a writer and that he taught sociology only to make a living. He quickly added, however, that this formulation was a way to "avoid the problem," which was "obviously more serious," noting that "one cannot be a novelist without taking into account the socio-political dimension," adding, "That is why I am a sociologist."[124] Much of Memmi's nonfictional work is situated squarely within sociology, including his essay on the sociology of literature in Gurvitch's field-defining *Traité de sociologie* (1960).[125] Also clearly located within sociology are Memmi's co-authored work *Les Français et le racisme* (chapter 5), his essay collection *Dominated Man*, and his *Portrait du colonisé*. The latter was "among the first to present the French reader with the viewpoint of the colonized,"[126] but it is also novel in *beginning* with the viewpoint of the colonizer. While many sociologists at the time called for relational studies of both sides of the colonial encounter, Memmi was the first to do so in a sustained way. Also important are the "narrative slippage, authorial intrusions, or impassioned rhetorical tactics" in Memmi's *Portrait du colonisé*, which recall the experimental texts by Balandier, Roland Barthes, Leiris, and Lévi-Strauss in this period.[127]

Perhaps most interesting for the present discussion, Memmi calls attention to the dilemma of the "colonized writer" forced to write in the language of the colonizer, and refers to the misrecognition of "colonized writers" by the metrocentric field of letters.[128] In light of Memmi's career as a sociology professor, we might also ask about the misrecognition of sociologists forced to write in the language and the stylistic genre of the colonizer. Memmi was ignored and sometimes harshly dismissed by other French sociologists, one of whom called him "a writer with a petty talent of observation" who "never thought of himself as a scientist."[129] Of course, the latter accusation may be accurate insofar as Memmi refused a naturalistic, positivist, "Americanized" definition of sociology, and aligned himself with the model of the *écrivain-sociologue* present among the colonial social scientists and intellectuals discussed in this book. It was perhaps this sensibility that made "scientific" French sociologists recoil from him. In an extreme example of presentism, histories of French sociology rarely even mention Memmi.[130]

We can draw several conclusions from these four cases and the rest of the "colonized" sociologists. First, this small group contributed some important analyses of social processes in colonial and postcolonial societies. Second, they have been ignored in the secondary literature on French and Francophone postwar sociology, with the partial and recent exception of Abdelmalek Sayad. Third, several of these sociologists discussed the need to *decolonize* intellectual life and sociology itself, echoing Berque and Bourdieu and anticipating contemporary discussions by more than five decades. Fourth, those who began publishing during the mid- to late 1960s referred explicitly to the continuing effects of colonialism into the postcolonial era. Finally, the case of Memmi suggests that a window was opened for indigenous sociologists by colonial sociology itself, but that this window was slammed shut by the processes of disavowal that set in during the 1960s. It is paradoxical that colonial sociology was open to highly original figures such as Memmi and created spaces for intellectual mixing, interaction, and interdisciplinarity across the colonial color line. These are some of the reasons that a "decolonization" of sociology—including sociological work actually produced under colonial conditions—needs to proceed with extreme caution and subtlety if it does not wish to align itself with an imperial Americanizing sociological positivism.

The foregoing discussion also underscores the importance of texts as the heart of a historical sociology of social science. A strategy of close textual reading is not a conservative strategy, but is instead the only approach that allows us to detect contradictory messages and slippages—indeed, the entire textual unconscious, as discussed by literary scholars from Pecheux to Jameson.[131] Only close reading can register the complicated presence of the contexts discussed so far in this book. Reponses to such contexts may take the form of explicit or oblique resistance, or acquiescence; it may take the form of a less conscious alignment, expressed as ideological "resonance" in the text. Resistance, especially within science, does not always, or even generally, take the form of calls to political action.

Before we turn to the detailed case studies of four sociologists, it is important to discuss a strategic level located between the purely textual and the overtly political. I am referring to strategies oriented toward challenging structural domination within the scientific field. Bourdieu's work has been salutary in calling attention to the ontological continuity between different forms of resistance to domination, without collapsing their differences. He called attention to a range of practical, partially unconscious strategies—from revolutionary action to fatalistic adjustment—used by actors within fields. To remind ourselves: Field theory is about strategy, agency, and dynamic change, as much as it is about the sometimes paradoxical or at least unpredictable and surprising reproduction of social structures and stabilized distributions of power.

Practical strategies are also textual, of course, especially in the case of writers. This means that textual and nontextual practices cannot be separated in analyzing social science. As chapter 13 will show, Balandier's practical orientation toward the colonial empire that existed in 1945, and his decision to go to Africa and socialize with African politicians and intellectuals as well as colonial officials, have to be considered at the same time as his orientation toward creating institutions, journals, and book series for social scientific research, and also at the same time as his experimental textual strategies or his analytic arguments about crisis, dynamism, and social novelty.

Toward a Theory of Colonial Sociological Practice

We might expect colonial specialists to have been located at the margins of their scientific fields, given their overall heteronomy and social marginality. But as we glimpsed in the preceding chapter, colonial specialists broadly resembled the rest of the sociology discipline in terms of their educational credentials, employment, publication patterns, professional memberships, and overall recognition, and some of them were located at the center of the field. What explains the relative success of some of them?

One explanation of the fact that colonial specialists were present in all sectors of the sociology field is grounded in the theory of practice. Agents with similar salient social properties, located in comparable social positions, may pursue completely different strategies. Social practices, including scientific ones, are not a direct function of structures.[132] Nor are they entirely legible in terms of an individual's history and embodied habitus. Bourdieu replaced the simplifications of "blissful structuralism" with his "theory of practice." A basic premise of the human sciences, including Bourdieu's version, is that agency and strategy play a central role, within structured limits.[133]

This section will examine the strategies used by sociologists of colonialism to overcome some of the structural encumbrances and disadvantages discussed above. Sociologists who had worked overseas for prolonged periods of time could point to their empirical knowledge and claim to be even *more* advanced scientifically than their office-bound colleagues. The older traditions of armchair anthropology and dispatching short-term research missions to colonies could be decried as "too centralized and old-fashioned."[134] Another strategy was to move from sociology (back) into anthropology or to build bridges to philosophy or the intellectual, literary, or artistic fields. Some sociologists sought to increase their scientific margin of maneuver in an effort to carry out research that was less administrative and socially reproductive, or to counter the reputational damage of bureaucratic complicity. We can examine each of these strategies in a bit more detail.

MOVING FROM SOCIOLOGY INTO ANTHROPOLOGY

Whereas many colonial social researchers declared their intellectual independence from ethnology after 1945, a reverse trend set in starting in the 1960s. Some of those whose careers were just beginning after 1960 and whose work would have seemed closer to sociology a decade or two earlier now became anthropologists. Augé, Balandier, Bekombo, Berque, Favret-Saada, Maquet, and Mercier were among the scholars who identified as sociologists at the beginning of their careers before gravitating into ethnology. Some were lured into anthropology by its greater cosmopolitanism or openness to theory and interpretive methods, or by its fashionable allure of scientificity during the structuralist era. Others felt themselves being pushed out of sociology by their more metrocentric and Americanized colleagues. Balandier described a combination of push and pull factors. Anthropology began to seem to him "less divided into sectors and less linked to methodological constraints, methodological formalism, compared to sociology," he recalled. It "permitted an intellectual and scientific perspective that was more open, more comprehensive, in the sense of approaching things according to a greater number of different aspects."[135]

French sociology also turned away from Balandier, as is suggested by the contributions to the journal he edited for almost six decades, *Cahiers internationaux de sociologie*. Most of the leading French social scientists contributed to the journal during its first decade, before Gurvitch passed it on to Balandier.[136] During Balandier's first two decades of editing *Cahiers*, he published articles by most of the French sociologists working on colonialism,[137] and by sociologists working on Africa and Asia who entered the discipline after decolonization.[138] Leading metrocentric sociologists such as Boudon and Touraine also still published occasionally in *Cahiers* until the end of the 1960s. Nonetheless, there was a noticeable shift. Although *Cahiers* remained one of just three generalist sociology journals in France until 1975 (when Bourdieu created a fourth, *Actes de la recherche en sciences sociales*), it no longer seemed to be an attractive venue for sociologists associated with Boudon, Bourdieu, Crozier, or Touraine, whom Heilbron identifies as the leading figures in the discipline at this time.[139] Rather than being specifically international and focused on global and imperial topics, the journal tilted toward anthropology, while also publishing some of the (neo)Marxists who did not work on industrial sociology, such as Baudrillard, Castells, and Lefebvre. In the case of Balandier's *Cahiers*, we can see how a strategy of resisting disciplinary domination could result in both marginalization and migration into another discipline. The fact that this could happen to someone who seemed so influential in the 1950s speaks volumes about French sociology's turning inward toward the national homeland in the next decade.

FORGING RELATIONS WITH THE INTELLECTUAL, CULTURAL, AND PHILOSOPHICAL FIELDS

Postwar sociologists were generally unconnected to intellectual and cultural fields, as Heilbron argues, yet this was less true of the colonial specialists. I want to examine three strategies, associated respectively with Balandier, de Dampierre, and Bourdieu, for breaking out of sociology's non-intellectual culture. The approach first involved reestablishing bridges between sociology and the arts. This was a bridge to (anti)colonial fiction, art, and poetry, and to interwar surrealism. Memmi and Pierre Naville were both writers before beginning their careers as social scientists. Balandier pursued an aesthetic approach that bridged the gap between colonial fieldwork and metropolitan cultural and intellectual fields, following his mentor Leiris.

A different strategy combined fieldwork with philosophy. Eric de Dampierre combined "bush ethnography," aesthetics, and sophisticated discussions of social science epistemology. Before his first trip to Africa in 1954, Dampierre was already an up-and-coming sociologist. He had studied for two years at the University of Chicago's Committee on Social Thought (1950–1952) and coordinated a UNESCO study of a village in the Paris region.[140] In 1952, Dampierre created a book series, *Recherches en sciences humaines*, with the prestigious editor Plon. The frontispiece of each book in this series included a page with the Latin phrase "Veh soli" (Woe to the Solitary) and the Greek text of section 528 of *The Republic*, where Plato argues that abstract thinking is more powerful than empirical observation. This can be seen as a gesture of warding off the charge of atheoretical empiricism often leveled at ethnography. The first book in Dampierre's series was a translation of Hayek's blistering antipositivist polemic, "Scientism and the Study of Society."[141] This positioned Dampierre politically to the right of many of his colleagues (though not Aron, as we will see in chapter 11), but it also sent a signal to the French sociologists who had focused on the sociology department rather than social thought and anthropology during their student exchange with Chicago. Dampierre also published a translation of Leo Strauss, another of the harshest critics of social scientific positivism at the time.[142] Dampierre personally translated Hegel's "Who Thinks Abstractly?" for the journal *Mercure*.[143] Hegel's attempt to overcome the division between abstraction and empirical concreteness appealed to Dampierre, whose diplomas were in letters and law, and in political science from *Sciences Po*. Dampierre also aligned himself closely with Weber's epistemology.[144] This was significant, since Weber walked a tightrope between theory and empirical exactitude, rejecting both of the dominant poles in the late-nineteenth-century German social scientific field—the idealism of Dilthey and the positivistic naturalism of Lamprecht and others—in favor of Heinrich Rickert's neo-Kantianism, which allowed Weber to define sociology as both explanatory and interpretive, and as oriented toward explaining unique, individual events as well as recurrent ones.[145] Aron's initial attraction to Dampierre was based on their shared appreciation of Weber. In 1958, Aron invited Dampierre to be his editorial assistant on the newly founded journal *Archives européennes de sociologie*, whose title was meant to resonate with Weber's *Archiv der Sozialwissenschaft*.[146]

Dampierre also promoted original works on race and colonialism in his Plon book series. He published E. Franklin Frazier's *Bourgeoisie noire* in French in 1955, two years before it appeared in English as *Black Bourgeoisie*.[147] This was followed by *Nomades noirs du Sahara*, by the former colonial officer Jean Chapelle; *Œdipe africain*, by colonial psychoanalyst Marie Cécile Ortigues (chapter 6); and Dampierre's own doctoral thesis on the Bandia polity of the Upper Ubangi from the precolonial to the postcolonial era.[148]

The scion of a famous aristocratic family, Dampierre was oriented toward "universal culture" and erudition.[149] He undertook "a veritable apprenticeship in typography" to increase the beauty of the books in his series.[150] His publications on harps in Equatorial Africa are lavishly illustrated and include photographs taken by Dampierre himself.[151] In short, Dampierre was developing a critique of empiricist social science at the same time as he was embarking on a lengthy program of highly particularistic fieldwork, his "sociological mission to the Upper Ubangi." And he was combining all of this with work that signaled cultural distinction.

The literature on Bourdieu, including his own writing, usually focuses on social class, language, and provincialism as the key disadvantages he faced. Bourdieu and Dampierre differed starkly in terms of their social origins. I will discuss Bourdieu in greater detail in chapter 14. The focus of the present discussion is to ask how sociologists dealt with the increasingly stigmatized background of having started their research careers in colonial settings. In this respect, the comparison between Bourdieu and Dampierre is enlightening. The two sociologists intersected around 1960, when Aron recruited them to his Center of European Sociology. They were two of the first French sociologists to establish close collaborative professional relations and friendships with sociologists born as colonial subjects—Bourdieu with Sayad and Dampierre with Bekombo.[152] The main difference is that Bourdieu was able to reorient his work in completely different empirical directions after 1964, even if he continued to refer to his Algerian research as the crucible of his thinking. Dampierre, by contrast, had spent a great deal of time, effort, and money installing his "sociological mission in the Upper Ubangi" before decolonization. The independent Central African Republic was happy to allow Dampierre to continue working there, and he remained an Africanist.

A second difference relates to Bourdieu's philosophical training. Much of Dampierre's work had an epistemological bent, as we have seen. Unlike Bourdieu, however, he was not a philosophy *agrégé*. Much of Bourdieu's brilliance has to do with his reworking of core philosophical concepts and questions, such as Kant's *Critique of Judgment* or Bachelard's "epistemological break," as sociological problems, and conversely, his reframing of sociological discussions of culture through the critical redeployment of philosophical concepts (as with his theory of *habitus*). The key point in the present context is that Bourdieu's philosophical background and orientation already characterized his empirical Algerian writings, distinguishing his work from most applied colonial sociology even when it was ostensibly on the same topics, such as unemployment (see chapter 14).

STRATEGIES FOR INCREASING SCIENTIFIC AUTONOMY

Although some colonial sociologists willingly served colonial powerholders and a few worked to overthrow European rule, a larger group worked to enhance their scientific autonomy in an effort to illuminate social structures as a means of reforming or transforming them. European social science faced several main threats to its autonomy after 1945. The first was the intense pressure to make useful contributions to rebuilding the war-torn continent and putting capitalism on a more stable basis, just as there was pressure to solve the mounting crisis in the colonies. This was accompanied by a shift from a model of "unattached cultural producers" to one of "salaried cultural producers, integrated into research teams endowed with expensive equipment and involved in long-term projects."[153]

The pressure on sociologists to provide Cameralistic advice was counterbalanced in several different ways. Perhaps most important was the fact that the scientific and political fields tend to become independent from one another in non-authoritarian societies.[154] It was also important that the leaders of ORSTOM and most other colonial research offices did not insist that all of their researchers conduct immediately applicable research.[155] Another countervailing factor was the intense emphasis on academic and scientific freedom, which came to be seen as a specific and urgent problem after the war. Concern with science was driven by the experience of Nazism and Vichyism, the ongoing revelations about Stalinism, and an array of threats within the democratic countries, including McCarthyism, the atom bomb, the growing role of the state in financing research, "the financial requirements of contemporary science," and the penetration of West German universities by former Nazis.[156] UNESCO created the journal *Impact of Science on Society*; the Congress of

Cultural Freedom published *Science and Freedom*.[157] Scientific research in the colonies raised such concerns urgently. The expansion of academic employment opportunities and research funding served as a counterweight to scientific heteronomy. Colonial researchers were able to play off different funding agencies against one another or to move from one employer to another. There was also a generalized expansion of freedom of expression in the colonies, which had conventionally been run like petty dictatorships.[158]

The postwar colonial context allows us to explore the dialectic of external pressure on sociological autonomy and strategies of counter-resistance. Colonial sociologists reveal a wide spectrum of stances on the question of autonomy. According to Abdelmalek Sayad, many of the French academics in colonial Algeria "leaned toward the side of political or administrative power, toward the side of the General Government, and, in fact, toward the side of the colonial order . . . in that way abdicating their intellectual independence . . . with the reward or compensation of colonial recognition for their allegiance."[159] Other academics had a sophisticated understanding of the relationship between politics and science. Bourdieu concluded from his experiences between 1956 and 1960 that social research requires maximum independence from government, business elites, scientific administrators, political parties and movements, and other external forces and fields. Bourdieu's abhorrence for Sartre's posture as "prophetic" or "total" intellectual did not lead him to reject participation in politics, but to develop an alternative vision of the "collective intellectual" that went beyond Foucault's model of the "specific intellectual."[160] Simplistic critiques of Bourdieu argue that his concern with relative autonomy is linked to a *depoliticization* of social science, but this is a distortion of Bourdieu's more subtle model of "engaged knowledge," which requires a first stage of autonomous knowledge production prior to engagement.[161] Bourdieu rejected the dichotomy of "scholarship" and "commitment," countering that "you have to be an autonomous scholar who works according to the rules of *scholarship* to be able to produce an engaged knowledge" or "*scholarship with commitment.*"[162] Bourdieu's own work demonstrates that it is possible to combine scientific autonomy and political engagement. Bourdieu suggested, for example, that his research with Sayad in Algeria was a form of "bearing witness" as well as a scientific contribution, arguing that "what we can quite justifiably demand of the ethnologist is that he do his best to restore to other men the meaning of their behaviours, a meaning of which, among other things, they have been dispossessed by the colonial system."[163] His insistence on protecting his own autonomy from the French colonial administration laid the groundwork not just for his theoretical breakthrough to the sociological theory of fields, but to the specific emphasis on the axis of autonomy versus heteronomy as a structural characteristic of fields in general (chapter 14).

Bourdieu believed that it was already possible during the 1950s to maintain the relative autonomy of the scientific field, even in the colonies. He was able to mobilize the support of agencies that were not directly controlled by the General Government. The Algiers branch of the French statistical office provided an official stamp of approval for Bourdieu's study of Algerian workers in 1960. His project on the resettlement camps was made possible by financial and logistical support from the director of the Algiers-based *Association pour la recherche démographique, économique et sociale*, Jacques Breil, who "always defended the autonomy of [his] researchers and their research," and with whom Bourdieu established a "relation of confidence."[164] Bourdieu created research teams that were half Algerian and half French, which helped to resist cooptation by colonial ideologies and distrust by different groups of inhabitants.

The case of Éric de Dampierre suggests a different approach to resistance to scientific subjugation. Dampierre's original fieldwork in Equatorial Africa during the mid-1950s was financed by ORSTOM and the *Conseil supérieur des recherches sociologiques outre-mer*. He was instructed to focus on explaining declining birthrates in the colony. The director of the *Conseil supérieur* and ORSTOM's Social Sciences Division, Hubert Deschamps (chapter 5), berated Dampierre in a letter, demanding that he stop pursuing historical studies of the colony and redirect his attention to the demographic question, writing that "it is the *present* and the *future* that are essentially at stake; the past should only intervene in an auxiliary role for explaining, in a certain measure, contemporary tendencies." Dampierre responded that "this is none of the Governor's business!" Deschamps insisted Dampierre focus on "demographic and sociological work"; Dampierre wrote in the margins of this letter: "demo. No. Socio. Yes" (i.e., no demographic research, only sociological research).[165]

Dampierre's resistance was not restricted to scribbled ripostes. Postwar colonial researchers faced a different situation than earlier researchers who had depended entirely on the colonial administration.[166] Dampierre was able to piece together funding from a variety of different organizations—UNESCO, CNRS, the *Centre d'études sociologiques*, the *École pratique des hautes études*, and the *Musée de l'homme*, in addition to the two mentioned earlier. This enabled him to avoid coming under the control of a single master. It is also notable that Dampierre began to defend the Weberian doctrine of *Wertfreiheit* at this time and published a French translation of Max Weber's *Science as a Vocation* and *Politics as a Vocation*.

Field Strategy and Beyond

This chapter has detailed the ways in which fields shape intellectual practice and are transformed by practice. Jockeying for position within scientific fields should be a means toward a different end: the production of knowledge. Where field positioning becomes an end in itself, scientific practice veers toward heteronomy and is overcome by non-scientific logics, including administrative and political ones. Figures such as Flaubert, Heidegger, and Manet, all analyzed by Bourdieu, are ultimately less interesting for their strategic moves in creating new fields, or new positions within fields, than for their work. Yet their work cannot be fully understood without analyzing their positions within fields. Bourdieu's own thinking evolved over time not simply in response to its internal logic or the wider sociopolitical environment but to the intermediate-level dynamics within the sociological and social scientific fields. Powerful examples of the inextricable intertwining of intellectual innovation and strategic maneuvering are evident in the case studies of Aron, Berque, Balandier, and Bourdieu in the final section of this book. Aron confronted the dominant Durkheimian establishment in French interwar sociology with a challenge from German historicism; Berque attacked the traditional Orientalists from the position of a historical ethnography; Balandier attacked French ethnology, still dominated in 1945 by Griaule, from the standpoint of "sociology." And, as we will see in chapter 14, Bourdieu was pulled into the wake of French structuralism during the mid-1960s before positioning himself against structuralism later in that decade. All of these field strategies were connected to genuine intellectual battles. Questions of structural domination and strategic practice in cultural fields are most interesting when they are related to cultural and intellectual innovation.

Four of the most dramatic examples of French sociologists affirming their autonomy and intellectual freedom in the face of fascism and colonial administration were Raymond Aron, Jacques Berque, Georges Balandier, and Pierre Bourdieu. The next four chapters will examine these sociologists' writings on colonialism and empire and the imbrications of these works with distant and proximate social contexts, with their authors' biographies and habituses, and with intertexts and paratexts.

PART V

Four Sociologists

CHAPTER ELEVEN

Raymond Aron as a Critical Theorist of Empires and Colonialism

European civilization, with its North American extension, has circled the globe and compelled recognition of its superiority . . . by the peoples of other continents. Chinese, Hindus, Moslems have been subjugated, humiliated, and exploited.

—ARON (1953)[1]

The Fourth Republic . . . died of colonial wars.

—ARON (1958)[2]

RAYMOND ARON HAS RARELY been discussed as a theorist of empires, imperialisms, and colonies, despite the sizable secondary literature devoted to him.[3] The neglect of this aspect of Aron's work is combined with his relative invisibility in his own discipline, sociology. Aron's "reputational eclipse" has several causes.[4] The most obvious reason is that Aron's legacy has been seized upon by conservatives and hawkish liberals, whereas sociology is overwhelmingly left wing.[5] The left mistakenly understands anti-imperialism as an inherently left-wing position, making it difficult for them to perceive Aron's critique of imperialism. Moreover, Aron's general support for American anti-Soviet foreign policies sometimes clashed with his anti-imperialism.

Aron's politics were also misunderstood in France. Born in 1905, he was part of the "non-conformist" crisis generation that came of age in France in the 1920s and 1930s and that rejected the conventional polarizations of Third Republic politics.[6] As a student at the *École normale supérieure*, Aron was a pacifist and member of the Socialist Party. In 1935, Aron declared himself to be "neither of the right nor of the left."[7] After 1945, Aron positioned himself against the USSR and the French Communist Party, and wrote for *Le Figaro* until 1977 and later for *Commentaire*. He was a founding member of the Congress for Cultural Freedom (CCF) in the 1950s and an active participant in its meetings and its French language journal, *Preuves*.[8] Aron resigned from the Congress in September 1967, after its financing by the CIA—already "an open secret" before that time—became impossible to ignore.[9] Aron argued that the Congress did not tell its members what to say or pay them to do it, and he noted that it embraced the entire non-communist political spectrum, from the extreme left to the right. This argument is supported by recent research, which finds that the CCF's membership was politically heterogeneous, due to the CIA's belief that "anti-communist leftists" were "Washington's most valuable allies in this fight," and that "the CIA could not always predict or control the actions of the musicians, writers, and artists it secretly patronized."[10] Aron was at the center of a renewed liberal anti-totalitarianism that gained strength in France after 1968, although he never embraced economic (neo)liberalism and remained, in his own words, "more of a left-wing Aronian than a right-wing one."[11] He became increasingly conservative after 1968 in political terms.[12] Yet, during the period I am exploring in this book, Aron advanced positions associated with the left on a number of questions, especially around imperialism. Most notably, his last book on imperialism, *République impériale* (1973), which I discuss in this chapter, suggests that his lifelong skepticism about imperialism continued to trouble his increasingly conservative politics.

A different set of obstacles to sociology's appreciation of Aron's anti-imperialism stem from the fact that most of his writing is historical and focused on international and transnational political processes. This fits poorly with sociology's overwhelming presentism, methodological nationalism, and methodological homelandism. Presentism blinds sociology even to the historical roots of contemporary phenomena; methodological nationalism posits nation-states as the natural containers for social processes; methodological homelandism further restricts analysts' vision to their *own* nation-state.[13] Aron explicitly rejected these epistemic and ontological premises.[14]

Aron's rejection of epistemic positivism was linked to his membership in a generation of graduates of the *École normale supérieure* who engaged intensively with German philosophy and culture.[15] Aron lived in Cologne, the capital of German positivist sociology in the Weimar Republic, and then in Berlin, between 1930 and 1933. He immersed himself in the writings of Max Weber, Georg Simmel, Karl Mannheim, Wilhelm Dilthey, and the Southwest German neo-Kantian philosophers, and witnessed the Nazis' rise to power. Aron's first book, *La sociologie allemande contemporaine* (*German Sociology*, 1935), is an excellent introduction to Weber and the German neohistoricist sociologists.[16] Aron's primary doctoral thesis dealt with the recent German "philosophy of history"; his complementary thesis focused on Dilthey, Rickert, Simmel, and

Weber. German sociology at the time was described, and described itself, as a *Krisenwissenschaft*, a "crisis science." This meant, first, that sociology was a symptom of the crisis of epistemic and political relativism. The sociology of knowledge, or *Wissenssoziologie*, which emerged in late imperial Germany and flourished in the Weimar Republic, explained all forms of thought, including science, in terms of social contexts. This generated anxious discussions of the dangers of relativism.[17] Sociology was also understood as a *Krisenwissenschaft* insofar as it explicitly thematized and theorized crisis. Leading German sociologists foregrounded the idea of contingency and criticized definitions of sociology as a science of general laws.[18] Aron embraced the "decline of scientism" heralded by these trends in the human sciences.[19] He rejected definitions of social causality patterned on the natural sciences and defended the broadly neohistoricist approach associated with Mannheim, Scheler, Troeltsch, Hans Freyer, Siegfried Landshut, and others. Aron criticized universal theories of history and epistemological positivism and defended value pluralism and the idea of the "limits of historical objectivity." "True history," Aron argued, should pay attention to both "regularities and accidents," and should not seek a "synthesis" of the two but should rather investigate their "interweaving."[20] Historical events need to be explained as the result of a conjunction of historical contingencies and decisionistic choices, intersecting with historical series that might remain autonomous from one another or converge.[21] Aron remained committed to this broadly Weberian understanding of historical sociology throughout most of his life, and continued to argue that the "solidarity of history and sociology" was the "centerpiece of the epistemological doctrine of Max Weber."[22]

Aron's professional academic career began with a heated debate around these crucial philosophical stakes in social science. He defended his doctoral theses in 1938 before a roomful of French scholars who were uniformly hostile to these ideas. Aron was the first French sociologist to challenge the hegemony of positivism à la Comte and Durkheim, and he did so as a student. He was pressured to abandon his plans to write a follow-up volume to his main doctoral thesis, *Introduction à la philosophie de l'histoire*, in which he planned to discuss the ideas of Troeltsch, Scheler, and Mannheim in more detail.[23] Yet, despite the hostility of mainstream French human scientists to these ideas, Aron received the "supportive tolerance of his teachers." They recognized his "claim to academic originality" based on his "epistemological innovations"—the recognized hallmarks of brilliance among philosophy *agrégés*.[24] Crucially, Aron was supported by the institutionally powerful sociologist Célestin Bouglé, and served as "general secretary" of Bouglé's *Centre de documentation sociale* (chapter 9) between 1934 and 1939. Aron contributed a number of book reviews to the Durkheimian journal *Annales sociologiques*, and was invited to participate in the annual ten-day meetings of influential French intellectuals, the *Décades de Pontigny*. In 1937, Aron filled in for Max Bonnafous, sociology professor at the University of Bordeaux. Two years later, he was recruited to a position as sociology professor at the University of Toulouse.

Aron was thus one of the leading younger figures in French sociology when the Germans invaded France in 1940. After serving in a meterological unit in the French army, Aron fled Nazi-occupied France for England, where he joined the Gaullist forces. While training in England, Aron was offered a position as deputy editor of a new review initially associated with de Gaulle, *La France Libre*. Aron wrote steadily for *La France Libre* from 1940 through 1945, with his wife and daughter joining him in London in July 1943. In 1945, they returned to Paris.[25] Aron immediately turned down an offer for the sociology chair at Bordeaux, and he did not press for restitution of his previous job at Toulouse. Instead, he continued working as a journalist, writing for *La France Libre* until September 1945 and Camus's left-of-center *Combat* from 1944 to 1947, when he joined the conservative daily, *Le Figaro*. Aron lectured during this time at the *École normale supérieure* and *Sciences Po*, but he spent most of his time as a journalist.

In 1955, Aron reentered his academic career after a 15-year hiatus by being elected to a sociology chair at the Sorbonne. Five years later, he was appointed to a professorship at the Sixth Section of the *École pratique des hautes études*. In 1969, Aron received a chair in "the sociology of modern civilization" at the *Collège de France*. Aron exercised an enormous intellectual and institutional influence over postwar French sociology, occupying positions at the three most important French academic institutions for the social sciences. He played a central role in consolidating sociology's place in the French university system and academic field. He created the sociology *licence* degree in 1958, served as president of the sociology committee of the *Centre national de la recherche scientifique* for four years, created the *Centre européen de sociologie*, and co-founded the trilingual *Archives européennes de sociologie* (*European Journal of Sociology*) with Tom Bottomore and Ralf Dahrendorf.[26] He promoted the careers of a number of rising figures in sociology, including Bourdieu.

Aron's wartime experience catalyzed a radical shift in his scholarly interests. As he wrote in his *Memoirs*, "the epistemological questions that had excited me before 1939 barely interested me in 1945."[27] What attracted him now were political themes, especially international politics, imperialism, colonialism, and totalitarianism. Aron's thinking about empire between the mid-1930s and the mid-1970s covered three main cases: Nazism, French colonialism, and American hegemony. During the first period, starting in 1936, Aron analyzed Nazi Germany as a specific form of imperialism. In the second period, Aron focused on French colonialism, analyzing the French war in Vietnam, the Suez crisis, Tunisian and Moroccan independence, the Algerian war, and anticolonialism in sub-Saharan Africa. Aron's third imperial theme was the reconfigured international system resulting from World War II, characterized by the decline of French power and the European states system and the emergence of the United States and USSR as the two great powers. Although Aron understood the Soviet Union as the greater threat and the United States as Europe's essential ally, he devoted more sustained attention to American foreign policy. The culmination of this third theme was *La république impériale* (*The Imperial Republic*) in 1973. Although this book takes us beyond our time frame here, its arguments had been emerging in Aron's writing since the 1940s.

Aron's Analysis of Nazi Imperialism (1936–1945)

According to Alan Bloom, Hitler remained "the obsessive puzzle of [Aron's] life."[28] It is crucial to begin our discussion with Aron's writings on Nazism because they informed all of his later thinking about imperialism and his entire framework of international relations theory. His wartime writing belongs to an intellectual conjuncture in which Nazism was being discussed as a novel form of imperialism, in works such as Franz Neumann's *Behemoth* and Hannah Arendt's *The Origins of Totalitarianism*.[29]

Aron's first significant intervention in this discussion was his 1936 article on Nazism as an "anti-proletarian revolution." Aron began by reminding readers that "Hitlerism has always been anti-Semitic" and that Germany was pressing toward war, since the "advantages" Germany sought were "not accessible peacefully."[30] Three years later, in an article discussing Elie Halévy's *The Era of Tyrannies* (1939), Aron introduced the notion of Nazi imperialism for the first time. At this point, Aron had already distanced himself from Marxism, though not Marx. He began by responding to Halévy's discussion of fascism as a form of tyranny linked to imperialism and war. This argument was directed against the popular "Leninist" theory that explained imperialism as a function of "aging capitalism" seeking to "enlarge its market." Aron deepened his critique of the Leninist account in subsequent publications.[31]

For Aron and Halévy, tyrannical fascism resulted from "strictly political" determinants, especially geopolitical ones.[32] Countries like Germany and Italy that did not "extend over an entire continent . . . tilted naturally toward imperialism."[33] The "new imperialisms," Aron insisted, granted "clear primacy to exterior policy"—i.e., to war. The totalitarian state, he continued, "has violently suppressed internal social conflicts and tends to project the country's dynamism into exterior adventures."[34] Germany's imperialist ambitions were "global," i.e., oriented toward world domination.[35]

Aron pursued several other analytic pathways in his efforts to understand Hitler. One of these led to a construction of Nazism as a modern form of Machiavellianism.[36] In 1940, Aron published an article on "Machiavellianism as the doctrine of modern tyrannies" in *La France Libre*. Here, he argued that violent elites had revolutionized politics and taken control of states during the modern era. With their "pessimistic view of human nature" and their "exaltation of human will and action," modern tyrants were inherently oriented toward war.[37] One technique recommended by Machiavelli and deployed by Hitler was the "extermination of the conquered peoples," or more specifically, the destruction of the elites in subjected nations. Aron pointed to the "concentration camps" as an expression of the Nazis' Machiavellian approach to power.[38]

Aron deepened his understanding of Nazi imperialism in 1942 and 1943. He discussed Hitlerism as "plebiscitary Caesarism," drawing on Weber's studies of Caesarism.[39] His essay on the "threat of the Caesars" (1942) proposed a typology of three types of "large conquests." In the first variant, a higher civilization subdues less developed cultures by virtue of military and technological superiority. Aron illustrated this first form with the example of the European colonization of Africa in the nineteenth century. In the second approach, a "barbarian" culture that is militarily superior but otherwise less developed overcomes a higher civilization. In the third approach, a state conquers rivals of *equal* power. The classical example of this third type was the Roman "unification of the ancient world"; the present-day example was Nazi Germany.[40] The comparison between the Roman empire and Nazi Germany, as Julia Hell has shown, was ubiquitous across different national and political contexts.[41]

Aron went on to suggest that there was a core contradiction within Nazi imperialism stemming from a source of "fragility" found in all conquest empires.[42] During the early phase of conquest, a dialectic ensued in which each act of conquest reinforced the next. This dynamic process was a function of enthusiasm and the addition of new combatants, manpower, and supplies contributed by vanquished countries.[43] This modern form of imperial warfare was "hyperbolic" and "technological," led by a militarized warrior elite, and characterized by pure, violent action.[44] Such frenzied imperialism was not a function of capitalism or any other coherent ideology but of "myth"—the "demon of adventurism," the "madness of seeking greatness," and so on.[45] Hitler's war, oriented "first toward the conquest of Europe, then the entire world," followed this frenzied model.[46]

Nazi imperialism contained an inherent weakness, however, stemming from the reduction of the vanquished to slavery. Nazism defined the German conqueror a priori as the master race. By contrast, "in the Roman empire, in the empire of Napoléon, every person retained the hope of becoming the equal of a Roman citizen, a French citizen."[47] The "genuine imperial tradition in Russia as in Great Britain involves bringing together many different peoples, each one according to its original essence, without the pretention of assimilating or unifying them."[48] In contrast, Hitlerism was unlikely to succeed in "attracting people it reduced to the status of slaves."[49] Aron did not yet recognize at this point that the contradiction he was describing was also inscribed into the constitution of other European colonial empires as the racist "rule of difference," although he did come to this realization when analyzing Algeria, as we will see below.

Nazi imperial rule also represented a *hybrid* form of governance, according to Aron.[50] Germany used different approaches to ruling different parts of the empire, revealing "expertly plotted gradations of subjection," with differing degrees of "autonomy" and "methods of rule." Imperial techniques ranged from direct administration in occupied countries to the almost complete independence granted to the Italian and Hungarian governments.[51] Defeated France was the most complex case, separated into many different parts—the annexed, forbidden, occupied, and unoccupied zones, the prisoners of war, and the overseas colonies.[52] The fact that Germany allowed France to keep its colonies underscored the singularity of this case. The French, as a population, were "condemned to a subordinated status" but they also "oscillate[d] between the status of slaves and that of free subjects."[53] German views of France were divided between a military tendency favoring the enslavement and destruction of the population and a "political" camp oriented toward cultivating French collaborators. Aron discussed the emergence of a "Europeanist" Nazi discourse that envisioned a new "Charlemagnian" empire, in which "the Franks of the east" would rule the Franks of the west.[54]

Aron developed several additional themes in his early reflections on Nazi imperialism. Turning to the theories of bureaucracy developed by Max and Alfred Weber, Aron analyzed the Nazi empire as a hypertrophic bureaucracy spread "across all territories" but remaining attached to "the metropole."[55] This version of bureaucracy entailed the "*administration of persons*" rather than the "government of societies."[56] Aron also immersed himself in the geopolitical writings of Mackinder, Haushofer, Schmitt, and other theorists of "Great Spaces" (*Grossräume*). He read Franz Neumann's *Behemoth* in 1942, which relied heavily on Schmitt.[57] Aron suggested that German imperialism was inherent in the very idea of the German state as *Reich*, even in Bismarckian, Wilhelmine, and Weimar Germany, and that this contrasted with the nation-state format of other European countries.[58]

After Liberation, Aron discussed the "return to favor" of the idea of empire in some French circles.[59] Alexandre Kojève, the Russian-born émigré philosopher whose lectures on Hegel had fascinated the Parisian intellectual world between 1933 and 1939, was now promoting the idea of a "Latin Empire." This would be a vast "imperial" union of culturally similar nations, to replace the supposedly obsolescent construct of the nation-state.[60] Aron rejected this idea of a Latin empire in *L'Âge des empires* (*The Age of Empires*, 1945), arguing that it had been "discredited in France due to the use made of [it] by rightwing parties."[61]

Although Aron explored different theoretical approaches, all of his analyses of Nazism were undergirded by a similarly historicist epistemology. He approached imperialism as an historical, dialectical process driven by contradictions and riven by crisis—all central ideas in Weimar-era sociology. Aron's rejection of the Leninist theory of imperialism questioned not only the primal role of capitalism therein, but universalizing, monocausal social theories in general. Aron argued that each imperial conquest or episode was the result of contingently intersecting historical series and decisions, yielding events that were "unique, irreversible, and linked."[62] Aron borrowed his specific notion of the meeting of independent causal series from the "theory of chance occurrences" developed by nineteenth-century French thinker Antoine Cournot.[63]

Aron, French Colonialism, and Decolonization (1945–1962)

Aron referred only episodically to France's overseas colonies in his wartime writings for *La France Libre*. He discussed the colonies' contributions to provisioning the metropole and Germany, the Nazis' effort to attract collaborators by allowing France to retain its empire, and the use of the colonies as a base for military and political operations by the Allies and the Free French. Aron still seemed to believe that France should retain its colonies in West Africa and the western Mediterranean, albeit with "reforms of a liberal nature."[64] At the same time, Aron recognized already in 1943 that France no longer had the resources to function as a Great Power.[65]

Aron's postwar discussions of colonialism emerged directly from his wartime thinking about Nazism and redeployed some of the same concepts. In 1945, Aron wrote that the colonial empire and the German question were the two key foreign policy issues facing France.[66] He analyzed colonialism, like Nazism, in terms of relations between conquerors and conquered, racism, and humiliation. He called attention to the hollowness of colonizers' claims to assimilate the colonized, just as he had attacked Nazi discourses about a "European peace" and French collaboration. Still, Aron insisted that "despite the bloodshed," Europe's "colonial conquests in Asia and Africa do not belong to the same category as Hitler's project."[67]

Aron abhorred colonialism on moral grounds. In a 1981 interview he recalled that he had been "in Tunisia and hated the colonial regime." As Aron explained, "[m]y temperament, my nature, contradicts the role of an occupier."[68] Nonetheless, Aron focused on developing arguments against empire that were grounded in economic rationality and political *raison d'état*, in order to convince those who still believed in the colonies' viability, rather than preaching to the converted.[69] Aron extended his earlier critique of the Marxist account of Nazism to colonialism.[70] Lenin's equation of "economic imperialism" with imperialism per se was empirically flawed, Aron insisted: Europe's conquest of Africa was not a function of capitalist expansion. Wars in general had not been provoked by colonial disputes. Colonialism was neither profitable nor economically necessary for the functioning of modern industrial European economies.[71] He observed sardonically that it "would be futile to hunt for 'compelling reasons of economic necessity' to explain those military and naval expeditions which planted the tricolore at . . . Brazzaville." Critics should stop "prating about 'monopoly capitalism.'" German colonialism before World War I had been driven by "jealous bitterness inspired by the conquests of other nations"; the impulse behind the French conquests was "military logic" and "the pioneering spirit of adventure and exploration." Empire "offered a field of glory for the fighting services rather than an outlet for economic products." It stemmed from "the will to power among nations."[72] Agreeing with Joseph Schumpeter, Aron argued that modern colonialism resurrected atavistic elites and practices from precapitalist eras.[73] This echoed Aron's earlier "Machiavellian" interpretation of Nazism. Inverting "Leninist" arguments, which claim to unmask the real economic reasons for colonialism lurking behind official rhetoric, Aron countered that statesmen often deploy "Leninist" arguments about the economic profitability of empire "to disguise their dreams of political grandeur."[74] It is remarkable how often theorists proclaimed the necessity of inverting the orthodox Marxist model of base and superstructure in order to make sense of colonial politics.

In 1945, Aron conceded that France had been reduced to the status of a "second-rate power" located between the "Great Powers" and "satellite countries."[75] France's diminished stature cast immediate doubt on the viability of its empire. Colonialism, Aron wrote, "from now on belongs to a bygone era." There was "no task more urgent than to elaborate a program to take the place of colonialism." He did not yet advocate immediate "independence pure and simple," which he believed would only "deliver territories to another form of imperialism"—i.e., the Soviet Union.[76] Nonetheless, the "movement of the victims of colonialism toward freedom" was an inevitable process:

> The European nations' loss of power and prestige, the diffusion of ideas borrowed from the colonizers themselves, the awakening or reawakening of political conscience among the indigenous populations, the distant or proximate propaganda from the grand empires of the 20th century, the USSR and the United States, whose contradictory ideologies equally reject the maintenance of the status quo—all of these "realist" reasons are sufficient to condemn the absurd pretense of prolonging the [colonial] order, without even invoking moral arguments.[77]

Aron's blunt conclusion was that "this system"—colonialism—"is dead."[78]

Aron returned to colonial problems during a journalistic trip to Asia in 1953. Aron's reporting in *Le Figaro* first invoked "moral" objections to the French war in Indochina, before turning to political and economic arguments. Here again he concluded that "our resources are no longer equal to the effort," despite American aid that covered most of the costs.[79] Aron argued that France should grant independence to Vietnam and ally with Saigon against the communist threat.[80] Like the leading faction in the US State Department at the time, Aron's anticolonialism was closely tied to anti-communism.

In 1954, Aron turned his attention to the emerging crisis of French rule in North Africa. He supported "autonomy" for Tunisia and Morocco, while specifying that France should continue to work for the "peaceful coexistence of the different communities in North Africa and accelerating economic development."[81] The Suez crisis in 1956 convinced Aron that the United States was now willing to turn against its European allies in order to lure countries like Egypt away from Soviet influence.[82] The Suez episode humiliated France, reducing it to the status of a "protected state" that could not even "lay claim to freedom of external military action."[83] Aron was more convinced than ever that France could no longer maintain a colonial empire. France might continue to radiate global power through its intellectual and cultural life as long as the country did not "ruin itself in sterile adventures" of the imperial sort.[84]

Aron still believed at this time that Algeria was a different and more difficult case, however. This was due to the presence of "a million French citizens and the inextricable intermixing of diverse communities."[85] Yet Aron ultimately concluded that Algeria should be treated like the other colonies. In May 1956, Aron signed a petition supporting military action and calling for the "renewal of French Algeria."[86] But later the same year, in a private interview with the French president, he argued that France should grant independence to Algeria.[87] Aron went on to defend Algerian independence in two short books, *La tragédie algérienne* (1957) and *L'Algérie et la République* (1958). These controversial publications brought Aron into conflict with his editor at *Figaro*, with Algeria's former governor Jacques Soustelle, and with most of the French political center and right.[88] Aron wrote in his memoirs that the Algerian struggle was the most intense "political uproar" of his life.[89]

Aron introduced *La tragédie algérienne* by quoting Montesquieu to the effect that while "every citizen is obligated to die for his country, no one is obligated to lie for it."[90] The revolt of the African and Asian people was less a struggle for individual rights than a struggle against foreign domination. The "people of color, whom the West humiliated, are using the western vocabulary to express their demands," Aron wrote.[91] He then shifted into a practical register, pointing out that the "reformist" program of assimilating Algeria into France would lead to 150 Algerian deputies in the *Assemblée nationale*.[92] Aron warned that the integration of millions of impoverished Muslim citizens would bankrupt France.[93]

A year later, in *L'Algérie et la République*, Aron elaborated upon his argument about the "disparity between great empires and mid-sized states and nations." He began by establishing that colonial empires "are now widely seen as losing ventures."[94] Aron completed this book following the failed "coup d'état" of May 1958 and de Gaulle's ascension to power with the backing of the French Army. These events lay behind Aron's statement that "the Fourth Republic died of... colonial wars."[95] Aron developed a sociological explanation of the 1958 "revolution from above" as an expression of the increasing precariousness of institutions and France's sequence of national defeats. France might have consented to the loss of empire or at least to some version of free association with the colonies if it had not been so badly humiliated by invasion and occupation.[96] Foreign policy was being driven more by "ideology" than by the sorts of rational calculations central to the Leninist and realist international relations theories. Industrial capitalism had made economic arguments for colonies even more untenable.[97]

Aron then turned to the question of anticolonialism. The national liberation movements were not the product of Soviet, American, or Egyptian interference, as conservatives were suggesting at the time. Aron defended the young Arab nationalist revolutionaries as rebels against misery and *"la situation coloniale"*—using the phrase introduced by Mannoni and Balandier.[98] He then listed several "causes internal to Africa itself" that were driving the rising tide of anticolonialism:

1. The divergence between demographic growth and economic torpor, and the system of vast inequalities between the "disinherited" and the "privileged"—i.e., the French.[99]
2. The "disaggregation of traditional frameworks and the concentration of masses in the cities."
3. The monopolization of lower and mid-level civil service posts in colonial administrations by the French. Aron suggested that colonial states should only have allowed top experts to immigrate while limiting the number of "petits Français," thereby opening up government jobs to the colonized.[100]
4. The fact that the French proclaimed a "fiction" of assimilation "without according the substance." European colonial rulers tended, in fact, to protect traditional customs and rely on indirect forms of colonial rule rather than pursuing resolute assimilation policies. Aron noted, for example, that polygamy was never banned in Tunisia by the French but by the Tunisians themselves after independence.[101]
5. The fact that the French gave "young men from the colonies" an education in metropolitan universities, providing them with a "taste of liberty" and teaching them to revolt.
6. The racism permeating colonial structures. Racism was the very foundation of empire, Aron insisted—the racism of countries inhabited by allegedly "superior people" conquering and ruling over "inferior people."[102] "Africa was considered as an *object*, rather than as a subject of history."[103] The colonizers justify their disdain for the colonized by embracing "racist ideologies," entering into a "vicious circle of hatred."[104] As we will see in the chapters to follow, all of the French sociologists placed racism at the center of their models of colonialism.

Aron also developed a useful typology of empire. Europeans define three kinds of political entities as empires, he argued: the Roman type; multinational empires like the Hapsburgs; and colonial empires.[105] Contemporary colonial empires consisted of "non-independent territories—non-autonomous territories, to use the United Nations jargon—which are, for the most part, underdeveloped, and which are under the sovereignty of a developed country."[106] The European colonial empires differed from continental or *terrestrian* empires, such as Russia. Colonial overseas empires tended to be transitory, even in terms of their own self-understanding, whereas empires such as the Russian one could last much longer. Continental empires were potentially more stable than modern colonies because they allowed the elites of conquered populations access to administrative positions.[107]

Aron distinguished further between colonialism and imperialism. Imperialism refers to the policies of a political unit that subjects foreign populations to its rule.[108] *Political* imperialism involves the usurpation of sovereignty. Imperialism is a political form that "encourages and thrives upon a sense of inequality between the conquering and the subject peoples," while colonialism is an "especially brutal form of imperialism."[109] Aron went on to distinguish four different subtypes of colonial rule in Africa, and argued that settler colonies were prone to greater violence and resistance to decolonization.[110]

Aron's Theory of Empire and the Rise and Fall of the American Empire

"We are living through an era of imperial wars," Aron wrote in 1942.[111] The following year, he argued that World War II was an "imperial war," not a European hegemonic war in the conventional sense.[112] An imperial war, as Aron defined it, is carried out in order to obtain *empire* over its rivals.[113] The new Great Powers were empires; the present moment was an "age of empires."[114] The nineteenth-century "concert of Europe," grounded in a system of equal nation-states, was being replaced by a "world system" dominated by vast empires.[115] The United States and the USSR were both empires insofar as both were "multinational states" or "heterogeneous political units that included a variety of nations, peoples and communities."[116] The new "great powers," Aron wrote in 1945, "don't simply have vaster dimensions than the other countries; they are constituted according to different principles. They are themselves empires."[117]

Aron observed in 1945 that "[a]lready in the last war, some prescient thinkers recognized that the hegemony of the United States was as inevitable as Rome's after the Second Punic War."[118] The reason for the inevitability of American hegemony, he suggested, was American "economic supremacy," although political hegemony could not be assumed to follow automatically.[119] As an empire, the United States was defined as military power and conqueror.

According to Aron, "the major historical fact of the past half century is the decline of Europe, especially western Europe," and the "rise of the peripheral states, Russia and the United States."[120] These two trends were closely connected. Europe had been reduced to a "fragment of the empire involuntarily created by the United States."[121] Every attempt to create a European empire in response to these pressures had failed.[122] Aron's reporting on Vietnam emphasized that the French war would have been impossible without the United States, which assumed 80 percent of the costs starting in 1954, even while the French continued to supply all of the soldiers.[123] Aron compared the demands that the Kremlin placed on its Chinese allies to American demands on their European allies, emphasizing the parallels between the two empires and their relations to their "protectorates."[124] For Aron, the polarization between the United States and the USSR constituted a "great schism." The balance between the two great powers produced a global condition that was neither war nor peace, but a "warlike peace" (*une paix belliqueuse*)—Aron's term for the Cold War. Indeed, the Soviets' acquisition of nuclear weapons in 1949 made "a return to total war unlikely."[125]

The United States and the USSR may both have been empires and nuclear powers, but they were not identical. Aron had used the concept of *totalitarianism* as early as 1934, and in 1936 he began describing the USSR as totalitarian.[126] There was "a kinship" between the Nazi and fascist regimes and the Soviet Union, he suggested, "despite their differences."[127] The totalitarian phenomenon consisted of five elements: (1) monopoly of a single party; (2) an ideology of official truth; (3) monopolization by the state of the means of persuasion; (4) state control of most economic and professional activities; and (5) transfiguration of all possible individual crimes into political and ideological ones.[128] Aron never described the United States as totalitarian. Yet, as Claude Lefort has argued, Aron tended over time to "dissolve the notion of a totalitarian regime and to relativize the opposition between democracy and totalitarianism."[129] The key point for the present discussion is that for Aron, *imperialist states were not necessarily totalitarian, but totalitarian states were always imperialist.*[130]

Aron analyzed American foreign policy in a series of newspaper articles between 1952 and 1958. He believed US military hegemony was necessary to protect Europe and its former colonies from communism, yet he expressed exasperation with particular American policies. Aron's criticism of the United States reached a peak during the Suez crisis, although he later regretted his anger.[131] The Americans, he wrote at the time, were "bad allies" who "chase us out of our colonies faster than our enemies."[132] He criticized Truman's Point Four program and Kennedy's Alliance for Progress as "myopically prioritiz[ing] an American ideology over the particularity of geographical, political, cultural, and religious conditions."[133] He criticized the modernization-theoretic doctrines of American policy as being "shocking to the historian"—shockingly stupid, that is.[134] Modernization and IR theories were predicated on notions of universal forms of rationality and universally valid social "laws," ideas that Aron had already demolished in his doctoral theses. In an article criticizing UNESCO's "Tensions" project, which attempted to develop a universal theory of war, Aron countered that war cannot be "treated mathematically" or by using game theory.[135] Since these were the social science approaches that informed US foreign policy, Aron's epistemological critiques were simultaneously critiques of American policy.

Aron turned his full attention to the United States with the publication of *La république impériale*. This book opens with a discussion of the two leading interpretations of US foreign policy at the time: the "realist school" and the "paramarxist" approach represented by William Appleman Williams, Gabriel Kolko, and Harry Magdoff. Both perspectives were similar to the theories of imperialism that Aron had been criticizing for more than three decades at this point. Against the first approach, he argued that US policy was not typically dictated by an amoral *raison d'état* but by a moralizing ideology. Indeed, the United States was typically "guilty not of any will to power, but of a failure to recognize the role imposed on it by destiny," especially in its hesitation to enter World War II. Echoing Carl Schmitt, Aron argued that there was a perennial American refusal to recognize the very "existence of the inter-state universe."[136] The Korean War led the United States to resign itself finally "to the European practice of maintaining a large standing army, not merely a navy and air force." It "precipitated the formation in Europe of two military blocs, and in Asia the quarantining of Communist China."[137] American policy in the Vietnam War then became openly imperialist, "reviving the ancient practice of 'punishment'—attacking the adversary's territory to weaken his morale even more than to destroy his resources."[138] Although Aron supported the containment of communism, he was harshly critical of the ways in which the United States was pursuing the war, and cannot therefore be considered as a straightforward supporter of America's Vietnam War.

Echoing a theme of C. Wright Mills, Aron also developed a critique of the pervasive influence of American academics on US defense policy. According to Aron, the "armaments race was spawned by scientists, not the armed forces" or the capitalists.[139] Aron argued that "the initiative throughout the period lay with the politicians, civilians, and academics rather than the generals," even if it was "undeniable" that "corporations used lobbyists to obtain defense contracts." There had been a "militarization of the . . . thinking of the civilian policymakers."[140] The mobilization of liberal intellectuals for the Cold War and the movement of academics into the Pentagon from universities represented more important policy determinants than "capitalism," the defense industry, or the "hiring of retired generals by General Dynamics."[141] The current "paramarxist" theories of American imperialism were therefore just as misleading as the earlier wave of "Leninist" theories of European imperialism.[142]

Aron went on to distinguish between the American approach to empire and European colonialism. While the latter represented a kind of "Paleo-Imperialism," the former was a "Neo-Imperialism" insofar as it did not attempt to replace the sovereign rulers of independent states with its own rulers.[143] Europeans, including the French, generally perceived the American presence in Europe as an *imperial* but not an *imperialist* form of power, since the United States was protecting Europeans at their own request rather than forcing a protectorate upon them.[144] By contrast, in the Caribbean and Central America, where the United States intervened to create or to uphold pro-American regimes and to overthrow or frustrate hostile ones, American policy was straightforwardly "imperialist" according to Aron.[145] The United States should therefore be described most accurately as a "quasi-imperator of a quasi-empire."[146]

The American imperial structures identified by Aron were beginning to crumble just as *La république impériale* was published in 1973. Aron was acutely aware of the "economic and military decline of the United States" in the following years. He believed that "US military failures in Vietnam, the collapse of the Bretton Woods systems, and Nixon's détente policies had resulted in *la fin du système bipolaire*."[147] Aron now lambasted *détente* policy and attacked the United States for "giving up its imperial responsibilities."[148] This analysis of the end of the US empire, notably appearing in the final and most conservative decade of Aron's life, echoes Immanuel Wallerstein's account, which situates the onset of US hegemonic decline at exactly the same historical moment while explaining it in more economic terms.[149]

Aron, Postcolonial Theorist?

Aron's imperial studies continued for almost two decades after the period analyzed in this book. His long-standing focus on totalitarianism made him the central figure on the "right flank of the liberal revival" around "anti-totalitarianism" in the wake of 1968, a movement whose effects resonated across the French intellectual scene. This moment is exemplified by Aron's partial support for the creation of the journal *Contrepoint* in 1970.[150] This was a different conjuncture, in which a new set of authors from the French liberal canon such as Montesquieu and Tocqueville became important for Aron. But in other respects, Aron remained faithful to his earlier themes: the primacy of ideology, politics, and geopolitics, and a non-positivist, historicist epistemology. Aron insisted in 1967 that he actually owed "nothing to the influence of Montesquieu and Tocqueville, whose work I have only studied seriously over the course of the last ten years," and that he had "arrived at Tocqueville via Marxism, German philosophy and my observation of the contemporary world."[151] These ideas sit uneasily with those who focus their attention on the older, more conservative Aron.

Aron's writing on empire contains a number of original elements. He attempted to develop historically sensitive definitions and explanations of Nazi imperialism, French colonialism, continental and settler empires, and American imperial politics. He helped to revive the concept of empire itself in discussions of contemporary politics. He provided an overarching concept of empire within which the other social theorists and researchers discussed in this book could situate their analyses of colonial phenomena. He showed that not all empires were imperialist, much less colonialist, at least in the sense of "colonial imperialism" or "Paleo-Imperialism," as he defined it. Aron's insistence on the primacy of politics served as a salutary counterweight against the perennially popular theories of imperialism as capitalism. Aron examined numerous causal factors in his typically moderate and judicious way in trying to explain the origins, dynamics, and endings of empires and colonies. His imperial studies were embedded within a larger theory of international relations, which allowed him to discern a continuous spectrum of diplomatic forms. Aron's imperial writings bring together Weimar-era epistemology with an insouciance toward disciplinary boundaries.

By foregrounding the importance of humiliation, racism, and the seizure of sovereignty in modern colonialism, Aron's writing anticipates some of the more recent discussions in postcolonial and decolonial theory. This connects Aron's work to that of the other French sociologists of colonialism, including those I discuss in the subsequent three chapters. Jacques Berque, to whom I turn next, advocated a form of knowledge he called "transcolonial," defined as a practice of "reciprocal knowledge."[152] Aron almost seemed to echo Berque in 1957 when he suggested that a full accounting (*bilan*) of European colonialism could only be "established later, once . . . masters and slaves, having become equal, can engage in an equitable dialogue about the meaning of their shared experience."[153] Aron as a postcolonial, post-imperial, self-reflexive theorist? Given what we now know about Aron's intellectual context, influences, and interlocutors, and about his political and intellectual nonconformism, this is not too far-fetched.

CHAPTER TWELVE

Jacques Berque

A HISTORICAL SOCIOLOGIST OF COLONIALISM AND "THE DECOLONIAL SITUATION"

An underdeveloped country is an under-analyzed country.
—BERQUE, "SCIENCES SOCIALES ET DÉCOLONISATION" (1962)[1]

Most of the historical initiatives that made the world move from the colonial situation to the decolonial situation proceeded from [a] dialectic of affirmation, rather than from Hegelian negativism.
—BERQUE, "DÉCOLONISATION INTÉRIEURE ET NATURE SECONDE" (1968)[2]

JACQUES BERQUE WAS BORN IN 1910 in Molière, Algeria. His childhood was spent in the Algerian *bled*, a word used by French colonial émigrés to refer to the rural, isolated interior of the country.[3] Berque was, in his own words, an "*homme de bled*" or man of the *bled*.[4] He also grew up in close proximity to the colonial field of power, "[i]ssuing from a colonial milieu," in his own words.[5] Berque recalled visiting a large number of "*bureaux*" or government offices during his Algerian childhood, including some of the famous *Bureaux Arabes* in which proto-sociological analyses of colonized society were carried out and from which colonial native policy was locally administered.[6] Augustin Berque, Jacques Berque's father, moved to Algeria as a child with his own father, who was a veterinarian with the *Chasseurs d'Afrique*, the light cavalry corps of the French Army of Africa. Augustin was a lifelong colonial administrator, though an unusual one. An expert in Islamic law, his writing focused on the transformative impact of French colonialism on Algerian social structures and religious and political movements.[7] Augustin wrote a report on the Algerian Muslim brotherhoods in 1919 that "caught the attention of the director of the

Native Affairs department," and he was transferred to Algiers to work in the office of the General Government. In 1940, Augustin became the director of the colony's "Muslim Affairs" department.[8]

Augustin had a decisive effect on his son's career in many other ways. He sent Jacques to the *lycée* in Algiers in order to obtain a "classical French education in the humanities." One of the young Berque's *lycée* teachers was none other than Fernand Braudel, the historian and future leader of the *Annales* school. Augustin made sure his son studied Arabic as his first foreign language at school, and sent Jacques to a "local Qur'ānic school" where he was "educated in classical Arabic" and developed some "fluency in the local Arab dialect and culture."[9] In the first half of the 1930s, Augustin helped his son gain employment in the colonial administration of Morocco. Jacques recalled later that his own *"ressentiment"* against his "severe and powerful father" led him to "harmonize with the revolts of humiliated peoples." His life "continued" that of his father, he observed, "in defying it, contradicting it, but finally also perhaps in completing it."[10]

Jacques Berque's mother, Florentine Migon, was the daughter of Spanish immigrants to Algeria. In Berque's own words, his mother was from the milieu of poor colonial settlers, a "small White" (*petit blanc*). This social position did not drive either Berque or his mother into political conservatism, however. Their democratic politics stemmed from the "rancorous aversion toward the colonial bureaucracy" that Berque argued was typical of the "Latin" colonial settler.[11] Berque's social origins had a decisive impact on his emergence as a scholar of Muslim Arab societies and their transformations under the impact of colonialism, as a theorist of colonialism and decolonization, and as a self-described "mutineer at the heart of the colonial system."[12]

Berque earned a *licence* and a *Diplôme d'études supérieures* in humanities at the University of Algiers, where he was particularly influenced by the Durkheimian Hellenist Louis Gernet.[13] Berque moved to Paris in November 1930 to work toward the *agrégation* in Letters. According to his memoirs, Berque felt "exiled" in the metropole. He got to know only a few other Algerian students, both "Muslims and neo-Latins," who lived together at the *Cité internationale universitaire de Paris*, the housing complex for foreign students in the South of Paris. At best, Berque recalled, he felt like an "exotic being" (*un exote*) and, at worst, like the "son of no one, a neo-Latin immigrant." Berque described his initial stay in Paris as the "failure of my youth."[14]

Berque abandoned his plans to pass the *agrégation* a few weeks before the exam and returned from Paris to Algeria in the spring of 1932.[15] For two months he served under the administrator of the Arab Bureau in the Hodna region, making rounds on horseback and "perfecting his Arabic (Maghrebi and classical)."[16] Berque then spent a year of obligatory French military service in Morocco. In 1934, his father helped him obtain a post as a *contrôleur civil* of indigenous courts in Morocco.[17] This was the beginning of a career in colonial administration that lasted more than 20 years. Berque was first posted to El Borouj, near Casablanca, to observe the legal proceedings of the Beni Meskine tribe. In late 1935, he was transferred to the town of Had Kourt in the Gharb, in the plains of northwestern Morocco. Berque's scholarly career began at the same time, although his job did not require him to conduct research. In 1936, Berque published a study of pastoral contracts in the Hodna region.[18] As Alain Mahé points out, the article revealed how much Berque had been influenced by the Durkheimian school—first and foremost by Mauss, but also by Davy, Gernet, and Halbwachs. Berque immersed himself in Durkheimian discussions of legal sociology, rites and contracts, and collective memory.[19]

In 1936, the colonial administrator-cum-sociologist published his first book, a short study of rural contracts among the Beni Meskine.[20] Berque's book was read and annotated by Mauss.[21] Berque did not pay much attention here to the effects of colonialism, although he noted that the Beni Meskine had been less "sociologically decomposed" than the social structures of the Gharb, which had been thoroughly "shaped by French law."[22] By organizing this initial comparison, Berque pointed to one of the central topics and strengths of his future research: comparatively studying responses by the colonized to capitalism and colonization.

Berque's Historical Sociology of Moroccan Society

The first breakthrough in Berque's scientific career occurred in 1937, when he published the lead article in *Annales* on the origins and transformations of the seigneurial system of land distribution in Morocco. Marc Bloch wrote an introduction to Berque's article.[23] Berque's second book, published the next year, was *Études d'histoire rurale maghrébine* (*Studies in Rural Maghrebi History*). In this book, Berque connected the *seigneurie* system to broader changes in Moroccan social structure.[24] *Études d'histoire rurale maghrébine* illustrates the mix of history, sociology, and social theory that typified much of Berque's work. It is based on deep historical and ethnographic knowledge, participant observation, familiarity with languages and dialects, and hitherto untapped indigenous archival sources. *Études* is also one of the first systematic empirical studies of the social and cultural transformations wrought by modern colonialism. The book is structured around a contrast between the society of the Gharb in 1900 and 1937. This design is meant to illuminate the "evolution of a rural Maghrebi society in contact with European economy" and the "struggle of ideas" (*lutte d'idées*) accompanying socioeconomic change.[25] Berque was especially interested in the emergence of new forms of property, law, and employment, and the genesis of atomized, individualized forms of subjectivity among the peasantry.

Berque also compared Moroccan forms of feudalism with European ones, in a move that appealed to Bloch, who wrote extensively on the comparative method and feudal history.[26] In North Africa, Berque found, there was a phenomenon dating to Roman days of peasants giving part of their harvest to a *Caïd*.[27] The Moroccan master, like his European analogues, offered "protection to the serfs" in return, although customary rights were rarely expressed openly here, and were "perhaps not even conscious." In contrast to western feudalism, the Moroccan lord lived in the city. The Moroccan seigneur was also sometimes a Marabout, exerting magico-religious influence over the peasants.[28] In this society, the individual was "emotionally submerged" into the collective, Berque argued. The only way to become an individual was through sainthood or theft, or by obtaining a great deal of land.[29] In 1900, collectivism was still "singularly strong," although the rural milieu was already situated "halfway between archaism and invading modernity."[30]

Berque went on to describe the effects of capitalism and colonialism. The "good old days" of "Qur'anic equilibrium" had been followed by the "iron age" of the French administration," which was "stamped onto the country" (*plaquée sur le pays*).[31] The colonizer arrived with his surveyors, who laid down boundary stones and borders, his "administrator," imbued with an "occidental concept of property," and "his threshing machines, his tractor."[32] There were now "fewer collectives" in the countryside and more great domains than in 1900.[33] The result was a "clash of cultures" (in English in the text) and wholesale "societal uprooting" (*déracinement*). French colonialism was producing a more individualized species of "new men" (*hommes nouveaux*) and an overall "swarming of individuals" (*pullulement d'individus*).[34] The system of feudal ties had been mortally wounded by the "French occupation," and the Gharb had become a "degraded milieu."[35] Although "no new order can emerge without destruction of the old," Berque warned against also "replacing the dead."[36] Foreshadowing the postwar emphasis on colonialism as crisis, Berque concluded that French colonization had engendered a total "crisis of the moral person."[37] Berque was the first European to paint such a systematic and damning portrait of colonialism's effects, writing as a sociologist and historian, and also as a colonial administrator.

Berque's Historical Sociology of Colonial Urbanism

In January 1937, Berque was assigned to the municipal administration of Fez, one of the most distinctively Islamic North African cities. His official assignment was to build bridges between the French administration and Moroccan urban elites and to organize the city's artisanal trades. This posting allowed Berque to become familiar with a completely different dimension of North African society and to write the first of his important series of publications on urban and spatial questions. This was his article in *Annales* on the

Qarawiyîn Mosque, known as the oldest university in the world. Qarawiyîn was an emerging center of the Moroccan nationalist movement at the time.[38] Once again, Berque's study was structured around a contrast between the before and after of the French incursion. He carefully reconstructed the origins and development of Qarawiyîn, and then examined the introduction of modern organizational forms and administrative practices under the protectorate. Berque called attention to the creation of a "humanities" section alongside "religious sciences," a move that "sanction[ed] the division between the sacred and the profane" that was central to French culture but anathema to Islam. As discussed in chapter 6, customary law was codified, relativized, and often replaced in colonial contexts. According to Berque, the new "master of arts" program at Qarawiyîn contributed to the marginalization of the ancient Moroccan juridical culture and its theologians and jurists.[39] Berque was the first non-Muslim to be invited to lecture at Qarawiyîn.[40]

Berque distinguished among three different forms of urbanization in the Maghreb. One was the traditional North African city, the *medina*. Here, the city was cut off from the countryside. It was defined by "ritual equipment" and "ritual prayer," materialized in an "architectural complex" of mosques, etc., and bolstered by a solid legal order.[41] This was an "urbanism of signs" in which historical memory was written in the language of the built environment. The version of capitalism at home in the medina was inextricably linked to the names of particular families.[42] The second form of North African urbanism was the *villeneuve*—the "new city" or colonial city. This was a *quantitative* form of urbanism.[43] Like the medina and unlike metropolitan cities, the colonial *villeneuve* was sharply delineated from its surrounding exterior. The new city was either superimposed on the old city, dismembering and replacing it, or located outside the ramparts of the medina, an entirely separate space, as in the projects initiated by Resident-General Lyautey.[44] In the present, Berque wrote, the "struggle" between *medina* and *villeneuve* was coming under pressure from a third urban-spatial phenomenon, the *bidonville* or shantytown. Located on the peripheries of cities, shantytowns represented a force of "wild urbanism" that exerted an "often decisive" counterpressure against the established urban order. They deviated not only from the modern city but also from the medina, as they were no longer organized around "ritual prayer materialized in an architectural complex and an economic system."[45] Berque's observations were confirmed in studies of colonial shantytowns across Africa.

From Colonial Reformer to Mutineer Inside the Colonial Administration (1939–1953)

Berque was mobilized for the French war effort in September 1939. He briefly entered the war cabinet of Charles Noguès, Resident General of Morocco at the time and Commander in Chief of the French theater of operations in

FIGURE 12.1. Jacques Berque in Had Kourt ca. 1940.
From Jacques Berque, *Mémoires des deux rives*
(Paris: Seuil, 1989).

North Africa. After the armistice, Berque returned to Had Kourt (figure 12.1). In 1943, he carried out various functions for the Protectorate's Political Section and Office of Native Affairs, and in 1944, he was invited to attend the Brazzaville Conference. Berque's politics moved steadily leftward during the war. He joined the Communist-oriented *Confédération générale du travail* and attempted to unionize colonial administrators. He began to argue for a socialist Morocco. The idea of a socialist approach to colonialism was not an absurdity at the time. The left-wing French parties still favored reforming rather than abandoning the empire, and some, including Berque, envisioned partially Soviet-style approaches, as we will see in a moment.

Berque also immersed himself in studies of Muslim jurisprudence between 1940 and 1944. He published translations and analyses of the eighth-century Islamic legal scholar and martyr Zayd ibn 'Alī' and the twentieth-century Moroccan Islamic jurist Al-Mahdi al-Wazzani. He wrote a short book on "legal methods in the Maghreb."[46] Berque's *Essai sur la méthode juridique maghrébine* (1944) began by establishing the existence of a traditional Muslim jurisprudence that was bound to universalism and transhistorical continuity.[47] He examined the ways in which the French Protectorate was codifying and "modernizing" these approaches.[48] During the past century, Berque wrote, North Africa had "experienced the sorts of evolutions that sociologists examined under the heading 'problems of contact.'" New "mores were being born under the influence of French habits and attitudes, along with a French lifestyle that has in some instances completely enveloped local institutions."[49] In certain sites, a form of "neo-Maghrebi Muslim law" had been created by using "reorganized institutions or entirely new ones." France had "jealously maintained the local culture even while trying to help it evolve along its own spontaneous lines."[50] Berque still believed at the time that the French legal approach consisted "first in a loving exploration of the richness of local law." The next step was to regularize local law and to introduce new elements understood as requirements for a developed economy. Finally, the French engaged in educational efforts that involved professionalizing the role of the *cadi* and Moroccan judges. In the book's conclusion, Berque conjured up an image of "the implantation of the French in the country through ideas, blood, and land," combined with the "simultaneous blossoming of the autochthone."[51] At this point, Berque had not yet given up on reforming colonialism.

In 1944, Berque briefly embarked on a quixotic campaign to "reconcile indigenous emancipation with the French presence."[52] In 1945, Berque was put in charge of a *Bureau d'études*, a policy-oriented research office, in Rabat. Together with an agricultural engineer, Berque developed a plan for a network of modernized agricultural collectives, labeled *Secteurs de modernisation du paysannat* (Sectors of the Modernization of the Peasantry), or SMPs. Berque's plan was inspired by Fourier's cooperative communities, the *phalansteries*, and by the Tennessee Valley Authority, but his most important inspiration was the Soviet *Kolkhoz* or collective farm, which he hoped to combine with the traditional North African *djema'a*, the assembly of village notables and elders.[53] The project's centerpiece was technological modernization. Berque described the goal as "putting the *djema'a* on a tractor" (figure 12.2).[54] This was also a "synthetic" or "integral" approach, in which technical development would be combined with social and cultural reform. The SMPs also included "compulsory education, preventative health care, social assistance, civil status, workers insurance, etc."[55] The leading figures in the SMP world, Berque wrote, were a "trio" comprised of "teacher, nurse, and social worker."[56] It is noteworthy that he did not include technician or agriculturalist, much less administrator or soldier, in this "trio."

The political conjuncture at the end of the war in France and the protectorate was favorable to such projects, as we saw in Chapter Four. The French Resident in Morocco between 1943 and 1946, Gaston Puaux, set in motion plans for "progressive structural reforms," including a Franco-Muslim Superior Council of the Peasantry. The minister plenipotentiary to the French

FIGURE 12.2. "The representatives of the *djema'a* observe with interest the yield produced by a tractor and its multi-disc plow." *Source:* Jacques Berque and Julien Couleau, "Vers la modernisation du fellah marocain," *Bulletin économique et social du Maroc* 7, no. 26 (1945): 18–24, 22.

Residency in Morocco, Léon Marchal, defended these policies as responding to the "needs of people, not profits."[57] French officials expressed a desire to see "*welfare* descend into the cottage of the *fellah*."[58] Berque also convinced the Moroccan Sultan and Grand Vizier to approve the plan. The result was that by the end of 1946, twenty SMPs had been created. Berque presided over the SMPs' Executive Council.[59]

The *Secteurs de modernisation du paysannat* were remarkable in several respects. First, the project was located at the progressive extreme among all colonial-era development projects in terms of its indifference to questions of profitability, rejection of large-scale private agriculture, and guiding ethos of "peasants working for the common good under the benevolent leadership of an agricultural expert" combined with an elected council. The plan's overriding aim was to reverse the ongoing dispossession of Moroccan land by Arab landowners and French settlers and capitalists. Berque believed that agricultural conditions in Morocco were amenable to collectivization due to the central role of irrigation in a desert landscape.[60] The *Secteurs* were also unusual in being the brainchild of a historical sociologist imbued with the ideas of Comte, Durkheim, and Marx. Berque's plans may seem superficially similar to the progressivist demiurgism and romantic social engineering that had already proven disastrous in the USSR, or to the gigantic colonial infrastructural projects in which entire populations were uprooted and resettled (chapter 10). By the time he created the SMPs, however, Berque had already criticized an earlier project in La Tadl among the Beni Amir for its "authoritarian and statist," top-down approach. Non-elite Moroccans did not resist the SMP collectivization plan, at least during the short life span of the program.

The SMP program demonstrated that colonial sociologists could shape official policy under certain conditions. Yet Berque had much less power within the colonial field of power than the combined might of the protectorate's officials, French investors and settlers, Moroccan landowners (who opposed the emergence of an independent small peasantry), and "conservative forces in France who were trying very hard to patiently regain the terrain lost in the immediate aftermath of the Liberation."[61] These groups launched a "furious campaign against the modernization of the peasantry." Berque resigned from the Executive Council board. The experiment was scaled back and given the narrower focus of making the collective farms profitable.[62]

At the end of 1946, Berque wrote a memo titled "For a new French political method in Morocco" that expressed his loss of confidence in the possibility of reforming the colony.[63] Here, he assailed the administration's "authoritarianism" and the "impasse of assimilationist policies," according to which "Muslims could only have freedom in identifying with us." The memo ended with this startling claim: genuine order could only exist in Morocco if the French left. In Berque's words, *"le vrai ordre ici serait que nous n'y fussions pas"* ("true order would only exist here if we were not present").[64] This left little doubt about the direction of Berque's politics. By 1956, he publicly supported independence for Algeria and all other colonies, and began analyzing the process of decolonization.

Berque's 1946 memo also contained his first explicit critique of heteronomous science. He argued that government elites typically tried to dictate researchers' agendas, promoting a top-down approach to ethnography. According to Berque, political rule could become *genuinely* scientific only if it was guided by the autonomous findings of researchers and by the voices of the colonized, via studies operating "from the bottom to the top," that is, beginning from questions the colonized ask about themselves and their self-interpretations.[65] This is the first articulation of the idea that the sociology of colonized societies needs to be written, or co-authored, by the colonized. The very implausibility of this proposal for an autonomous, reflexive social science written by members of the (post)colonized as the basis of (post)colonial rule underscores the limits on the so-called *scientization of colonialism* (*Verwissenschaftlichung des Kolonialen*), even in the late colonial era.[66]

The memo marked another crucial caesura in Berque's career. The Residency responded to Berque's criticism by dispatching him to a remote and "archaic canton in the High Atlas," *Imintanoute*, among the Berber Seksawa people, giving him "explicit instructions never to leave."[67] Located far from government supervision, more than 400 kilometers from the colonial capital,

Berque was able to carry out the extended fieldwork that became the basis of his primary doctoral thesis and that catapulted him into a metropolitan scientific career. The 1946 memo also signaled that Berque had broken free of the influence of his father, who incarnated for him the idea that colonial rule could be reformed and made humane on the basis of expert research. Berque began drafting his memo soon after his father's death in September 1946. As Jacques Frémaux writes, Berque's "loyalty" to his father "emancipated itself" at this point from the narrative of "reproduction." The idea of a "synthesis between respect for the natives and maintenance of French sovereignty" suddenly appeared "completely anachronistic" to Berque.[68]

Berque's "Structures sociales du Haut-Atlas"

Berque's doctoral thesis, *"Structures sociales du Haut-Atlas"* (Social Structures of the High Atlas), was published in 1955.[69] On the surface, this study seeks to show that Seksawa social structures, legal forms, and religious beliefs and practices are systematically related to their natural environment. Berque argues that the orchestration of land and irrigation only appeared to be "piecemeal," but was in fact highly organized.[70] He demonstrates that territorial divisions correspond "to a system of names and to a scansion of the calendar of irrigation."[71] The explanation for "this society's peculiarity," including its appearance of being completely unchanging, should not be sought in any "supposed state of nature, or a conserved archaism," but rather in "a historical evolution that is partly organized and conscious."[72] According to Berque, the presentation of an endless repetition of ancient traditions was the product of intense collective effort. He rejected the view that any "mass of ancient traits is frozen in a system of survivals." A number of elements that seemed to have persisted despite conquest and the passage of time, such as the systems of irrigation, property, and law, were actually active *reconstructions*.[73] "Everything seems as if this society were seeking to reestablish its equilibrium and autonomy via internal compensations."[74] Seksawa society revealed not so much "archaism" as an intense "desire for archaism."[75] According to Moroccan sociologist Paul Pascon, Berque's thesis showed "through subtle touches" how, in fact, a number of "profound changes were emerging" like a "smoldering fire beneath the ashes."[76] Ethnologists had previously studied cultures like the Seksawa as if they existed "outside of time," Berque wrote, but researchers now realized they should situate customs in historical evolution.[77] This approach was as remote from conventional accounts of the functional reproduction of social structures as it was from anthropological primitivism. In an article published in 1953, Berque explicitly rejected the "search for the primitive," arguing it had led researchers astray.[78]

Berque developed his argument about the intensive sociocultural labor required to produce the façade of continuity in a celebrated critique of the notion of the Moroccan tribe. More precisely, Berque rejected the definition of a tribe as "a group descended from a common father." Berque repudiated the "fake histories of tribes" that were written by the protectorate's officer-sociologists and embraced by some tribal leaders. He called his alternative account an *onomastic* theory, i.e., relating to the history and origins of names. According to Berque, "the plurality of sometimes remote origins invoked by a given group does not correspond to a historical given in every case, but may be little more than an onomastic differentiation."[79] Berque understood the tribal name as an "identitary banner" that allowed a group to "position itself in a larger society" and to persist despite "perpetual recomposition."[80] Tribes were not so much pure fictions as they were dynamic cultural performances that created social structures. There was a stark difference between Berque's account of the primacy of performance and the Durkheimian vision of social structures producing culture. Berque's description of the colonized as continuously creating their own traditions also contrasts with more recent studies of the invention of tradition.

Berque also explored the ways French colonialism and western modernity were affecting even this remote region, appearances to the contrary. Berque often used the term *precolonial* in preference to *traditional*, in order to call attention to the central importance of this historical transition and to problematize the idea of unchanging tradition.[81] Berque argued against "contemporary sociologists" who "describe acculturation ... via contact of one society with another, expansive or superior," where the "vanquished culture instinctively simulates even the most intimate realities and seeks out its arguments" from the foreign "model." The reaction by Moroccan societies to Oriental and European conquerors, Berque countered, "reveals many examples" in which "problems of reinterpretation, opposition, or transposition have superseded all others." The result was not an acculturated society but a "mixed, adulterated" one. The Maghreb "draws from this ... a strong personality."

What Berque meant by a "strong personality" was revealed in his analyses of specific social regulations and legal and religious texts. Berque argued that the sheer "volume" of these societies' "social apparatus" contrasted sharply with their material poverty.[82] The indigenous legal system, for example, was a "rich bastard ensemble," characterized by "complexity, multiplicity, and the displacement of its elements."[83] This approach was closer to the nuanced analyses of Afro-Brazilian culture by Bastide than to the acculturation theorists and cultural diffusionists who posited a modular, unidirectional process of cultural encompassment.

Berque's work was distinguished by methodological pluralism and by an extreme version of the indifference to disciplinary identity that we saw in Aron's case and will also encounter in the discussion of Balandier and Bourdieu. Berque relied on fieldwork and direct observation, including "participant observation," and he was especially interested in his subjects' *self*-interpretations.[84] Berque's position as *contrôleur civil* required him to supervise and comment on local legal decision-making, and he scrutinized indigenous court cases and legal texts written in Arabic.[85] His doctoral research was based on "long chats along the paths, at legal disputes, festivals, funeral vigils," as well as "direct investigation, *tournées*"—official tours to check on the people under his jurisdiction—"and research into traditions and in local archives."[86] Berque rejected "American techniques" of social research based on "quantitative excess" and "naïve numeric aspects," noting that "we Europeans, and especially French sociologists, remain skeptical about this approach."[87] Qualitative fieldwork and individualizing observation were indispensable to the social sciences, although quantitative data could sometimes be a useful supplement.[88] Given the lack of good data on the Arab and Muslim world, Berque recommended reading their novelists and poets and interpreting Islamic aesthetics.[89]

One other factor may explain why Berque omitted a more explicit discussion of the effects of colonialism from his doctoral thesis. He was composing a text that was meant to conform to existing scholarly standards, and he had been shaken by his earlier academic failure in Paris. The scholarly standards in question included the approaches he was revising or rejecting, namely, classical Orientalism, "Muslim sociology," acculturation theory, and conventional ethnology. As a complete outsider to academia at this point, Berque may have suppressed overt criticism of these approaches in order to give the superficial impression that he was indeed describing a timeless culture, untouched by the outside world. His attempt to trace structural resonances or homologies between nature and culture, and his treatment of culture as a system of "signs," aligned his book broadly with Lévi-Straussian structuralism.

In fact, Berque's thesis opened the door overnight to his appointment to the Sixth Section of the *École pratique des hautes études* in 1955, quickly followed by a chair at the *Collège de France*. Like Bourdieu, but with a much longer—20-year—delay, Berque had moved from the periphery of the periphery to the center of the French academic world.

The End of Berque's Colonial Service

Berque resigned from colonial service in 1953. The final tipping point was his strong disagreement with the French Residency's decision to exile the Moroccan Sultan, Mohammed V, and replace him with a puppet monarch. Berque took up a research position with the United Nations Educational, Scientific and Cultural Organization (UNESCO), and spent two years in Egypt and Lebanon.[90] This was an important interlude for his future work, in several respects. It provided him with an opportunity to extend his analysis beyond Morocco and Algeria to the whole of North Africa and the Arab world. In *Le Maghreb entre deux guerres* (1962) and *L'Egypte, impérialisme et révolution*

(1967), Berque surveyed the devastation caused by Western imperialism and the beginnings of anticolonial uprisings. In *Les Arabes* (1959), Berque presented a sweeping overview of postcolonial Arab politics.[91] He learned new dialects of Arabic and returned to his studies of non-western urbanism in a short book on an Egyptian village.[92] Berque also began to contribute more directly to the decolonizing movement. In 1956, he created a University Committee for the Solution of the Algerian Problem (*Comité universitaire pour la solution du problème algérien*), which called for Algerian independence. He also intensified his interaction with intellectuals from the colonized countries.[93]

Berque's first sustained discussion of decolonization appeared in a series of articles published in 1956. At that point, he supported the creation of an autonomous Algerian Republic, although he hoped that the French settler population could remain. Berque initially proposed that France assume a mandatory role to lead Algeria toward its "national vocation" of independence, and suggested that Morocco and Tunisia, which were already independent, should be involved in exercizing this mandate. This governing structure could be used to educate Algerians, complete a more thorough infrastructural upgrading of the country, and lay the groundwork for "cohabitation" between the French and Algerian communities. This would not be a weak "compromise," he argued, "but a revolutionary passage from one order to another." There was "primitivism" emerging on both the French and Algerian sides, Berque wrote, with the colonizer turning into the very "terrorist" he hates, and a reawakening of residual "archaic violence" among the colonized.[94] In order to find a solution, Europeans would have to "give up their colonial traits," and Muslims would have to abandon their *ressentiment*.[95] This was written five years before Fanon's paean to violence as "absolute praxis."[96]

Two years later, in an interview in *Le Monde*, Berque returned to the idea of a "unity of Europeans and Muslims in a Maghrebi unity." This outcome would represent a "brilliant reconversion of our colonial era." Berque was beginning to acknowledge, however, that French settlers in Algeria were unlikely to support such a reconciliation. He painfully severed his ties with his Algerian relatives after recognizing that they had "detached themselves from the metropole which they both idealize and condemn."[97]

From Colonialism to "the Decolonial Situation"

As the colonial era drew to a chaotic end, Berque had already been analyzing the effects of colonial rule on North Africa for more than two decades. During the second half of the 1950s, Berque began to synthesize his thinking about colonialism, imperialism, decolonization, neocolonialism, and postcolonialism. In his 1960 book *Les Arabes* (*The Arabs*), he broached the theme of anticolonial revolt and the general transition from the "domination effect" to "de-domination."[98] This book began with the thesis that colonialism was the "object and motive force of the Arab Revolt."[99] According to Berque, colonialism "played in the Arab world, and indeed throughout the Eastern world, the part played among ourselves by original sin!"[100] The result was an enduring mixture of *resentment* and *attraction* directed toward the west. Berque traced "two great conflicting themes in the Arab world" across various realms: "the symbol against the machine" and "the sense of the cosmic" or sacred against "the sense of history."[101] He traced a succession of different "types of resistance," "successive reactions to the installation of foreign powers." The earliest movements were identified "almost everywhere with religious and social conservatism" in the guise of "holy war" or "tribal risings." More recent movements led by "the intelligentsia" were marked by the "attraction, as well as the horror, it feels for the alien, the 'Other.'"[102] Berque noted that Arab writers between the wars posed the problem in terms of "a distinction between the East, as the realm of the spirit, and the West, as the realm of matter and imperious causality."[103] Berque framed the difference differently: Arab behavior was more influenced than "our own" by "emotion and an ethical sense." The "material elements of economic growth must be repudiated if they are incompatible with justice."[104] In Arab societies, the "symbol has tended to beget the fact rather than being supported by it"; the "superstructure" is more powerful than "the base."[105]

Berque began here to define his political concepts more deliberately. *Imperialism* as used by Berque refers to the expansion of a small group of nations, the West, undergirded by their technical superiority. *Colonialism* is defined by the presence of both economic domination and foreign seizure of power (*mainmise étrangère*).[106] Berque emphasizes the racializing practices that Partha Chatterjee later referred to as the colonial "rule of difference."[107] Epithets were widely used to label the colonized. Those who tried to remain separate were treated as archaic or backwards. The "Moslems, though actually in the majority" in the colonies, "ranked as a minority group in legal procedure."[108] Colonialism, Berque wrote, represented *"the structural nighttime of the planet"* (*la nuit structurale de la planète*).[109] Colonialism devalues and "decultures" all aspects of local life.[110] It "devastates and remakes everything under the mask of progress."[111]

Nonetheless, Berque saw colonialism as both destructive and creative, insofar as the practices and morals that it introduced became more and more incompatible with its ongoing reproduction, leading the colonized to emancipate themselves.[112] Berque was the first writer to use the neologism *"decolonial"* as an adjective, speaking of "the *decolonial* situation," along with "the man of decolonization."[113]

Berque's most sustained analysis of decolonization is *Dépossession du monde*, published in 1964. Berque described this book as a "sociology of decolonization."[114] It is the first sustained theoretical analysis of decolonization per se. The first thing to notice about *Dépossession du monde* is its evocative title. *Dépossession* has a dual meaning here. First, colonialism involved a massive *dispossession (dépossession)* of land and an uprooting (*déracinement*) of people; in an extended sense, colonialism brought a dispossession of culture, politics, and identity. Decolonization would thus have to involve a *repossession* (*réposession*) of lands seized by the foreigner and a "re-rooting" (*réenracinement*) in the land. Second, colonization induced a kind of *possession* in the religious sense, as Fanon and many others also argued. In the eyes of its victims, the western conqueror was "the colonial devil." The Arabs framed their struggle as a "triumph over absolute evil." Decolonization therefore required rites of *de-possession*, or exorcism, to rid the colony of evil spirits. Berque's notion of *dépossession* thus encompasses the material, symbolic, psychic, and spiritual dimensions of decolonization. Berque preferred the term *dépossession* to decolonization, because the latter suggested that it was possible to unmake the mixed conditions created by colonization.

Berque's approach to the history of decolonization is one that historians would call "ex-centric," insofar as it argued that the "initiative of the colonized" had become an increasingly "important factor" over time.[115] At the present moment, he wrote in *Dépossession du monde*, colonialism was being destroyed by a "Golem"—by "*beings* that it had created or awakened."[116] The "deepening of the colonial situation" over time had rendered Arabs' reality thoroughly "dialectical," meaning that their identities were defined by and against the Other. This argument was familiar from Hegel's phenomenology of the dialectical relationship between master and bondsman, Sartre's *Anti-Semite and Jew* (1946), and Fanon's *Black Skin, White Masks* (1952). However, Berque's dialectic differed in two respects. For Hegel, the bondsman does not *reject* being recognized and defined through mutual recognition by the Other, but Berque argues that the Arab refuses to be defined by the Other.[117] He also suggested that the Hegelian model was less applicable to Arabs since Islam forbids the enslavement of Muslims.[118]

Berque argued further that the "role that the classics [Marxism] arrogated to the proletariat" had been "largely taken over by today's former colonial subjects."[119] During the nineteenth century, the working-class movement provided Marx with the materials to "renew the logic" of Hegel's philosophy. The "uprising of the colonial world" today offered philosophy "something analogous," but with a difference.[120] In contrast to Marx's historical context, the scale of the anticolonial movement had become more immediately "planetary" because every colony or postcolony was linked to the entire world.[121] Empire's assault on the colonized was more encompassing and radical than the changes capitalism had imposed on European peasants and workers.[122] Imperialism in the colonies "differs from capitalism at home, because it blocks potentialities rather than mobilizing" them. It is a "short-term profiteer, grabbing windfalls . . . exploiting the superficial and the immediate." At the same time, the European "dominator" blankets the colonized with its "values."[123] Colonialism demolishes the relationship between the colonized and their "nature." The colonized are "ethnically humiliated"; they "suffer metaphysically." Their "religion becomes superstition"; their "law becomes custom"; their "art becomes folklore."[124] Even the term "native" becomes "extremely pejorative." The European working class, by contrast, may be alienated and deracinated, but it did not become so thoroughly "de-natured" as the victims of colonization.[125]

There was a vast political and scholarly debate at the time around identifying the vanguard of the decolonizing movement. Did these movements emerge from groups produced by colonization, such as the indigenous proletariat, intelligentsia, or comprador bourgeoisie, or were they rooted in populations that were relatively untouched by "exterior forces"?[126] Berque pointed to various aspects of indigenous life in "the interior Maghreb" that had partially escaped the reach of western colonization. For Berque, the word *interior* included not just geographic but social and psychic coordinates as well.[127] Various sites had remained "heterogeneous to industrial civilization." They were "linked to *landscapes of excess* marked by their *singularity* and wild *vitality*: the desert, the bush, the virgin forest."[128] The "[d]omains that had been spared, neglected, abandoned" became sites and symbols of resistance.[129] This was closer to Fanon and, later, Deleuze and Guattari, than to Marxists or Bourdieu.

Berque underscored the existence of "plural logics of development," foreshadowing more recent theories of alternative modernities.[130] Postcolonial societies were advancing toward singular new arrangements rather than converging upon a universal model or returning to precolonial traditions. Of course, it was also true that liberation movements often tried to repossess land and other resources and to redeploy European ideologies, daring colonizers to live up to their own ideals. Yet even where decolonizing movements took the form of a dialectical sublation of the inherited system, they produced entirely unforeseen results in which "all of the elements of the program" were rearranged "in their relations to one another."[131] Egypt's nationalization of the Suez Canal, for example, was "the most radical act in thousands of years," representing the "reappropriation by Oriental man of his own geography."[132] The problem for any decolonized people was to cultivate the specific local contents of their culture and identity while simultaneously positioning themselves within global modernity.[133] Decolonization's overarching accomplishment was to impose a recognition of the "diversity of the world, its pluralism, and the basic dignity of all cultures and ethnicities."[134]

Berque admired Fanon, whom he met in Tunis and eulogized after his death in *Présence africaine*.[135] He praised Fanon for thematizing the *unconscious* aspects of colonized subjectivity, which is surely Fanon's greatest accomplishment.[136] Berque embraced Fanon's idea of colonialism as inducing rites of *possession* and his concept of *depersonalization*. Fanon had used the notion of depersonalization in a technical, psychiatric sense in his medical thesis before extending it to the general condition of the colonized "Arab" as living "in a state of absolute depersonalization."[137] Berque wrote that "Fanon understood in a particularly tragic manner" that the worst thing about colonialism was "the *depersonalization* of the individual, groups, classes, and cultures."[138] Berque preferred to speak of depersonalization rather than alienation, which he associated with Hegelian Marxism and therefore with a more limited, European geohistorical context.

Berque's Theoretical, Epistemological, and Methodological Position in the French and International Context

One of Berque's most famous quotations is "an underdeveloped country is an under-analyzed country."[139] This should not be understood simply as a call for more research on the non-west. It also contains a critique of Orientalism and a program of reflexivity. Colonized and non-western societies need to be analyzed using indigenous sources and paying attention to their self-interpretations. They should not be approached in terms of their approximation to supposedly universal western models, which leads inevitably to a verdict of "underdevelopment."[140] In other words, these societies are called underdeveloped because they are understood in western, positivist terms. Berque's statement is also sometimes understood as suggesting that the administration of non-western societies needs to rely on social science, i.e., "analysis." Yet Berque's understanding of "analysis" differed from the standard forms of scientific sociology "in the West."[141]

Berque intervened in a number of scientific discussions and touched on epistemological and methodological questions.[142] As noted above, he rejected the primitivism of leading French specialists in Morocco and the Islamic world, as well as the functionalism of Durkheimian sociology. Rather than focusing on traditional lifeworlds and their simple reproduction, Berque developed a dynamic, historical approach. He rejected traditional Orientalism's focus on the archaic, sacred, and exotic, rather than contemporary history. In his earliest publications, Berque criticized Edmond Doutté for exaggerating the omnipotence of magic in Moroccan culture and seeing only a "land of spirits linked to ruins or grottos," while ignoring the creation of magical rites of possession by colonialism.[143] Berque admired Louis Massignon, calling him "the admirable Sheikh," yet Berque described himself as someone who related to "Islam not as religious thinker but as a man of the social sciences." Massignon refused to recognize the desacralization of much of Arab life and "emphasized effervescent and paradoxical experiences."[144]

Another target was Robert Montagne, the leading French expert on Morocco and holder of the *Collège de France* chair to which Berque was elected in 1956.

Montagne depicted the societies of the High Atlas as being continuously reproduced through an "alternation between oppressive power and equilibrated anarchy."[145] The politics of the High Atlas were structured by the dualism of Berber clans, the *leffs*.[146] Berque countered that the *leff* system had declined in importance and was "now little more than a classification system."[147] Where Montagne distinguished among four social states in Arab countries—archaic, medieval, premodern, and modern—Berque argued that all four conditions coexisted in Arab societies and even "within each individual."[148] He hinted that Montagne was unable to understand "the interpretation this society gives of itself" because he did not study indigenous law.[149] Berque was thus subtly critical of Doutté, Massignon, and Montagne, providing a critique of Orientalism that resonates with the later criticisms of Anouar Abdel-Malek and Edward Said.

Another critical strand of Berque's thought involves his relationship to Marxism. Berque's publications devoted a great deal of space to questions of agriculture and irrigation, leading some to understand him as a crypto-Marxist. Yet while Berque was certainly more sympathetic to Marxism than were Aron or Bourdieu, he always insisted on the inadequacy of a one-sidedly materialist or economistic Marxism for understanding Morocco, Arabs, Islam, colonialism, and decolonization. He quipped that he had become "such a specialist in the Third World that it was impossible to be a Marxist in the western style." The implication was that Marxism was a local theory of capitalist and western lands, and that when it took a universalizing form it could only mislead.[150] Berque analyzed the colonized by comparing them to, and differentiating them from, the (western) proletariat. He argued that Marxism was unable to acknowledge that "culture is now the motor of collective identities."[151] Asked about his relationship to Marxism, Berque responded with a question: "Is there a single economic act from which language, symbolism, psychism, and therefore structures and values, are absent?"[152]

Berque also rejected the social sciences' "general alignment on the American model" and its "caricatural scientism."[153] In this respect, he concurred with most of the prominent French sociologists in this period, including those specialized in colonial societies. Berque's description of the American project he was involved with in Egypt in 1953 illustrates his amusement about this mindless positivism, which was buttressed by US geopolitical supremacy. UNESCO, which was in the sway of "American triumphalism," had created a program for the "basic education" of Egyptians. Sixty interns recruited from various Oriental countries were led by 20 "experts" from the west. The Americans' "ridiculous pedagogy," Berque recalled, included a course in home economics taught by a specialist "newly arrived from Illinois, who taught the bewildered girls of the fellah" to make meringue by whipping egg whites. A scientific and culinary expression of "Pax Americana" was "being imposed in the region" in place of the previous British hegemon.[154] Berque rejected versions of sociology that worked with cookbook recipes, turning the inhabitants of postcolonies into "things" and "inserting them into statistics."[155] The imperial powers had dragged the colonies into "the era of quantity," but this could not be the final word in social science. The *quantification of the social* was itself an historical problem that needed to be studied and explained, but it should not be taken for granted as a scientific starting point.[156]

A Political and Epistemological Mutiny

Berque described himself as having committed "mutiny at the heart of the colonial system."[157] This mutiny was epistemological as well as political. Alongside his rejection of colonialism and American-style scientism, Berque expressed a profound aversion to scientific heteronomy. Indeed, one of the demi-regularities[158] that we can glean from the present study is that scholars who experience intense pressure to align their research with external powers often embrace scientific freedom most emphatically, especially if this desire for autonomy resonates with other elements of their personality.[159] Berque understood heteronomy as particularly threatening to researchers like himself, particularly in colonial settings, where scientific freedom has fewer guarantees. In 1955, he wrote that his own discipline, Orientalism, "is no longer, or can no longer be, the intellectual counterpart to political expansion."[160] The sociology and history of the Islamic world have to become a "fundamental discipline, free of all compromises with journalism, politics, and information-gathering (*le renseignement*)."[161]

Berque was the first sociologist to call for a systematic decolonization of the social sciences. Scientific decolonization required carefully working through the archive of previous scholarly literature rather than simply denouncing or burying it. Berque's approach to scientific self-reflexivity is similar to the program that emerged in the work of Pierre Bourdieu and his colleagues many years later. According to Edward Said, Berque was distinguished by his "methodological self-consciousness." Berque and Maxime Rodinson displayed "a direct sensitivity to the material before them, and then a continual self-examination of their methodology and practice, a constant attempt to keep their work responsive to the material and not to a doctrinal preconception."[162] For Berque, it was crucial to revisit the history of colonial sociology itself, since this was the tradition out of which his own early research had emerged. In contrast to some of the recent calls to "decolonize the social sciences," Berque's writings do not take the form of "summary accusations" against historical figures.[163] He recognized that the writers in colonial contexts differed enormously in terms of the quality of their research. In his inaugural lecture at the *Collège de France* in 1956, Berque argued that

> most of our scholars were upright. The culture that supported them had invented the ideas of critique, objectivity, and history. Yet their research

was also inevitably shaped by the tendencies of its milieu and its historical moment. A question of perspective, of moderation, of the range of options (*Question d'angle de vue, de mesure, d'options*).[164]

Berque's views have been confirmed by subsequent research. Alain Messaoudi, in a comprehensive study of French Arabists through 1930, concludes that "among the scholars involved in the colonial project, the perceptions of the Arabic language and literature are far from all being identical."[165]

However, Berque was unsparing in his criticism of intellectuals who subordinated their thinking to the requisites of colonization. This was partly a practice of rigorous self-criticism. Berque acknowledged that he had behaved at one time like a "Jacobin of the conquering species."[166] Later in life, he rejected the authoritarianism and dirigisme of this earlier "Jacobin" self, and moved into the role of a traveler between "two shores" as he suggested in the title of his memoirs (*Mémoires des deux rives*). Berque now understood that the artist, scholar, hero, and saint were all "apostles of respect," but that each had also "contributed to the penetration of the colony." They "exalt the values of the man they destroy."[167] The French "triumphed" in North Africa using "scientific investigation" to complement "conquest."[168] As colonial penetration deepened, the "native" came to be "understood in his relation to us" and not on his own terms. The colonizer's "*élan*" consisted in "the liquidation of the diverse in the world."[169] The French law faculties operated as an "*arsenal of the liquidation of the heterogeneous*" by "degrading Muslim law to customary law."[170] The Arab Bureaus in Algeria produced hundreds of anecdotes around stereotypes such as the Berber and the Arab, the nomadic and the sedentary, the European and the native. From 1870 on, "the Arab" came to be seen as "romantic, poetic, and nonchalant"; the Kabyle as a "practical and proud peasant"; the Mozabite as a "puritan shopkeeper." The position favoring the Berber became dominant, and the French came to see "all problems as coming from the Orient," i.e., from Arabs.[171] Professionals from "the universities of Paris and Algiers came to love the primitive—just as the English school still does—turning to less explored zones, those reputed to be more 'intact' and 'pure.'"[172] These scientific visions were closely related to government "native policies."

Berque's epistemology was oriented toward contingency and historicization, and he leaned toward methods of symbolic and semi-psychoanalytic interpretation. He defended "a sociological theory of *ensembles*" and a "logic of *assemblage*" over simple statistical causalities or general laws of historical change, which he qualified as "sophism."[173] In an era of "stylistic ruptures," researchers should not hesitate to experiment with radical forms of "mixed methods" combining history, sociology, and poetry.[174] Rather than implementing participant observation, Berque suggested a form of collaborative research. It had become impossible and objectionable to study any aspect of

Arab civilization, he argued, without working with Arabs.[175] Berque took his own advice in his extensive research on law. This work was sociological in tracing the connections between law and social structure, and it was "collaborative" in that it involved Berque apprenticing himself to Islamic teachers and participating in legal hearings presided over by Arab or Berber judges. Berque used the word "*transcolonial*" to describe the emerging era of "reciprocal knowledge."[176]

Berque's Position in the Disciplinary Fields

In 1988, Berque resumed his career, stating that at the outset, "I considered myself a sociologist . . . then a social historian, and now, I am doing Islamology," before asking rhetorically, "isn't it all the same thing?"[177] Berque's earliest and most durable disciplinary identity was as a sociologist. His first field of study at the university was Hellenism, which channeled him toward Durkheimian sociology. In a tribute to Gernet, Berque recalled that he left for his first posting in the colonial service in 1934 with a copy of the eleventh volume of the *Année sociologique* under his arm. Gernet's courses, he wrote, had produced a "decisive shock" in him that allowed him "to break with the particularism in which the sociology of the Maghreb was trapped" and to place it in a comparative and historical perspective.[178] The specialists Berque took the most seriously—those with whom he published, and those whose work he reviewed positively or prefaced—were mainly associated with sociology.[179] UNESCO asked Berque to report on the establishment of social science teaching and research in Tunisia and Lebanon in 1959, and his reports focused on sociology.[180] Berque gained recognition in the leading circles of French sociology. His 1954 doctoral thesis was supervised by the Sorbonne sociology professor Georges Davy, the most loyal of the surviving Durkheimians, and published in the *Centre d'études sociologiques* series of the *Bibliothèque de sociologie contemporaine*. Berque was also close to the group around Gurvitch and Balandier, publishing in their *Cahiers internationaux de sociologie*.[181] In 1959, Berque joined the *Association internationale des sociologues de langue française* (chapter 9), which brought together many of the sociological specialists in colonial and postcolonial societies.[182]

Berque also identified as a historian. His chair at the *Collège de France* was in the "Social History of Contemporary Islam." Berque may have avoided the word "sociology" in renaming his chair due to the association with the older school of "Muslim sociology." The historians of *Annales* saw Berque's work as fitting closely with their project. Berque suggested that history could be "a remedy" for versions of "sociology" that reduce complexity and diversity,[183] writing that "the social history of Marc Bloch and Lucien Febvre is perhaps the most authentic daughter of Durkheim."[184] Berque rejected the atheoretical, event-focused approaches that the *Annales* school called "historicizing history" as "only having indirect relations to *our* disciplines" in the social sciences.[185] Here again, Berque suggests that his core discipline was located in the social sciences.

One of Berque's descriptions of his own work during the 1960s was "historical sociology" (*sociologie historique*) or "historicizing sociology" (*sociologie historisante*).[186] Scholars of the non-west, he argued, need to "scrutinize contemporary realities in light of [the] layer immediately anterior to our own"—that is, to the "epoch immediately prior to European implantation."[187] The "upheavals produced by colonialization," Berque suggested, would then become central, and this is where sociology and history became identical.[188] Historical sociology as Berque defined it involved an equal relationship between the two components, history and sociology, rather than subordinating one to the other.

If Berque was recognized as a sociologist, historian, and historical sociologist during his lifetime, his identity has often been narrowed to Orientalism and ethnology in the intervening period.[189] Berque sometimes called himself an historian-anthropologist after the late 1970s. This was the same historical context in which others made the same transition for reasons explained by Balandier: sociology had become too constraining, presentist, and positivistic (chapter 13). The discipline changed, driving some of the scholars out. Ethnology, however, was a self-description that Berque rarely used. He noted that ethnology was a "troublemaker" that had "humiliated" the colonized and "underdeveloped countries."[190]

Berque was most famously an Arabist or Islamologist. He mastered classical Arabic and North African dialects, became a specialist in Arabic poetry and fiction,[191] and translated and commented on the Qur'an and medieval Islamic texts.[192] He wrote a well-known article on the motif of the "starred polygon" (*polygone étoilé*) in Islamic art. It is important, however, that Berque's analysis of these aesthetic objects was always fully historical and sociological. In his discussion of the "starred polygon," for example, Berque emphasizes its "refusal of closed forms," its "centrifugal élan," and its outward movement in all directions from an internal axis. Berque then contrasts this with western aesthetic forms such as the European city, which he describes as a "concentration, a solidification that could also be called imperialism."[193] This approach is closer to Said's postcolonial epistemology than to conventional Orientalism. Indeed, Said praised Berque for reorienting the study of the Orient toward the "broad field of all the human sciences."[194]

Berque's last major historical book, *Ulémas, fondateurs, insurgés du Maghreb* (*Ulemas, Founders, Insurgents of the Maghreb*), brings together all of these components of his work. It is a study of the political-religious struggles in seventeenth-century Morocco that gave rise to the Alouite ('Alawid) dynasty, which reached its greatest extension and power under Sultan Moulay Ismail in the early eighteenth century.[195] This book is recognizably "Berquian" in comparing the Alouite and French states, both of which "fortified the monarchy, developed the nation-state, strengthened centralism at the expense of urban and regional franchises" in the eighteenth century.[196] Berque focuses on Moulay Ismail's "introduction of a state" separated from the people via a system of 66 fortresses and a "Pretorian army of Blacks."[197] He also emphasizes the "opponents of the sharifs" and "the contestation against the official, the peripheral against the central."[198] This work relies on rarely used Alouite archives alongside reports by European consuls, missionaries, captives, adventurers, and traders.

Decolonial Social Science beyond Borders

Berque's rural North African background and fluency in Arabic seem to have guided him toward imaginary ego identifications with traditional Moroccan scholars of Islamic erudition. Berque was powerfully attracted to figures such as Zayd ibn 'Alī' and the seventeenth-century Moroccan Islamic scholar Al Yousi, who was the subject of Berque's complementary doctoral thesis.[199] Like Al Yousi, who "considered linguistic acumen and taste for eloquence" to be an "essential... aspect of the traditional man of Islamic letters," Berque's writing was characterized by stylistic flourishes and resonant phrases. Al Yousi had been banished to Fez, Marrakesh, and Meknes by the Alawite leader Mulay al-Rashīd, who destroyed the Zāwiyah (religious school) of Dilā'iyyah in Central Morocco, where Al Yousi was teaching between 1653 and 1669. Al Yousi had then been "ordered back" to "the ruins of the Dilā'iyyah Zāwiyah" in 1684, where he wrote "two of his most important works."[200] This story resonated with Berque, who had been posted to Fez and "banished" to Imintanoute.

There is a stunning discrepancy between the importance of Berque's work and contemporary lack of awareness of it in discussions of postcolonial theory and decolonizing social science. Berque hinted that his rural background as a *pied noir* might have tainted the reception of his work. Yet this cannot explain his disappearance globally, given the counterexamples of Albert Camus and Louis Althusser, who were both sons of Algerian settlers and are both still famous.[201] Nor is it a problem of overspecialization, given Berque's more general works.

A more compelling set of reasons for Berque's scientific "obscurity" are located within the scientific field. The first is the dislocation of the Orient between the social sciences and the older philological approaches. Berque's work was too "sociological" for Arabist journals and too "Orientalist" for sociological journals. He believed that his own "humanist" and interdisciplinary style was seen as "outmoded" in a technicized, "positivist" world.[202] He argued that even the non-west was succumbing to numeric scientism "borrowed from abroad," an observation that was true of "Arab sociology written by Arabs" at the time. The "obsession with quantity," Berque ventured, "tends to perpetuate the colonial era."[203] However, it is important to recognize that Aron and Bourdieu, both of whose work was neither scientistic nor technicist, remained prominent. Berque's obscurity therefore probably has more to do with the repression of the colonial era after the 1960s and the redefinition of French sociology as the science of the metropole.

The next chapter will examine Balandier, who is in many ways the Africanist analogue to Berque. Berque and his second wife, Julia Berque, were close to Balandier and his wife, Claire Balandier.[204] Berque and Balandier both taught at the Sixth Section, where Balandier directed African studies and Berque directed studies of North Africa and the Muslim and Arab worlds. Balandier had a decisive impact on African studies at the time, yet in many respects he is as obscure today as Berque. Both Berque and Balandier remained tied to the colonial aura through their identification with southern geographic areas. Aron and Bourdieu escaped this fate of obscurity in part by reorienting their work away from the colonial matrix.

CHAPTER THIRTEEN

Georges Balandier

A DYNAMIC SOCIOLOGY OF COLONIALISM
AND ANTICOLONIALISM

Then came Balandier.

—EMMANUEL TERRAY[1]

Georges Balandier wanted to decolonize sociology in order to produce a sociology of decolonization.

—GABRIEL GOSSELIN[2]

The sociology that I attempted to do à propos of Africa, you have tried to do à propos of Europe. It is good that these things are reciprocal.

—GEORGES BALANDIER[3]

Foundations of a Dynamic Sociology

Georges Balandier was born in 1920 in Ailleville-et-Lyaumont, a village in the Franche-Comté region in eastern France. His father was a socialist railway worker and active supporter of the Popular Front, while his mother came from a conservative Catholic background. His two grandfathers were artisanal laborers, but the "family's imaginary was marked by the image" of the imperial adventures of one of Balandier's paternal great-grandfathers.[4] Balandier's fantasies were sparked not just by his ancestors' exotic adventures but also by the familial memory of his maternal grandfather, who had achieved top marks in the cantonal examination for the *certificate d'études*—the last year of elementary school—but had died young. Balandier later wrote that in his career he was trying to continue his maternal grandfather's unfinished work.[5]

Balandier's family moved to Noisy-le-Sec in the eastern Paris suburbs when he was nine years old.[6] He obtained a scholarship to attend *lycée* in Paris, earning a *baccalauréat* in philosophy. At the age of 16 and at the moment of the Popular Front government, Balandier joined the French Communist Party's youth organization.[7] He went on to study at the Sorbonne, where he worked toward a *licence* degree in Letters (philosophy).[8] This included a certificate in ethnology, which Balandier obtained through an internship at the Africa Department of the *Musée de l'homme*, starting in 1942. In spring 1943, he earned a diploma from the *Institut d'ethnologie*. It was at the *Musée de l'homme* that Balandier came under the influence of the surrealist novelist and ethnographer Michel Leiris, who "fascinated" him more than anyone else and became his "guide."[9] Balandier began to imagine a colonial career focused on "adventure, not administration, not hierarchy."[10] As he wrote in 1947,

> I launched myself into chimerical constructions, imagining . . . a renewed humanism that would help European civilization to move out of its impasse thanks to borrowings from primitive peoples. . . . I saw myself contributing to the liberation of indigenous nations. . . . I felt the "call of Africa."[11]

Balandier began teaching history in elementary school under the Vichy government but soon left this job.[12] In 1943, he received a draft notice from the *Service du travail obligatoire* and was assigned to work as a longshoreman at the port of Oslo.[13] Balandier evaded the draft and fled to his relatives in eastern France, where he worked as a teacher of refugee children from Paris. It was there that Balandier made contact with the Resistance. He participated in a military *maquis* unit starting in spring 1944.[14] Balandier then returned to Paris, where he reentered the *Musée de l'homme*. Thanks to Leiris, Balandier also began at this time to penetrate Parisian intellectual circles. The *Musée de l'homme* served as a site of intellectual initiation, an experience Balandier referred to repeatedly in his writing.[15] This was the context in which Balandier published a semi-autobiographical, 236-page novel, *Tous comptes faits*, in 1947.[16]

BALANDIER AND LEIRIS: *TOUS COMPTES FAITS*

A historical socioanalysis of social science has to pay attention not only to social and textual contexts but also to individual biography.[17] Many of the sociologists discussed in this book wrote memoirs, but Balandier was the most engaged in autobiographical reflection. Of course, this does not mean that we should take his self-analyses at face value. Balandier warned that "societies are never what they appear to be or what they say they are," arguing that we need "a sort of socioanalysis, a type of work in anthropology and sociology analogous to what Freud did in the universe of psychology."[18] The same is true of texts, including autobiographies and the distinctive genre of the fictional autobiographical novel. Balandier endorsed psychoanalytically oriented social science starting in 1948, although he never wrote directly on psychoanalysis like Bastide, and his vocabulary never became saturated with psychoanalytic terminology like Bourdieu's.[19] A historical socioanalysis of a social scientific text must pay attention to what its author intends it to be, the ideological project it pursues, both consciously or unconsciously. I interpret *Tous comptes faits*, first and foremost, as a text intended to launch Balandier's career as a project. The novel thematizes a fateful biographical turning point. It signals that Balandier is above all an intellectual, attuned to aesthetics, even though he will soon be employed as an applied colonial social scientist and then as a university professor.[20] The novel can also be understood as an attempt to prove that the metropolitan intellectual field is connected to colonial service, social research, and anticolonial engagement.

Balandier wrote *Tous comptes faits* in 1945-1946, before leaving for Africa.[21] The book appeared as the first in a new series, *Le chemin de la vie*, created by a prominent editor and critic, Maurice Nadeau.[22] *Tous comptes faits* had a small print run, even though it was featured in a full-page advertisement in *Présence africaine*, and the publisher destroyed the unsold copies "fairly soon" after publication.[23] Its publication nonetheless aligned Balandier with the avant-garde French traditions that linked ethnography to surrealism, existentialism, and aesthetics.

The novel creates a strong sense of ambivalence about the rupture between Balandier's life before and after the war. This transition can be read in three ways. First, *Tous comptes faits* maps a caesura between the narrator's youth as a budding poet and novelist and his professional adulthood. In this reading, the book's closing lines become something like an existentialist declaration of liberty, marking a sharp break with the narrated events:

> I have to want to be a new person without any residue of my past errors, facing my fortune alone. So I draw a line [*je tire un trait*], I add it up, and I put down *zero*.[24]

The expression "*je tire un trait*" has the double meaning of "to make a break with the past" and "to draw a line." A second possibility is to read the novel as a form of self-analysis, in which the narrator's excavation of his past serves the understanding of the present. The third possibility, and the one I find most compelling, is to understand it as a sort of a dialectical *Aufhebung* (sublation) of the narrator's earlier life.[25] This allows the narrator to maintain a continuity with his artistic and militant past, while "sublating" both histories in a new project that hinges on recognition of the African Other, cultural difference, cultural syncretism, and decolonization. This interpretation also connects Balandier with his ego ideal, Leiris, who was making a parallel declaration of independence from his prewar apoliticism and narcissism at the time. Indeed, Leiris read *Tous comptes faits* in manuscript and helped Balandier to publish it. Afterwards, Balandier continued to publish on African art, literature, music, and dance.[26] He was a co-creator of *Présence africaine*, the journal that combined literature and social and political thought. He also returned to his own biography at regular intervals, in books and interviews.[27] Later, in *Afrique ambiguë* (*Ambiguous Africa*, 1957), discussed below, he combined autobiography and ethnography.

This reading of *Tous comptes faits* as an *Aufhebung* of his artistic and militant period resonates with Balandier's understanding of the relation between politics and intellectual work. Balandier noted that postwar French intellectuals were divided between communists and Marxists on one side, and those oriented toward the colonial question and themes of liberation on the other. He assured his readers: "I chose the latter."[28] Balandier's anticolonialism was located in a non-communist political spectrum that encompassed Bourdieu, Berque, and even Aron. By continuing to remind readers of his participation in the Resistance, Balandier was also implicitly refusing to allow the French Communists to monopolize that legacy.

The cover of *Tous comptes faits* calls the book a novel ("*roman*"; figure 13.1). At various moments in his life, Balandier calls *Tous comptes faits* a "fake novel," a "raging autobiography," an "arranged autobiography," a "balance sheet," a "book that marks a break, and a sometimes obscene revolt."[29] Such characterizations locate the book in a French literary tradition reaching back to Rousseau, in which autobiography and fiction are mixed, and to the "obscenities" of interwar surrealism. The most immediate influence on Balandier's novel was Leiris's own autobiographical novel *L'âge d'homme* (figure 13.2), which was often described as part of the "literature of confession." Leiris's earlier book, *Phantom Africa* (1934), opened with a quotation from Rousseau's *Confessions*: "If I am not more deserving, at least I am different."[30] Leiris explained that *L'âge d'homme* was animated by the self-imposed rule of speaking truthfully, "frankly," "without artifice," and "only of what I know from experience and what touched me closely."[31] Leiris's approach to writing the self was "massively influenced" by his participation in the surrealist movement and his relation to psychoanalysis, both as a reader of Freud and as an analysand. The young Leiris was thrilled by Bataille's "violently materialist disarticulation of selfhood," which relocated identity "within the corporeal mass" and focused on "de-idealized body parts, indecency, and degradation."[32] Leiris eventually became more critical of Bataille, but he continued to share the latter's fascination with the unconscious, the interpenetration of the political and the sacred, and the abolition of exploitation through sacrificial, revolutionary "expenditure."[33]

According to literary critic Séan Hand, the dominant thrust of *L'âge d'homme* is to explain all events in the narrator's life as being derived "from a tyrannical norm . . . taught to the young Leiris by a powerful socio-cultural machine."[34] *L'âge d'homme* begins with several pages of clinically brutal

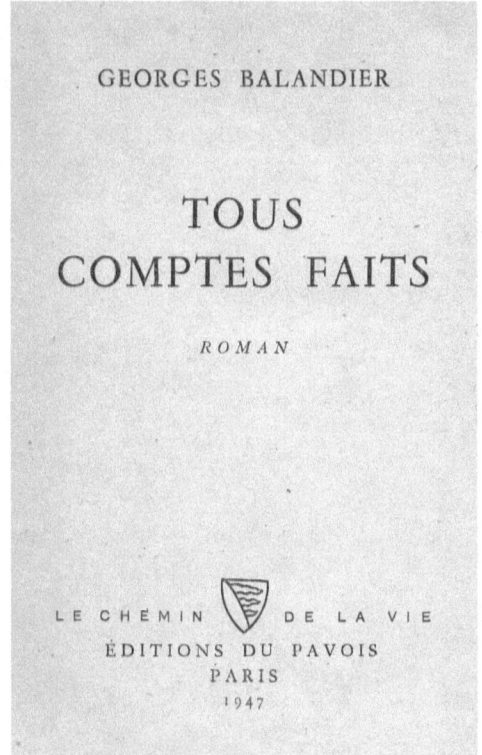

FIGURE 13.1. Georges Balandier, *Tous comptes faits* (1947).

self-objectification. The narrator describes himself as "humiliatingly ugly" and details a number of unappealing habits and traits. Much of the novel focuses on fantasies and anxieties around sexual impotence, humiliation, cowardice, death, and degradation. Leiris explained that when he wrote the novel, "sexuality then seemed to me to be the cornerstone in the structure of the personality."[35] Thematically, the novel is organized around the "obsessive repetition of certain figures," especially female figures from classical antiquity, Christianity, theater, and opera. Although many of the narrator's phobias and anxieties are traced to his early childhood, the novel's temporal structure resembles memory, psychoanalysis, and dreaming in its use of nonlinear condensations, displacements, compressions, and elongations of events. The narrator's efforts over the course of the novel to gain control over these emotions and memories are upended by the final chapter, entitled "The Raft of the Medusa," which presents three dream sequences. Hand argues that these dreams "lie outside the story of the struggle to achieve manhood" and "signify precisely those irreconcilable elements that must be noted but expelled from the autobiographical act of

FIGURE 13.2. Michel Leiris, *L'âge d'homme* (Gallimard, 1939, Collection "Blanche," cover art by Mario Prassinos).

L'âge d'homme." The desires expressed in these dreams "move in the opposite direction to *L'âge d'homme*'s conscious progress towards 'the banal reality' and 'dead calm' of heterosexual maturity."[36] At the end of the book, therefore, we are "still in the clinic, and the book remains under analysis."[37]

Leiris completed *L'âge d'homme* in 1935. When he published it four years later, he included a new 17-page preface, "Literature considered as a bullfight." This essay reframes the entire novel along the lines of politically "engaged" literature. Leiris now explains that his gaze had been "entirely fixed on [him]self" when writing *L'âge d'homme*, but that he would now transcend himself, "in the direction of something more broadly human."[38] The writer today, Leiris insists, "must contribute evidence to the trial of our present system of values and tip the scales . . . toward the liberation of *all* men, without which none can achieve his own."[39] Leiris also added a footnote in which he explains that his turn toward "more broadly human" values means that he now rejects the psychoanalytic method that structures the novel.[40] By publishing the novel in its original version—thoroughly permeated by psychoanalysis, but now combined with this self-critique—Leiris foreshadowed Balandier's gesture of "drawing a line" and marking a break with the past, while still allowing us to read the ideas that have come under erasure.

Balandier's novel echoes this dualistic structure, displaying both the disavowed aspects and the ideology of a political reframing. The first sections of *Tous comptes faits* dwell on the narrator's childhood, which is driven by implacable, external forces and chaotic libidinal energies. As the narrative progresses, its protagonist is subjected to ideologies of war, heroism, imperialism, masculinism, and racism. The narrator seems to exemplify Bataille's theory, according to which fascism channels the explosive energy of heterogeneity back into alignment with capitalism.[41] In the novel's final pages, the narrator declares himself a *tabula rasa*, breaks his ties with a world that "disgusts" him, and embarks on a career that will paradoxically be both colonial and anticolonial. Here, there are parallels with Leiris and a few innovations.

Leiris's narrator in *L'âge d'homme* describes his "chief activity" as literature, but adds that he is also "obliged to work" as an ethnographer.[42] Balandier's narrator explains that he is "an ethnographer, not an exhibitionist," which in this context means that Balandier's auto-analysis will be a kind of clinical, non-exhibitionist ethnography of the self. Balandier compares his self-ethnography to a scientific dissection, proposing to apply the "method of classification and schemas" to the phenomenon *"moi-même"* (myself). This is the *only* way, he notes, to gain a "historical consciousness of reality."[43] Here, we find three of the core themes in Balandier's future thinking: self-reflexivity, ethnography, and history.

A number of passages echo Leiris's novel. Balandier's narrator informs us that he is losing his hair, although he is only 25 years old; that his teeth are rotting; and that his habits include fainting at the sight of blood and laughing in a way that masks his teeth, producing a "rictus" effect.[44] He is a petty bourgeois, in his own words, an *"épicier manqué"* or shopkeeper frustrated in the fulfillment his aspirations.[45] The narrator is plagued by anxieties concerning such varied objects as uniforms, North African workers, and mud, and he is fascinated by "African orgies," "violence," and "battles." He is prone to alienating and denigrating descriptions of women.[46] As time advances to the early 1940s, the narrator briefly expresses an attraction to Vichyism and monarchism.[47] The narrator's father calls him a *"girouette"* (weathercock) and *"tourne-veste"* (turncoat).[48] These hints of fascist temptation are startling in a text published just after Liberation by a participant in the Resistance, but they are indicative of Balandier's willingness to adopt Leiris's dictum of speaking with clinical frankness of the self. They also should not be taken at face value, given Balandier's familiarity with Bataille's theory of fascism.

As the narrator of *Tous comptes faits* enters adolescence, the external world and political events begin to impinge on him more ineluctably, causing him to try to seize control of his life. This move from fantasy to iron compulsion to agency emplots the narrator's entrance onto the "path of liberty"—the title of Sartre's wartime trilogy—and the "path of life," the title of the series in which the book appeared. The narrative of coming to grips with "dangerous freedom" (Camus) is accompanied by a discourse of generalized revolt.[49] Gradually, the narrator's world becomes less self-centered and he becomes less prone to describing his life as determined by random events and inexorable structural determinants, "essences within which one is enclosed."[50] The novel's ending signals a declaration of independence from contingencies and structures. This personal revolt is already adumbrated when the narrator decides to escape from mobilization by the *Service du travail obligatoire*.[51] The choice to join the Resistance was dangerous and non-conformist, yet the narrator does not describe it in these terms. Indeed, he describes his entry into the Resistance as an almost random event, an existentialist *acte gratuit* stemming from a chance encounter. We know from other interviews that this was not, in fact, a random or gratuitous event. Before he left for Eastern France, Balandier knew about the defeated resistance network at the *Musée de l'homme*, although he had not been openly informed about it.[52] We learn from a much later text that Balandier's close friend and longtime intellectual collaborator Paul Mercier accompanied him into the *maquis*.[53] Balandier's deliberately anti-heroic treatment of these events is itself a political statement and a philosophical choice.

Balandier resembles Leiris in other respects. Like Leiris, Balandier attempts to encompass desire rather than repressing it.[54] We can trace the residue of this effort in Balandier's later writings that integrate psychoanalysis with sociology.[55] Both writers motivate their colonial engagements by tying them to their intimate lives and family backgrounds. Leiris discusses an uncle who was a "faithful aide-de-camp of a great colonial leader"; Balandier discusses his great-grandfather who was involved in an African military operation and was in Mexico during Napoléan III's campaign.[56] Both writers attack anthropology's relationship to colonialism. Leiris rejected an ethnography that attaches itself "by preference to peoples one can qualify as relatively intact, either out of a love of a certain 'primitivism' or ... exoticism" and called for a counter-ethnography of the colonizer by the colonized.[57] Balandier developed a more sustained critique of ethnology and an alternative approach he called "sociology," as we will see below.

Balandier's tone also recalls Camus, whom Balandier had met through Leiris. In Camus's *Myth of Sisyphus* (1942), "revolt gives life its value."[58] Camus was no longer a communist when Balandier met him, but he was a veteran of the Resistance, editor of the Resistance journal *Combat*, and an ardent anticolonialist.[59] Like Camus, Balandier suggests in *Tous comptes faits* that life is shaped by a clash of decisionistic acts with the "implacable reign of necessity."[60] The world in which these actions are taking place is absurd, lacking metaphysical guidance or universal standards.

The final pages of Balandier's novel mark another consequential decision. Only here does he gesture toward a future "project": the narrator joins the Organization of Colonial Research—a fictional name that was just one word removed from the real Organization of Colonial Scientific Research—and becomes a "sociologist of Black Africans," or an "ethnographic official."[61] This transformation is connected to the idea of becoming a "new person, without a residue of my past errors, facing my fortune alone."[62] According to the narrator, the move to Africa will mark a "break with a world that disgusts me, an order I no longer believe in."[63] Years later, Balandier summarized this moment as one in which he sought an "experience of an absolute cultural break," embarking on a project that would "impose upon [him] a series of moral requirements and also requirements in the realm of knowledge."[64] As mentioned, the novel concludes with an existential decision to "draw a line," "add it up," and "put down zero."[65] The zero in this instance suggests the bankruptcy or unprofitability of all of his previous experiences, and also alludes to the end of the war—"zero hour." It is not just Balandier but the entire nation, including "greater France" and indeed all of Europe, that has reached zero hour.

From Dakar to Brazzaville, via Conakry

Balandier left Paris in June 1946 for a research position with ORSC, the Organization of Colonial Scientific Research (*Office de la recherche scientifique coloniale*). ORSC was not yet well established in Africa at the time, so Balandier was seconded to IFAN, the *Institut Français d'Afrique noire*. Balandier was thus a colonial civil servant, an "ethnographic official," but he had no administrative duties.

During his first year in Africa, Balandier worked closely with his friend Paul Mercier, who also joined ORSC in 1946 and was also stationed at IFAN headquarters in Dakar. Balandier published his first social scientific articles that year in *Notes africaines*, IFAN's journal. His first publication was a study of older African women who sold salt excavated from lagoons.[66] The second article was a study of traditions of inheritance before and after the Lébou fishermen of the Dakar region were converted to Islam.[67] Balandier observed that many Lébou cultural traits and organizations preserved maternal ties, while Islam was dominant among the male population. These themes were developed in greater detail in Balandier's 1952 book with Mercier, discussed below.

Dakar, as Balandier later explained, was not a "place of absolute unfamiliarity" but was "a city," indeed, "a capital city," i.e., a "very organized" social space, where "civility was very coded and where the African part was in fact partially mixed" (*métissée*).[68] Balandier was unable to find lodging in Dakar and initially slept on a cot in the IFAN headquarters. Soon, he was invited to the home of Alioune Diop, an African political leader he had met at Leiris's apartment in Paris.[69] This friendship separated Balandier from French colonial elites, who practiced what Balandier called "unconditional white supremacy" (*la suprématie inconditionnelle de la blanchitude*).[70] Balandier collaborated with Alioune Diop and Diop's wife Christiane Yandé Diop, and with other Africans and Europeans to launch the literary-scholarly journal *Présence africaine* in 1947. Diop was editor-in-chief; the journal's advisory committee included Sartre, Leiris, Richard Wright, André Gide, Aimé Césaire, and the West African writer Paul Hazoumé. The editorial board consisted of Diop, Balandier, Mercier, the writer Abdoulaye Sadji, and the future Senegalese politician, Mamadou Dia. The editorial introduction to the first issue explained that the journal was "open to the collaboration of all men of goodwill (white, yellow, and black) who are willing to help us define the African's creativity and to hasten his integration in the modern world." The journal would focus on three areas:

> The first part will contain authoritative studies of the culture and civilization of Africa by well-known scholars. There will also be searching examinations of the methods of integrating the black man in western civilization. The second part, which is the most important in our eyes, will be composed of texts by Africans (novels, short stories, plays, etc.). Finally, part three will be devoted to a review of art and thought concerning the black world.[71]

Balandier was very involved in *Présence africaine* and briefly became its co-editor with Bernard Dadié, Ivoirian writer and future cultural minister of Côte d'Ivoire.[72]

The first issue of *Présence africaine* included a manifesto-like essay by Balandier, "Le noir est un homme" ("The Black is a Man"). Here, Balandier discussed the historical evolution of European racism in the context of colonialism. Balandier unflinchingly presents some of the most rebarbative racist stereotypes and slurs and draws examples from his own earlier views. During the first period of colonial conquest, he writes, Europeans spoke "disdainfully" of "blacks, reds, and yellows." During the intermediate period between the wars, Europeans "became more tender" and shifted to a discourse of the exotic and the "noble savage."[73] In the most recent past, the participation of colonial subjects in the French army had led some politicians "to transform them ... into citizens, representatives, counsellors."[74] Indeed, many colonial administrators today are "conscientious and honest people who want to get to know and understand the people for whom they bear responsibility, to speak their language and speak with them, man-to-man."[75] This essay recalls *Tous comptes faits* in its synthesis of self-scrutiny and social-historical analysis.

Balandier published several other articles in early issues of *Présence africaine*. He reviewed the prose-poem *Cahier d'un retour au pays natal* by Aimé Césaire, the Martinican writer who had been Frantz Fanon's *lycée* teacher.

Balandier presented Césaire's text as inaugurating a "renaissance of the literature of violence" and restoring connections with the interwar surrealism movement that had been "buried by the recent events."[76] These comments underscored Balandier's interest in African and colonized intellectuals as well as his continued attachment to the mix of literature and social theory characteristic of the interwar period.

Another of Balandier's articles in *Présence africaine*, "Erreurs noires" ("Black Mistakes"), was a follow-up to "Le noir est un homme." The title suggested that French views of Africans were fundamentally erroneous. Here again, Balandier engaged in a masochistic practice of self-exposure reminiscent of Leiris. The article begins with a jolting description of the racist views of Balandier's uncle, who spent time in a military hospital with a Senegalese soldier.[77] Balandier then presents the stereotypes about Africans that he himself brought with him to Africa—stereotypes that, he explains, "shaped my responses to real blacks."[78] One stereotype, drawn from his childhood geography books, divided the world into four races and placed Blacks at the bottom of the hierarchy. Balandier then discussed his encounters with Alioune Diop, his "first Negro friend," and Mamadou Madeira Keita, whom he called "*mon ami*."[79] In conclusion, Balandier observed that Africans were beginning to refer to traditional chiefs who were installed by the French administration as "collaborators," and that some Africans were labeling the French "occupiers." Colonialism was being delegitimized using a vocabulary forged in the Resistance.[80] This association of colonialism with Nazism certainly dampened any remaining hope Balandier might have had for reforming rather than expunging colonialism.

BALANDIER AND MERCIER ON THE LÉBOU

Balandier's most sustained research project during his first months in Africa was a collaborative study with Mercier of the "encounter between tradition and change" among the Lébou, the Dakar area's original residents.[81] Balandier and Mercier argued that the Lébou were ideally suited for a project of "*sociologie vivante*" (living sociology). The Lébou were "a well-defined and delimited group ... particularistic and coherent." Rather than assuming that cultural coherence was the norm, however, the authors took this relative stability as a puzzle to be explained, asking how this community had been able to preserve its integrity in the face of centuries of incursions by Islamic conquerors and French colonizers, and despite its close proximity to the modern urban centers of Dakar and Rusfique.[82] The authors concluded that Lébou "ethnic identity," while unified on the surface, "masks multiple forms of *métissage* (biological, social, cultural)."[83]

This way of posing the problem inverted the dominant approach to Africanist ethnology, which paid preferential attention to cultures that seemed to be traditional and unchanging, and that took such stasis for granted. Ethnologists tended to dismiss as unattractive societies like the Lébou that were syncretic and undergoing dynamic transformations. Balandier was following in the footsteps of Leiris in rejecting this approach, which viewed Africa "in light of timeless forms."[84] Leiris's 1948 essay on the French Antilles elevated the notion of syncretism to the very principle of poetry itself.[85]

Balandier and Mercier reframed this entire discussion in their seemingly modest study of the Lébou. Rather than focusing on linear processes of "acculturation," as in the research on "culture contacts" that Balandier criticized elsewhere, the authors argued that the Lébou played a complex game of "conservation and innovation" in which they "filtered and measured outside influences." Rather than allowing themselves to "be assimilated," the Lébou selectively assimilated certain cultural elements.[86] Such a flexible practice of cultural stabilization and conservation was "very different from conservatism" *tout court*. The borrowed elements were not simply grafted onto the extant culture but were fully integrated into it.[87] The Lébou therefore continued to change "without revolutionizing their social order."[88]

Two aspects of Balandier and Mercier's discussion of Lébou religious "syncretism" differed from other studies of acculturation. First was the gendered division of religious labor, which Balandier and Mercier argued proved highly functional to societal cohesion.[89] Islam, which was "durably installed" among the Lébou during the second half of the nineteenth century, was borne by men and correlated with power.[90] Lébou women remained "obstinately loyal" to pre-Islamic religious traditions, even while "theoretically claiming to be Muslims."[91] Women retained "rights and control over everything linked to assuring fecundity, power, and wealth."[92] Inheritance continued to pass through the female line, in contradiction to Islam.[93] Not only were the two religions able to "coexist at the same moment," but in some areas, elements from different religions were "mixed, imbricated."[94]

The second unique feature of Lébou society was that the gendered balance between traditional religion and Islam was maintained through a carefully organized system of socialization that shaped the psychological makeup of Lébou males. All boys lived in the female milieu for many years, "longer than the time required by mere biological dependence." During this time, they were exposed to women's rites, songs, and dances, "which are forbidden to men."[95] Every boy acquired "fundamental disciplines and common attitudes" from adult women, and as a result became "more affectionate" and formed "an idealized image of women" that lasted into adulthood.[96] Between the ages of nine and thirteen, in the traditional system, boys were circumcised, which afforded "access to normal sexual life at a precise moment."[97] After the liminal period of healing, each boy moved in with a maternal uncle. Because education took place first "inside the society of women, then passing to the men," males became "rooted in the group's past and its present," both in the religious traditions linked to female power, and in Islam, which was linked to men and male power. The relative "equilibrium in gender relations" explained the fact that Lébou culture was able to change and adapt "smoothly" in an arrangement that "reconcile[d] conservatism and innovation."[98] Balandier and Mercier concluded that the Lébou were taking advantage of "all of the gods and 'recipes' that might prove helpful" to them.[99]

Yet, while the Lébou had long succeeded in resisting political domination and "cultural colonization," the authors raised the possibility of a "grave crisis" in the future.[100] A certain degree of freedom of choice in marriage was emerging, destabilizing the gender-based division of religious labor.[101] Lébou men were pressing to eliminate maternal control of inheritance.[102] For the time being, however, the Lébou were continuing to navigate the threats of external invasion, colonization, urbanization, proletarianization, and individualization.

The Lébou became a model for Balandier's study in his doctoral thesis of the Bakongo, who were also relatively successful in warding off the threats of cultural disintegration.[103] The Lébou study was the first time he discussed colonialism in the context of explaining African culture.

FROM MAURITANIA TO GUINÉE

Later in 1946, Balandier spent three months in Mauritania, where he pursued similar themes. He became interested in the way the shock of colonial conquest had led to a "hibernation of history" in which tradition assumed a static, "immemorial" guise.[104] As this formulation suggests, Balandier recognized that African societies were inherently historical; colonialism stopped history rather than starting it. As Balandier wrote in 1950, "African societies are dynamic in themselves. Their original dynamism was *disrupted* by colonialism." It is a complete distortion of Balandier's thinking to suggest that he saw change in African societies as being solely the product of external interventions.[105] An entire section of Balandier's book *Sens et Puissance* is entitled "Dynamiques 'du dedans' et 'du dehors'" (dynamics of inside and outside).[106]

Balandier caught typhus in Mauritania. IFAN's director, Théodore Monod, had Balandier moved from the hospital in Dakar, where he seemed close to death, to Dalaba, a health resort in Fouta Djallon in the highlands of French Guinea. Monod asked Balandier to remain in Guinea after his recovery in order to build up a new IFAN center in Conakry.[107] The first steps toward the creation of this IFAN center had been taken by Madeira Keita, an IFAN employee, trained archivist-librarian, and anticolonial activist who belonged to a ruling family in Mali, where he held several ministerial posts after independence.[108]

Balandier arrived in Guinea in October 1946, and carried out several research projects in Conakry (figure 13.3). These included a study of indigenous gold miners in the Siguiri region. The mainly self-employed miners

FIGURE 13.3. Georges Balandier in *Institut français d'Afrique noire* jeep, Conakry, in 1946 or 1947. *Source:* Courtesy of Anne Balandier Rocha-Perazzo.

worked in pits for six months of the year, living in provisional camps, then returning to their fields for the winter.[109] The camps were "cosmopolitan," that is, multiethnic or multitribal. The customs that people brought with them to the worksite often gave way to customs that combined different ethnicities. This transformation foreshadowed the syncretic cultural forms that Balandier went on to analyze in Brazzaville several years later. Balandier discussed the rituals used to locate new mines, which included the interpretation of dreams and cola nuts and consultation of the Qur'an by marabouts (Muslim holy men).[110] The mine director was both an engineer and a ritual expert, and was required to carry out sacrifices when opening new mines for exploitation. When a worker found an unusually large chunk of gold, the mine director asked the police to fire their guns at the gold nugget "to dispel the *ginné* responsible for such dangerous generosity."[111] Miners sold their gold to Diola traders, who monopolized the sale of food and supplies at the camps, siphoning off two-thirds of miners' earnings. The resulting class division between merchants and miners was a harbinger of wider processes of class formation and struggle that Balandier went on to study.[112]

During his stay in Guinea, Balandier also studied demographic questions, African housing practices, and relations between towns and the agricultural countryside. Balandier designed a model village of 300 people in Guinea. This suggests that he was involved in some of the tasks typically associated with colonial administrators.[113] Balandier dressed in "African style" clothing while in Guinea and was soon expelled from the colony for suspiciously pro-African sympathies. Yet he also drove around in an IFAN jeep, often with a chauffeur, and sometimes wore a pith helmet. Balandier wrote at the time that some Africans assumed he was a "commander."[114]

While he was in Conakry, Balandier launched the journal, *Études guinéennes*, in which he and his collaborator Keita published several articles. In his introduction to the first issue, Balandier presented a rough sketch of his distinctive research program. This included a focus on African history, to be based as much as possible on African sources. *Études guinéennes* also published documents from the colonial archives. Historical investigations, Balandier argued, should be combined with ethnographic, psychological, and geographical research carried out by interdisciplinary teams. The moment had arrived, Balandier insisted, to "transcend the stage of picturesque tales and colonial novels" and "infantile decorations."[115] Every detail about Africa was "interesting"—even the "most humble" details of "everyday life," including technical and economic facts and levels of socioeconomic well-being.[116] This emphasis on everyday practices and objects was in line with the program of the *Musée de l'homme*.[117] Nor was the idea of multidisciplinary teams studying colonial phenomena unique to Balandier, as we have seen. What *was* unique was the particular group of disciplines he brought together. In addition to history, Balandier was interested in ethnology, sociology, and psychology, including the newer social psychology he attributed to Erich Fromm and others, which integrated sociology with psychoanalysis.[118]

Balandier became better informed about African resistance while in Guinea. Through Keita, he "met some of the Guinean partisans" and "became the observer and the ally of a liberation movement."[119] Balandier and his future wife Claire, who was directing the girl's school (*collège de jeunes filles*) at Conakry, were expelled from the colony in August 1947.[120] French colonial officials had become wary of Balandier, arguing "he is an anticolonialist" and "he has influence, he is sabotaging the Empire."[121] Only Keita accompanied the Balandiers to the airport when they left.[122] Balandier had already become an anticolonial employee of the colonial state.

IN EQUATORIAL AFRICA

Balandier's most extended African posting was in Brazzaville, the capital of French Equatorial Africa. There, he created and directed the sociology section of the *Institut d'études centrafricaines* (IEC) from 1948 until 1951, and was interim director of the entire institute in 1950.[123] During this highly productive period, Balandier carried out various research projects in Gabon and the French Congo, and directed projects by other researchers at the IEC.

He distributed a typewritten document to incoming researchers entitled "Recommendations for the historical study of the historical societies of Black Africa."[124] This memo guided researchers to focus, as Balandier did, on the rapid transformations of societies and mentalities. It emphasized social institutions, which, according to Balandier, "bear the marks of history." Researchers were urged to study a specific set of "transformations of social organization":

a. Slackening of the political function at the level of the tribe, the clan, and "specialized" families;
b. Transformations of religious, moral, administrative, political, and economic solidarity of the inhabitants (also, the emergence of social classes);
c. Reactions to the administrative structures imposed by European nations (especially administrative and traditional chiefs, politico-religious organizations with a more or less marginal character; displacements of villages provoked by administrative orders; awakening of cooperative, syndical, and political life, etc.)
d. The attraction to urban centers.

Colonial sociologists would analyze the degeneration of older forms of social solidarity and, perhaps, social reconstitution along new lines. They would study emerging forms of economic behavior, from individual budgets to the impact of technical changes in the labor process on African workers, to the emergence of labor unions.[125] The third and fourth points were central to Balandier's most sustained research projects, which gave rise, in turn, to his doctoral theses (see below).

Each of these items could be read as suggesting that sociology was offering useful services to colonial administration. In fact, two of Balandier's projects were initiated by the High Commissioner of French Equatorial Africa: the study of regrouping Fang villages in Gabon and the study of the African districts in Brazzaville. Yet, as we will see, Balandier managed to maintain his scientific autonomy and to make new discoveries even when conducting these official investigations.

"THE COLONIAL SITUATION" AND THE "SOCIOLOGY OF DEPENDENCY"

Balandier's most famous article was on the "colonial situation" in 1951.[126] Together with an article on the theory of dependency in 1952, this established Balandier's reputation as a leading theorist of colonialism. According to Balandier, his article was meant as a "provocation."[127] It was as heretical to colonial officials as it was eye-opening to social scientists:

> It was simply scandalous. It couldn't be accepted. I could understand that it was not accepted by conservative milieux, the police, and other political circles, but I could not understand that it was not accepted by fellow anthropologists. It showed exactly that there was a completely

unrealistic anthropology, without any relation to the present historical moment. It was as if, for example, in Africa, Africa was eternal, as if it could not really change in a genuine way. As if Africans were constructed once and for all as Africans with mental structures and cultural configurations that basically could barely change at all.[128]

Balandier approached the theme by first defining colonialism as a system that combines the *economic* dimension of exploitation, the *political* dimension of subjection and loss of sovereignty, and the *sociological* dimension of minority status for the majority of the population, a status grounded in systemic racism. To this he added a fourth dimension, which he called "spiritual domination."[129] Analyzing the colonial situation, Balandier argued, requires attention to a variety of factors, none of which can be assumed to be causally primary.

Having defined colonialism as a totality shaped by heterogeneous determinants, Balandier turns to the notion of "situation." Balandier first used the phrase "colonial situation" in 1950, arguing that it referred to the "double dynamic" of the colonizing and the colonized society.[130] Why did "situation" seem appropriate here? In that 1950 article, Balandier argued that the word situation was not the exclusive property of existentialist philosophers, even while acknowledging existentialism as its most obvious origin.[131] When I asked Balandier about this, he responded:

> I said "situation," but I could have said "a configuration." But why situation? In 1951, . . . I was quite close to Sartre, Simone de Beauvoir, and Camus. There was the way Sartre theorized about situations; and with Gluckman in anthropology it means something else. Gluckman, I was very close to him, I brought him to speak here, I knew him. It turns out that we discovered that we had something in common and in particular this dynamic approach which emphasizes conflicts, which does not think that the social universe is working out that well, but that on the contrary it is always on the move.[132]

Balandier's choice of the word situation underscores the fact that he did not abandon his earlier aesthetic-philosophical orientation but tried to articulate it with a conception of modern social science. Balandier noted that Bronislaw Malinowski had spoken of "contact situations" in colonial contexts; Max Gluckman had analyzed the multifaceted "social situation" in Zululand; and Octave Mannoni had used the phrase "colonial situation" in his book *Psychologie de la colonisation*, where he theorized colonies as "the meeting point of two societies," jointly producing one another as Prospero and Caliban (chapter 6).[133] The idea of the colonial situation signaled that colonialism had to be analyzed relationally, conflictually, processually, and historically, in terms of subjectivities and objectivities.

The colonial situation is particularly complex due to the fact that colonialism is a configuration of two separate societies existing within a single geospace. This does not mean that colonial societies represent anything like a shared community. They are radically hierarchical, fragmented, and antagonistic. The original racism of nineteenth-century colonial rule, which underwrote native policy, was transformed in the twentieth century by the resistance, messianism, prophetism, and nationalism of the colonized. These responses converted the older forms of European racism into a "new racism" that was more latent than manifest and was oriented toward a more "technical" approach to rule.[134]

According to Balandier, the responses of each colonized and colonizing group are conditioned by internal and external factors—the internal history of the colonized and the external history of the foreign power. The sociologist should analyze colonized societies as the product of this "dual history."[135] This distinguishes Balandier's approach from Hegelian immanentism and methodological nationalism. Sociologists should attend to the "social surgery" that imperial powers carry out on colonized societies. Balandier argues further that colonialism always drives colonized societies into a state of latent or manifest *crisis*.[136] Colonies are not spaces of "culture contact" but are conflictual arenas in which radically differing, antagonistic, and racialized groups meet within a political framework dominated by the colonizer. European society is itself internally divided, and each European sector "has its own native policies."[137]

Colonialism had to be studied "dynamically," in Balandier's terminology. Indeed, "dynamic sociology" became one of the main catchwords associated with Balandier. He defined dynamism as the "study of movements," in contrast to "an ethnology that studied frozen institutions."[138] Dynamism suggested a historical process permeated by inequality and conflict.[139] The word *situation* suggested an alternative to positivist or totalitarian conceptions of historical closure, processes with a telos or endpoint. The alternative was an insistence on perpetual change and a universal condition of societal "inachievement" (*inachèvement*) or incompleteness. As Balandier explained in an interview,

> My claim is that there is a continuous "struggle against incompleteness." The reason is that societies are never complete, they always have something to conquer, to acquire, one more perfection to achieve. But when perfection is affirmed despite this situation, we are in totalitarianism.... For me, history is this continuous advance to try to achieve this inachievement, to try to complete what cannot be completed. This touches a bit on the idea of situation, but in the sense of configuration: continuously in motion.[140]

Like Aron, Berque, and Bourdieu, Balandier concluded that the sociologist must also become a historian. Historical research, he insisted already in 1951, provides us with our "first and indispensable frame of reference."[141] Balandier did, in fact, become a historian, especially in *The Kingdom of the Kongo*, as we will see below. Several of Balandier's students, including Emmanuel Terray and Pierre Philippe Rey, engaged in a form of historical ethnography that differed sharply from the ahistorical forms of structuralist anthropology dominating the French academy at the time. This historical approach combined archival research with ethnographic fieldwork in African settings and a neo-Marxist theoretical framework of "modes of production" indebted to Louis Althusser (see chapter 6). The Paris *Centre d'études africaines*, which Balandier created in 1957, became the first center of African history in France.

"The Colonial Solution" is also the first essay in which Balandier assails methodologies that bracket the coloniality of the cultures under investigation. Balandier granted that "all of the knowledge we had" of colonized societies came "from ethnologists," but argued that while ethnologists "should not have ignored colonialism," in fact, "they did." They were "obsessed with the pursuit of the ethnologically pure, with the unaltered fact miraculously preserved in its primitive state." Within cultural anthropology, colonialism only appeared as "a disturbing factor," and even in applied anthropology, it never appeared "as a force acting in terms of its own totality."[142] Although Balandier did not accuse European "colonial anthropologists" of racism, he noted that they "paid little attention to racial facts and problems," ignoring the "centrality of race relations, the racial coloration of political and economic facts" in colonial systems.[143]

Balandier's colonial situation essay had an enormous echo across the field of African studies, in France and across Europe. According to Gérald Gaillard, this essay inaugurated the third phase of French Africanism, following the founding era of military and administrative studies and the second period of university ethnology represented by Marcel Griaule.[144] The essay was translated into English in 1952, and appeared in an improved translation in 1966 in a volume edited by Immanuel Wallerstein.[145] Balandier's critique had an immediate impact on French African studies, due to his position as director of the Sociology Department at the IEC and his engagement at *Sciences Po*, the Sixth Section of the *École pratique des hautes études*, and the Sorbonne.

Another article by Balandier in 1952 on the "sociology of dependency" complemented the essay on the colonial situation.[146] He begins by arguing that all human freedom is limited and relative, and that a certain degree of "dependency" is common to all social relations. There are passive and active forms of dependency. The passive form is necessary for security: citizens are in certain respects "dependent" upon the state, for example. The active forms of dependency, however, provoke resistance. The analysis of active dependency in Marx and Hegel was limited to ancient slavery and the capital-labor relation, but it is now being extended to colonialism. As the colonized become ever more dependent, they become "globally alienated" and experience colonialism as "material and spiritual dispossession" (*dépossession*).

Balandier then sketches a typology of responses to colonialism. This is the key contribution of the article, and it paved the way to his doctoral dissertation, where he examined differing responses in great detail. The first response is "active acceptance," which can take the form of an attitude of "collaboration," in the "special sense that this word assumed during the past war." The second and most common response is "passive acceptance," where loyalty is exchanged for paternalistic dependence. A third response, "passive opposition," assumes a range of forms, from the "refusal to exist" to utopian refuge in messianic movements. Finally, there is direct opposition. Here, anticolonial leaders frame the movement at a universalizing level in order to counter the colonizer's divide-and-rule strategy. Direct resistance takes both modernist forms, such as political parties, and traditionalist forms, such as the revival of Islam. Citing Kojéve, Balandier also compares colonialism to Hegel's analysis in the *Phenomenology of Mind*, in which the slave transforms himself in the "struggle for recognition." In the end, the slave (here: the colonized) is prepared for change, while the master (here: the colonizer) remains "frozen in his mastery." With this article, Balandier emerged as a theorist of anticolonial resistance and, indeed, of social practice in general.

SOCIOLOGY AND POPULATION RESETTLEMENT IN GABON

Gabon and Congo are unintelligible if you ignore their colonial and precolonial antecedents.... Many of the most significant characteristics are the result of negative events—the destruction of populations, mass emigration, failed agricultural experiments, economic failures—whose only traces in the landscape are void and absence.

—GILLES SAUTTER (1966)[147]

Three years after his arrival in Africa, Balandier was asked to direct a study of the effects of a new program for village regrouping in Gabon. From 1900 through the 1950s, the French administration had embarked on periodic campaigns to rearrange the scattered and highly mobile populations of French Equatorial Africa and to fix them in place. Their aims were to eliminate "nomadism," undercut resistance movements, bolster security and social control, and make the population more accessible for tax collection, health policies, labor recruitment, and road construction and maintenance.[148] This involved relocating people to villages situated along the emerging grid of transportation routes. There were many obstacles to success. Resettled villagers continuously escaped back into the bush and forest.[149] One official in Gabon described a situation in which Africans would interact with French officials in the official village, the "village for the commander," and retreat to encampments far removed from government observation the rest of the time.[150] Still, colonial space in Gabon became increasingly linear and organized, with ever larger portions of the population living in stabilized villages and traveling along "state-controlled axes."[151]

The early resettlement efforts in Gabon were undertaken "without a lot of consideration of the sociological functioning of the villages," and individuals from different clans were thrown together haphazardly. A similar resettlement program in the French Middle Congo in 1931 and 1932 destroyed social structures by "mixing clans and families without taking their affinities into account," "altering the groups' relationship to land," and "perverting the political system," according to Balandier.[152] This socially disorganizing approach began to be reformed around 1934, when the administrator of one subdivision attempted to base a new settlement initiative on prior research into "clans and families." The result was a collection of new villages that were more internally homogenous in terms of clan ties.[153]

Social scientists were introduced into resettlement planning after World War II. In 1949, the High Commissioner of French Equatorial Africa, Bernard Cornut-Gentille, commissioned a "sociological mission" to investigate the idea of a new round of village regrouping in Gabon.[154] Balandier described Cornut-Gentille as a "governor of an age of Enlightenment" who had expressed "interest in the social scientific activities I was facilitating."[155] Balandier led this mission between January and March 1949, with the help of geographer Gilles Sautter.[156] Together with the sociologist Jean-Claude Pauvert, Balandier carried out a second study between January and March 1950. Balandier managed to transcend the genre of applied sociology and to produce an exemplary work of sociological theory and empirics on this question.

One key difference from prewar regrouping endeavors was that the postwar project was initiated by Africans—specifically, by a Gabonese Fang Deputy in the French National Assembly, Jean-Hilaire Aubame.[157] This project was centered on "a program of practical demands (for schools, dispensaries and markets) and reforms," and was also motivated by the political goal of reconstituting the unity of the atomized Fang people at the level of the *ayong* or tribe.[158] Aubame believed that "it was now necessary to build villages comparable to those in the French countryside."[159] Sociologists described the Fang movement in favor of *regroupement* as deeply "ambivalent," simultaneously "conservative and progressive, religious and political, nationalist and federalist."[160] A tribal hierarchy began to be created at the level of the district, canton, and village, with the aim of replacing the chiefs appointed by the French with chiefs chosen by the Fang.[161]

Balandier's first study was based on "observations and suggestions" made by French "functionaries " and African chiefs. At this point, Balandier had favorable views of the project. His views changed, however, as a result of his second survey. This time, the sociologists interviewed everyday Gabonese subjects rather than governing elites in three different regions. Balandier and

Pauvert concluded that regrouping should not be applied universally. Their second report begins with a demographic analysis of the three regions. Their results challenge one of the core justifications for resettlement: the belief that Gabon's population was declining. In fact, they argued, there was no evidence of overall decline, although the colony remained underpopulated and its population was stagnant.[162] Instead, the authors pointed to the exodus of most working-age men and some women from the villages to the towns, due mainly to labor recruitment. The apparent population decline was thus the result of a "certain form of colonization" based on large-scale logging and mining operations and cocoa plantations. Colonialism, coming on the heels of two centuries of slave trading, was the source of "the veritable disorganization of the family," the decimation of the "indigenous economy," and the "spread of [other] social illnesses." The Gabonese village could no longer function as a "family, religious, and economic cell," but had become a "cell 'in the colonial situation.'"[163] The report was a unique blend of applied, theorized, and critical colonial social science. Its closest analogue was Berque's analysis of the *Secteurs de modernisation du paysannat* in 1945–46 in Morocco, discussed in the previous chapter.

Balandier and Pauvert's survey of attitudes in the three regions identified large differences in African support for the regrouping project. In Aubaume's region, Woleu-N'Tem, there was widespread support among the younger "modernizing" sections of the population and older groups who believed that reconsolidation would promote political unification of the Fang. The Bapounou of Nyanga rejected regrouping, while the Bapounou of N'Gounié accepted limited forms. The final report therefore contradicted the all-encompassing resettlement plan.[164] The result was a limited experiment with voluntary "centers of attraction" in the N'Gounié region and two potential sites for voluntary centers in Nyanga. Only in Woleu-N'Tem were entirely new, regrouped villages created—and this was an African initiative.[165] As Balandier told me in 2015:

> The idea that the administration could take charge of a regroupment led to regroupments that were initiated spontaneously and regroupments with very limited local resources. . . . Regrouping was provoked, but not really supervised. . . . Africans themselves took the initiative to create them. They . . . built by themselves, structures for work, for classes, for schools. They tried to make the roads approximately accessible, so that villages would not be isolated. There was the clan grouping. . . . it was on the basis of the clan. . . . it was a modernization based on the recovery of categories that were categories of the already existing tradition.[166]

In their first report in 1950, Balandier and Pauvert could not find a convincing way to express their disapproval of the general plan, only noting in their conclusion that "regrouping is not a simple affair that can be implemented by a simple administrative decision.... its realization, even if gradual, threatens to overtax the administrator's schedule, already weighed down with duties."[167] In their report in 1952, they voiced strong disapproval for the project. By revising his initial support for the plan, Balandier became another researcher who refutes the thesis that modern colonial science "could never revise itself."[168]

Colonial Quintet

Balandier's career advanced rapidly between 1952 and 1962. In 1952, he became a member of the CNRS and the *Centre d'études sociologiques*. In 1954, Balandier was elected professor (*directeur d'études*) at the Sixth Section of the *École pratique des hautes études*. In 1957, he created the *Centre d'études africaines*. In 1960, he became head of the Human Sciences section of ORSTOM.[169] In 1962, he was elected to a chair in Ethnology and Sociology of Black Africa at the Sorbonne; in 1967, he took over Georges Gurvitch's chair in "general sociology."[170] Balandier also assumed a number of editorial responsibilities. He assumed the post of "editorial secretary" of *Cahiers internationaux de sociologie* from Georges Gurvitch in 1954. Whereas the journal had foregrounded social theory under Gurvitch's editorship, under Balandier it focused on colonial, postcolonial, and non-European studies. Balandier also edited the book series "*Sociologie d'aujourd'hui*" with *Presses universitaires de France*, along with the journal *Informations dans les sciences sociales*.[171]

Balandier published five important books between 1955 and 1968. The first two are his primary and complementary doctoral theses, both published in 1955: *Sociologie actuelle de l'Afrique noire* (*The Sociology of Black Africa*) and *Sociologie des Brazzavilles noires* (*The Sociology of the Black Brazzavilles*). The third book is *Afrique ambiguë* (*Ambiguous Africa*, 1957). I will discuss each of these in turn. I will then discuss his little known study, *La vie quotidienne au royaume de Kongo du XVIe au XVIIIe* (*Daily Life in the Kingdom of the Kongo*, 1964), one of the first political histories of a precolonial Black African polity. Finally, I will turn to Balandier's best known book, *Anthropologie politique* (*Political Anthropology*, 1967).

THE SOCIOLOGY OF BLACK AFRICA

The Sociology of Black Africa was Balandier's main doctoral thesis, based on his research in Gabon and Congo between 1948 and 1951. In contrast to his studies of village resettlement, the administrative origins of Balandier's research are invisible here. The book reconstructs the precolonial history of Gabon and Congo, tracks the effects of conquest across a range of different practices and institutions, and maps emerging forms of resistance to colonialism. *The Sociology of Black Africa* is structured around a comparison between the Gabonese Fang and the Bakongo of the French Congo. Both societies had been divided by arbitrarily placed colonial boundaries. The Fang were located in Gabon, Cameroon, and Spanish Guinea; the Bakongo were situated on both banks of the Congo River in the Belgian and French colonies, and in Portuguese Angola. The puzzle structuring Balandier's thesis is that the Fang and the Bakongo had both been subjected to the same French colonizer, but had responded in very different ways. Fang society had been shattered. The main response by Fang leaders after 1945 consisted in efforts to reconstruct their society, including the village regrouping schemes discussed above. Bakongo social structure had emerged from the onslaught of colonialism fairly intact and were uniting at the time behind neo-Christian churches with an explicitly anticolonialist, nationalist agenda. Balandier's analytic puzzle was that colonized societies "react differently to the experience of transformation begun by colonization."[172]

Balandier went on to argue that colonized societies tend to respond in the sphere in which they are most threatened in their basic beliefs and activities, but that they also tend to focus resistance in arenas where there were more "opportunity structures," in contemporary social science jargon. The Fang, whose very existence was being thrown into question at the tribal and clan levels, ended up focusing on societal reconstitution as their primary goal. Given the willingness of French rulers to entertain ideas like village regrouping and social development, it is not surprising that Fang leaders themeslves began to emphasize these ideas. The Bakongo, by contrast, concentrated their resistance in the realm of religion.

The first part of the book focuses on the Fang and shows that various aspects of Fang culture were radically transformed by colonization. In a report to the Industrial Sociology group of the *Centre d'études sociologiques* in 1952, Balandier described the creation of an "uprooted proletariat that has broken off all contacts with its ancestral customs."[173] Precolonial Fang society was based on an economy of "conquest rather than production." This specialization in fighting initially enabled the Fang "to resist colonialism [but] was later to be the cause of their complete subjection to it."[174] The Fang were reduced to the status of "out-of-work conquerors."[175] Fang villages, once large, were now microscopic, as there was no longer any need for self-defense due to the French peace.[176] The effects of French rule on Fang social organization were thus "exceptionally grave." The Fang were widely subjected to forced labor recruitment during the colony's early decades. This was combined with the monetization of their economy and the growth of chartered companies and other private enterprises involved in logging, copper mining, oil drilling, rubber tapping, and building roads and railways.[177] These businesses had an "insatiable demand for labor." Fang marriage systems were eroded by the distorted demographic structure discussed above. Men were drawn into work camps and cities, and the young and old, and most women, were left in the backcountry. The motivations for Fang males to enter the colonial economy included the need to pay the colonial hut tax, the growing demand for European commodities, and the marriage dowry, which was now entirely monetized. The customary marriage payment was linked to exogamy among different clans, forging connections among villages and clans that might otherwise have gone to war with one another. The monetization of the economy, including bridal dowries, led to the erosion of boundaries between clans, whose members now mingled at work sites and in the cities. The monetization of dowries diminished the pressure to marry outside the clan. Urban Fang men, according to Balandier, sometimes did not even realize they were marrying women from their own clans.

Balandier also detailed the ways in which French rule degraded the traditional Fang political system. Fang society before colonization was decentralized and "stateless," but that did not mean that there was no political system. A village council sharply limited the ability of any chief to accumulate power or to make power hereditary.[178] There was not a trace of "feudalism" in precolonial Fang society, Balandier wrote. There was not even a word for the function of "chief."[179] The Fang had a legal system based on oral tradition, with trials by judge and jury.[180] There was also an organization, the Ngil, whose function was to restore order in times of crisis.[181] The French disrupted and replaced this entire political system. Since there were no traditional Fang chiefs with sovereignty linked to specific territories, the French drew up a map of "cantons" and "territories" and organized their political-legal structure around this novel political geography.[182] "Administrative chiefs" were appointed at the head of each of unit and were granted authority to arbitrate legal disputes. Their judgments could only be overruled by French officials. This system of appointing chiefs violated Fang custom, according to which the leader at any moment was the best speaker, the fiercest warrior, or the leading genitor.[183]

Balandier's research alerted him to the importance of one particularly important development in the struggle against colonialism: social movements grounded in syncretic and messianic religions, such as the Bwiti cult in Gabon and the Matswa movement and Kibangism in the French Congo. These religions emerged in more or less direct response to the corrosive effects of colonialism and missionary Christianity. Missionaries were at the forefront of cultural colonization, attacking the "indispensable cults" of African societies, just as they had been responsible for the torment of Amerindians accused of idolatry or unwilling to convert to Christianity.[184] One assiduous missionary in Gabon told Balandier that he had personally destroyed around 6,000 Bakongo "fetishes."[185] The Christian onslaught targeted Africans' basic ontologies, personalities, and social structures. The new African religions analyzed by Balandier combined elements of Christianity with remnants of the old cultures and entirely new symbols.

Balandier had already touched on the argument that the new African churches were not simply protests against religious "dispossession" but represented a "total reaction . . . against the [entire] situation created by the White colonizers" in his 1952 article on the "sociology of dependency."[186] He was encouraged to study messianic religions by Maurice Leenhardt, who had been his teacher at the Fifth Section of the *École pratique des hautes études* before the war.[187] According to Balandier, Leenhardt argued that Ethiopianism was a "*total* reaction to the political situation, to the inequality existing between the races and to the ill-conceived approach of the missionaries."[188] Griaule dismissed studies of African messianic movements such as Balandier's, insisting that only traditional religions were worthy of scholarly attention.[189] Once again, Balandier decided to ignore Griaule.

The number of people in the "negro churches" was greatest in places where the colonial situation had been experienced most harshly, he argued, but also where resistance was most plausible. The same conditions explained the birth of African nationalism.[190] It was inaccurate to see these churches simply as religious movements, since they were channeling protest against "colonial economics" and were at the heart of emerging nationalism. Their sacred texts represented "a literature of resistance."[191] The first presidents of independent Gabon and French Congo were leaders of messianic movements. In more "developed" colonies like Algeria or Egypt, opposition to foreign rule took a more directly political form.[192]

In the study of religion, Balandier differentiated again between the Fang and the Bakongo. The Fang had first been contacted by American Protestant missionaries in 1842.[193] The Americans were replaced by French Catholic and Protestant missions once France seized power over the colony.[194] The most important form of syncretic religious expression among the Fang was the Bwiti cult. This was initially a response to "the need for change" and involved a "reworking by the Fang themselves of their ancestral cult."[195] In a report to the High Commissioner in 1952, Balandier argued that the Bwiti cult was a "reactionary and frustrated response to the Fang crisis."[196] At this point, Balandier still grouped Bwiti with magic, sorcery, and an increase in suicide as responses to the devalorization of old beliefs. To describe such calamitous conditions, Balandier used the term "social death," foreshadowing the famous concept developed by Orlando Patterson in his theory of slavery.[197]

In his doctoral thesis, Balandier reframed Bwiti as a "syncretistic" movement with "modern aspects."[198] Bwiti's main base was the uprooted, homeless African.[199] Bwiti had secret aspects: there were often two temples, one in the village and another in the bush.[200] The Bwiti church preserved a body of traditional customs that had been attacked by the Christian missions, while also presenting certain Christian "aspects or ideas."[201] Bwiti was directed against the fragmenting effects of colonial divide-and-rule policy, and favored tribal unification. Bwiti was part of the movement for Fang unification described above. It had no limits on clan or family membership. Even Europeans could become members "on the understanding that they would obey the rules strictly."[202]

In the second half of the thesis, Balandier discussed the Bakongo and their resistance. At the moment when the Bakongo relinquished sovereignty to the French, they had already been dealing directly or indirectly with European colonizers, missionaries, and slave traders for four centuries. The Kongo and Loango Kingdoms fought with some success to retain their sovereignty during this period, although Kongo finally accepted Portuguese suzerainty in 1888 and was abolished by Portugal in 1914. The Loango Kingdom, located in the territory that became part of the French Middle Congo, ceded power to French explorer Pierre Savorgnan de Brazza in 1883.[203] The Bakongo of the French colony were all "historically attached to the Kingdom of San Salvador"—that is, the Kongo Kingdom.[204] Balandier discovered that "the Bakongo did not, like the Fang, adapt the model of the colonial administration to their projects for renewing their society, but rediscovered a form of response to the crisis resulting from colonization that had already been applied in the course of the history of the Kongo kingdom, notably at the beginning of the eighteenth century."[205] Followers of the Bakongo messianic leaders Kimbangu and Matswa called them "kings of Kongo."[206]

The first sign of political resistance was that the Bakongo retained their crowned chiefs alongside the official chiefs appointed by the French, resulting in a dual-power situation.[207] Bakongo chieftainship was organized into three levels. At the top was the king or chief (*mfumu mpu*); in the middle was the head of the lineages (*mfumu nkâda*); and at the bottom were the administrative chiefs appointed by the French, who were mainly responsible for technical tasks.[208] In places where there was no Bakongo chief, tribal elders conducted legal arbitration and educated the young in customs.[209] The Bakongo had stable marketplaces and were strongly rooted in particular locations, unlike the Fang.[210] By the 1950s, more than 30 percent of the Bakongo were urban dwellers, but most of them circulated between the cities and their natal villages. In his complementary doctoral thesis, Balandier revealed that the villages still maintained strong connections to the city and had not been undermined by urban migration.

Bakongo culture had also been destabilized, however, Balandier found. Traditional hierarchies were weakened by the abolition of internal slavery and the installation of official chiefs, many of whom came from "minor lineages, or who had bought their freedom, with administrative authority."[211] Individualism and patriarchy had been strengthened, with the result that "children's property was increasingly being transferred to the father, instead of being in the hands of the maternal uncle as hitherto." Consequently, "land must eventually cease to belong to the clan and become private property."[212] The intermixing of legal systems and incompatible clan fragments in the cities sapped the traditional chiefs' authority.[213] These sources of cultural decomposition were less advanced than among the Fang, but Balandier predicted that the Bakongo could not resist the colonial crisis forever.

The new Bakongo churches were the most important response to these combined pressures. These movements were at the heart of "a kind of sacred nationalism" that was emerging as the most powerful challenge to foreign rule.[214] The first movement in the French Congo was led by Simon Kimbangu (1887–1951) in the early twentieth century. A second messianic movement was founded by André Matswa, a Congolese veteran of the French colonial army in the Rif War who created an "amicalist" organization to provide economic assistance to Africans living in Paris. When Matswa's secular movement migrated to the Congo, it "rapidly acquired messianic overtones."[215] Matswa was imprisoned twice by French authorities and transformed into a martyr when he died in prison in 1942. Matswa's followers worshipped him as Christ, while "combining Christian elements with traditional forms of ancestor worship."[216] A third messianic movement appeared in 1939, led by Simon-Pierre Mpadi, who "claimed to be the reincarnation of Kimbangu" as well as "Matswa's local deputy."[217] This movement was modeled on the Salvation Army and was known as the Khakists, due to their khakhi-colored uniforms. These religions enabled the Bakongo "to emerge from a state of religious decline that had been brought about by the proliferation of magic and sorcery" and provided them with "a solution, albeit illusory, to the state of subjection resulting from colonialism."[218] Balandier was not the first to study African millenarianism, as he acknowledged, but he explored its links to colonialism and connected it to the new versions of nationalism emerging at the time.

The other aspect of *Sociology of Black Africa* that stands out is its concluding chapter, titled "Colonial Situation and Social Change" in the 1955 edition, and "Dynamic Sociology and Social Change" in the second edition. The emphasis on the colonial situation signaled that this was a "relational" form of sociology focusing on the totality of the colonial context—on all groups in relation to one another.[219] It was essential to encompass all of the colonized groups in the sociological field of vision, including the most urbanized and Europeanized populations and the so-called *métis* populations, rather than exclusively studying rural and traditional groups as in conventional anthropology.[220] It was also crucial to study the ruling Whites and settlers, and their indigenous collaborators. Balandier's use of the phrase *dynamic sociology* signaled that this was an historical and processual sociology, in Aron's sense. The study of colonized societies had to be organized around the investigation of distinct and interacting "historical series," both internal and external, colonized and colonizing, African and European.

SOCIOLOGIE DES BRAZZAVILLES NOIRES

Balandier's first immersion in urban Africa took place in Dakar, which was in many ways anomalous. As one historian writes, "of all the colonial cities that the French constructed along the African coastline, none was less African... than Dakar."[221] Dakar was established by the French in 1857, and until 1946, it was an imperial headquarters directly administered by the Governor General of French West Africa. Dakar was also atypical in being one of the "four communes," older Senegalese coastal towns whose original inhabitants, "known as *originaires*, were considered French citizens and legally enjoyed the same civil and political rights as Frenchmen."[222] Balandier also wrote extensively about another African city, Mbanza Kongo, formerly the capital of the Kongo kingdom. In contrast to both Dakar and Mbanza Kongo, Brazzaville corresponded to geographer Jacques Dresch's definition of the archetypical colonial African city as one "created by whites, but populated by blacks."[223] Brazzaville grew up around the military barracks, the originating point of the colonial state and of colonial urban space, according to some analysts.[224] Also at the center of Brazzaville were the administrative center for the entire federative colony of Equatorial Africa and the commercial district. Most Africans lived in neighborhoods located outside the city's core. The city was named after the colony's European founder.

Sociologie des Brazzavilles noires focuses on the city's African districts, described by Balandier as hyper-complex social spaces. This is a comprehensive survey of Africans living in a colonial metropole. Like some of Balandier's other investigations, this one was initiated by a request from the High Commissioner. Together with several other members of the sociology department at the *Institut d'études centrafricaines*, Balandier applied a variety of methods to the project. These included: a census; a study of the constitution of the families living in one hundred residential units; examination of records of disputes in African customary courts; collection of 150 biographies of educated Africans (so-called *évolués*); administration of Rorschach, intelligence, and sociometric tests; and interviews and observations.

Balandier rejected an earlier description of Brazzaville as a "Euro-African" city, since it was divided into separate White and Black sections.[225] Although there was no "rigid discriminatory legislation" preventing Africans from living in the European district—unlike the Belgian Congo—there was a systematic avoidance of contact, stemming from the "hierarchical character of relations between Blacks and Whites, which expresses a sort of natural order."[226] While "there is no regulation" preventing an African from "sitting on a cafe terrace" in the "White city," no African could do so "without risking an incident."[227] Despite this social-spatial segregation, contact between Whites and Blacks was more direct, sustained, and intense in Brazzaville than in the countryside. In 1950, 6,000 Whites lived in Brazzaville, in a population of around 80,000.[228] "The white city . . . weighs heavily . . . on black society," Balandier writes. "In his professional, . . . political, . . . or spiritual life, the Black finds himself in the presence of totally imported social models, over which he has little influence."[229] This colonial urban situation unified the colonized, who were ethnically mixed in the city, against the colonizers, to whom Africans attributed their poverty and political weakness.[230]

Balandier's study of Brazzaville is structured partly around a comparison between the two African residential districts: Bacongo, which had around 18,500 inhabitants, and Poto-Poto, with a population of 56,000. Bacongo was located west of the European residential sector, Poto-Poto on the city's east side, bordering the commercial and industrial sector. By 1950, one-fifth of French Middle Congo's population lived in Brazzaville, and a tenth of the colony's entire population lived in Poto-Poto. There was a much higher percentage of urban-born residents in Bacongo (35%) than in Poto-Poto (7%). Bacongo had a normal age-sex distribution, while Poto-Poto had a disproportionate number of young men. Both of the African districts had a grid structure of streets with identical administrative buildings.[231] Bacongo was more ethnically homogenous, consisting almost entirely of members of the Bakongo tribe, and was more modernized, with many of its residents working in the business district or in administration. Bacongo had a small number of model homes built in the European style, whereas all of the African homes in Poto-Poto were huts.[232] Streets in Bacongo were paved and named after French heroes. The Bakongo were more urbanized than other groups in the colony—more than 30 percent of the Bakongo were urban dwellers by 1950. Poto-Poto's residents included representatives from more than 60 different ethnic groups, many from different colonies and different European empires. The streets of Poto-Poto were unpaved and were named after the places from which its residents hailed.

Balandier discussed the Bakongo in *Sociology of Black Africa*, including town dwellers. He observed that urbanized Bakongo did not abandon their traditions or connections to their rural countrymen, but forged strong linkages to the countryside, counteracting some of the supposed negative results of urbanization.[233] The Bakongo were open to "modernity," but they integrated innovations into traditions. Any cultural innovation needed to appeal to both urban and rural Bakongo in order to take hold among the people as a whole.[234] Bakongo were not averse to accumulating wealth, Balandier argued, but they used money mainly in pursuit of traditional goods such as status, power, and authority.[235] Traditional social relations remained largely intact in the Bacongo district.[236] This combination of elements among the Bakongo of Brazzaville led Balandier to declare the categories of modern and traditional inadequate.[237]

In his complementary thesis, Balandier focused on the district of Poto-Poto.[238] He was concerned with the ways Africans' lives were being transformed by urban life and the ways they were responding culturally, socially, and politically. Balandier first traced the weakening of ethnic and family ties and the effects of individualization and participation in capital, labor, and consumer markets. He then examined the ways Africans were reappropriating the city, recreating cultural cohesion, turning the city into an "experimental space, a kind of laboratory where tradition . . . and modernity . . . are combined in unstable but provocatively creative" ways.[239] Cultural innovation was not limited to the imitation of European forms, but included wholly new groupings, cultural practices, and religious and political phenomena.[240]

The population of Poto-Poto was highly fluctuating, consisting predominantly of young males. City dwellers came from rural places where social organization was primarily a function of ethnicity, the extended family, gender, and age. Migration to the city entailed a "sociological expatriation" (*dépaysement sociologique*) that was embraced by some and rejected by others.[241] The city liberated Africans from their family and customary constraints.[242] This was particularly true of women, who gained power vis-à-vis men by moving to the city.[243] At the same time, urbanized Africans experienced destabilization as their points of reference disappeared.[244] Work was precarious and the minimum wage was barely adequate to support an individual. There was a great deal of shared housing.[245] Men experienced heightened competition for women and a rising cost of bride payments.[246] Family ties among the poor remained one of the only ways to survive and find work.[247]

Balandier wanted to show in this book "that African cities were laboratories of modern social relations, modern cultures, of the search for modern forms of expression."[248] He hoped to demonstrate that the colonial city was co-created by Africans, who drew upon ideas about "relations of kinship, alliance, cooperation, solidarity, and certain ritual models" in organizing a tolerable form of urban life.[249] The need for social reorganization in anomic urban space led to a blossoming of associations and groups, ranging from ethnic mutual aid societies to political parties, to forms of cultural experimentation, including fashion and modernist art.[250]

AMBIGUOUS AFRICA

With *Afrique ambiguë* (*Ambiguous Africa*), Balandier's writing experimented with a new mixed genre combining autobiography and social science. *Ambiguous Africa* appears at first glance like a response to Leiris's *Phantom Africa*, which it recalls not only in its title but in its combination of ethnography and self-criticism in a colonial setting. The word *ambiguous* in the title, however, suggests that Africa is no longer an indecipherable "phantom," as in Leiris. Balandier refers at the beginning of the book to his yearning for an "old Africa with a passion fed by Conradian reminiscences, with the illusion that the *Heart of Darkness* was still a guide." Once in Dakar, however, he writes, "I felt cheated on finding myself so much at home."[251] In the rest of the book, Africa is neither a Conradian phantom nor a real "home," but an "ambiguous" space in which modernity bleeds into tradition and vice versa, and where images of political hope blend into scenarios of ruin.

Ambiguous Africa appeared in the most prestigious collection for French anthropology, *Terre humaine*, founded by ethnologist Jean Malaurie and published with Plon.[252] The most famous book in this series was, and still is, *Tristes tropiques* by Claude Lévi-Strauss. If Leiris's *L'âge d'homme* was the main intertext for Balandier's *Tous comptes faits*, *Tristes tropiques* is a key intertext for *Ambiguous Africa*. *Tristes tropiques* and *Ambiguous Africa* were two of the five "foundation stones" of the *Terre humaine* series, according to Malaurie. Jean Duvignaud compared the series to Diderot's *Encyclopédie* in terms of its ambition.[253] It is worth noting that Malaurie did not include Griaule in the series. Balandier may have continued to hammer Lévi-Strauss for his "undynamic" structuralism, but he recognized that Lévi-Strauss would soon wield enormous influence over the French human sciences, and that his work was therefore well worth engaging.

Balandier's lifelong polemic against ahistorical, decontextualized, static forms of ethnology crystallized in his polarization vis-à-vis Lévi-Strauss. Balandier suggested that the formal and technical character of Lévi-Strauss's structuralism resonated with the technicism of postwar French society.[254] Whereas Balandier attacked approaches to non-western societies as static and unchanging, Lévi-Strauss insisted that anthropology was precisely about "frozen societies," even repeating this in a review of Balandier's *Brazzavilles noires*.[255] Sociology, Lévi-Strauss argued polemically, was a narrowly applied discipline; anthropology was the only "true sociology."[256] The tensions between the two men were heightened by the fact that Lévi-Strauss had started his career as a sociologist and protégé of Célestin Bouglé, whereas Balandier had started as a protégé of Leiris, a much more modern and prestigious figure in ethnology. Lévi-Strauss began *Structural Anthropology* by accepting the classical Durkheimian classification of ethnology as a branch of sociology, but he didn't discuss the critique of ethnology that had been mounted by Leiris and Balandier in the preceding period. Lévi-Strauss also dedicated a harsh footnote to Balandier in *The Savage Mind*.[257] Notably, Balandier is the only one of my four case studies who was not elected to the *Collège de France*, a fact that is often attributed to Lévi-Strauss's insistence that Balandier would never set foot there.[258]

Ambiguous Africa and *Tristes tropiques* are both presented by their authors as ironically updated versions of the "philosophical travel narrative" genre.[259] Both books combine subjective first-person narrative with passages written in the empirically objective voice of the scientific ethnographer. Both authors distance themselves from the conventional tropes of escaping European modernity through the discovery of exotic otherness or criticizing Europe via comparison with virtuous "noble savages." As Lévi-Strauss said to an interviewer who asked why he did not accept job offers in the United States, "it is one thing to have a passion for the New World before 1492 and another to uproot yourself to live in the New World of today."[260] Lévi-Strauss seems open in *Tristes tropiques* to the varieties of *métis* cultures that Leiris and Balandier favored more expressly. In a passage that strongly recalls Balandier, or for that matter any of the other ethno-sociologists discussed in chapter 8 (especially Soustelle), Lévi-Strauss argues that the Tibagy culture "was an individual mixture, made up on the one hand of ancient traditions which had withstood the influence of the whites ... and on the other of borrowings from modern civilization." Lévi-Strauss notes that the study of this mixed culture, "however deficient in the element of the picturesque, was to prove no less instructive than that of the pure Indians I was subsequently to encounter."[261] As can be seen in figures 13.4 and 13.5, the two books had similar cover designs. Yet that is where the similarity ends. Even while providing evidence of cultural decay and mixing, Lévi-Strauss's text still clearly prefers "true Indians," "virtuous savages," "comparatively untouched" native cultures, and the "Neolithic" way of life.[262] He still "orientalises the tropics."[263] And then there is the word "triste" in the title. At a time when the world was enthralled by anticolonial revolution and postcolonial energy, Lévi-Strauss finds the contemporary tropics "sad" or "unhappy" (*triste*). His subsequent work focused entirely on undiluted, "primitive" cultures.

Balandier's text can also be read as an oblique response to *Tristes tropiques*, even though his rivalry with Lévi-Strauss had not yet emerged into the open. Balandier distinguishes his approach from that of Lévi-Strauss in at least five ways. The first concerns cultural syncretism and the structuralist preference for "pure" cultures. Lévi-Strauss declares on the first page of *Tristes tropiques*, "I hate travelling and explorers," and on the last page he bids a "fond farewell to savages and explorations."[264] Balandier also dismisses the conquering, imperialist forms of ethnographic traveling, yet his own text seems to revel in traveling, covering vast amounts of territory by airplane, jeep, and boat in the French and British African colonies.[265] Balandier echoes Lévi-Strauss's "I hate travelling" with a more paradoxical statement: "I hate objects." More specifically, Balandier writes,

> I hate objects, above all those regarded as works of art, when they are divorced from the human context which gives them their full significance; objects under glass, as helpless in the presence of sightseers as the dead in the presence of the crowds on All Saints' Day.

This refers ostensibly to Balandier's apprenticeship at the *Musée de l'homme* as a classifier of dead, stolen, and decontextualized ethnographic objects. Yet the close analysis of exotic objects also became a hallmark of Lévi-Strauss's

FIGURE 13.4. Cover of Georges Balandier's *Afrique ambiguë* (1957), in the *Terre humaine* collection. Courtesy of PLON.

"non-travelling" version of anthropology. The cover of the first edition of *Tristes tropiques* features an image that merges a human head with a pottery vase. *Afrique ambiguë* also discusses objects, but it distinguishes between traditional, syncretic, and modern approaches to African art. The cover of the first edition of *Afrique ambiguë* shows the face of a statue of a Cameroonian Bamileké chief. Balandier argues that traditional art persists and flourishes where the colonial situation is weakest, for example, among the Bamileké. By contrast, African art has been most likely to disappear where the "shock" of colonization is greatest and the "colonial situation" most totalizing, that is, where the social structures that necessitate and sustain traditional art are swept away.[266] Balandier also discusses syncretic cultural forms, illustrated in the text with drawings of a Bwiti temple and cult objects and a photograph of the contiguous graves of an African chief and a Christian missionary (figure 13.6).[267] Balandier was fascinated by even the most degraded aesthetic forms, such as the "ornamental use of certain of our waste products" in Bwiti temples. These European signifiers, he argues, are coming to constitute an "African baroque," taking on new meanings that are "difficult to define in terms of our own criteria." This resignification constitutes an "alienation and 'Africanization' of our familiar objects," thereby contributing to the emergence of "an aesthetic perspective specific to modern Africa."[268] Balandier's

FIGURE 13.5. Cover of Claude Lévi-Strauss's *Tristes Tropiques* (1955), in the *Terre humaine* collection. Courtesy of PLON.

analysis of the resignification of mass culture anticipates subsequent critiques of structuralism.[269]

Balandier's professed "hatred" of objects is linked to his rejection of decontextualizing and ahistorical accounts. The phrase "I hate objects" appears in a chapter titled "Lost Arts." The chapter begins with a scene of "masks lined up in my office at Conakry . . . inert, ready for the descriptive labels and the obscurity of museum files."[270] Balandier goes on to describe the "decline of the gods," the mask-makers, and the masks. Everywhere, he encounters the "inferior execution of the newer masks and their commercialization."[271] Balandier mentions that his colleague, Bohumil Holas, rescued discarded masks from garbage heaps. He tells the story of a French administrator who has in his office a crate in which skulls and *bieri*—figurative sculptures produced for the Fang ancestor cult—are thrown together with canned goods.[272] Balandier did not literally hate these objects, in other words; what he hated is what they were communicating about colonialism, capitalism, ethnology, and the European disdain for Africa. Balandier was enthusiastic about contemporary forms of African art, including the "modernist school" that was emerging at the time, which demonstrated an interest in making culture more *"imperishable."*[273]

The second difference from Lévi-Strauss relates to the status of colonialism as an analytic object. Lévi-Strauss registered the depredations of Portuguese

FIGURE 13.6. Graves of Bwiti chief (left) and Christian missionary (right), from original edition of *Afrique ambiguë*. Balandier, *Afrique ambiguë* (Paris: Plon, 1957), 248–49. Courtesy of PLON.

colonialism in *Tristes tropiques* and supported French withdrawal from Algeria as early as 1956.[274] In contrast to Balandier, however, who placed colonialism at the center of his analytic frame, Lévi-Strauss never explicitly analyzed colonialism after *Tristes tropiques*. Lévi-Strauss criticized racism in *Race and History* (1952), but even here he avoided naming colonialism, despite the fact that colonialism had been widely cited as a central source of racism by this time.[275] For Balandier, the *tristesse* of the tropics was the specific effect of the destruction of indigenous cultural and social forms caused by "contact with our economic, administrative and religious imperatives."[276]

Balandier's focus on resistance marks a third difference from Lévi-Strauss. In Balandier's account, African history during the colonial era is driven by dialectical intersections between internal and external forces. This is explored in chapter 7 of *Ambiguous Africa*, titled "Opposing Movements." Here, Balandier discusses activities that "revealed a desire to alter the social relations imposed by colonization." The "antagonisms arising from colonialism and the opposition of two not only different but unequal civilizations" take on "the quality of religious war."[277] Christianity unintentionally promoted movements of collective emancipation, due to its monotheism, which "contributed a principle of unification," and its "example of a Messiah" who was "sacrificed by the public powers." Christianity "brought all the revolutionary force it possessed at the time of its origins, together with the expectation inherited from Jewish messianism."[278]

A "dialectical" approach is evident even in Balandier's discussion of his own "saddest" tropical colony, Gabon. He perceives the entire country as "drab and gray" and as "haunted by the theme of isolation." For Balandier, the town of Lambaréné was "one of the most oppressive sites I have ever known," where "everything conspires to unnerve as well as to depress." Gabon is a place where colonial officials "succumb to exhaustion" and doctors are "reduced to a state of delirious frenzy."[279] The ultimate symbol of African hopelessness in Balandier's Gabonese travel narrative is "a young madwoman" who "accompanied our party constantly during its final stages. . . . howling incoherent songs."[280] Yet, even at moments like this, Balandier always brings the discussion back to the colonial situation and African resistance. One might assume that "all human endeavor seems doomed to come to a sudden end" in such a desolate land. But Balandier emphasizes that the Gabonese Fang are attempting, through their religiously based uprising, to arrive "by a kind of dialectical movement . . . at the epoch of modern civilization," despite French opposition to all forms of tribal unity.[281] More generally, Balandier assures his reader, Africa has a "humble fabric of everyday life [that] has held fast in spite of . . . wars and colonial conquests," and this "resembles that very flag of civilization which no defeat can utterly destroy."[282] Even the movements that seem most marked by foreign Christianity or the artworks that seem most alienated from the past maintain embers of precolonial culture that may be reignited into revolutionary flames.

The fourth difference between the two scholars concerns practices of self-reflexivity. Balandier was 12 years younger than Lévi-Strauss, but he had a head start in this domain due to his discussion of his own "making" as a "sociologist of Black Africans" in *Tous comptes faits*. Lévi-Strauss similarly included a chapter in *Tristes Tropiques* on "the making of an anthropologist." Balandier revisits the question in the first chapter of *Ambiguous Africa*, where he observes that "to explain foreign peoples . . . is, inevitably, to explain oneself." In all ethnography, he writes, a "kind of self-criticism . . . becomes necessary."[283] Balandier justifies his use of the first person pronoun in *Ambiguous Africa*—"however obnoxious it may be"—in terms of the imperative of self-reflexivity.[284] Lévi-Strauss is often described as presenting a self-reflexive discussion of the anthropologist in *Tristes tropiques*, but this is far from the scathing, clinical self-revelation of Leiris or Balandier. Balandier's narrative practice in *Ambiguous Africa* is also interesting in this regard. In most of the chapters, a chronological travel narrative is periodically interrupted by analytical and thematic discussions. This continuous cycling between objective and subjective voices reminds the reader that even the objective, scientifically presented ethnography stems from a particular, situated observer.

Fifth, Balandier's approach is explicitly constructed as a history of the present. As his student Emmanuel Terray wrote, "Balandier's primary characteristic, in my view, is to give history its rightful place."[285] Fabienne Samson comments that "Balandier's objective was to reinscribe African societies in history."[286] Balandier's approach is historical in its overdetermined, processualist refusal of closure, telos, and societal "achievement." *Ambiguous Africa* is also historical in its narrative form. The book's overall narrative structure moves from the "play of memory" (the title of chap. 1), through a series of African *impasses* (the title of chap. 5), to oppositional movements (chap. 7), portraits of African leaders (chap. 8), and African intellectual formations (chap. 9), to a final chapter, "Landmarks," added to the second edition in 1962, on the postcolonies as "'laboratories' of decolonization."[287]

Balandier's publications in the decade after *Ambiguous Africa* moved in three principal directions. First, he became the leading French sociologist of underdevelopment. In 1952, he began lecturing at *Sciences Po* on theories of development. The same year, Balandier popularized Sauvy's term "*Tiers-monde*" (Third World), discussed in chapter 7. In 1953, Balandier became the director of the International Office on the Social Implications of Technological Change. Although this work was important at the time, it was too closely linked to ongoing policies of development to make lasting theoretical contributions. Balandier's second path was into African studies and, specifically, African history. Although he had long argued for a "dynamic" sociology, *Daily Life in the Kingdom of the Kongo* introduced a fully historical approach. This book was linked to Balandier's third strand of research, which inaugurated the political sociology and anthropology of African and non-western states and societies.

DAILY LIFE IN THE KINGDOM OF THE KONGO

After several years focusing on questions of development, Balandier turned his attention to African politics, asking specifically "how Africa elaborated a conception of politics." This was a *political* sociology, history, and anthropology of Africa.[288] His first historical intervention in this arena was *Daily Life in the Kingdom of the Kongo*.[289] Balandier relied here on published sources in several European languages, accumulated over four centuries of contact with the Kongo kingdom, and his own field research. Although the book has been surpassed by more recent histories, Catherine Coquery-Vidrovitch credits it with initiating the French field of African history.[290] This is a remarkable statement from one of France's leading African historians.[291] Balandier's methods represented a novel approach to the history and historical sociology of Africa.

Daily Life in the Kingdom of the Kongo tells the story of the formation of an African state and its resistance to increasingly aggressive efforts by the Portuguese to limit the kingdom's sovereignty and subject it to Portugal's will. This is a historical sociology of state formation, international relations, and movements of resistance to European hegemony. Balandier defines the kingdom as a particular type of polity based on war and slavery. He describes the ways in which the kingdom's development was transformed by Portugal, which first established a trading presence along the coast, then became the colonizer of Angola, adjacent to the Kongo kingdom, and finally claimed sovereignty over the Kongo kingdom itself.

Portuguese influence was initially heightened by the slave trade, which undergirded the expansion of the Kongo kingdom. The Europeans transformed the kingdom's economy, which was "partly geared toward survival and partly to the service of the state and the aristocracy, into an economy that was mercantile and fundamentally inhuman, since the prime commodity became the slave destined for exploitation."[292] Kongo was then further transformed by European missionaries, who converted its entire ruling elite. The result was an evolving mixture of Christianity and traditional religion. The Portuguese then moved to tie the hands of Kongo's rulers and stifle the kingdom's growth. Portuguese kings intervened to prevent Kongo from forging independent relations with the Holy See. Portugal seized the island from which the kingdom gathered the *zimbu* shells that were its currency, strangling the Kongo treasury.[293] In 1665, Kongo's King António I was killed in a battle with a Portuguese force, which decapitated him and brought his severed head, scepter, and crown to Luanda, the Angolan capital, as a prize.[294]

In the last part of the book, Balandier discusses several aspects of Kongolese resistance to European infringement. First was the Antonian movement, led by the young African noblewoman Beatriz Kimpa Vita at the beginning of the eighteenth century. Beatriz was possessed by Saint Anthony of Padua, who commanded Kongo to unite and reoccupy the kingdom's now abandoned capital city. Beatriz tried "to restore the kingdom to its greatness."[295] Balandier ends the book with the observation that in the present, more than "two centuries later, the mystical heirs of Dona Beatriz would rediscover, without even knowing her name, the road to the ideal kingdom of liberty and fullness in life."[296] These were the nationalist, revolutionary movements Balandier studied in the 1950s, discussed in his previous books. *Daily Life in the Kingdom of the Kongo* is thus not only a foundational contribution to African history but a genealogy of the anticolonial movements and history of the present.

This book also made further contributions to African art history and urban sociology. The topography of Kongo's capital city, Mbanza Kongo—called São Salvador between 1570 and 1975—anticipated the colonial cities of the nineteenth and twentieth centuries with its landscape of "racial division."[297] There were essentially two cities—a European one, whose constructions were built solidly in order to endure, and an African city, which had the appearance of "overgrown villages." This was reminiscent of Balandier's description of Brazzaville in the 1950s. Balandier also discussed the art of the Kongo kingdom, which had "degenerated" but was still admirable.[298] This discussion recalled Balandier's treatment of the Poto-Poto school of art in Brazzaville. Balandier praised Kongo sculptural graves, called *mitandi*. Each one of these pieces was unique, and unlike much African art, they were asymmetrical in form.[299] Artists had "succeeded in Kongolizing the Christian images," Balandier wrote, in a "process of Africanization."[300] With the "modifications of form imposed upon Christian symbolism and changes of meaning, the art of the Kongo has sometimes produced extraordinary works," he concluded.[301]

POLITICAL ANTHROPOLOGY

Although it was published just after the end of the period examined in this book, *Political Anthropology* is in many ways the *summa* of Balandier's previous work and has to be considered here. It is an attempt to make sense of the entire range of historical and contemporary politics in the "Third World," from social movements to the foundation of states.

The book begins from a premise that Balandier forcefully rejected between 1945 and 1960—the definition of anthropology as the study of the non-western or "exotic" other. This apparent backsliding reveals Balandier's migration out of sociology but also serves his analytic purposes here. One of his themes is the "traditional state," which had long been seen as being fundamentally different from modern states.[302] Many non-western societies were characterized as stateless, or, in the dubious terminology of the time, "acephalous."[303] A more serious challenge from some anthropologists was the idea that traditional or non-western societies did not even have politics. Balandier counters that political anthropology is the study of "'other,' exotic political forms."[304] The "traditional state" is part of this subfield but is not exhaustive of "other" forms of politics, which also include social movements. These can exist outside the state and in stateless situations.

The first six chapters rely heavily on work on non-western politics by European, African, and Indian anthropologists and sociologists. Balandier begins with the hypothesis that even lineage or kinship societies have politics (chap. 3), and argues that social stratification is strongly correlated with political hierarchies (chap. 4). Chapter 5 returns to the theme of the interfusing of religion and politics, explored in *Sociology of Black Africa*. Balandier connects this to the surrealist discussion of "sacred sociology" and a wide array of anthropological studies of political ritual and myth. The sacred, he argues, is "one dimension of the political sphere."[305] Political rituals present "a sort of résumé of society as a whole," an "enacted social system."[306] In societies without a centralized state, mythology becomes a social charter that explains and justifies the existing order.[307] Where there is a state, mythical knowledge is "often held by a body of specialists whose work is secret."[308] The sacred can also exist separately from political power and serve to "limit and challenge" it.[309] Balandier's sociology of "elementary forms of the religious life" moves beyond Durkheim, whose theory does not encompass pluralism, divisions, and conflicts within the realm of the sacred and does not thematize the sociology of ritual specialists.

At this point, the reader familiar with Balandier's earlier writing may wonder about the lack of attention to colonialism. Balandier seems to be deliberately ignoring the political role of colonial officials and missionaries, collaborating native chiefs, syncretic and messianic churches and nationalist movements, and the wholesale destruction and transformation of the political structures of the colonized. Chapter 6 of *Political Anthropology*, "Aspects of the Traditional State," examines the organized polities of non-western societies, but again ignores colonialism.

In the final chapter, however, Balandier discusses five main effects of colonialism on contemporary politics in the "Third World." First is the "denaturation of traditional political units." The national frontiers that were "created by the accidents of colonization do not coincide with the political frontiers established in the course of African history, or with areas possessing cultural similarities."[310] The second effect is "degradation by depolitization." Colonizers destroyed preexisting states or reduced them to the status of lower-level administrative bureaucracies. As a result, genuine political life became clandestine or indirect, or reemerged during the transfer of political power.[311] The third effect of colonialism is its destruction of "traditional systems of *limiting* power." Colonial governors were not responsible to their subjects, while native sovereigns, if they remained in power after colonial conquest, were oriented toward "the acquiescence of the colonial power" rather than attaining the "good-will of the governed." The legitimacy of these traditional rulers was corroded as the colonized masses began appealing directly to colonial rulers for help in resisting their own leaders' policies.[312] The fourth lasting effect of colonialism after independence is that what was characterized as loyalty in the old system becomes nepotism in the new system, for example.[313]

Balandier's fifth and most original point is that colonialism introduces a "partial desacralization of power." The loss of power by traditional political authorities is due in large part to the actions of missionaries, who "break the spiritual unity of which sovereigns or chiefs were symbols, and often the guardians."[314] This explains efforts to resacralize political power by the

Bwiti, Matswa, and Kibangist movements. Balandier argues further that colonized societies react differently to the desacralizing impetus of colonialism depending on whether they have a centralized state. Stateless societies are more vulnerable to colonial bureaucratization, but their sacred spheres are less threatened because they are immediately linked to politics.[315]

Balandier's Shifting Disciplinary Identities

Balandier's works are a manifestation of the movement from a classic ethnology to a total sociology.

—EUGÈNE ENRIQUEZ (1958)[316]

Sociology was the first discipline with which Balandier identified, during the crucial first two decades of his career. In his 1947 novel, the narrator calls himself a "sociologist of Black Africans." In a 1948 article, Balandier approvingly cited Charles Le Coeur to the effect that sociology explains and does not simply describe.[317] In 1950, he insisted on the importance of a politically active (*engagé*) *sociology*.[318] His study of the Fang in 1950 was labeled a "sociological mission." Balandier published a critique of René Maunier's work for being "closed to modern sociology" in 1954, and he praised the contemporary sociology of Gurvitch and others, even publishing a short book on Gurvitch.[319]

Balandier explained his preference for the identity of "sociologist" on multiple occasions. In 1950, Balandier argued that "ethnology, centered on the notion of the primitive, is giving way to a sociology preoccupied by the evolution of African societies and the current problems posed by these changes."[320] I asked Balandier why he had insisted on the term sociology. He replied that sociology

> was a theoretical position, a militant position. It was a way of saying that I wanted to do something current, so it's sociological. It is not this timeless way of speaking about peoples and civilizations.... Sociology in the 1950s, as I said, referred to my dissenting position. It was a position of contradiction: I could not consider myself satisfied with that timeless ethnology at that time, in France, after taking into account what I had seen and experienced in societies that were engulfed in the currents of decolonization. Therefore, I spoke of sociology, not ethnology, with that meaning.[321]

Sociology had a more radical political reputation than ethnology in the immediate postwar context (chapter 7), heightening its attractiveness to people like Balandier. In my last interview with Balandier in 2015, he repeated that his choice of the label sociology had been a "polemical" and "combative" move. His struggle with Lévi-Strauss overdetermined his alignment with sociology, he argued, allowing him to "demarcate" himself.[322]

Most of Balandier's external markers of recognition also located him within sociology. His organization in Brazzaville was a "sociology" institute while he was directing it. He entered the CNRS in 1952 through the sociology division and joined the *Centre d'études sociologiques*, France's leading sociological research organization. Although Balandier's original job title at the *Office de la recherche scientifique coloniale* also included the word "ethnology," that disappeared when he moved to the Brazzaville center. Balandier's original chair at the Sorbonne included ethnology, but he held a chair in "general sociology" there from 1967 until 1985. Between 1963 and 1973, Balandier directed the sociology section of the *Office de la recherche scientifique et technique outre-mer*.[323] During the colonial era, and in the five or ten years following decolonization, the majority of Balandier's articles were published in sociology journals—above all, *Cahiers internationaux de sociologie*. Several dozen were published in intellectual journals without a disciplinary identity, such as *Les temps modernes*, and a smaller number appeared in interdisciplinary journals such as *Présence africaine* and *Cahiers d'études africaines*. Most tellingly, Balandier did not publish a single article in the leading French anthropology journals such as *L'homme*, which was edited by Lévi-Strauss.[324] Three *festschriften* were published in Balandier's honor, in 1985, 1993, and 1997, the first two edited by sociologists (Marc Maffesoli and Gabriel Gosselin), the third by a group called *Rencontres sociologiques de Besançon* (Sociological Encounters at Besançon) at the Université de Franche-Comté. One notable feature of these collections is that the titles of the first two refer to anthropology, not sociology, while the third calls Balandier a "socio-anthropologist."[325] Given that the editors of all three volumes are closer to sociology, their insistence on Balandier's identity as anthropologist seems to be a response to his own desire to be identified with that discipline, later in his life.

Balandier's solidarity with sociology remained strong until the early 1970s. He introduced *Sens et puissance (Meaning and Power)* in 1971 as "a new conception of . . . the sociological enterprise."[326] In the following years, however, the language of anthropology began to predominate.[327] There was, however, another aspect of Balandier's late work, which Jean Copans calls his "second paradigmatic career," in which he published books on broad social theoretical topics such as "accelerated globalization" and "super-modernity" (*surmodernité*).[328] This actually seems to mark a third, not a second career, insofar as it differs from both his earliest work as a "sociologist of black Africans" and his self-described anthropological orientation afterwards.

Following Balandier's death in 2016, several positive articles about him appeared in French anthropological journals. Ironically, the leading professional French sociology journal since 1960, *Revue française de sociologie*, never published an article by or about Balandier.[329] There are several reasons for Balandier's invisibility in histories of French sociology. The first is the disavowal of colonial research during the immediate postcolonial period, which carved a gaping hole in the discipline's collective memory. A second reason is the unfamiliarity of Balandier's field sites, located in what are today some of the poorest countries in Africa and the world. Third, Balandier never created a unified theoretical system comparable to Lévi-Straussian structuralism or Bourdieusian field theory. Finally, Balandier rejected the "positivist" approach based on universal law-like causal statements and "scientific" orientations centered around technological fixes and large datasets. Although appreciative of many trends in American social science, especially anthropology, Balandier agreed with Gurvitch, whom he described as a bulwark against American "scientific imperialism."[330] Colonialism has only started to be accepted as a sociological topic in France in recent years, after a decades-long abeyance, and mainly among Bourdieusians, a group with which Balandier had few contacts.

Another Intellectual Mutiny

As we will see in the next chapter, Balandier has gotten off lightly compared to Bourdieu in terms of polemical misreadings. The sheer indifference of most French sociologists to Africa, and colonialism, especially after the 1960s, has made Balandier a less important target. Balandier's critics come from other disciplines. Historian John K. Thornton, for example, states that Balandier's methodology "assumed a static structure."[331] This can only be read as the projection of a stereotype about unhistorical sociologists onto a body of work that was defined, as we have seen, by its historicism and dynamism. Art historian Cécile Froment asserts without citing any evidence that Balandier was "ethnocentric." This disregards Balandier's explicit arguments against ethnocentrism and racism throughout his entire career and his participation in *Présence africaine* and other ventures that defied enthocentrism.[332] Perhaps Froment was disturbed by Balandier's critique of certain French art historians who ignored colonialism's devastation of African art.[333]

The critiques by Thornton and Froment rehearse a familiar trope of the agency of the oppressed, and the related insinuation that foregrounding structural constraints in social science is the intellectual equivalent of suppressing agency. Viewed as a whole, however, Balandier's work is focused on the dialectics of structure and agency. As Jean-Paul Colleyn observes, "far from emphasizing Africa's curses and sufferings *ad nauseam*, Georges Balandier never stopped insisting on Africa's creativity."[334] Beginning with his youthful novel, Balandier suggested that imperious structures and contingent external events are crushing and unavoidable, but that it is still sometimes possible to forge a *project* that maneuvers through and around these constraints.

CHAPTER FOURTEEN

Pierre Bourdieu

THE CREATION OF SOCIAL THEORY IN THE CAULDRON OF COLONIAL WAR

In my view, the history of sociology, understood as an exploration of the scientific unconscious of the sociologist through the explication of the genesis of problems, categories of thought, and instruments of analysis, constitutes an absolute prerequisite for scientific practice.

—PIERRE BOURDIEU (1992)[1]

Texts that are inertly of their time stay there: those which brush up unstintingly against historical constraints are the ones we keep with us, generation after generation.

—EDWARD SAID, *FREUD AND THE NON-EUROPEAN*[2]

IN MAKING SENSE OF the sociology produced in and around French colonies in this book, I have drawn extensively on Bourdieu's theory of the dynamics of social fields.[3] Seen from a different angle, the present book has reconstructed some of the conditions of possibility for the genesis of Bourdieu's analytic framework, and thus my own. We now have assembled the tools with which to analyze the genesis of Bourdieu's theoretical framework.

Bourdieu is the most widely cited sociologist and the second-most widely cited author in the human and social sciences in the world today.[4] It would be impossible to do justice to the ever-expanding ocean of literature on Bourdieu without devoting an entire book to it. Yet the majority of the secondary literature on Bourdieu focuses on his empirical studies of metropolitan France.[5] The influence of Bourdieu's Algerian research on his mature thinking has not yet been fully understood. One commentator notes that "Bourdieu first came to the attention of scholars in what he often referred to as an 'Anglo-Saxon,'

English-speaking academic world ... [who] read Bourdieu with little reference to his voluminous work on Algeria carried out in the 1950s and early 1960s," and adds "if we had done so, we may have understood" Bourdieu better.[6]

After a brief biographical discussion, the first section of this chapter examines Bourdieu's research on Algeria and colonialism between 1957 and 1964 in order to situate it within the contexts of social research on colonialism at the time. This early work falls into four main parts. *Sociologie de l'Algérie* is a brief, systematic analysis of the impacts of colonialism on Algeria's colonized populations. Second, in a series of articles, Bourdieu develops a theory of modern colonial war and analyzes the post-independence Algerian government. Third, in the book *Travail et travailleurs en Algérie* and a series of essays, Bourdieu analyzes the sense of temporality among Algerian proletarians, unemployed, and underemployed workers. In a final set of writings, Bourdieu analyzes the French army's mass resettlement of Algerians during the war. The key publications here, coauthored with Abdelmalek Sayad, are *Le déracinement* (*Uprooting*) and "*Paysans déracinés*" ("Uprooted Peasants"). Bourdieu and Sayad focus on the spatial and social-technical effects of colonialism on peasants who have been "depeasanted" in the context of the war.

In the chapter's second section I examine a specific line of criticism that goes to the heart of my arguments about Bourdieu's Algerian work. Bourdieu's prominence has made him the target of a stunning array of attacks. Some of these barely merit a response, as with the claims that Bourdieu was an "intellectual terrorist,"[7] a self-help guru for academics,[8] a leftist activist posing as a scholar,[9] a theorist of "order and social reproduction,"[10] or an anti-Semite.[11] Some commentators mischaracterize Bourdieu's thinking by relating it to the traditions of Anglo-American social science with which they are most familiar.[12] The omnipresence of Bourdieu, especially in France, means that these various postures and positions vis-à-vis his thought could be used to map entire sociological fields. I ignore these criticisms in this chapter and focus on the claim that Bourdieu reiterated the ages-old colonial vision of the Kabyle as noble primitives.

The chapter's third section tracks the influence of Bourdieu's colonial-era studies on his mature concepts and theories. I examine the colonial origins of Bourdieu's concepts of habitus, practice, strategy, and domination, cultural and symbolic capital, and social fields. I conclude with a discussion of Bourdieu's approach to questions of social epistemology.

Biographical Notes

Bourdieu was born on August 1, 1930 in Denguin, a village in the Béarn region of the Pyrénées-Atlantique in southwestern France. Bourdieu's mother completed her schooling until the age of 16; his father was able to advance to the position of local postmaster despite never completing the *certificate d'études*.

Bourdieu excelled in school and was sent to *lycée* in Pau as a boarder, where his stellar performance led to his admission to the most prestigious secondary school in France, the *Lycée Louis-le-Grand* in Paris. After completing his *baccalauréat*, Bourdieu passed the examination to enter the *École normale supérieure* in 1951. He was initially interested in earning an *agrégation* degree in Spanish, with a second preference for the study of Letters.[13] He soon reoriented himself toward philosophy. His thesis was a critical translation of Leibniz's *Animadversiones [Remarks] on the General Part of Descartes' Principles of Philosophy*.[14] In 1954, Bourdieu passed the *agrégation* examination in philosophy at the top of his class. He terminated his education at the *École normale supérieure* after three years, rather than continuing on toward a further degree, and spent a year teaching philosophy at a *lycée* in Auvergne (1954-1955). During this year, the philosopher Georges Canguilhem agreed to supervise Bourdieu's doctoral thesis. The working title of the thesis, as reported by Canguilhem, was "L'émotion comme structure temporelle: essai d'interprétation des données physiologiques" (Emotions as Temporal Structure: Interpretation of Physiological Facts).[15] Here, we see one of the crucial sources of Bourdieu's analytic framing of his study of Algerian workers (discussed below), which focused on their subjective sense of time.

Bourdieu was drafted into the army in 1955, a year after the start of the Algerian War. He spent three months in military classes in Chartres, and then entered the army's psychological service in Versailles. After vigorous disagreements with his superiors due to his opposition to the war, Bourdieu joined the air force and was sent to Algeria. He was punished with additional months of military service for his resistance to the war, serving a total of 30 months at a time when the required service was two years.[16] Bourdieu was first posted to the Chélif valley, where he later conducted some interviews and observations in resettlement camps. In Orléansville, Bourdieu was put in charge of guarding munitions. Thanks to his mother's contact with an officer from the Béarn region who was posted in Algeria, Bourdieu was detached to the office of the General Government. His recognized brilliance due to his *agrégation* examination played a role in his assignment to the colony's Information Service in the role of "Editor-Creator" (*Rédacteur concepteur*). He was put in charge of tracking international public opinion about Algeria and writing reports for the media and the United Nations. More specifically, Bourdieu was involved in drafting parts of a report that was internally referred to as "the Bible,"[17] whose purpose was to call into question the legitimacy of any international intervention in Algeria and to call attention to the crimes committed by Algerian rebels and the aid given to them by communist countries. Amín Pérez has determined Bourdieu's authorship of specific sections of the report concerning the University of Algiers, reforms in mass education, and French contributions to social progress in the colony.[18] The focus of Bourdieu's contributions is important in light of the role of developmentalist reforms in colonial sociology (chapter 4) and the importance of Bourdieu's criticism of public educational systems starting in the 1960s. In April 1957, Bourdieu was involved in updating a dossier for the United Nations. Here, he argued that Algeria was not a stereotypical "exploitation colony" in which the dominant power focuses only on "good investments," but that Algeria represented a "humanistic endeavor." The agrarian population, Bourdieu wrote, was moving into industrial and commercial employment. This was presented as evidence that Algeria was not a conventional colony in which modern employment was reserved for settlers.[19]

These activities directly influenced Bourdieu's research interests and ideas after the completion of his military service. Between 1958 and 1964, Bourdieu argued systematically against all of the points he had developed in the reports for the Information Service. He demonstrated that the war was brutally accelerating the decimation of Algerian social structures, and that white settlers monopolized the best working-class jobs in the colony. His earlier involvement in producing government propaganda led him to insist vehemently on the separation between scholarship and politics, and to reject Sartre's definition of the committed intellectual. Ultimately, these experiences were channeled into Bourdieu's model of scientific fields as divided between autonomous and heteronomous poles, his concept of the collective intellectual, and his decolonizing critique of colonial sociology. I will develop each of these arguments below.

Rather than returning to France at the end of his military service, Bourdieu began lecturing at the University of Algiers in the fall of 1957. At least a portion of his teaching covered sociology as part of the relevant philosophy certificate. At the University of Algiers, Bourdieu was known to support "the handful of progressive students," who included Sayad and the future sociologist Alain Accardo.[20] In 1958, Bourdieu published *Sociologie de l'Algérie* and an article on the Algerian Mozabites. This work was based mainly on library research, but all of his subsequent Algerian publications were based on firsthand empirical research. Bourdieu returned to France in 1960, and his direct involvement in Algerian fieldwork dwindled after a few additional research visits during school vacations to complete his study of the resettlement camps. In the following years, however, Bourdieu drew repeatedly on his Algerian research in an array of projects.

Between 1957 and 1960, Bourdieu was embarking on his scholarly career, and the discipline he chose was sociology. As a philosophy student socialized into that discipline's traditional disdain for the social sciences, Bourdieu may have required the shock of Algeria in order to begin paying attention to such an "ignoble" discipline and to such mundane empirical objects. According to Bourdieu, his Algerian episode was "the pivotal moment" in his "transition from philosophy to sociology."[21] While this transition seemed improbable to Bourdieu himself at the time, and while he often commented on the low prestige of sociology relative to philosophy, there are certainly some reasons for his disciplinary move that he did not seem to recognize. In the 1950s, sociology was the academic discipline most critical of colonialism and most interested in the effects it was having on colonized societies. There was an elective affinity between Bourdieu's anticolonialism and sympathy for Algerians and the "pariah" discipline of sociology.

For the rest of his life, Bourdieu remained first and foremost a sociologist. When he returned to Paris in 1960, he joined Aron's *Centre de sociologie européenne*, and became Aron's teaching assistant at the Sorbonne during the 1960-1961 academic year.[22] In 1961, Bourdieu took up a post for three years teaching sociology at Lille. In 1964, he assumed a position as *Directeur d'études* at the Sixth Section of the *École pratique des hautes études*. In 1968, he took over the *Centre de sociologie européenne*. In 1981, Bourdieu was awarded the Sociology chair at the *Collège de France*, previously held by Halbwachs and Aron.[23]

Bourdieu's Research in Late Colonial Algeria

Bourdieu's military experience seems to have increased his determination to explain the Algerian situation accurately to the French public. As he stated pointedly in the introduction to his "sociological essay" in *Travail et travailleurs en Algérie*, "everyone knows that to describe is to denounce" in situations like the present one.[24] The time Bourdieu spent in the Information Service also seems to have made him more critical of reformers like Germaine Tillion, who argued for Algeria's assimilation to France rather than its independence. The most important evidence for Bourdieu's rejection and critical analysis of colonialism is contained in three books—*Sociologie de l'Algérie*, *Travail et travailleurs en Algérie*, and *Le déracinement*—and a handful of essays written at the time.[25] These publications develop an unsparing critique of colonialism's racism and its destruction of Algerian lives and social structures.

FRENCH COLONIALISM AS A RACIAL ORDER: *SOCIOLOGIE DE L'ALGÉRIE* AND "THE CLASH OF CIVILIZATIONS"

Sociologie de l'Algérie is the place to begin a reconstruction of Bourdieu's thought. It is, however, an anomalous publication in his oeuvre. *Sociologie de l'Algérie* appeared in the popular *Que sais-je* series, a collection of short introductory texts written for students and a lay readership published by the Presses Universitaires de France. In 1986, Bourdieu described his decision to publish this book as one of a "range" of his "bizarre actions" at the time, which also included his abandonment of philosophy for sociology. Bourdieu also suggested that the book made "no impact at all," but this is dubious.[26] Such retrospective judgments do not do justice to the historical context of the war, when reaching a mass audience was crucial. *Sociologie de l'Algérie* was Bourdieu's only book from the Algerian period that appeared in English until 1979, and it is still in print in its eighth French edition. Bourdieu obviously cared enough about the book to continue revising it. Soon after the book was published, Bourdieu wrote in a letter to the historian André Nouschi, a founder of the modern history of colonial Algeria, that he had "the feeling" that he had "done something useful," despite having heard "a thousand venomous and bilious remarks" from the Algiers "specialists."[27] Nouschi praised the book for its "moderate but incisive approach."[28] Nouschi also recalled that *Sociologie de l'Algérie* was received with "ironic distance by those who regarded themselves as connoisseurs of Algerian society," especially the established scholars at the University of Algiers. The book was "political" and "intended to undermine the schemas that the sociologists of the *École d'Alger* continued to disseminate," according to Nouschi.[29] *Sociologie de l'Algérie* represents Bourdieu's first critical analysis of colonialism and contains some of the germs of his eventual conceptual apparatus.

The first chapter in the first edition of the book, published in 1958, argues that it is better to speak of Berberophones and Arabaphones than "Berbers and Arabs."[30] Even this approach was something of a simplification, however, as Bourdieu explained in a later interview, as many Algerians were bilingual in Arabic and one of the Berber languages.[31] Nevertheless, he steadfastly resisted cultural reification, not to mention any language of race, which is entirely absent from his thinking.

With this caveat regarding terminology in mind, the next four chapters offer portraits of four somewhat distinct Algerian cultures. This is particularly true of the second edition from 1961, and all subsequent editions. In each chapter, Bourdieu discusses the "changes introduced by colonialism." Moreover, he notes that each of the Algerian civilizations had "already been changing before the war."[32] This refutes the claim that these chapters construct a reified "time before a time."[33] Bourdieu uses a combination of synchronic and diachronic discourse, briefly reconstructing social "mutations" during both the precolonial and colonial eras. The first two chapters deal with the Kabyles and the Chaoui. Bourdieu points out that these Berber civilizations had been in contact with various "imperialisms" for many centuries. This made it impossible for Bourdieu to indulge in any portrait of eternal traditions or to traffic in the "Kabyle myth" (see below).[34] Nonetheless, the Chaoui in the Aurès mountains had been isolated enough to preserve certain "ancient social structures."[35] As we will see below, Bourdieu went on to analyze the brutal military dislocation of even the most isolated Berber communities during the forced resettlements.

Chapter 4 of *Sociologie de l'Algérie* deals with the Mozabites, a Berber civilization of Ibadi Muslims living in ancient cities in the Mzab region at the edge of the Sahara in Algeria's south.[36] In a discussion that recalls Balandier's analyses of the Lébou and Bakongo (chapter 13), Bourdieu describes the Mozabites as continuously responding to external interventions in ways that modify "secondary elements" of their culture while maintaining their "fundamental values."[37] The secondary values in question, significantly, are economic ones, while the more fundamental values, Bourdieu argues, are religious. According to Bourdieu, the Mozabites' cultural survival depended on having a large number of their men working as financiers in cities and towns outside their homeland. Mozabite women, on the other hand, were forbidden to leave the Mzab, thereby constituting a force for cultural preservation. This gendered division of labor, which strategically modulated outside perturbations, was perfected over centuries. Bourdieu mentions the Mozabites' subjection to French rule, their response to the colonizer's requirement to select indigenous indirect administrators (*cadis*), and their exposure to the rationalized, technical, capitalist world.[38]

This discussion already refutes the argument that Bourdieu forced Algerian society into a straightjacket of immobile traditionalism and denied Algerians the "reflexive and critical capacities to navigate successfully between . . . worlds."[39] To the contrary, Bourdieu pointed to the Mozabites as illustrating that "the maintenance of stability, far from excluding change, presupposes the capacity to modify oneself to adapt to new situations."[40] His analysis here anticipates both his later theory of practice as simultaneously strategic and unconscious, and his critical refutation of structuralist theories of social reproduction. It also illustrates the paradoxical importance of the money economy for maintaining tradition, both before and during the colonial era. Capitalism, Bourdieu argues, was a precondition for the reproduction of *precapitalist* traditions. The importance of this example for Bourdieu at the time is suggested by the fact that his only other publication in 1958 was a pamphlet on the Mozabites.[41]

The book's next chapter turns to the Arabic-speaking peoples of the high plateaus and cities.[42] Bourdieu distinguishes among three groups: city dwellers, nomads (whose numbers declined following the French conquest), and the "new sedentary people." The 1863 *Senatus Consulte* and other colonial laws were aimed at hastening "the disintegration of the tribal structure," and they had largely succeeded.[43] The Arabic speakers were located in the regions most desirable for European settlement; as such, they experienced "most directly and most deeply the shock of colonization."[44] This chapter is again quite remote from suggesting any fantasy of a "time before a time" or of a society reproducing itself without change.

In the penultimate chapter, Bourdieu examines the emergence of a *common Algerian culture* before French rule and during the colonial era.[45] While noting that "it is obvious that Algeria, considered in isolation from the rest of the Maghreb, does not constitute a true cultural unit," Bourdieu argues that something like a distinctive Algerian civilization emerged over the *longue durée* through interactions among Berbers, Arabs, and Jews. No group escaped Algeria's "intense cultural interpenetration."[46] Just as there is a "Berber rock . . . just beneath the surface of Muslim legislation," by the same token, Kabyle law is shaped by "the invasion of Qur'anic law."⁴⁷ He suggests that while Islam permeates Algeria, this cannot be understood in terms of cultural conquest. Instead, there is a general "structural affinity" between Islam and Algerian society. Islam enunciates "tacit rules of conduct" that existed before Islamicization. "Algerian society has retained those answers which consecrate, that is to say corroborate and ratify, sanction and sanctify, the answer that it had already provided by the fact of its existence." Islam added to this by giving "Algerian traditionalism its specific character."⁴⁸ This is Bourdieu's first discussion of the invention of tradition, which will become more elaborate over time, as discussed below. Bourdieu also suggests here that colonialism and war have intensified Algerian nationalism and religiosity. Muslim religious observance has become a way of "defending personal identity." Echoing Balandier's study of Equatorial Africa just a few years earlier, Bourdieu argues that the new nationalist and religious movements were essentially anticolonial.

The last chapter of *Sociologie de l'Algérie* is called "Disintegration and Distress" (*Désagrégation et désarroi*).⁴⁹ This title amplifies Bourdieu's statement that Algeria has experienced a form of "social vivisection" by the French for 130 years. This chapter is a direct critique not only of the pro-colonial professors and students at the University of Algiers, but of liberals such as Tillion. In the 1961 revised edition, this concluding chapter also discusses the ways in which revolution was simultaneously accelerating colonialism's destructive effects while laying the groundwork for a new society. The chapter is subdivided into three sections, on "the colonial system," "the colonial society," and "the total disruption of a society." The first section rephrases Balandier's argument that colonial society is a "situation" (Bourdieu cites Balandier in the book's first edition), encompassing both the "colonial system" and "colonial society." Paraphrasing Balandier, Bourdieu defines the colonial system as giving "meaning to all forms of behavior."⁵⁰

Bourdieu proposes several different "laws" of colonialism, although it is important to keep in mind that he did not use the word law in the positivist or modernization theoretic sense.⁵¹ Instead, these "laws" refer to theses about formations of cultural change under colonialism. Bourdieu argues that: (1) certain aspects of the cultural system change more rapidly than others, leading to social disequilibrium; (2) there are limits on possible borrowings between cultures; (3) borrowed items are reinterpreted and altered in the new setting by the receiving culture; (4) all cultural elements are interconnected. These ideas are familiar from Mauss, Bastide, Balandier, and Aron, revealing the extent to which Bourdieu was immersed in French intellectual history and French colonial studies.

The chapter's second section analyzes "colonial society," which refers here to the colonizers. Though short, this section is significant, since social studies of colonialism rarely encompassed the colonizers. Bourdieu argues that the colonizers tend to adhere to a pervasive "racism" that produces "natives" and rationalizes "the existing state of affairs so as to make it appear to be a lawfully instituted order." A racist rule of difference is so powerfully embedded within the colonial system that it transforms even nonracist Frenchmen into racists: "it is the colonial situation that makes the racist."[52] Racism, for Bourdieu, is the core structure of the colonial polity.[53] The colonial system, he writes, "creates the 'contemptible' person at the same time as it creates the contemptuous attitude" that defines him.[54]

In the last section, Bourdieu summarizes his overarching argument about the disaggregation of Algerian culture. Colonialism has created a dualistic society in which every institution and individual is internally divided. For example, in Kabylia and the Aurès, the "djemaâ of the kharrouba" (fraction) "continues to function at the same time as the djemaâ of the douar"—i.e., the official colonial village.[55] This final section also focuses on the revolutionary war itself. Bourdieu argues that the war, with its "population regroupings, rural exodus, and atrocities," is aggravating divisions.

In the 1958 edition, Bourdieu refers to the war euphemistically as the "current conflict." This is part of what he meant by the "cautious tone" his publisher forced him to adopt. Bourdieu promised Nouschi at the time that he would go "very much further in [his] conclusions" in the book published by the Secrétariat social d'Alger the following year. Indeed, he also went "much further" in the 1961 edition of *Sociologie de l'Algérie*. The 1958 edition concludes that the "conflict" was "objectively grounded in . . . the deregulation of a vital order and the destruction of a universe of values." This indicated to any careful reader that Bourdieu was referring to a process that could not be contained by liberal reforms.[56] The 1961 edition argues that "[it] is only if the colonial system is *radically destroyed*" that a "new social ensemble" based on the "active, creative, and deliberative participation" of all Algerians becomes possible.[57] Bourdieu continued to update the concluding section in subsequent editions, taking into account changes in Algerian politics after independence.

Bourdieu sharpened his critique of colonialism in "The Clash of Civilizations," an essay published in 1959 in a volume edited by the Secrétariat social d'Alger, an organization created and directed by the Jesuit social researcher Henri Sanson.[58] The essay begins by comparing the conquest of Algeria, American Indians, and Black Africans. If Bourdieu had been forced in 1957 to argue that Algeria was not a colony, and had referred in 1958 euphemistically to the war, his opening lines in 1959 struck a profoundly different chord. Bourdieu now argued that while there were different styles of "native policies" in different colonies, including assimilation and reservations, the basic principles of colonialism were universal. Like Balandier, he criticized the acculturation literature (Herskovits, Linton, and Redfield) for ignoring colonialism. Using the example of the Algerian Chaoui, he argued that their civilization had indeed been disrupted by the processes discussed by the American acculturationists: a demographic burst, the exhaustion of cultivable soil, influx of market society, and so on. At the same time, the destructuring impact of acculturation was accentuated by colonial policies such as the replacement of existing political structures with *douars*, which imitated the metropolitan municipality, and the individualization of land ownership, which led to a decline in collective property.[59] In colonial situations, Bourdieu concluded, social changes express an interaction between "external forces," including colonial overrule and the "incursion of western civilization," and "internal forces" stemming from the preexisting structures of the "autochthonous civilization." The explicit comparison of internal and external causal factors again immediately recalls Balandier's framework. What Bourdieu added to this was the argument that the interaction between external and internal forces is "effected within a field, whose originality cannot be overlooked."[60] Here, we see Bourdieu already alluding to something like a colonial field of power; I will return in a moment to these early traces of his field concept.[61]

It is difficult to find any evidence in these early writings that Bourdieu was beguiled by images of timeless, repetitive, or "cold" cultures. It is equally unconvincing to argue that Bourdieu's analysis is politically neutral, given its merciless description of colonialism's devastation of Algerian society and his explicit support for the revolution.[62] As we will see below, Bourdieu argued that the Algerian proletariat, rather than peasants and the unemployed, were the true revolutionary force—a theme that was far from politically neutral.

BOURDIEU'S ESSAYS ON COLONIAL WAR AND REVOLUTION: FROM ANTICOLONIAL STRUGGLE TO THE THEORY OF PRACTICE

Bourdieu wrote three important essays in the 1958–1964 period that developed a theory of modern colonial warfare and analyzed the post-independence Algerian government. The first is "*Guerre et mutation sociale en Algérie*" (War and Social Change in Algeria) from 1960. In this piece, Bourdieu presents the idea of a specifically colonial form of war and its effects, along with a theory of decolonization. The sociological results of colonial war take both direct and indirect forms, he argues. Directly, the war provides the "dominated caste" with a language and a voice, disrupting the colonial "logic of humiliation." Indeed, the war was leading the Algerian people to assume responsibility for their own destiny. Indirectly, war reinforced existing disorder and decay. A nebula of small, highly structured communities was replaced by a dust storm of fragmented individuals without attachments to others or to their own past. The old values of honor collapsed under the onslaught of the war's cruelties and atrocities. Thousands of Algerian men joined the maquis, fled into exile, or were sent to prison or internment camps. Algerian women became more independent as they were compelled to take on responsibilities that had previously belonged to men. The new Algeria would thus have to be based on Algerians' active, creative, and deliberative participation in a common program, not on a chimera of ancient traditions, now irretrievably lost.

In "*Révolution dans la révolution*" (The Revolution Within the Revolution), published in *Esprit* in 1961, Bourdieu constructs *revolutionary war* as a distinct analytic object. "Only a revolution," he argues, "can abolish the colonial system." War reveals the true basis of the colonial order: a system in which the dominant caste maintains its dominance through violence. Anticolonial revolution cannot be theorized as a class struggle, because colonialism is a *caste* system, not a class system. Although the war reinforced social disorder, it simultaneously served to partly overcome the fragmentation of the Algerian people.

The most original aspect of this essay is its sophisticated theory of traditionalism. Bourdieu's discussion of this topic further invalidates claims that he adhered to an old-fashioned tradition-vs.-modernity framework. First, he argues, there is "traditional traditionalism"—Algerian cultures as they existed before colonialism. Second is "colonial traditionalism," an invented version of traditionalism used by colonial rulers to dominate, humiliate, divide and conquer, and rule indirectly. Third, he refers to a "pathological traditionalism" or a "traditionalism of despair." Fourth is "anticolonial traditionalism," a neotraditionalism that emerges within anticolonial resistance movements. Bourdieu develops the example of the veil and the fez as everyday vestments that became signs used to express resistance during the war. Elimination of the veil was a prime objective of French assimilation policies. For Algerians, the veil became the ultimate symbol of non-reciprocity, breaking the "logic of humiliation" by refusing recognition. This was neotraditionalism, not "traditional traditionalism." In *Travail et travailleurs en Algérie*, published two years after this essay, Bourdieu suggests that class differentiation and inequality had proceeded so far that traditionalism itself was now "sometimes a luxury."[63] By calling attention to these different forms of traditionalism—and by speaking of *traditionalism* rather than *tradition*—Bourdieu was anticipating and even going beyond the literature on the invention of tradition that emerged three decades later.[64]

A third essay, published in 1962, "*De la guerre révolutionnaire à la revolution*" (From Revolutionary War to Revolution), represents Bourdieu's first attempt at analyzing post-independence Algeria. He begins with an argument for rejecting the idea of a "revolutionary revolution," that is, the mythical hope that revolution would transform Algerian society entirely. The first critique of this mythical argument is a sociological one. A huge number of Algerians had left their customary lives for the shantytowns and regroupment centers, and many were currently "floating between two cultures." In his parallel research on the unemployed, Bourdieu examined the phenomenon of "doubled" subjectivity in great detail. As the primary "victims of colonialism," the peasantry could not become a true revolutionary force, Bourdieu argued. The masses of unemployed and underemployed also represented a problematic social base for the post-independence state. Due to their economic insecurity, they did not have the material stability that would allow them to create plans and project their consciousness into the future. Their social views tended therefore to be incoherent and steeped in *ressentiment*. They did not understand colonialism as a system, but as a sort of evil god. Proletarians who were regularly employed and socially insured were better positioned to forge attitudes based on a rational conduct of life and a planned orientation toward the future. Here, Bourdieu reasonably assumes that the ability to plan one's personal life is relevant for the ability to understand government policies and participate in politics. The stably employed did not tend to regard the colonial era as a "poisoned chalice," all traces of which had to be eliminated after independence. Bourdieu suggested that the postcolonial government should not roll back social programs simply because they were created by the French during their "developmentalist" period. The proletariat would likely prefer that the regime downplay attacks on colonialism's legacies and focus on the internal contradictions of Algerian society instead.[65]

TRAVAIL ET TRAVAILLEURS EN ALGÉRIE: THE SOCIOLOGY OF COLONIAL LABOR

In the colonial situation, work is the pre-eminent locus of conflict between traditional models and those imported and imposed by colonization.

—BOURDIEU (1963)[66]

Bourdieu developed these ideas about the differences between proletarians and the unemployed and underemployed at greater length in his contributions to *Travail et travailleurs en Algérie*. This is a hybrid text. It is based on a large research project Bourdieu carried out in 1960 with the statisticians Alain Darbel, Jean-Paul Rivet, and Claude Seibel from the Algiers-based *Association pour la recherche démographique, économique et sociale* (Association for Demographic, Economic and Social Research), an organization partly staffed by researchers from the metropolitan statistics office. The statisticians carried out a questionnaire survey of 12,376 European and Muslim inhabitants of Algeria. Bourdieu used a research team drawn from his University of Algiers students, including Sayad, in a series of projects, including a study of the material conditions and political views among those who had been resettled in the "new villages." *Travail et travailleurs en Algérie* begins with a short introduction by Bourdieu titled "Statistics and Sociology," followed by 250 pages of survey results presented by the statisticians. The second half of the book is a 300-page "*Étude sociologique*" (Sociological Study) by Bourdieu that combines photographs by Bourdieu, open-ended interviews, data analysis, and theoretical reflection. This "sociological study" begins with a second "introduction" that discusses the epistemological, political, and methodological problems raised by research in colonial settings.

The first introduction, "Statistics and Sociology," is essentially an argument in favor of interdisciplinarity that defines the different tasks of the two disciplines. The discussion reveals, first, that social science disciplines were already firmly enough established for the question of interdisciplinarity to be posed explicitly. Bourdieu is also affirming the value of team research, which he continued to emphasize throughout his career and reframed using the category of the "collective intellectual." Most important, however, he is arguing that statistical empiricism has little value unless it is integrated into a theoretical (sociological) framework. The statistical method, he writes, allows researchers to grasp certain "causal linkages" that the sociologist then endows "with meaning," using "interpretive hypotheses." In other words, "statistical data" are only actually "'explained' if they are interpreted in a manner which reclothes the particular case with meaning." Bourdieu refers back to his earlier approach in *Sociologie de l'Algérie*, where he argued that "only knowledge of previous cultural models can allow us to grasp the meaning of behaviors that always refer back to these models, even when they betray them, transform them, or recreate them as a function of new situations."[67] This essentially restated Bachelard's argument for an objectivizing break with commonsense categories and perceptions—via statistics, in this case—while also insisting on the need for a further epistemic break in order to give meaning to those objectified facts. The emphasis on epistemic breaks, combining quantitative and qualitative methods, and integrating explanation and interpretation, are recurrent leitmotifs in all of Bourdieu's writing.

The section by Darbel, Rivet, and Seibel first examines family structures among Algeria's Muslim population. The authors then describe patterns of employment, unemployment, and migration both within Algeria and between Algeria and metropolitan France. The statisticians then turn their attention to the colony's European population. This is interesting in two respects. First, sociologists and ethnologists were inclined to ignore colonial settlers and administrators. Statisticians were more deeply ensconced within a scientific ethos of value-free research than sociologists. In their discussion of the European population, the statisticians attributed the migration of most of the Europeans into Algeria's largest cities and towns to the war, which they followed official French usage in referring to as "the events."[68]

Bourdieu's overarching argument in the subsequent section, "*Étude sociologique*," is that colonialism has produced massive unemployment by uprooting Algerian peasants and propelling them into cities and resettlement camps. His guiding question asks how these deracinated masses and the more stabilized proletarians relate differently to the project of overthrowing the colonial regime and building a new society. The first chapter in this section examines hiring processes among Europeans and Muslims. Directly contradicting the reports he had written for the colony's information service, Bourdieu presents evidence of rampant discrimination against Algerians in hiring practices, which is one reason for their higher rates of unemployment. He describes European settlers as having stronger internal ties of "caste" solidarity, leading them to favor one another in hiring decisions. Bourdieu finds that Europeans living and working in a given city typically know one another personally, whereas Algerians generally don't socialize with co-workers outside the workplace.[69]

Bourdieu goes on to analyze attitudinal differences between employed, underemployed, and unemployed Algerians. The underemployed workers tend to direct their revolt against individual situations or persons, not against the entire colonial organization. They tend to have distinctive stereotypical views of their workplace superiors. The French boss is regarded as a kind of second father; the foreman is disdained as "white trash" if he is Spanish or Italian, or as a caste "traitor" if he is Algerian. Work also generates catastrophic and despairing forms of subjectivity and a belief in magic among the under- and unemployed. They see the economic and social world as being dominated by a malignant and all-powerful will.[70]

Among highly qualified Algerian workers, there is often a narrowing of the "field of social relations," a "forced individualism," and an overall "*embourgeoisement*."[71] Bourdieu quotes a manual laborer from Oran who states, "[a]t work, it's everyone for himself, and after work everyone stays in his own home."[72] Bourdieu argues that the more materially stable working class is detached enough from their social situation to constitute it as an object in thought and action. They are able to conceptualize and plan for the future both in their individual lives and in terms of the revolutionary project of building a new society. Bourdieu's sociology of Algerian subjectivity is thus situated between the poles of structural determinism and an untethered free will—just as subjectivity in general will be, in his mature social theory.

In a related article, "Traditional Society's Attitude towards Time and Economic Behavior" (1963), Bourdieu analyzes the temporal structure of emotions and the emotional basis of the sense of time. This is a classic theme in phenomenological and Bergsonian philosophy, and is very close to Bourdieu's original thesis topic, "emotions as temporal structure." Bourdieu distinguishes here between two words meaning "future" in French: *avenir* and *futur*. He renders the first as *a-venir*, meaning, "to come." This orientation is dictated by the imitation of the past and faithfulness to the values of forebears, which configures time as endless repetition. This can be distinguished from an orientation toward the future as "*futur*," which is related to predictions and risk-taking improvisation. These categories of *futur* versus *avenir* map onto the difference between proletarians, who are planning, predicting, and improvising "entrepreneurs" of their own lives, and the unemployed and

FIGURE 14.1. "In [photography and anthropology] there was this type of rapport that was both objectifying and affectionate at the same time"–Bourdieu. Source of photo: Jérôme Bourdieu; Fonds Pierre Bourdieu. Quote from Bourdieu, "Photographie d'Algérie. Entretien avec Pierre Bourdieu du 26 juin 2001 au Collège de France par Franz Schultheis," in Bourdieu, *Images d'Algérie* (Arles: Actes Sud, 2003), 28.

underemployed, who fall back on versions of traditionalism as foresight. This is a "forced regression," and it involves retreat into a mental state Bourdieu calls *mens momentanea*.[73] Bourdieu uses the same term, *mens momentanea*, in his final book of social theory, *Pascalian Meditations*, to describe an overly adaptive, unstable habitus.[74] The basic outlines of the theory of unstable and divided forms of habitus were thus already present in Bourdieu's Algerian research.

LE DÉRACINEMENT: THE SOCIOLOGY OF COLONIAL DISPOSSESSION

Le déracinement (*Uprooting*) is a study of the uprooting and resettlement of Algerians during the war of independence.[75] Bourdieu co-authored *Le déracinement* with Abdelmalek Sayad, who had just arrived in Paris in 1964 when the book came out and was trying to enter the *Centre national de la recherche scientifique*, with Bourdieu's support. Their collaboration represents, I believe, the first instance of co-authored sociological work on colonialism by a metropolitan citizen and a former colonial "subject." *Le déracinement* remains the most important account of the resettlement camps. The authors painted such a devastating picture of the relocation processes that the French government barred the book from being published until after the war. The book is based on a series of case studies, carried out between June and September of 1960. The goal was to contrast local variations among camps located in three regions: Collo, Kabylia, and the Chélif Valley.[76]

The book begins with an overview of the resettlement policies, which started in 1954 and became systematic after 1957. By 1961, more than a quarter of Algeria's Muslim population had been regrouped, and at least half of the rural population had left for the towns and cities, since most of the fighting was in the countryside. The expulsion was typically effected by military force.[77] The first chapter frames the uprooting as a continuation of nineteenth-century laws that displaced peasants to create land for settlers. The "depeasanted" peasants turned to raising cattle for immediate cash rather than sowing grain. The poorest peasants lost the forms of foresight that were once grounded in tradition. This was the origin of a "traditionalism of despair."[78] Some of the Kabyle regions in the high mountains that had remained almost untouched by colonialism were being emptied out. Resettlement was the limit form of the disruptive onslaught of colonialism, revealing the ultimate "*truth* about the colonial system."[79] Colonialism produced a *pathological acceleration* of cultural change, preventing any dialogue between permanence and alteration, assimilation and adaptation.[80] The war completed Algeria's subjection, 130 years after the initial conquest, while also digging colonialism's grave.

Bourdieu and Sayad used the same verb as Berque to describe the reterritorializing impetus of colonization, writing that the army *stamped* its structures onto the terrain.[81] The colonizer began by disciplining space as if, in doing so, they could also discipline human beings. Bourdieu and Sayad compared this to the Roman practice of centuration, a "system of coordinates marked on the ground" at the start of colonization. In this way, "Rome made a tabula rasa of the past by imposing the new framework on its conquests: either by indifference, or out of contempt, it ignored the pre-existing administrative organization and marked eminent property rights by minutely measuring its territorial conquest."[82]

The colonizer was following the rule according to which "the reorganization of the habitat" can transform an entire cultural system: "forced resettlement affects the whole of social life by transforming the organization of inhabited space (a schema projected onto the ground of social structures) and by breaking the ties of familiarity that unite individuals to their environment."[83] Bourdieu and Sayad's interviews in the Kerkera regroupment found that the inhabitants had three distinct images of the new settlements: a prison; nakedness; night-time darkness. Discussing the regroupment of Aïn-Aghbel, the authors describe a street that did not even have a name, as if the inhabitants refused to make the village familiar.[84] The resettlement program "pushed forward a homogenization of Algerian society" by "systematically imposing an identical organization of dwelling, even in the most remote regions."[85] Houses were laid out along wide roads that resembled a Roman *castrum*. In the center of the Algerian camp was "the triad characteristic of French villages" with a school, mayoral office, and monument to the French war dead.[86] Bourdieu and Sayad described the camp at Oum-Toub in the Collo region, where the transplanted population was "subjected to military order." The resettled were awakened by a bugle call; they left for work in the fields at set hours; curfew was announced by the ringing of a bell; a daily "report" informed the population of decisions taken from above, in "a caricature of both democratic consultation and the traditional assembly."[87]

French officials believed that a systematic "destructuration" of the Muslim population was the best way to break their resistance.[88] The goal was to produce "solidarities of a new type based above all on an identity of conditions of existence."[89] Populations from very different origins were therefore jumbled together. The camps furnished "a favorable terrain for cultural contagion," since "transplanted groups are prone to accelerated cultural change because they are too disorganized to be able to engage in regulatory activities."[90] The camps also stimulated the emergence of individualism. After a century of ambivalent policies toward Algerian assimilation, the camps were unambiguously geared toward making "the Algerian population 'evolve' toward social structures and attitudes of a Western type":

> [T]heir intention was to substitute for the clan or family unit (with a genealogical basis) a village unit (with a spatial base). The extended family, composed of several generations living according to a property and inheritance regime of indivision, would be replaced by a Western type of household. Thus in many places the "resettled" were obliged to construct as many houses as there were households.[91]

The "household in the Western sense" was to replace the conventional household form.[92]

One of the book's recurrent themes is the splitting or *dualism* of all aspects of colonial life. Chapter 2 is called "Two Societies, Two Histories," and chapter 8, "The Cultural Sabir." Sabir was a pidgin language used as a lingua franca in the Mediterranean Basin. The idea of a "cultural sabir" therefore refers to a hybrid culture, a "coexistence of contraries."[93] As we have seen throughout this book, many observers of colonial settings described practices of cultural mixing, doubling, and syncretism. *Le déracinement* expands on the theme in Bourdieu's *Sociologie de l'Algérie* of the *dédoublement* of the colonized subject. The "models of behavior and the economic ethos imported by colonization coexist, in each subject's mind, with the models and ethos inherited from

FIGURE 14.2. Example of individualized family homes in Algerian resettlement camp (ca. 1961). Xavier de Planhol, *Nouveaux villages algérois. Atlas blidéen, Chenoua, Mitidja occidentale* (Paris: Presses universitaires de France, 1961), plate 14. © Presses universitaires de France / Humensis, 1961.

FIGURE 14.3. Rectangular resettlement camp Sainte-Marguerite, Algeria (ca. 1961). Xavier de Planhol, *Nouveaux villages algérois*, plate 12. © Presses universitaires de France / Humensis, 1961.

ancestral tradition."[94] The authors compare Algerian perceptions of work to "the ambiguous forms in *Gestalttheorie*," which "might have two quite different readings, depending on the frame of reference used to interpret it."[95] In order to make sense of a social reality that is "objectively contradictory," they summarize, one "must simultaneously resort to two contradictory analytical grids; our fidelity to the contradictory reality forbids choosing between the contradictory aspects that make up this reality."[96] The destruction of traditional structures in Arab-speaking regions leads to an "anguish of individuals who are adrift between the ancient structures . . . and the modern structures."[97] Elsewhere, Bourdieu writes that every behavior "may be the object of a double reading, as it bears within itself reference to both logics," capitalist and

FIGURE 14.4. Le Mazdour camp, in style of French seventeenth-century Vauban fortifications (1960). Photo courtesy of Marc Garanger.

FIGURE 14.5. S'bara resettlement camp being built by its future inhabitants (June 1960). Photo courtesy of Marc Garanger.

traditional.[98] The attitude of the peasant of the Chélif valley, for example, was dominated by the feeling of incommensurability between the two universes. A peasant was "disinclined to transfer into his familiar universe everything he saw and experienced as the colonist's waged worker, such as the notions of return and profitability, and more generally, the convertibility of work into money."[99] Cultural dualism permeated the resettlement camps, where peasants who had "already taken certain liberties with tradition" were "placed in continuous contact" with "peasants attached to the traditional system of values."[100]

Le déracinement also discusses resistance and its variations. Resistance was much more intense in the more "integrated" Collo region than in the Chélif.[101] By 1960, the Algerian Liberation Army (ALN) had become "ensconced in the mountains," which were now "emptied of inhabitants."[102] By passively resisting the French military authorities and maintaining continuous contact with the ALN, the community in the resettlement camp reinforced the "self-esteem" of each individual, allowing "him to experience resettlement as a temporary ordeal." Revolt was an "index of integration" and a "force for integration, because it unites individuals in refusal and in hope."[103]

The "Two Algerias" Thesis

One slice of the critical literature on Bourdieu is important in the present discussion: the debate about whether there are "two Algerias" in Bourdieu's work—one historical, the other mythical; one emphasizing dynamic change, the other based on a static view; one "Occidentalist" or "Eurocentric," the other "Orientalist."[104] This is relevant here because the vision of Algeria as a mythical, eternal Orient was an essential tenet of the *École d'Alger*, the conservative bastion of Algerian studies at the University of Algiers against whom Bourdieu's earliest work was directed.[105]

The most extreme version of the "two Algerias" thesis argues that Bourdieu was taken in by the "Kabyle myth" that underwrote French colonial policies of divide and rule in Algeria.[106] Colonna asserts that Bourdieu believed that "history had not touched the Algerian peasants over the centuries."[107] Silverstein and Goodman suggest that Bourdieu's writing embraced "anthropology's colonial legacy"—"the fantasy of primordial cultural unity that underwrote the Kabyle Myth."[108] However, Bourdieu was highly critical of any "nostalgia for the agrarian paradises," which he called "the principle of all conservative ideologies."[109]

Another dubious claim is that the "doubling" of Bourdieu's own habitus can be mapped on to differing visions of Algeria. Bourdieu may indeed have had a divided habitus, as he himself suggested. This *habitus dédoublé* may even have helped him to understand Algeria.[110] Yet it is not evident which of the purported two bodies of literature on Algeria should be associated with the "rural" Bourdieu and which with the scholarly, Parisian Bourdieu. After all, many of the anthropologists who posed as connoisseurs of rural, indigenous cultures came from the upper classes and were embedded within Parisian institutions. A careful reading of Bourdieu's texts has to remain attentive to their proximate and distant contexts, to the evolution of texts through different rewritings, and to their internal logic and contradictions. None of this can justify the argument about a simple dualism in his views of Algeria, much less a correlation of these views with two sides of his split personality.

Some writers suggest that Bourdieu expressed "romanticizing" views of the Kabyle in interviews.[111] Leaving aside the point that off-the-cuff comments should not be taken as more decisive evidence than scholarly publications, the more important point is that even these interviews are being misinterpreted. Silverstein and Goodman criticize Bourdieu, for example, for agreeing with the Kabyle writer Mouloud Mammeri that images which "contain a bit of mythic millenarianism can have a political utility."[112] Yet Bourdieu should be taken literally here: mythic or millenarian images can be *politically* useful. This says nothing about their *scientific* validity. It is also highly significant that Bourdieu makes this statement in the course of a dialogue in which both participants sharply reject the mythology of a proverbial Kabylia. Mammeri criticizes "Kabyle intellectuals who are trying in a way to recuperate Kabyle society, a society that is, how shall I put it, that is ideal or mystical," who are "greatly drawn towards the ideal re-creation of [their] own society, particularly in reaction to the devaluing images that people who deny it try to give of it." Bourdieu replies that "this original state, *doubtless very mythical*, has been totally abolished." This means that "original Kabyle-ness" would represent "a kind of fantasy of return to origin," a "populist exaltation of the past" that is "both very understandable and very dangerous." Bourdieu concludes that "it is completely naïve or dangerous to hope to restore the old social order."[113] In a different interview, Bourdieu states unequivocally that "[i]n my view it was not at all helpful, even for an independent Algeria, to feed a mythical conception of Algerian society."[114] It is hard to imagine a sharper rejection of the Kabyle myth.

The two Algerias approach also ignores the very different contexts of Bourdieu's colonial-era writing and his subsequent uses of his Algerian material, which were mainly deployed in developing general theoretical arguments. Bourdieu did describe the Kabyle using a version of the "anthropological present tense" after the mid-1960s, but this always occurs in contexts where he is using his older ethnographic material to develop theory. At this point, he was no longer interested in describing the changes effected by colonialism—which had ended. He did not comment on developments in post-independence Algeria. Bourdieu's books *Outline of a Theory of Practice* (*Esquisse d'une théorie de la pratique*, 1972) and *Logic of Practice* (*Le sens pratique*, 1980) are not ethnographies of the Kabyle but works of social theory that draw on his earlier Algerian research.

[336] CHAPTER 14

Three case studies in which Bourdieu redeploys his Kabyle material underscore this point. First, in *Outline of a Theory of Practice*, Bourdieu discusses Kabyle marriage practices in order to criticize structuralist accounts of practice as rule-following, and to present a theory of practice as strategic and open-ended—as "regulated improvisation." Deviations from the prescribed rule of parallel-cousin marriage are theorized as strategic practice. This discussion shows how even the most traditional forms of traditionalism do not involve the simple execution of rules.

A second case is the discussion of sentiments of honor. Here again, Bourdieu mobilizes material from his Kabyle research. Practices around honor are not depicted as archaic and unchanging, but as a contradictory mix of older and colonial-contemporary traits. Bourdieu's essay "The Sentiment of Honour in Kabyle Society" (written in 1960 and first published in English in 1965) begins with several examples of transformations of Kabyle traditions of honor stemming from colonialism. One example involves a confrontation between a Kabyle "who was completely master of the [traditional] dialectic of challenge and riposte" and another who "had forgotten the technique and spirit of what he called 'Kabyle rhetoric'" because he had "lived for a long time outside Kabylia and . . . acquired certain western values." Another example depicts a Kabyle city dweller, "ignorant of the nuances of 'Kabylian rhetoric,'" who enters a dispute with a sharecropper who is better versed in Kabyle folkways. In a third case, a rich Kabyle family builds "a family tomb in European style . . . transgressing the rule which imposes anonymity and uniformity upon tombs."[115] Discussing a conflict around honor between two village factions, Bourdieu begins by pointing out that these factions only exist in "degenerated form." This reference to a "degenerated form" is deleted from the version of this essay published in *Algeria 1960*, again showing how important it is to compare versions published in different periods and different argumentative contexts.[116] Rather than depicting an Edenic view of the Kabyle, Bourdieu's discussions of honor recall the work of other colonial sociologists in the preceding decades who had described unstable cultural mixtures leading to constant, crisis-ridden change.

The third case is Bourdieu's renowned essay on the Kabyle house. This is apparently a clear exception in which Bourdieu embraces of a model of unified tradition. The essay is an elegant presentation of a set of symbolic oppositions that appear to be eternal, existing in a continuous cycling between subjects and their objects. However, we must pay close attention to the contexts in which Bourdieu produced and redeployed this essay. Drafted in 1960, the essay was first published in a *festschrift* for Lévi-Strauss in 1970.[117] In other words, it was written near the start of the period in which Bourdieu was, in his own account, fascinated with structuralism, and published at the end of that decade. It is an homage to a thinker Bourdieu credited with "ennobling" anthropology and for whom he had enormous respect.[118] The essay also demonstrates that

Bourdieu could perform as a virtuoso structuralist even at the moment when, in his other writing, he was explicitly transcending structuralism. In short, this essay stands out in Bourdieu's oeuvre because it was written for a unique, and uniquely structuralist, purpose. At the same time, it is the swan song of "blissful structuralism" in Bourdieu's thinking.

It is also interesting to examine Bourdieu's redeployment of the Kabyle house essay as an "Appendix" in the *Logic of Practice*, which was published after Bourdieu had fully developed his theory of fields and reflexivity. Here, the Kabyle house essay is used to illustrate the series of epistemological "breaks" discussed above. Bourdieu now presents the essay precisely as evidence for the evolution of his theory as an ongoing process moving from pre-notions to scientific objectification, and from there to a transcendence of the original objectification. Bourdieu argues that the static structural analysis of "The Kabyle House" represents a necessary first stage of "objectivist reconstruction" en route to the "more complete and complex" "final interpretation" centered on practice as strategy.[119] In other words, the essay is presented here as an example of the intermediate, objectifying, epistemic "break," and thus has the same function as statistical tables in *Travail et travailleurs*. In sum, there is much more than meets the eye, even in this example of a seemingly pure mythical Kabylia.

Bourdieu frequently presents a model of a unified habitus that is perfectly synchronized with its environment. Given Bourdieu's insistence in his colonial-era writing on *mismatches* between habitus and environment, this cannot be understood as a description of Kabyle culture. Bourdieu needed to posit such a "cold" ideal-type of the habitus in its simple, non-divided form in order to understand various axes and degrees of divergence between habitus and its social *Umwelt*.[120] In all of Bourdieu's empirical studies, starting with his Algerian research, the ideal-type of stability, of a habitus perfectly aligned with social structures, is disrupted by forces that open up gaps between habitus and world, divide habitus, and prevent some actors from even forming a coherent habitus.[121]

Colonial Tributaries of Bourdieu's Mature Theory

Excavating the Algerian origins of Bourdieu's categories is by no means intended to downplay the importance of other factors and intellectual traditions in the formation of his thought. At the most general level, Bourdieu's entire *Denkstil* is clearly that of a philosophy graduate from the *École normale supérieur* at the mid-twentieth century.[122] Bourdieu's concepts continued to evolve as a function of his ongoing research projects and the inner dialectics of his thought, and also his changing position within the constellations of the intellectual and scientific fields and the wider contexts discussed in this book. Bourdieu worked assiduously to maximize his own scientific autonomy, and to monitor and control the effects of non-scientific contexts on his thinking. Yet such scientific closure even in the best of cases could only be partial or "relative." This is illustrated by examples from Bourdieu's thinking. For instance, psychoanalytic concepts became increasingly prevalent in his vocabulary and guided his thinking in many ways, yet Bourdieu's overt relation to psychoanalysis, especially the dominant "French school," was hesitant and often hostile. This pattern can be explained by the powerful position of Lacanian psychoanalysis within the postwar French intellectual field and Bourdieu's perception of that formation as elitist and conservative.[123]

In addition to such uncontrolled influences on Bourdieu's thinking, each of his concepts was indebted to additional sources that Bourdieu acknowledged and that were situated outside of his Algerian experiences. This includes his concepts of *habitus*, *field*, and *cultural capital*, his *depth-realist ontology*, and his conception of the *role of the intellectual*.

Bourdieu was exposed to the idea of *habitus* in his philosophical training before leaving for Algeria. As discussed by Héran and Wacquant, the concept is an ancient one, traced back to Aristotle and translated into Latin as *habitus* by Thomas Aquinas, before entering early sociological theory (Durkheim, Weber, Mauss) and phenomenology, especially in the writings of Husserl, with which Bourdieu was closely familiar. Bourdieu's Algerian-era conceptualization of habitus was given a new direction by reading and commenting on Erwin Panofsky's *Gothic Architecture and Scholasticism*.[124] I have mentioned Bachelard's influence on Bourdieu's rethinking habitus as a spatially situated concept. Bourdieu's attunement to the idea of a *cleft* habitus was overdetermined by his own "doubled" experience of social class in addition to the even more intense doubling of colonial existence in Algeria.

The most immediate source of Bourdieu's *field theory* is Kurt Lewin, inventor of psychological field theory, whom Bourdieu was already reading and referring to in the late 1950s.[125] Bourdieu first tried to deploy Lewin's field approach in his Algerian research. Bourdieu's concept of the structuring of social space also owes much to Lévi-Straussian structuralism, even while Bourdieu elaborated his praxeology or practice theory in direct confrontation with structuralism.

The idea of *cultural capital* is indebted to Bourdieu's reading of Marx and Weber, the idea of classification struggles to his reading of Durkheim, and the notion of status competition to Veblen and others. Bourdieu's *depth-realist ontology* and his *critical epistemology* are explicitly indebted to the critique of pre-notions by Durkheim and Bachelard.[126] Bourdieu developed his theory of the *role of the intellectual* in politics in opposition to the notion of the "total intellectual" associated with Sartre and also to the kinds of intellectuals he associated with the French Communist Party, which he viewed as subordinating science to politics.

That said, Bourdieu's Algerian formulations are more than mere "pseudo-anticipations" of his later ideas. At the very least, they are "adumbrations" of his mature concepts, and sometimes they are much more than that.[127]

Without denying the importance of noncolonial intellectual sources and additional contextual influences on Bourdieu's work, I will focus here on the specifically Algerian and colonial origins of his thought.

Bourdieu's processual, historical version of sociology was born of his experience of an ongoing, catastrophic demolition of social structures, an all-encompassing social crisis, and a military revolution.[128] Of course, objective experience is not transmitted directly into thought but is mediated through cognitive categories, classificatory grids, and collective communications. Thus, while historians may generally agree on the characterization of the late colonial world as one of crisis, the key point for Bourdieu was that it was being described in these terms by many other critical thinkers at the time. It is a shortcut to argue that Bourdieu's own divided habitus operated like an epistemic "standpoint," allowing him to perceive the ubiquitous social divisions of colonial society. Bourdieu's perceptions of Algeria were filtered through the work of the writers discussed in this book, some of whom he read even before leaving for Algeria. Once there, Bourdieu witnessed policies of extreme symbolic and physical violence directed against Algerians. His sociology of conflict, antagonism, revolution, and change emerged from this experience. Bourdieu witnessed displays of extreme racism and rightwing settler discourse. This focused his attention on what he described as the core *racist* structure of the colonial regime and the role of academic scholarship in perpetuating it. Bourdieu's "initial discovery of radical deprivation of the weakest" in Algeria "opened the way to his theory of domination as [the] keystone of all social relations."[129] Direct political interference with his research lent additional vehemence to Bourdieu's argument for scientific autonomy. Bourdieu was able to discuss politics with Muslim students at the University of Algiers who supported the revolution, and to meet the Kabyle family of his coworker Abdelmalek Sayad. He was able to break through the colonizer-colonized barrier within academia and science in a more systematic way than even Balandier or Berque. Bourdieu's fieldwork brought him face to face with forms of cultural difference that made a mockery of economic models of "homo economicus," ethnological models of "traditional tradition," and schemas of tradition versus modernity rooted in classical social theory and modernization approaches—all of which he explicitly rejected.

COLONIAL ORIGINS OF THE CONCEPT OF HABITUS

It was not by chance that the relationship between structures and habitus was constituted as a theoretical problem in relation to a historical situation in which that problem was in a sense presented by reality itself, in the form of a permanent discrepancy between agents' economic dispositions and the economic world in which they had to act.

—BOURDIEU, "TRADITIONAL SOCIETY'S ATTITUDE TOWARDS TIME"[130]

The notion of habitus was present in rough outline in Bourdieu's earliest Algerian analyses. The essay "Traditional Society's Attitude towards Time" discussed gift exchange, barter, and the entire temporal orientation of traditional society as being rooted in a form of "pre-perceptive anticipation" that guided practice.[131] The idea of pre-perceptive anticipation is exemplified by Bourdieu's discussion in *Travail et travailleurs en Algérie* of the ways in which relatively secure material conditions shaped workers' ability to project their own action into the future. In *Le déracinement*, Bourdieu and Sayad used the term habitus, which they defined as follows: "the peasant's being is above all a certain *manner* of being, a *habitus*, a permanent and general disposition before the world and others." Habitus as defined here is, on the one hand, a bodily habitus. For the peasant, "the familiar world is . . . the native world" and "his whole *corporeal habitus* is 'made' within the space of his customary movements." At the same time, habitus is described as a durable set of predispositions. Because habitus is incorporated, it is able to survive changes in external conditions. Bourdieu later called this persistence the "hysteresis of habitus." The peasant "can remain a peasant even when he no longer has the possibility of behaving like one." Body and soul come together in their discussion of the habitus of the "authentic peasant," the "*bu-niya* peasant," who exudes "*niya*"—a Kabyle word meaning "a certain manner of being and acting, *a permanent, general and transposable disposition* in the face of the world and other men."[132] The formulation here—"*a permanent, general and transposable disposition*"—is almost identical to Bourdieu's "mature" definition of habitus as "*systems of durable, transposable dispositions*."[133] Kabyle *niya*, and the difficulties of continuing to negotiate a world brutally transformed by colonialism on the basis of *niya*, is a key adumbration of the concept of habitus.[134]

In *Le déracinement*, Bourdieu and Sayad show how habitus is linked to *habitat*, or social space. The Kabyle house is described as a space of precisely organized relations, locations, and functions. The peasant's entire "bodily habitus" is inculcated in interaction with the house, later described in *Outline of a Theory of Practice* as a "'book' from which children learn their vision of the world," a book that they "read with the body."[135] The authors cite Bachelard's *Poetics of Space*, published just a few years earlier but already a *locus classicus* of the phenomenology of the house.[136] If the house is a space of customary movements, practices, and meanings, so is the village. Peasants sometimes attempt to reestablish old patterns in their new habitation. Bourdieu and Sayad describe the entry to the Djebabra resettlement camp, where

> one could see (already marked on the ground) a path running from the main road to the upper part of the village where the men gather; thus two types of organization of space and two types of attitude to the world were superimposed: on one hand is the *castrum*, traversed by two intersecting wide avenues that surrendered intimacy by directly

introducing the stranger into the heart of the inhabited universe, and on the other is the closed world, the sanctuary of *ḥurma* (honor) that the roads leading to the outside skirted round, as in Kabylia, so that the stranger should continue on his way without entering. As if they bore in their bodies the schema of their familiar displacements, the men never took the most direct route, meaning one or the other broad avenue, to get back to their houses; first taking the peripheral path, they invented detours via the small alleys that ran between the houses and they walk furtively, staying close to the walls.[137]

Yet, even as the resettled peasant tries to reassert customary resonances between habitus and the built environment, the resettlement camp, with its modern, individualized family houses, decouples these synergies. Colonialism prohibits cultural reproduction, continuously rearranging any temporarily stabilized relations between habitus and its social environment. Bourdieu and Sayad discussed a peasant in the Chélif valley who was "disinclined to transfer into his familiar universe everything he sees and experiences as the colonist's waged worker."[138] Different forms of habitus therefore continued to coexist within a single individual. According to Bourdieu, "the model of behavior and the economic ethos imported by colonization coexist, in each subject's mind, with the model and ethos inherited from ancestral tradition."[139] Bourdieu was prodded toward the idea of the split habitus through his immersion in the colony's radical forms of social splintering, combined with his reading of the extant literature on cultural mixing discussed throughout this book.

Habitus is also therefore an example of a social scientific concept that was generated in a colonial setting and reimported back into the study of metropolitan society. In reversing the standard direction of the circulation of ideas—turning the arrow from North→South to South→North—Bourdieu was part of a wider tendency in postwar colonial social science. Some sociologists spoke explicitly about "anthropologizing" or "primitivizing" the European or North American self.[140] Norbert Elias argued that anthropology was obsolete, since the same set of sociological categories could be used to analyze all human societies.[141] Arriving on the scene when these discussions were already well under way, Bourdieu did not hesitate to redeploy concepts back to Europe in a counter-imperial direction.

COLONIAL ORIGINS OF THE CONCEPTS OF SYMBOLIC AND CULTURAL CAPITAL, PRACTICE, AND STRATEGY

Cultural capital is another idea that Bourdieu adumbrated in his analyses of colonized cultures and then redirected back to Europe. In Algeria, Bourdieu began to think about prestige and honor as resources, or forms of capital. In the first edition of *Sociologie de l'Algérie*, he argues that colonialism destroys Algerians' "ancient values, above all the values of prestige and honor," which are replaced by "monetary values, impersonal and abstract." Once Bourdieu returned to France, he began to identify a similar disjuncture between value systems grounded in "prestige and honor," which he began calling cultural capital, and systems grounded in economic capital.

The importance of the Algerian foundation becomes even clearer if we reconsider Bourdieu's discussion of *onomastic* differentiation among Arab tribes. Echoing Berque (chapter 12), Bourdieu discusses the ways Arab tribes are distinguished by their *names* and "by the ascendency that this name confers on the group that bears it." According to Bourdieu, the name is a resource that confers "ascendency" on the group, an "immense prestige," contributing to the accumulation of a "*capital* of combined *power and prestige.*"[142] This discussion recalls Berque's study of tribal names as "signs, regulated by their own laws," in an article that Bourdieu later credited with providing him with "countless starting points and invaluable points of reference."[143] The traditional French versions of cultural capital in the ancient régime were *titles of nobility*, while the new titles of cultural nobility were linked to education, the *institutionalized* state of cultural capital, that is, to a version of cultural capital linked to the names of universities and university degrees. Bourdieu was well aware of the onomastic power of the *agrégation* degree, or the power of the *doctorat d'état* as opposed to a *doctorat de 3ᵉ cycle*—even if he described the "embodied" state of cultural capital as more legitimate, because it was less pedantic and scholastic.[144] Contemporary sociologists refer to Bourdieu's theory of the "power to name" without recognizing the origins of this concept in his Algerian research, and in colonial sociology more broadly.[145]

Bourdieu's discussion of the strategic manipulation of names in his Algerian research is another path to his discussion in *Outline of a Theory of Practice* of the movement "from rules to strategies," i.e., from structuralism to a non-utilitarian praxeology. There, he suggests that he first introduced the idea of symbolic capital by discussing "the form of prestige and renown attached to a family and a name."[146] Bourdieu recognized that his own concept of symbolic capital originated in his Algerian studies. In accounting for his break with structuralism, Bourdieu focuses on his studies of Kabyle marriage strategies, specifically the "strategic uses of genealogy for legitimating social units." The entire discussion of strategy, performative discourse, and group formation through classification struggles in his later work can be traced to his early discussion of onomastic differentiation and marriage and kinship strategies in Algeria.[147] Bourdieu's exposure to the massive social upheaval of colonial war made it impossible for him to understand history as repetition, even though government policymakers and structuralist theorists were doing their best to make it seem so. His exposure to the collective self-affirmation of the Algerian people in the revolution provided the raw material for his successful overthrow of Lévi-Straussian structuralism.[148]

TRACES OF THE FIELD CONCEPT IN BOURDIEU'S ALGERIAN WRITINGS

Bourdieu first engaged with field theory in his Algerian work. In 1958, he argued that the interaction between external and internal forces in shaping activity in colonial situations "is effected within a field."[149] The following year, in a letter to Sayad, Bourdieu wrote that he was rethinking his treatment of honor in Kabyle culture through "a Lewinian perspective, by trying to demonstrate the type of personality corresponding to a society of honor."[150] Kurt Lewin, the founder of psychological field theory, extended Einstein's field theory to the social sciences.[151] Bourdieu's first article using the word "field" in the title was published six years later.[152]

There is an additional source of Bourdieu's field theory in his colonial research. One of the main principles "governing the oppositional structures of fields" in his mature theory is the the distinction between their autonomous and heteronomous poles.[153] Bourdieu was made acutely aware of the problem of heteronomy and censorship during his military service, at the University of Algiers, and in his fieldwork. His personal exposure to these issues resonated with the wider discussions of academic and scientific freedom at the time (chapter 10). Colonial scholars, Bourdieu argued, often exhibited a *"double dependence"* on the "colonial power" and the "central intellectual power, that's to say the metropolitan science of the day."[154] The colonial state represented a source of scientific heteronomy insofar as scholars oriented themselves toward the criteria governing the internal logics of that political field.[155]

COLONIALISM AND EPISTEMOLOGY

The discussion of scientific autonomy is closely related to Bourdieu's thinking about social epistemology in general and his response to his colonial experience. Bourdieu's epistemology is grounded first in the Bachelardian idea of the necessity of "constructing" the social scientific object in order to control the influence of spontaneous pre-notions. The object of science has to be actively and consciously constructed in all situations, colonial and otherwise, due to the ontological layering of reality and the resulting divergence between empirical appearances and underlying structures.[156]

Epistemic caution becomes particularly urgent in colonial situations, where social reality is covered in additional layers of obfuscation. Bourdieu argued that a "Gestalt switch" was necessary even to perceive empirical colonial reality. Added to this was the intense swirling of ideologies of racism, "caste," "traditionalism," etc. One of Bourdieu's tasks during his military service was to write reports that *obscured* Algeria's very coloniality. Bourdieu's publications after 1957 reversed course, *emphasizing* the imbrication of knowledge production with colonial ideology. While this might seem obvious to us today, in the wake of decades of postcolonial theorizing, this contextual determinant of knowledge was ignored by most social scientists at the time.[157] For Bourdieu, what "follows from" the fact of colonialism is "an absolute imperative, not ethical but scientific: there is no behavior, attitude or ideology which can be described, understood or explained objectively without reference to the existential situation of the colonized as it is determined by the action of economic and social forces characteristic of the colonial system."[158]

Bourdieu approached his analysis of Algerian workers and the unemployed and sub-proletarians in explicitly epistemological terms. As we have seen, he describes Algerians as knowledge-seeking subjects. The unemployed and underemployed were "not sufficiently detached from their condition to posit it as an object," and their "aspirations and demands, even their revolt, are expressed within the framework and logic of the system," i.e., in terms of pre-notions or spontaneous ideologies.[159] The fully employed workers, who are more detached from their immediate condition, might therefore be able to construct it consciously and express their aspirations, demands, and revolts within an alternative logic outside the colonial system. The Algerian proletariat becomes a stand-in for the sociologist or epistemologist. This discussion also returns to the theme of autonomy. Knowledge depends upon a certain degree of "autonomy"; as Bourdieu puts it, "In order for a systematic and rational vision of the colonial system to be formed, the economic pressure has to let up in a way that allows one to break the fascination of the current condition."[160]

Bourdieu returned to the question of colonial social science in 1975, 1980, and 1985, and in his posthumous "sketch for a self-analysis." He did not fundamentally change the views set out in his 1963 text, although he became more appreciative of some of the advantages offered by "insider" positions when they were combined with practices of "self-objectification."[161] He revised his earlier, more rigorous objectivism and was now increasingly open to the idea that "[t]here are extraordinary advantages in the fact of being native, on condition one knows what this implies, that is, everything it hides."[162] He argued in *Outline of a Theory of Practice* that researchers should make not just a first break with spontaneous knowledge, but also a second break with their objectivist descriptions.[163] In fact, as Pels points out, Bourdieu advocates not two but three epistemic "breaks" in the research process. The researcher first needs to break with their own pre-notions; second, they should break with the spontaneous views of the historical or contemporary actors being studied; third, there has to be a break with the researcher's initial objectivizing descriptions, whether statistical or ethnographic.[164] The implication for "standpoint epistemologists" and other advocates of "spontaneous" knowledge is that prenotions may be useful if they can be controlled and reconstructed via epistemic breaks, but they are poor guides on their own.

Bourdieu continued to call attention to anthropology's genetic entanglement with colonial systems.[165] In 1975, at a conference on Orientalism and colonialism, Bourdieu argued that the "question of the privileged viewpoint needs to be replaced by the question of scientific control of the relation to the object of science," that is, to ask "what it means to be an observer or an agent."[166] Here, he sketches a historical project of reconstructing the colonial-era "Algiers School" of "Muslim sociology," which was closely aligned with the colonial government, in order to understand the genesis of contemporary prenotions involved in the study of Algeria, Islam, and colonialism.[167] Bourdieu also reaffirmed his argument against Leiris from 1963, while acknowledging the value of a nuanced historical reconstruction of actual ethnography and sociology. Colonial science was thus one of the first intellectual formations to which Bourdieu applied his field theory, along with German philosophy in his study of Heidegger, published at the same time as his lecture on "decolonizing sociology."[168] The title of this essay in the French original is lost in the English translation: "sociologie coloniale et décolonisation de la sociologie," or "colonial sociology and decolonization of sociology." Bourdieu is thus one of the first sociologists, along with Berque, to call explicitly for a "decolonization of sociology." What is equally important is the relevance to "decolonizing sociology" of the specific approach to reflexivity developed by Bourdieu. I will return to this problem in the concluding chapter.

Transition

Bourdieu's oeuvre demonstrates that colonial situations, despite their injustice, could be extremely generative in intellectual terms. This was particularly true of the late colonial era, since this was also marked by the increased involvement of social thinkers in firsthand fieldwork and observation. The contradictions and multiple forms of *doubling* that characterized colonial social existence could be generative of insight. Every situation presented itself as a dualistic or kaleidoscopic one, open to conflicting interpretations. Such fracturing of reality could lead alert observers toward a glimpse of the contingency of social reality and the relativity of any particular view of the social. Bourdieu was ideally equipped to grasp the ways colonialism could destabilize European classification schemes, and he was able to integrate this insight into his epistemology and theory of reflexivity. This revolutionary dynamic guided Bourdieu to a social ontology of constant change, *tous azimuts*. Such change made it seem urgent to theorize agentic praxis.

Bourdieu suggested that the aim of his research on Algerian workers was to "restore to other men the meaning of their behaviours."[169] Three decades later, in his project on "social suffering," Bourdieu argued that his aim was "helping interviewees discover and state the hidden principle of their extreme tragedies or ordinary misfortunes."[170] Amín Pérez writes that "the project Bourdieu and Sayad took on in Algeria was one of speaking truth to power."[171] These scientific goals are not specific to colonial situations, but the latter sometimes brought the importance of these ideas into sharp relief.[172]

CHAPTER FIFTEEN

Conclusion

THE HISTORY OF SOCIOLOGY, REFLEXIVITY, AND DECOLONIZATION

In colonial studies, it is no longer the time for summary accusations and capital condemnation, but for a calmer examination and evaluation of a shared heritage.

—GIANNI ALBERGONI (2001)[1]

You read a historic writer not for what they failed to see, not for the ideological blindspots of their writing—too easy, too programmatic in the literary academy of recent years—but for the as-yet-unlived, still-shaping history which their vision—which must mean including the limitations of that vision—partially, tentatively, forsees and provokes.

—JACQUELINE ROSE (2003)[2]

COLONIAL SITUATIONS ARE HORRIFYING and unjust. I am writing at a moment when Russia is recolonizing Ukraine, recalling the American war in Vietnam, the French war in Algeria, the German war in Southwest Africa, the Spanish conquest of the Aztec Empire, and the Romans' Punic Wars with Carthage. Modern French colonialism involved conquest and subjugation; slavery; expropriation of land, property, sovereignty, and identity; racist policies of rule; and brutal campaigns to ward off independence. But colonial situations could also be generative of startling insights. Starting in the 1930s, the racist asymmetry of the rule of difference increasingly brought the injustice of colonialism to the level of consciousness, leading to revolutionary action by the colonized and critical anticolonialism among some Europeans. Empires are always culturally multiplex, pushing intellectuals beyond their culturally bound categories, as we have seen in many of the cases discussed in this book.

One of the important results of these processes was the genesis of a historical sociology. The fact that empires are always riven by anti-imperial pressures alerted some social scientists to the implausibility of static, ahistorical models. Colonialism's careening crisis made it difficult for thinkers to apply the ahistorical models of unilinear change and frozen repetition that had been prevalent in Comptian positivism and interwar ethnology, and that characterized Talcott Parsons's American sociology, Lévi-Strauss's anthropology, and much of western neo-Marxism. Empire's very evanescence, which was evident to Aron, Berque, Balandier, Bourdieu, and others, focused attention on the historicity of sociopolitical formations. This sense of the decline of empire helped push these thinkers to develop a historical sociology, before that idea had been established in French sociology.

A second result was the creation of a critical sociology that was not limited to the categories of capitalism and social class and that rejected the primacy of economic determinism. The fact that anti-imperialism developed dialectically along with imperialism, especially in the early years ("primary resistance") and again during the middle decades of the twentieth century, helped observers to perceive the importance of social movements based on ethnic or tribal identity, religion, and nation. Colonialism's hierarchical and racist dualism led these thinkers to construct theories with multiple axes of domination—"intersectional" theories before that term had been coined.

The experience of late colonialism helped immunize French sociologists against the opposing errors of static social theories and theories of inexorable social progress. The appearance of social reproduction was approached as a puzzle to be explained rather than an ontological constant. Witnessing the long-term destructiveness of European "development" programs on colonized societies diminished the allure of American-manufactured modernization theory. The plurality and mixing of cultures in the colonies revealed the shortcomings of American theories of "marginal man." The impossibility of predicting the direction of social change in colonial settings undermined the plausibility of social scientific positivism.

These comments should not be misconstrued as a call for recolonizing sociology, much less for recolonization *tout court*. History does not repeat itself. A singular confluence of factors and "historical series" allowed the sociology of colonialism discussed in this book to emerge, in one particular geospatial context. Any attempt to recreate late colonial conditions, even if it were desired, would be doomed to failure.[3] The context analyzed in this book should not even be defined strictly as colonial, since it was also already decolonizing. Moreover, as we have seen, the most prescient sociologists discussed in this book rejected any doctrine of axiological neutrality. Most of them rejected even a highly reformed version of colonialism, whose shattering effects on societies and individuals they had closely examined.

Summary of the Book's Argument

This book has presented a revisionist history of French social thought, arguing that colonial research represented a crucial part of the renascent academic discipline of sociology between the late 1930s and the 1960s. This scientific formation encompassed sociologists from several generations, born between the 1870s and the 1930s. The final years of the colonial era and the period that followed saw the first collaborative research between sociologists born as colonized subjects and sociologists born as French citizens. The effects of this repressed disciplinary unconscious can be felt throughout the modern social sciences, just like the individual unconscious, whose tendrils reach into consciousness in ways that are unpredictable, startling, even shocking. Many of our current categories originated in colonial contexts. Most important, this sociology of colonialism laid the foundations for many of the subfields of contemporary French sociology and for the mature thinking of Pierre Bourdieu, the most influential sociological theorist today. This does not mean that we should purge these colonial origins and ideas, subjecting them to a second round of repression. Nor does it mean that we should try to recreate the contradictory mix of colonizing and decolonizing dynamics that allowed these ideas to emerge. What it means is that we should examine these stories of intellectual emergence in detail, paying attention to their contexts and contents.

In order to study this formation, this book proposed a methodology that I call the historical socioanalysis of social science. This approach to intellectual history combines attention to broadly contextual factors, adjacent fields, dynamics within the narrower microcosm of the sociology discipline, the more immediate sites of intellectual production, and close readings of sociological texts. We move gradually inward toward the postwar sociologists of colonialism and their writings. And we need to closely interpret the works themselves—their internal structure and meanings, and their relations to other works. Finally, I argue that the historical sociology of sociology is justified by the needs of scientific reflexivity, in addition to providing intellectual resources for current social research.[4]

We can now revisit the overview of the book. Chapter 2 demonstrates that historians of French sociology have ignored the existence of this formation of colonial specialists. Chapter 2 also explores the reasons for this repression of disciplinary memory. Chapters 3–5 explore the most macroscopic contexts shaping postwar colonial sociology. Chapter 3 discusses the postwar "re-occupation" of the French empire, elites' belief in the empire's longevity, the permeation of the empire by experts, including sociologists, and the intense commitment to the empire among most of the French public after 1945. Chapter 4 examines the turn to colonial developmentalist policies, including infrastructural and social policies, which created a demand for new forms of social scientific expertise. Chapter 6 reconstructs the importance of colonialism in French higher education, demonstrating that sociological instruction was increasingly linked to colonial thematics. I then discuss the creation after 1945 of an archipelago of research institutions and universities across the entire empire. Social scientists, including sociologists, worked in these institutions. They worked alongside scholars from the natural sciences and other social sciences. These contexts were much less committed to disciplinary divisions than was the case in the metropole.

The next section focuses on the intellectual contexts shaping postwar colonial sociology. Chapters 6 and 7 show that colonialism was an important focus in the social scientific fields with close connections to sociology: law, economics, psychology, history, statistics and demography, and anthropology. Chapter 8 explores theoretical, methodological, and empirical developments within interwar French sociology. These discussions provided the most direct intellectual platform for postwar sociological studies of colonialism. A few of the sociologists discussed in chapter 8 also carried out fieldwork in colonial and postcolonial sites between the wars. The careers of several of these figures continued into the postwar era, providing a bridge to earlier discussions.

Chapter 10 presents a field-theoretic analysis of postwar sociology and its colonial subfield. This entails, first, a prosopography of the entire sociological discipline and its colonial subgroup. Here, I establish that the colonial specialists constituted around half of the entire disciplinary field between 1945 and 1965. A field analysis also requires that we examine the main lines of internal polarization within the discipline. A central part of this discussion is the comparison between colonial sociologists and their metrocentric counterparts. I argue that the colonial specialists were beginning to constitute a proper subfield in the years after World War II. They had their own recognized intellectual leaders, such as Raymond Aron, Jacques Berque, Roger Bastide, and Georges Balandier, as well as institutional *patrons* who were not specialized in colonialism but who promoted the colonial specialists, such as Georges Davy and Georges Gurvitch. Colonial sociology was autonomous enough to have its own internal debates and research agendas, research institutes, journals, conferences, and networks. At the same time, the colonial researchers were distributed across the entire sociological field, rather than being concentrated in the dominant or dominated sector. Their overall disciplinary status, or average level of symbolic capital, was equivalent to that of their metrocentric colleagues. That said, some groups of colonial sociologists faced daunting obstacles to achieving disciplinary recognition. These disadvantaged groups included researchers who spent their entire careers in remote overseas settings, colonial officials who became scholars, and above all, indigenous or "colonized" sociologists. The final section of chapter 10 examines the strategies some colonial sociologists used to overcome their marginalization, such as seeking to enhance their scientific autonomy or building bridges to the fields of literature, philosophy, and ethnology.

The next four chapters trace the interweaving of context, field, author, and text in the writing of four of the main figures in French postwar sociology. These four intellectuals epitomize the discipline-defining moment examined in this book. Aron created a sociology of empires and integrated Weimar historicist sensibilities into a French sociology hitherto committed to Comtian/Durkheimian positivism and ahistoricism. Aron integrated German historicism and political theory into an incisive historical and comparative sociology of empire. Aron's political position as a non-Marxist socialist before the war and an anti-totalitarian liberal during and after the Occupation underwrote his global vision of politics, which was unique in French sociology. His early abhorrence for imperialism was closely tied to his experience of the Nazi Occupation, which forced him into exile. Aron diagnosed the French Empire's unviability in the mid-1940s and argued for decolonization of Indochina and Algeria before anticolonialism became consensual among French sociologists and before independence became inevitable. Together with Georges Gurvitch and other leading figures in the renascent discipline, Aron promoted the early careers of some of the sociologists of colonialism, thus also indirectly helping to transfer their ideas about colonial societies into a sociology of "Northern" societies.

Berque created a non-Orientalist historical sociology of North Africa and initiated the critique of Orientalism. Berque's biography and social properties had a decisive effect on his intellectual writings. He felt ostracized by the metropole and was more at home among Muslim Moroccans, both elite and plebian. Berque flourished in urban Fez and among the Seksawa in the upper Atlas Mountains. His intense interest in these cultures drove him to push the historicization of sociology in a different direction than Aron's German historicism. Berque joined forces early on, in the 1930s, with the leading *Annales* school of French historiography. He analyzed various North African social and cultural systems in ways that broke with the powerful *École d'Alger*—the politically conservative specialists in Islam at the University of Algiers. Berque tapped into novel indigenous archival sources and combined this evidence with extended periods of ethnographic observation. The result was a thoroughly transdisciplinary mix of history, sociology, ethnology, and social theory. Like Aron's epistemic historicism, Berque's unique approach represented an alternative to the scientistic positivism that was promoted across the world by US scholarly and official agencies after 1945—the scientific "Pax Americana," in his words.[5]

Balandier was also innovative, doing more to create a properly sociological approach to colonized societies than anyone else, while also founding the sociology of the modern African church and making an early contribution to the history of African state formation. Balandier created an entire vocabulary for analyzing colonialism. In understanding how Balandier became himself, I discussed his childhood in the French provinces, his participation in the Resistance, and his adoption of the surrealist writer and ethnologist Michel Leiris as an ego ideal. The evidence for the importance of this identification with Leiris is impressive, including Balandier's early novel, *Tous comptes faits*, which emulates Leiris's *L'âge d'homme* (*Manhood*), and Balandier's *Afrique ambiguë*, which resonated with Leiris's *L'Afrique fantôme*. Balandier's autobiographic writings, including his semi-fictional autobiographical novel, and his personal papers and numerous interviews, allow us to relate self-perception and self-presentation to objective social structural analysis, and to bring both together in interpreting his textual production. Another crucial feature of Balandier's life and work is a series of new, expanding opportunities from which he was able to profit. He arrived in Senegal just as the scientific expansion was getting under way as part of French reoccupation and developmentalism. His non-elite status led him to associate early on with African intellectuals and politicians, leading to his participation in the journal *Présence africaine*. He began teaching at *Sciences Po* just as it was opening its doors to more critical voices; he entered the Sixth Section of the *École pratique des hautes études* just as it was plunging into "area studies," with student interest turning toward Africa. He moved to a sociology professorship at the Sorbonne at the start of the decade in which student interest in sociology was greatest—the 1960s.

If I pay more attention to Bourdieu in this book than to the other thinkers, it is because his theoretical framework has been so important for my own work, and for sociology and social theory in general. This detailed analysis is in part my own effort to come to grips with the partly colonial origins of my own theoretical framework. All sociologists living in the United States are, in one sense, complicit with the imperial politics of this country, including those writing on colonialism and decolonizing sociology. In a future volume, I will examine contemporary American sociology. But the French social scientists had to be studied first.

What I have shown here is that Bourdieu's mature thinking was shaped not just by the sources that have been discussed in the voluminous secondary literature, but also by his experiences in late colonial Algeria, and his reading of the sociologists of colonialism. Bourdieu's Algerian concepts were then cycled back into his analysis of metropolitan social structures, moving in a counter-imperial direction. Arriving in sociology and in the colonies near the end of the centuries-long era of overseas European empires, Bourdieu was ideally positioned to transform the best ideas that had emerged from these imperial contexts and to combine them with the best ideas from his philosophical training, giving rise to a general sociology and social theory that transcended the colonial context. Bourdieu's processual social ontology emerged from his observation of the crushing of Algerian social structures by the colonial state and the military, of the sweeping social crisis that engulfed Algerian society, of Algerians' practical improvisations in these conditions, and of the revolutionary war. Bourdieu's emphasis on conflict, antagonism, domination, revolution, and change emerged from this foundational experience. His fieldwork brought him face to face with forms of cultural difference that debunked models of "homo economicus" and anthropologies premised on notions of "traditional tradition." He explicitly rejected rational choice models, ahistorical models of the social, and conventional theories of progress from "tradition" to "modernity." Bourdieu's theory of habitus was indebted not just to his study of phenomenology but also to his study of the Kabyle concept of *"niya,"* which he summarized as "a certain manner of being and acting, a permanent, general and transposable disposition in the face of the world and other men."⁶ Bourdieu's concept of *cultural capital* originated in his discussion of *onomastic* differentiation among Arab tribes in which names figure as resources that confer "an ascendency" on the group, an "immense prestige," contributing to the accumulation of a "capital of combined power and prestige."⁷ Bourdieu first discussed the social scientific field theory of Kurt Lewin in an analysis of honor in Kabyle culture. He discovered the importance of the distinction between fields' autonomous and heteronomous poles during his time in Algeria, where he was exposed to the thinking of scholars who were doubly dependent on the colonial state and the "metropolitan science of the day."⁸

Bourdieu's mature epistemology was linked to his experience of colonialism, in which social reality was so obscured by racism and ontological doubling that the researcher was required to execute a "Gestalt switch" to even perceive the empirical social situation, much less to pierce its surface. Although Bourdieu had learned from Bachelard and Durkheim that it was crucial to make a break with spontaneous pre-notions, this point was decisively brought home by his Algerian experiences. He approached Algerian workers and the unemployed and sub-proletarians as knowledge-seeking subjects, and argued that the employed were better able to posit their condition "as an object" and to step outside the "framework and logic of the system."⁹ Here, Bourdieu perceived that knowledge depends upon a certain degree of "autonomy": "the economic pressure has to let up in a way that allows one to break the fascination of the current condition."¹⁰

Bourdieu sketched a model of colonialism and a methodology for studying colonial scientists. He argued that colonialism was socially and epistemically bifurcated and inherently racist, producing racists. Colonialism was an all-pervasive system. This means that "there is no behavior, attitude or ideology which can be described, understood or explained objectively without reference to the existential situation of the colonized as it is determined by the action of economic and social forces characteristic of the colonial system."¹¹ Bourdieu was able to break through the colonizer-colonized barrier in science. His study of the resettlement camps showed how deracinated peasants tried to reassert customary resonances between habitus and the built environment and how the modern, individualized family houses of the camps undercut these synergies.

The Question of "Decolonizing" Sociology

This book has shown that it would be an enormous mistake to re-entomb all of the social science produced under colonial conditions. The intellectual formations reconstructed here were internally stratified and differentiated; its members varied enormously in terms of their social properties, their politics, and their writing. The political and intellectual differences between a René Maunier and an Albert Memmi, a Jacques Soustelle and an Abdelmalek Sayad, or a Georges-Henri Bousquet and a Pierre Bourdieu, are vast. Indeed, most of the 20th-century French practitioners of the sociology of colonialism rejected colonialism, and some of them introduced the idea of "decolonizing sociology." Berque argued that most of the French scholars in the colonies embraced "the ideas of critique, objectivity, and history." It was a question of individual perspective and moderation as well as the "range of choices" available.[12] Anouar Abdel Malek endorsed Berque's argument that Orientalism had adopted the "the optic of the Arab bureau" and was animated by "Europeocentrism" in which the "Oriental" was treated as the Other, emphasizing language and religion and ignoring or denigrating Arab scientific achievements. Abdel Malek credited Louis Massignon with "generosity" in his treatment of the Orient, despite "profoundly erroneous" views that were "capable of pernicious extensions."[13] Abdel Malek's aim was to "'dis-orientalize' the studies relative to Asia" by defining "a new attitude towards the problem of the relationships between orientalism and every one of the human sciences, each of them conceived in its planetary universality."[14]

The first sociologist to call explicitly for "decolonizing sociology," using those exact terms, was Bourdieu.[15] Bourdieu echoed Berque in criticizing those "who set themselves up as judges and distribute praise and blame among the sociologists and ethnologists of the colonial past." He insisted that they should try "to understand what it was that prevented the most lucid and best intentioned of those they condemn from understanding things which are now self-evident for even the least lucid and sometimes the least well-intentioned observers."[16] Bourdieu went further than Berque in suggesting that a decolonization of sociology should take the form of a historical sociology of science, and in demonstrating what such a method would look like in practice.[17] This is the reflexive historical socioanalysis of science pursued in the present book.

This approach intervenes in discussions of "decolonizing sociology" in several ways. First, colonial-era thinkers should not be condemned without careful reading of all of their work, situating writing in its historical contexts and relations to earlier writing. For every text, we need to pay attention to exact formulations and arguments, narrative structures and argumentative aporias, intertexts and paratexts.¹⁸ I have shown how problematic it is to assume that any scholar who came in contact with colonialism was inherently complicit with that system, or to assume that their work does not need to be read carefully and taken seriously.

The danger of focusing on just one aspect of a sociologist's oeuvre, or just one sentence or passage within a specific text, applies with special force to someone like Durkheim. While Durkheim failed to discuss colonialism explicitly (with a few exceptions, discussed in chapter 8), in other respects his framework was antiracist and anticolonial. This is particularly true of his sociology of morality.¹⁹ By the same token, Bourdieu's writings are often cherry-picked for statements that seem to support the claim that his theory is one of "order and social reproduction,"²⁰ even though his most important works and concepts deal with process and historical change as the more fundamental aspects of social reality.

Second, some of the literature on decolonizing sociology proceeds in a distinctly unsociological manner, failing to contextualize writing or to situate it within the relevant dynamics of fields. Two examples, relating to Balandier and Max Weber, illustrate the importance of careful reading and contextualization. Chapter 13 discussed Balandier and his study of a resettlement program in Gabon. As we saw, Balandier revised his views completely after his more extensive research, reversing his initial policy recommendation. Those who only read the earlier statement could be led to think that Balandier favored resettlement. The historical context of this discussion is also crucial, since it was African Fang leaders who initiated this call for regrouping.

Max Weber's comments on Confucianism and Chinese culture in his *Religionssoziologie* seem at first glance to provide evidence of racism.²¹ A sociological approach sheds a different light on this matter, without providing an *apologia* for Weber's comments. Weber's scientific habitus led him to align his views with the intellectual positions of the dominant professors in leading German universities, especially Berlin's. The two leading specialists on China at Berlin University when Weber was writing on China were Ferdinand von Richthofen and J. J. de Groot. Weber endorsed these writers' Sinophobic visions.²² By contrast, Weber's analysis of India does not depict the country as stagnant, despotic, or racially inferior. Here, Weber oriented his analysis toward the "outstanding German Indologists" at Berlin University, who were more enthusiastic about their analytic object.²³ In other words, there was not a generalized Weberian view of the non-European other, nor a uniformly "racist" Weber.²⁴ Weber's strategy of aligning his views with dominant professorial positions led him to adopt contradictory positions when the relevant experts were divided. This can be seen in his writings on methodology, which vacillate between historicist, cultural, interpretivist, and hermeneutic models rooted in the (neo)historicism of German economics and neo-Kantian epistemology, on the one hand, and more "modern" rational actor models, on the other. The two positions jostle for primacy in the "Methodological Foundations" section of Weber's *Wirtschaft und Gesellschaft*.[25] His China writings can only be grasped by placing them within Weber's entire oeuvre and placing the latter within the relevant fields and contexts.

A third problem with some of the literature on decolonizing sociology is its orientation toward unearthing writers who remain "inertly of their time" (Said) rather than those who "partially, tentatively, foresee and provoke," despite their "ideological blindspots" (Jacqueline Rose). Forgotten sociologists are thus reanimated, only to be stricken with anathema and reburied. It is paradoxical that such underwhelming figures as Franklin Giddings, Albert Keller, Benjamin Kidd, William Graham Sumner, and Lester Ward, whose books have not been seriously studied for a century, are now being made more familiar by the decolonizing literature.[26] Of course, some of this "inert" thought may be relevant if one is interested in writing the history of American imperialism. This is particularly the case for modernization theory, a banal and lifeless framework that was actually put into practice overseas by the United States.[27] A field analysis of American social science in the Cold War obviously needs to include such figures.[28] However, none of the decolonizing literature so far has carried out a proper field analysis or compiled a prosopography of sociologists.

A fourth difficulty arises when intellectual historians fail to differentiate between scholarly, political, and private genres of writing. Of course, intellectual history may need to consider all of these sources, but it also needs to think carefully about how they differ and how they are related to one another. Sometimes non-academic writing provides the key to understanding more scientific work. Private correspondence and political statements have played a central role in interpreting the theoretical frameworks of Carl Schmitt and Martin Heidegger. Schmitt's most explicit anti-Semitic comments are found in his personal diaries, and in public statements made during the Nazi era. Raphael Gross has argued that Schmitt's basic conceptual apparatus is anti-Semitic, and that his private and political statements elucidate seemingly abstract concepts such as *Nomos* and *Grossraumordnung*.[29] On the other hand, the dangers of failing to distinguish between scholarly and extra-academic statements can be seen in the violations of academic freedom at numerous campuses across the United States in the past decade.[30]

A final set of problems with the extant literature on decolonizing sociology relates to questions of epistemology, reflexivity, and method. Some decolonizing writers characterize western sociology as just another "provincial" theory of a specific geospace and reject its claims to universal validity.[31] "Southern" epistemologies sometimes seem to collapse into the argument that social processes outside the global North can only be explained in terms of causal mechanisms specific to those regions. This is a familiar argument from cultural anthropology, which suggested long ago that India might need to be analyzed through Hindu categories or Chinese society through Chinese ones.[32] This is the same critique raised by Charles Le Coeur (chapter 8), Georges Balandier, Paul Mercier, and others discussed in this book. The argument that social structures and causal mechanisms are not universal in scope is fully compatible with the most compelling philosophies of the social science. Critical realism, for example, argues that all causal mechanisms in the human sciences are time- and space-dependent.[33] Yet the question whether social change in non-western sites needs to be explained in terms of structures or mechanisms that do not exist in Europe or the United States cannot be answered by epistemic fiat. The question whether the conceptual languages used to describe such local mechanisms can be applied beyond their region of origin has to remain an open one, subject to empirical investigation. Bourdieu's field theory, for example, may be of limited use outside highly differentiated societies. His concepts of habitus and symbolic capital, by contrast, may have a broader reach, though still not necessarily a universal one. After all, these latter concepts are in a sense "Southern" ones, insofar as they were created by abstracting features of Kabyle culture. The sociologists of colonialism described in this book suggested that concepts could circulate in a counter-imperial direction. Le Coeur urged sociology to open itself to the possibility that "Aboriginal social concepts" could be used to analyze metropolitan social phenomena.[34] Balandier suggested that the sociology he conducted in Africa should be tried "à propos of Europe."[35]

A different approach to the question of decolonizing knowledge argues for a non-western or "Southern" episteme. Here, it is unclear whether the proposed alternatives are in fact incompatible with "western" philosophy per se or only with *particular* western philosophies.[36] The rise of antipositivist neohistoricism in late-nineteenth-century Germany put an end to the thesis of a monolithic "western" epistemology. It is worth recalling that German neohistoricism emerged from a cultural space that understood itself as being located on the periphery of Europe that was opposed to the "west."[37] The first non-western sociologies were created in India by the likes of André Béteille, G. S. Ghurye, Benoy Kumar Sarkar, and Rabindranath Tagore, whose epistemological views were rooted in British social anthropology and, in Sarkar's and Tagore's cases, in German social scientific historicism.[38] Disciplines like anthropology and social science epistemologies such as German historicism have moved farther from the stereotypical "western episteme" than most of the sociological decolonizers.

Some of the American literature on decolonizing sociology adopts a conventional view of science that prioritizes universal, general theory. Julian Go advocates a "postcolonial sociology," but also insists that "social knowledge requires generalizability," and argues that "Yoruban concepts" and "other theories of concepts derived from local contexts" cannot speak to "global social processes."[39] Michael Burawoy worries about a "plethora of particularisms," and suggests that the "nineteenth-century Positivist dream of universal knowledge that will rescue humanity is now, for the first time, on the horizon."[42] Both of these statements suggest that intellectual "decolonizing" can go hand in hand with positivist epistemology. This seems more epistemically conservative than Bourdieu and the other sociologists of colonialism discussed in this book. The fact that Kabyle concepts helped Bourdieu make sense of social practices far beyond Algeria or France already refutes this argument, as does the very fact that "local" European theories such as Marxism have been used to great avail by sociologists to explain historical phenomena in other "local" contexts, including the Philippines (Go), India (Chibber), and Zambia (Burawoy).[40] Raewyn Connell concludes that "the only possible future for social science on a world scale involves a principle of unification," which includes "a capacity for generalization" and embraces the idea that "social sciences in the periphery" can make "some use of concepts or techniques from the metropole."[41]

In fact, the sociology of colonialism discussed in this book was capacious and secure enough to encompass the historicists of the Weimar Republic, the surrealists of the interwar *Collège de sociologie*, and experimental genres such as *littérature-sociologie* and *cinéma vérité*. Sociology should easily be able to encompass an interpretive method based on Yoruba oral poetry, as proposed by the American-trained Nigerian sociologist Akinsola A. Akiwowo.[43] Ideas of scientific "unification" and "universal knowledge" are not necessarily compatible with decolonizing sociology.

A much more promising approach to the questions raised by the decolonizing literature is one that takes seriously the questions of methodology, epistemology, and reflexivity raised by the sociologists discussed in this book. But what, exactly, is reflexivity?

Reflexivity as Epistemic Vigilance

Bourdieu describes reflexivity as a practice of "epistemic vigilance."[44] He argues further that scientific reflexivity requires the history of science, and that the history of science requires a reflexive approach. Scientific reflexivity pushes us to reconstruct the historical evolution of the disciplines and other fields in which we are participating in order to understand the genesis of our own concepts and theories.[45] As Camic notes, "investigating the contingent historical processes by which certain forms of knowledge were institutionalized at the expense of others" can "free[] us from the present."[46] The historical socioanalysis of science is itself a practice of scientific reflexivity in which science "bends back" upon itself and makes the collective and historical processes of science itself into a crucial part of the explanation of knowledge.[47]

Scientific reflexivity involves at least four epistemic breaks. The first is a break with one's own spontaneous pre-notions, as advocated by Durkheim and Bachelard. This marks a difference from simple standpoint epistemologies. The second, irreducible to the first, is a break with the empirical level of surface appearances. Bourdieu is not an empiricist; his ontology is a stratified one, like that of critical realism. The empirical level of practice and ideology hides as much as it reveals. Third is a break with the pre-notions of the people one is studying. This moves us beyond the anthropological distinction between "etic" and "emic" perspectives. Fourth, there is a break with one's initial, objectivizing scientific constructions, which may reify reality, as in the statistical findings of *Travail et travailleurs en Algérie*, or the structuralist analysis of the Kabyle house. These objectifying practices express a scholastic or intellectualist bias. Moving beyond scholasticism is the fourth face of reflexivity.

Sociological reflexivity differs from standpoint theory, without rejecting it outright. The idea of a knowledge perspective or standpoint based on firsthand experience is only one part of reflexivity, and is inadequate on its own. The spontaneous standpoint is likely to encode societal and field-level ideologies. Of course, Georg Lukács's original formulation of this position, in his discussion of proletarian standpoint epistemology, was not oriented toward the proletarian's spontaneous perspectives, which are mired in reification. In its original formulation, the possibility of attaining scientific knowledge of capitalism stemmed from the proletarian's shared ontological status with the commodities that constitute the essential structure of capitalism. The proletarian's consciousness, Lukács argued, is the "self-consciousness of the commodity" and the "self-knowledge ... of capitalist society."[48] Later standpoint epistemologies tended to abandon this distinction between potential and actual perspectives on reality linked to social positions.[49] Bourdieu's model is not a repudiation of standpoint theory, but builds this epistemology into its own approach.

Reflexivity as defined here is neither an "exercise of introspection,"[50] a confession of intimate secrets, or a posture referring to the speaker's demographic properties. Nor is reflexivity as understood here a form of "postmodern" skepticism about knowledge, or a narcissistic mirror-gazing focused uniquely on the analyst.[51] Bourdieusian reflexivity differs from psychoanalysis—even though a more adequate approach to reflexive socioanalysis would require deeper probing into the individual unconscious.[52] Reflexivity does not involve tracing simple correlations between a thinker's social origins or demographic properties and their ideas. Social origins are rarely irrelevant for current intellectual work, but they may be less important than the history of the thinker's socialization and the history of the fields in which their scientific work is being carried out. The role of a writer's social origins can be best understood when the latter are relocated within disciplinary fields and broader social contexts. This consideration guides us to investigate the field's history of battles, revolutions, and settlements, and the field's precise configuration at the moment of the gestation of the ideas, theories, or texts under analysis. We should try to identify the social location of the speaker within the given field and the hidden presuppositions and arrangements of power within that field.

Bourdieusian reflexivity is therefore an essential part of any program for decolonizing sociology. It is an essential component of the methodology I have presented in this book: a reflexive and historical socioanalysis of knowledge. Reflexivity requires the history of science, and the history of science requires reflexivity.

APPENDIXES

APPENDIX ONE

Sociologists Whose Academic Careers Started before 1965 in France or the French Overseas Empire and Were Active in Colonial Research between the Late 1930s and the 1960s

1. Abdel-Malek, Anouar. 1924 (Cairo, Egypt)–2012.
2. Accardo, Alain. 1934 (Algeria)–.
3. Adam, André. 1911 (Saint-Lô, France)–1991.
4. Agblémagnon, François N'Sougan. 1929 (Ahépé, Togo)–2008.
5. Althabe, Gérard. 1932 (Gelos-Pau, France)–2014.
6. Aron, Raymond. 1905 (Paris)–1983.
7. Balandier, Georges. 1920 (Aillevillers-et-Lyaumont)–2016.
8. Bastide, Roger. 1898 (Nîmes, France)–1974.
9. Bekombo, Manga. 1932 (Bonéléké, Douala, Cameroon)–2004.
10. Berque, Jacques. 1910 (Molière, Algeria)–1995.
11. Biffot, Laurent Marie. 1925 (Nkovié, Ogooué Maritime, Gabon)–2015.
12. Binet, Jacques. 1916 (Gretz, France)–2009.
13. Bonnafous, Max. 1900 (Bordeaux)–1975.
14. Bourdieu, Pierre. 1930 (Denguin, France)–2002.
15. Bourricaud, François. 1922 (Saint-Martin-du-Bois, France)–1991.
16. Bousquet, Georges-Henri. 1900 (Meudon, France)–1978.
17. Bureau, René. 1929 (Nantes, France)–2004.
18. Cazeneuve, Jean. 1915 (Ussel, France)–2005.
19. Chaulet, Claudine (née Guillot). 1931 (Longeau, France)–2015.

20. Chombart de Lauwe, Paul-Henry. 1913 (Cambrai)–1998.
21. Clément, Pierre. 1915–2002.
22. Clignet, Rémi. 1931 (Reims, France)–.
23. Condominas, Georges. 1921 (Haïphong)–2011.
24. Cuisenier, Jean. 1927 (Paris)–2017.
25. Dampierre, Eric de. 1928 (Paris)–1998.
26. Darbel, Alain. 1932–1975.
27. Davy, Georges. 1883 (Bernay)–1976.
28. Descamps, Paul. 1872–1946.
29. Descloitres, Robert Jean Denis. 1928 (Paris)–.
30. Desroche, Henri. 1914–1994.
31. Devauges, Roland. 1923 (Trappes)–1982.
33. Diop, Abdoulaye Bara. 1930 (Saint-Louis, Senegal)–2021.
34. Dumont, René. 1904 (Cambrai)–2001.
35 Duvignaud, Jean. 1921 (La Rochelle)–2007.
36. Fougeyrollas, Pierre. 1922 (Mont-de-Marsan)–2008.
37. Frère, Suzanne.
38. Gosselin, Gabriel. 1939–.
39. Gouellain, René. 1928 (Paris)–.
40. Goussault, Yves. 1923–2003.
41. Granai, Georges. 1923–1981.
42. Hauser, André. 1921 (Paris)–1994.
43. Hoffmann, Michel. 1929–.
44. Jamous, Haroun. 1934–.
45. Jullien, Michel.
46. Kohler, Jean-Marie. 1936 (Mulhouse)–.
47. Lapierre, Jean-William. 1921 (Mans)–2007.
48. Le Cœur, Charles. 1903 (Paris)–1944.
49. Leenhardt, Maurice. 1878 (Montauban)–1954.
50. Lesne, Marcel. 1916–2012.
51. Maquet, Jacques Jérôme Pierre. 1919 (Brussels)–2013.
52. Marié, Michel. 1931–.
53. Marthelot, Pierre. 1909 (Joigny [Yonne])–1995.
54. Massé, Louis. 1925–.
55. Massignon, Louis. 1883 (Nogent-sur-Marne)–1962.
56. Maucorps, Paul-Henri. 1911 (Constantinople)–1969.
57. Maunier, René. 1887 (Niort)–1951.
58. Meister, Albert. 1927 (Basel)–1982.
59. Memmi, Albert. 1920 (Tunis)–2020.
60. Mercier, Paul. 1922 (Paris)–1976.
61. Mersadier, Yvon. 1927 (Ussel, Corrège)–2007.
62. Michel, Andrée (Andrée Vielle). 1920–2022.
63. Montagne, Robert. 1896 (Mans)–1954.

64. Morin, Edgar (Edgar Nahoum). 1921 (Paris)-.
65. Naville, Pierre. 1903 (Paris)-1993.
66. Nguyễn Văn Huyên. 1908 (Hanoï)-1975.
67. Pascon, Paul. 1932 (Fez, Morocco)-1985.
68. Pauvert, Jean-Claude. 1923-.
69. Petit, Joseph. 1924-.
70. Petit, Odette. 1926 (Cairo)-.
71. Reverdy, Jean-Claude. 1933 (Fontaine-Grenoble)-2012.
72. Rodinson, Maxime. 1915 (Paris)-2004.
73. Rondot, Pierre. 1904 (Versailles)-2000.
74. Sauvy, Alfred. 1898 (Villeneuve de la Raho, Catalan)-1990.
75. Sayad, Abdelmalek 1935-1998.
76. Schwartz, Alfred B. 1937-.
77. Sebag, Paul. 1919 (Tunis)-2004.
78. Servier, Jean Henri. 1918 (Constantine, Algeria)-2000.
79. Sicard, Émile. 1909-1978.
80. Soret, Marcel. 1920 (Chevroux-Ain)-2010.
81. Sorre, Maximilien. 1880 (Rennes)-1962.
82. Thomas, Louis-Vincent. 1922 (Paris)-1994.
83. Thoré, Luc. 1926 (Paris)-.
84. Touma, Toufic. 1919 (Hadeth-el-Jobbé, Lebanon)-1998.
85. Trystram, Jean-Paul. 1912 (Paris)-.
86. Wilbois, Joseph. 1874-1952.
87. Xydias, Nelly. 1908-2001.
88. Zghal, Abdelkader. 1932 (Tunisia)-2015.

APPENDIX TWO

Greater French Sociology Field in 1946

Noncolonial Sociologists in 1946:

1. Arbousse-Bastide, Paul
2. Bayet, Albert
3. Bourgin, Hubert
4. Bouthoul, Gaston
5. Caillois, Roger
6. Cuvillier, Armand
7. Davy, Georges
8. Dumazedier, Joffre
9. Duprat, Guillaume L.
10. Friedmann, Georges
11. Gernet, Louis
12. Girard, Alain
13. Gurvitch, Georges
14. Le Bras, Gabriel
15. Stoetzel, Jean
16. Victoroff, David

Colonial Sociologists in 1946:

1. Aron, Raymond
2. Balandier, Georges
3. Bastide, Roger
4. Bousquet, Georges Henri
5. Chombart de Lauwe, Paul-Henry
6. Dumont, René
7. Leenhardt, Maurice
8. Lévy-Bruhl, Henri
9. Massignon, Louis
10. Maunier, René
11. Mercier, Paul
12. Montagne, Robert
13. Pauvert, Jean-Claude
14. Sicard, Emile
15. Wilbois, Joseph

APPENDIX THREE

Greater French Sociology Field in 1949

Noncolonial Sociologists in 1949:

1. Bayet, Albert
2. Bettelheim, Charles
3. Bourgin, Georges
4. Bouthoul, Gaston
5. Brams, Lucien
6. Cuvillier, Armand
7. Davy, Georges
8. Duveau, Georges
9. Friedmann, Georges
10. Gernet, Louis
11. Gurvitch, Georges
12. Isambert-Jamati, Viviane
13. Le Bras, Gabriel
14. Lévy-Bruhl, Henri
15. Stoetzel, Jean
16. Victoroff, David

Colonial Sociologists in 1949:

1. Adam, André
2. Aron, Raymond
3. Balandier, Georges
4. Bastide, Roger
5. Bousquet, Georges
6. Caillois, Roger
7. Chombart de Lauwe, Paul-Henry
8. Clément, Pierre
9. Condominas, Georges
10. Dampierre, Eric de
11. Dumont, René
12. Froelich, Jean-Claude
13. Maucorps, Paul-Henri
14. Mercier, Paul
15. Montagne, Robert
16. Naville, Pierre
17. Pauvert, Jean-Claude
18. Sicard, Emile
19. Soret, Marcel
20. Wilbois, Joseph

APPENDIX FOUR

Greater French Sociology Field in 1955

Noncolonial Specialists in 1955:

1. Andrieux, Cecile
2. Barthes, Roland
3. Bayet, Albert
4. Berger, Ida
5. Bettelheim, Charles
6. Bouthoul, Gaston
7. Brams, Lucien
8. Callois, Roger (no longer working on colonial topics)
9. Couvreur, Louis
10. Crozier, Michel
11. Cuvillier, Armand
12. Davidovitch André
13. Davy, Georges
14. Dofny, Jacques
15. Dogon, Mattei
16. Dumazedier, Joffre
17. Duveau, Georges
18. Fouilhé, Pierre
19. Friedmann, Georges
20. Frisch-Gauthier, Jacqueline
21. Gernet, Louis
22. Guilbert, Madeleine
23. Gurvitch, Georges
24. Isambert, François
25. Isambert-Jamati, Viviane
26. Jenny, Jacques
27. Labbens, Jean
28. Lambert, Roger
29. Lefebvre, Henri
30. Le Bras, Gabriel
31. Lévy-Bruhl, Henri
32. Maisonneuve, Jean
33. Maître, Jacques
34. Maucorps, Paul-Henri (no longer working on colonial topics)
35. Mendras, Henri
36. Mitrani, Nora
37. Modigiliani, Jeanne
38. Montuclard, Maurice
39. Oeconomo, Constantin
40. Pagès, Robert
41. Poulat, Emile
42. Raymond, Henri
43. Reynaud, Jean-Daniel
44. Rubel, Mamilien
45. Schoen, Ariane
46. Stoetzel, Jean
47. Touraine, Alain
48. Tréanton, Jean-René
49. Van Bockstaele, Jacques
50. Victoroff, David
51. Vincienne, Monique

Colonial Specialists in 1955:

1. Adam, André
2. Aron, Raymond
3. Balandier, Georges
4. Bastide, Roger
5. Berque, Jacques
6. Binet, Jacques
7. Bourricaud, François
8. Bousquet, Georges
9. Boutillier, Jean-Louis
10. Cazeneuve, Jean
11. Chombart de Lauwe, Paul-Henry
12. Clément, Pierre
13. Condominas, Georges
14. Cuisenier, Jean
15. Dampierre, Eric de
16. Desroche, Henri
17. Devauges, Roland
18. Dumont, René
19. Frère, Suzanne
20. Froelich, Jean-Claude
21. Girard, André (begins work on colonial immigrants in 1953)
22. Gouellain, René
23. Granai, Georges
24. Hauser, André
25. Hoffmann, Michel
26. Laude, Jean
27. Marié, Michel
28. Marthelot, Pierre
29. Massé, Louis
30. Memmi, Albert
31. Mercier, Paul
32. Mersadier, Yvon
33. Michel, Andrée
34. Molet, Louis
35. Montagne, Robert
36. Morin, Edgar
37. Naville, Pierre
38. Pauvert, Jean-Claude
39. Sebag, Paul
40. Sicard, Emile
41. Soret, Marcel
42. Sorre, Maximillian
43. Stoetzel, Jean (working on colonial immigrants by 1953)

APPENDIX FIVE

Greater French Sociology Field in 1960

Noncolonial Specialists in 1960:

1. Andrieux, Cecile
2. Arbousse-Bastide, Paul
3. Barthes, Roland
4. Bassoul, Rene
5. Berger, Ida
6. Bettelheim, Charles
7. Bouthoul, Gaston
8. Brams, Lucien
9. Couvreur, Louis
10. Crozier, Michel
11. Cuvillier, Armand
12. Davidovitch, André
13. Davy, Georges
14. Dofny, Jacques
15. Dogon, Mattei
16. Dumazedier, Joffre
17. Fouilhé, Pierre
18. Friedmann, Georges
19. Gamond, Jean
20. Gauthier, Jacqueline
21. Gernet, Louis
22. Girard, André
23. Goldmann, Lucien
24. Guilbert, Madeleine
25. Gurvitch, Georges
26. Isambert, François
27. Isambert-Jamati, Viviane
28. Jean, Suzanne
29. Labbens, Jean
30. Lahalle, Dominique
31. Lambert, Roger
32. Le Bras, Gabriel
33. Lefebvre, Henri
34. Legoux, Yves
35. Lévy-Bruhl, Henri
36. Maget, Marcel
37. Maisonneuve, Jean
38. Maître, Jacques
39. Marenco, Claudine
40. Maucorps, Paul-Henri
41. Mendras, Henri
42. Mitrani, Nora
43. Modigliani, Jeanne
44. Montuclard, Maurice
45. Moscovici, Marie
46. Mottez, Bernard
47. Moulin, Raymonde
48. Oeconomo, Constantin
49. Pagès, Robert
50. Peyre, Christiane

Noncolonial Specialists in 1960:

51. Poulat, Emile
52. Rambaud, Placide
53. Raymond, Henri
54. Reynaud, Jean-Daniel
55. Rolle, Pierre
56. Rubel, Maximilien
57. Stoetzel, Jean
58. Touraine, Alain
59. Tréanton, Jean-René
60. Van Bockstaele, Jacque
61. Vergnaud, Mme Marguerite
62. Victoroff, David
63. Vincienne, Monique

Colonial Specialists in 1960:

1. Abdel-Malek, Anouar
2. Adam, André
3. Agblémagnon, François N'Sougan
4. Althabe, Gérard
5. Aron, Raymond
6. Balandier, Georges
7. Bastide, Roger
8. Bekombo, Manga
9. Berque, Jacques
10. Biffot, Laurent Marie
11. Binet, Jacques
12. Bourdieu, Pierre
13. Bourricaud, François
14. Bousquet, Georges
15. Cazeneuve, Jean
16. Chaulet, Claudine
17. Chombart de Lauwe, Paul-Henry
18. Clément, Pierre
19. Clignet, Rémi
20. Condominas, Georges
21. Cuisenier, Jean
22. Dampierre, Eric de
23. Desroche, Henri
24. Devauges, Roland
25. Diallo, Ousmane Poreko
26. Diop, Abdoulaye Bara
27. Dumont, René
28. Duvignaud, Jean
29. Frère, Suzanne
30. Froelich, Jean-Claude
31. Gosselin, Gabriel
32. Gouellain, René
33. Goussault, Yves
34. Granai, Georges
35. Hauser, André
36. Hoffmann, Michel
37. Jamous, Henri
38. Jullien, Michel
39. Kohler, Jean-Marie
40. Lesne, Marcel
41. Maquet, Jacques Jérôme Pierre
42. Marié, Michel
43. Marthelot, Pierre
44. Massé, Louis
45. Meister, Albert
46. Memmi, Albert
47. Mercier, Paul
48. Michel, Andrée
49. Morin, Edgar
50. Naville, Pierre
51. Pascon, Paul
52. Pauvert, Jean-Claude
53. Rondot, Pierre
54. Sayad, Abdelmalek
55. Sebag, Paul
56. Servier, Jean
57. Sicard, Emile
58. Soret, Marcel
59. Sorre, Maximillian
60. Thomas, Louis-Vincent
61. Touma, Toufic
62. Trystram, Jean Paul
63. Xydias, Nelly
64. Zghal, Abdelkader

APPENDIX SIX

Belgian Colonial Sociologists

Benoît, J. (Mlle.). Member of mission for recruiting inhabitants to experimental village; Researcher in Sociology, Centre d'étude des problèmes sociaux indigènes (CEPSI), late 1950s.

Bernard, Guy. Researcher in Sociology, Lovanium University, Kinshasa, 1960s; then Sociology Professor, Laurentian University, Canada.

Bernard, Stéphane.

Brausch, Georges. Member of CEPSI General Council, 1960; Lecturer in Sociology and Social Anthropology, University of Khartoum.

Caprasse, Pierre. Sociology intern under Malengreau in Congo, then Professor, Lovanium and University of Louvain.

Clémens, René. Professor of Sociology, Liège, 1937–1980; Director, Solvay Institute of Sociology.

Comhaire, Jean Louis Léopold. Taught at University of Haiti; Seton Hall University, New School for Social Research; Université d'Ibadan; and Université de Nsukka, Nigeria, Department of Sociology and Anthropology.

Dethier, Robert. Sociology Professor, Liège.

Doucy, Arthur. Director of Sociology Institute, University of Brussels.

Feldheim, Pierre. Researcher, Institute of Sociology Solvay.

Forthomme, Georges. Sociology, Liège; Comité de Direction, CEPSI, 1958–1960.

Halkin, Joseph. Professor, Liège, Geography and Sociology.

Hennin, R. Sociological researcher, Elisabethville, 1959–1961.

Ivanitzky, Nadine.

Janne, Henri. Director of Institute of Sociology Solvay; Professor of Sociology, Bruxelles.

Lebrun, E. Sociological researcher in Elisabethville, 1959–1961.

Loeb-Mayer, Mme. Licence in social sciences, intern at CEPSI, 1958–1960.

Mahaim, E. Sociology Chair, Liège, 1892–1935.

Malengreau, Guy. Sociology professor, Louvanium, Congo.

Maquet, Jacques. Director, Rwanda-Burundi Center, IRSAC (1952–1957); University of the Congo, Elisabethville, Professor of Anthropology 1957–1960; Sixth Section of the EPHE, professor of "Sociology of Black Africa" (1962–1968); Case Western Reserve, Professor of Anthropology (1968–1970); UCLA, Professor of Anthropology (1970–1990).

Minon, Paul. Researcher, Sociology Professor, Liège.

Hockers (Perin-Hockers), Maryse. Researcher, Institute of Sociology Solvay (1960).

Poupart, Robert. Full-time researcher, Institute of Sociology Solvay (1959–1960).

Smets, Georges. Director of Institute of Sociology Solvay.

Van Overberghe, Cyriel.

Verhaegen, Benoit. Professor of Sociology and Political Science, Lovanium University, Congo, 1959–1964.

Waxweiler, Émile. Director of Institute of Sociology Solvay; Professor of Sociology and Bruxelles.

NOTES

Chapter One: Writing the Historical Sociology of Colonial Sociology in a Postcolonial Situation

1. Fanon, *The Wretched of the Earth* (New York: Grove Press, [1964] 2004), 58.

2. This argument is developed in sweeping historical detail and theoretical depth by Julia Hell, *The Conquest of Ruins: The Third Reich and the Fall of Rome* (Chicago: University of Chicago Press, 2019); also Idem., "Imperial Ruin Gazers, or Why did Scipio Weep?," *Germanic Review* 84, no. 4 (2009): 283–326.

3. Mark Katz, "The Legacy of Empire in International Relations," *Comparative Strategy* 12, no. 4 (1993): 365–83.

4. On "state culture," see my essay "Culture and the State,"in *State/Culture: Historical Studies of the State in the Social Sciences*, ed. George Steinmetz, (Ithaca, NY: Cornell University Press, 1999) 1–49; for (post)colonial case studies of state culture, see Nayanika Mathur, *Paper Tiger: Law, Bureaucracy and the Developmental State in Himalayan India* (Delhi: Cambridge University Press, 2016); Yael Berda, "Colonial Legacy and Administrative Memory: The Legal Construction of Citizenship in India, Israel and Cyprus" (PhD diss., Princeton University, 2014).

5. Deborah Durham, "Images of Culture: Being Herero in a Liberal Democracy (Botswana)" (PhD diss., University of Chicago, 1993); Karima Lazali, *Colonial Trauma: A Study of the Psychic and Political Consequences of Colonial Oppression in Algeria* (Cambridge: Polity, 2020).

6. Immanuel Wallerstein, *The Modern World-System*, vol. 1 (New York: Academic Press, 1974).

7. W. E. B. Du Bois, "Whites in Africa after Negro Autonomy," in *Albert Schweitzer's Realms: A Symposium*, ed. A. A. Roback (Cambridge, MA: Sci-Art Publishers, 1962), 243–55, 250–51; Du Bois, *Black Reconstruction in America* (New York: Oxford University Press, [1935] 2007).

8. Antony Anghie, *Imperialism, Sovereignty and the Making of International Law* (Cambridge: Cambridge University Press, 2004); George Lawson, "Colonial Origins—and Legacies—of International Organizations," in *The Presence of the Past*, ed. Klaus Schlichte and Stephan Stetter (Cambridge: Cambridge University Press, forthcoming); George Steinmetz, "The State of Emergency and the New American Imperialism: Toward an Authoritarian Post-Fordism," *Public Culture* 15, no. 2 (Spring 2003): 323–46; Steinmetz, "Return to Empire: The New US Imperialism in Theoretical and Historical Perspective," *Sociological Theory* 23, no. 4 (2005): 339–67; Samir Puri, *The Shadows of Empire: How Imperial History Shapes our World* (New York: Pegasus, 2021); Léonard Colomba-Petteng, *La coopération militaire franco-africaine: une réinvention complexe (1960–2017)* (Paris: L'Harmattan, 2019).

9. For an overview of the many ways in which the global North continues to be permeated with signs, practices, and objects traceable to the colonial era, see George Steinmetz, "The Afterlives of Empires: Notes toward an Investigation," in *The Presence of the Past*, eds. Klaus Schlichte and Steffan Stetter (Cambridge: Cambridge University Press, forthcoming).

10. Victor Klemperer, *The Language of the Third Reich: LTI—Lingua tertii Imperii. A Philologist's Notebook* (London: Athlone Press, 2000).

11. On the inseparable nexus of colonialism and racism, see Fanon, *Wretched*; Pierre Bourdieu, "The Revolution within the Revolution," chap. 7 in Bourdieu, *The Algerians* (Boston: Beacon Press, 1961); and, more recently, Joseph Wouako Tchaleu, *Le racisme colonial: analyse de la destructivité humaine* (Paris: L'Harmattan, 2015).

12. Ali Meghji, *Decolonizing Sociology: An Introduction* (Cambridge: Polity Press, 2021).

13. George Steinmetz, "Empire et domination mondiale," *Actes de la recherche en sciences sociales* 171–72 (March 2008): 4–19; J. Lanxade, "Le stand de l'Institut national de la statistique et des études économiques à la Foire coloniale et internationale de Bordeaux," *Bulletin de l'INSEE*, no. 9 (Novembre 1947): 47–64.

14. Felwine Sarr and Bénédicte Savoy, *The Restitution of African Cultural Heritage. Toward a New Relational Ethics* (Paris: Ministère de la Culture, 2018), 4.

15. Guido Gryseels, Gabrielle Landry, and Koeki Claessens, "Integrating the Past: Transformation and Renovation of the Royal Museum for Central Africa, Tervuren, Belgium," *European Review* 13 (2005): 637–47.

16. Steinmetz, "The Afterlives of Empires."

17. Ana Lucia Araujo, "Toppling Monuments Is a Global Movement," *Washington Post* (June 23, 2020).

18. Oluwaseun Tella and Shireen Motala, eds., *From Ivory Towers to Ebony Towers: Transforming Humanities Curricula in South Africa, Africa and African-American Studies* (Auckland Park: Jacana, 2020).

19. Important works in these fields include: Eric Stokes, *The English Utilitarians and India* (Oxford: Clarendon Press, 1959); John Cunningham Wood, *British Economists and the Empire* (London: St. Martin's Press, 1983); Gerard Leclerc, *Anthropologie et colonialisme: essai sur l'histoire de l'africanisme* (Paris: Fayard, 1972); Talal Asad, ed., *Anthropology and the Colonial Encounter* (London: Ithaca Press, 1973); Edward Said, *Orientalism: Western Conceptions of the Orient* (New York: Pantheon Books, 1978); Richard C. Keller, *Colonial Madness: Psychiatry in French North Africa* (Chicago: University of Chicago Press, 2007); Erik Linstrum, *Ruling Minds: Psychology in the British Empire* (Cambridge, MA: Harvard University Press, 2016); Anne Godlewska and Neil Smith, eds., *Geography and Empire* (Oxford: Blackwell, 1994); Kristin Mann and Richard Roberts, eds., *Law in Colonial Africa* (Portsmouth, NH : Heinemann Educational Books, 1991); Fassil Demissie, ed., *Colonial Architecture and Urbanism in Africa: Intertwined and Contested Histories* (Burlington, VT: Ashgate, 2011); Tomoko Masuzawa, *The Invention of World Religions, or, How European Universalism Was Preserved in the Language of Pluralism* (Chicago: University of Chicago Press, 2005); Patrick Petitjean and Catherine Jami, eds., *Science and Empires: Historical Studies about Scientific Development and European Expansion* (Dordrecht: Kluwer, 1992); Megan Vaughan, *Curing Their Ills: Colonial Power and African Illness* (Cambridge: Polity Press, 1991); Helen Tilley, *Africa as a Living Laboratory: Empire, Development, and the Problem of Scientific Knowledge, 1870–1950* (Chicago: University of Chicago Press, 2011); Pierre Singaravélou, *Professer l'Empire: Les sciences coloniales en France sous la IIIe République* (Paris: Publications de la Sorbonne, 2011); Sophie Dulucq and Colette Zytnicki, eds., *Décoloniser l'histoire? De l'histoire coloniale aux histoires nationales en Amérique latine et en Afrique, XIXe-Xxe siècles* (Saint-Denis: Société française d'histoire d'outre-mer, 2003); Jennifer Pitts, ed., *Alexis de Tocqueville, Writings on Empire and Slavery* (Baltimore, MD: Johns Hopkins University Press, 2001).

20. Only recently have scholars begun to examine sociology's colonial entanglements. See R. W. Connell, "Why Is Classical Theory Classical?," *American Journal of Sociology* 102 (1997): 1511–57; George Steinmetz, "Decolonizing German Theory: An Introduction," *Postcolonial Studies* 9, no. 1 (2006): 3–13; Steinmetz, "The Imperial Entanglements of Sociology in the United States, Britain, and France since the Nineteenth Century," *Ab*

Imperio 4 (2009): 23–78; Steinmetz, *Sociology and Empire* (Durham, NC: Duke University Press, 2013); Steinmetz, "The Sociology of Empires, Colonialism, and Postcolonialism," *Annual Review of Sociology* 40 (July 2014): 77–103; Gurminder Bhambra, *Rethinking Modernity. Postcolonialism and the Sociological Imagination* (New York: Palgrave, 2007); E. Gutiérrez Rodríguez, Manuela Boatcă, and Sergio Costa, eds., *Decolonizing European Sociology: Transdisciplinary Approaches* (Burlington, VT: Ashgate, 2010); Julian Go, *Postcolonial Thought and Social Theory* (New York: Oxford University Press, 2016); Meghji, *Decolonizing Sociology*.

21. For evidence that the heads of the leading US sociology departments insist that graduate students study the present-day United States rather than foreign countries or earlier historical periods, see Mitchell L. Stevens, Cynthia Miller-Idriss, and Seteney Khalid Shami, *Seeing the World: How US Universities Make Knowledge in a Global Era* (Princeton, NJ: Princeton University Press, 2018).

22. This is the important second, and often ignored, section of J. A. Hobson, *Imperialism: A Study* (London: James Nisbet, 1902); Aimé Césaire, *Discourse on Colonialism* (New York: Monthly Review Press, [1950] 2000), 36.

23. US sociologists specializing in Native Americans *before* the 1960s included B. W. Aginsky, John Collier, James Owen Dorsey, William Henderson, Alfred P. Parsell, Jr., and Murray L. Wax.

24. See "Preface" in Steinmetz, *Sociology and Empire*, i–xvi, xv, notes 7 and 8.

25. I have tried to diagnose the contours of this spectral form of positivism that lurks in most corners of US sociology, rarely expressing itself openly. I have also proposed an alternative epistemology that can allow sociologists to grapple with the sorts of singular events that are often ethically and politically more important than the endlessly repeated, usually trivial regularities that lend themselves to law-like generalizations of the "if A, then B" variety. My first discussion of this alternative epistemology is in *Regulating the Social: The Welfare State and Local Politics in Imperial Germany* (Princeton, NJ: Princeton University Press, 1993), 15–18; see also my "Critical Realism and Historical Sociology," *Comparative Studies in Society and History* 40, no. 1 (1999): 170–86; and most recently, "Historicism and Positivism in Sociology: From Weimar Germany to the Contemporary United States," in *Historicism: A Travelling Concept*, eds. Herman Paul and Adriaan van Veldhuizen (London: Bloomsbury, 2020), 57–95.

26. Connell, "Why Is Classical Theory Classical?"

27. The first publication that singles out and reconstructs this mid-twentieth-century sociological formation is Steinmetz, "The Imperial Entanglements of Sociology." See also my essays on British and French mid-century sociology: "A Child of the Empire: British Sociology and Colonialism, 1940s–1960s," *Journal of the History of the Behavioral Sciences* 49, no. 4 (2013): 353–78; "British Sociology in the Metropole and the Colonies, 1940s–1960s," in *The Palgrave Handbook of Sociology in Britain*, ed. John Scott and John Holmwood (Houndsmills: Palgrave Macmillan, 2014), 302–37; "Sociology and Colonialism in the British and French Empires, 1940s–1960s," *Journal of Modern History* 89, no. 3 (September 2017), 601–48; "Soziologie und Kolonialismus: Die Beziehung zwischen Wissen und Politik," *Mittelweg 36* 29, no. 3 (June–July 2020): 17–36. Wiebke Keim's excellent book examines South African labour studies, including sociology, through the end of Apartheid: Wiebke Keim, *Vermessene Disziplin: zum konterhegemonialen Potential afrikanischer und lateinamerikanischer Soziologien* (Bielefeld: Transcript, 2008).

28. George Steinmetz, "American Sociology and Colonialism, 1890s–1960s," in *Reconsidering American Power: Pax Americana and Social Science*, ed. John Kelly, J. K. Jacobsen, and Marston H. Morgan (Oxford: Oxford University Press, 2019), 273–93.

29. David Levering Lewis, *W. E. B. Du Bois*, 2 vols. (New York: H. Holt, 1993–2000); Eric Porter, *The Problem of the Future World: W. E. B. Du Bois and the Race Concept at*

Midcentury (Durham, NC: Duke University Press, 2010); George Steinmetz, "Présentation de W. E. B. Du Bois," *Actes de la recherche en sciences sociales* 171–172 (March 2008): 75–77.

30. I will analyze American and Nazi German imperial sociology in future volumes. On the latter, see Jörg Gutberger, *Volk, Raum, und Sozialstruktur: Sozialstruktur- und Sozialraumforschung im "Dritten Reich"* (Munster: LIT Verlag, 1996); Ingo Haar and Michael Fahlbusch, eds., *German Scholars and Ethnic Cleansing (1920–1945)* (New York: Berghahn Books, 2005); Carsten Klingemann, "Ostforschung und Soziologie während des Nationalsozialismus," in *Deutsche Ostforschung und polnische Westforschung im Spannungsfeld von Wissenschaft und Politik*, ed. Jan M. Piskorski, Jörg Hackmann, and Rudolf Jaworski (Osnabrück: Fibre, 2003), 161–203; George Steinmetz, "Scientific Autonomy and Empire, 1880–1945: Four German Sociologists," in *German Colonialism in a Global Age*, ed. Geoff Eley and Bradley Naranch (Durham, NC: Duke University Press, 2014), 46–73; Idem., "Neo-Bourdieusian Theory and the Question of Scientific Autonomy: German Sociologists and Empire, 1890s–1940s," *Political Power and Social Theory* 20: 71–131. On Austrian social science during Nazi occupation, see Andre Gingrich and Peter Rohrbacher, eds., *Völkerkunde zur NS-Zeit aus Wien (1938–1945)*, vol. 1 (Vienna: Österreichische Akademie der Wissenschaften, 2021).

31. Waast was taught by Balandier, Aron, and Gurvitch, and the young Pierre Bourdieu (as an assistant) at the Sorbonne between 1960 and 1965, and was then employed by the *Office de la recherche scientifique et technique outre-mer* (ORSTOM) to work with a *bureau d'études* in Madagascar. He became a full-time ORSTOM researcher and directed its "Département H" (Stratégies du développement) from 1982 to 1986, and then led an ORSTOM team on "pratiques et politiques de science" (1987–2004). My interview with Waast took place in Paris on Feb. 15, 2012.

32. The University of Dakar, which opened in 1960, had a French Rector until 1971 and a French Dean in the Letters Faculty until 1976, when the Senegalese philosopher Alassane Ndaw stepped into the post. Ndaw, "Philosopher en Afrique, c'est comprendre que nul n'a le monopole de la philosophie," *Critique* 771–72 (2008): 624–25; Ebrima Sall and Jean-Bernard Ouedraogo, "Sociology in West Africa: Challenges and Obstacles to Academic Autonomy," in *The ISA Handbook of Diverse Sociological Traditions*, ed. Sujata Patal (Los Angeles: Sage), 225–34, 228.

33. Université de Dakar, *Livret de l'étudiant. Année scolaire 1962–1963* (n.p., 1962), 510, 520, 532; Moustapha Tamba, "La sociologie au Sénégal," *La sociologie aujourd'hui: une perspective africaine*, ed. Nga Valentin Ndongo and Emmanuel Kamdem (Paris: L'Harmattan, 2010), 347–61, 353.

34. Lilia Ben Salem, "'Propos sur la sociologie en Tunisie,'" Entretien avec Sylvie Mazzella, *Genèses: sciences sociales et histoire* no. 75 (2009): 125–42, 128; George Steinmetz, "An Oblique Encounter with Sociology: Frantz Fanon's *Les damnés de la terre*," *Soziopolis* (December 2021), https://www.soziopolis.de/. Ben Salem's notes on Fanon's course are reproduced as "Rencontre de la société et de la psychiatrie," in Fanon, *Oeuvres*, vol. 2 (*Écrits sur l'aliénation et la liberté*), ed. Jean Khalfa and Robert Young (Paris: La Découverte, 2015), 430–56.

35. Jules Falquet, "Avant-propos" to Andrée Michel, *Féminisme et antimilitarisme* (Donnemarie-Donilly, 2012), 11; H. Maus and H. L. Krämer, "Sicard, Emile," in *Internationales Soziologenlexikon*, ed. Wilhelm Bernsdorf and Horst Knospe, vol. 2, 2nd ed. (Stuttgart: Enke, 1980), 789–90; Maison des sciences de l'homme, *Répertoire national*, 204; Sicard dossier, Archives de l'école des hautes études en sciences sociales, Clemens Heller papers.

36. On methodological nationalism, see Herminio Martins, "Time and Theory in Sociology," in *Approaches to Sociology*, ed. John Rex (London: Routledge & Kegan Paul, 1974),

246–94; Tanja Bogusz, "Ende des methodologischen Nationalismus?," *Soziologie. Forum der Deutschen Gesellschaft für Soziologie* 47, no. 2 (2018): 143–56; on the distinct concept of methodological homelandism, which restricts researchers to studies of their own country, see Steinmetz, "Methodological Homelandism," *Contemporary Sociology* 48, no. 3 (2019): 244–48.

37. This does not lead us back to an older historiography emphasizing national styles of colonialism. In fact, different colonial powers often pursued similar policies in the same zones of the global periphery vis-à-vis the same non-western populations, while a single power like Germany engaged in very different native policies in its various colonies. See George Steinmetz, *The Devil's Handwriting: Precolonial Ethnography and the German Colonial State in Qingdao, Samoa, and Southwest Africa*. (Chicago: University of Chicago Press).

38. For example, the German-American-British tridominium that ruled Samoa from 1889 to 1900 was premised on equality among the three powers. This can be contrasted with the "coalition of the willing" in the Iraq War, which was dominated by the United States.

39. Steinmetz, *The Devil's Handwriting*.

40. Susan Buck-Morss, *Hegel, Haiti and Universal History* (Pittsburgh, PA: University of Pittsburgh Press, 2009).

41. For an excellent study of the long-term effects of such a division, see William F. S. Miles, *Hausaland Divided* (Ithaca, NY: Cornell University Press, 1994).

42. Andrew Jamison, *National Components of Scientific Knowledge: A Contribution to the Social Theory of Science* (Lund: Research Policy Institute, 1982).

43. Peter Wagner and Björn Wittrock, "States, Institutions, and Discourses: A Comparative Perspective on the Structuration of the Social Sciences," in *Discourses on Society. The Shaping of the Social Science Disciplines*, ed. Peter B. Wagner and Björn Wittrock (Dordrecht: Kluwer Academic Publishers, 1991), 331–58, 342.

44. Michael Pollak, "Paul F. Lazarsfeld, fondateur d'une multinationale scientifique," *Actes de la recherche en sciences sociales* 25, no. 1 (1979): 45–59, 57; see also Johannes Weyer, *Westdeutsche Soziologie 1945–1960. Deutsche Kontinuitäten und nordamerikanischer Einfluß* (Berlin: Duncker & Humblot, 1984), ch. 4; Uta Gerhardt, *Denken der Demokratie. Die Soziologie im atlantischen Transfer des Besatzungsregimes* (Stuttgart: Franz Steiner Verlag, 2007).

45. Report by N. J. Demerath, Research Professor at the Institute for Research in Social Science at UNC–Chapel Hill, April 27, 1948 to Joseph Willits, Director of the Social Science Division at the Rockefeller Foundation, on his visit to the University of Birmingham, where he ascertained that the "faculty of commerce and social science at Birmingham is the most likely 'beachhead' for the establishment of sociology, social psychology, social anthropology as we in the United States know them." Rockefeller Archive Center, RG1.2, series 401.S, box 66, Folder 578, "University of Birmingham—Visits—(Sociology), 1948–1950."

46. Steinmetz, "A Child of the Empire"; "British Sociology in the Metropole and the Colonies."

47. J. W. Schoorl, "Sociology of Development: Focus of a New Profession," *Netherlands Journal of Sociology* 6, no. 2 (1970): 175–83, 177–80. The difference between non-western sociology and cultural anthropology was distilled in an information booklet for students: Peter Kloos, "Anthropology and Non-Western Sociology in the Netherlands," in *Current Anthropology in the Netherlands*, ed. Peter Kloos and Henri J.M. Claessen (Rotterdam: NSAV, 1975), 10–29, 17.

48. Claudia Castelo, "Scientific Research and Portuguese Colonial Policy: Developments and Articulations, 1936–1974," *História, Ciências, Saúde—Manguinhos* 19, no. 2

(2012); Frederico Ágoas, "Social Sciences, Modernization and Colonialism and Late Colonialism: The Centro de Estudos da Guiné Portuguesa," *Journal of the History of the Behavioral Sciences* 56 (2020): 278–97, 292, n. 2.

49. Carmelo Viñas, "Actividades culturales: De sociología colonial," *Revista internacional de sociología* 3, no. 11 (1945): 426–29.

50. Corrado Gini, *Corsi di Sociologia* (Rome: Edizioni Ricerche, 1957).

51. Pierre Fonçin, "La France extérieure," *Annales de Géographie* 1 (1891): 1–9; Aldrich Robert, *Greater France: A History of French Overseas Expansion* (Basingstoke: Macmillan, 1996).

52. Exposition universelle internationale de 1900, *Congrès international de sociologie coloniale*, 2 vols. (Paris, 1900); René Maunier, *Sociologie coloniale*, 3 vols. (Paris: Domat-Montchrestien, 1932–1942).

53. Eugène Enriquez, "De la sociologie coloniale à la sociologie de la colonisation et des pays sous-développés: l'œuvre de Georges Balandier," *Critique* 134 (1958) : 641–51.

54. Jacques Berque, *Dépossession du monde* (Paris: Seuil, 1964), 92.

55. In a private communication with the author, the socio-ethnologist Jean Copans argued that the expression "colonial sociology" is misleading because only Maunier used it, and only before the war. Yet the phrase was obviously widely used, as suggested by the references in notes 52 and 53. Maunier published the second volume of *Sociologie coloniale* in 1949.

56. I have argued elsewhere that modern colonialism is defined by (1) the coercive seizure of sovereignty over foreign territories, and (2) discursive and social practices of civilizational hierarchy, a *rule of colonial difference*. Critics of the phrase "rule of colonial difference" object that colonial policies were not always followed; hence, there was no "rule" of difference but a "politics" of difference. This criticism is overly literalist. The language of "rules" need not imply that rules are universally followed but underscores the fact that there is a dominant structure, such as a legal code or a more implicit set of norms. Rules exist, in other words, but they are not always followed. See Steinmetz, "The Colonial State as a Social Field," *American Sociological Review* 73, no. 4 (2008): 589–612. For the original formulation of the idea of the rule of difference, see Partha Chatterjee, *The Nation and Its Fragments* (Princeton, NJ: Princeton University Press, 1993), 14, 20.

57. Pierre Boiteau, "Le colonialisme et la recherche scientifique dans l'Union française," *La Pensée* n.s. 18 (May–June 1948): 116–20, 120. Boiteau was a scientist in French Madagascar, a member of the French Communist Party's "colonial committee," and an elected Councilor in the Assembly of the Union française (1949–1958). See "Boiteau, Pierre Louis" (https://maitron.fr/spip.php?article17097).

58. Maurice Faivre, "Un ethnologue de terrain face à la rebellion algérienne," *Mondes et cultures* 63 (2003): 448–60; Camille Lacoste-Dujardin, *Opération "Oiseau bleu": des Kabyles, des ethnologues et la guerre en Algérie* (Paris: Découverte, 1997), 277. Servier became a lecturer in 1957 at Montpellier University and a professor of ethnology and sociology in 1962.

59. According to Catherine Perlès, in an interview with the author, Nanterre, January 2014; also Margaret Buckner, "Eric de Dampierre and the Art of Fieldwork," in *Out of the Study and into the Field: Ethnographic Theory and Practice in French Anthropology*, ed. R. Parkin and A. de Sales (New York: Berghahn, 2010), 103–24.

60. The *porteurs de valises* or suitcase carriers were left-wing French supporters of the Algerian FLN who were involved in carrying money, papers, and sometimes weapons for the Algerians. Hervé Hamon and Patrick Rotman, *Les porteurs de valises. Le résistance française à la guerre d'Algérie* (Paris: Albin Michel, 1979). On Michel's work in Algiers after 1962, see her correspondence with Pierre Naville, in Naville Papers, Musée Social (Paris), especially the letter from Michel to Naville, May 20, 1964.

61. Pierre and Claudine Chaulet, *Le choix de l'Algérie: deux voix, une mémoire* (Alger: Barzakh, 2012); Jules Falquet, "Avant-propos," 11.

62. See the superb study by Lyn Schumaker, *Africanizing Anthropology: Fieldwork, Networks, and the Making of Cultural Knowledge in Central Africa* (Durham, NC: Duke University Press, 2001); see also Andrew Bank and Leslie J. Bank, eds., *Inside African Anthropology: Monica Wilson and her Interpreters* (Cambridge: Cambridge University Press, 2013).

63. Nguyễn Văn Huyên, *La civilisation annamite* (Hanoi: Direction de l'Instruction Publique de l'Indochine, 1944); Văn Huyên, *Le culte des immortels en Annam: Bois tirés du Hội Chân Biên* (Hanoii: Impr. d'Extrême-Orient, 1944). Nguyễn rallied to Ho Chi Minh and served as Education Minister in the Democratic Republic of Vietnam from 1946 until his death in 1975. Văn Huyên and Pierre Singaravélou, "Nguyên Van Huyên," in *Dictionnaire des orientalistes de langue française*, ed. Francois Pouillon, 2nd ed. (Paris: Karthala, 2012), 764; Singaravélou, *L'École française d'Extrême-Orient*, 342–43.

64. Pierre Bourdieu and Abdelmalek Sayad, *Le déracinement. La crise de l'agriculture traditionelle en Algérie* (Paris: Les Éditions de Minuit, 1964). Bourdieu's sponsorship of Sayad and the friendship between the two has been analyzed in detail by Amin Perez, "Rendre le social plus politique. Guerre coloniale, immigration et pratiques sociologiques d'Abdelmalek Sayad et de Pierre Bourdieu" (PhD diss., École des hautes études en sciences sociales, 2015); Perez, *Combattre en sociologues. Abdelmalek Sayad et Pierre Bourdieu dans une guerre de libération coloniale* (Paris: Agone, 2022); see also Yves Jammet, "Abdelmalek Sayad, les années d'apprentissage," in *Abdelemalek Sayad. La découverte de la sociologie en temps de guerre*, ed. Tassadit Yacine, Yves Jammet, and Christian de Montlibert (Nantes: Defaut, 2013), 17–127.

65. Efram Sera-Shriar, "What Is Armchair Anthropology? Observational Practices in Nineteeth-Century British Human Sciences," *History of the Human Sciences* 27, no. 2 (2013): 26–40.

66. René Hubert, author of a sociology manual used by French teachers and students at all levels, discussed colonialism but did not carry out fieldwork. Hubert, *Manuel élémentaire de sociologie*, 5th ed., revised (Paris: Delalain, 1949).

67. A number of sociologists were born as colonial subjects, analyzed African and Arab societies against the backdrop of colonialism but had research careers that started after decolonization, and therefore fall outside my study. For example, the Tunisian sociologist Abdelwahab Bouhdiba earned his agrégation in philosophy in 1959 and his State doctorate in 1972, and wrote on decolonization and other topics in Tunisian history. Another Tunisian sociologist, Abdelbaki Hermassi, born in 1937, received a PhD in Sociology from the Sorbonne in 1966 and from the University of California in 1971, and published extensively on comparative colonialism in the Maghreb. Sociologist Honorat Aguessy, born in Benin in 1934, wrote his State doctorate on the precolonial state under King Guezo in Dahomey.

68. Suzanne Marchand, "Has the History of the Disciplines Had Its Day?," in *Rethinking Modern European Intellectual History*, ed. Darrin M. McMahon and Samuel Moyn (Oxford: Oxford University Press, 2014), 131–52.

69. E.g. Bert Hardin, *The Professionalization of Sociology. A Comparative Study: Germany–USA* (Frankfurt: Campus, 1997); Christian Fleck, *Transatlantische Bereicherungen: zur Erfindung der empirischen Sozialforschung* (Frankfurt am Main: Suhrkamp, 2007), 189.

70. Bourdieu, *Microcosmes: Théorie des champs* (Paris: Raisons d'agir, 2022).

71. It is clear for example that the followers of Ferdinand Le Play constituted an alternative and dominated lineage of French sociology; see chapter 8.

72. Pierre Bourdieu, *Sociologie générale*, vol. 2 (Paris: Seuil, 2015), 1083–89.

73. The CNRS classification scheme grouped sociology with psychology and demography in our period, and more recently with legal studies.

74. Pierre Bourdieu, *The Rules of Art* (Cambridge, UK: Polity Press, 1996), 226.

75. Conversely, those who hold sociology doctorates may fail to find employment in the discipline or move into other disciplines and professions. From a field-theoretic standpoint, they will usually not be counted as members unless they continue publishing and participating in the disciplinary field. Field theory does not argue that individuals can only participate in a single specialized field, although it is impossible to participate fully in a large number of different fields given the costs of admission, the psychic burden of investment, and the corporeal tasks of adjusting habitus to each new domain.

76. This certificate was divided into four sections: general sociology, social psychology, demography, and ethnology.

77. To some extent, we have to apply the same "recognition" criterion to institutions as to individuals. In France, the state functions as the supreme arbiter of the legitimacy of research organizations. All of the institutes that supported colonial sociological research were licensed by the state; most received funding from the French or the relevant colonial state.

78. Almost all CNRS sociologists belonged to the *Centre d'études sociologiques*, but the converse was not true.

79. Consider two cases, Pierre Naville and Jacques Maquet. Naville, who started as a surrealist poet and Trotskyist activist between the wars, moved into psychology during World War II, and shifted from the CNRS psychology section into sociology and demography between 1950 and 1955. It is clear that most French sociologists in the postwar period, and today, see Naville as one of their own. Michel Huteau, "Pierre Naville, le marxisme, la psychologie, et l'orientation professionelle," *L'orientation scolaire et professionnelle* 26, no. 2 (1997): 195–220, 196; Pierre Rolle, "Pierre Naville: De la psychologie à la sociologie," *L'orientation scolaire et professionelle* 26, no. 2 (1997): 221–47; Michel Burnier, Sylvie Célérier, and Jan Spurk, eds., *Des sociologues face à Pierre Naville, ou, L'archipel des saviors* (Paris: L'Harmattan, 2007). Maquet was a sociologist in Belgium in the late 1940s, with a doctoral thesis on a classical sociological topic, the sociology of knowledge. He was then an anthropologist at the London School of Economics in the early 1950s, a professor of sociology at the University of the Congo and Rwanda-Urundi in Elisabethville and at the Sixth Section of the Paris *École pratique des hautes études* from the 1950s to 1968, and an anthropologist after moving to the United States in 1968. University of California Los Angeles Library, Special Collections, Maquet papers; E. L. Cerroni-Long, "Jacques Maquet: Pioneer of Cross-Cultural Research," *International Journal of Anthropology* 26, nos. 1–2 (2015): 67–71.

80. ORSOM, *Courrier des chercheurs*, vol. 4 (1951).

81. Georges Condominas, "Dans quelle mesure les asiatiques et les africains participant-ils aux recherches menées sur les divers aspects des civilisations africains et orientales?," in *État et perspectives des études africaines et orientales*, ed. Association des universités partiellement ou entièrement de langue française (Montreal: Therien freres, 1966), 105–13, 112.

82. Michel-Rolph Trouillot, "Anthropology and the Savage Slot. The Poetics and Politics of Otherness," in *Recapturing Anthropology. Working in the Present*, ed. Richard Fox (Santa Fe, NM: School of American Research Press, 1991), 18–44; Vineeta Sinha, "Annihilating the 'Savage Slot' from Anthropology: Materializing Reflexive Practices," *HAU. Journal of Ethnographic Theory* 11, no. 1 (2021): 264–72.

83. In the United States, graduate students writing PhDs are usually considered part of the disciplinary field due to their presumed trajectory into it. This is why field analysis also

has to have a prospective dimension, very much like the phenomenology of temporality discussed by writers from Husserl to Bourdieu (chapter 14).

84. Samer Frangie, "Bourdieu's Reflexive Politics. Socio-Analysis, Biography and Self-Creation," *European Journal of Social Theory* 12 (2009): 213–29.

85. Pierre Bourdieu, *Science of Science and Reflexivity* (Chicago: University of Chicago Press, 2004), 45–55.

86. Karl Mannheim, "Conservative Thought," in *Essays on Sociology and Social Psychology*, ed. Paul Kecskemeti (New York: Oxford University Press, 1953), 74–164, 76.

87. Mannheim, "Conservative Thought"; Mannheim, "The Problem of a Sociology of Knowledge," in Mannheim, *Essays on the Sociology of Knowledge*, 134–90.

88. George Steinmetz, "Ideas in Exile: Refugees from Nazi Germany and the Failure to Transplant Historical Sociology into the United States," *International Journal of Politics, Culture, and Society* 23, no. 1 (2010): 1–27; Sven Papke, "'Deutsche' Soziologie im Exil," in *Handbuch Geschichte der deutschsprachigen Soziologie*, vol. 1, ed. Stephan Moebius and Andrea Ploder (Wiesbaden: Springer, 2017), 149–68.

89. George Steinmetz, "The Genealogy of a Positivist Haunting: Comparing Prewar and Postwar U.S. Sociology," *boundary2* 32, no. 2 (2005): 107–33.

90. Ernst Robert Curtius, *Deutscher Geist in Gefahr* (Stuttgart: Deutsche Verlags-Anstalt, 1932); Ernst Wilhelm Eschmann, "Die Stunde der Soziologie," *Die Tat* 25, no. 12 (1934): 953–66.

91. George Steinmetz, "Concept-Quake: Toward a Historical Sociology of Social Science," in *The Social Sciences Through the Looking-Glass. Studies in the Production of Knowledge*, ed. Didier Fassin and George Steinmetz (Durham, NC: Duke University Press, 2022, 20–80).

92. Alan Sica, "Merton, Mannheim, and the Sociology of Knowledge," in *Robert K. Merton: Sociology of Science and Sociology as Science*, ed. Craig Calhoun (New York: Columbia University Press, 2010), 164–81, 164, 175.

93. Robert K. Merton, "Foreword," in *Science and the Social Order*, ed. Bernard Barber (Glencoe, IL: Free Press, 1952), 7–20, 15.

94. Henrika Kuklick, "The Sociology of Knowledge: Retrospect and Prospect," *Annual Review of Sociology* 9 (1983): 287–310, 291; Steve Fuller, *The Knowledge Book: Key Concepts in Philosophy, Science and Culture* (Stocksfield: Acumen, 2007), 20; Fuller, *Thomas Kuhn: A Philosophical History for Our Times* (Chicago: University of Chicago Press, 2010).

95. Bourdieu, *The Rules of Art*.

96. Pal Ahluwalia, "Origins and Displacement: Working Through Derrida's African Connections." *Social Identities* 13, no. 3 (2007): 325–36; Ahluwalia, "Post-Structuralism's Colonial Roots: Michel Foucault," *Social Identities* 16, no. 5 (2010): 597–606.

97. On situating fields within broader epochal social formations, see George Steinmetz, "Scientific Authority and the Transition to Post-Fordism: The Plausibility of Positivism in American Sociology since 1945," in *The Politics of Method in the Human Sciences: Positivism and its Epistemological Others*, ed. George Steinmetz (Durham, NC: Duke University Press, 2005), 275–323.

98. George Steinmetz, "The Octopus and the *Hekatonkheire*: On Many-Armed States and Tentacular Empires," in *The Many Hands of the State*, eds. Kimberly Morgan and Ann Orloff (New York: Cambridge University Press, 2017), 369–94.

99. On spatializing field theory, see Pascale Casanova, *The World Republic of Letters* (Cambridge, MA: Harvard University Press, 2004); Steinmetz, "The Colonial State as a Social Field"; Steinmetz, "Social Fields, Subfields, and Social Spaces, at the Scale of Empires: Explaining the Colonial State and Colonial Sociology," in *Fielding Transnationalism*, ed. Julian Go and Monika Krause (Chichester, West Sussex, UK: John Wiley Sons, 2016), 98–123.

100. On psychoanalysis, habitus, and the theory of the subject, see George Steinmetz, "Toward Socioanalysis: The 'Traumatic Kernel' of Psychoanalysis and Neo-Bourdieusian Theory," in *Bourdieu and Historical Analysis*, ed. Phil Gorski (Durham, NC: Duke University Press, 2013), 108–30; Steinmetz, "Bourdieu's Disavowal of Lacan: Psychoanalytic Theory and the Concepts of 'Habitus' and 'Symbolic Capital'," *Constellations* 13, no. 4 (2006): 445–64; Muriel Darmon, "Bourdieu and Psychoanalysis: An Empirical and Textual Study of a *pas de deux*," *Sociological Review* 64 (2016): 110–28.

101. Bourdieu did not invent the term socioanalysis, and indeed, the word had an unstable meaning in his discourse.

102. Johan Heilbron, "Practical Foundations of Theorizing in Sociology: The Case of Pierre Bourdieu," in *Social Knowledge in the Making*, eds. Charles Camic, Neil Gross, and Michèle Lamont (Chicago: University of Chicago Press, 2011) 181–208; Bourdieu, *Outline of a Theory of Practice*.

103. See chapter 14 and George Steinmetz, "Colonialism, Crisis, and Change: The Algerian Origins of Bourdieu's Concepts and His Rejection of Social Reproductionism," *Rassegna Italiana di Sociologia*, 63, n. 2 (2022): 323–348.

104. George Steinmetz, "Bourdieu, Historicity, and Historical Sociology," *Cultural Sociology* 5, no. 1 (2011): 45–66.

105. George Steinmetz, "Colonialism, Crisis, and Change."

106. Heilbron, "Practical Foundations"; Bourdieu, *Outline of a Theory of Practice*.

107. Bourdieu, *Manet*. See for example Bourdieu's brief discussion of Manet's "signature brushstroke" on p. 83.

108. Gérard Genette, *The Architext: An Introduction* (Berkeley: University of California Press, 1992): Roland Barthes, "Introduction to the Structural Analysis of Narratives," in *Image-Music-Text* (New York: Hill and Wang, 1977), 79–124.

109. Pierre Bourdieu, *L'intérêt au désintéressement. Cours au Collège de France 1987–1989* (Paris: Raisons d'agir/Seuil, 2022), 25.

110. Bourdieu, in Bourdieu and Wacquant, *An Invitation to Reflexive Sociology*, 68.

111. George Steinmetz, intervention at the conference "Sociologie, histoire. Histoire, sociologie. Journée d'étude autour de George Steinmetz," Maison Suger, Paris, March 30, 2007; along similar lines, see Sourabh Singh, "Anchoring Depth Ontology to Epistemological Strategies of Field Theory: Exploring the Possibility for Developing a Core for Sociological Analysis," *Journal of Critical Realism* 17, no. 5 (2018): 429–48.

112. The differences between German neohistoricism and British critical realism lie in the former's neo-Kantian epistemology, but ultimately this makes little difference for historical or social research. On the similarities and differences, see George Steinmetz, "From Ideal Types to Ontological Realism: Reconstructing Weber's Logic of Comparative-Historical Sociology." Keynote lecture, conference sponsored by Max-Weber-Network, at the Hamburg Institut for Social Research, Nov. 29, 2017.

113. Bourdieu, in Bourdieu and Wacquant, *An Invitation to Reflexive Sociology*, 194.

114. Bourdieu, in Bourdieu and Wacquant, *An Invitation to Reflexive Sociology*, 199.

115. Bourdieu, in Bourdieu and Wacquant, *An Invitation to Reflexive Sociology*, 199, 183–84. On the notion of explanatory critique in critical realism, see Hugh Lacey, "Explanatory Critique," in *Dictionary of Critical Realism*, ed. Mervyn Hartwig (London: Routledge, 2007), 196–201.

116. Aron was the leading French expert in German neohistoricism; see chapter 11 on Antoine Cournot's "theory of chance occurrences" and Aron's studies of German historicist sociology; see also Steinmetz, "Historicism and Positivism," 57–95.

117. As discussed in the concluding chapter of this book, Bourdieu's methodology actually entails four breaks, including a break with surface appearances in general and with one's initial "scholastic" construction of the analytic object. For a sociology of knowledge

grounded in the emic-etic distinction, see André Kieserling, *Selbstbeschreibung und Fremdbeschreibung: Beiträge zu einer Soziologie soziologischen Wissens* (Frankfurt: Suhrkamp, 2004).

118. Sourabh Singh, "Science, Common Sense and Sociological Analysis: A Critical Appreciation of the Epistemological Foundation of Field Theory," *Philosophy of the Social Sciences* 49, no. 2 (2019): 87–107.

119. An example of the failure to reflexively analyze one's own spontaneous categories or to analyze the historical contexts of knowledge is the dispute in 2021 within the "Comparative Historical Sociology" section of the American Sociological Association around naming a lifetime achievement award after Ibn Khaldun, who was accused of committing twenty-first-century political sins in the fourteenth century. See Şahan Savaş Karataşlı and Derek Clark, "Labor, Race, and Antinomies of Modernity: Non-debates between Ibn-Khaldun and Modern Social Theory," paper presented at the Social Theory Workshop, University of Michigan Department of Sociology, March 2022.

120. Bourdieu, *Outline of a Theory of Practice*, 1–30.

121. Robert K. Merton, "Insiders and Outsiders: A Chapter in the Sociology of Knowledge," *American Journal of Sociology* 78, no. 1 (1972), 9–47, 13. Merton pointed out that the Nazi regime propounded a "special application of the Insider doctrine" (ibid., 12).

122. Steinmetz, "The Colonial State as a Social Field."

123. Gaston Bachelard, *The Formation of the Scientific Mind* (Manchester: Clinamen, [1938] 2002).

124. Frantz Fanon, *A Dying Colonialism* (New York: Grove Press, 1967), 140.

125. Indeed, this had been the case for some scientists even during the era of high imperialism before 1914. In my analysis of the notorious study of the Namibian Rehebothers by the future Nazi eugenicist Eugen Fischer, I found that Fischer was forced by his own evidence to reject his initial hypothesis that race mixing led to biological degeneration. Fischer concluded that the Basters' "alleged inferiority" was due "almost entirely to the social milieu." Eugen Fischer, *Die Rehobother Bastards und das Bastardierungsproblem beim Menschen* (Jena: Verlag von Gustav Fischer, 1913), 16–17; Steinmetz, *The Devil's Handwriting*, 232–37.

126. For the analytic distinction between internalist and externalist explanatory accounts in the sociology of knowledge and the need to combine them along a continuum, see my "Scientific Authority and the Transition to Post-Fordism."

127. Pierre Bourdieu, "Les professeurs de l'Université de Paris à la veille de Mai 1968," in *Le Personnel de l'enseignement supérieur en France aux XIXe et XXe siécles*, ed. Christophe Charle and Régine Ferré (Paris: Éditions du Centre national de la recherche scientifique, 1985), 177–84, 177.

128. Of course, French sociologists were not exclusively focused on French scholarship. Relevant inputs from other national fields will be discussed when necessary. Aron in particular was shaped by German historical social science (chapter 11).

129. Raymond Aron, "What Empires Cost and What Profits They Bring," in *The Dawn of Universal History* (New York: Basic Books, [1962] 2002), 407–18.

130. Jacques Berque, "Décolonisation intérieure et nature seconde," *Etudes de sociologie tunisienne* 1 (1968) : 11–27, 13, 19, 24; Berque, "Préface," *Ibla: Revue de L'institut des belles lettres arabes* 79 (1960): 351–56, 352.

131. Syed F. Alatas, "Academic Dependency and the Global Division of Labour in the Social Sciences," *Current Sociology* 51, no. 6 (2003): 599–613; Alatas, "The Autonomous, the Universal and the Future of Sociology," *Current Sociology* 54, no. 1 (2006): 7–23; Bourdieu, *Science of Science and Reflexivity*.

132. Harald Weinrich, *Lethe: The Art and Critique of Forgetting* (Ithaca, NY: Cornell University Press, 2004).

Chapter Two: Constructing the Object, Confronting Disciplinary Amnesia

1. Sigmund Freud, "A Disturbance of Memory on the Acropolis (1936)," in Freud, *Standard Edition*, vol. 22 (London: Hogarth, 1964), 239-48, 246.

2. Jean Copans, *Critiques et politiques de l'anthropologie* (Paris: Maspero, 1974), 98.

3. The exceptions are biographies of individual sociologists, such as Balandier, Bastide, Berque, and Bourdieu, and the work of a few exceptional researchers such as Edmund Burke III, Alice Conklin, Benoît de L'Estoile, Amin Perez, Emmanuelle Sibeud, and Pierre Singaravélou (see bibliography).

4. See Roger Bastide, ed., *Contributions à la sociologie de la connaissance* (Paris: Ed. Anthropos, 1967). The editor of this collection and five of the eight contributors (Berque, Cazeneuve, Memmi, Maucorps, and Roumeguère-Eberhardt) were specialists in non-western, colonized, and postcolonial cultures. Their contributions focused on topics, such as "knowledge of the other" (Maucorps) and "sociology of African epistemology" (Roumeguère-Eberhardt), that had not been addressed by Scheler, Mannheim, and other founders of the sociology of knowledge in Weimar Germany.

5. On colonial shantytowns, see Paul Sebag, "Le bidonville de Borgel," *Cahiers de Tunisie* 23-24 (1958): 267-309; Robert Descloitres, Jean Claude Reverdy, and Claudine Descloitres, *L'Algérie des bidonvilles* (Paris: Mouton, 1961). On urban-rural circulation, see Georges Balandier, *Sociologie des Brazzavilles noires* (Paris: A. Colin, 1955). On new cultural mélanges across the colonizer-colonized boundary, see René Maunier, "L'action du 'primitif' sur le 'civilise,'" *Revue de l'Institut de Sociologie* 10, no. 3 (1930): 451-70; Frantz Fanon, *Peau noire, masques blancs* (Paris: Seuil, 1952), and the work by Bastide, Le Coeur, Métraux, and Soustelle discussed in later chapters.

6. Georges Balandier, "The Colonial Situation: A Theoretical Approach," in *Social Change. The Colonial Situation*, ed. Immanuel Wallerstein (New York: Wiley, 1966): 34-61, 47.

7. Georges Balandier, "Sociologie dynamique et histoire à partir de faits africains," *Cahiers internationaux de sociologie* 34 (1963): 3-11; see Christian Giordano, "Jenseits von Emile Durkheims Erbschaft: Die dynamische Sociologie und Anthropologie Georges Balandiers," in *Französische Soziologie der Gegenwart*, ed. Stephan Moebius and Lothar Peter (Konstanz: UVK, 2004), 213-36. On the impact of Balandier on Portuguese colonial sociologists and Dutch "non-western" sociology, see chapter 1.

8. Jean Duvignaud, "La pratique de la sociologie dans les pays décolonisés," *Cahiers internationaux de sociologie* 34 (1963): 165-74, 170. Duvignaud taught sociology at the University of Tunisia (1960-1965), wrote on the sociology of theater, and carried out a detailed ethnography of a village in southern Tunisia. Duvignaud, *Chebika—mutations dans un village du Maghreb. Étude sociologique* (Paris: Gallimard, 1968).

9. Joseph Wilbois, *Le Cameroun, les indigènes, les colons, les missions, l'administration française* (Paris: Payot, 1934); Robert Montagne, "Afrique noire et Afrique blanche," *L'Afrique et L'Asie* 4, no. 32 (1951): 90-97; Albert Memmi, *Portrait du colonisé, précédé du portrait du colonisateur* (Paris: Corrêa, 1957); Paul Mercier, "Le groupement européen de Dakar: orientation d'une enquête," *Cahiers internationaux de sociologie* 19 (1955): 130-46; Jean Cuisenier, *L'Ansarine. Contribution à la sociologie du développement* (Paris: Presses universitaires de France, 1960); Paul Mercier, *Dakar dans les années 1950* (Aubervilliers: CTHS, 2021), 154-73. See also, Pierre Nora, *Les français d'Algérie* (Paris: Julliard, 1961); Frantz Fanon, "Algeria's European Minority," in *A Dying Colonialism* (New York: Grove Press 1965), 147-62. Nora is a historian most famous for *Les lieux de mémoire*, 3 vols. (Paris: Gallimard, 1996-1998). His study of Algerian *pied noirs* has been criticized for not being a work of history based on original research and "the usual scholarly apparatus"

but as a "personal account." David Prochaska, *Making Algeria French: Colonialism in Bône, 1870–1920* (Cambridge: Cambridge University Press, 1990), 6. Fanon, discussed in chapter 6, also dedicated few pages to analyzing the colonizers.

10. Steinmetz, "Ideas in Exile."

11. Georges Balandier, *Sociologie actuelle de l'Afrique noire. Dynamique des changements sociaux en Afrique centrale* (Paris, PUF, 1955).

12. Georges Balandier, *Daily Life in the Kingdom of the Kongo from the Sixteenth to the Eighteenth Century* (New York, Pantheon Books, [1965] 1968); John K. Thornton, "Afro-Christian Syncretism in the Kingdom of Kongo," *Journal of African History* 54 (2013): 53–77, 53.

13. Paul Mercier, "Aspects des problèmes de stratification sociale dans l'Ouest Africain," *Cahiers internationaux de sociologie* 17 (1954): 47–65, 48, 59; Mercier, "Les classes socials et les changements politiques récents en Afrique noire," *Cahiers internationaux de sociologie* 38 (1965): 143–54, 144.

14. Mercier, "Le groupement européen de Dakar," 130.

15. Mercier, "Les classes sociales," 146.

16. Mercier, "Aspects des problèmes de stratification sociale," 58.

17. Mercier, "Les classes sociales," 146.

18. Mercier. "Aspects des problèmes de stratification sociale," 57, 65.

19. Mercier, *Histoire de l'anthropologie* (Paris: Presses universitaires de France, 1966), 168, note 1.

20. Mercier, "Les classes sociales," 145.

21. Mercier, "On the Meaning of 'Tribalism' in Black Africa," in *Africa: Social Problems of Change and Conflict*, ed. Pierre L. Van den Berghe (San Francisco: Chandler, 1965), 483–501, 493.

22. Éric de Dampierre, *Un ancien royaume Bandia du Haut-Oubangui* (Paris: Plon, 1967); Dampierre, "Soutenance, thèse de doctorat ès lettres," University of Paris. Unpublished document at Bibliothèque Éric-de-Dampierre, Nanterre, France. See also, Paul Mercier, *Tradition, changement, histoire. Les "Somba" du Dahomey septentrional* (Paris: Editions Anthropos, 1968).

23. Pierre Philippe Rey, "Sociologie economique et politique des Kuni, Punu et Tsangui de la région de Mossendjo et de la Boucle du Niari (Congo-Brazzaville)," (Thèse de doctorat de recherche ès-sociologie, University of Paris, 1969), 519; see also Idem., *Les alliances de classes: sur l'articulation des modes de production* (Paris: Maspero, 1973). Another student of Balandier who combined ethnography with history, and who was associated with both sociology and ethnology in his teaching appointments during the 1960s, was Claude Meillassoux. Balandier's student Alfred Schwartz, discussed in chapter 10, included a historical section in his doctoral thesis and published several systematic historical accounts of French colonial policies in Upper Volta (Burkino Faso).

24. Kamal Chachoua, "Fanny Colonna, chercheure essentielle," *El Watan*, Nov. 21, 2014. https://www.elwatan.com/edition/contributions/fanny-colonna-chercheure-essentielle-21 -11-2014.

25. Fanny Colonna, *Instituteurs algériens, 1883–1939* (Paris: Presses de la Fondation nationale des sciences politiques, 1975): 168–69.

26. See, for example, Julia Adams, Elisabeth Clemens, and Ann Orloff, eds., *Remaking Modernity: Politics, Processes and History in Sociology* (Durham, NC: Duke University Press, 2005), which ignores the original formation of genuinely historical sociology in Imperial and Weimar Germany.

27. Leroi-Gourhan, "Qu'est-ce que c'est . . . l'ethnologie?," *Bulletin du Centre de formation aux recherches ethnologiques*, no. 5 (Janvier 1953): 1–7, 1; Gerald Gaillard, *Répertoire de l'ethnologie française: 1950–1970*, 2 vols. (Paris: Editions du Centre national de

la recherche scientifique, 1990), vol. 2, 30–31; Jacques Gutwirth, "La professionnalisation d'une discipline: Le centre de formation aux recherches ethnologiques," *Gradhiva* no. 29 (2001): 25–41.

28. Marcel Maget, "Remarques sur l'ethnographie metropolitaine," *Bulletin de la Société neuchâteloise de géographie* 60, no. 2 (1948): 39–58; Maget, *Ethnographie métropolitaine: Guide d'étude directe des comportements culturels* (Paris: Civilisations du Sud, 1953).

29. Éric de Dampierre, "Malvire-sur-Desle. Une commune aux franges de la region parisienne," *L'information géographique* 20 (1956): 68–73; Lucien Bernot and René Blancard, *Nouville, un village français* (Paris: Institut d'ethnologie, 1953); Pierre Clément and Nelly Xydias, *Vienne sur le Rhône, la ville et les habitants, situations et attitudes. Sociologie d'une cité française* (Paris: A. Colin, 1955).

30. Laura Ann Twagira, "'Robot Farmers' and Cosmopolitan Workers: Technological Masculinity and Agricultural Development in the French Soudan (Mali), 1945–68," *Gender & History* 26 (2014): 459–77, 460.

31. Alice Conklin, *In the Museum of Man: Race, Anthropology, and Empire in France, 1850–1950* (Ithaca, NY: Cornell University Press, 2013), 203.

32. F. Morvan, "Le premier bateau français consacré à l'ethnologie va partier pour le Niger. M. Marcel Griaule, conseiller de l'Union française dirigera l'expédition," *France-tropiques. Organe de l'Intergroupe parlementaire de la France d'Outre-mer* (August 5, 1955), 5.

33. Marcel Griaule, "L'avion au service des sciences humaines," *Atomes* 4 (1946): 7–10; Paul Henry Chombart de Lauwe, "Chez les Fali. Mission ethnographique Griaule-Sahara-Cameroun," *La Géographie* 68, nos. 2–3 (1937): 97–104, 98; Chombart de Lauwe, "La photographie aérienne et les sciences humaines," *Comptes rendus sommaires des séances de l'Institut français d'anthropologie* 3, no. 54 (1946): 19–20; Chombart de Lauwe, *La découverte aérienne du monde* (Paris: Horizon de France, 1948); Chombart de Lauwe, "Vision aerienne et civilization," *Atomes* 45 (1949): 429–41; Chombart de Lauwe, *Photographies aériennesmethode, procédés, interpretation. L'étude de l'homme sur la terre* (Paris: Colin, 1951); Chombart de Lauwe, *Un anthropologue dans le siècle* (Paris: Descartes & Cie, 1996), 26–28.

34. Jeanne Haffner, *The View from Above: The Science of Social Space* (Cambridge, MA: MIT Press, 2013), 72. Chombart de Lauwe's ethnographic mission in Northern Cameroon in 1936 was inspired by Mauss and carried out with Marcel Griaule. His two-year ethnographic mission in Northern Tonkin and Southern China, funded by CNRS in 1939, was aborted due to the war. He planned a research mission in French West Africa for ORSOM during the Occupation and carried out two missions on nomads in the Algerian Grand Erg Occidental in 1950. Only then did he begin to focus on metropolitan urban sociology, creating the *Groupe d'ethnologie sociale* (later called *Centre d'ethnologie sociale*). André Grelon, "Paul-Henry Chombart de Lauwe."

35. P. F. Gonidec, *L'évolution des territoires d'outre-mer depuis 1946* (Paris: Librairie générale de droit et de jurisprudence, 1958), 26.

36. Jacques Berque, "Cent vingt-cinq ans de sociologie maghrébine," *Annales. Economies, sociétés, civilisations* n.s. 10, no. 3 (1956): 296–324; and especially "Vers une étude des comportements en Afrique du Nord," *Revue africaine* 100 (1956): 523–36; Edward Said, *Orientalism* (New York: Vintage Books, 1979). Another precursor of Said was Anouar Abdel Malek, "Orientalism in Crisis," *Diogenes* 11, no. 44 (1963): 103–40.

37. Jacques Berque, "Décolonisation intérieure et nature seconde," *Etudes de sociologie tunisienne* 1 (1968): 11–27, 19, 13, 24.

38. Steinmetz, "An Oblique Encounter with Sociology."

39. Georges Balandier and Paul Mercier, *Particularisme et évolution. Les pêcheurs Lébou du Sénégal* (Saint-Louis: Senegal, 1952), 131, 212.

40. Pierre Bourdieu, "La culture Mozabite," *Documents Algériens, Série monographies*, no. 23 (Nov. 20, 1958).

41. Roger Bastide, "Le principe de coupure et le comportement afro-brésilien," in *Anais do XXXI Congresso Internacional de Americanistas, São Paulo*, vol. 1 (São Paulo: Anhembi, 1955), 493–503; Bastide, "L'acculturation formelle," in *Le prochain et le lointain* (Paris: Cujas, 1970), 137–48, 138.

42. Octave Mannoni, "The Decolonisation of Myself," *Race* 7, no. 4 (1966): 327–35; Mannoni, *Psychologie de la colonisation* was translated as *Prospero and Caliban: The Psychology of Colonization* (Ann Arbor: University of Michigan Press, [1950] 1990).

43. For the rejection of a separate science for the colonized, see Paul Mercier, *Les tâches de la sociologie* (Dakar: Institut français d'Afrique noire, 1951); also D. G. MacRae, "Sociology in Transitional Societies," *Universitas* (Accra) 2 (1956): 107–9; Norbert Elias, "Sociology and Anthropology," presented at the annual conference of the Ghana Sociological Association, April 1963. Norbert Elias archive, file MISC—E XI = SOC-Anthrop. For the second approach, see Mercier, "Aspects des problèmes de stratification sociale dans l'Ouest Africain."

44. Most of these themes were developed before 1945 by the surrealists and the *Collège de Sociologie*; see Denis Hollier, ed., *The College of Sociology (1937–39)* (Minneapolis: University of Minnesota Press, 1988); Stephan Moebius, *Die Zauberlehrlinge. Soziologiegeschichte des Collège de Sociologie* (Konstanz: UVK Verlagsgesellschaft, 2006); Simonetta Falasca-Zamponi, *Rethinking the Political: The Sacred, Aesthetic Politics, and the Collège de Sociologie* (Montréal: McGill-Queen's University Press, 2011).

45. Bourdieu and Sayad, *Le déracinement*, 88.

46. François N'Sougan Agblémagnon, "La différence de psychologie et de sensibilité provoque-t-elle une différence de comportement entre occidentaux d'une part, africaines de l'autre, quant aux méthodes de la recherche et quant à l'interprétation des résultats?," in Association des universités partiellement ou entièrement de langue française, *État et perspectives des études africaines et orientales* (Montréal: Therien frères, 1965), 128–44.

47. Fanon, "On Violence," in *Wretched*, 1–62, 13.

48. The Weimar era sociology of knowledge did not inaugurate an era of self-reflexivity in sociology. This is probably because of the brutal curtailment of discussions of the sociology of knowledge in Germany with the advent of Nazism. The Americanized offshoot of the sociology of knowledge, led by Robert Merton, was uninterested in self-reflexivity. George Steinmetz, "The History of Sociology as Disciplinary Self-Reflexivity," in *The Palgrave Handbook of the History of Human Sciences*, ed. D. McCallum (London: Palgrave Macmillan, 2022), pp. 833–864.

49. Comments by M. S. Benyahi in 1971, quoted in Fanny Colonna, "Une fonction coloniale de l'ethnographie dans l'Algérie de l'entre deux-guerres: la programmation des élites moyennes," *Libyca* 20 (1972): 259–67.

50. Kamel Chachoua, "Pierre Bourdieu et l'Algérie : le savant et la politique," in *L'Algérie sociologique: hommage à Pierre Bourdieu (1930–2002)*, ed. Kamel Chachoua (Alger: CNRPAH, 2012), 9–23, 17.

51. On historical forgetting, see Lucian Hölscher, "Geschichte und Vergessen," *Historische Zeitschrift* 249 (1990): 1–17; Weinrich, *Lethe*. Ann Stoler's concept of "aphasia" is inadequate for grasping this process, since aphasia has an individual and linguistic focus. By contrast, repressed material, including repressed social science, takes embodied, emotional, visual, and material forms, not just linguistic ones, and is collective as well as individual. Aphasia also elides the *moral* dimension in discussions of burying memory, discussed by Paul Ricœur in *Memory, History, Forgetting* (Chicago: University of Chicago

Press, 2004): 412–56. See Ann Laura Stoler, "Colonial Aphasia: Race and Disabled Histories in France," *Public Culture* 23, no. 1 (2011): 121–56.

52. Johan Heilbron, "Pionniers par défaut? Les débuts de la recherche au Centre d'études sociologiques (1946–1960)," *Revue française de sociologie* 27, no. 3 (1991): 365–79; Heilbron, *French Sociology* (Ithaca, NY: Cornell University Press, 2015).

53. Philippe Masson, *Faire de la sociologie: les grandes enquêtes françaises depuis 1945* (Paris: Découverte, 2008).

54. Osama Abi-Mershed, *Apostles of Modernity: Saint-Simonians and the Civilizing Mission in Algeria* (Palo Alto, CA: Stanford University Press, 2011), 106–7, 115.

55. Françoise Arnault, *Frédéric Le Play. De la métallurgie à la science sociale* (Nancy: Presses universitaires de Nancy, 1993), 72; Frédéric Le Play, *Les ouvriers européens* (Paris: L'Imprimerie impériale, 1855).

56. Frédéric Le Play, *Les ouvriers des deux mondes* (Paris: Au Sécretariat de la Société d'économie sociale, 1858–1908); H. Higgs, "Frederic Le Play," *Quarterly Journal of Economics* 4, no. 4 (1890): 408–33, 419.

57. "Les grandes enquêtes en Afrique du Nord," *Bulletin économique du Maroc* 3, no. 12 (1936): 159–60; Edmund Burke, III, "The Sociology of Islam: The French Tradition," in *Islamic Studies: A Tradition and Its Problems*, ed. Malcolm H. Kerr (Santa Monica, CA: Undena Publications, 1980), 73–88, 86.

58. Louis Massignon, "Enquête sur les corporations d'artisans et de commerçants au Maroc (1923–1924) d'après les réponses au questionnaire transmis par circulaire du 15 Novembre 1923 sous le timbre de la Direction des affaires indigènes et du service des renseignements," *Revue du Monde Musulman* 58 (1924): 1–250.

59. Robert Montagne, *Naissance du prolétariat marocain. Enquête collective exécutée de 1948 à 1950* (Paris: Peyronnet, 1951); ORSTOM, *Organisation-Activités 1944–1955* (Paris, 1955).

60. Paul Henry Chombart de Lauwe, *Pour retrouver la France, Enquêtes sociales en équipes* (Uriage: École nationale des cadres d'Uriage, 1941). Chombart initially worked for the Vichyist elite training school "Uriage," but soon moved into the Resistance. Antoine Delestre, *Uriage: une communauté et une école dans la tourmente 1940–1945* (Nancy: Presses Universitaires de Nancy, 1989).

61. Abdelmalek Sayad, *Histoire et recherche identitaire: suivi de entretien avec Hassan Arfaoui* (Saint-Denis: Bouchène, 2002), 71.

62. Pierre Monbeig, *La crise des sciences de l'homme* (Rio de Janeiro: Edição da Casa do estudante do Brasil, 1941), 59–60.

63. Michel Amiot, *Contre l'état, les sociologues. Élements pour und histoire de la sociologie urbaine en France (1900–1980)* (Paris: Editions de l'Ecole des hautes études en sciences sociales, 1986); Eric Le Breton, *Pour une critique de la ville: la sociologie urbaine française: 1950–1980* (Rennes: Presses universitaires de Rennes, 2012).

64. Paul Lapie, *Les civilisations tunisiennes (musulmans, israélites, européens). Étude de psychologie sociale* (Paris: Félix Alcan, 1898). Although Lapie's study took the entire colony as its analytic frame, it begins with a striking image of the "violent contrasts" that made Tunis a "sort of living absurdity," in which "incompatible elements" somehow manage to coexist (ibid., p. 2). Jean Le Chatelier, *Alfred Le Chatelier, 1855–1929: sa carrière africaine* (Paris: Service historique de l'Armée de terre, 1987).

65. Kenneth L. Brown, *People of Salé: Tradition and Change in a Moroccan City, 1830–1930* (Manchester: Manchester University Press, 1976), 195; Burke, III, "The Sociology of Islam," 73–88.

66. André Adam, *La Société rurale et la société urbaine au Maroc. Deux leçons de sociologie marocaine pour la classe de première* (Rabat: Impr. françaises et marocaines, 1954), 52.

67. Jean Guiart, *Recherches de sociologie urbaine dans le Pacifique français* (Paris: ORSTOM, 1958).

68. Mercier, *Dakar dans les années 1950.*

69. Michel Marié, *Les terres et les mots. Une traversée des sciences sociales* (Paris: Editions Méridiens-Kliencksiek, 1989), 58.

70. Georges Balandier, *L'action en faveur des populations rurales: le regroupement des villages au Gabon* (Brazzaville: I.E.C., 1950).

71. Balandier, "The Colonial Situation," 34–61, 44.

72. Balandier, *Sociologie des Brazzavilles noires*; Balandier, "Évolution de la société et de l'homme" in *Afrique équatoriale française*, ed. Eugène Léonard Guernier (Paris, Encyclopédie Coloniale et Maritime, 1950), 125–132, 130.

73. Balandier, *Daily Life in the Kingdom of the Kongo*, 151.

74. Chapoulie and Rose ignore the colonial origins of sociology of labor; Jean-Michel Chapoulie, "Sur le developpement en France d'un programme de recherche unissant perspective historique et travail de terrain," in *Observer le travail: histoire, ethnographie, approches combinées*, ed. Anne-Marie Arborio et al. (Paris: La Découverte, 2008), 265–80; see also, Michael Rose, "Retrospection and the Role of a Sociology of Work," in *Work in the French Tradition*, ed. Claude Durand (London: SAGE Publications, 2007), 1–29. An important exception is Maxime Quijoux, ed., *Bourdieu et le travail* (Rennes: Presses universitaires de Rennes, 2015), which discusses Bourdieu's sociology of labor in Algeria.

75. Lucie Tanguy, *La sociologie du travail en France. Enquête sur le travail des sociologues, 1950–1990* (Paris: La Découverte, 2011), 77. French sociologists who carried out *enquêtes* on industrialization and labor conditions in the colonies include Balandier, Bourdieu, Montagne, Gérard Althabe, Jacques Binet, Pierre Clément, Jean Cuisenier, Robert Descloitres, Roland Devauges, Eric de Dampierre, Jean-Claude Froehlich, André Hauser, Paul Mercier, Yvon Mersadier, Jean-Claude Reverdy, Marcel Soret, and Jean-Paul Trystram. See, for example, Marcel Soret, *Main d'oeuvre fixe et main d'oeuvre saisonnière dans la vallée du Niari* (Brazzaville: Institut d'études centrafricaines, 1953); Jean Paul Trystram, "Quelques aspects des relations industrielles au Maroc," *Annales. Économies, Sociétés, Civilisations* n.s. 7, no. 3 (1952): 361–70; Trystam, "Le mineur marocain. Contribution statistique à une étude sociologique" (PhD diss., Faculté des lettres de l'Université de Paris, 1955); Eric de Dampierre, "Coton noir, café blanc: Deux cultures du Haut-Oubangui à la veille de la loi-cadre," *Cahiers d'Études Africaines* 1, no. 2 (1960): 128–47.

76. See, for example, Jean-L. Trochain, "Les études poursuivies par l'Institut d'études centrafricaines, depuis sa création, sur le territoire de la République du Congo," *Bulletin de l'Institut d'études centrafricaines*, n.s, nos. 19–20 (1960): 127–88, 173.

77. Jean Copans, "Une relecture actuelle," in Georges Balandier, *Sociologie des Brazzavilles noires*, 2nd ed. (Paris: Presses de la Fondation Nationale des Sciences Politiques, 1985), 281–96.

78. Roland Devauges, *Les chômeurs de Brazzaville et les perspectives du barrage du Kouilou* (Brazzaville: ORSTOM, 1959); Gérard Althabe, *Le chômage à Brazzaville: étude psychologique* (Paris: ORSTOM, 1959).

79. Pierre Bourdieu, "La hantise du chômage chez l'ouvrier algérien. Prolétariat et système colonial," *Sociologie du travail* 4, no. 4 (1962) : 313–31, 325.

80. François Perroux, "'L'ordonnance' de J. M. Keynes et les pays sous-développés," *Bulletin de l'Union des exploitations électriques en Belgique* no. 3 (July 1953): 1–18.

81. Balandier, *Sociologie des Brazzavilles noires*; Michael Banton, *The Coloured Quarter. Negro Immigrants in an English City* (London: Jonathan Cape, 1955); Andrée Michel, *Les travailleurs algériens en France* (Paris: CNRS, 1956); Robert Montagne, *Étude sociologique de la migration des travailleurs musulmans d'Algérie en métropole*, 8 vols.

(Paris: Ministère de l'interieur, Direction des affaires d'Algérie, Bureau des affaires sociales musulmanes, 1957); Abdoulaye Bara Diop, "Enquête sur la migration Toucouleur à Dakar," *Bulletin de l'Institut français d'Afrique noire*, série B, vol. 22 (1960): 393–418; Bara Diop, *Société toucouleur et migration, l'immigration toucouleur à Dakar* (Dakar: IFAN, 1965).

82. Montagne, *Naissance du prolétariat marocain*; Montagne, *Étude sociologique de la migration*.

83. See note 23.

84. Abdelmalek Sayad and Alain Gillette, *L'immigration algérienne en France* (Paris: Éditions Entente, 1976); Abdelmalek Sayad, *La double absence. Des illusions de l'émigré aux souffrances de l'immigré* (Paris: Seuil, 1999).

85. Paul-Henri Maucorps, Albert Memmi, and Jean-Françis Held, *Les français et le racisme* (Paris: Payot, 1965), 170.

86. Patrick Crowley, "Albert Memmi: The Conflict of Legacies," in *Postcolonial Thought in the French-Speaking World*, ed. Charles Forsdick and David Murphy (Liverpool: Liverpool University Press, 2009), 126–35, 134.

87. Meghji, *Decolonizing Sociology*, 23–24.

88. On the sociology of religious syncretism, Black Islam, and other non-Christian religious phenomena in colonial settings, see Roger Bastide, *Éléments de sociologie religieuse* (Paris: A. Colin, 1935); Bastide, *The African Religions of Brazil: Towards a Sociology of the Interpenetration of Civilizations* (Baltimore, MD: Johns Hopkins University Press, [1960] 1978), 221.

89. The first two volumes of *Histoire des religions* were dominated by articles on non-western religions by the sociologists Wilbois and Leenhardt, in addition to essays by Indologists, Japanologists, Sinologists, Africanists, and other Orientalists. Articles on non-European religions were published during the first ten years (1956–1965) of the *Archives de sociologie des religions* by the sociologists Syed Hussein Alatas, Robert Attal, Balandier, Bastide, Berque, René Bureau, Kofi Busia, Pierre Marthelot, Pereira de Queirox, Maxime Rodinson, and Peter Worsley. Non-European religions were also discussed in *Archives de sociologie des religions* by ethnologists Jeanne Cuisinier, Germaine Dieterlen, Louis Dumont, Luc de Heusch, Alfred Métraux, and Jean Guiart.

90. Desroche's chair at the Sixth Section of the EPHE, starting in 1958, was in "sociology of cooperation and development."

91. Anon., "Le groupe de sociologie des religions. Quinze ans de travail," *Archives de sociologie des religions* 14, no. 28 (1969): 3–92, 21.

92. "Le groupe de sociologie des religions," 6.

93. Bastide, *The African Religions of Brazil*, 383; Bastide, *Les religions africaines au Brésil* (Paris : Presses universitaires de France, 1960), 529.

94. Bastide, *The African Religions of Brazil*, 221.

95. Georges Balandier, *The Sociology of Black Africa. Social Dynamics in Central Africa* (New York: Praeger, [1955] 1970), 403.

96. Compare Henri-Charles Puech and Paul Viganux, "La science des religions," in *Les sciences sociales en France. Enseignement et recherche*, ed. Centre d'études de politique étrangère (Paris: P. Hartmann, 1937), 134–62.

97. Danièle Hervieu-Léger, "Objet perdu et retrouvé: de quelques singularités de la scène française de la sociologie des religions," in *Les sociologies françaises: héritages et perspectives: 1960-2010*, ed. Catherine Paradeise, Dominique Lorrain, and Didier Demazière (Rennes: Presses universitaires de Rennes, 2015), 209–20; Jean-Paul Williame, *Sociologie des religions* (Paris: Presses universitaires de France, 2012), 40–60; Pierre Lassave, *La sociologie des religions: histoire d'une communauté de savoir* (Paris: Ecole des hautes études en sciences sociales, 2019); Émile Poulat, "Sociologie religieuse," in *La*

sociologie et les sciences de la société, ed. Jean Cazeneuve and André Akoun (Paris: CEPL, 1975), 309–414.

98. Fanon, "On Violence," 19–20.

99. See *Memoires du CHEAM 1937-2000. Classement par auteurs* (Paris: Académie des Sciences d'Outre-Mer, 2002).

100. Pierre Rondot, "Contacts sociaux dans l'armée d'Afrique," *Cahiers Charles de Foucauld* 17, no. 1 (1950): 88–94.

101. Gaston Bouthoul, *Ibn-Khaldoun, sa philosophie sociale* (Paris: Librairie Orientaliste Paul Guethner, 1930).

102. Paul Henry Chombart de Lauwe and Marie-José Chombart de Lauwe, eds., *Images de la femme dans la société* (Paris: Éditions ouvrières, 1964).

103. Theodore Porter and Dorothy Ross, "Introduction. Writing the History of Social Science," in *The Modern Social Sciences*, vol. 7, ed. Theodore Porter and Dorothy Ross (Cambridge: Cambridge University Press, 2003), 1–10, 6; George Steinmetz, "Begriffsbeben. Von der Geschichte der Wissenschaft zur historischen Soziologie der Sozialwissenschaften," *Mittelweg* 36 (May 2020): 94–115.

104. J. Stuart Hughes, *Consciousness and Society. The Reorientation of European Social Thought, 1890-1930* (New York: Knopf, 1958), ch. 2.

105. George Steinmetz, "The Relations between Sociology and History in the United States: The Current State of Affairs," *Journal of Historical Sociology* 20, nos. 1–2 (2007): 1–12.

106. Charles Camic, "Uneven Development in the History of Sociology," *Swiss Journal of Sociology* 23 (1997): 227–33, 230; see also Camic, *Veblen* (Cambridge, MA: Harvard University Press, 2020), a brilliant model for writing the historical sociology of social science.

107. Strategic and legitimatory uses of the disciplinary past are, of course, not absent among professional historians. Yet historians are more likely to encounter pushback if they engage in egregious presentism or anachronism, overt teleology, or celebratory hagiography. David Hackett Fischer, *Historians' Fallacies: Toward a Logic of Historical Thought* (New York: Harper & Row, 1970).

108. Monique Hirschhorn, "The Place of the History of Sociology in French Sociology," *Schweizerische Zeitschrift fur Soziologie* 23, no. 1 (1997): 3–7, 5.

109. See Christophe Charle and Laurent Jeanpierre, eds., *La vie intellectuelle en France* (Paris: Éditions du Seuil, 2016), a volume edited by a historian and a sociologist, respectively.

110. Charles Camic, "Periphery toward Center and Back: Scholarship on the History of Sociology, 1945–2012," in *Historiography of the Social Sciences*, ed. Roger Backhouse and Philippe Fontaine (New York: Cambridge University Press, 2014), 99–143, 108.

111. George Steinmetz, "Positivism and Its Others in the Social Sciences," in *The Politics of Method in the Human Sciences: Positivism and its Epistemological Others*, ed. George Steinmetz (Durham, NC: Duke University Press, 2005), 1–56. Unfortunately, my analysis of sociology's spontaneous philosophy in this book has not become dated.

112. Alfred North Whitehead, *The Organisation of Thought, Educational and Scientific* (London: Williams and Norgate, 1917), 115; Pasteur, "The Pasteur Institute," *Nature* 40, 1029 (July 18, 1889), 278. On the importance of images of natural sciences for sociology, see Johan Heilbron, "Social Thought and Natural Science," in Theodore Porter and Dorothy Ross, eds., *The Cambridge History of Science*, 40–56.

113. Brigitte Nagel, *Die Welteislehre: ihre Geschichte und ihre Rolle im "Dritten Reich"* (Stuttgart: Verlag für Geschichte der Naturwissenschaften und der Technik, 1991).

114. Alatas, "Academic Dependency."

115. Berque, *Dépossession du monde*, 93, note 6.

116. Georges Balandier, *Histoire d'autres* (Paris: Stock, 1977), 190.

117. George Steinmetz and Julia Hell, "The Visual Archive of Colonialism: Germany and Namibia," *Public Culture* 18, no.1 (2006): 141–82; Patricia M. E. Lorcin, "Imperial Nostalgia; Colonial Nostalgia: Differences of Theory, Similarities of Practice?," *Historical Reflections/Réflexions Historiques* 39, no. 3 (2013): 97–111; Lorcin, "The Nostalgias for Empire," *History and Theory* 5, no. 2 (June 2018): 269–85.

118. Joachim Zeller, *Kolonialdenkmäler und Geschichtsbewußtsein* (Frankfurt am Main: IKO, 2000). On the difference between collective melancholia and collective nostalgia, see my "Colonial Melancholy and Fordist Nostalgia: The Ruinscapes of Namibia and Detroit," in *Ruins of Modernity*, ed. Julia Hell and Andreas Schoenle (Durham, NC: Duke University Press, 2010), 294–329.

119. According to Jean-Louis Boutellier, an economist and anthropologist who worked for the *Office de la recherche scientifique et technique outre-mer*, the 1960s was a "bizarre" and in-between era with respect to colonialism, lodged between the "hard colonial period" and the "no-less-hard postcolonial one." Jean-Louis Boutillier, "C'était une sorte de bulle," *L'homme* 185–86 (2008): 33–37, 36; for a similar recollection, see the remark by Roland Waast in chapter 1.

120. As Patricia Lorcin points out, there are "theoretical and practical differences between colonial and imperial nostalgia," in Lorcin, "The Nostalgias for Empire," 269. Idealized empires can thus appear as sites of multiculturalism.

121. The repression of colonial research is reminiscent of the ways postwar German sociologists long refused to acknowledge the discipline's continuing existence after 1933 in Nazified forms, but see Carsten Klingemann, *Soziologie im Dritten Reich* (Baden-Baden: Nomos-Verlag, 1996); Klingemann, *Soziologie und Politik: Sozialwissenschaftliches Expertenwissen im Dritten Reich und in der frühen westdeutschen Nachkriegszeit* (Wiesbaden: VS Verlag für Sozialwissenschaften, 2009). A similar refusal to admit the very existence of sociology in fascist Italy is discussed by Marco Santoro, "Empire for the Poor," in *Sociology and Empire: The Imperial Entanglements of a Discipline*, ed. George Steinmetz (Durham, NC: Duke University Press, 2013), 106–65.

122. Bourdieu, "Méthode scientifique et hiérarchie sociale des objets," *Actes de la recherche en sciences sociales* 1 (1975), 4–6.

123. Methodological nationalism is implicit in all forms of scientific metrocentrism, but is not the same thing. Social scientists in peripheral states may also engage in methodological nationalism, for example, yet they are clearly not metrocentric, since their national states do not belong to the global core.

124. Fabien Sacriste, *Germaine Tillion, Jacques Berque, Jean Servier et Pierre Bourdieu: des ethnologues dans la guerre d'indépendance algérienne* (Paris: L'Harmattan, 2011). See chapters 12–14 for sustained discussion of the disciplinary identities of Berque, Balandier, and Bourdieu.

125. Philippe Masson and Cherry Schrecker, *Sociology in France after 1945* (London: Palgrave, 2016), 57. Masson and Schrecker arrive at a census of 20 French sociologists in 1950, compared to the 35 counted here; they count about a hundred sociologists in "the 1950s and 1960s" (pp. 40, 47), whereas our census reveals around 130 sociologists by 1960 (see appendixes 2, 3 in this text). They attribute the growth of sociology to French planification after 1963, ignoring colonial planning and developmentalism in the 1950s. Masson and Schrecker discuss Chombart de Lauwe, but overlook his colonial research and read his ethnography entirely in terms of an appropriation of the Chicago school, completely missing its colonial past and his close connections to Griaule.

126. Olivier Godechot, "La formation des relations académiques au sein de l'EHESS," *Histoire et mesure* 26 (2011): 223–60.

Chapter Three: Colonial Reconquest, Scientification, and Popular Culture

1. Quoted in Véronique Dimier, "For a New Start? Resettling French Colonial Administrators in the Prefectoral Corps," *Itinerario* 28, no. 1 (2004): 49–66, 49 (translation altered).
2. Tyler E. Stovall, *France since the Second World War* (New York: Longman, 2002), 46.
3. Frederick Cooper, "'Our Strike': Equality, Anticolonial Politics and the 1947–48 Railway Strike in French West Africa," *Journal of African History* 37, no. 1 (1996): 81–118.
4. Michael Crowder, *West Africa under Colonial Rule* (London: Hutchinson, 1968), 499.
5. On US support for French and British colonialism after 1945, see the classic analysis by William Roger Louis and Ronald Robinson, "The Imperialism of Decolonization," *Journal of Imperial and Commonwealth History* 22, no. 3 (1994): 462–511; see also John Gallagher and Ronald Robinson, "The Imperialism of Free Trade," *Economic History Review* 6, no. 1 (1953): 1–15; William Roger Louis, *Imperialism at Bay: The United States and the Decolonization of the British Empire, 1941–1945* (Oxford: Clarendon Press, 1977). The USSR did not develop tools for engaging in sub-Saharan Africa until 1957; see Alessandro Iandolo, "The Rise and Fall of the Soviet Model of Development in West Africa, 1957–1964," *Cold War History* 12, no. 4 (2012): 683–704; Iandolo, *Arrested Development: The Soviet Union in Ghana, Guinea, and Mali, 1955–1968* (Ithaca, NY: Cornell University Press, 2022).
6. Julia Hell, "Katechon: Carl Schmitt's Imperial Theology and the Ruins of the Future," *Germanic Review: Literature, Culture, Theory* 84, no. 4 (2009): 283–326.
7. D. Anthony Low and John Lonsdale, "Introduction: Towards the New Order, 1945–1963," in *History of East Africa*, vol. 2, ed. D. A. Low and Alison Smith (Oxford: Clarendon Press, 1989), 1–62. Georges Balandier discussed the postwar colonial reconquest and noted that it was a "technical phase." Balandier, "La situation coloniale: approche théorique," *Cahiers internationaux de sociologie* 11 (1951) : 44–79. European historians tend to ignore this second colonial occupation, narrating the entire postwar period as one leading inexorably to decolonization. See, for example, Tony Judt, *Postwar. A History of Europe since 1945* (New York: Penguin, 2006), 278–301.
8. W. E. B. Du Bois, *The World and Africa; and, Color and Democracy* (New York: Oxford University Press, 2007), 245.
9. Frederick Cooper, *Citizenship between Empire and Nation: Remaking France and French Africa, 1945–1960* (Princeton, NJ: Princeton University Press, 2014), 27.
10. John Gallagher, "The Decline, Revival, and Fall of the British Empire," in *The Decline, Revival, and Fall of the British Empire: The Ford Lectures and Other Essays* (Cambridge: Cambridge University Press, 1982), 73–153, 144.
11. Gérard Bossuat, *La France, l'aide américaine et la construction européenne, 1944–1954* (Paris: Comité pour l'histoire économique et financière de la France, 1992), ch. 14.
12. Gallagher, "The Decline, Revival, and Fall of the British Empire," 145.
13. Jean-Charles Fredenucci, "La brousse coloniale ou l'anti-bureau," *Revue française d'administration publique* 108 (2003): 603–615, 604.
14. Quoted in Dimier, "For a New Start?," 49.
15. Julien Meimon, "L'invention de l'aide française au développement. Discours, instruments et pratiques d'une dynamique hégémonique," *Questions de recherche* 21 (2007): 1–43, 15.
16. Véronique Dimier, "Recycling Empire. French Colonial Administrators at the Heart of European Development Policy," in *The French Colonial Mind*, ed. Martin Thomas (Lincoln: University of Nebraska Press, 2011), 251–74, 263; William B. Cohen, *Rulers of Empire: The French Colonial Service in Africa* (Stanford, CA: Stanford University Press, 1971), 173.
17. Meimon, "L'invention de l'aide," 20.

18. Salem Chaker, "Algérie 1962–1974. La refoulement des études berbères," in *Le temps de la coopération: sciences sociales et décolonisation au Maghreb*, ed. Jean-Robert Henry and Jean-Claude Vatin (Paris, 2012), 109–118, 113, note 10.

19. Virginia Thompson and Richard Adloff, *The Malagasy Republic: Madagascar Today* (Stanford, CA: Stanford University Press, 1965), 222. In addition to the French sociologists at Algiers University discussed in chapter 1, Louis-Vincent Thomas taught sociology at Dakar from 1951 to 1958 and Pierre Fougeyrollas did so from 1956 until the early 1970s; René Bureau taught sociology at the University of Abidjan between 1968 and 1971; sociologist Jean Cuisenier was Professor of Philosophy at Carthage (Tunisia) and then at the *Institut des Hautes Études* in Tunis (1954–1959); ethno-sociologist Jean Poirier became head of the Department of Human Sciences at the University of Madagascar in the 1960s. Philippe Laburthe-Tolra, "René Bureau (1929–2004)," *Journal des africanistes* 75 (2005): 306–8; Rachide Sidi Boumedine, "L'enseignement de la sociologie à l'université d'Alger entre 1962 et 1976. Quels enjeux?," in *Le temps de la coopération: Sciences sociales et décolonisation au Maghreb*, ed. Jean-Robert Henry and Jean-Claude Vatin (Paris: Karthala, 2012), 285–94.

20. George Steinmetz, "Colonialism, Crisis, and Change: The Algerian Origins of Bourdieu's Concepts and His Rejection of Social Reproductionism," *Rassegna Italiana di Sociologia*, 63, n. 2 (2022): 323–348.

21. Charles-Robert Ageron, *France coloniale ou parti coloniale?* (Paris: PUF, 1978), 283.

22. Frederick Cooper, *Decolonization and African Society: The Labor Question in French and British Africa* (Cambridge: Cambridge University Press, 1996).

23. Raymond F. Betts, "Dakar: Ville impériale (1857–1960)," in *Colonial Cities*, ed. Robert J. Ross and Gerard J. Telkamp (Boston: Kluwer Academic, 1985), 193–206, 201.

24. Cooper, *Citizenship between Empire*.

25. Enrico Bellone, *A World on Paper: Studies on the Second Scientific Revolution* (Cambridge, MA: MIT Press, 1980). On the previous transition from explorers to conquerors in the French African sphere of influence, see Emmanuelle Sibeud, *Une science impériale pour l'Afrique? La construction des savoirs africanistes en France 1878–1930* (Paris: EHESS, 2002).

26. See Anne Kwaschik, "Die Verwissenschaftlichung des Kolonialen als kultureller Code und internationale Praxis um 1900," *Historische Anthropologie* 28, no. 3 (2020): 399–423.

27. On German colonial social science in general, see Felix Brahm, *Wissenschaft und Dekolonisation: Paradigmenwechsel und institutioneller Wandel in der akademischen Beschäftigung mit Afrika in Deutschland und Frankreich, 1930–1970* (Stuttgart: Franz Steiner Verlag, 2010); Lewis Pyenson, *Cultural Imperialism and Exact Sciences. German Expansion Overseas, 1900–1930* (New York: Lang, 1985). The image of Germany as a particularly scientific colonizer is undermined by the fact that scientists' views rarely prevailed in the internally competitive dynamics within German colonial states, even if those views were used selectively by the elite groups who actually forged native policies; Steinmetz, *The Devil's Handwriting*. That said, other policy realms, including some scientific ones, were relatively autonomous from these inter-imperial struggles over native policy,

28. Jean-Charles Fredenucci, "L'entregent colonial des ingénieurs des Ponts et Chaussées dans l'urbanisme des années 1950–1970," *Vingtième Siècle* 79 (2003): 79–91; Fredenucci, "La brousse coloniale"; Sabine Clarke, "A Technocratic Imperial State? The Colonial Office and Scientific Research, 1940–1960," *Twentieth-Century British History* 18, no. 4 (2007): 453–80; Brett M. Bennett and Joseph M. Hodge, eds., *Science and Empire: Knowledge and Networks of Science across the British Empire, 1800–1970* (New York: Palgrave Macmillan, 2011); Hodge, *Triumph of the Expert*.

29. Tilley, *Africa as a Living Laboratory*, 20, 9.

30. Robert Chambers, *Settlement Schemes in Tropical Africa* (London: Routledge, 1969), 17.

31. For an overview of research in colonial Africa, see Peter Duignan and Lewis H. Gann, *Colonialism in Africa, 1870-1960*, vol. 5, *A Bibliographical Guide to Colonialism in Sub-Saharan Africa* (London: Cambridge University Press, 1973), 1-32.

32. On the most *geisteswissenschaftliche* pole of colonial experts, see Alain Messaoudi, *Les arabisants et la France coloniale: savants, conseillers, médiateurs, 1780-1930* (Lyon: ENS, 2015).

33. See, for example, the praise for "impartial science" seeking "scientific laws of colonization" in Marcel Dubois, "Leçon d'ouverture du cours de géographie coloniale," *Annales de Géographie* 10, no. 3 (1894): 121-37, 125.

34. Letter from French Colonial Minister Moutet to the Governor General of Indochina in 1936, quoted in Singaravélou, *Professer l'Empire*, 106.

35. ORSC, *Rapport d'activité pour l'année 1945* (Paris: ORSTOM, 1945), 12, 14.

36. Pierre Singaravélou, "Le moment 'impérial' de l'histoire des sciences sociales (1880-1910)," *Mil neuf cent. Revue d'histoire intellectuelle* 27, no. 1 (2009): 87-102, 96.

37. Roger Duveau, Secretaire d'État à la France d'Outre-Mer, "Inauguration du cours de sciences sociales," *Colo/ENFOM* 53, no. 165 (October 1954): 1-3, 1-2.

38. George Steinmetz, "The Crisis of History and the History of Crisis: Sociology as a 'Crisis Science,'" *Trajectories: Newsletter of Comparative and Historical Sociology* 29, no. 1 (2017): 1-5.

39. Catherine Coquery-Vidrovitch, "Selling the Colonial Economic Myth (1900-1940)," in *Colonial Culture in France Since the Revolution*, ed. Pascal Blanchard et al. (Bloomington: Indiana University Press, 2014), 180-88; Sandrine Lemaire, "Manipulation: Conquering Taste (1931-1939)," in ibid., 285-95.

40. Jacques Berque, *Mémoires des deux rives* (Paris, Seuil, 1989), 31.

41. Georges Balandier, *Civilisés, dit-on* (Paris: PUF, 2003), 22; see chapter 13.

42. Georges Balandier, *Tous comptes faits* (Paris: éditions du Pavois, 1947), 231.

43. Martin Thomas, *The French Empire at War, 1940-45* (Manchester: Manchester University, 1998), 71.

44. Eric T. Jennings, *Vichy in the Tropics: Pétain's National Revolution in Madagascar, Guadeloupe, and Indochina, 1940-44* (Stanford, CA: Stanford University Press, 2001), 9.

45. Pascal Blanchard and Gilles Boëtsch, "Races et propagande coloniale sous le régime de Vichy 1940-1944," *Africa: Rivista trimestrale di studi e documentazione dell'Istituto italiano per l'Africa e l'Oriente* 49, no. 4 (1994): 531-61, quotations from 532, 557.

46. Jennings, *Vichy in the Tropics*, 12, 14.

47. Ian S. O. Playfair et al., *The Mediterranean and Middle East*, vol. 4 (London: H.M.S.O., 1966), 109-36.

48. Charles de Gaulle, *The Call to Honour, War Memoirs* (New York: Viking Press, 1955), 105.

49. Thomas, *The French Empire at War*; Jennings, *Vichy in the Tropics*, 9.

50. On French North Africa during the war, see Christine Levisse-Touzé, *L'Afrique du Nord dans la guerre, 1939-1945* (Paris: A. Michel, 1998); on French West Africa, see Catherine Akpo-Vaché, *L'AOF et la seconde guerre mondiale: la vie politique (septembre 1939-octobre 1945)* (Paris: Karthala, 1996). On wartime French Africa as a whole, see Jean-Noël Vincent, *Les forces françaises dans la lutte contre l'Axe en Afrique* (Paris: Ministère de la défense, 1983-1985).

51. Allied forces intelligence report from January 1944, quoted in Thomas, *The French Empire at War*, 224.

52. Raymond-Marin Lemesle, *La Conférence de Brazzaville de 1944* (Paris: C.H.E.A.M., 1994); Tony Smith, "A Comparative Study of French and British Decolonization," *Comparative Studies in Society and History* 20, no. 1 (1978): 70-102, 73.

53. Thomas, *The French Empire at War*, 135.

54. See the essays in John M. MacKenzie, ed., *European Empires and the People: Popular Responses to Imperialism in France, Britain, the Netherlands, Belgium, Germany and Italy* (Manchester: Manchester University Press, 2011); compare Stuart Ward, "Introduction," in *British Culture and the End of Empire*, ed. Stuart Ward (Manchester: Manchester University Press, 2001), 1–20.

55. Thomas, *The French Empire at War*, 24; Thomas, *The French Empire between the Wars: Imperialism, Politics and Society* (Manchester: Manchester University Press, 2005), 204.

56. Pierre-Henri Simon, "Du sens impérial," *Revue des troupes coloniales* 47, no. 275 (March 1946): 32–40, 32. Simon later polemicized against the Algerian War in *Contre la torture* (Paris: Le Seuil, 1957).

57. Ageron, *France coloniale*.

58. Jürgen Klöckler, *Abendland—Alpenland—Alemannien. Frankreich und die Neugliederungsdiskussion in Südwestdeutschland 1945–1947* (München: R. Oldenbourg, 1998), 29.

59. Charles-Robert Ageron, "L'opinion publique face aux problèmes de l'Union française," in *Les Chemins de la décolonisation de l'empire colonial français*, ed. Charles-Robert Ageron (Paris: CNRS, 1986), 33–48.

60. See *Bulletin intérieur de l'INSEE*.

61. Pierre Abramovici, *Le putsch des généraux: De Gaulle contre l'armée, 1958–1961* (Paris: Fayard, 2011).

62. Quotes from Robert Aldrich, *Greater France: A History of French Overseas Expansion* (Basingstoke: Macmillan, 1996), 283; Ageron, "L'opinion publique, 38, 41, 43. See also Anon., "Le sondage d'opinion sur l'Union française," *Bulletin d'information (INSEE)* no. 11 (Nov. 1949): 1–8; P. F. Gonidec, *L'évolution des territoires d'outre-mer depuis 1946* (Paris: Librairie générale de droit et de jurisprudence, 1959), 49.

63. Gonidec, *L'évolution*, 48.

64. Didier Fischer, *L'histoire des étudiants en France, de 1945 à nos jours* (Paris: Flammarion, 2000), 195. The journal "Anticolonial Students" (*Étudiants anticolonialistes*) was created in 1949 (Ibid., 196).

65. Ageron, "L'opinion publique," 47.

66. Interview with Alain Accardo, a French settler from Algeria who was a university student in Algiers in the 1950s, in Amin Perez, "Rendre le social plus politique," 44.

67. Jacques Lanxade, "Le Stand de l'Institut National de la Statistique et des Études Économiques à la Foire Coloniale et Internationale de Bordeaux," *Bulletin de l'INSEE* no. 9 (Nov. 1947): 47–64.

68. For a fascinating evocation of the colonial atmosphere of Paris in the early 1960s, see Ulrike Ottinger, *Paris Calligrammes: Eine Erinnerungslandschaft* (Ostfildern: Hatje Cantz, 2019).

69. Kristin Ross, *Fast Cars, Clean Bodies: Decolonization and the Reordering of French Culture* (Cambridge, MA: MIT Press, 1995).

Chapter Four: Colonial Developmentalism, Welfare, and Sociology

1. Michel Marié, *Les terres et les mots. Une traversée des sciences sociales* (Paris: Editions Méridiens-Kliencksiek, 1989), 30.

2. Paul V. Dutton, *Origins of the French Welfare State: The Struggle for Social Reform in France, 1914–1947* (Cambridge: Cambridge University Press, 2012), 223.

3. Eric Jabbari, *Pierre Laroque and the Welfare State in Postwar France* (Oxford: Oxford University Press, 2012), 107.

4. Herrick Chapman, *France's Long Reconstruction: In Search of the Modern Republic* (Cambridge, MA: Harvard University Press, 2018), 2.

5. Chapman, *France's Long Reconstruction*, 120, 112. The so-called Laroque Plan of October 1945, named after its author and the director of social insurance in de Gaulle's provisional government, Pierre Laroque, combined the existing social insurance plans with family allowances to create a "unified system of benefits." Jabbari, *Pierre Laroque*, 107.

6. Bruno Valat, *Histoire de la sécurité sociale (1945-1967)* (Paris: Économica, 2001), 496.

7. Chapman, *France's Long Reconstruction*, 278; see also Daniel Lefeuvre, *Chère Algérie: comptes et mécomptes de la tutelle coloniale, 1930–1962* (Saint-Denis: Société française d'histoire d'outre-mer, 1997), 283–326.

8. Marié, *Les terres et les mots*, 30.

9. Eric Williams, *Capitalism and Slavery* (Chapel Hill: University of North Carolina Press, 1944); Immanuel Wallerstein, *The Modern World-System*, vol. 3: *The Second Great Expansion of the Capitalist World-Economy, 1730–1840s* (San Diego, CA: Academic Press, 1989); Christopher A. Bayly, *Imperial Meridian: The British Empire and the World, 1780–1830* (London: Longman, 1989); for the French case, see David Todd, "A French Imperial Meridian, 1814–1870," *Past and Present* 210, no. 1 (2011): 155–86.

10. Frederick Cooper, *Decolonization and African Society: The Labor Question in French and British Africa* (Cambridge: Cambridge University Press, 1996); Babacar Fall and Richard L. Roberts, "Forced Labour," in *General Labour History of Africa: Workers, Employers and Governments, 20th–21st Centuries*, ed. Stefano Bellucci and Andreas Eckert (Melton: Boydell & Brewer, 2019), 77–115; S. Morandeau-Couderc, "Le travail obligatoire dans les colonies françaises," in *La justice et le droit: instruments de strategie coloniale*, vol. 3, ed. Bernard Durand (Montpellier: CNRS, 2001), 959–95.

11. C. W. Newbury, *Patrons, Clients and Empire: Chieftaincy and Over-Rule in Asia, Africa and the Pacific* (Oxford: Oxford University Press, 2003).

12. Frederick Lugard, *The Dual Mandate in British Tropical Africa* (London: W. Blackwood, 1922); Lugard, *Representative Forms of Government and "Indirect Rule" in British Africa* (London: W. Blackwood & Sons, 1928).

13. Hubert Lyautey, *Lettres du Tonkin et Madagascar (1894–1899)*, 2nd ed. (Paris: A. Colin, 1921), 71; William B. Cohen, *Rulers of Empire: The French Colonial Service in Africa* (Stanford, CA: Stanford University Press, 1971), 116.

14. Steinmetz, *The Devil's Handwriting*.

15. Catherine Coquery-Vidrovitch, "L'impérialisme français en Afrique noire: Idéologie impériale et politique d'équipement, 1924–1975," *Relations internationales* 7 (1976): 261–82, 269.

16. Jean Copans, *Sociologie du développement*, 2nd ed. (Paris: Armand Colin, 2016), 10; Roy MacLeod, "Introduction," *Osiris* 15 (2000): 1–13, 12.

17. C. H. Filgueria, "Development: Social," in *International Encyclopedia of the Social & Behavioral Sciences*, ed. Neil J. Smelser and Paul B. Baltes (Amsterdam: Elsevier, 2001), 3583–87, 3583.

18. Jean Duvignaud, *La sociologie: guide alphabétique* (Paris: Denoël, 1972), 131–38.

19. Ekkehard Geib, "Ausbildung des Nachwuchses für den höheren Verwaltungsdienst unter besonderer Berücksichtigung der Geschichte der Justiz- und Verwaltungsausbildung in Preußen," *Archiv des öffentlichen Rechts* 80 (1955/56): 307–45, 322.

20. An exception is Erik S. Reinert, who traces development economics to Central European traditions: see his "German Economics as Development Economics," in *The Origins of Development Economics: How Schools of Economic Thought Have Addressed Development*, ed. Jomo KS and Erik S. Reinert (London: Zed, 2005), 48–68. Foucault discusses

Polizeiwissenschaft, which he relabels governmentality, but he ignores its modern evolution into colonial developmentalism. Michel Foucault, "Governmentality," in *The Foucault Effect. Studies in Governmentality*, ed. Graham Burchell, Colin Gordon, and Peter Miller (Chicago: University of Chicago Press, 1991), 87–104.

21. On the separate genealogies of the concepts of progress and development, compare Wolfgang Wieland, "Entwicklung, Evolution," in *Geschichtliche Grundbegriffe. Historisches Lexikon zur politisch-sozialen Sprache in Deutschland*, vol. 2, ed. Otto Brunner, Werner Conze, and Reinhart Koselleck (Stuttgart: Klett-Cotta, 1975), 199–228; Reinhart Koselleck, "'Progress' and 'Decline': An Appendix to the History of Two Concepts," in *The Practice of Conceptual History: Timing History, Spacing Concepts* (Stanford, CA: Stanford University Press, 2002), 218–35.

22. On the use of the terms transitive and intransitive in social theory, see Mervyn Hartwig, *Dictionary of Critical Realism* (London: Routledge, 2007), 263–65.

23. George Steinmetz, "German Exceptionalism and the Origins of Nazism: The Career of a Concept," in *Stalinism and Nazism: Dictatorships in Comparison*, ed. Ian Kershaw and Moshe Lewin (Cambridge: Cambridge University Press, 1997), 251–84; Steinmetz, "Historicism and Positivism."

24. Henri, Comte de Saint-Simon, *Catéchisme des industriels* (Paris: Sétier, 1823–1824), quotes from 186, 165, 91, 188.

25. Michael Cowen and Robert Shenton, *Doctrines of Development* (London: Routledge, 1996), 22.

26. Richard Vernon, "Auguste Comte and 'Development': A Note," *History and Theory* 17, no. 3 (1978): 323–26, 324; Comte, *Cours de philosophie positive* (1830–1842), Part 2 in *Auguste Comte and Positivism*, ed. Gertrud Lenzer (New York: Harper, 1975), 71–308.

27. John Stuart Mill, *Auguste Comte and Positivism* (Ann Arbor: University of Michigan Press, [1866] 1961), 114.

28. Joseph M. Hodge and Gerald Hödl, "Introduction," in *Developing Africa: Concepts and Practices in Twentieth-Century Colonialism*, ed. Joseph M. Hodge, Gerald Hödl, and Martina Kopf (Manchester: Manchester University Press, 2014), 1–34, 6.

29. Alice Conklin, *A Mission to Civilize: The Republican Idea of Empire in France and West Africa, 1895–1930* (Stanford, CA: Stanford University Press, 1997).

30. Albert Sarraut, *La mise en valeur des colonies françaises* (Paris: Payot, 1923).

31. Van Beusekom, *Negotiating Development*, 7–12; Emil Schreyger, *L'office du Niger au Mali, 1932 à 1982: la problématique d'une grande entreprise agricole dans la zone du Sahel* (Wiesbaden: Steiner, 1984), 33–34. That said, the Office du Niger involved uprooting and resettlement and forced labor, as discussed in chapter 10.

32. Christophe Bonneuil, "Development as Experiment: Science and State Building in Late Colonial and Postcolonial Africa, 1930–1970," *Osiris* 15, no. 1 (2000): 258–81, 259. This statement ignores the developmentalist policies already being undertaken in the French North African colonies, although these were directed more toward the benefit of Europeans than natives. Prochaska, *Making Algeria French*; Jonathan Wyrtzen, *Making Morocco: Colonial Intervention and the Politics of Identity* (Ithaca, NY: Cornell University Press, 2016), 88.

33. This was the *Fonds national pour l'outillage public de la France d'outre-Mer* (National Fund for the Public Infrastructure of Overseas France). *Conférence économique de la France métropolitaine et d'outre-mer* 1935: vol. 2, 7.

34. Arturo Escobar, *Encountering Development. The Making and Unmaking of the Third World* (Princeton, NJ: Princeton University Press, 1995), 26.

35. Quotes from Cowen and Shenton, *Doctrines of Development*, 3; Hodge and Hödl, "Introduction," 2.

36. Charles-Robert Ageron, "La deuxième guerre mondiale," in *Histoire de la France coloniale*, ed. Jacques Thobie, Jean Meyer, Catherine Coquery-Vidrovitch, and Charles-Robert Ageron (Paris: Armond Colin,1990–1991), vol. 2, 311–54, 344; Nancy Lawler, "Reform and Repression under the Free French: Economic and Political Transformation in the Côte d'Ivoire, 1942–45," *Africa: Journal of the International African Institute* 60, no. 1 (1990): 88–110; Thomas, *The French Empire at War*, 153

37. Jennings, *Vichy in the Tropics*, 22.

38. Document quoted in Jacques Marseille, "La conférence des gouverneurs généraux des colonies (novembre 1936)," *Le mouvement social* 101 (1977): 61–84, 70.

39. The Vichy government also resumed the use of coerced labor at the Office du Niger. Van Beusekom, *Negotiating Development*, xxxi, 63.

40. Cooper, *Decolonization*, 152.

41. Daniel Lefeuvre, "Vichy et la modernisation de l'Algérie: intention ou réalité?" *Vingtième siècle* 42 (Apr.–June 1994): 7–16, 8; Thomas, *The French Empire at War*, 179.

42. Thomas, *The French Empire at War*, 246

43. République Française, *Conférence africaine française. Brazzaville. 30 janvier 1944–8 février 1944* (Paris: Ministère des Colonies, 1945), 45, 49; John D. Hargreaves, *Decolonization in Africa*, 2nd ed. (London: Routledge, 1996), 69.

44. République Française, *Conférence africaine française*, 11–13.

45. Thomas, *The French Empire at War*, 251–52.

46. Cooper, *Decolonization*, 203.

47. Thomas, *The French Empire at War*, 179.

48. Thomas, *The French Empire at War*, 244.

49. "Development Crusade," *Empire: Journal of the Fabian Colonial Bureau* 10, no. 4 (Dec. 1947): 3–4.

50. Cohen, *Rulers of Empire*, 173. FIDES accounted for more than 50% of all direct spending on French colonies during the 1950s; Ministère de la France d'outre-mer, Service des statistiques, *Outre-Mer, 1958* (Paris: Presses universitaires de France, 1960), 570.

51. Hubert Deschamps, *The French Union* (Paris: Berger-Levrault, 1956), 209.

52. Joseph-Roger de Benoist, *L'Afrique occidentale française, de la Conférence de Brazzaville (1944) à l'Indépendance (1960)* (Dakar: Nouvelles Editions Africaines, 1982), 136–38, 243–63; Martin-René Atangana, *French Investment in Colonial Cameroon: The FIDES era (1946-1957)* (New York: Peter Lang, 2009).

53. Cooper, *Decolonization*, 203.

54. Coquery-Vidrovitch, "L'impérialisme français," 269.

55. Barry J. Eichengreen, *The European Economy Since 1945: Coordinated Capitalism and Beyond* (Princeton, NJ: Princeton University Press, 2007), chs. 3–4.

56. Richard F. Kuisel, *Capitalism and the State in Modern France: Renovation and Economic Management in the Twentieth Century* (Cambridge: Cambridge University Press, 1981), 194, 203. Kuisel, *Capitalism and the State*, 225, 241. The metropolitan *Fonds de modernisation et d'équipement*, precursor of future French funds for public equipment programs, was established in January 1948; in 1955, it was replaced by the *Fonds de développement économique et social*. Kuisel, *Capitalism and the State*, 240, 254.

57. Anon., "Loi no. 46-860 du 30 avril 1946 tendant à l'établissement, au financement et à l'exécution de plans d'équipement et de développement des territoires relevant du ministère de la France d'outre-mer," *Journal official* 78, no. 102 (May 1, 1946): 3365–66.

58. Kuisel, *Capitalism and the State*, 225, 241.

59. Philippe Masson, "Le financement de la sociologie française: les conventions de recherche de la DGRST dans les années soixante," *Genèses* 62 (2006): 110–28; Masson and Schrecker, *Sociology in France after 1945*, 44–45.

60. Samir Saul, *Intérêts économiques français et décolonisation de l'Afrique du Nord (1945-1962)* (Genève: Librairie Droz S.A., 2016), 90–110.

61. Catherine Coquery-Vidrovitch, *Le Congo au temps des grandes compagnies concessionnaires: 1889-1930*, vol. 2 (Paris: EHESS, 2001), 131, 174.

62. Laurence Monnais-Rousselot, *Médecine et colonisation: l'aventure indochinoise 1860-1939* (Paris: CNRS, 1999), 66, 442.

63. Wyrtzen, *Making Morocco*, 55.

64. Patricia Lorcin, "Imperialism, Colonial Identity, and Race in Algeria, 1830–1870: The Role of the French Medical Corps," *Isis* 90 (1999): 653–79, 654.

65. Gary Wilder, *The French Imperial Nation-State: Negritude and Colonial Humanism between Two World Wars* (Chicago: University of Chicago Press, 2005), 50.

66. William B. Cohen, "The Colonial Policy of the Popular Front," *French Historical Studies* 7, no. 3 (1972): 368–93, 374. But only half of the authorized loans had actually been paid off by the end of the 1930s. Coquery-Vidrovitch, "L'impérialisme français," 267.

67. Cohen, *Rulers of Empire*, 138; Marseille, "La conférence"; Cooper, *Citizenship*, 68–69; Armelle Mabon, *L'action sociale coloniale: l'exemple de l'Afrique occidentale française du Front populaire à la veille des indépendances* (Paris: L'Harmattan, 2000), 14, 19–34.

68. Christopher J. Gray, *Colonial Rule and Crisis in Equatorial Africa: Southern Gabon, c. 1850-1940* (Rochester, NY: University of Rochester Press, 2002), 188.

69. "Opérations de placement," *Bulletin économique et social du Maroc* 1, no. 1 (1934): 56. On the origin of the metropolitan placement offices, see Peter Schöttler, *Die Entstehung der "Bourses du Travail". Sozialpolitik und französischer Sydikalismus am Ende des 19. Jahrhunderts* (Frankfurt: Campus, 1982).

70. Ellen J. Amster, *Medicine and the Saints: Science, Islam, and the Colonial Encounter in Morocco, 1877-1956* (Austin: University of Texas Press, 2013), 207.

71. See, for example, Marcelle Zeys, "Oeuvres d'assistance et de prévoyance sociales au Maroc," *Bulletin économique et social du Maroc* 2, no. 8 (1935): 169–71.

72. Mabon, *L'action sociale colonial*, 67.

73. Cooper, *Citizenship*, 55.

74. Mabon, *L'action sociale colonial*, 62.

75. Commissariat Général du Plan, *Rapport annuel sur l'exécution du plan de modernisation et d'équipement (Métropole et Outre-Mer)* (Paris: Le Commissariat, 1956), 527; Deschamps, *The French Union*, 208; "Grand Conseil de l'A.E.F.," *Marchés coloniaux* (June 26, 1954), 1759. The percentage of FIDES credits channeled into social spending was highest in French Equatorial Africa and Togo. Institut national de la statistique et des études économiques, *Outre-Mer 1958. Tableau économique et social des états et territoires d'outre-mer à la veille de la mise en place des nouvelles institutions* (Paris: PUF, 1960), 592–93.

76. J. Maréchal, R. Garnier, and R. de Montvalon, *Un sécretariat social en Oubangui* (Bangui: Cercle d'Etudes et d'Action sociales, 1956), 1. See also the journals *Servir-Outre-mer: notes documentaires du Secrétariat social l'Union française* (1949–1953) and *Notes documentaires du Secrétariat social d'outre-mer* (1954–1962).

77. "Les assemblés dans l'Union française," *Marchés coloniaux*, July 3, 1954, 1818; "Legislations coloniales," *Marchés coloniaux*, July 3, 1954, 1864; F. de Danville, "Incidences marocaines de la défaite française," *En terre d'Islam* 5 (1941): 61–71, 65.

78. International Labour Organisation, Social Policy (Non-Metropolitan Territories) Convention, 1947 (No. 82), http://www.ilo.org/dyn/normlex/en/f?p=NORMLEXPUB:12100:0::NO::P12100_INSTRUMENT_ID:312227. Also Cooper, *Decolonization*, 218.

79. Mabon, *L'action sociale coloniale*, 64.

80. Commission for Technical Co-operation in Africa and Scientific Council for Africa South of the Sahara, *Rural Welfare: Inter-African Conference, 2nd meeting, 1957* (London/Bukavu: CCTA/CSA).

81. Joseph Wilbois, *L'action sociale en pays de missions* (Paris: Payot, 1938); Idem., "Les conditions du service social en France et en Afrique noire," in *Le service social dans les colonies françaises d'Afrique noire* (Paris: Éditions SPES, 1947), 9–32.

82. Mabon, *L'action sociale colonial*, 70; Simone Crapuchet, ed., *Politique sociale d'outre-mer: un devoir de mémoire à l'égard des pionnières* (Ramonville Saint-Agne: Erès, 1999), 30.

83. Marie-Thérèse Sainz née Cueff, "Création d'un service social dans une entreprise agricole, la Cotonfran, en Afrique équatoriale française," in Crapuchet, ed., *Politique sociale d'outre-mer*, 161–65.

84. Idrissa Abdourahmane and Samuel Decalo, *Historical Dictionary of Niger*, 4th ed. (Lanham, MD: Scarecrow Press, 2012), 102–103; Edmond Séré de Rivières, *Histoire du Niger* (Paris: Berger-Levrault, 1965), 278.

85. PROHUZA, *Problèmes humains posés par l'implantation des familles en régions désertiques. Colloque, Alger, 20–21 Mai 1960* (Paris: Prohuza, 1960).

86. Centre d'études et d'informations des problémes humains dans les zones arides, *Les Mekhadma. Étude sur l'évolution d'un groupe humain dans le Sahara moderne* (Paris: Arts et métiers graphiques, 1960).

87. Retel-Laurentin dossier, *Archives de l'école des hautes études en sciences sociales*, Clemens Heller papers, "Afrique" section.

88. Dampierre and Clément to Governor of Ubangi-Chari and Deschamps, General Secretary of the Superior Council of Overseas Sociological Research, December 3, 1954, in Bibliothèque Éric-de-Dampierre, Mission sociologique du Haut Oubangui papers, Folder "Note MSHO, 1961."

89. Retel-Laurentin dossier, op. cit. On Retel-Laurentin, see also Nancy Rose Hunt, *A Nervous State: Violence, Remedies, and Reverie in Colonial Congo* (Durham, NC: Duke University Press, 2016), 248–49.

Chapter Five: Colonialism, Higher Education, and Social Research

1. "La rentrée de l'Université de Paris. Discours de M. S. Charléty, recteur de l'Académie de Paris, president du Conseil de l'Université," *Revue internationale de l'enseignement* 52, no. 86 (Jan. 15, 1932): 47–55, 53.

2. Marcel Griaule, "L'action sociologique en Afrique noire," *Présence africaine* 3 (1948), 388–391, 390.

3. Peter Wagner and Björn Wittrock, "States, Institutions, and Discourses: A Comparative Perspective on the Structuration of the Social Sciences," in *Discourses on Society. The Shaping of the Social Science Disciplines*, ed. Peter B. Wagner and Björn Wittrock (Dordrecht: Kluwer Academic Publishers, 1991), 331–58, 331. This volume is an excellent introduction to the role of institutions in analyzing the sociology of the social sciences.

4. Émile Durkheim, *The Evolution of Educational Thought: Lectures on the Formation and Development of Secondary Education in France* (London: Routledge & Kegan Paul, [1938] 1977); Robert Gilpin, *France in the Age of the Scientific State* (Princeton, NJ: Princeton University Press, 1968); Antoine Prost, *Histoire de l'enseignement en France, 1800–1967* (Paris: Colin, 1968); Terry Shinn, "The French Science Faculty System, 1808–1914: Institutional Change and Research Potential in Mathematics and the Physical Sciences," *Historical Studies in the Physical Sciences* 10 (1979): 271–332; Harry W. Paul, *From Knowledge to Power: The Rise of the Science Empire in France, 1860–1939* (Cambridge: Cambridge University Press, 1985); Bourdieu, *Homo Academicus* (Cambridge: Polity Press, 1988); Charles Gillispie, *Science and Polity in France: The Revolutionary and Napoleonic Years* (Princeton, NJ: Princeton University Press, 2004).

5. Roger L. Geiger, "Prelude to Reform: The Faculties of Letters in the 1860s," *Historical Reflections/Réflexions Historiques* 7, no. 2 (1980): 337-61, 339.

6. Prost, *Histoire de l'enseignement*, 248.

7. There was a concerted effort by Law professors to annex the new discipline of sociology in the 1890s. The "invasion of the Faculties by sociology" appeared "very dangerous" to the Law Faculty's representative on the General Council of the Faculties. George Weisz, "L'idéologie républicaine et les sciences sociales. Les durkheimiens et la chaire d'histoire d'économie sociale à la Sorbonne," *Revue française de sociologie* 20, no. 1 (1979) : 83-112, citing discussions in 1893-1894; see also Paul Gerbod, "Le personnel enseignant des facultés des lettres et sa contribution à la recherche et au changement culturel (1870-1939)," in *Le personnel de l'enseignement supérieur en France aux XIXe et XXe siècles*, ed. Christophe Charle and Régine Ferré (Paris: Editions du Centre National de la Recherche Scientifique, 1985), 187-204, 189; Roger Lewis Geiger, "The Development of French Sociology, 1871-1905" (PhD diss., University of Michigan, 1972).

8. The Latin thesis had taken up most of the students' time and had been required in all faculties. F. Lot, "La licence ès lettres," *Revue Internationale de l'Enseignement* 34 (1930): 19-29.

9. Theodore Zeldin, "Higher Education in France, 1848-1940," *Journal of Contemporary History* 2 (1967): 53-80, 65.

10. Pierre Singaravélou, *Professer l'Empire: Les sciences coloniales en France sous la IIIe République* (Paris: Publications de la Sorbonne, 2011), 14.

11. Singaravélou, *Professer l'Empire*, 31, n. 71, 102. On private colonial institutes and schools, see Laurent Morando, *Les instituts coloniaux et l'Afrique, 1893-1940. Ambitions nationales, réussites locales* (Paris: Karthala, 2007).

12. L. Gray Cowan, James O'Connell, and David G. Scanlon, *Education and Nation-Building in Africa* (New York: Praeger, 1965), 10-11.

13. Jean Roche, "Institut des hautes études de Tunis," *Annales de l'Université de Paris* 23, no. 1 (1953): 59-61.

14. François Siino, *Science et pouvoir dans la Tunisie contemporaine* (Paris: Karthala, 2004), 91.

15. Because Madagascar had an institution of higher education but no full-fledged university prior to decolonization, with no social sciences, I do not discuss it here. The *Université de la Polynésie française* was not founded until 1987. French Martinique had a law school in 1881 and a research institute in legal, political, and economic sciences after 1949—the Institut Henri-Vizioz—but this former colony had become an "overseas department," exiting from colonial status, and is thereby also bracketed here. H. Perret, "L' Institut Henri-Vizioz et le développement de l'institution universitaire aux Antilles-Guyane Françaises," in *Mélanges offerts à André Garrigou-Lagrange*, ed. André Garrigou-Lagrange (Bordeaux: Impr. Drouillard, 1974), 253-61.

16. Amín Pérez, "Rendre le social plus politique. Guerre coloniale, immigration et pratiques sociologiques d'Abdelmalek Sayad et de Pierre Bourdieu" (PhD diss., École des hautes études en sciences sociales, 2015), 70.

17. "Situation de l'enseignement supérieur en Algérie,"*Bulletin économique et social du Maroc* 4, no. 16 (1937): 177.

18. Pierre Singaravélou, "Enseignement supérieur coloniale: Un état des lieux," *Histoire de l'éducation*, no. 122 (2009): 71-92, 82.

19. Louis Paoli, "L'enseignement supérieur à Alger," *Revue internationale de l'enseignement* 35 (1898): 226-32, 228; *Annuaire de l'Université d'Alger, Livret de l'étudiant, année scolaire 1929-1930* (Alger: l'Université, 1929), 45-129.

20. "Pour la création d'un institut de criminologie en Afrique du Nord," *Bulletin économique et social du Maroc* 1, no. 6 (1934): 461-62; Paoli, "L'enseignement supérieur à Alger," 228; *Annuaire de l'Université d'Alger (1929-1930)*, 339-97.

21. On the Kabyle myth, see Patricia Lorcin, *Imperial Identities: Stereotyping, Prejudice, and Race in Colonial Algeria* (London: Tauris, 1995); for an example of Masqueray's thinking on this topic, see his article "Impressions de voyage: La Kabylie et le pays berbère," *Revue politique et littéraire*, Feb. 19 and 26 (1876), 177-83, 203-7.

22. Louis Paoli, letter to the editor, *Revue Internationale de l'Enseignement* 36 (1898): 560-61, 561.

23. George Steinmetz, "The Imperial Entanglements of Sociology in the United States, Britain, and France since the 19th Century," *Ab Imperio* 4 (2009): 23-78, 53-55.

24. Jeanne Favret-Saada, *Algérie 1962-1964: essais d'anthropologie politique* (Saint-Denis: Bouchène, 2005), 9.

25. This organization was originally called *Institut d'études administratives nord-africaines et coloniales* but was renamed in 1941. The Institute's teachers included Roger Le Tourneau, Georges Henri Bousquet, and Philipp Marçais—members of the École d'Alger whom Bourdieu criticized in his lecture on decolonizing sociology (see chapter 14). Jacques Peyrega, "L'Institut des Sciences Administratives et Sociales de l'Université d'Alger," *Documents Algériens*, série culturelle, no. 29 (June 20 1948).

26. Florence Renucci, "La 'décolonisation doctrinale' ou la naissance du droit d'outremer (1946-début des années 1960)," *Revue d'histoire des sciences humaines*, no. 24 (2011): 61-76, 70, note 43.

27. Phuong Ngoc Nguyen, *À l'origine de l'anthropologie au Vietnam: Recherche sur les auteurs de la première moitié du XXe siècle* (Aix-en-Provence: Presses universitaires de Provence, 2012), 202.

28. Pierre Singaravélou, *L'École française d'extrême-orient, ou, L'institution des marges, 1898-1956: essai d'histoire sociale et politique de la science coloniale* (Paris: L'Harmattan, 2009), 75-77.

29. On Nguyên Van Huyên, see chapter 1; on Lê Du, see Yufen Chang, "Emulation, Differentiation, and Syncretization in Colonial Vietnam's Development of National Written Language, National Literature, and National Learning, 1900-1945" (PhD diss., University of Michigan, 2013), ch. 6.

30. Jean Roche, "Institut des hautes études de Tunis," *Annales de l'Université de Paris* 23, no. 1 (1953): 59-61.

31. Jean Roche, "Bilan de l'année universitaire 1949-1950 à l'Institut des hautes études de Tunis," *Bulletin économique et social de la Tunisie*, no. 47 (1950): 57-60, 57.

32. "Population scolaire," *Bulletin économique et social de la Tunisie* 23 (1948): 68-69. See also "La scolarisation en Tunisie" in the *Bulletin économique et social de la Tunisie*, no. 48 (1951): 71, (1952): 84, (1954), and (1956): 96.

33. "Le Centre tunisien de documentation scolaire et universitaire," *Bulletin économique et social de la Tunisie* 76 (1953): 91-97.

34. Jacques Berque, *Rapport de M. Jacques Berque, professeur au Collège de France, sur la mission qu'il a effectuée en Tunisie de novembre à décembre 1959, en vue du développement de l'enseignement et de la recherche dans le domaine des sciences sociales, au titre du programme de participation aux activités des États membres de l'Unesco*. UNESCO/ss/Mission/Tunisie 59. Paris, Feb. 19, 1960. Chaulet was in Tunis in 1958-1959. Pierre and Claudine Chaulet, *Le choix de l'Algérie: deux voix, une mémoire* (Alger: Barzakh, 2012).

35. See the notes on Fanon's course taken by Lilia Ben Salem, "Rencontre de la société et de la psychiatrie," in Fanon, *Oeuvres*, vol. 2 (*Écrits sur l'aliénation et la liberté*), ed. Jean

Khalfa and Robert Young (Paris: La Découverte, 2015), 430–56; also Berque, *Rapport de M. Jacques Berque* (1960), 2, 11.

36. The school's official name until 1945 was *École libre des sciences politiques*.

37. Thomas R. Osborne, *A Grande École for the Grands Corps: The Recruitment and Training of the French Administrative Elite in the Nineteenth Century* (Boulder, CO: Social Science Monographs, 1983), 53–54.

38. Dominique Dammame, "Genese sociale d'une institution scolaire, l'École libre des sciences politiques," *Actes de la recherche en sciences sociales* 70 (1987) : 31–46, 45.

39. Osborne, *A Grande École for the Grands Corps*, 63.

40. Singaravélou, *Professer l'Empire*, 46–47.

41. My estimates of course offerings cover the entire period; estimates of *Annales* publications are from Singaravélou, *Professer l'Empire*, 47. Singaravélou estimates that "a fifth of the courses of the École were devoted to colonial studies" by the end of the 1880s.

42. http://www.sciencespo.fr/stories/#!/fr/frise/33/de-l-ecole-libre-a-sciences-po/. The school was renamed *Institut d'études politiques (Institute of Political Studies)* but continues to be referred to as *Sciences Po* colloquially.

43. Jean-Louis Tissier, "Jean Dresch," in *Dictionnaire des intellectuels français*, ed. Jacques Julliard and Michel Winock (Paris: Seuil, 1996), 370–71.

44. Georges Balandier, *Conjugaisons* (Paris: Fayard, 1997), 317.

45. Singaravélou, *Professer l'Empire*, 55, 205.

46. Roy Jumper, "The Recruitment and Training of Civil Administrators for Overseas France: A Case Study of French Bureaucracy" (PhD diss., Duke University, 1955), 128.

47. Georges Hardy, "Discours de M. Georges Hardy, Directeur de l'École coloniale," *Bulletin de la société des anciens élèves de l'Ecole coloniale* 30, no. 109 (1931): 15–19, 18.

48. Jumper, "Recruitment and Training," 80–87, 186; William B. Cohen, *Rulers of Empire: The French Colonial Service in Africa* (Stanford, CA: Stanford University Press, 1971), 87–89.

49. Robert Louis Delavignette, "L'école coloniale," *Bulletin de la société des anciens élèves de l'Ecole coloniale* 38, no. 123 (1938): 21–27, 22–23. See Véronique Dimier, "Enjeux institutionnels autour d'une science politique des colonies en France et en Grande-Bretagne, 1930–1950," *Genèses* 37 (1999) : 70–92; Dimier, "Formation des administrateurs coloniaux français et anglais entre 1930 et 1950 développement d'une science politique ou science administrative des colonies" (Thèse de doctorat, Sci. pol., Grenoble 2, 1999), vol. 1, 16–17.

50. *École nationale de la France d'outre-mer* (Paris: Librairie Vuibert, 1955), 7.

51. Armelle Enders, "L'école nationale de la France d'outre mer et la formation des adminstrateurs coloniaux," *Revue d'historie moderne et contemporaine* 40, no. 2 (1993): 272–88, 274; also Béatrice Grand, *Le 2 avenue de l'Observatoire, de l'École cambodgienne à l'Institut international d'administration publique* (Paris: La Documentation française, 1996), 77–78. On Hardy's claim to have invented oral history, see Singaravélou, *Professer l'Empire*, 98.

52. "Mesures prises ou projetées par M. Marius Moutet, Ministre des Colonies, en ce qui concerne l'ENFOM," Dec. 14, 1937, Archives Nationales d'Outre-Mer, *École coloniale*, Box 17, folder 1, p. 9; Cabinet du Ministère de l'Éducation Nationale, May 27, 1945, "Création d'une Licence d'Études Coloniales (Décret du 17 octobre 1945)," in Archives nationales, F/17/17708; Braillon, Cabinet du Ministère de l'Éducation Nationale, May 27, 1945, Archives nationales, file F17/17708. The degree was renamed *Licence d'études des populations d'outre-mer* in 1950.

53. The *licence* in colonial studies could also be earned at regular universities, which allowed students who were not accepted into the *École coloniale* to work toward colonial

careers in "offices, agencies, banks, shops," or even "in colonial administration itself." Ministère des Colonies, Direction de l'enseignement et de la jeunesse, to Director of Cabinet of Ministère de l'éducation nationale, May 2 and May 26, 1945. In Archives nationales, F/17/17770, "École coloniale."

54. "Note à l'attention de M. le Ministre (des colonies) au sujet de la creation d'une licence d'études coloniales," p. 6. Ministère des colonies, Direction de l'enseignement et de la jeunesse, to Director of Cabinet of Ministère de l'éducation nationale, May 2 1945, in AN F/17/17708.

55. "Mesures prises ou projetées par M. Marius Moutet, Ministre des colonies, en ce qui concerne l'ENFOM," Dec. 14, 1937, in Archives nationales d'outre-mer, École coloniale collection, Carton 17, doss. 1, pp. 4, 8; notice on organization of African studies in France, in Archives de l'école des hautes études en sciences sociales, Clemens Heller papers, Afrique, Georges Balandier, folder "Note IV-1956 Balandier."

56. Colonial Ministry to Director of ENFOM, July 23, 1951. Archives nationales d'outre-mer, *École coloniale* collection.

57. Susan Bayly, "Conceptualizing Resistance and Revolution in Vietnam: Paul Mus' Understanding of Colonialism in Crisis," *Journal of Vietnamese Studies* 4, no. 1 (2009): 192–205; David Chandler, "Paul Mus (1902–1969): A Biographical Sketch," *Journal of Vietnamese Studies* 4, no. 1 (2009): 149–91; Laurent Dartigues, "Paul Mus et l'expérience de la guerre. La pensée d'un orientaliste sur la violence de la situation colonial," in *Ethnologues en situations coloniales*, ed. Christine Laurière and André Mary, vol. 11, *Les Carnets de Bérose* (n.p.: Bérose, 2019), 182–205.

58. Pierre Laubriet, "'A la conquête des coeurs' par l'École de la France d'outre-mer," *Mer-Outre-mer* 1 (June–July 1947), 8–9.

59. Jean Clauzel, *La France d'outre-mer (1930–1960): témoignages d'administrateurs et de magistrats* (Paris: Karthala, 2003), 44.

60. Enders, "L'école nationale de la France d'outre mer," 278; *Le Monde* Feb. 12–13, 1956, p. 2, quoted in Cohen, *Rulers of Empire*, 154.

61. These included Africanist Jean-Claude Froelich, whose career started in colonial service, followed by a position as professor and director of the *Centre des hautes études d'administration musulmane* (discussed below). Jean-Claude Froelich, "De quelques anciens élèves de l'École qui se sont illustrés dans les sciences humaines," *Latitudes: Revue de l'Association des anciens élèves et élèves de l'Ecole nationale de la France d'outre-mer* (1963): 10–16.

62. Christophe Charle, "Savoir durer," *Actes de la recherche en sciences sociales* 86, no. 1 (1991): 99–105, 99.

63. http://www.sciencespo.fr/stories/#!/fr/frise/33/de-l-ecole-libre-a-sciences-po/

64. Jumper, "The Recruitment and Training," 32.

65. École nationale d'administration, *Promotions*, no. 35, Special Issue, X^e anniversaire de l'Ordonnance du 9 octobre 1945 (1955): 114–15. On the interns of the École nationale d'administration in Algeria, see Noara Omouri, *La connaissance sociale dans l'administration française entre 1954 et 1962. Enquête documentaire* (Paris: École des hautes études en sciences sociales, 1996).

66. Hélène Grandhomme, "Connaissance de l'Islam et pouvoir colonial: L'exemple de la France au Sénégal, 1936–1957," *French Colonial History* 10 (2009) : 171–88, 186, n. 23. On Montagne, see François Pouillon and Daniel Rivet, eds., *La Sociologie musulmane de Robert Montagne* (Paris: Éditions Maisonneuve & Larose, 2000); and Pierre Rondot, "Robert Montagne et le Levant," *L'Afrique et l'Asie* 4, no. 32 (1955): 36–43. On CHEAM, see Noara Omouri, "L'institutionnalisation d'une nouvelle anthropologie coloniale. Le Centre de hautes études administratives sur l'Afrique et l'Asie modernes (CHEAM) 1937–1962"

(Paris: DEA thesis, École normale supérieure, EHESS, 1997) and Pierre Vermeren, *Misère de l'historiographie du Maghreb post-colonial: 1962-2012* (Paris: Publications de la Sorbonne, 2012), 57-59.

67. Robert Montagne, *Les Berbères et le Makhzen dans le sud du Maroc* (Paris, Félix Alcan, 1930).

68. "Un plan d'enquêtes sociologiques—démographie et questions sociales marocaines," *Bulletin économique du Maroc* 3 (January 1936): 75-76; Robert Montagne, "L'évolution moderne des pays arabes," *Annales sociologiques* series A, no. 2: 29-76.

69. Omouri, "L'institutionnalisation, 15.

70. Omouri, "L'institutionnalisation," 22.

71. Général Catroux, "Hommage à Robert Montagne," *L'Afrique et l'Asie* 29, no. 1 (1955), 5-8, 7; Philippe Marçais, "Robert Montagne et l'Algérie," *L'Afrique et l'Asie* 29, no. 1 (1955): 9-15, 11.

72. Brigitte Mazon, "La Fondation Rockefeller et les sciences sociales en France 1925-1940," *Revue française de sociologie* 26 (1985): 311-42, 333.

73. Ernst Gellner, "Introduction" to Robert Montagne, *The Berbers. Their Social and Political Organization* (London: Cass, 1973), xiii-xl; François Pouillon and Daniel Rivet, "Présentation: La sociologie musulmane de Robert Montagne," in *La Sociologie musulmane de Robert Montagne*, ed. François Pouillon and Daniel Rivet (Paris: Éditions Maisonneuve & Larose, 2000), 9-18. On Mauss's expressed admiration for Montagne as the equal of the Durkheimian Sinologist Marcel Granet, see Jacques Berque, "Cent vingt-cinq ans de sociologie maghrébine," *Annales. Economies, sociétés, civilisations* n.s. 11, no. 3 (1956): 296-324, 310. Berque was much more critical of Montagne (see chapter 12).

74. CHEAM remained an "institute" rather than becoming a university or *grande école*. Montagne, "La formation des spécialistes des affaires musulmanes." *Bulletin économique du Maroc* 5, no. 19 (1938): 3-7, 7.

75. Omouri, "L'institutionnalisation," 39; Montagne, "La formation," 6.

76. Montagne, "La formation," 6.

77. Montagne, "La formation," 5. The largest collection of *mémoires* by students at the *Centre des hautes études d'administration musulmane* is held by the *Académie des sciences d'outre-mer*.

78. Omouri, "L'institutionnalisation," 22; *Annuaire de l'éducation nationale 1962* (Paris: Ministère de l'Éducation Nationale, 1962), 137.

79. Pouillon and Rivet, "Présentation," 11.

80. Pouillon and Rivet, "Présentation," 12.

81. Claude Liauzu, *Dictionnaire de la colonisation française* (Paris: Larousse, 2007), 159.

82. Montagne, "La formation."

83. Roger Le Tourneau, "Robert Montagne," *L'Afrique et l'Asie* 29, no. 1 (1955): 57-60, 58-59.

84. The Fifth Section of the *École pratique des hautes études*, created in 1886, was dedicated to religious science and encompassed specialists in non-western civilizations. Colonial material was present in lectures by Mauss, Leenhardt, Georges Condominas, Louis Massignon, Paul Mus, Jean-Paul Trystram, Jean Guiart, and Claude Tardits.

85. Brigitte Mazon, *Aux origines de l'École des hautes études en sciences sociales: Le rôle du mécénat américain, 1920-1960* (Paris: Cerf, 1988); Jacques Revel and Nathan Wachtel, eds., *Une école pour les sciences sociales: de la VIe section à l'École des hautes études en sciences sociales* (Paris: Les Editions du Cerf, 1996).

86. Of the 48 *Directeurs d'études* at the Sixth Section in 1955, six were colonial specialists (12.5% of total); 9 of 68 in 1958-59 (13.2%); 14 of 91 in 1964-65 (15.4%). See the online

prosopography of colonial sociologists for the names of professors and lecturers at the Sixth Section.

87. Olivier Godechot, "La formation des relations académiques au sein de l'EHESS," *Histoire et mesure* 26 (2011): 223–60.

88. Osama Abi-Mershed, *Apostles of Modernity: Saint-Simonians and the Civilizing Mission in Algeria* (Palo Alto, CA: Stanford University Press, 2011), 89; Jacques Frémeaux, *Les bureaux arabes dans l'Algérie de la conquête* (Paris: Denoël, 1993), 106–7, 115; Terry Shinn, *L'École polytechnique: 1794-1914* (Paris: Presses de la Fondation nationale des sciences politiques, 1980); Fritz K. Ringer, *Education and Society in Modern Europe* (Bloomington: Indiana University Press, 1979), 114–15; Marcel Emerit, *Les saint-simoniens en Algérie* (Paris: Les Belles lettres, 1941).

89. Collège de France professors involved in colonial or imperial work included Pierre Levasseur, Gabriel Tarde, Alfred Le Chatelier, Louis Massignon, Alfred Martineau, Edmond Chassigneux, Pierre Gourou, Françoise Héritier, Henri Laoust, Paul Mus, Alfred Sauvy, as well as Montagne, Aron, Berque, Bourdieu, and Lévi-Strauss, all discussed below.

90. "Le budget de l'instruction publique à la Chambre des députés de France," *Revue internationale de l'enseignement* 34 (1897): 531; "Le budget de l'instruction publique à la Chambre des députés de France," *Revue internationale de l'enseignement* 35 (1898): 151, 154; Florence Deprest, "Le Collège de France en situation coloniale? Autour de quelques chaires (fin XIXe siècle—début XXe siècle)" (unpublished paper presented at the conference "Dans l'atelier des intitulés. A propos de la singularité du Collège de France," Paris, Nov 2014); abstract at https://hal-paris1.archives-ouvertes.fr/halshs-01091708/fr/.

91. On the relations between French science and empire before the 1880s, see George N. Vlahakis et al., *Imperialism and Science: Social Impact and Interaction* (Santa Barbara, CA: ABC-CLIO, 2006), 19–49.

92. Singaravélou, *Professer l'Empire*, 109.

93. Université de Paris, *Livret de l'étudiant, 1920-1921* (Paris: Bureau des renseignements scientifiques, 1922), 155.

94. *Diplôme de médecin colonial. Instructions et programme de l'enseignement. Première série d'études avec le concours de l'Institut colonial de Bordeaux (novembre 1901-février 1902)* (Bordeaux: Gounouilhou, 1902).

95. Singaravélou, *Professer l'Empire*, 141.

96. Dr. Noël Bernard, "L'Œuvre coloniale de l'Institut Pasteur," *Académie des sciences coloniales, Comptes rendus des séances, communications* 29 (1938): 68–75.

97. Louis Genet, "L'école coloniale d'agriculture de Tunis," *Bulletin économique et social de la Tunisie*, no. 25 (1949): 48–49.

98. François Pouillon, *Dictionnaire des orientalistes de langue française*, 2nd ed. (Paris: Karthala, 2012), 724.

99. Agbenyega Adedze, "In the Pursuit of Knowledge and Power: French Scientific Research in West Africa, 1938–65," *Comparative Studies of South Asia, Africa and the Middle East* 23, nos. 1–2 (2003): 335–44, 336.

100. Li-Chuan Tai, *L'anthropologie française entre sciences coloniales et décolonisation (1880–1960)* (Paris: Publications de la Societe française d'histoire d'outre-mer, 2010), ch. 3; Christophe Bonneuil and Patrick Petitjean, "Les chemins de la creation de l'Orstom, du Front populaire à la Libération en passant par Vichy, 1936–1945. Recherche scientifique et politique colonial," in *Les sciences coloniales: Figures et institutions*, ed. Patrick Petitjean (Paris: ORSTOM, 1996), 113–62, 116.

101. Christophe Bonneuil, *Des savants pour l'empire: La structuration des recherches scientifiques coloniales au tems de 'la mise en valeur' des colonies françaises 1917-1945*

(Paris: Editions de l'ORSTOM, 1991); Albert Sarraut, *La mise en valeur des colonies françaises* (Paris: Payot, 1923), 342.

102. Bonneuil, *Des savants*, 52.

103. Bonneuil, *Des savants*, 50.

104. Jean-Hervé Jézéquel, "Les professionnels africains de la recherche dans l'état colonial tardif. Le personnel local de l'Institut français d'Afrique noire entre 1938 et 1960," *Revue d'histoire des sciences humaines*, no. 24 (2011): 35–60, 48.

105. "Compte rendu de l'activité du CNRS de Septembre 1944 à Octobre 1945," Archives du Centre national de la recherche scientifique, fonds documentaire.

106. Bonneuil and Petitjean, "Les chemins de la creation de l'Orstom," 144; 160 note 182. On postwar French planning, see Richard F. Kuisel, *Capitalism and the State in Economic Management in the Twentieth Century* (Cambridge: Cambridge University Press, 1981).

107. Commissariat général du plan, *La recherche scientifique et technique: quatrième plan, 1962–1965* (Paris: La Documentation Française, 1961); "Scientific and Technological Research in France Fourth Plan 1962–1965," *Minerva* 1, no. 4 (1963): 493–507; République Française, *Conférence africaine française. Brazzaville. 30 janvier 1944–8 février 1944* (Paris: Ministère des colonies, 1945), 47.

108. Commissariat général du plan, *Rapport annuel sur l'exécution du plan de modernisation et d'équipement (métropole et outre-mer)* (Paris: 1956), 476; Hubert Deschamps, *The French Union. History, Institutions, Economy, Countries and Peoples, Social and Political Changes* (Paris: Berger-Levrault, 1956), 209; Mission démographique de Guinée, *Étude démographique par sondage en Guinée, 1954–1955. 1ère Partie: Technique d'enquête*, 74–75.

109. IFAN, *Rapport annuel 1950*, 2, 52–53; Martin-René Atangana, *French Investment in Colonial Cameroon: The FIDES Era (1946–1957)* (New York: Peter Lang, 2009), 69–70, table 5.5. On local and FIDES contributions to the African research projects organized by INSEE, see M. Théodore, "Rapport sur un programme d'enquêtes statistiques agricoles et démographiques en Afrique noire française," *Bulletin intérieur de l'INSEE*, no. 10 (Dec. 1954): 17–28, 24.

110. INSEE, INED, and the Alexis Carrell foundation are discussed in chapter 7, in the context of the statistical and demographic disciplines surrounding sociology.

111. This became the CNRS in 1939. Gilpin, *France in the Age of the Scientific State*, 154–59; Antoine Prost, "Les origines de la politique de la recherche en France, 1939–1958," *Cahiers pour l'histoire du CNRS 1939–1989* 1 (1988), 41–62; Paul, *From Knowledge to Power*.

112. Gilpin, *France in the Age of the Scientific State*, 160.

113. H. W. Paul and Terry Shinn, "The Structure and State of Science in France," *Contemporary French Civilization* 6 (1981–1982): 153–93, 166; also Jean François Picard and Elisabeth Pradoura, "La longue marche vers le CNRS (1901–1945)," *Cahiers d'histoire du CNRS* (1988); rev. version (2009) online: http://www.vjf.cnrs.fr/histcnrs/pdf/cahiers-cnrs/picard-pradoura-88.pdf; Alain Chatriot and Vincent Duclert, "Fonder une politique de recherche. Les débuts de la DGRST," in *L'État à l'epreuve des sciences sociales. La function recherche dans les administrations de la Vème République*, ed. Philippe Bezes (Paris: Découverte, 2005), 23–36.

114. Picard and Pradoura, "La longue marche," 14.

115. Denis Guthleben, *Histoire du CNRS de 1939 à nos jours: une ambition nationale pour la science* (Paris: Armand Colin, 2009), 115, 139.

116. Guthleben, *Histoire du CNRS*, 108, 141; Gilpin, *France in the Age of the Scientific State*, 161–62; The Delegate General and the Consultative Committee on Scientific and Technological Research of France, "Scientific and Technological Research in France Fourth plan 1962–1965," *Minerva* 1, no. 4 (1963): 493–507, 475; Prost, *Histoire de l'enseignement*, 457.

117. Girolamo Ramunni, ed., "Le CNRS au temps de Charles de Gaulle," *La revue pour l'histoire du CNRS* (1999), special issue. Online: https://doi.org/10.4000/histoire-cnrs.480.

118. There was a CNRS research center at Beni Abbès in the Algerian Sahara, for instance, with laboratories for geophysics, zoology, and botany. Centre de recherches sahariennes, *Centre de recherches sahariennes* (Paris: CNRS, 1961); Pierre Chouard, "Le centre de recherches sahariennes de Beni Abbès et les recherches biologiques et agronomiques au Sahara," *Comptes rendus des séances de l'Académie d'Agriculture de France* 43 (1957): 477–88.

119. Data on sociologists' lifelong employment in online prosopographic database.

120. For an interview with ORSTOM's founder Jeannel, see Charles Gastaut, "Pour la prosperité de l'empire, l'Institut colonial de recherches scientifiques va etre crée," *L'œuvre*, no. 9.702, July 21 (1942), 1. ORSTOM was renamed *Institut de recherche pour le développement* in 1998.

121. Gérald Gaillard, "Chronique de la recherche ethnologique dans son rapport au centre national de la recherche scientifique 1925–1980," *Cahiers pour l'histoire du CNRS* 3 (1989): 85–123, 92.

122. Letter from the CNRS Director, Charles Jacob, to the Vice President of the Council, Jardel, March 3, 1942, Archives Nationales F/60/609 (Secrétariat général du gouvernement et services du premier ministre, Recherche scientifique), reproduced in Alain Drouard, *Une inconnue des sciences sociales: la fondation Alexis Carrel* (Paris: Editions de la Maison des Sciences de l'Homme, 1992), 460.

123. Bonneuil and Petitjean, "Les chemins de la creation de l'Orstom," 139.

124. The idea of *équipement* was criticized by radical French urbanists, who opposed it to "public space." Eric Le Breton, *Pour une critique de la ville: la sociologie urbaine française: 1950–1980* (Rennes: Presses universitaires de Rennes, 2012), 151–53.

125. ORSC, *Rapport d'activité pour l'année 1945* (Paris: ORSC, 1945), 1, 8–12.

126. Simone Crapuchet, *Politique sociale d'outre-mer: un devoir de mémoire à l'égard des pionnières* (Ramonville Saint-Agne: Erès, 1999), 166.

127. Marie-Lise Sabrié, *Sciences au Sud. Dictionnaire de 50 années de recherche pour le développement* (Paris: ORSTOM, 1994), 56.

128. Michel Gleizes, *Un regard sur l'ORSTOM 1943–1983. Témoinage* (Paris: Éditions de l'ORSTOM, 1985), 23, 28–29.

129. ORSTOM, *Organisation-Activités 1944–1955* (Paris: ORSTOM, 1955), 34, 8; Gleizes, *Un regard sur l'ORSTOM*, 94.

130. Gastaut, "Pour la prosperité de l'empire."

131. Marie-Hélène Durand, "La lente progression des femmes chercheuses à l'IRD (ex-ORSTOM)," *L'homme et la société* 176–177 (2010): 213–45, 219.

132. The IEC "took on a separate existence" in Brazzaville following decolonization, and the subsidiary centers in Bangui and Pointe Noire became autonomous institutions. Renaud Paulian, "L'Institut de recherches scientifiques au Congo, Brazzaville," *Journal of Modern African Studies* 2, no. 3 (1964): 431–32, 431.

133. Jean-L. Trochain, "Compte rendu d'activité (Septembre 1950–Août 1952) et programmes de recherche (Août 1951–Août 1952)," *Bulletin de l'Institut d'études centrafricaines*, n.s., no. 3 (1952): 5–74, 19.

134. Hubert Deschamps, *Roi de la brousse: mémoires d'autres mondes* (Paris: Berger-Levrault, 1975), 298; Deschamps, "Les sciences humaines et l'ORSTOM," in Organisation d'études pour l'expansion de la recherche scientifique, *Actes du colloque sur la recherche scientifique et technique et le développement économique et social des pays africains* (Dakar, 14–17 décembre 1959, Abidjan, 17–20 décembre 1959), 318–22; ORSTOM, *Courrier des chercheurs* 10 (1953–1954): 11; Gaillard, "Chronique de la recherche ethnologique," 108; ORSTOM, *Bulletin de liaison, sciences humaines*, no. 2 (July 1965), p. I.

135. Jean-Louis Boutillier and Yves Goudineau, *Trente ans* (Paris: Éditions de l'ORSTOM, 1993), 5.

136. *Annales de l'Université de Paris* 28, no. 1 (1958), 65; *Courrier des chercheurs* 10 (1953–54), 11.

137. See below for a discussion of the license diploma in colonial studies.

138. Charles Bettelheim and Suzanne Frère, *Auxerre en 1950, une ville française moyenne. Étude de structure sociale et urbaine* (Paris, A. Colin, 1950); Johan Heilbron, *French Sociology* (Ithaca, NY: Cornell University Press, 2015), 136. According to Heilbron, French sociologists at the time said that the Auxerre book was mainly Suzanne Frère's work. Private communication with the author, March 31, 2016.

139. Suzanne Frère, "Panorama de l'Androy. Enquête socio-démographique à Madagascar, mai-décembre 1955" (Thèse d'université, Lettres, Paris, 1957); Frère, *Madagascar: Panorama de l'Androy* (Paris: Éditions Aframpe, 1958). Frère's research was also supported by the Statistical Office in Madagascar. See Service des archives économiques du Ministère des finances (Savigny-le-Temple), Statistiques-Outre-mer, B-0057585/1, Travaux statistiques, Madagascar, "statistiques, étude démographique dans le pays d'Androye (1955) par Suzanne FRÈRE, sociologue, chargée de mission à Madagascar pour préparer une enquête décidée par le Conseil supérieur de la recherche sociologique Outre-mer (1955-1958)."

140. Albert Charton, "Création de l'IFAN," *Bulletin du Comité d'études historiques et scientifiques de l'Afrique occidentale française* 1 (1936): 385–86; Anon., "Création de l'Institut français d'Afrique noire," *Journal de la Société des africanistes* 7, no. 2 (1937): 234–35.

141. Philip L. Ravenhill, "The Passive Object and the Tribal Paradigm," in *African Material Culture*, ed. Mary Jo Arnoldi, Christraud M. Geary, and Kris L. Hardin (Bloomington: Indiana University Press, 1996), 265–82, 265.

142. Institut français d'Afrique noire, *Rapport annuel 1956*, 22; Alice Conklin, *In the Museum of Man: Race, Anthropology, and Empire in France, 1850-1950* (Ithaca, NY: Cornell University Press, 2013), 228.

143. See "Liste de membres," Comité d'études historiques et scientifiques de l'Afrique occidentale française, *Annuaire et mémoires du Comité d'études historiques et scientifiques de l'Afrique occidentale française* 1 (1917): 13–16, 15.

144. Institut français d'Afrique noire, *Rapport annuel 1948*.

145. Charton, "Creation de l'IFAN," 385–86; Marie-Albane de Suremain, "L'IFAN et la 'mise en musée' des cultures africaines," *Outre-mers* 95 (2007): 356–57, 356. Sociology was renamed "Department of societies and cultures" in 1962–1963, but it remained separate from the IFAN ethnology department. IFAN, *Rapport annuel 1962–63*, 34–42.

146. Université de Dakar, *Livret de l'étudiant. Année scolaire 1962-1963*, 510, 513–14, 520. The *diplôme d'études supérieures*, introduced in 1896, was intended to assess a student's capacity for independent scholarship, thereby providing a triage point and stepping stone toward the *doctorat d'état*.

147. Université de Dakar, *Annales de la Faculté des lettres et sciences humaines*, no. 5 (1975): 296; cf. Moustapha Tamba, *Sociologie au Sénégal* (Paris: Harmattan, 2014).

148. George Steinmetz, "Sociology and Colonialism in the British and French Empires, 1940s-1960s," *Journal of Modern History* 89, no. 3 (2017): 601–48.

149. Victor Karady, "Le problème de la légitimité dans l'organisation historique de l'ethnologie française," *Revue française de sociologie* 23 (1982): 17.

150. Paul Rivet, "L'ethnologie en France," *Bulletin du Muséum nationale d'histoire naturelle*, 2nd ser., 12 (1940): 38–52; Éric Jolly and Marianne Lemaire, eds., *Cahier Dakar-Djibouti* (Meurcourt: Les Cahiers, 2015).

151. Conklin, *In the Museum of Man*, 194.

152. Marcel Fournier, *Marcel Mauss: A Biography* (Princeton, NJ: Princeton University Press, 2006), 166.

153. Fournier, *Marcel Mauss*, 237.

154. Alice Conklin, "Civil Society, Science, and Empire in Late Republican France: The Foundation of Paris's Museum of Man," *Osiris* 2nd series, 17 (2002): 255–90, 271.

155. Paul Lapie, "L'Université de Paris aujourd'hui et demain," *Annales de l'Université de Paris* 1, no. 5 (1926): 449–61, 460.

156. Lucien Lévy-Bruhl, "L'Institut d'ethnologie de l'université de Paris," *Revue d'ethnographie et de traditions populaires* 23–24 (1925): 1–4; Conklin, "Civil Society," 287; Benoît de l'Estoile, "Science de l'homme et 'domination rationnelle'. Savoir ethnologique et politique indigène en Afrique coloniale française," *Revue de synthèse*, 4th ser., nos. 3–4 (2000): 294–95.

157. Conklin, *In the Museum of Man*, 32–33; Nélia Dias, *Le Musée d'ethnographie du Trocadéro, 1878-1908: anthropologie et muséologie en France* (Paris: Editions du CNRS, 1991); Benoît de L'Estoile, "Le musée, laboratoire de la science de l'homme" in *Le goût des autres: de l'exposition coloniale aux arts premiers* (Paris: Flammarion, 2007), 103–36.

158. Conklin, "Civil Society," 281, 287.

159. Paul Rivet to Minister of Higher Education, Oct. 27, 1937, in Archives nationales, F/17/17770, "École coloniale"; Cabinet du Ministère de l'éducation nationale, May 27, 1945, "Création d'une licence d'études coloniales (Décret du 17 octobre 1945)," in Archives nationales, F/17/17708; Braillon, Cabinet du Ministère de l'éducation nationale, May 27, 1945, in Ibid.

160. Serge Bahuchet, "Hommes, natures et sociétés: la construction de l'interdisciplinarité," in *Le Musée de l'homme. Histoire d'un musée laboratoire*, ed. Claude Blanckaert (Paris: Muséum national d'histoire naturelle/Éditions Artlys, 2015), 124–39.

161. Conklin, *In the Museum of Man*, 88–90.

162. Conklin, *In the Museum of Man*, 60–69.

163. Marcel Mauss, "Lévy-Bruhl sociologue," *Revue philosophique de la France et de l'étranger* 127, nos. 5/6 (1939): 251–53.

164. Lucien Lévy-Bruhl, *Les fonctions mentales dans les sociétés inférieures* (Paris: F. Alcan, 1910); translated as *How Natives Think* (New York: A.A. Knopf, 1925). See Frédéric Keck, *Lucien Lévy-Bruhl: entre philosophie et anthropologie: contradiction et participation* (Paris: CNRS éditions, 2008).

165. See Gerald Gaillard, *The Routledge Dictionary of Anthropologists* (London: Routledge, 2004), ch. 8.

166. Stefan Esselborn, *Die Afrikaexperten: das Internationale Afrikainstitut und die europäische Afrikanistik, 1926-1976* (Göttingen: Vandenhoeck & Ruprecht, 2018), 290.

167. Rockefeller subsidized overseas research trips by Marcel Griaule (1931, 2 years) for research in French Congo, Soudan, and Ethiopia; Denise Paulme (1935, 2 years) for a research trip to French Sudan; and Charles Le Coeur (1932, 2 years) for studies in Britain and research in Chad.

168. George Steinmetz, "A Child of the Empire: British Sociology and Colonialism, 1940s–1960s," *Journal of the History of the Behavioral Sciences* 49, no. 4 (2012): 353–78; Steinmetz, "American Sociology and Colonialism, 1890s–1960s," in *Reconsidering American Power: Pax Americana and Social Science*, ed. John Kelly, J. K. Jacobsen, and Marston H. Morgan (Oxford: Oxford University Press, 2019), 273–93.

169. William R. Pendergast, "French Policy in UNESCO" (PhD diss., Columbia University, 1971); Julia Buhrle, "La France et l'UNESCO de 1945 à 1958," *Revue histoire diplomatique* 2, no. (2008): 117–33; Chloé Maurel, *Histoire de l'UNESCO* (Paris: L'Harmattan, 2010); Chloé Belloc, "La création du Conseil International de la Philosophie

et des Sciences humaines, 1946-1949," *Bulletin de l'Institut Pierre Renouvin* 25 (2007): 17-41. The social sciences had the smallest budget of all UNESCO programs, rarely exceeding 6% of the total. Total spending was just over one million USD in 1953, peaking at 2 million USD in 1965-1966, and then declining precipitously. Peter Lengyel, *International Social Science: The Unesco Experience* (New Brunswick, NJ: Transaction, 1986), 2.

170. UNESCO, *Records of the General Conference*, Proceedings (1947, 8; 1949, 320; 1950, 320; 1958, 89; 1960, 110); *UNESCO Chronicle* (Nos. 1-2, 1959), 37; *Rapport de M. Jacques Berque, professeur au Collège de France, sur la mission qu'il a effectuée en Tunisie de novembre à décembre 1959, en vue du développement de l'enseignement et de la recherche dans le domaine des sciences sociales, au titre du programme de participation aux activités des États membres de l'Unesco*. UNESCO Archives, document "UNESCO/ss/Mission/Tunisie 59."

171. Lengyel, *International Social Science*, 38.

172. Maurel, *Histoire de l'UNESCO*.

173. Jennifer Platt, *A Brief History of the ISA: 1948-1997* (Montréal: International Sociological Association, 1998), 26.

174. UNESCO archives, document 338.924: 3(6)(666.8) "54", IVORY COAST—Meeting 1954—Social Impact of Technological Change.

175. Daryll Forde, ed., *Social Implications of Industrialization and Urbanization in Africa South of the Sahara* (Paris: UNESCO, 1956).

176. Anthony Q. Hazard, *Postwar Anti-Racism: The United States, UNESCO, and "Race," 1945-1968* (New York: Palgrave Macmillan, 2012), 37.

177. Claude Lévi-Strauss, *Race and History* (Paris: UNESCO, 1958).

178. Paul Sebag, Abdelwahab Bouhdiba, and Carmel Camilleri, *Les préconditions sociales de l'industrialisation dans la région de Tunis* (Tunis: Centre d'études et de recherches économiques et sociales, 1968).

179. UNESCO, *Four Statements on the Race Question* (Paris: UNESCO, 1969), 51-52.

180. Commission for Technical Co-operation in Africa, *Inter-African Conference on Social Sciences* (London: Commission for Technical Co-operation in Africa, 1955).

181. Commission for Technical Co-operation in Africa, *Inter-African Conference*, 9; Commission for Technical Co-operation in Africa, *Inter-African Scientific and Technical Co-operation, 1948-1955* (London: Commission for Technical Co-operation in Africa, 1956), 67.

Chapter Six: The Earliest Colonial Social Sciences and Their Engagement with Sociology: Geography, Law, Economics, and the Sciences of the Psyche

1. Inter- and transdisciplinarity can be favorable to scientific flourishing, but may threaten scientific autonomy. George Steinmetz, "Field Theory and Interdisciplinarity: Relations between History and Sociology in Germany and France during the Twentieth Century," *Comparative Studies in Society and History* 59, no. 2 (2017): 477-514.

2. Philosophy is not discussed here as a general field due to its general lack of interest in colonialism, even though it was a key interdiscipline for French sociology during its first century. The key exception, philosopher Lucien Lévy-Bruhl, is discussed below and in chapter 7.

3. P. Matter, "Préface," in Pierre Dareste, *Traité de droit colonial*, vol. 1 (Paris: Impr. Robaudy, 1931-1932), vi.

4. Michael Worboys, "Germs, Malaria and the Invention of Mansonian Tropical Medicine: From 'Diseases in the Tropics' to 'Tropical Diseases,'" *Clio Medica* 35 (1996): 181-207.

5. Saïd Almi, *Urbanisme et colonisation: présence française en Algérie* (Sprimont, Belgium: Mardaga, 2002); Fassil Demissie, ed., *Colonial Architecture and Urbanism in Africa*:

Intertwined and Contested Histories (Burlington, VT: Ashgate, 2011); Mia Fuller, *Moderns Abroad: Architecture, Cities, and Italian Imperialism* (New York: Routledge, 2004); Michael Hofmann, *Deutsche Kolonialarchitektur und Siedlungen in Afrika* (Petersberg: Imhof, 2013); Hannah le Roux, "The Networks of Tropical Architecture," *Journal of Architecture* 8, no. 3 (2003): 337–54; Itohan Osayimwese, *Colonialism and Modern Architecture in Germany* (Pittsburgh, PA: University of Pittsburgh Press, 2017); Gwendolyn Wright, *The Politics of Design in French Colonial Urbanism* (Chicago: University of Chicago Press, 1991); Michael Falser, "Von Windhuk bis Tsingtau und Samoa: Deutsch-koloniale Architektur aus globaler Perspektive," *Kunstchronik* 74, no. 7 (2021), 390–99.

6. Pierre Singaravélou, "Le moment 'impérial' de l'histoire des sciences sociales (1880–1910)," *Mil neuf cent. Revue d'histoire intellectuelle*, no. 27 (2009): 87–102, 98.

7. INSEE, *INSEE, 1946–1956* (Paris: INSEE, 1956), 33.

8. Matter, "Préface," v.

9. On the "colonial mode of production" and the "articulation of modes of production," see Pierre Philippe Rey, "Sociologie économique et politique des Kuni, Punu et Tsangui de la région de Mossendjo et de la Boucle du Niari (Congo-Brazzaville)" (PhD diss., University of Paris, 1969), 519; the notion of the "colonial situation" was first introduced by Georges Balandier, "La situation coloniale: approche théorique," *Cahiers internationaux de sociologie* 11 (1951): 44–79; "colonial system" and "colonial society" are developed as analytic concepts by Pierre Bourdieu, *Sociologie de l'Algérie*, new ed. (Paris: Presses Universitaires de France, 1961); for "colonial traditionalism," see Bourdieu, "Étude sociologique," in *Travail et travailleurs en Algérie*, ed. Pierre Bourdieu, Alain Darbel, Jean-Paul Rivet, and Claude Seibel (Paris: Mouton, 1963), 253–562, 382.

10. J. Bastier, "L'image de Rome et le modèle du droit romain dans la construction du droit colonial français," in *Droit romain, jus civile et droit français*, ed. Jacques Krynen (Toulouse: Presses de l'Université des sciences sociales, 1999): 67–86; J. H. Elliott, "Iberian Empires," in *The Oxford Handbook of Early Modern European History, 1350–1750*, ed. Hamish Scott, vol. 2 (Oxford: Oxford University Press, 2015), 4.

11. René Maunier, *Des comptoirs aux empires* (Paris: Sirey, 1941), 18; Maunier, *L'empire français, Propos et projects* (Paris: Sirey, 1943), 32.

12. Maunier, *L'empire français*, 31–39.

13. Partha Chatterjee, *The Nation and Its Fragments* (Princeton, NJ: Princeton University Press, 1993), 14, 20.

14. Contrary to official French mythology, there was no universal form of French law or citizenship, no generalized *jus solis*, even in Algeria, even though Algeria was officially part of France. René Maunier, "Citoyenneté et nationalité dans l'Empire français," *Académie des sciences coloniales, Comptes rendus des séances*, n.s. 2 (1942): 50–67; Emmanuelle Saada, *Empire's Children: Race, Filiation, and Citizenship in the French Colonies* (Chicago: University of Chicago Press, 2012), 253. Ironically, the German Empire had fewer restrictions on colonial subjects gaining German citizenship than the French Empire until the turn of the twentieth century; Steinmetz, *Devil's Handwriting*.

15. Maunier, "Citoyenneté et nationalité," 56; Maunier, *L'empire français*, 54, 81.

16. For the definition of the modern colonial state, see George Steinmetz, "The Colonial State as a Social Field," *American Sociological Review* 73, no. 4 (August 2008): 589–612. Modern colonial states tended to have all of the characteristics of metropolitan states, with the exception of legitimacy vis-à-vis the colonized portion of the population, and the ability of the colonial state to represent itself in foreign policy. However, these criteria are also unevenly present among metropolitan nation-states.

17. Elliott, "Iberian Empires," 18.

18. Matter, "Préface," vi; Pierre Singaravélou, *Professer l'Empire: Les sciences coloniales en Cœur sous la IIIe République* (Paris: Publications de la Sorbonne, 2011), 308, and 301–13.

For the argument that colonies require a distinct type of legal regime, see J.-C. Paul Rougier, *Précis de législation et d'économie coloniale* (Paris: L. Larose, 1895), 66.

19. Carine Jallamion, "Le juge français face aux collectivités indigènes," in *Le juge et l'outre-mer. Les roches bleues de l'Empire colonial*, ed. Bernard Durand and Martine Fabre (Lille: Publications du centre d'histoire judiciare, 2004), 385–419, 402–3. For a case of the role of customary law in a colonial court of appeals, see Mamadou Badji, "Considerations sur l'application de la coutume devant les magistrats de la Cour d'appel de Dakar, de 1903 à 1960," in *La justice et le droit: instruments de strategie coloniale*, ed. Bernard Durand, vol. 3 (Montpellier: CNRS, 2001), 1075–110.

20. Matter, "Préface," v.

21. Bernard Durand, "En guise de conclusion," in *Le juge et l'outre-mer*, ed. Bernard Durand and Martine Fabre (Lille: Publications du centre d'histoire judiciare, 2004), 457–63, 457–58.

22. Olivier Le Cour Grandmaison, *De l'indigénat* (Paris: Zones, 2010), 7.

23. "Arrêté du 23 juillet portant réorganisation de l'agrégation des Facultés de droit," *Revue internationale de l'enseignement* 32 (1896) 282–84, 283.

24. *Annuaire de l'Université d'Alger, Livret de l'étudiant, année scolaire 1930–1931* (Alger: La Maison des livres, 1930).

25. René Maunier, *Les lois de l'empire (1940–1942)* (Paris: Domat-Montchrestie, 1942), 59; Maunier, *L'empire français*, 84–97; Florence Renucci, "L'élaboration du Code du travail outre-mer et la durée du travail en Afrique occidentale française," in *Les politiques du travail (1906–2006)*, ed. A. Chatriot, O. Join-Lambert, and V. Viet (Rennes: Presses Universitaires de Rennes, 2006), 59–68, 59.

26. Florence Renucci, "La 'décolonisation doctrinale' ou la naissance du droit d'outremer (1946–débat des années 1960)," *Revue d'histoire des sciences humaines* 24 (2011): 61–76; on the reforms leading to eventual independence, see Frederick Cooper, *Citizenship between Empire and Nation: Remaking France and French Africa, 1945–1960* (Princeton, NJ: Princeton University Press, 2014).

27. Singaravélou, *Professer l'empire*, 308; Emmanuelle Chevreau, *Henri Lévy-Bruhl: juriste sociologue* (Paris: Editions Mare & Martin, 2018).

28. Maunier, "Vision d'une Eurafrique," in *L'empire français*, 135–46.

29. René Maunier, *L'empire français. Propos et projets* (Paris: Librarie du Receuil Sirey, 1943), 141. See Florence Renucci, "La 'décolonisation doctrinale' ou la naissance du droit d'outremer (1946–débat des années 1960)," *Revue d'histoire des sciences humaines* 24 (2011): 61–76; on Naumann and German geopolitics, see George Steinmetz, "Geopolitics," in *The Wiley-Blackwell Encyclopedia of Globalization*, ed. George Ritzer, vol. 2 (Malden, MA: Wiley-Blackwell, 2012), 800–22.

30. Frédéric Audren, "Un interlocuteur français: René Maunier," *Les études sociales*, nos. 153–154 (2011): 213–16. On the ideological framework of "Eurafrica," see the contributions to Marie-Thérèse Bitsch, ed., *L' Europe unie et l'Afrique: de l'idée d'Eurafrique à la convention de Lomé I* (Bruxelles: Bruylant, 2005); also Frederick Cooper, *Citizenship between Empire and Nation*, 202–10. Some jurists continued to cite Maunier after the war, e.g. François Luchaire, *Manuel de droit d'outre-mer* (Paris: Sirey, 1949), 12.

31. Henri Lévy-Bruhl, "Allocution," *Annales de l'Université de Paris* 30, no. 1 (Jan–March 1960): 40–46.

32. P. F. Gonidec, *L'évolution des territoires d'outre-mer depuis 1946* (Paris: Librairie générale de droit et de jurisprudence, 1958).

33. Maurice A. Glélé, "Introduction aux mélanges offerts à P.-F. Gonidec," in *Mélanges offerts à P.-F. Gonidec* (Paris: Libraire générale de droit et de jurisprudence, 1985), 17–19, 17.

34. François Luchaire, *Droit d'outre-mer et de la coopération* (Paris: PUF, 1966), 7–8, 79–112. Luchaire directed ENFOM, the former *École coloniale*, in 1960, guiding its

transition from training colonial officials to educating indigenous administrators of African and Asian nations. Gérard Conac, "François Luchaire, décolonisateur," in *François Luchaire, un républicain au service de la république*, ed. Didier Maus and Jeanette Bougrab (Paris: Publications de La Sorbonne, 2005), 109–20.

35. George Steinmetz, "Geopolitics," in *The Wiley-Blackwell Encyclopedia of Globalization*, vol. 2, ed. George Ritzer (Malden, MA: Wiley-Blackwell, 2012), 800–822.

36. This is the slogan of the Verband deutscher Schulgeographen (Association of German Academic Geographers); Heinz Peter Brogiato, *"Wissen ist Macht—Geographisches Wissen ist Weltmacht": die schulgeographischen Zeitschriften im deutschsprachigen Raum (1880–1945) unter besonderer Berücksichtigung des Geographischen Anzeigers* (Trier: Geographische Gesellschaft, 1998).

37. Michael Heffernan, "The Spoils of War: The Société de Géographie de Paris and the French Empire, 1914–1919," in *Geography and Imperialism, 1820–1940*, ed. Morag Bell (Manchester: Manchester University Press, 1995), 221–64, 222.

38. The *Parti colonial* wielded "an influence over [colonial] policy out of proportion to their limited public support," due to "public indifference" to the empire. Heffernan, "The Spoils of War," 225.

39. Jean-Marie Mayeur and Madeleine Rebérioux, *The Third Republic from Its Origins to the Great War, 1871–1914* (Cambridge: Cambridge University Press, 1987), 94.

40. Pierre Singaravélou, "The Institutionalisation of 'Colonial Geography' in France, 1880–1940," *Journal of Historical Geography* 37 (2011): 149–57.

41. *Bulletin de la Société de géographie* and *Revue de géographie*.

42. Singaravélou, "The Institutionalisation of 'Colonial Geography.'"

43. *Annales de l'Université de Paris* 5 (1930): 207.

44. Yves Lacoste, "Postface," in *L'empire des géographes. Géographie, exploration et colonisation XIXe–XXe siècle*, ed. Pierre Singaravélou (Paris: Belin, 2008), 235–41, 240. On Dresch, see Michel Coquery and Catherine Coquery-Vidrovitch, "Jean Dresch, un géographe au déclin des empires," *Annales de Géographie* 89, no. 492 (1980): 239–40; on Lacoste, see Steinmetz, "Geopolitics," 16–17.

45. Maximilien Sorre, who taught colonial geography at Bordeaux between the wars, directed the *Centre d'études sociologiques* (1951–1956) and entitled his memoirs *Encounters of Geography and Sociology*. Maximilien Sorre, *Rencontres de la géographie et de la sociologie* (Paris: Marcel Rivière, 1957).

46. Chantal Blanc-Pamard and Roland Pourtier, "Gilles Sautter ou le bonheur d'être géographe," *Annales de géographie* 606 (1999): 201–6.

47. Gilles Sautter, *De l'Atlantique au fleuve Congo. Une géographie du sous-peuplement* (Paris: Mouton, 1966).

48. Alain Clément, "French Economic Liberalism and the Colonial Issue at the Beginning of the Second Colonial Empire (1830–1870)," *History of Economic Ideas* 21, no. 1 (2013): 47–75, 51; Clément, "La question coloniale et les économistes français," *L'Économie politique* 64 (2014): 72–82.

49. These arguments were also developed by Jules Duval, *Les colonies et la politique coloniale de la France* (Paris: A. Bertrand, 1864) and Charles Gide, "À quoi servent les colonies?," *Revue de géographie* 18 (Jan. 1886–Feb. 1886): 36–52, 141–47.

50. Clément, "French Economic Liberalism," 63–64, n. 1; Nicolas Villiaumé, *Nouveau traité d'économie politique* (Paris: Guillaumin, 1857); see also Jules Duval, *Réflexions sur la politique de l'empereur en Algérie* (Paris: C. Ainé, 1866), 130.

51. Paul Leroy-Beaulieu, *De la colonisation chez les peuples modernes* (Paris: Guillaumin, 1874); 2nd ed. (1882).

52. Dan Warshaw, *Paul Leroy-Beaulieu and Established Liberalism in France* (DeKalb: Northern Illinois University Press, 1991), 78–105.

53. Singaravélou, *Professer l'empire*, 317; Yves Breton, "The Société d'économie politique of Paris (1842–1914)," in *The Spread of Political Economy and the Professionalisation of Economists: Economic Societies in Europe, America and Japan in the Nineteenth Century*, ed. Massimo M. Augello and Marco E. L. Guidi (London: Routledge, 2001), 53–69.

54. Jean Copans, *Sociologie du développement*, 2nd ed. (Paris: Armand Colin, 2016), 10.

55. Emile Durkheim, "Value Judgments and Judgments of Reality," in *Sociology and Philosophy* (New York: Free Press, 1974), 80–97, 86; Phillipe Steiner, "La tradition française de critique sociologique de l'économie politique," *Revue d'histoire des sciences humaines* 18 (2008): 63–84.

56. Philippe Steiner, *Durkheim and the Birth of Economic Sociology* (Princeton, NJ: Princeton University Press, 2011), chs. 1–2.

57. Steiner, *Durkheim and the Birth of Economic Sociology*, 70.

58. Thierry Pouch, *Les économistes français et le marxisme. Apogée et déclin d'un discours critique (1950–2000)* (Rennes: Presses universitaires de Rennes, 2001).

59. John Bellamy Foster, "Samir Amin at 80: An Introduction and Tribute," *Monthly Review* 63, no. 5 (2011): 1–7; I. H. Kvangraven, "A Dependency Pioneer: Samir Amin," in *Dialogues on Development*, vol. 1, *Dependency*, ed., Ingrid Harvold Kvangraven et al. (Harare: University of Zimbabwe, 2017), 12–17, 15.

60. Samir Amin, *Les effets structurels de l'intégration internationale des économies précapitalistes: une étude théorique du mécanisme qui a engendré les économies dites sous-développées* (Paris: Université de Paris, 1957).

61. Copans, *Sociologie du développement*, 33.

62. Samir Amin, "The Class Struggle in Africa," *Revolution Africa Latin America Asia* 1, no. 9 (1964): 23–47. Amin's ideas had a formative influence on Immanuel Wallerstein's world system theory.

63. Balandier lectured on colonial development and underdevelopment at *Sciences Po* during the 1950s; Georges Balandier, ed., *Le Tiers-Monde, sous-développement et développement* (Paris: PUF-INED, 1957).

64. Julien Meimon, "L'invention de l'aide française au développement. Discours, instruments et pratiques d'une dynamique hégémonique," *Questions de recherche* 21 (2007): 1–43; Véronique Dimier, "Recycling Empire: French Colonial Administrators at the Heart of European Development Policy," in *The French Colonial Mind*, ed. Martin Thomas (Lincoln: University of Nebraska Press, 2011), 251–74; Dimier, "For a New Start? Resettling French Colonial Administrators in the Prefectoral Corps," *Itinerario* 28, no. 1 (2004): 49–66, 49. On "sociology of development" at Vincennes University in 1968–69, see Charles Soulié, "De Vincennes à Saint-Denis . . . Journée de réflexion de l'UFR textes et sociétés. Jeudi 24 mai 2012, Paris 8, amphithéâtre D 001," 42. At http://www2.univ-paris8.fr/sociologie/fichiers/soulie2012-documents-vincennes.pdf. Accessed Jan. 18, 2022.

65. François Perroux, "L'effet de domination et les relations économiques," *Hommes et techniques* 5 no. 49 (1949) : 9–17; Perroux, "Esquisse d'une théorie de l'économie dominante," *Économie appliquée* 1, nos. 2–3 (1948): 243–300; Perroux, "'L'ordonnance' de J. M. Keynes et les pays sous-développés," *Bulletin de l'Union des exploitations électriques en Belgique*, no. 3 (July 1953): 1–18 (cited by Bourdieu in "Le choc des civilisations," in *Le sous-développement en Algérie*, ed. Secrétariat social d'Alger [Alger: Éditions du Secrétariat social d'Alger, 1959], 52–64, 56–57). Perroux taught at Lyon and Paris between 1928 and 1955, and was named to a chair at the Collège de France. He championed corporatism during the early Vichy regime and promoted Keynsianism and mathematicization of economics after the war.

66. Philippe Hugon, "Retour sur une cinquantaine d'années d'économie du développement dans la Revue Tiers Monde," *Revue Tiers Monde* 191 (2007): 717–41, 722.

67. Hugon, "Retour sur une cinquantaine," 720.

NOTES TO CHAPTER SIX [421]

68. Hugon, "Retour sur une cinquantaine," 718.

69. Rey taught in the *départment de sociologie* at Vincennes-St-Dénis between 1971 and 1985, at which time he initiated the creation of a separate anthropology department. Terray taught "sociology of development" at Vincennes in 1968–1969. Christelle Dormoy-Rajmanan, "Sociogenese d'une invention institutionnelle: le Centre universitaire experimental de Vincennes" (PhD diss., Université de Paris Ouest Nanterre la Défense, 2014), 675 note 1; Soulié, *De Vincennes à Saint-Denis*, 42, 44.

70. On psychology in British colonies, see the superb study by Erik Linstrum, *Ruling Minds: Psychology in the British Empire* (Cambridge, MA: Harvard University Press, 2016).

71. Emile Durkheim, "Représentations individuelles et représentations collectives," *Revue de métaphysique et de morale* 6, no. 3 (1898): 273–302, 274.

72. Laurent Mucchielli, *La découverte du social: naissance de la sociologie en France (1870–1914)* (Paris: La Découverte, 1998), 317; Marcel Mauss, "Real and Practical Relations between Psychology and Sociology," in Mauss, *Sociology and Psychology: Essays* (London: Routledge and K. Paul, 1979),1–34.

73. Paul Fauconnet, review of G. Tarde, *L'opinion et la foule*, in *Année sociologique*, ser. 1, 5 (1900–1901): 160–66, 163; Paul Fauconnet and Marcel Mauss, "Sociologie," *La grande encyclopédie* 30 (1901): 165–76, 171.

74. Laurent Mucchielli, "Pour une psychologie collective: l'héritage durkheimien d'Halbwachs et sa rivalité avec Blondel durant l'entre-deux-guerres," *Revue d'histoire des sciences humaines* 1, no. 1 (1999): 103–14, 104.

75. Jean Piaget, "Logique génétique et sociologie," *Revue philosophique de la France et de l'étranger* 105 (1928): 167–205, 168; Thomas Hirsch, *Le temps des sociétés, d'Émile Durkheim à Marc Bloch* (Paris: Éditions de l'EHESS, 2016), 131.

76. Charles Blondel, *La conscience morbide: essai de psychopathologie générale* (Paris: Librairie F. Alcan, 1914), 250.

77. Blondel, *La conscience morbide*, 250–51.

78. Mucchielli, "Pour une psychologie collective," 104–105; Mauss, "Real and Practical Relations."

79. Report on the complementary doctoral thesis by Essertier in *Annales de l'Université de Paris* 2 (1927), 379; Daniel Essertier, *Psychologie et sociologie: essai de bibliographie critique* (Paris: F. Alcan, 1927).

80. Hirsch, *Le temps des sociétés*, 142; Charles Blondel, *Introduction à la psychologie collective* (Paris: A. Colin, 1928).

81. Theodor W. Adorno, "Einleitung zu Emile Durkheim, 'Soziologie und Philosophie,'" in *Soziologische Schriften I* (Frankfurt am Main: Suhrkamp, 1972), 245–79, 257.

82. Lucien Lévy-Bruhl, *How Natives Think* (New York: A. A. Knopf, 1925), 18..

83. Dominique Merllié, "Durkheim, Lévy-Bruhl et la 'pensée primitive': quelle différend?," *L'Année sociologique* 62 (2012): i–xiii, iv.

84. Adorno, "Einleitung zu Emile Durkheim," 258.

85. René Hubert, *Manuel élémentaire de sociologie*, 5th ed., revised (Paris: Delalain, 1949). Hubert may not have been aware of Lévy-Bruhl's revisions, which were first published posthumously in 1949: Lucien Lévy-Bruhl, *Les carnets* (Paris: Presses universitaires de France, 1949).

86. Lévy-Bruhl, *Les carnets*, 131. Translation mine, based partly on Lucien Lévy-Bruhl, *The Notebooks on Primitive Mentality* (Oxford: Blackwell, 1975), 101. On the differences between Durkheim and Lévy-Bruhl, see Stanislas Deprez, *Lévy-Bruhl et la rationalisation du monde* (Rennes: Presses Universitaires de Rennes, 2010); Frédéric Keck, *Lévy-Bruhl: Entre philosophie et anthropologie* (Paris: CNRS Éditions, 2008); Merllié, "Durkheim, Lévy-Bruhl."

87. Jan Goldstein, "The Advent of Psychological Modernism in France: An Alternate Narrative," in *Modernist Impulses in the Human Sciences, 1870-1930*, ed. D. Ross (Baltimore, MD: Johns Hopkins University Press, 1994), 190-209, 194; Serge Nicolas, *Histoire de la philosophie en France au XIXe siècle: naissance de la psychologie spiritualiste (1789-1830)* (Paris: L'Harmattan, 2007), 242-60.

88. Jan Goldstein, "Foucault and the Post-Revolutionary Self," in *Foucault and the Writing of History*, ed. Jan Goldstein (Oxford: Blackwell, 1994), 99-115, 102.

89. Goldstein, "The Advent of Psychological Modernism," 200.

90. Geneviève Vermès, "La recherche en psychologie au CNRS, son institutionnalisation de ses début aux années cinquante. Construction d'une unité disciplinaire," *Bulletin de psychologie* 52, no. 440 (1999): 213-22, 217-21; Serge Nicolas, *Histoire de la psychologie française: naissance d'une nouvelle science* (Paris: In Press Éditions, 2002), 262.

91. Office de la recherche scientifique coloniale, *Rapport d'activité pour les années 1946-1947* (Paris: ORSC, 1947), 81, 112.

92. As a Naval College graduate, Maucorps had spent time in French Oceania, and after the war he carried out research for the French military. Paul H. Maucorps, "Les recherches de psychométrie ethnologique et leurs perspectives océaniennes," *Journal de la Société des Océanistes* 4, no. 4 (1952): 87-113. See chapter 2 for discussion of Maucorps's text on the causes of racism.

93. William L. Thomas and Anna M. Pikelis, eds., *International Directory of Anthropological Institutions* (New York: Wenner-Gren Foundation for Anthropological Research, 1953), 105.

94. Jean Paul Trystram, "La psychotechnique au Maroc," *Cahiers nord-africains* 20 (1952): 71-74; Trystram, "Recherches psychotechniques au Maroc. Principes et applications," *Bulletin économique et social du Maroc* 57, no. 1 (1955): 219-25. The Société des Mines de Zellidja was founded in 1929 to extract lead ore at Bou Beker in Morocco, and was a beneficiary of the US Marshall Plan. Partnership with two American companies led to the participation of American engineers and the use of American technologies for the extraction of lead, manganese, and zinc. Samir Saul, "Harnessing Americanisation: The Case of the Zellidja Mining Company," in *Americanisation in Twentieth-Century Europe*, vol. 2, ed. Matthias Kipping and Nick Tiratsoo (Villeneuve-d'Ascq: Université Charles-de-Gaulle Lille 3, 2002): 339-55.

95. Pierre Fougeyrollas, "De la psychotechnique à la sociologie policière," *La nouvelle critique* (July-August 1951): 25-40. Mental testing in the French empire has been largely ignored, but for the British Empire, see Linstrum, *Ruling Minds*, ch. 3.

96. Jacques Berque, "The North of Africa," *International Social Science Journal* 13, no. 2 (1961): 177-96, 195, n. 50.

97. Richard C. Keller, *Colonial Madness: Psychiatry in French North Africa* (Chicago: University of Chicago Press, 2007), 9.

98. Jean-Michel Bégué, "French Psychiatry in Algeria (1830-1962): From Colonial to Transcultural," *History of Psychiatry* 7, no. 28 (1996): 533-48, 534; Keller, *Colonial Madness*, 41-43.

99. Jean-Michel Bégué, "Genèse de l'ethnopsychiatrie, un texte fondateur de la psychiatrie coloniale française: le Rapport de Reboul et Régis au Congrès de Tunis en 1912," *Psychopathologie africaine* 28, no. 2 (1997): 177-220; René Collignon, "La psychiatrie coloniale française en Algérie et au Sénégal: esquisse d'une historisation comparative," *Revue Tiers Monde*, no. 187 (2006): 527-46; Keller, *Colonial Madness*, 49.

100. Jock McCulloch, *Colonial Psychiatry and the "African Mind."* (Cambridge: Cambridge University Press, 1995), 44.

101. Keller, *Colonial Madness*, ch. 4.

102. Jalil Bennani, *La psychanalyse au pays des saints: les débuts de la psychiatrie et de la psychanalyse au Maroc* (Rabat: Editions Le Fennec, 1996), 80–8; Alice Bullard, "The Critical Impact of Franz Fanon and Henri Collomb: Race, Gender, and Personality Testing of North and West Africans," *Journal of the History of the Behavioral Sciences* 41, no. 3 (2005): 225–48.

103. J. J. Moreau de Tours, "Recherches sur les aliénés en Orient," *Annales Médico-psychologiques* 1 (1843): 103–32, 128.

104. J. C. Carothers, "A Study of Mental Derangement in Africans, and an Attempt to Explain Its Peculiarities, More Especially in Relation to the African Attitude to Life," *Journal of Mental Science* 93, no. 392 (1947): 548–97, 577.

105. S. Davidson, "Psychiatric Work among the Bemba," *Rhodes-Livingstone Journal* 7 (1949): 75–86, 76.

106. Bégué, "French Psychiatry," 542.

107. Henri Aubin, *L'homme et la magie* (Paris: Desclée de Brouwer, 1952), 222.

108. Bégué, "French Psychiatry, 537.

109. P. Gallais and L. Planques, "Étude sur les déficiences mentales dans les territoires d'outre-mer: perspectives ethno-psychiatriques dans l'Union française," *Médicine tropicale* 11, no. 1 (1951): 5–33; Geoffrey Cuthbert Tooth, *Studies*.

110. A. Donnadieu, "Psychose de civilisation," *Annales medico-psychologiques* 15th ser., 97, no. 1 (1939): 30–37, 37; see also Marianna Scarfone, "'Psychosis of Civilization': A Colonial-Situated Diagnosis," *History of Psychiatry* 32, no. 1 (2020): 52–68.

111. Andras Zempleni, "La dimension therapeutique du culte des *rab, Ndöp, tururu* et *Samp*. Rites de possession chez les Lebou et les Wolof," *Psychopathologie africaine* 2, no. 3 (1966): 291–439, 291.

112. Pierre Maréschal, "Réflexions sur vingt ans de psychiatrie en Tunisie," *La raison* 15 (1956): 68–79, 75.

113. Bégué, "Un siècle."

114. Bégué, "French Psychiatry," 541–42.

115. The open service continued to be combined with asylums for the chronically mentally ill. Frantz Fanon, "Day Hospitalization in Psychiatry: Value and Limits," in Frantz Fanon, *Alienation and Freedom*, ed. Jean Khalfa and Robert J. C. Young (London: Bloomsbury, 2015): 473–94.

116. Bullard, "The Critical Impact," 231.

117. Maréschal, "Réflexions," 70–71; A. Ammar, "L'assistance aux alienés en Tunisie (quelques étapes)," *L'information psychiatrique* 31, no. 4 (January 1955): 24–27, 26.

118. Bullard, "The Critical Impact," 231.

119. Jean Khalfa, "Fanon, Revolutionary Psychiatrist," in Frantz Fanon, *Alienation and Freedom*, ed. Jean Khalfa and Robert J. C. Young (London: Bloomsbury, 2015), 167–202, 167; George Steinmetz, "An Oblique Encounter with Sociology: Frantz Fanon's *Les damnés de la terre*," *Soziopolis* (December 2021). https://www.soziopolis.de/.

120. Frantz Fanon, "L'Œil se noie," in Fanon, *Écrits sur l'aliénation et la liberté*, ed. Jean Khalfa and Robert J. C. Young (Paris: La Découverte, 2018), 65–90.

121. Camille Robcis, *Disalienation: Politics, Philosophy, and Radical Psychiatry in Postwar France* (Chicago: University of Chicago Press, 2021), 62.

122. Frantz Fanon and Charles Geronimi, "TAT in Muslim Women: Sociology of Perception and Imagination," in Frantz Fanon, *Alienation and Freedom*, ed. Jean Khalfa and Robert J. C. Young (London: Bloomsbury, 2015), 427–32.

123. Frantz Fanon and Jacques Azoulay, "Social Therapy in a Ward of Muslim Men," in Frantz Fanon, *Alienation and Freedom*, ed. Jean Khalfa and Robert J. C. Young (London: Bloomsbury, 2015), 353–72.

124. Steinmetz, "An Oblique Encounter."

125. Fanon and Azoulay, "Social Therapy," 363.

126. Jean Khalfa, "La bibliothèque de Frantz Fanon," in Frantz Fanon, *Alienation and Freedom*, ed. Jean Khalfa and Robert J. C. Young (London: Bloomsbury, 2015), 587–655.

127. Frantz Fanon, "Conducts of Confession in North Africa," in Frantz Fanon, *Alienation and Freedom*, ed. Jean Khalfa and Robert J. C. Young (London: Bloomsbury, 2015), 409–16, 414.

128. Lilia Ben Salem, "'Propos sur la sociologie en Tunisie.' Entretien avec Sylvie Mazzella," *Genèses: sciences sociales et histoire* 75 (2009): 125–42, 127–28; see also Ben Salem's notes on Fanon's 1959–1960 course, "The Meeting between Society and Psychiatry" in Fanon, *Alienation and Freedom*, ed. Jean Khalfa and Robert J. C. Young (London: Bloomsbury, 2015), 511–30. See also Khalil Zamiti, "Aux origines de la sociologie en Tunisie," in *Abdelkader Zghal: l'homme des questions*, ed. Mohamed Kerrou (Tunis: Cérès éditions, 2017), 229–38.

129. Quotes in this paragraph from Fanon, *Black Skin White Masks* (New York: Grove Press, 1967).

130. We should also not discount the impact of Fanon's early infatuation with surrealism. As Balandier noted in his review of Aimé Césaire's *Cahier d'un retour au pays natal* in *Présence africaine*, this text inaugurated a "renaissance of the literature of violence," restoring connections with the interwar surrealist movement, which had been "buried by the recent events." This aspect of the surrealist context was also important for Fanon, as is clear from his early unpublished play "L'Œil se noie" (*The Drowning Eye*), in Frantz Fanon, *Alienation and Freedom*, ed. Jean Khalfa and Robert J. C. Young (London: Bloomsbury, 2015), 65–90, which resonates with Bataille's famous "Histoire d'un œil."

131. Octave Mannoni, "Sociologie et psychanalyse," *Présence africaine* 10/11 (1957): 211–15; Fanon (1952) devoted an entire chapter to attacking Mannoni's thesis of the existence of a Malagasy "inferiority complex . . . that antedates colonization." Fanon counters, implausibly, that colonization completely erases the preexisting personality of the colonized.

132. Neither Fanon nor Mannoni refer to W. E. B. Du Bois, who deployed the metaphor of the veil in describing a similar context in *Darkwater: Voices from within the Veil* (New York: Harcourt, Brace and Howe, 1920), but Mannoni discusses Richard Wright at length, and refers to the French version of a lecture by Wright in *Les temps modernes*. Wright's novella *The Man Who Lived Underground*, which uses the metaphors of veiling and masking as well as Plato's cave, was published in *Les temps modernes* in 1951. For Mannoni's discussion of social masks and veils in colonial situations, see *Prospero and Caliban: The Psychology of Colonization* (Ann Arbor: University of Michigan Press, [1950] 1990), 41, 51, 76; Mannoni, "La plainte du noir," *Esprit* (May 1951): 734–49. On Du Bois, Wright, and the veiling metaphor, see Rebecka Rutledge Fisher, *Habitations of the Veil: Metaphor and the Poetics of Black Being in African American Literature* (Albany: State University of New York Press, 2014); on Mannoni and Fanon, see Boni Livio, "La condition (post)coloniale entre marxisme et psychanalyse: l'apport d'Octave Mannoni," *Actuel Marx* 61 (2017): 153–67.

133. In his excellent biography of Fanon, David Macey writes that *L'an V de la révolution algérienne* (1959) was reissued "rather misleadingly" under the title *Sociologie d'une révolution*, "even though it is obviously not an exercise in sociology in any real sense." This statement suggests that Macey does not know what French sociology looked like at the time. However, Macey elsewhere describes Fanon as engaging in "sociological analysis" and as combining "sociology" with "phenomenological" and "psychiatric." David Macey, *Frantz Fanon* (New York: Picador, 2000), 398, 485, 232, 473. Joby Fanon actually writes that his brother Frantz studied for a *licence* degree in sociology. Although the sociology *licence* did not exist until 1958, after Fanon had already completed his studies, his brother's mistaken memory is evidence of the perception of Fanon's work as "sociological" even by those closest to him.

134. Frantz Fanon, *The Wretched of the Earth* (New York: Grove Press, [1961] 2004), 17, 20, 172, 15. On the statue metaphor in the colonial context, see Julia Hell, "Triumphs and Laments: Peter Weiss's Pergamon Altar and William Kentridge's Tiber Mural" (forthcoming).

135. René Collignon, "Les conditions de développement d'une psychiatrie sociale au Sénégal," *Présence africaine*, no. 129 (2004): 3–19; Henri Collomb, "Collaboration interdisciplinaire (réflexions à propos d'une expérience médicale)" (Dakar, unpublished paper, 1965).

136. Quotes from unpublished papers by Collomb in Stéphane Boussat and Michel Boussat, "À propos de Henri Collomb (1913–1979): De la psychiatrie coloniale à une psychiatrie sans frontiers," *L'Autre* 3, no. 3 (2002): 411–24, 413–16.

137. On the more recent turn at Fann toward universal approaches to the human psyche and pharmaceutical strategies, abandonment of Collomb's psychodynamic approaches, and provision of a "new 'VIP' level of patient accommodation," see Katie Kilroy Marac, *An Impossible Inheritance: Postcolonial Psychiatry and the Work of Memory in a West African Clinic* (Berkeley: University of California Press, 2019), 11.

138. See various issues of *Psychopathologie Africaine*, and Andras Zempleni, "Du symptôme au sacrifice. Histoire de Khady Fall," *L'homme* 14, no. 2 (1974): 31–77.

139. Marie Cécile Ortigues and Edmond Ortigues, *Œdipe africain* (Paris: Librarie Plon, 1966).

140. Danielle Storper-Perez, *L'Hospitalisation en milieu psychiatrique occidental: fait et facteur d'acculturation chez les Wolof du Sénégal* (3rd cycle doctorate, Sixth Section, E.P.H.E., 1968); Storper-Perez, *La folie colonisée* (Paris: Maspero, 1974).

141. Ashis Nandy, *The Intimate Enemy: Loss and Recovery of Self under Colonialism* (New York: Oxford University Press, 1988).

142. Mrinalini Greedharry, *Postcolonial Theory and Psychoanalysis* (New York: Palgrave Macmillan, 2008), 53.

143. Jacqueline Rose, "Wulf Sachs's Black Hamlet," in *The Psychoanalysis of Race*, ed. Christopher Lane (New York: Columbia University Press, 1998), 333–52.

144. Edward W. Said, *Freud and the Non-European* (London: Verso, 2003), 15.

145. Julia Hell, "On the Way to the London Mithraeum: Freud's Archaeo-Analysis and the Habsburg Empire's Neo-Roman Mimesis," *American Imago* 78, no. 2 (2021): 245–74.

146. Sigmund Freud, "An Autobiographical Study," *The Standard Edition*, vol. 20, 7–74, 62.

147. Caillois, a student of Mauss, was identified before and during the war as a sociologist and taught sociology while in exile in Argentina during the war, from 1939 to 1944. On Leiris, see chapter 13.

148. For a psychoanalytic discussion of theatrical metaphors in imperial contexts, see Julia Hell, *The Conquest of Ruins* (Chicago: University of Chicago Press, 2019); on psychoanalysis and masks, see Joan Rivière, "Womanliness as a Masquerade," *International Journal of Psycho-Analysis* 10 (1929): 303–13; for Mannoni's discussion of social masks in colonial situations, see Mannoni, *Prospero and Caliban*, 41, 51, 76.

149. The first book on this topic, to my knowledge, was Aurel Kolnai, *Psychoanalyse und Soziologie* (Leipzig: Internationaler Psychoanalytischer Verlag, 1921). Norbert Elias's *Über den Prozeß der Zivilisation* (Basel: Haus zum Falken, 1939) was published earlier, but Elias was strikingly reticent about his debt to Freud. This means that the book's essential identity as a historicization of Freud is completely obvious to some and invisible to others.

150. Ulrike Bokelmann, "Georges Devereux," in *Die wilde Seele. Zur Ethnopsychoanalyse von Georges Devereux*, ed. Hans Peter Duerr (Frankfurt am Main: Suhrkamp, 1987), 9–31.

151. J. C. Carothers, *The African Mind in Health and Disease. A Study in Ethnopsychiatry* (Geneva: World Health Organization, 1954), 161; Fanon, "Racism and Culture," in Fanon, *Toward the African Revolution* (New York: Grove Press, 1967), 31–44, 32.

Chapter Seven: Other Neighboring Social Sciences and Their Engagement with Sociology and Colonialism

1. Olivier Dumoulin, "Le professionalization de l'histoire en France (1919–1939)," in Société française de sociologie, *Historiens et sociologues aujourd'hui* (Paris: Centre national de la recherche scientifique 1986), 49–60; Gérard Noiriel, "Naissance du métier d'historien," *Genèses* 1 (1990): 58–85.

2. Report by Lucien Febvre to the meeting of deliberation on candidates at the Collège de France, cited by Sophie Dulucq, *Écrire l'histoire de l'Afrique à l'époque coloniale: XIXe-XXe siècles* (Paris: Karthala, 2009), 227.

3. Henri Froidevaux, *Les études d'histoire coloniale en France et dans les pays de colonisation française* (Paris: Honoré Champion and Émile Larose, 1913), 12–15.

4. Colette Zytnicki, "La maison, les écuries. L'émergence de l'histoire coloniale en France (des années 1880 aux années 1930)," in *Décoloniser l'histoire? De l'histoire coloniale aux histoires nationales en Amérique latine et en Afrique, XIXe-XXe siècles*, ed. Sophie Dulucq and Colette Zytnicki (Saint-Denis: Société française d'histoire d'outre-mer, 2003), 9–24, 11; Pierre Singaravélou, *Professer l'empire: Les sciences coloniales en France sous la IIIe République* (Paris: Publications de la Sorbonne, 2011), 270.

5. Sophie Dulucq, *Écrire l'histoire de l'Afrique*.

6. Singaravélou, *Professer l'Empire*, 271.

7. Singaravélou, *Professer l'Empire*, 279–80. Singaravélou does not tally the number of books in colonial history published in the Fourth and early Fifth Republics, the period examined here.

8. Singaravélou, *Professer l'Empire*, 284, 275, 280; Robert Dauvergne, "Les aspects de l'histoire coloniale," *Revue de synthèse* 5, no. 1–3 (1933): 59–67, 147–58, 281–95.

9. Singaravélou, *Professer l'Empire*, 288.

10. Claude Singer, *L'université libérée, l'université épurée (1943–1947)* (Paris: Les Belles Lettres, 1997), 24–25, note 2.

11. Georges Hardy, *Les éléments de l'histoire coloniale* (Paris: La Renaissance du livre, 1921).

12. Singaravélou, *Professer l'Empire*, 288.

13. Singaravélou, *Professer l'Empire*, 281.

14. Daniel Rivet, "De l'histoire coloniale à l'histoire des états independents," in *L'Histoire et le métier d'historien en France 1945–1995*, ed. F. Bédarida (Paris: MSH, 1995), 369–78, 370, quoted in Singaravélou, *Professer l'Empire*, 281, n. 60.

15. Quoted in M. Lakroum, "De l'histoire coloniale à l'histoire africaine (1921–1960)," in C. Coquery-Vidrovitch, ed., *L'Afrique occidentale au temps des Français colonisateurs et colonisés (c. 1860–1960)* (Paris: La Découverte, 1992), 37–47, 43.

16. Henri Labouret, "Irrigations, colonisation intérieure et main-d'œuvre au Soudan français," *Annales d'histoire économique et sociale* 1, no. 3 (1929): 365–76. Labouret was a former colonial administrator, *École coloniale* instructor, and a precocious critic of colonialism. See Henri Labouret, *Colonisation, colonialisme, décolonisation* (Paris: Larose, 1952); Romuald Fonkoua, "Robert Delavignette et Henri Labouret: régards et approaches du fait colonial," in *Robert Delavignette, savant et politique: 1897–1976*, ed. Bernard Mouralis and Anne Piriou (Paris: Karthala, 2003), 73–89.

17. Braudel is discussed in Jean Alazard et al., *Histoire et historiens de l'Algérie* (Paris: Alcan, 1931).

18. *Revue africaine* was edited in Algiers by the *Société historique algérienne*, a learned society founded in 1856 by Algeria's Governor General.

19. Fernand Braudel, "En Algérie: problèmes généraux et problèmes d'Oranie," *Annales d'histoire économique et sociale* 10, no. 54 (1938): 509–12, 510.

20. The social scientists who published articles on colonial themes in *Annales* before 1965 included Balandier, Berque, Bastide, Caillois, Devereux, Dresch, Pierre Gourou, Jean Laude, Pierre Marthelot, Tillion, and Trystram.

21. Jean Despois, Marcel Emerit, Gabriel Esquer, Charles Le Tourneau, Henri Terrasse, Xavier Yacono, and Georges Yver.

22. Claude Liauzu, *Les intellectuels français au miroir algérien* (Nice: Université de Nice, 1984), 19.

23. The first articles were by Jean Meyer, Henri Moniot, Henri Brunschwig, and Catherine Coquery-Vidrovitch.

24. Catherine Coquery-Vidrovitch, *Enjeux politiques de l'histoire coloniale* (Marseille: Agone, 2009), 26–27.

25. Dulucq, *Ecrire l'histoire de l'Afrique*, 247, 210, 242.

26. M. Lakroum, "De l'histoire coloniale"; Daniel Rivet, "De l'histoire coloniale," 369–78.

27. Coquery-Vidrovitch, *Enjeux politiques*, 26–27; Ruth Grosrichard, "Charles-André Julien, Le Maghrébin," *Zamane: l'histoire du Maroc* 20 (2012): 68–73; Daniel Rivet, "De l'histoire coloniale," 369–78, 370.

28. André Nouschi, *Enquête sur le niveau de vie des populations rurales constantinoises de la conquête jusqu'en 1919. Essai d'histoire économique et sociale* (Paris: Presses Universitaires de France, 1961).

29. On the relationship between Nouschi and Bourdieu, see "Letters to André Nouschi," in Pierre Bourdieu, *Algerian Sketches* (Cambridge: Polity, 2013), 317–22.

30. Abdoulaye Ly, *Dialogue avec Abdoulaye Ly: historien et homme politique sénégalais* (Dakar: IFAN, 2001), 44; Institut français d'Afrique noire, *Rapport annuel 1952* (Dakar: IFAN, 1952), 16; Université de Dakar, *Livret de l'étudiant. Année scolaire 1962–1963* (Dakar: Université de Dakar, 1962), 549; Abdoulaye Ly, "La Compagnie du Sénégal de 1673 à 1696. L'évolution du commerce français d'Afrique noire dans le dernier quart du XVIIe siècle" (PhD diss., University of Bordeaux, 1955). See also Anne Piriou, "Intellectuels colonisés et écriture de l'histoire en Afrique de l'Ouest (c. 1920–c.1945)," in *Décoloniser l'histoire? De l'histoire coloniale aux histoires nationales en Amérique latine et en Afrique, XIXe–XXe siècles*, ed. Sophie Dulucq and Colette Zytnicki (Saint-Denis: Société française d'histoire d'outre-mer, 2003), 59–81.

31. J. H. Hexter, "Fernand Braudel and the *Monde Braudellien*," *Journal of Modern History* 44, no. 4 (1972): 480–539, 491.

32. Olivier Godechot, "La formation des relations académiques au sein de l'EHESS," *Histoire et mesure* 26 (2011): 223–60, 231.

33. Desrosières, *The Politics of Large Numbers*, 147.

34. Jacques Dupâquier and Eric Vilquin, "Le pouvoir royal et la statistique démographique," in INSEE, *Pour une histoire de la statistique*, vol. 2, 2nd ed. (Paris: Economica-INSEE, 1987), 83–104, 85.

35. Alain Desrosières, "L'histoire de la statistique comme genre: style d'écriture et usages sociaux," *Genèses* 39, no. 2 (2002): 121–37, 123; Desrosières, *The Politics of Large Numbers*, 152; Alfred Sauvy, "Statistique générale et service national de statistique de 1919 à 1944," *Journal de la société statistique de Paris* 116 (1975): 34–43, 35; Béatrice Touchelay, "L'INSEE, histoire d'une institution," in *L'ère du chiffre: systèmes statistiques et traditions nationales*, ed. Jean-Pierre Beaud (Saint-Foy: Presses de l'Université du Québec, 2000), 153–87, 156–57.

36. Sauvy, "Statistique générale," 40; Touchelay, "Le développement de la statistique d'outre-mer du début du siècle aux indépendances: l'accomplissement d'une tâche de souveraineté," in Ministère de l'économie, des finances et de l'industrie, ed., *La France et l'outre-mer. Un siècle de relations monétaires et financières* (Paris: Comité pour l'histoire économique et financière de la France, 1998), 259–80, 265–69.

37. Touchelay, "L'INSEE," 170, 154.

38. Alain Desrosières, "The Economics of Convention and Statistics: The Paradox of Origins," *Historical Social Research* 36, no. 4 (2011): 64–81, 65.

39. See the cover of INSEE, *Bulletin d'information*, 1947.

40. Dupâquier and Vilquin, "Le pouvoir royal," 92.

41. Dupâquier and Vilquin, "Le pouvoir royal," 93–94.

42. Dupâquier and Vilquin, "Le pouvoir royal," 97.

43. Béatrice Touchelay, "L'émergence des statistiques du travail entre 1891 et 1967 ou la construction d'une réalité économique, politique et sociale" (unpublished report, at https://travail-emploi.gouv.fr/IMG/pdf/Rapport_Touchelay.pdf), 11. Accessed June 26, 2022. L'émergence des statistiques," 11; Touchelay, "Le développement de la statistique d'outre-mer."

44. Pierre Sanner, "Contribution à un memorial du Service colonial des statistiques, 1923–1958," *Journal de la société statistique de Paris* 135, no. 1 (1994): 73–99, 75.

45. Albert Ficatier, *Un certain regard sur une des fonctions de l'INSEE: de la statistique coloniale à la coopération technique* (Paris: INSEE, 1981), 5–6; Gérard Théodore, "Rapport sur un programme d'enquêtes statistiques agricoles et démographiques en Afrique noire française," INSEE, *Bulletin d'information* 10 (December 1954): 17–28, 10, 18.

46. INSEE, *INSEE, 1946–1956* (Paris: INSEE, 1956), 31; Sanner, "Contribution," 95; Ficatier, *Un certain regard*, 15; "Catalogues des publications reçues de l'Union française," *Bulletin intérieur de l'INSEE*, no. 5 (May 1951): 75–85.

47. Ficatier, *Un certain regard*, 11; Théodore, "Rapport sur un programme," 23.

48. No census of the entire population was undertaken due to the country's "administrative complexity," the "lack of precision in the orthography of localities," and sometimes even "incertitude about these localities' existence." Georges Bournier, "Les services de statistique d'outre-mer (1). IV. Le service des statistique du Maroc," *Bulletin intérieur de l'INSEE*, no. 12 (Dec. 1949): 55–62, 58–59.

49. Kamel Kateb, *Européens, "indigènes" et juifs en Algérie (1830–1962), représentations et réalités des populations* (Paris: INED, 2001), ch. 6; Touchelay, "Le développement de la statistique," 16.

50. Théodore, "Rapport sur un programme," 22.

51. Georges Bournier, "Le service de statistique générale d'Algérie," *Bulletin intérieur de l'INSEE* no. 8 (September 1948): 3–9; Claude Seibel, "Les liens entre Pierre Bourdieu et les statisticiens à partir de son expérience algérienne," in *La liberté par la connaissance. Pierre Bourdieu (1930–2002)*, ed. Jacques Bouveresse and Daniel Roche (Paris: Odile Jacob, 2004), 105–20.

52. Kateb, *Européens*, 59, 227–29.

53. Andrés Horacio Reggiani, *God's Eugenicist: Alexis Carrel and the Sociobiology of Decline* (New York: Berghahn Books, 2007), 71, 95.

54. According to Reggiani, the Rockefeller Foundation did not give Carrel approval to use the Paris venue. Reggiani, *God's Eugenicist*, 104, 113.

55. Alain Drouard, *Une inconnue des sciences sociales: la fondation Alexis Carrel* (Paris: Editions de la Maison des Sciences de l'Homme, 1992), 177–80; Andrés Horacio Reggiani, "Alexis Carrel, the Unknown: Eugenics and Population Research under Vichy," *French Historical Studies* 25, no. 2 (2002): 331–56; Alain Girard, *L'Institut national d'études démographiques: histoire et développement* (Paris: Éditions de l'INED, 1986), 67.

56. Reggiani, *God's Eugenicist*, 119.

57. Paul-André Rosental, *L'intelligence démographique: sciences et politiques des populations en France (1930–1960)* (Paris : Odile Jacob, 2003), 133; Reggiani, "Alexis Carrel, the Unknown," 354. INED also replaced the Vichy *Service de démographie*.

58. Monica M. Van Beusekom, *Negotiating Development: African Farmers and Colonial Experts at the Office du Niger, 1920-1960* (Portsmouth, NH: Heinemann, 2000), 178 ; Gilles Sautter, *De l'Atlantique au fleuve Congo. Une géographie du sous-peuplement* (Paris: Mouton, 1966).

59. Alain Girard and Joseph Leriche, *Les Algériens en France, Étude démographique et sociale* (Paris: INED, 1955); Alfred Sauvy, *La vie en plus: souvenirs* (Paris: Calmann-Lévy, 1981), 143-44; Louis Henry, "Perspectives relatives a la population musulmane de l'Afrique du Nord," *Population* 2, no. 2 (1947): 267-80.

60. Rosental, *L'intelligence démographique*, 133, 144.

61. Alfred Sauvy, "Préface," in *Le tiers-monde, sous-développement et développement*, ed. Georges Balandier (Paris, PUF-INED, 1956), 11.

62. Georges Balandier, "Introduction," in *Le tiers-monde, sous-développement et développement*, ed. Georges Balandier (Paris, PUF-INED, 1956), 13-22, 15.

63. Alfred Sauvy, "Trois mondes, une planète," *L'Observateur*, August 14, no. 118 (1952): 14. The phrase was popularized by Balandier and was imported into English by the British colonial sociologist Peter Worsley.

64. Olivier Gilg, "Gessain, Robert," in *Encyclopedia of the Arctic*, vol. 2, ed. Mark Nutall (New York: Routledge, 2015), 730-32; Andre Burguière, "Plozévet, une mystique de l'interdisciplinarité?," *Cahiers du Centre de recherches historiques* 36 (2005): 231-63, 237.

65. Louis Chevalier, *Le problème démographique nord-africain* (Paris: INED, 1947); Chevalier, *Madagascar: Populations et ressources* (Paris: INED, 1952). Chevalier is best known as the author of *Classes laborieuses et classes dangereuses* (Paris: Plon, 1958).

66. John E. Craig, "Sociology and the Related Disciplines between the Wars: Maurice Halbwachs and the Imperialism of the Durkheimians," in *The Sociological Domain: The Durkheimians and the Founding of French Sociology*, ed. Philippe Besnard (Cambridge: Cambridge University Press, 1983), 263-89, 263; Annette Becker, *Maurice Halbwachs: un intellectuel en guerres mondiales, 1914-1945* (Paris: A. Viénot, 2003), 79-92; Maurice Halbwachs, "La statistique en sociologie" in *La statistique, ses applications, les problèmes qu'elle soulève* (Paris: Presses universitaires de France, 1944), 113-34.

67. Alain Desrosières, *The Politics of Large Numbers: A History of Statistical Reasoning* (Cambridge, MA: Harvard University Press, 1998), 155; Jean Bouvier, "François Simiand, la statistique, et les sciences humaines," in INSEE, *Pour une histoire de la statistique*, vol. 1, 2nd ed. (Paris: Economica-INSEE, 1987), 431-43.

68. Jean Stoetzel, "L'esprit de la sociologie contemporaine," *Revue française de sociologie* 32, no. 3 ([1946] 1991): 443-56, 455.

69. Jon Cowans, "Fear and Loathing in Paris. The Reception of Opinion Polling in France, 1938-1977," *Social Science History* 26, no. 1 (2002): 71-104, 75.

70. Loïc Blondiaux, *La fabrique de l'opinion: une histoire sociale des sondages* (Paris: Editions du Seuil, 1998); H. Riffault, "L'Institut français d'opinion publique 1938-1978," in *Science et théorie d'opinion publique: Hommage à Jean Stoetzel*, ed. R. Boudon et al. (Paris: Retz, 1981), 231-46; Jean Stoetzel, "La doxométrie française a un an," *Sondages* 2 (1939): 2-4. Stoetzel's IFOP ceased operations during the Occupation and reopened in 1944.

71. Touchely, "L'INSEE," 162; Drouard, *Une inconnue*, 274, note 3. The employers' organization was *Commission générale de l'organisation scientifique*.

72. Loïc Blondiaux, "Comment rompre avec Durkheim? Jean Stoetzel et la sociologie française de l'après-guerre (1945-1958)," *Revue française de sociologie* 32, no. 3 (1991): 411-41.

73. Stoetzel's most extensive praise for Le Play was expressed in an unpublished lecture in Tokyo in 1952, quoted *in extenso* in Blondiaux, "Comment rompre," 429.

74. Letter from de Dampierre to Stoetzel, July 8, 1958, in Bibliothèque Éric-de-Dampierre, Mission sociologique du Haut Oubangui papers, folder "Correspondence Génerale 1954–1967/1958–1959."

75. Alain Girard and Jean Stoetzel, *Français et immigrés. Institut national d'études démographiques* (Paris: Presses universitaires de France, 1953); Girard and Stoetzel, "Nouveaux documents sur l'immigration en France," *Population* 9, no. 1 (1954): 43–50.

76. Emmanuelle Saada, *Empire's Children: Race, Filiation, and Citizenship in the French Colonies* (Chicago: University of Chicago, 2012), ch. 4.

77. Abdelmalek Sayad, *La double absence. Des illusions de l'émigré aux souffrances de l'immigré* (Paris: Seuil, 1999).

78. Jean Stoetzel, "Une enquête sur l'opinion du personnel saharien et des familles," in *Problèmes humains posés par l'implantation des familles en régions désertiques*, ed. Centre d'études et d'informations des problèmes humains dans les zones arides (Paris: Prohuza, 1961), 79–87, 87.

79. "Recensements démographiques recents des pays d'outre-mer de l'Union française," *Bulletin intérieur de l'INSEE* 5 (May 1956): 43–63, 55.

80. Robert Blanc, *Handbook of Demographic Research in Under-Developed Countries* (London: CCTA, 1959), 56–57, 61; Ministère de la France d'Outre-Mer, Service des statistiques, *Manuel d'agent recenseur dans le cadre d'une enquête démographique en pays sous-développé* (Paris: Ministère de la France d'Outre-Mer, 1955).

81. Mission démographique de Guinée, *Étude démographique par sondage en Guinée, 1954–1955. 1ère Partie: Technique d'enquête* (Paris: Ministère de la France d'Outre-Mer, Service des statistiques, 1956), 4, 13.

82. Pascal-Gaston Marietti, "Présentation," in Mission démographique de Guinée, *Étude démographique par sondage en Guinée, 1954–1955. 1ère Partie: Technique d'enquête* (Paris: Ministère de la France d'Outre-Mer, Service des statistiques, 1956), i–iii, ii; Théodore, "Rapport sur un programme," 28.

83. Marietti, "Présentation," i–iii, ii.

84. "Recensements démographiques recents," 57.

85. Massé had an advanced degree in Public Health from Harvard. Other social scientists on loan from IFAN to the Guinée survey included the geographer Edmond Bernus and the anthropologist Pierre Cantrelle. Marietti, "Présentation," ii, note 1; Théodore, "Rapport sur un programme," 19.

86. Blanc, *Handbook of Demographic Research*, 65.

87. Christian Faure, *Le projet culturel de Vichy: Folklore et révolution nationale, 1940–1944* (Paris: CNRS, 1989).

88. See, for example, Julius Lips, *The Savage Hits Back, Or The White Man Through Native Eyes* (London: Dickson, 1937), and the discussion of Michel Leiris in chapter 13, below.

89. On Broca, see Claude Blanckaert, *De la race à l'évolution. Paul Broca et l'anthropologie française* (Paris: Harmattan, 2009).

90. Charles Letourneau, *Sociology based upon Ethnography* (London: Chapman and Hall, 1881).

91. Laurent Mucchielli, *La découverte du social: naissance de la sociologie en France (1870–1914)* (Paris: La Découverte, 1998), 459.

92. Louis Thomas, *Arthur de Gobineau. Inventeur du racisme. 1816–1882* (Paris: Mercure de France, 1941).

93. Mucchielli, *La découverte du social*, 278–79.

94. Alice Conklin, *In the Museum of Man: Race, Anthropology, and Empire in France, 1850–1950* (Ithaca, NY: Cornell University Press, 2013), 30.

95. Steinmetz, *The Devil's Handwriting: Precolonial Ethnography and the German Colonial State in Qingdao, Samoa, and Southwest Africa* (Chicago: University of Chicago Press), 301–5; Jean Louis Armand Quatrefages de Bréau, *Les Polynésiens et leurs migrations* (Paris: A. Bertrand, 1864).

96. Li-Chuan Tai, *L'anthropologie française entre sciences coloniales et décolonisation (1880–1960)* (Paris: Publications de la Société Française d'Histoire d'Outre-mer, 2010), 32, citing Théodore Reinach, *Notice sur la vie et les travaux de M. Ernest Hamy* (Paris: Firmin-Didot, 1911), 57.

97. These journals were *Revue d'ethnographie* and *L'Anthropologie*. Conklin, *In the Museum*, 39–40.

98. Christopher Johnson, *Claude Lévi-Strauss: The Formative Years* (Cambridge: Cambridge University Press, 2003), 12–13.

99. Conklin, *In the Museum*, 37.

100. Emmanuelle Sibeud, *Une science impériale pour l'Afrique? La construction des savoirs africanistes en France 1878–1930* (Paris: EHESS, 2002), 36; Elizabeth A. Williams, "Anthropological Institutions in Nineteenth-Century France," *Isis* 76, no. 3 (1985): 331–48, 338–39; R. Lacombe, "Essai sur les origines et les premiers développements de la société d'ethnographie," *L'ethnographie* 76 (1980): 329–41.

101. Frederick C. Beiser, *The German Historicist Tradition* (Oxford: Oxford University Press, 2011); George Steinmetz, "Historicism and Contingency: Beyond Positivism in the Social Sciences," in *Historicism: A Travelling Concept*, ed. Herman Paul and Adriaan van Veldhuizen (London: Bloomsbury, 2020), 57–95.

102. Williams, "Anthropological Institutions," 345; Tai, *L'anthropologie*, 42, n. 89.

103. George Stocking, "What's in a Name? (II) The Société d'ethnographie and the Historiography of 'Anthropology' in France," in *Delimiting Anthropology: Occasional Essays and Reflections* (Madison: University of Wisconsin Press, 2001), 207–18, 213, 215.

104. Williams, "Anthropological Institutions," 331, 344, 339.

105. Paul Rivet, "L'ethnologie," in *La science française*, ed. Henri Bergson et al., vol. 2, 2nd ed. (Paris: Larousse, 1934), 5–12; Conklin, *In the Museum*, 59, 87.

106. Tai, *L'anthropologie*, 178.

107. Stocking, "What's in a Name?," 213, 215.

108. Tai, *L'anthropologie*, 33, 37–38.

109. Tai, *L'anthropologie*, 40–42.

110. Steinmetz, "Field Theory and Interdisciplinarity: Relations between History and Sociology in Germany and France during the Twentieth Century," *Comparative Studies in Society and History* 59, no. 2 (2017): 477–514.

111. Marcel Cohen, "Sciences humaines," *La Pensée* n.s., no. 4 (1945): 58–64, 61; Johnson, *Claude Lévi-Strauss*, 63.

112. See the recollections of the ethnologist Paul-Émile Victor, *La mansarde* (Paris: Stock, 1981), 304.

113. Marcel Mauss, "Note de méthode sur l'extension de la sociologie, énoncé de quelques principes à propos d'un livre recent," in Mauss, *Oeuvres*, vol. 3 (Paris: Minuit, 1969), 283–97, 291.

114. Marcel Griaule, "Notes sur l'organisation de l'ethnologie en France," AN, F17 13358, dossier "ethnologie et anthropologie," cited in Tai, *L'anthropologie*, 179.

115. Nathan Glazer, "What Is Sociology's Job?," *Commentary* 4 (Jan. 1947): 181–86, 181. This definition of sociology's domain as "dribs and drabs" or "nuts and sluts" is only found in the United States. Alexander Liazos, "The Poverty of the Sociology of Deviance: Nuts, Sluts, and Preverts," *Social Problems* 20, no. 1 (1972): 103–20.

116. Mauss, "La sociologie en France," 36; Conklin, *In the Museum*, 91.

117. *Races et racisme: Bulletin du Groupement d'étude et d'information.* This journal's advisory and editorial committees included Lévy-Bruhl, Bouglé, Leenhardt, Maunier, and Rivet.

118. Paul W. Vogt, "Durkheimian Sociology versus Philosophical Rationalism: The Case of Célestin Bouglé," in *The Sociological Domain: The Durkheimians and the Founding of French Sociology*, ed. Philippe Besnard (Cambridge: Cambridge University Press, 1983), 231–47, 242; Guillaume-Léonce Duprat, *La solidarité sociale. Ses causes, son évolution, ses consequences* (Paris: O. Doin, 1907).

119. Robert Marjolin, "French Sociology-Comte and Durkheim," *American Journal of Sociology* 42, no. 5 (1937): 693–704, 700.

120. For further development of this argument see George Steinmetz, *The Devil's Handwriting*; and Steinmetz, "The Colonial State as a Social Field," *American Sociological Review* 73, no. 4 (August 2008): 589–612.

121. Paul Le Coeur, *Le rite et l'outil—Essai sur le rationalisme social et la pluralité des civilisations*, 2nd ed. (Paris: Presses universitaires de France, 1969 [1939]), 33, 51.

122. Frantz Fanon, *Wretched of the Earth* (New York: Grove Press, 2004), 20.

123. Memoirs of European colonial officials, travelers, traders, and social scientists reveal that many were fascinated with worlds that differed as strongly as possible from their familiar homelands. A fascination with contemporary "archaic" cultures also served aesthetic interests in modern art's turn toward primitivism.

124. The German infatuation with Polynesia in the late eighteenth century was expressed in utopian plans for emigration to Tahiti by a group of German writers associated with the Pietistic *Empfindsamkeit* (sentimentality) movement in 1777, for example. Steinmetz, *The Devil's Handwriting*, 269.

125. See especially chapter 13 on Georges Balandier. Balandier's publications after 1946 soon began to focus on the cultural, social, and psychological spoliation of Africa by colonialism, leaving behind his earlier exoticist dreams.

126. Jack Flam and Miriam Deutch, eds., *Primitivism and Twentieth-Century Art* (Berkeley: University of California Press, 2003); Daniel J. Sherman, *French Primitivism and the Ends of Empire, 1945–1975* (Chicago: University of Chicago Press, 2011).

127. Marcel Griaule, "Introduction méthodologique," *Minotaure* 2 (1933): 7–12, 7; Jean Jamin, "La mission ethnographique et linguistique DAKAR-DJIBOUTI," *Cahiers Ethnographiques*, n.s. 5 (1984): 7–86; Éric Jolly and Marianne Lemaire, eds., *Cahier Dakar Djibouti* (Meurcourt: Éditions les Cahiers, 2015). The Ethnological Institute sponsored more than 100 expeditions before 1940, the majority of which went to French colonies. James Clifford, *The Predicament of Culture* (Cambridge, MA: Harvard University Press, 1988), 62.

128. Marcel Griaule, *Conversations with Ogotemmêli. An Introduction to Dogon Religious Ideas* (London: Oxford University Press, 1965).

129. Michael Rothberg, "The Work of Testimony in the Age of Decolonization: *Chronicle of a Summer*, Cinema Verité, and the Emergence of the Holocaust Survivor," *PMLA* 119, no. 5 (2004): 1231–46.

130. Marcel Griaule, "Les problèmes de la colonisation et les sciences de l'homme," in *De la banquise à la jungle*, ed. H. Lauga (Paris: Plon, 1952), 157–62, 159.

131. Clifford, *The Predicament of Culture*, 78; see Marcel Griaule, *Burners of Men: Modern Ethiopia* (Philadelphia: J. B. Lippincott, 1935), 24.

132. Hubert Deschamps, "Griaule, Mandel et l'Ethiopie," *Journal of Ethiopian Studies* 4, no. 1 (1966): 71–73; Isabelle Fiemeyer, *Marcel Griaule, citoyen dogon* (Arles: Actes sud, 2004), 48–53.

133. James I. Lewis, "The MRP and the Genesis of the French Union, 1944–1948," *French History* 12, no. 3 (1998): 276–314, 299.

134. Marcel Griaule, "L'action sociologique en Afrique noire," *Présence africaine* 3 (1948): 388–91, 390; also Griaule, *Méthode de l'ethnographie* (Paris: Presses universitaires de France, 1957), 82–83.

135. Benoît de l'Estoile, *Le goût des autres. De l'exposition coloniale aux arts premiers* (Paris: Flammarion, 2007), 148.

136. Rivet in 1932, quoted in Conklin, *In the Museum*, 232.

137. According to Denise Paulme, who accompanied Griaule on his third ethnographic mission to the Dogon. Denise Paulme, "Sanga 1935," *Cahiers d'études africaines* 17, no. 65 (1977): 7–12, 9. Haffner underscores the continuity between Griaule's work in World War I as an aerial spotter and navigator and the military character of his research methods; Jeanne Haffner, *The View from Above: The Science of Social Space* (Cambridge, MA: MIT Press, 2013), 32.

138. Leiris, Letter from Jan. 5, 1932, in *Miroir de l'Afrique* (Paris: Gallimard, 1996), quoted in de l'Estoile, *Le goût des autres*, 149.

139. Georges Balandier, *Civilsés, dit-on* (Paris: PUF, 2003), 81.

140. Griaule, *Méthode de l'ethnographie*, 57.

141. Steinmetz, *The Devil's Handwriting*.

142. Marie-Albane de Suremain, "Faire du terrain en AOF dans les années cinquante," *Ethnologie française* 34, no. 4 (2004): 651–59, 654.

143. Denise Paulme, "Quelques souvenirs," *Cahiers d'études africaines* 19, no. 73 (1979): 9–17, 12. On Métraux's Easter Island expedition, see Christine Laurière, "L'Odyssée pascuane. Mission Métraux-Lavachery, Île de Pâques (1934–1935)," at http://www.berose.fr/?L-Odyssee-pascuane-Mission-Metraux.

144. Denise Paulme, *Organisation sociale des Dogon* (Paris: Domat-Montchrestien, 1940); Marianne Lemaire, "A Journey through many Fields. Denise Paulme's Scientific Itinerary," *L'homme* 193, no. 1 (2010): 51–73.

145. Seán Hand, *Michel Leiris. Writing the Self* (Cambridge: Cambridge University Press, 2002), 54; Denis Hollier and Jean Jamin, eds., *Leiris Unlimited* (Paris: CNRS Éditions, 2017).

146. Jolly and Lemaire, *Cahier Dakar Djibouti*, 1294; Michel Leiris, "La jeune ethnographie," *Masses* 3 (March 1933): 10–11.

147. Michel Leiris, *C'est-à-dire: entretien avec Sally Price et Jean Jamin; suivi de titres et travaux* (Paris: J.-M. Place, 1992), 46; also Claude Arditi, "Michel Leiris devant le colonialism," *Bulletin, Association française des anthropologues* 42 (1990): 95–99, 95; Fournier, *Marcel Mauss*, 282.

148. Michel Leiris, *L'Afrique fantôme* (Paris: Gallimard, 1981), 13.

149. Michel Leiris, "The Ethnographer Faced with Colonialism," in *Brisées = Broken Branches*, trans. Lydia Davis (San Francisco: North Point, 1989), 112–31.

150. Clifford, *The Predicament of Culture*, 89.

151. Arditi, "Michel Leiris," 97. See Michel Leiris, *Contacts de civilisations en Martinique et en Guadeloupe* (Paris: UNESCO/Gallimard, 1955).

152. Leiris, *C'est-à-dire*, 19.

153. Leiris, "The Ethnographer Faced with Colonialism," 125.

154. Ministère de l'éducation nationale, CNRS, *Séance plénière du Comité national de la recherche scientifique 2 juin 1948* (Paris, 1948), 5.

155. Anne Dhoquois, "Introduction," in *Comment je suis devenu ethnologue*, ed. Anne Dhoquois (Paris: Cavalier bleu, 2008), 9–16, 15.

156. André Leroi-Gourhan, "Qu'est-ce que c'est ... l'ethnologie?," *Bulletin du Centre de formation aux recherches ethnologiques*, no. 5 (Jan 1953): 1–7, 1; Jacques Gutwirth, "La professionnalisation d'une discipline: Le centre de formation aux recherches ethnologiques," *Gradhiva* 29 (2001): 25–41.

157. Mauss lost his post at the Fifth Section; Aron, Balandier, Joffre Dumazédier, Georges Friedmann, Paul-Henri Maucorps, and Boris Vildé joined the resistance. Ethnologists Tillion and Yvonne Oddon, Head Librarian at the Musée de l'Homme, were deported to Nazi camps and survived. Ethnologist Deborah Lifchitz was killed at Auschwitz; sociologist Maurice Halbwachs died at Buchenwald. Régis Meyran, "Écrits, pratiques et faits. L'ethnologie sous le régime de Vichy," *L'homme* 39, no. 150 (1999): 203–12, 203–4.

158. Carole Reynaud-Paligot, *Races, racisme et antiracisme dans les années 1930* (Paris: Presses universitaires de France, 2007), 56; Martin S. Staum, *Nature and Nurture in French Social Sciences, 1859–1914 and Beyond* (Montreal: McGill-Queen's University Press, 2011), 203.

159. See the essays in *Anamnese*, no. 7 (March 2012), Special Issue: "Les sociologues sous Vichy," ed. Jean Ferrette. Max Bonnafous and Marcel Déat were direct collaborators. Bonnafous, who held the sociology chair at Bordeaux, was named to several important posts in the Vichy government, although he began helping the resistance in 1943 when he became convinced of the Allies' immanent victory. Déat, who entered politics after a brief career in sociology, founded and directed one of the two main French fascist parties, the *Rassemblement national populaire*. See Justinien Raymond, "Bonnafous Max, Jean-Marie, Antoine," https://maitron.fr/spip.php?article17171 (consulted Jan. 22, 2022); Mathieu Hikaru Desan, "Order, Authority, Nation: Neo-Socialism and the Fascist Destiny of an Anti-Fascist Discourse" (PhD diss., University of Michigan, 2016).

160. Conklin, *In the Museum*, 308, note 82, ff.; Laurent Joly, *Vichy dans la "solution finale": Histoire du commissariat général aux questions juives (1941–1944)* (Paris: Grasset, 2006), 555; Yves Laplace, *L'Exécrable* (Paris: Fayard, 2020). Herman Lebovics, "Le conservatisme en anthropologie et la fin de la Troisième République," *Gradhiva* 4 (1988): 3–17; Marc Knobel, "L'ethnologue à la dérive. George Montandon et l'ethnoracisme," *Ethnologie et racismes* 18, no. 2 (1988): 107–13. On Eugen Fischer, see Steinmetz, *The Devil's Handwriting*, 232–37.

161. Fredrik Petersson, *Willi Münzenberg, the League Against Imperialism, and the Comintern, 1925–1933* (Lewiston: Queenston Press, 2013); Michael Goebel, *Anti-Imperial Metropolis: Interwar Paris and the Seeds of Third-World Nationalism* (New York: Cambridge University Press, 2015).

162. Marcel Cornu, "Les journées d'Ivry," *La Pensée* n.s. 48–49 (1953): 161–74, 169; Henri Lefebvre, "Intervention au Cercle des sociologues," *La nouvelle critique* 5, no. 45 (1953): 247–50, 250. See also A. Gersaint, "Chronique sociologique," *La penseé*, n.s. 60 (1955): 99–114.

163. Parti communiste français, *Journal de la cellule Paul Eluard du Centre d'études sociologiques* (Jan. 1961).

164. Quotes from interviews by the author with Georges Balandier, Feb. 9, 2007, Paris, and Roland Waast, Feb. 15, 2012, Paris.

165. Jacques Berque, "Sciences sociales et décolonisation," *Tiers-Monde* 9–10 (1962): 1–15, 3; Berque, "The North of Africa," *International Social Science Journal* 13, no. 2 (1961): 177–96, 184.

166. Bernard Mouralis, *Comprendre l'œuvre de Mongo Beti* (Issy les Moulineaux: Classiques africains, 1981), 11, 16–17.

167. Owen Sichone, "The Social Sciences in Africa," in *The Modern Social Sciences*, ed. Ted Porter and Dorothy Ross, vol. 7 of *The Cambridge History of Science* (Cambridge: Cambridge University Press, 2003), 466–81, 478.

168. See "Resolution de sociologie," *Présence africaine* 24–25 (Feb.–March 1959): 405–6. The sociology subcommission called for studies of traditional Africa *and* social change in Africa.

169. Paul Rivet, "Des risques qu'il faut accepter," *Le Monde*, June 12–13, 1955.

170. Germaine Tillion, *L'Algérie en 1957* (Paris: Éditions de Minuit, 1957).

171. Comments by M. S. Benyahi in 1971, quoted in Fanny Colonna, "Une fonction coloniale de l'ethnographie dans l'Algérie de l'entre deux-guerres: la programmation des élites moyennes," *Libyca* 20 (1972): 259–67.

172. The resonances between scientific and literary writing have been fruitfully explored by Devin Griffiths, *The Age of Analogy: Science and Literature between the Darwins* (Baltimore, MD: Johns Hopkins University Press, 2016); see also Vincent Debaene, *Far Afield: French Anthropology between Science and Literature* (Chicago: University of Chicago Press, 2014).

173. François Dosse, *History of Structuralism*, 2 vols. (Minneapolis: University of Minnesota Press, 1997).

174. Balandier, *Histoire d'autres*, 187.

175. Pierre Bourdieu, *Sketch for a Self-Analysis* (Cambridge: Polity, 2007), 40; Steinmetz, "The Colonial Origins of Bourdieu's Dynamic Sociology. Beyond "Social Reproduction Theory" and the Thesis of Bourdieu's "Two Algerias," *Rassegna Italiana di Sociologia*, 63, n. 2 (2022): 323–348.

Chapter Eight: Theoretical Developments in Interwar Sociology as a Context for Postwar Colonial Sociology

1. Karl Mannheim, "The Problem of a Sociology of Knowledge," in Karl Mannheim, *Essays on the Sociology of Knowledge*, ed. Paul Kecskemeti (London: Routlege and Kegan Paul, 1952), 134–90, 135–36.

2. Cited in Alice Conklin, *In the Museum of Man: Race, Anthropology, and Empire in France, 1850–1950* (Ithaca, NY: Cornell University Press, 2013), 234; see also Mauss's remarks in *Revue de synthèse historique* n.s. 1, no. 2 (1931): 202–3.

3. John E. Craig, "Sociology and the Related Disciplines between the Wars: Maurice Halbwachs and the Imperialism of the Durkheimians," in *The Sociological Domain: The Durkheimians and the Founding of French Sociology*, ed. Philippe Besnard (Cambridge: Cambridge University Press, 1983), 263–89, 263.

4. The philosopher Raymond Polin did fieldwork on rural cooperatives while he was associated with Bouglé and published *Les coopératives rurales et l'état en Tchécoslovaquie et en Roumanie* (Paris: F. Alcan, 1934).

5. Mauss in Dirk Käsler, *Sociological Adventures: Earle Edward Eubank's Visits with European Sociologists* (New Brunswick, NJ: Transaction Publishers, 1991), 143.

6. Johan Heilbron, *French Sociology* (Ithaca, NY: Cornell University Press, 2015), 119.

7. Robert Marjolin, "French Sociology—Comte and Durkheim," *American Journal of Sociology* 42, no. 5 (1937): 693–704, 700.

8. Georges Davy, "Sociology," *The Monist* 36 (1926): 456–76.

9. Paul Bureau, *Introduction à la méthode sociologique* (Paris: Bloud & Gay, 1923). Daniel Essertier discussed contemporary Le Playsians in *La sociologie* (Paris: F. Alcan, 1930).

10. Bernard Karaola, "Le mysticisme technique de Joseph Wilbois," in *Les chantiers de la paix sociale*, ed. Yves Cohen and Remi Badoui (Fontenay: ENS editions, 1996), 185–94, 189–90.

11. Célestin Bouglé, "La sociologie française et l'éducation nationale," *Archives pour la science et la réforme sociale* 13, no. 1 (1936): 39–46, 41.

12. Edmund Burke, III, "The Sociology of Islam: The French Tradition," in *Islamic Studies: A Tradition and its Problems*, ed. Malcom H. Kerr (Santa Monica, CA: Undena Publications, 1980), 73–88, 86.

13. François Pouillon, *Dictionnaire des orientalistes de langue française* (Paris: Karthala, 2008), 681; Kenneth L. Brown, *People of Salé: Tradition and Change in a Moroccan City, 1830–1930* (Manchester: Manchester University Press, 1976), 195.

14. Tayeb Chenntouf, "La sociologie au Maghreb: Cinquante ans après," *Revue Africaine de Sociologie* 10, no. 1 (2006): 1–30, 3.

15. Essertier, *La sociologie*, 281–83; Alain Mahé, "Un disciple méconnu de Marcel Mauss: René Maunier," *Revue européenne des sciences sociales-Cahiers Vilfredo Pareto* 34, no. 105 (1996): 237–64.

16. Marcel Mauss, "Fragment d'un plan de sociologie générale descriptive (1934)," in Mauss, *Oeuvres*, vol. 3 (Paris: Ed. Minuit, 1969), 303–58, 353–54. See also Mauss's comments on René Maunier in Mauss, "Les peuples mixtes dans le monde moderne," *Bulletin de l'Institut français de sociologie* 2, no. 4 (1932): 131–46, 146.

17. Catherine Bruant, "L'Orient de la science sociale," *Revue du monde musulman et de la Méditerranée*, nos. 73–74 (1994): 295–310, 305.

18. H. Higgs, "Frederic Le Play," *Quarterly Journal of Economics* 4, no. 4 (1890): 408–33, 419.

19. Frederic Le Play, *Les ouvriers des deux mondes* (Paris: Au Sécretariat de la Société d'économie sociale, 1858–1908) contains case studies in Algeria, Cambodia, Réunion, the Ivory Coast, Syria, and Tunisia, all of which were or would become French colonies.

20. Three examples: M. L. Simonin, "Mulâtre affranchi de l'Ile de la Réunion," *Les ouvriers des deux mondes* ser. 1, 4, no. 31 (1862), 159–94; M. M. Cos, "Précis d'un monographe du paysan colon du Sahel (Algérie)," *Les ouvriers des deux mondes* ser. 2, 2, no. 57 *bis* (Firmin-Didot, 1890); M. E. Delaire, "Petit fonctionnaire de Pnom-Penh (Cambodge)," *Les ouvriers des deux mondes* ser. 2, 5, no. 44 (1899), 437–83.

21. Frédéric Le Play, *La réforme sociale en France déduite de l'observation comparée des peuples européens*, vol. 1, 4th ed. (Tours: A. Mame, 1872), 73, note 2.

22. Frédéric Le Play, *Frédéric le Play d'après lui-même* (Paris: V. Giard & E. Brière, 1906), 451–53.

23. Stewart Clegg and Robert van Krieken, "A Post-Colonial Comment on Collins," unpublished paper at https://ses.library.usyd.edu.au/handle/2123/900 (accessed Jan. 22, 2022); C. C. Zimmermann and M. E. Frampton, "Theories of Frédéric Le Play," in *Kinship and Family Organization*, ed. Bernard Farber (New York: Wiley, 1966), 14–23, 19.

24. Louis Tauxier, for example, was a colonial administrator in French West Africa, later an archivist and librarian for the *Société des africanistes*, and author of numerous books on African cultures. Edmond Bernus, "Introduction," in Louis Tauxier, *Les états de Kong (Côte d'Ivoire)* (Paris: Karthala, 2003), 7–14, 12.

25. Pierre Escard, *Précis d'un monographie d'un cultivateur-pêcheur-porte-canne du pays Adioukrou-Bouboury, Côte d'Ivoire* (Paris: Au Sécretariat de la Société d'économie sociale, 1910), 140, 111, 113, 122–23.

26. Joseph Wilbois, *Le Cameroun, les indigènes, les colons, les missions, l'administration française* (Paris: Payot, 1934), 256.

27. Wilbois, *Le Cameroun*, quotes at 10, 20, 69, 71, 42, 91, 101; emphasis added.

28. I discuss the internal heterogeneity of European texts on non-European cultures in *The Devil's Handwriting: Precoloniality and the German Colonial State in Qingdao, Samoa, and Southwest Africa* (Chicago: University of Chicago Press, 2007). For Said's claim that all of the diverse "idioms" at the surface of this discourse converged at a deeper level concerning "essential aspects of the Orient," see *Orientalism* (New York: Vintage, 1978), 203. Said tempers his earlier account with respect to certain thinkers in his *Freud and the Non-European* (London: Verso, 2003).

29. Edward Said, *Freud and the Non-European*, 26.

30. Émile Durkheim, "Préface," *L'Année sociologique* 1 (1898): i–vii, ii–iii.

31. Émile Durkheim, "Debate on Explanation in History and Sociology," in *The Rules of Sociological Method*, ed. Steven Lukes (London: Macmillan, 1982), 211–228, 224.

32. George Steinmetz, "Field Theory and Interdisciplinarity: Relations between History and Sociology in Germany and France during the Twentieth Century," *Comparative Studies in Society and History* 59, no. 2 (2017): 477–514, 499; Jean Meuvret, "Histoire et sociologie," *Revue historique* 183, no. 2 (1938): 193–206.

33. Henri Berr and Lucien Febvre, "History," in *Encyclopedia of the Social Sciences*, ed. Edwin Seligman and Alvin Johnson, vol. 7 (New York: Macmillan, 1935), 357–68; Steinmetz, "Field Theory and Interdisciplinarity."

34. Lewis A. Coser, "Introduction," in Maurice Halbwachs, *On Collective Memory* (Chicago: University of Chicago Press, 1992), 1–34, 8.

35. Steinmetz, "Field Theory and Interdisciplinarity."

36. Célestin Bouglé, Review of *Revue de synthèse*, *Année sociologique* ser. 1, no. 5 (1901–1902): 138–40, 140.

37. Célestin Bouglé, "Histoire et sociologie: remarques générales," *Annales sociologiques*, ser. A, no. 1 (1934): 172–84, 180.

38. Célestin Bouglé, *Bilan de la sociologie française contemporaine* (Paris: Alcan, 1935), 91. See also Bouglé, "Rapports de la sociologie avec l'histoire," in Bouglé, *Cours de sociologie générale* (Paris: Centre de Documentation Universitaire, 1935), n.p.; Bouglé, "Histoire et sociologie. Note sur la synthèse historique," *Annales sociologiques*, ser. A, no. 2 (1936), 105–23.

39. Charles Le Coeur, *Le rite et l'outil. Essai sur le rationalisme social et la pluralité des civilisations* (Paris: Presses universitaires de France, 1969 [1939]), 9.

40. Nicolas Baverez, *Raymond Aron: un moraliste au temps des ideologies* (Paris: Flammarion, 1993), 76, 80.

41. Raymond Aron, *German Sociology* (Glencoe: Free Press, [1935] 1964), 111.

42. Raymond Aron, "Conflict and War from the Viewpoint of Historical Sociology," in International Sociological Association, *The Nature of Conflict. Studies on the Sociological Aspects of International Tensions* (Paris: UNESCO, 1957), 177–203.

43. Émile Durkheim, *Sociologie et philosophie* (Paris: Alcan, 1924).

44. Adorno perceived this connection between critical theory and Durkheim, but insisted that Durkheim's moral theory could not point beyond the ethics inherent in extant, capitalist social structures. Theodor W. Adorno, "Einleitung zu Emile Durkheim, 'Soziologie und Philosophie,'" in Adorno, *Soziologische Schriften I* (Frankfurt am Main: Suhrkamp, 1972), 245–79; see also Titus Stahl, *Immanente Kritik: Elemente einer Theorie sozialer Praktiken* (Frankfurt: Campus, 2013).

45. Steven Lukes, *Émile Durkheim* (New York: Penguin, 1973), 425. See also Tobias Garde Hagens, "Conscience Collective or False Consciousness?," *Journal of Classical Sociology* 6, no. 2 (2006): 215–37.

46. The phrase "rational critique" is from Durkheim, "Sociologie morale et juridique," *Année sociologique*, ser. 1, no. 10 (1905–1906): 352–69, 356.

47. Durkheim, *Sociology and Philosophy* (New York: Free Press, 1974), 72, 40.

48. Durkheim, *Sociology and Philosophy*, 35–36.

49. Durkheim, *Sociology and Philosophy*, 77; Émile Durkheim, *Moral Education: A Study in the Theory and Application of the Sociology of Education* (New York: Free Press of Glencoe, 1961), 244.

50. Durkheim, *Sociology and Philosophy*, 37.

51. Durkheim, *Sociology and Philosophy*, 93.

52. Durkheim, *Moral Education*, 87.

53. Henri Lévy-Bruhl, *Ethics and Moral Science* (London: A. Constable, 1905), 160.

54. Émile Durkheim, *The Elementary Forms of the Religious Life* (New York: The Free Press, 1915), 418. This book, mainly known for its analysis of the social origins of the ideas of time, space, and cause, concludes with a discussion of the genesis of modern morality.

55. Célestin Bouglé, *The Evolution of Values. Studies in Sociology with Special Applications to Teaching* (New York: H. Holt, [1922] 1926), 131. Bouglé's text is organized around a contrast between "primitives"—said to "fail in distinguishing kinds and instituting logical relations among judgments"—and moderns. Ibid., 61.

56. Durkheim, *Moral Education*, 87.

57. Durkheim, "Sociologie morale," 368.

58. The doctoral thesis by Durkheimian sociologist Paul Fauconnet followed this template, arguing that primitive societies have a *collective* sense of responsibility, which becomes more *individualized* over the course of social evolution. Paul Fauconnet, *La responsabilité* (Paris: F. Alcan, 1920), 330.

59. Durkheim, "Sociologie morale," 362.

60. Durkheim, "Sociologie morale," 368.

61. Durkheim, "Sociologie morale," 356.

62. Max Weber, "The Economic Foundations of 'Imperialism,'" in Weber, *Economy and Society*, vol. 2 (Berkeley: University of California Press), 913–21.

63. Pierre Favre, "The Absence of Political Sociology in the Durkheimian Classifications of the Social Sciences," in *The Sociological Domain: The Durkheimians and the Founding of French Sociology*, ed. Philippe Besnard (Cambridge: Cambridge University Press, 2009), 199–216.

64. Georges Davy, *Éléments de sociologie. I. Sociologie politique appliquée à la morale de à l'éducation*, 3rd ed. (Paris: Delagrave, 1932); Hüseyin Nail Kubali, *L'idée de l'état chez les précurseurs de l'école sociologique française* (Paris: Domat-Montchrestien, 1936); Georges Gurvitch, *L'Idée du droit social* (Paris: Sirey, 1931).

65. Émile Durkheim, "Morale professionnelle," *La Revue de metaphysique et morale* 44, nos. 3–4 (1937): 527–44, 711–38; Durkheim, *Leçons de sociologie. Physique des moeurs et du droit* (Paris: Presses universitaires de France, 1950). On Mauss's efforts to publish Durkheim's essays on the state, politics, and morals, and Kubali's role in this, see Ivan Strenski, "Hüseyin Nail Kubali and Durkheim's *Professional Ethics and Civic Morals*," *Scripta Instituti Donneriani Aboensi* 19 (2006): 358–73.

66. Durkheim, *Moral Education*, 79.

67. Durkheim, *Moral Education*, 77.

68. Favre, "The Absence of Political Sociology," 213.

69. Alexandre Moret and Georges Davy, *From Tribe to Empire: Social Organization among Primitives and in the Ancient East* (New York: A. A. Knopf, 1926), 359, 135.

70. Henri Berr, Foreword to Moret and Davy, *From Tribe to Empire* (New York: A. A. Knopf, 1926), ix–xxx, xix, xxiv.

71. Georges Davy, *Éléments de sociologie. I. Sociologie politique* (Paris: Delagrave, 1924).

72. René Hubert, *Manuel élémentaire de sociologie*, 5th ed., revised (Paris: Delalain, 1935), 183–84, 215–17, 255–57, 263–64, 447–49, 454–56. Compare the unrevised version, Hubert, *Manuel élémentaire de sociologie*, 5th ed. (Paris: Delalain, 1935), which is missing the discussion of colonies and empires.

73. Durkheim, *Moral Education*, 193.

74. Wendy James, "The Treatment of African Ethnography in *L'Année sociologique* (I–XII)," *Année sociologique* ser. 3, 48, no. 1 (1998): 193–207, 198.

75. Dominick La Capra, *Émile Durkheim: Sociologist and Philosopher* (Ithaca, NY: Cornell University Press, 1972), 120; Armand de Quatrefages, *Les Polynésiens et leurs migrations* (Paris: Arthus Bertrand, 1864), 75.

76. Alice Conklin, "De la sociologie objective à l'action. Charles Le Coeur et l'utopisme colonial," *Les Carnets de Bérose* 11 (2019), 46–79.

77. All quotes in this section from Le Coeur, *Le rite et l'outil*.

78. On the *Kulturkreis* concept, see Julia Hell, *The Conquest of Ruins: The Third Reich and the Fall of Rome* (Chicago: University of Chicago Press, 2019), 289, 500, note 62.

79. Jacques Berque, "Une perte pour la sociologie française: Charles Le Coeur," *Annales ESC* 7, no. 1 (1952): 143.

80. Edward Said, *Freud and the Non-European*, 27.

81. René Maunier, "Leçon d'ouverture d'un cours de sociologie 'algérienne,'" *Hespéris* 2, no. 2 (1922): 93–108, 98.

82. René Maunier, "Bericht über die soziologische Literatur seit 1900 und die soziologische Gesellschaften. B. Die Soziologie in Frankreich seit 1900," *Monatsschrift für Soziologie*, nos. 1–2 (Feb. 1909): 100–14; Maunier, *L'économie politique et la sociologie* (Paris: V. Giard & E. Brière, 1910).

83. Maunier also served as secretary of the *Société française d'ethnographie* and edited the *Revue française d'ethnographie et des traditions populaires*. Santi Nova, "René Maunier, sociologue de la colonization," *Revue internationale de sociologie* 47 (1939): 177–84; Jean-Robert Henry, "Approches ethnologiques du droit musulman," in *L'enseignement du droit musulman*, ed. M. Flory and J.-R. Henry (Paris: CNRS, 1989): 133–71; Thierry Paquot, "Du lu avec du vu, la méthode de René Maunier (1887–1951)," *Urbanisme* 324 (2002): 78–83.

84. Daniel Cefaï and Alain Mahé, "Échanges rituels de dons, obligation et contrat. Mauss, Davy, Maunier: trois perspectives de sociologie juridique," *Année sociologique* ser. 3, 48, no. 1 (1998) : 209–28.

85. Mahé, "Un disciple."

86. Maunier, *The Sociology of Colonies* (London: RKP, 1949), xii.

87. Maunier, *The Sociology of Colonies*, 5–6.

88. Maunier, *The Sociology of Colonies*, 7.

89. Maunier, *The Sociology of Colonies*, 29, 19.

90. Paquot, "Du lu avec du vu," 80, note 4.

91. Maunier, *The Sociology of Colonies*, 201.

92. Henry, "Approches ethnologiques," 143, citing René Maunier, "Préface," in Robert Randau et Abdelkader Fikri, *Les compagnons du jardin* (Paris: Domat-Montchrestien, 1933), 9–16.

93. Steinmetz, *The Devil's Handwriting*.

94. Maunier, *The Sociology of Colonies*, 535, 118–28; René Maunier, "L'action du 'primitif' sur le 'civilisé,'" *Revue de l'Institut de sociologie* 10, no. 3 (1930): 451–70.

95. Maunier, "L'action du 'primitif,'" 453.

96. Melville Herskovits, *The Myth of the Negro Past* (New York: Harper, 1941), 184–85. See also Melville Herskovits, *Life in a Haitian Valley* (New York: Knopf, 1937), and Herskovits, *Acculturation: The Study of Culture Contact* (New York: J. J. Augustin, 1938).

97. Melville J. Herskovits and Frances S. Herskovits, *Trinidad Village* (New York: Octogon Books, 1947), vi, 6. See Robert Baron, "Amalgams and Mosaics, Syncretisms and Reinterpretations: Reading Herskovits and Contemporary Creolists for Metaphors of Creolization," *Journal of American Folklore* 116, no. 459 (2003): 88–115.

98. A few legal scholars continued to refer to Maunier's work (chapter 6), and Karl Mannheim published an English translation of Maunier's *Sociologie coloniale* in 1949.

99. Zoltán Rostás, "L'histoire d'un congrès qui n'a pas eu lieu: le XIVe congrès international de sociologie (Bucarest 1939)," *Les études sociales* 153–154 (2011): 195–212. Conze's paper called for German colonization of Poland and the active *"Entjudung"* (dejudaization) of Polish cities and towns. Werner Conze, "Die ländliche Überbevölkerung in Polen," in *Travaux du XIVe congrès international de sociologie Bucuresti (1939), Communications,* Série B, vol. 1, *Le village* (Bucharest: Institut international de sociologie, 1940), 40–48.

100. Frédéric Audren, "Un interlocuteur français: René Maunier," *Les études sociales* 153–54 (2011): 213–16.

101. Maunier, *Sociologie coloniale*, vol. 3, *Le progrès du droit* (Paris: Domat-Montchrestien, 1949). This volume was printed with the number "II" rather than "III" on the cover; as Rodinson pointed out, the very "numbering" of the volumes was "already ambiguous," and there were "numerous repetitions." Maxime Rodinson, review of Maunier, *Sociologie coloniale*, vol. 2, in *Année Sociologique*, 3rd series, 1 (1948–1949): 271–75, quotes from 272, 275.

102. René Maunier, *Des comptoirs aux empires* (Paris: Sirey, 1941), 36.

103. One could also include Georges Devereux in this context, given his work among the Mohave Indians, but his work pointed in different directions, toward psychoanalysis, and did not engage sociology.

104. Alfred Métraux, "Les Indiens Uro-Cipaya de Carangas," *Journal de la Société des americanistes* n.s. 27 (1935–1936): 111–28, 325–415, 116, note 1; 326–27.

105. Métraux, "Les Indiens Uro-Cipaya," 124–26, 325, 113, 325–28.

106. Alfred Métraux, "Mes amis les paysans de Marbial," *Gradhiva* 1 (2005): 255–59; Christine Laurière, "D'une île à l'autre," *Gradhiva* 1 (2005): 181–207; Alfred Métraux, *Le vaudou haïtien* (Paris: Gallimard, 1958), 17.

107. Alfred Métraux, "Unesco and Anthropology," *American Anthropologist* n.s., 53, no. 2 (1951): 294–300, 295.

108. James D. Le Sueur, *Uncivil War: Intellectuals and Identity Politics during the Decolonization of Algeria* (Philadelphia: University of Pennsylvania Press, 2001); Bernard Ullmann, *Jacques Soustelle: le mal aimé* (Paris: Plon, 1995).

109. Jacques Soustelle, *The Four Suns. Recollections and Reflections of an Ethnologist in Mexico* (New York: Grossman Publishers, [1967] 1971), 6.

110. Jacques Soustelle, "La culture matérielle des Indiens Lacandons," *Journal de la société des américanistes* 29, no. 1 (1937): 1–96, 23; Sousetelle, "The Lacandone Indians of Southern Mexico," *Man* 43, nos. 88–91 (1943): 117, quote on 117.

111. Jacques Soustelle, "Note sur les Lacandon du Lac Peljá et du Río Jetjá," *Journal de la société des américanistes* 25, no. 1 (1933): 153–80, 177, 179; Soustelle, "Les idées religieuses des Lacandons," *La terre et la vie* 5, no. 4 (1935): 170–78, 170.

112. Soustelle, *The Four Suns*, 24, 27, 36, 43; "Les idées religieuses," 170.

113. Soustelle, "La culture matérielle," 85–86; Soustelle, *The Four Suns*, 70.

114. Jacques Soustelle, *La famille otomi-pame du Mexique central* (Paris: Institut d'ethnologie, 1937), 253, 488–510, 90, 99, 253.

115. Soustelle, *The Four Suns*, 100.

116. Jacques Soustelle, "Une danse dramatique mexicaine: 'le torito,'" *Journal de la société des américanistes* 33, no. 1 (1941): 155–64, 164; Idem., *The Four Suns*, 131–32.

117. Soustelle, *The Four Suns*, 132, 137; Soustelle, "Une danse dramatique," 164.

118. Soustelle, *The Four Suns*, 121, 137, 176, 155.

119. Leenhardt, *Le mouvement éthiopien au sud de l'Afrique de 1896 à 1899* (Paris: Académie des sciences d'outre-mer, [1902] 1976), 22–23.

120. Fournier, *Marcel Mauss*, 319.

121. James Clifford, *Person and Myth: Maurice Leenhardt in the Melanesian World* (Berkeley: University of California Press, 1982), 155, 159.

122. Jean Guiart, *Maurice Leenhardt: le lien d'un homme avec un peuple qui ne voulait pas mourir* (Nouméa: Le Rocher-à-la-voile, 1977), 106.

123. Jean Guiart, *Maurice Leenhardt: Missionaire et sociologue* (Paris: Office de la Recherche Scientifique et Technique d'Outre-Mer, 1955); Pierre Métais, "Sociologue parce que linguiste," *Journal de la Société des Océanistes* 10 (1954): 40–50; Métais, "L'oeuvre ethnologique et sociologique de Maurice Leenhardt," *Journal de la Société des Océanistes* 10 (1954): 51–69 ; Jean Poirier, "Maurice Leenhardt, océaniste et sociologue," *Le monde non chrétien* 33 (1955): 72–95; Pierre Teisserenc, "Science sociales, politique coloniale, stratégies missionaries. Maurice Leenhardt en Nouvelle-Calédonie," *Recherches de science religieuse* 65, no. 3 (1977): 389–442.

124. Raymond Polin, "La sociologie française pendant la guerre," *Synthèse* 5, nos. 3–4 (July–Aug. 1946): 117–29, 128.

125. See, for example, Maurice Leenhardt, "Modes d'expression en sociologie et en ethnologie," *Synthèse* 10, no. 1 (1953): 259–64; Leenhardt, *Gens de la grande terre*, 2nd ed. (Paris: Gallimard, 1953), 7, 223.

126. Quoted in Clifford, *Person and Myth*, 102.

127. Leenhardt, *Gens de la grande terre*, 213, 221–23.

128. William S. F. Pickering, "A Note on the Life of Gaston Richard and Certain Aspects of His Work," in *Durkheim on Religion*, ed. W.S.F. Pickering (London: Routledge & K. Paul, 1989), 343–59. Gaston Richard was a contemporary of Durkheim, co-founder of the *Année sociologique*, and heir of Durkheim's University of Bordeaux position, but he distanced himself from Durkheim starting in 1907. Bastide, Lasbax, and Essertier were Richard's most prominent students.

129. Denys Cuche, "Roger Bastide, le 'fait individuel', et l'école de Chicago," *Cahiers internationaux de sociologie* 124 (2008): 41–59, 41.

130. Bastide published 58 reviews in the *RIS* between 1926 and 1938. Françoise Morin, "Les inédits et la correspondance de Roger Bastide," in *Roger Bastide ou le réjouissement de l'abîme*, ed. Phillipe Laburthe-Tolra (Paris: L'Harmattan, 1994): 21–42, 34, note 7.

131. Letter from Gaston Richard to Roger Bastide, August 19, 1924, reproduced in Cécil Rol, "Dix-neuf lettres de Gaston Richard (1898–1939)," *Lendemains: études comparées sur la France* 41, nos. 158–159 (2015): 113–40, 123.

132. Roger Bastide, *Initiation aux recherches sur l'interpénétration des civilisations* (Paris: Centre de documentation universitaire, 1948), 2–3.

133. Michel Despland, *Bastide on Religion: The Invention of Candomblé* (London: Equinox, 2008), 42.

134. Roger Bastide and P. Verger, "Contribution à l'étude sociologique des marchés Nagô du Bas-Dahomey," *Cahiers de l'Institut de science économique appliquée*, no. 95 (1959): 33–65; Roger Bastide and F. Raveau, "Contribution à l'étude de l'adaptation des Noirs en France," in *Transactions of the Sixth World Congress of Sociology. Actes du sixième congrès mondial de sociologie. Evian, 4–11 September 1966*, vol. 4 (Genève: International Sociological Association, 1966), 279–88.

135. Bastide's views summarized by Despland, *Bastide on Religion*, 70.

136. Paul Gilroy, *The Black Atlantic: Modernity and Double Consciousness* (Cambridge, MA: Harvard University Press, 1993).

137. Despland, *Bastide on Religion*, 59.

138. Bastide, *Initiation aux recherches*; Bastide, *Le prochain et le lointain* (Paris: Cujas, 1970), 11.

139. Denys Cuche, "Le concept de 'principe de coupure' et son évolution dans la pensée de Roger Bastide," in Philippe Laburthe-Tolra, *Roger Bastide ou le réjouissement de l'abîme: échos du colloque tenu à Cerisy-la-Salle du 7 au 14 septembre 1992* (Paris: L'Harmattan, 1994), 69–84, 73–74.

140. Roger Bastide, "Contribution à l'étude de la participation," *Cahiers internationaux de sociologie* 14 (1979): 30-40, 39; Bastide, "Le principe de coupure et le comportement afro-brésilien," in *Anais do XXXI Congresso Internacional de Americanistas, São Paulo*, vol. 1 (São Paulo: Anhembi, 1955), 493-503, 503; Maria Isaura Pereira de Queiroz, "Principe de participation et principe de coupure. La contribution de Roger Bastide à leur définition sociologique," *Archives de sciences sociales des religions* 47, no. 1 (1979): 147-57.

141. Robert E. Park, "Human Migration and the Marginal Man," *American Journal of Sociology* 33 (1928): 881-93; Everett V. Stonequist, *The Marginal Man: A Study in Personality and Culture Conflict* (New York: Scribner, 1937).

142. Roger Bastide, "L'acculturation formelle," in *Le prochain et le lointain* (Paris: Cujas, 1970), 137-48, 138.

143. Maria Isaura Pereira de Queiroz, "Les Années brésiliennes de Roger Bastide," *Archives de sciences sociales des religions* 40 (1975): 79-87, 85; Françoise Morin, "Roger Bastide ou l'anthropologie des gouffres," *Archives des sciences sociales des religions* 40, no. 1 (1975): 99-106, 103.

144. Roger Bastide, *Initiation aux recherches sur l'interpénétration des civilisations* (Paris: Centre de documentation universitaire, Tournier et Constan, 1948), 4-5.

145. Roger Bastide, "Sociologie et psychanalyse," *Cahiers internationaux de sociologie* 2 (1947): 108-22; Bastide, *Sociologie et psychanalyse* (Paris: Presses universitaires de France, 1950); Bastide, "Rêves de noirs," *Psyché. Revue international des sciences de l'homme et de psychanalyse* 5, no. 49 (1950): 802-11; Halbwachs, "Le rêve et le langage inconscient dans le sommeil," *Journal de psychologie normale et pathologique* 39 (1946): 11-64.

146. Despland, *Bastide on Religion*, 46.

147. Bourdieu diagnosed "professionalism" as a peculiarly Anglo-American sociological theme and one that obscures more than it reveals. Pierre Bourdieu and Loïc Wacquant, *An Invitation to Reflexive Sociology* (Chicago: University of Chicago Press, 1992), 242-45.

Chapter Nine: The Sociology of Sociology and Its Colonial Subfield (France and Belgium, 1918-1965)

1. The difference between *field* and *network* is that those located in similar positions within a field, or in homologous positions in different fields, may resemble one another in terms of their social properties, practices, or beliefs without being linked by any direct network connections. While I am arguing that colonial sociology was a subfield, this does not exclude the possibility that it also contained one or more networks. Indeed, colonial sociologists were connected directly in networks, as I have shown. Establishing the *fieldness* (or *subfieldness*) of a practice requires more evidence, and a different kind of evidence, than establishing the existence of network ties.

2. The phrase *finis sociologiae* was used by Henry Michel, in a letter to Célestin Bouglé in 1897, referring to Durkheim's failure to obtain the new *Collège de France* chair. Quoted in George Weisz, "L'idéologie républicaine et les sciences sociales. Les durkheimiens et la chaire d'histoire d'économie sociale à la Sorbonne," *Revue française de sociologie* 20, no. 1 (1979): 83-112, 103.

3. Jean-Christophe Marcel, *Le durkheimisme dans l'entre-deux guerres* (Paris: PUF, 2011), 298-299; Victor Karady, "Emile Durkheim, les sciences sociales et l'université: bilan d'un semi-échec," *Revue française de sociologie* 17:2 (1976), 267-311; Marcel Fournier, *Marcel Mauss* (Princeton, NJ: Princeton University Press, [1994] 2006), 246; Pierre-Jean Simon, "Roger Bastide et l'histoire de la sociologie," in Philippe Laburthe-Tolra, ed., *Roger Bastide ou le réjouissement de l'abîme: échos du colloque tenu à Cerisy-la-Salle du 7 au 14 septembre 1992* (Paris: L'Harmattan, 1994), 55-68, 55.

4. Johan Heilbron, *French Sociology* (Ithaca, NY: Cornell University Press, 2015), 96.

5. Raymond Polin, "La sociologie française pendant la guerre," *Synthèse* 5, nos. 3–4 (July–Aug 1946): 117–29, 120. Polin is discussed below.

6. Catherine Paradeise, Dominique Lorrain, and Didier Demazière, "Introduction générale: cinquante ans de sociologie française," in *Les sociologies françaises: héritages et perspectives: 1960-2010*, ed. C. Paradeise, D. Lorrain, and D. Demazière (Rennes: Presses universitaires de Rennes, 2015), 9–37. For an effort to limit the history of postwar French sociology to the group around Stoetzel, see Stefano Alpini, *La sociologia repubblicana francese: Émile Durkheim e i durkheimiani* (Milano: F. Angeli, 2004).

7. On empirical research in the CES, see Johan Heilbron, "Pionniers par défaut? Les débuts de la recherche au Centre d'études sociologiques (1946–1960)," *Revue française de sociologie* 27, no. 3 (1991): 365–79; and Patricia Vannier, "Un laboratoire pour la sociologie? Le Centre d'études sociologiques (1946–1968) ou les débuts de la recherche sociologique en France" (PhD diss., Université de Paris, 1999). On the French sociology of labor, see Lucie Tanguy, *La sociologie du travail en France. Enquête sur le travail des sociologues, 1950–1990* (Paris: La Découverte, 2011); on French postwar urban sociology, see Jeanne Haffner, *The View from Above: The Science of Social Space* (Cambridge, MA: MIT Press, 2013); on surveys and quantitative methods, see Loïc Blondiaux, *La fabrique de l'opinion: une histoire sociale des sondages* (Paris: Editions du Seuil, 1998); on Americanization in French sociology, see Jean-Christophe Marcel, *Éléments pour une analyse de la réception de la sociologie américaine en France (1945–1959)* (HDG thesis, Université de Paris-Sorbonne, 2010); on social psychology, see Olivier Martin and Patricia Vannier, "La sociologie française après 1945: places et rôles des méthodes issues de la psychologie," *Revue d'Histoire des Sciences Humaines* 1, no. 6 (2001): 95–122.

8. Heilbron, *French Sociology*, quotes from 143, 124, 125, 128, 125, 10; C. Laude, "Le Centre d'études sociologiques en 1959," *Revue française de sociologie* 32, no. 3 (1991): 405–09.

9. Victor Karady, "The Durkheimians in Academe. A Reconsideration," in *The Sociological Domain: The Durkheimians and the Founding of French Sociology*, ed. Philippe Besnard (Cambridge: Cambridge University Press, 1983), 79–91, 77.

10. Célestin Bouglé, "Comment étudier la sociologie à Paris?," *Annales de l'Université de Paris* 2, no. 4 (1926): 313–24, 316; Victor Karady, "Les sociologues avant 1950," *Regards sociologiques* 22 (2000): 5–22, 19.

11. Karady, "Les sociologues avant 1950."

12. Karady, "The Durkheimians in Academe," 75–6.

13. Karady, "The Durkheimians in Academe," 78.

14. Karady, "Les universités françaises de Napoléon à la deuxième guerre mondiale," in *Histoire des universités françaises*, ed. Jacques Verger (Toulouse: Privat, 1986), 261–365, 355.

15. See also Jean-Pierre Rioux, *The Fourth Republic, 1944–1958* (Cambridge: Cambridge University Press, 1987), 417.

16. Figures from *Annales de l'Université de Paris*, vols. 1–14 (1926–1939), annual reports of the Doyen, Faculté de Lettres. NB: These are the numbers of students successfully granted certificates, not the numbers enrolled.

17. For the breakdown of philosophy theses by theme before 1914, see, Jean-Louis Fabiani, *Les philosophes de la République* (Paris: Les Minuit, 1988), 85.

18. "Liste des sujets de thèses, déposés à la Faculté des Lettres du 1er janvier au 31 décembre 1938," *Annales de l'Université de Paris* vol. 14 (1939): 397–407, 399.

19. The authors of 9 of these 16 sociology theses were of non-European origin.

20. "Section d'ethnologie juridique," *Annales de l'Université de Paris* 13, no. 5 (1938): 431–32.

21. This paragraph is based largely on Heilbron, "Les métamorphoses du durkheimisme, 1920–1940," *Revue française de sociologie* 26 (1985): 203–37.
22. Bouglé, Simiand, Mauss, Fauconnet, Halbwachs, and Blondel. Dirk Käsler, *Sociological Adventures. Earle Edward Eubank's Visits with European Sociologists* (Newark, NJ: Transaction Publishers, 1991), 138.
23. Weisz, "L'idéologie républicaine," 92,
24. Weisz, "L'idéologie républicaine," 110.
25. Jean-René Tréanton, "Les premières années du Centre d'études sociologiques (1946–1955)," *Revue française de sociologie* 32, no. 3 (1991): 381–404, 383, note 4.
26. William S. F. Pickering, "A Note on the Life of Gaston Richard and Certain Aspects of his Work," in *Durkheim on Religion*, ed. William S. F. Pickering (London: Routledge & K. Paul, 1989), 343–59, 343.
27. Heinz Maus, "Lasbax, Émile," in *Internationales Soziologenlexikon*, ed. Wilhelm Bernsdorf and Horst Knospe, vol. 1, 2nd ed. (Stuttgart: Enke, 1980), 232.
28. Halbwachs actually held three different chairs at the Sorbonne, but the "methodology and logic of science" was the only chair that was newly created.
29. Massignon took over the chair that had been created for Charles Letourneau in 1885. This was the first sociology chair in the entire world, according to Terry Nichols Clark, *Prophets and Patrons: The French University and the Emergence of the Social Sciences* (Cambridge, MA: Harvard University Press, 1973), 118. Massignon was a founding member of the postwar *Centre d'études sociologiques*. Anon, "Centre d'Études Sociologiques," *Cahiers internationaux de sociologie* 1 (1946): 177–80, 179.
30. Bousquet stayed at Algiers until 1962 and then moved to Bordeaux, where he taught Muslim Sociology and the History of Economic Thought. According to his biographer, Bousquet was a sociologist *avant tout*. Michel Robine, "L'œuvre scientifique du Professeur Georges-Henri Bousquet," *Revue économique du sud-ouest* 27, no. 2 (1978): 115–21, 116.
31. Bernard Kalaora and Antoine Savoye, "La mutation du mouvement le playsien," *Revue française de sociologie* 26, no. 2 (1985): 257–76, 259.
32. Clark, *Prophets and Patrons*, 109–11; Bernard Kalaora and Antoine Savoye, *Les inventeurs oubliés. Le Play et ses continuateurs. Aux origins des sciences sociales* (Paris: Champ Vallon, 1989): 187–92; Isabelle Lespinet-Moret, "Pierre du Maroussem, un arpenteur de l'économique et du social," in *L'économie faite homme: Hommage à Alain Plessis*, ed. Olivier Feiertag and Isabelle Lespinet-Moret (Genève: Droz, 2011), 423–36.
33. Patrick Petitjean, "Autour de la mission française pour la création de l'université de Sao Paulo (1934)," in *Science and Empires: Historical Studies about Scientific Development and European Expansion*, ed. Patrick Petitjean and Catherine Jami (Dordrecht: Kluwer, 1992), 339–62.
34. "Travaux et publications de M. Emile Sicard," in *Archives de l'école des hautes études en sciences sociales*, Clemens Heller papers, Sicard file.
35. Heilbron, *French Sociology*, 96. Law professors who were strongly identified with sociology during the interwar years included Charles Gide, Paul Huvelin, Gabriel Le Bras, Emmanuel Lévy, Henri Lévy-Bruhl, René Maunier, and Louis Millot.
36. H. Maus and H. L. Krämer, "Worms, René," in *Internationales Soziologenlexikon*, ed. Wilhelm Bernsdorf and Horst Knospe, vol. 1, 2nd ed. (Stuttgart: Enke, 1980), 505. Worms died in 1926 and therefore is not included in appendix one. Worms was dismissed as inconsequential by the French sociologists interviewed by Eubank in 1934.
37. *Annales de l'Université de Paris* 11, no. 1 (1936), 14.
38. Fauconnet, "Amorce d'un programme sur l'enseignement de la sociologie," *Bulletin de l'Institut français de sociologie* 1 (1930): 69–72; Paul Fauconnet in Käsler, *Sociological*

Adventures, 120. Other philosopher-sociologists included the Durkheimians Dominique Parodi, Armand Cuvillier, and Achille Ouy.

39. Sociological Orientalists included Marcel Cohen, Marcel Granet, Claude-Eugene Maitre, Paul Masson-Oursel, Edmond Mestre, Jean Przyluski.

40. The Rockefeller Foundation subsidized Georges Gurvitch for two years of research in Europe, Philippe Schwob for a year in the United States, and at least eight other French sociologists (Aron, Bouglé, Friedmann, Maunier, Montagne, Polin, Stoetzel, and Duveau). Information from Brigitte Mazon, "La Fondation Rockefeller et les sciences sociales en France 1925–1940," *Revue française de sociologie* 26 (1985): 311–42, 330; Ludovic Tournès, *Sciences de l'homme et politique. Les fondations philanthropiques américaines en France au XXe siècle* (Paris: Classiques Garnier, 2008), 207–44; and Rockefeller archives.

41. On Chombart de Lauwe, see chapter 2.

42. "Mission du Recteur de l'Université de Paris aux États-Unis," *Annales de l'Université de Paris* 1 (1926): 524–25. See Paul W. Vogt, "Un durkheimien ambivalent," *Revue française de sociologie* 20 (1979): 123–29, 125.

43. Antoine Savoye, "Enquête sur les étudiants en sociologie de Célestin Bouglé et leur engagement en politique (1920–1940)," *Les études sociales* 165, no. 1 (2017): 111–56.

44. Sophie Coeuré, "Les centres de documentation sociale, 1920–1940," in *Albert Kahn, 1860–1940: Réalités d'une utopie*, ed. Jeanne Beausoleil and Pascal Ory (Boulogne: Musée Albert Kahn, 1995), 201–10, 204.

45. Brigitte Mazon, "La création du Centre de documentation sociale," *Études durkheimiennes* 9 (1983): 15–20; Jean-Christophe Marcel, *Le durkheimisme dans l'entre-deux guerres* (Paris: PUF, 2001), 223-ff.; Heilbron, *French Sociology*, 117–20; Rockefeller Archives, Foundation records, projects, RG 1.1, Box 24, Folder 237.

46. Heilbron, *French Sociology*, 119, quoting from a report by one of the officers in the Social Sciences division of the Rockefeller Foundation's Paris office before World War II; Tracey B. Kittredge, "Social Sciences in France, 1932," in Rockefeller Archive Center, RG 2, box 6, folder 101. See also "Centre de documentation sociale," *Annales de l'Université de Paris* 12, no. 4 (1937): 339–43.

47. Bouglé provided space for a small Paris branch of the Frankfurt Institut for Social Research when it was forced into exile in 1933. Martin Jay, *The Dialectical Imagination* (Boston: Little, Brown & Co., 1973), 30.

48. Mathieu Hikaru Desan and Johan Heilbron, "Young Durkheimians and the Temptation of Fascism: The Case of Marcel Déat," *History of the Human Sciences* 28, no. 3 (2015): 22–50, 44 note 78, 37.

49. Mazon, "La Fondation Rockefeller," 329, quoting from the same report listed in note 43. Polin moved into a philosophy professorship at Lille University in 1946 and then at the Sorbonne, in 1961; Bertrand Saint-Sernin, "Notice sur la vie et les travaux de Raymond Polin," http://www.asmp.fr/travaux/notices/polin_saint_sernin.htm (accessed June 8, 2017).

50. Friedmann was a Marxist specializing in the USSR and later an industrial sociologist; Marjolin was an economist and government official; Schwob wrote his doctoral thesis in 1934 on "investment trusts" in the United States. Isabelle Gouarné, "Engagement philosoviétique et posture sociologique dans l'entre-deux-guerres: le rôle politico-intellectuel de Georges Friedmann," *Sociologie du travail* 54 (2012): 356–74; Robert Marjolin, *Le travail d'une vie: mémoires 1911–1986* (Paris: Éditions Robert Laffont, 1986).

51. Johan Heilbron, "Note sur l'Institut français de sociologie (1924–1962)," *Études durkheimiennes* 9 (1983): 9–14, 10; Heilbron, 96; *Bulletin de l'Institut français de sociologie* 1 (1930).

52. Lapie (1867–1927) became Recteur of the University of Paris in 1925.

53. "Liste des membres," *Bulletin de l'Institut français de sociologie* 1 (1930): 74–75; "Institut français de sociologie. Liste des membres," *Synthese* 7, no. 3 (1948/1949): 190–95.

54. Roger Lewis Geiger, "The Development of French Sociology, 1871–1905" (PhD diss., University of Michigan, 1972), 185; *Annales de l'Institut international de sociologie* 15 (1928): 14–37; Guillaume L. Duprat, "The International Institute of Sociology," *American Sociological Review* 1, no. 3 (1936): 449–54.

55. The Institute also published the *Annales de l'Institut international de sociologie*, which carried the proceedings of its international meetings and published 16 volumes between 1894 and 1932.

56. Matthias Duller and Christian Fleck, "Sociology in Continental Europe," in *The Cambridge Handbook of Sociology*, Volume 1: *Core Areas in Sociology and the Development of the Discipline*, ed. Kathleen Korgen (Cambridge: Cambridge University Press, 2017), 5–17; Johannes Weyer, "Der 'Bürgerkrieg in der Soziologie.' Die westdeutsche Soziologie zwischen Amerikanisierung und Restauration," in *Ordnung und Theorie: Beiträge zur Geschichte der Soziologie in Deutschland*, ed. Sven Papcke (Darmstadt: Wissenschaftliche Buchgesellschaft, 1986), 280–304.

57. The only French members attending the 1950 meeting were demographer Alfred Sauvy, Le Playsian sociologists Lasbax and Bouthoul, and the loyal longtime members Achille Ouy and Roger Bastide.

58. On Gini's fascist colonial activities, see chapter 1 in this volume, and Marco Santoro, "Empire for the Poor: Colonial Dreams and the Quest for an Italian Sociology, 1870s–1950s," in *Sociology and Empire. The Imperial Entanglements of a Discipline*, ed. George Steinmetz (Durham, NC: Duke University Press, 2013), 106–65.

59. René Worms, *Études de sociologie coloniale* (Paris: V. Giard & E. Brière, 1908).

60. Colonial topics included French Indochina, "the indigenous populations of the French protectorate on the Somali coast," "the indigenous populations of Annam," Syria and Palestine, "Professional Social Types: The Colonial"; "Les Peaux-Rouges et les Nègres aux États-Unis"; and a plan to augment French settlement by transplanting orphans and children on public assistance to the colonies, where they would be trained as colonizers in special schools. G. Valran, "La colonisation par l'assistance," *Revue international de sociologie* 9 (1901): 514–20.

61. Santi Nava, "René Maunier, sociologue de la colonisation," *Revue internationale de sociologie* 47 (1939): 177–84.

62. Carl Schmitt, "Nehmen/Teilen/Weiden: Ein Versuch, die Grundfragen jeder Sozial- und Wirtschaftsordnung vom Nomos her richtig zu stellen," *Revue internationale de sociologie* ser. 2, no. 1 (1954): 59–72.

63. In 1950s West Germany, the IIS also represented former Nazi sociologists opposed to the more American-oriented *Deutsche Gesellschaft für Soziologie* (German Sociological Society). Stephan Moebius, "Kontroversen in der deutschsprachigen Soziologie nach 1945," in *Handbuch Geschichte der deutschsprachigen Soziologie*, vol. 1, ed. Stephan Moebius and Andrea Ploder (Wiesbaden: Springer VS, 2017), 289–314.

64. Jean Breton (alias Célestin Bouglé), *Notes d'un étudiant français en Allemagne. Heidelberg—Berlin—Leipzig—Munich* (Paris: Calman-Lévy, 1895), 127; Bouglé, *Qu'est-ce que la sociologie?*, 7th ed. (Paris: Alcan, 1939), 33.

65. A list of all French sociologists in 1944 is provided by Jean Ferrette, "La sociologie sous Vichy: rupture ou continuité? Retour sur un impensé historique," *Anamnese* 7 (2012): 9–26, 22–23. Ferrette's list should be treated with caution, however, since it contains names that were identified by contemporary academics as members of other disciplines, including ethnology (Dumézil, Giraule, van Gennep, Leiris, Rivet, Soustelle, and Boris Vildé), history

(Henri Berr, Bernard Faÿ, Lucien Febvre, and Édouard Dolléans), Sinology (Granet), and folklore (Varagnac). Conversely, Ferette's list overlooks sociologists working in French colonial and overseas institutions during the Vichy period, such as Robert Montagne, Maxime Rodinson, Émile Sicard, etc.

66. Patricia Vannier, "La relance de *L'Année sociologique* (1949–1960): un pari réussi," *Année Sociologique*, 3rd ser., no. 69 (2019): 181–207.

67. Jacques Lautman, "Chronique de la sociologie française après 1945," in *Science et théorie de l'opinion publique: hommage à Jean Stoetzel*, ed. Alain Girard, Francois Bourricaud, and Raymond Boudon (Paris: Retz, 1981), 269–84, 270.

68. Maximilien Sorre and F. A. Isambert, "L'activité sociologique en France," in *Transactions of the Third World Congress of Sociology*, vol. 6 (Paris: International Sociological Association, 1956), 69–76.

69. By 1968, there were 100 French university sociologists. Alain Chenu, "Une institution sans intention. La sociologie en France depuis l'après-guerre," *Actes de la recherche en sciences sociales* 141–142 (2002): 46–61, 49.

70. At least 11 scholars were employed as sociologists by IFAN between 1952 and 1960. Université de Dakar, IFAN, *Rapport Annuel 1959–60* (Dakar: IFAN, 1960), 57. Researchers employed as sociologists by IFAN between 1945 and 1960 included Balandier, Diallo, Diop, Froelich, Gouellain, Hauser, Holas, Massé, Mercier, Mersadier, and Thomas.

71. Balandier, Bekombo, Biffot, Binet, Chaumeton, Clément, Condominas, Dampierre, Devauges, Gouellain, Guiart, Hauser, Holas, Jullien, Kohler, Leenhardt, Massé, Mercier, Mersadier, Molet, Pauvert, Pelage, Schwartz, Soret, Thomas, and Trystram.

72. Lautman, "Chronique," 270.

73. A prosopographic list with additional information on all of the sociologists of colonialism between 1938 and 1965 is available on the author's personal website.

74. Jean-René Tréanton, "Professional activities and responsibilities of sociologists. *Bulletin international des sciences sociales*," 6, no. 1 (1954): 53–62, 55.

75. Other applied colonial research organizations with sociologists on staff included the *Centre algérien des sciences humaines appliquées* (CASHA) and the *Centre d'études et d'informations des problèmes humains dans les zones arides*. Sociologists also worked on temporary jobs for the *bureaux d'études* created for specific projects in the colonies. These applied sociologists included Michel Marié, Joseph Petit, Jean-Claude Reverdy, Nelly Xydias, and (immediately after decolonization) Roland Waast.

76. Abdel-Malek, Agblémagnon, Aron, Balandier, Bekombo, Berque, Bourricaud, Chelhod, Cuisenier, Cazeneuve, Chombart de Lauwe, Davy, Frère, Hoffmann, Jamous, Lebret, Maquet, Marthelot, Marié, Memmi, Michel, Naville, Servier, Sicard, Stoetzel, Trystram, and Xydias.

77. Aron, Balandier, Berque, Bourricaud, Chombart de Lauwe, Davy, Naville, Sauvy, Stoetzel, and Trystram. Section 30, for Sociology and Demography, had ten other members: Georges Friedmann, Henri Lefebvre, Jacques Maître, V. Isambert-Jamati, Alain Touraine, J. Carbonnier, Pierre George, J. Sutter, Poncin, and Gurvitch. List in Chenu, "Une institution," 47, note 2.

78. Anon., "Centre d'études sociologiques"; CNRS, *Rapport d'activité* (1961–1962), 409; ibid. (1962–1963), 483. This group already existed in 1958; see de Dampierre to Stoetzel, July 8, 1958, in Bibliothèque Éric de Dampierre, Dampierre papers, MSHO Correspondence Génerale 1954–1967, Folder 1958–1959.

79. Richard Swedberg, "Georges Gurvitch. The Unhappy Positivist," *Journal of the History of Sociology* 4, no. 1 (1982): 66–93, 76; Henri Lévy-Bruhl, "Le Centre d'études sociologiques," *Revue de sythèse* 5, nos. 3–4 (1946): 130–32, 130.

80. Anon., "Centre d'Études Sociologiques," 177–79.

81. Roger Bastide, *Initiation aux recherches sur l'interpénétration des civilizations* (Paris: CES, 1948); André Leroi-Gourhan, *Initiation aux recherches de la symbiose technique (Ainous et Japonais)* (Paris: CES, 1949), 5–9, 30–31, 42.

82. Raymond Aron, Georges Balandier, Roger Bastide, Jacques Berque, Pierre Bourdieu, Georges Condominas, Eric de Dampierre, Albert Memmi, Paul Mercier, and Maxime Rodinson. See EPHE, Section des sciences économiques et sociales, *Annuaire* (1956/57–1965/66).

83. Dampierre actually had the unusual title of "*sous-directeur d'études*," a rank between *chargé de cours* and *directeurs d'études*. See the longer online version of appendix one for information on employment and sources.

84. See document "Démande à la Ford (IIIe version)," in Archives de l'école des hautes études en sciences sociales, Clemens Heller papers, Sociologie, Centre de sociologie européenne, Aron file. This is a report on the *Le Centre de sociologie européenne*, in English, for the Ford Foundation.

85. Jean Cuisenier, "Le sous-développement économique dans une groupement rural en Tunisie: le Djebel Lansarine," *Cahiers de Tunisie* 6, nos. 23–24 (1958): 219–66; Pierre Marthelot, "L'avant-Granai: contribution à l'histoire de l'enseignement de la sociologie en Tunisie," in U.E.R. de Sociologie-Ethnologie (Université de Provence), *Hommage à Georges Granaï* (Aix-en-Provence: Université de Provence, 1985), 9–18, 16. Bourricaud is not listed as a member in early *Centre de sociologie européenne* reports but is included in Aron's memo concerning the creation of the Center in the late 1950s. Archives de l'école des hautes études en sciences sociales, Clemens Heller papers, Sociologie, Centre de sociologie européenne, folder labeled "Centre européen (son but)," undated.

86. Salah Bouhedja, "'Il était un parmi les dix', autour de l'enquête sur les camps de regroupement dans *Le déracinement*," *Awal* 27–28 (2003): 287–93; interview by the author with Françine Muel-Dreyfus, March 30, 2014; *Le Centre de sociologie européenne 1961–1965* (Paris: *Le Centre de sociologie européenne*, 1965).

87. Amin Perez, "Rendre le social plus politique. Guerre coloniale, immigration et pratiques sociologiques d'Abdelmalek Sayad et de Pierre Bourdieu" (PhD diss., École des hautes études en sciences sociales, 2015), 228, 232–40.

88. Heilbron, *French Sociology*, 138.

89. Bourdieu distinguishes embodied, objectified, and institutionalized states of cultural capital in "The (Three) Forms of Capital," *Handbook of Theory and Research in the Sociology of Education*, ed. John G. Richardson (New York: Greenwood Press, 1986), 241–58.

90. In four cases I was unable to ascertain the *licence* degree specialization; I count these as non-philosophy/letters.

91. Rodinson and Sicard contributed to this section until Bastide's death in 1974, after which it became more straightforwardly anthropological. It was eventually renamed "Social and Cultural Anthropology" (1986). This section disappeared entirely, along with the rest of the book review section, in 1995.

92. Wendy James, "The Treatment of African Ethnography in 'L'année sociologique' (I–XII)," *Année Sociologique* 48, no. 1 (1998): 193–207; J. Fabulée, "Description et analyse des sociétés appurtenant au domaine ethnographique," *Année sociologique*, ser. 3, 11 (1960), 285–306, 287.

93. M. Rodinson, M. Sorre, and G. Stresser-Péan, "Contacts de civilisations. Colonialisme," *Année sociologique*, ser. 3, 1 (1948–1949): 265–283.

94. Faublée et al., "Contacts," 265.

95. Louis Gernet, Review of P. Mercier, *Les tâches de la sociologie* (Dakar: Institut français d'Afrique noire, 1951), *Année sociologique*, ser. 3, 3 (1951) 255.

96. Jean Chesneaux, Review of Georges Taboulet, La geste française en Indochine (Paris: Maisonneuve, 1956), *Année sociologique*, ser. 3, 8 (1955–1956), 376–78, 378.

97. Maxime Rodinson, review of Maunier, *Sociologie coloniale*, vol. 2, in *Année Sociologique*, 3rd series, 1 (1948–1949): 271–75, 275.

98. Georges Balandier, "La situation coloniale: approche théorique," *Cahiers internationaux de sociologie* 11 (1951): 44–79; Albert Memmi, "Sociologie des rapports entre colonisateurs et colonisés," *Cahiers internationaux de sociologie*, 23 (1957): 85–96.

99. Swedberg, "Georges Gurvitch," 76.

100. Georges Gurvitch, ed., *Traité de sociologie* (Paris: Presses universitaires de France, 1958), 2 vols.

101. Phillip Bosserman, "Gurvitch, Georges: Social Change," in *Blackwell Encyclopedia of Sociology*, ed. George Ritzer (Malden, MA: Blackwell Publishing, 2007), 1–4.

102. Anon., "Les sociologues francophones et la décolonisation," *Le Monde*, November 8, 1965, p. 15.

103. Émile Durkheim, *Leçons de sociologie physique des moeurs et du droit* (Paris: Presses universitaires de France, 1950).

104. Archives nationales, F/17/17770, "École coloniale," folder "Création d'une licence d'études coloniales (Décret du 17 octobre 1945)."

105. Paul Mus, *Viêt-Nam, sociologie d'une guerre* (Paris: Éditions du Seuil, 1952); George Steinmetz, "The Imperial Entanglements of Sociology in the United States, Britain, and France since the Nineteenth Century," *Ab Imperio* 4 (2009): 23–78.

106. E. Deladrier, Review of Van Overbergh and De Jonghe, *Les Bangala* (1907), in *Bulletin de la Société royale belge de géographie* 31, no. 6 (1907): 477–79, 478.

107. Julien van Hove, *Histoire du Ministère des colonies* (Bruxelles: Académie royale des sciences d'outre-mer, 1968).

108. Developed by Joseph Halkin, geographer at Liège, and Cyrille Van Overberghe, sociologist. See Joseph Halkin, "L'enquête sociologique sur les peuples de civilisation inférieure," *Le movement sociologique* 6, no. 1 (1905): 102–03; "Questionnaire ethnographique et sociologique rédigé par Joseph Halkin," *Annales de sociologie* 2 (1905), 229–56; Overbergh, ed., *Collection de monographies ethnographiques* (11 volumes) (Bruxelles: A. de Wit, 1907–1914)

109. Halkin, "L'enquête sociologique," 102–03.

110. Marc Poncelet, "Colonisation, développement et sciences sociales. Éléments pour une sociologie de la constitution du champ des 'arts et sciences du développement' dans les sciences sociales francophones belges," *Bulletin de l'APAD* 6 (1993): 2–20, para 38; Marc Poncelet, *L'invention des sciences coloniales belges* (Paris: Karthala, 2008), 97–99.

111. Poncelet, "Colonisation," 44; Other organizations were *Institut royal colonial belge*, the *Institut colonial international*, and the state-sponsored *Institut pour la recherche scientifique en Afrique centrale*. Benjamin Rubbers and Marc Poncelet, "Sociologie coloniale au Congo belge. Les études sur le Katanga industriel et urbain à la veille de l'Indépendance," *Genèses* 99 (2015): 93–112, 96.

112. Jean-François Crombois, *L'univers de la sociologie en Belgique de 1900 à 1940* (Bruxelles: Ed. de l'Université de Bruxelles, 1994).

113. Poncelet, *L'invention*, 156, note 34, 158, 169

114. Crombois, *L'univers*, 84–89, 127.

115. Poncelet, *L'invention*, 151.

116. Crombois, *L'univers*, 129; L'Université libre de Bruxelles, Institut de sociologie Solvay, *Études coloniales* Vol. 1, *Comte rendu des journées interuniversitaires d'études coloniales organisées à l'Université libre de Bruxelles les 29–30 décembre 1952*.

117. Poncelet, "Colonisation"; P. De Bie, *Naissance et premiers développements de la sociologie en Belgique* (Louvain la Neuve: CIACO, 1988).

118. On Belgian colonial developmentalism, see Guy Vanthemsche, *Genèse et portée du "Plan décennal" du Congo belge (1949–1959)* (Bruxelles: Académie royale des sciences d'outre-mer, 1994).

119. Poncelet, "Colonisation," paragraphs 70, 89; Arthur Doucy and Pierre Feldheim, "Problèmes du Katanga," *Revue de l'Institut de sociologie* 27, no. 3 (1954): 393–416; Arthur Doucy, "Le rôle des influences coutumières sur les travailleurs indigènes du Congo belge," *Revue de l'Institut de sociologie Solvay* 27, no. 4 (1954): 819–30.

120. Poncelet, *L'invention*, 156, note 34, 158, 169

121. Gustav Spiller, ed., *Universal Races Congress. Papers on Inter-Racial Problems communicated to the First Universal Races Congress, held at the University of London, July 26-29, 1911* (London: P.S. King & Son, 1911); xviii; Poncelet, *L'invention*, 169.

122. L. Gillon, "Lovanium," *Progress: the magazine of Lever Brothers and Unilever Limited* 47, no. 265 (1954): 227–33.

123. Poncelet, "Colonisation," para 118.

124. Marcel Dubuisson, *Mémoires* (Liège: Éditions Vaillant-Carmanne, 1977), 141.

125. W. Promper, "Entwicklung der Universität Louvanium in Belgisch Kongo," *Zeitschrift für Missionswissenschaft und Religionswissenschaft* 42, no. 1 (1958): 68–69, 68.

126. Marc Poncelet, "René Clémens et la mobilization des universitaires liégois au Katanga dans les années 1955-1960. Fin de colonie, sociologie clinique et bricolages du développement," in *Généalogie des sociologues et anthropologues belges disparus*, ed. Jeanne Beausoleil and Pascal Ory (Paris: Harmattan, 2015), 205–22.

127. Rubbers and Marc Poncelet, "Sociologie coloniale," 97.

128. E. L. Cerroni-Long, "Jacques Maquet: Pioneer of Cross-Cultural Research," *International Journal of Anthropology* 26, nos. 1–2 (2015): 67–71. I am grateful to Professor Cerroni-Long for sharing with me her memories of Prof. Maquet.

129. On contingent, conjunctural forms of causal explanation in social science, see George Steinmetz, "Critical Realism and Historical Sociology," *Comparative Studies in Society and History* 40, no. 1 (1998): 170–86; Steinmetz, "Historicism and Positivism in Sociology: From Weimar Germany to the Contemporary United States," in *Historicism: A Travelling Concept*, ed. Herman Paul and Adriaan van Veldhuizen (London: Bloomsbury, 2020), 57–95.

130. Neither were the colonial sociologists located in the more complex categories of "dominant-dominated" or "doubly dominated," discussed by Christophe Charle, *Birth of the Intellectuals: 1880-1900* (Cambridge: Polity, 2015).

Chapter Ten: Outline of a Theory of Colonial Sociological Practice

1. Philip Burnham, "'Regroupement' and Mobile Societies: Two Cameroon Cases," *Journal of African History* 16, no. 4 (1975): 577–94, 583.

2. Bourdieu's best studies of such strategies include *The Rules of Art* (Cambridge: Polity, 1996); Bourdieu, *Manet: A Symbolic Revolution* (Cambridge: Polity, 2017).

3. Timothy Scott Johnson, "The French Revolution in the French-Algerian War (1954–1962): Historical Analogy and the Limits of French Historical Reason" (PhD diss., CUNY, 2016), 5.

4. Balandier observed that postwar French intellectuals were divided between communists and Marxists on the one hand, and those oriented toward the colonial question and themes of liberation on the other, adding: "I chose the latter." Georges Balandier, *Civilsés, dit-on* (Paris: PUF, 2003), 25.

5. Classic examples of the tainting of colonial careers can be found in the literary portrayal of abject male British colonizers by Somerset Maugham, in "Rain" and "The Pool"; see Maugham, *Collected Short Stories*, vol. 1 (New York: Penguin, 1951), 9–45, 110–43. The exemplary French novelist of abject colonial masculinity is Michel Leiris, who discovered

that his African travels did not function as a "means of escape" but only strengthened his "relative isolation—his narcissism, his worries, his obsessions." Leiris, *Manhood* (New York: Grossman, 1963), 140; Leiris, *Scratches* (New York: Paragon House, 1991), 197.

6. I discuss these fears in George Steinmetz, *The Devil's Handwriting: Precoloniality and the German Colonial State in Qingdao, Samoa and Southwest Africa* (Chicago: University of Chicago Press, 2007).

7. See the discussion of colonial psychiatry in chapter 6 and, for a non-scientific postwar example, the narrative of travel in French Gabon by British journalist Russell Warren Howe, *Theirs the Darkness* (London: Herbert Jenkins, 1956).

8. Gilles Aubagnac, "Armée d'Afrique et troupes coloniales: deux entités au service de l'empire, 1830–1914," in *1830–1914, de l'armée en Afrique à l'Armée d'Afrique: actes de la journée d'étude, 10 décembre 2012* (Paris: Riveneuve, 2012), 13–27; Eric Storm, *Colonial Soldiers in Europe, 1914–1945: "Aliens in Uniform" in Wartime Societies* (New York: Routledge, 2016).

9. Balandier hinted at this comparison in 1948, writing that a French journalist who visited the IFAN center in Conakry that shared a building with an old quarantine station had called it "Buchenwald." Balandier noted that the words "collaborateurs et occupants" were used in the colony, like in Nazi occupied France. Georges Balandier, "Erreurs noires," *Présence africaine* 3 (1948): 393–404, 401, 404.

10. Edward Said, *Orientalism* (New York: Vintage Books, 1979), 117.

11. For a study of the ways in which the "native policies" in German colonies were shaped by professional and amateur ethnographic representations, see Steinmetz, *The Devil's Handwriting*.

12. Edmund Burke, III, "La mission scientifique du Maroc," *Bulletin économique et social du Maroc*, nos. 138–139 (1979): 37–56; Burke, III, *The Ethnographic State: France and the Invention of Moroccan Islam* (Berkeley: University of California Press, 2014).

13. Alain Messaoudi, *Les arabisants et la France coloniale: savants, conseillers, médiateurs, 1780–1930* (Lyon: ENS, 2015).

14. Jean Schmitz, "L'Afrique par défaut ou l'oubli de l'orientalisme," in *Maurice Delafosse: entre orientalisme et ethnographie: l'itinéraire d'un africaniste, 1870–1926*, ed. Jean-Loup Amselle and Emmanuelle Sibeud (Paris: Maisonneve, 1998), 107–21, 109–10.

15. Daniel Rivet, "Exotisme et 'pénétration scientifique': L'effort de découverte du Maroc par les Français au début du XXe siècle," in *Connaissances du Maghreb, sciences sociales et colonisation*, ed. Jean-Claude Vatin (Paris : CNRS, 1984), 95–109, 104.

16. Claude Lefébure, "Spillmann Georges Joseph Roger André," in *Dictionnaire des orientalistes de langue française*, ed. François Pouillon, 2nd ed. (Paris: Karthala, 2012), 966–67.

17. Georges Spillmann, *Souvenirs d'un colonialiste* (Paris: Presses de la cité, 1968).

18. Romuald Fonkoua, "Robert Delavignette et Henri Labouret: régards et approaches du fait colonial," in *Robert Delavignette, savant et politique: 1897–1976*, ed. Bernard Mouralis and Anne Piriou (Paris: Karthala, 2003), 73–89, 84; see also Henri Copin, "Delavignette et l'émergence d'un humanisme colonial," in *Robert Delavignette, savant et politique: 1897–1976*, ed. Bernard Mouralis and Anne Piriou (Paris: Karthala, 2003), 13–28.

19. Robert Louis Delavignette, *Les paysans noirs* (Paris: Stok, 1931).

20. Robert Delavignette, *Mémoires d'une Afrique française: texte inédit*, 2 vol. (Paris: L'Harmattan, 2017).

21. Georges Malecot, "Jean-Claude Froelich (1914–1972)," *Revue française d'histoire d'outre-mer* 59, no. 217 (1972): 699–700, 699.

22. Première conférence internationale des africanistes de l'ouest, *Comptes rendus*, vol. 1 (Paris: Librarie d'Amérique et d'Orient, Adrien-Maisonneuve, 1950–1951), 1.

23. René Maunier, *Des comptoirs aux empires* (Paris: Sirey, 1941), 143.

24. Hubert Deschamps, *Roi de la brousse: mémoires d'autres mondes* (Paris: Berger-Levrault, 1975).

25. The sociologists in question were Binet, Clément, Devauges, Froelich, Hauser, Holas, Jullien, Kohler, Meister, Mersadier, Pauvert, Alfred B. Schwartz, and Soret.

26. Balandier wore a *casque colonial* during his early research stay in Africa, according to his own account, but no photographs of him wearing it have come to light, and he was unwilling to show it to me when I interviewed him at his home. A photograph of Jean-Paul Sartre with a colonial pith helmet in his hand in Dakar in 1950 is reproduced in Kristin Ross, *Fast Cars, Clean Bodies: Decolonization and the Reordering of French Culture* (Cambridge, MA: MIT Press, 1995), 129. This photo suggests that French colonial culture ca. 1950 was still largely continuous with the 1930s, although Ross also gives examples of countervailing trends in the 1950s.

27. Of course there was a second fiction of the colonial state: that the colonized were incapable of governing themselves, hence in need of colonial tutelage. Ethnologists oriented themselves toward one or the other of these fictions depending on the historical context and their scientific orientation and strategy.

28. Marcel Soret, *Travaux des chercheurs de la section des sciences humaines de l'ORSTOM-IEC* (unpublished document, Brazzaville, January 1960), p. 2. Fonds Marcel Soret, folder 1A1.

29. Marcel Soret, *Activité scientifique* (Brazzaville: IRSC, 1963), 3–4. Fonds Marcel Soret, folder 1A1.

30. Marcel Soret, *Les Kongo nord-occidentaux* (Paris: PUF, 1959).

31. Soret, *Les Kongo nord-occidentaux*, 114.

32. Soret does not refer to Balandier's publications on the resettlement scheme (chapter 13), nor does he cite Gilles Sautter, "Les Paysans noirs du Gabon Septentrional. Essai sur le peuplement et l'habitat du Woleu-N'Tem," *Les cahiers d'outre-mer* 4, no. 14 (1951): 119–59.

33. Marcel Soret, "Les Téké de l'est. Essai sur l'adaptation d'une population a son milieu." (Thèse de doctorat, Lettres, Université de Lyon, 1970).

34. Soret, *Activité scientifique*, 1.

35. "Académie des Sciences d'Outre-Mer 1976–1978." Fonds Marcel Soret, folder 1A4.

36. J.-C. Froelich, *La Tribu Konkomba du Nord Togo* (Dakar: IFAN, 1954).

37. Soret and Balandier applied for ORSC fellowships in 1946: Georges Balandier, *Histoire d'autres* (Paris: Stock, 1977), 49; Soret, *Activité scientifique*.

38. Georges Balandier, *Tous comptes faits (*Paris: Éditions du Pavois, 1947), 231. The exact quote is: "C'est pourtant vrai que je suis maintenant ethnographe officiel (et non plus amateur, 'bénévole' comme c'était indiqué lors de mes premières années d'études), sociologue des Noirs africains." Jean Copans describes Balandier's writing as *"buissonière"*; Copans, "Les soixante-dix ans (1946–2015) d'écriture buissonière de Georges Balandier," *Cahiers d'études africaines* 228 (2017): 833–63. The literal meaning of *buissonière* is "in the bushes."

39. Georges Balandier, "Approche sociologique des Brazzavilles noires," *Africa* 22, no. 1 (Jan. 1952): 23–34, 28.

40. ORSTOM, *Activités de l'ORSTOM en République du Gabon* (Libreville: ORSTOM, 1969), 32.

41. Georges Balandier, *Le dépaysement contemporain* (Paris: PUF, 2009), 128, 158.

42. Louis-Vincent Thomas, "De l'ethnologie à la sociologie: essai sur un programme de recherches en Afrique noire," in Organisation d'études pour l'expansion de la recherche scientifique, *Actes du colloque sur la recherche scientifique et technique et le développement économique et social des pays africains* (Dakar: Université de Dakar, 1959), 331–32.

43. Louis-Vincent Thomas, *Cinq essais sur la mort africaine* (Paris: Karthala, 2013).

44. René Gouellain, *New Bell Doula. Enquête sociologique, 1ere partie* (Youndé: IRCAM, 1956). This report is subtitled "Enquête urbaine demandée par Monsieur le Haut-Commissaire" (Urban survey requested by the High Commissioner).

45. René Gouellain, *Douala: ville et histoire* (Paris: Institut d'ethnologie, Musée de l'homme, 1975), 385; verbatim in René Gouellain, "Douala, Sociologie d'une ville coloniale" (Thèse de 3ème cycle, Paris, EPHE, 1966), 499. Historians have relied on Gouellain's book; see Andreas Eckert, *Grundbesitz, Landkonflikte und kolonialer Wandel: Douala 1880 bis 1960* (Stuttgart: Steiner, 1990), which has 43 references to Gouellain; also Ralph A. Austen and Jonathan Derrick, *Middlemen of the Cameroons Rivers: The Duala and Their Hinterland, c.1600–c.1960* (Cambridge: Cambridge University Press, 1999).

46. Alfred Schwartz, *Témoignage d'Alfred Schwartz, Directeur de recherche honoraire de l'IRD (Institut de recherche pour le développement, ex-ORSTOM). Promotion 1960*. http://www.iep-strasbourg.fr/en/9-octobre-2015-liep-a-fete-ses-70-ans/tranches-dhistoire-la-vie-de-linstitut-detudes-politiques-de-strasbourg-au-fil-du-temps/ (consulted Aug. 24, 2017).

47. Alfred Schwartz, "Ziombli: l'organisation sociale d'un village Guéré-Nidrou (Côte d'Ivoire)," *Bulletin de liaison sciences humaines—ORSTOM*, no. 4 (1966): 83–86.

48. Alfred Schwartz, *Ziombli: l'organisation sociale d'un village Guéré-Nidrou (Côte d'Ivoire)* (Adiopodoumé: ORSTOM, 1965). In 1966, Schwartz published a study of the Toulépleu sub-Prefecture in Ivory Coast, where he detailed French efforts at regrouping and consolidating villages as a precursor to the Ivoirian government's regrouping policies in 1960–1965. Schwartz, *Toulepleu: étude socio-économique d'un centre semi-urbain de l'Ouest ivoirien* (Adiopodoumé: ORSTOM, 1966).

49. Christopher Gray, "Territoriality and Colonial 'Enclosure' in Southern Gabon," in *Enfermement, prison et châtiments en Afrique. Du 19ᵉ siècle à nos jours*, ed. Florence Bernault (Paris: Karthala, 1999): 99–132, 102; Robert David Sack, *Human Territoriality: Its Theory and History* (Cambridge: Cambridge University Press, 1986).

50. Jeremy Ravi Mumford, *Vertical Empire: The General Resettlement of Indians in the Colonial Andes* (Durham, NC: Duke University Press, 2012).

51. On the political and geographic fashioning of Indian Territory between 1800 and 1830 in what is now Kansas and eastern Oklahoma, see James P. Ronda, "'We Have a Country': Race, Geography, and the Invention of Indian Territory," *Journal of the Early Republic* 19, no. 4 (1999): 739–55.

52. James E. Togerson, "Indians against Immigrants: Old Rivals, New Rules: A Brief Review and Comparison of Indian Law in the Contiguous United States, Alaska, and Canada," *American Indian Law Review* 14, no. 1 (1988): 57–103, 59; see also the forthcoming PhD dissertation by Juan Delgado, postdoctoral fellow and sociologist at the University of Michigan in Ann Arbor.

53. Steinmetz, *The Devil's Handwriting*.

54. For additional examples, see Moritz Feichtinger, "'A Great Reformatory': Social Planning and Strategic Resettlement in Late Colonial Kenya and Algeria, 1952–63," *Journal of Contemporary History* 52, no. 1 (January 2017): 45–72; Christophe Bonneuil, "Development as Experiment: Science and State Building in Late Colonial and Postcolonial Africa, 1930–1970," *Osiris*, ser. 2, 15 (2000): 258–81; Samuël Coghe, "Reordering Colonial Society: Model Villages and Social Planning in Rural Angola, 1920–45," *Journal of Contemporary History* 52, no. 1 (January 2017): 16–44; Bogumil Jewsiewicki, *Modernisation ou destruction du village africain: l'économie politique de la "modernisation agricole" au Congo Belge* (Brussels: Centre d'Etude et de Documentation Africaines, 1983).

55. Burnham, "Regroupement," 585.

56. Edward Said, *Orientalism*, 291.

57. David Brokensha, "Detailed Plan of Proposals and Estimates for Anthropological Research in the Volta Basin," May 7, 1962, Norbert Elias archive, File 294. On Elias's activities in Ghana, see George Steinmetz, "A Child of the Empire: British Sociology and Colonialism, 1940s–1960s," *Journal of the History of the Behavioral Sciences* 49, no. 4 (2013): 353–78.

58. Della E. McMillan, *Sahel Visions: Planned Settlement and River Blindness Control in Burkina Faso* (Tucson: University of Arizona Press, 1995), 175, note 6; Myron Echenberg and Jean Filipovich, "African Military Labour and the Building of the Office du Niger Installations, 1925–1950," *Journal of African History* 27 (1986): 533–51. Later settlers were attracted by "simple persuasion"; Jean-Yves Marchal, "Office du Niger: îlot de prospérité paysanne ou pôle de production agricole?," *Revue canadienne des études africaines* 8 (1974): 73–90, 79–80.

59. François Bourricaud and Guy Laserre, *Aménagement hydro-agricole de la Vallée du Sourou. Programme de recherches en sciences humaines* (Bordeaux: Institut des Sciences humaines et appliquées, 1957), 69; Françoise Izard-Héritier and Michael Izard, *Les Mossi du Yatenga. Étude de la vie économique et sociale* (Bordeaux: Institut des Sciences humaines et appliquées, 1959).

60. Paul Mercier, "Curriculum Vitae," in *Archives de l'école des hautes études en sciences sociales*, Clemens Heller papers, Afrique, Mercier files; Georges Balandier, *Conjugaisons* (Paris: Fayard, 1997), 325.

61. Paul Mercier to Georges Balandier, Conakry, Sept. 21, 1956. "Dossier Guinée," in *Fonds Georges Balandier*. The Konkouré dam was never built during the colonial era and became a *cause célèbre* after independence in the struggle between the United States and the USSR for influence over the Guinean government. In 1978, the *Electricité de France* "undertook to update the old colonial studies concerning the Konkouré hydroelectric scheme," but the project was set aside again. Bonnie K. Campbell, "Negotiating the Bauxite/Aluminium Sector under Narrowing Constraints," *Review of African Political Economy*, no. 51 (1991): 27–49, 36, 40; Sergey Mazov, *A Distant Front in the Cold War: The USSR in West Africa and the Congo, 1956–1964* (Stanford, CA: Stanford University Press, 2010), 132–33.

62. Pierre Marthelot, "L'avant-Granai: contribution à l'histoire de l'enseignement de la sociologie en Tunisie," in *Hommage à Georges Granaï* (Aix-en- Provence: Université de Provence, 1985), 9–18, 14; Marthelot, "Sur la terre algérienne: le point de vue d'un sociologue," *Annales* 20, no. 4 (1965): 809–11; Jean Roche, "Bilan de l'année universitaire 1949–1950 à l'Institut des hautes etudes de Tunis," *Bulletin économique et social de la Tunisie*, no. 47 (1950): 57–60, 58; A. Bessis et al., *Le territoire des Ouled Sidi Ali ben Aoun* (Paris: Presses universitaires de France, 1956).

63. Benjamin N. Lawrance, "Togo," in *New Encyclopedia of Africa*, ed. John Middleton and Joseph C. Miller, vol. 5, 2nd ed. (Scribner, 2008), 60–67. *Gale Ebooks*, https://link.gale.com/apps/doc/CX3049000658/GVRL?u=umuser&sid=GVRL&xid=b454656e. Accessed Sept. 22, 2019.

64. ORSTOM, *Elements de bilan* (1959), section "IRTO" (*Institut de Recherches du Togo*), 4.

65. Marcel Lesne, "Une expérience de déplacement de population: les centres de regroupement en Algérie," *Annales de géographie* 71, no. 388 (1962): 567–601, 588.

66. Centre de doctrine d'emploi des forces, *Les "Sections administratives spécialisées" en Algérie: un outil pour la stabilisation* (Paris: Ministère de la Défense, 2005), 27; Grégor Mathias, *Les Sections administratives spécialisées en Algérie: entre idéal et réalité (1955-1962)* (Paris: L'Harmattan, 1998), 37.

67. Noara Omouri, "Les Sections administratives spécialisées et les sciences sociales: études et actions sociales de terrain des officiers SAS et des personnels des Affaires

algériennes," in *Militaires et guérilla dans la guerre d'Algérie*, ed. Jean-Charles Jauffret and Maurice Vaïse (Bruxelles: Complexe, 2001), 383-98.

68. Michel Marié, *Les terres et les mots. Une traversée des sciences sociales* (Paris: Editions Méridiens-Kliencksiek, 1989), 39-42.

69. The Centres sociaux were created by Germaine Tillion in 1955; see Serge Jouin and Jean-Philippe Ould-Aoudia, "Les Centres sociaux éducatifs en Algérie, 1955-1962," *Cahiers du Centre fédéral* (Fédération de l'éducation nationale, Paris), no. 4 (Dec. 1992): 103-40; Nelly Forget, "Le Service des centres sociaux en Algérie," *Matériaux pour l'histoire de notre temps*, no. 26 (Jan.-March 1992): 37-47.

70. Marc Joly, *Devenir Norbert Elias. Histoire croisé d'un processus de reconnaissance scientifique* (Paris: Fayard, 2012), 201.

71. Lesne, "Une expérience de déplacement," 585.

72. Lesne, "Une expérience de déplacement," 572. Bourdieu and Sayad evoke the "*situation quasi-concentrationnaire des regroupés*" ("almost concentration camp situation") in *Le déracinement. La crise de l'agriculture traditionelle en Algérie* (Paris: Les Éditions de Minuit, 1964), 12, n. 3.

73. Michel Cornaton, *Les regroupements de la décolonisation en Algérie* (Paris: Éditions ouvrières, 1967); Cornaton, *Les camps de regroupement de la guerre d'Algérie* (Paris: L'Harmattan, 1998); Cornaton, *La guerre d'Algérie n'a pas eu lieu: du déni à l'oubli, chronique d'une tragédie* (Paris: L'Harmattan, 2018).

74. Cornaton did not mention Bourdieu for five decades after his thesis, but when a wave of attacks on Bourdieu appeared after his death, Cornaton leapt onto the bandwagon; see Michel Cornaton, *Pierre Bourdieu: une vie dédoublée* (Paris: L'Harmattan, 2010).

75. Bourdieu and Sayad, *Le déracinement*, 26-27.

76. Lesne, "Une expérience de déplacement," 573-74.

77. Pierre Bourdieu, "From Revolutionary War to Revolution," in Bourdieu, *Algerian Sketches*, ed. Tassadit Yacine (Cambridge: Polity, 2013), 85-91, 351-352, 352, note 10.

78. Pierre Bourdieu, "The Revolution within the Revolution," in Bourdieu, *The Algerians* (Boston: Beacon Press, 1962), 146.

79. Mohamed Talbi, *Penseur libre en Islam* (Paris: Albin Michel, 2001), 28.

80. Jules Brévié, "Travaux scientifiques dus à des indigènes," *Bulletin du Comité d'etudes historiques et scientifiques de l'Afrique Occidentale Française* 14 (1931): 184-86, 185.

81. Female sociologists were still a small minority in French sociology at the time. In 1960, there were 18 women in a field of 127 sociologists at all ranks in Greater France (appendix five); five women were colonial specialists: Andrée (Vielle) Michel, Claudine Chaulet, Suzanne Frère, Odette Petit, and Nelly Xydias. Chenu and Martin show empirically that the French sociology discipline was feminized over the subsequent half century even while maintaining a "glass ceiling" with respect to full professor positions. Women became majoritarian at all teaching ranks by 2001, but men were still three times more likely than women to be promoted to full professor from the *maître de conférences* rank. Women were 15% of the total numbers of CNRS sociology researchers in 2014. See Alain Chenu and Olivier Martin, "Le plafond de verre chez les enseignants-chercheurs en sociologie et démographie," *Travail, genre et sociétés* 36 (2016): 135-56, 148.

82. Jean Copans, "Intellectuels visibles, intellectuels invisibles," in Copans, *Un demi-siècle d'africanisme africain: terrains, acteurs et enjeux des sciences sociales en Afrique indépendante* (Paris: Karthala, 2010), 15-30

83. See the discussions of the interwar journal *Races et racisme* (ch. 7); Balandier's articles "Le noir est un homme" (1947) and "Erreurs noires" (1948); the 1950 UNESCO statement on race (ch. 5); and the 1965 study of French racial attitudes by Maucorps, Memmi, and Held (ch. 2).

84. Albert Memmi, "Présentation générale," in Jacques Nanet, ed., *Cercle ouvert: Culture et colonialisme. 8° Conférence-Débats* (Paris: La Nef, 1957), 1–2; my emphasis.

85. Georges Condominas, "Dans quelle mesure les asiatiques et les africains participant-ils aux recherches menées sur les divers aspects des civilisations afircains et orientales?," in Association des universités partiellement ou entièrement de langue française, *État et perspectives des études africaines et orientales*, ed. Pierre Louis (Montreal: Therien freres, 1966), 105–13, 111.

86. Raymond Aron, *The Imperial Republic. The United States and the World, 1945–1973* (Englewood Cliffs, NJ: Prentice-Hall, 1974), discussed in ch. 11; C. Wright Mills, "Crackpot Realism," *Fellowship. The Journal of the Fellowship of Reconciliation* 25, no. 1 (1959): 3–8.

87. See Jeffery M. Paige, *Agrarian Revolution: Social Movements and Export Agriculture in the Underdeveloped World* (New York: Free Press, 1975) for an example of a study that works symmetrically for insurgents and counter-insurgents.

88. The most thoroughly researched of these figures are Albert Memmi and Abdelmalek Sayad. See Jeanyves Guérin, ed., *Albert Memmi, écrivain et sociologue: actes du colloque de Paris X-Nanterre, 15 et 16 mai 1988* (Paris: L'Harmattan, 1990); Amín Pérez, "Doing Politics by Other Means: Abdelmalek Sayad and the Political Sociology of a Collective Intellectual," *Sociological Review* 68, no. 5 (2020): 999–1014; and Yves Jammet, "Abdelmalek Sayad, les années d'apprentissage," in Abdelemalek Sayad, *La découverte de la sociologie en temps de guerre*, ed. Tassadit Yacine, Yves Jammet, and Christian de Montlibert (Nantes: Éditions Cécile Defaut, 2013), 17–127.

89. Anouar Abdel-Malek, François N'Sougan Agblémagnon, Manga Bekombo, Laurent Marie Biffot, Ousmane Poreko Diallo, Abdoulaye Bara Diop, Albert Memmi, Nguyễn Văn Huyên, Abdelmalek Sayad, Paul Sebag, Toufic Touma, and Abdelkader Zgahl. Sociologists who were born as French subjects in the 1930s or 1940s and who had scholarly careers that started just after decolonization include Honorat Aguessy, Abdelwahab Bouhdibah, Abdelbaki Hermassi, Abdelkébir Khatiba, Abbès Lahlou, Lilia Ben Salem, Frej Stambouli, and Khalil Zamiti. See prosopographic Appendix (online) for biographic information.

90. Georges Condominas, "La contestation ethnologique. Entretien de Yves Goudineau avec Georges Condominas," in *Trente ans*, ed. Jean-Louis Boutiller and Yves Goudineau (Paris: ORSTOM, 1993), 37–42, 38; Condominas, "Danses du vodou de la foudre dans le Bas-Togo," *Science et nature, par la photographie et par l'image* 3 (1954): 19–24; Condominas, "Introduction à une étude sur l'émigration grecque à Madagascar," in *Contributions to Mediterranean Sociology*, ed. J.-G. Peristiany (Paris: Mouton, 1968), 215–34.

91. Condominas, "Dans quelle mesure," 111.

92. François N'Sougan Agblémagnon, "Les responsabilités du sociologue africain," *Présence africaine* 27–28 (1959): 206–14, 206; see also Agblémagnon, "La différence de psychologie et de sensibilité provoque-t-elle une différence de comportement entre occidentaux d'une part, africaines de l'autre, quant aux méthodes de la recherche et quant à l'interprétation des résultats?," in Association des universités partiellement ou entièrement de langue française, ed., *État et perspectives* (Montreal: Therien freres, 1965), 128–44.

93. See École pratique des hautes études, *Contributions à la sociologie de la connaissance* (Paris: Editions Anthropos, 1967); and Georges Balandier et al., eds., *Perspectives de la sociologie contemporaine. Hommage à Georges Gurvitch* (Paris: Presses universitaires de France, 1968), Part 2, "Sociologie de la connaissance."

94. François N'Sougan Agblémagnon, "La concept de crise appliqué à une société africaine. Les Éwés," *Cahiers internationaux de sociologie* 23 (1957): 157–66, 159.

95. Agblémagnon, "La concept de crise," 159 (my emphasis).

96. Robert Ezra Park, "Human Migration and the Marginal Man," *American Journal of Sociology* 33, no. 6 (1928): 881–93.

97. Georges Balandier, *Sens et Puissance* (Paris: PUF, 1971), 122.

98. Augé was a student of Balandier who earned a "licence libre de sociologie" in 1964–1965 with a certificate that specialized in the "sociology of tropical Africa." He worked with Balandier on his 3rd cycle thesis and his *thèse d'état*, based on research in Ivory Coast. In 1965, he was identified with ORSTOM's "Comité technique de sociologie et de psycho-sociologie," whose program he described in Augé, "Les communautés rurales. Problèmes de méthode et de définition," ORSTOM, *Bulletin de liasion des sciences humaines* 2 (1965): 1–20. Augé later turned his attention from Africa to Europe, following in the footsteps of dozens of earlier sociologists of colonialism. Marc Augé, "Marc Augé," in *Comment je suis devnenu ethnologue*, ed. Anne Dhoquois (Paris: Cavalier bleu, 2008), 17–29, 19; Augé, *Non-Places: Introduction to an Anthropology of Supermodernity* (London: Verso, 1995).

99. Memmi, *The Pillar of Salt* (Boston: Beacon, 1955), 108–09, 96.

100. Pérez, "Doing Politics," 1003; Sayad, *Le double absence*.

101. Alfred Adler, "Manga Bekombo Priso (1932–2004)," *Journal des africanistes* 75, no. 2 (2005): 131–38.

102. Adler, "Manga Bekombo Priso," 2.

103. Manga Bekombo-Priso, "La société familiale Dwàla" (Doctorat de 3e cycle d'Ethnologie, Université de Nanterre, 1969).

104. Charles Soulié and Brice Le Gall, "Sociologie et philosophie: étude comparée de leurs évolutions socio-démographiques à l'université depuis le début des années 1970," *Regards sociologiques* 36 (2008): 43–52, 49.

105. Manga Bekombo, "Incidences sociales de la modernisation en agriculture en Afrique noire," *Présence africaine* 55 (1965): 135–44, 135–37. Quotes in this paragraph are all from this article.

106. Bekombo, "Incidences sociales," 143.

107. Adler, "Manga Bekombo Priso," 2.

108. Congrès des hommes de culture noirs, "Resolution de sociologie," *Présence africaine* 24–25 (Feb.–March 1959): 405–06.

109. Manga Bekombo, "Brazzaville à l'heure de la télévision congolaise," *Revue française de sociologie* 7, no. 2 (1966): 188–200.

110. Bekombo-Priso, *La société familiale Dwàla*, 224.

111. Bekombo-Priso, *La société familiale Dwàla*, 222.

112. On the latter see Manga Bekombo, "Parole et persuasion," *Recherche, pédagogie et culture*, no. 62 (1983): 40–45; Bekombo, "Le regard des ethnologues," *Magazine littéraire*, no. 195 (May 1983): 37–38.

113. Biffot died at the age of 39 before starting to publish. http://www.webfuuta.net/bibliotheque/ousmane_poreko/index.html (accessed Aug. 27, 2017); Gerald Gaillard, *Répertoire de l'ethnologie française: 1950–1970*, 2 vols. (Paris: Editions du Centre national de la recherche scientifique, 1990), 199; Jean-Hervé Jézéquel, "Les professionnels africains de la recherche dans l'état colonial tardif. Le personnel local de l'Institut français d'Afrique noire entre 1938 et 1960," *Revue d'histoire des sciences humaines* 24 (2011): 35–60.

114. The Tunisian students in question are Abdelbaki Hermassi, Abdelkébir Khatiba, Abbes Lahlou, Lilia Ben Salem, Frej Stambouli, and Khalil Zamiti. See Khalil Zamiti, "Aux origines de la sociologie en Tunisie," in *Abdelkader Zghal: l'homme des questions: Hommage à Abdelkader Zghal, 5 avril 1931–22 février 2015*, ed. Mohamed Kerrou (Tunis: Cérès éditions, 2017), 229–38; Lilia Ben Salam, "'Propos sur la sociologie en Tunisie.' Entretien avec Sylvie Mazzella," *Genèses: sciences sociales et histoire* 75 (2009): 125–142.

115. Pierre Bourdieu, *Homo Academicus* (Cambridge: Polity Press, 1988), 152. The *maître-assistant* position was eliminated in 1984, at which time the majority of existing *maîtres-assistants* became *maîtres de conférences*.

116. Albert Memmi, *Portrait of a Jew* (New York: Orion Press, 1962), 3.

117. Lia Nicole Brozgal, *Against Autobiography: Albert Memmi and the Production of Theory* (Lincoln: University of Nebraska Press, 2013), xv.

118. Patrick Crowley, "Albert Memmi: The Conflict of Legacies," in *Postcolonial Thought in the French-Speaking World*, ed. Charles Forsdick and David Murphy (Liverpool: Liverpool University Press, 2009), 126–35, 127.

119. Brozgal, *Against Autobiography*, xv.

120. Guérin, *Albert Memmi*.

121. See the essays in *Academic Dependency in the Social Sciences: Structural Reality and Intellectual Challenges*, ed. Kathinka Sinha-Kerkhoff and Syed Farid Alatas (New Dehli: Manohar, 2010).

122. Patricia Vannier, "Un laboratoire pour la sociologie? le Centre d'Études Sociologiques (1946–1968) ou les débuts de la recherche sociologique en France" (PhD diss., University of Paris, 1999), 136, 147.

123. Brozgal, *Against Autobiography*, does not mention Memmi's contributions to sociology.

124. Albert Memmi in discussion, in Jean-Yves Guérin, ed., *Albert Memmi: Écrivain et sociologue* (Paris: L'Harmattan, 1990), 172.

125. Albert Memmi, "Problèmes de la sociologie de la littérature," in *Traité de sociologie*, ed. Georges Gurvitch, vol. 2 (Paris: PUF, 1960), 1221–44.

126. Crowley, "Albert Memmi," 129.

127. Brozgal, *Against Autobiography*, 150.

128. Memmi, "Présentation générale," 1–2, 110–11; Albert Memmi, *The Colonizer and the Colonized* (New York: Orion Press, [1957] 1965), 111. See also Guy Dugas, *Albert Memmi: du malheur d'être juif au bonheur sépharade* (Paris: Alliance israélite universelle, 2001).

129. These phrases are from sociologist Jacques Lautman, who chaired the sociology department at Nanterre University (1976–1980) when Memmi was director of the social sciences division there, and later directed CNRS's department of human and social sciences. Email from Lautman to the author, Jan 25, 2014.

130. An exception is Vannier's exhaustive study, *Un laboratoire*.

131. Michel Pêcheux, *Language, Semantics, and Ideology: Stating the Obvious* (London: Macmillan, [1975] 1982); Fredric Jameson, *The Political Unconscious: Narrative as a Socially Symbolic Act* (Ithaca, NY: Cornell University Press, 1981).

132. See especially Geoffrey Mead, "Sense of Structure and Structure of Sense: Pierre Bourdieu's Habitus as a Generative Principle" (PhD diss., University of Melbourne, 2013); Idem., "Forms of Knowledge and the Love of Necessity in Bourdieu's Clinical Sociology," *Sociological Review* 65, no. 4 (2017): 628–43.

133. Pierre Bourdieu, *Outline of a Theory of Practice* (Cambridge: Cambridge University Press, [1972] 1977).

134. Frederico Ágoas describes the use of this argument in Portuguese colonial social science, in "Social Sciences, Modernization and Colonialism at the Age of Decolonization: the Centro de Estudos da Guiné Portuguesa, 1945–1955," *Journal of the History of the Behavioral Sciences* 56 (2020): 278–97, 284.

135. Balandier, "Tout parcours scientifique comporte des moments autobiographiques (entretien). Interview with Georges Balandier, *Actes de la recherche en sciences sociales* 185 (2010): 44–61, 57–58.

136. Authors in issues published between 1946 and 1955 include Bastide, Berque, Bettelheim, Braudel, Caillois, Canguilhem, Crozier, Davy, Duvignaud, Gernet, Griaule, Gurvitch, Friedmann, Halbwachs, Le Bras, Lefort, Lefebvre, Lévi-Strauss, Lévy-Bruhl, Leenhardt, Massignon, Mercier, Morin, Mus, Naville, Paulme, Piaget, Sauvy, Sorre, and Touraine.

137. These specialists in colonialism and postcolonialism who continued to publish in *Cahiers* included: Abdel-Malek, Bastide, Berque, Bourricaud, Camilleri, Cazeneuve, Charnay, Clignet, Chombart de Lauwe, Condominas, Duvignaud, Gosselin, Guiart, Morin, Mus, Rodinson, Sauvy, Storper-Perez, and Thomas.

138. Lahouri Addi, Lilia Ben Salem, Abdelwahab Bouhdiba, Jean Copans, Didier Fassin, Claude Meillassoux, John Rex, Claude Tapia, Serge Thion, and Yaya Wane.

139. According to Johan Heilbron, *French Sociology* (Ithaca, NY: Cornell University Press, 2015), these were the key patrons of post-1960 French sociology.

140. Eric de Dampierre, "Malvire-sur-Desle: une commune aux franges de la region parisienne," *L'information géographique* 20 (1956): 68–73.

141. Friedrich Hayek, "Scientism and the Study of Society" (Parts I–III), *Economica* 9, no. 35 (1942): 267–91; 10, no. 37 (1943): 34–63; 11, no. 41 (1944): 27–39.

142. Leo Strauss, "An Epilogue," in *Essays on the Scientific Study of Politics*, ed. Herbert J. Storing (New York: Holt, Rinehart and Winston, 1962): 306–27.

143. G. W. F. Hegel, "Qui pense abstrait?," translation by Eric de Dampierre of Hegel, "Wer denkt abstrakt?," *Mercure de France* 349 (Dec. 1963): 746–51.

144. Max Weber, *Le savant et le politique*, trans. Julien Freund (Paris: Plon, 1959); Freund, the translator, was an expert in Carl Schmitt and Max Weber.

145. Max Weber, *Collected Methodological Writings*, ed. Hans Henrik Bruun and Sam Whimster (London: Routledge, 2012); Ola Agevall, "Science of Unique Events: Max Weber's Methodology of the Cultural Sciences" (PhD diss., Uppsala University, 1999).

146. Aron successfully nominated de Dampierre for the *médaille d'argent du CNRS*, emphasizing the latter's exemplary editorial activity and arguing that Dampierre worked "also and especially for others." Dossier Éric de Dampierre in Raymond Aron papers, box 49, quoted in Michael Gemperle, "La fabrique d'un classique français: le cas de 'Weber,'" *Revue d'Histoire des Sciences Humaines*, no. 18 (2008): 159–77, 164, note 30.

147. E. Franklin Frazier, *Bourgeoisie noire* (Paris: Plon, 1955).

148. Eric de Dampierre dossier, Archives de l'école des hautes études en sciences sociales, Clemens Heller papers; Frazier, *Bourgeoisie noire*; Jean Chapelle, *Nomades noirs du Sahara* (Paris: Plon, 1958); Marie-Cécile Ortigues, *Œdipe africain* (Paris: Librarie Plon, 1966); Eric de Dampierre, *Un ancien royaume Bandia du Haut-Oubangui* (Paris: Plon, 1967).

149. Gemperle, "La fabrique," 168.

150. Henri Mendras, "Dampierre, Éric de (1928–1998)," https://www.universalis.fr/encyclopedie/eric-de-dampierre/.

151. Eric de Dampierre, *Harpes zandé* (Paris: Klincksieck, 1992); Dampierre, *Une esthetique perdue: harpes et harpistes du Haut-Oubangui* (Paris: Presses de l'École normale supérieure, 1995); Dampierre, *Harpes d'Afrique centrale : la parole du fleuve* (Paris: Cité de la musique, 1999).

152. Manga Bekombo, "Celui qui va là-bas ne parle plus," *L'homme* 28, no. 148 (1998): 11–13; Amín Pérez, "Rendre le social plus politique. Guerre coloniale, immigration et pratiques sociologiques d'Abdelmalek Sayad et de Pierre Bourdieu" (PhD diss., EHESS, 2015).

153. Pierre Bourdieu, *The State Nobility* (Stanford, CA: Stanford University Press, 1996), 337.

154. Pierre Bourdieu, "The Force of Law: Toward a Sociology of the Juridical Field," *Hastings Law Journal* 38, no. 5 (1987): 814–53, 831.

155. This point was made by Balandier, who was employed by ORSTOM and later directed its Division of Human Science; see his comments in Georges Balandier, *Autour de Georges Balandier* (Paris: Fondation d'Hautvillers pour le dialogue des cultures, 1981), 55.

156. Michael Polanyi, "Preface," in Congress for Cultural Freedom, ed., *Science and Freedom. The Proceedings of a Conference Convened by the Congress for Cultural Freedom and Held in Hamburg on July 23rd–26th, 1953* (London: M. Secker & Warburg, 1955), 10. The

journal *Science and Freedom* focused on relations between science and the state in Britain and the United States in issues 2 (1955) and 7 (1956); issue 3 (1955) discussed the resistance to the appointment of the neo-Nazi politician Leonhard Schlüter at Göttingen University.

157. Audra J. Wolfe, "Science and Freedom: The Forgotten Bulletin," in *Campaigning Culture and the Global Cold War: The Journals of the Congress for Cultural Freedom*, ed. Giles Scott-Smith and C. Lerg (London: Palgrave Macmillan, 2018), 27–45.

158. The Algerian war was a partial exception, with the government seizing "leftist newspapers whose editorial line supported the self-determination policy," and bloody "police actions against anti-OAS demonstrators" in metropolitan France. In 1960, however, "the government began to allow publication of books that were extremely critical of the war effort." Ian Lustick, *Unsettled States, Disputed Lands. Britain and Ireland, France and Algeria, Israel and the West Bank-Gaza* (Ithaca, NY: Cornell University Press, 1993), 527, note 40.

159. Abdelmalek Sayad, *Histoire et recherche identitaire suivi de Entretien avec Hassan Arfaoui* (Saint-Denis: Bouchène, 2002), 60.

160. Pierre Bourdieu, "Il faut que l'intellectuel donne la parole à ceux qui ne l'ont pas!," *L'événement du Jeudi*, 10–16 (September 1992): 114–16.

161. Geoffroy de Lagasnerie, *Sur la science des oeuvres: questions à Pierre Bourdieu (et à quelques autres)* (Paris: Cartouche, 2011); compare Franck Poupeau and Thierry Discepolo, eds., *Pierre Bourdieu, Interventions, 1961-2001* (Marseille: Éditions Agone, 2002).

162. Pierre Bourdieu, "Les chercheurs et le mouvement social," in *Bourdieu, Interventions, 1961-2001*, ed. Franck Poupeau and Thierry Discepolo (Marseille: Éditions Agone, 2002), 465–66, 465. Italicized text in English in the original.

163. Pierre Bourdieu, "For Abdelmalek Sayad," in Bourdieu, *Algerian Sketches*, 295–300, 296; Pierre Bourdieu, "Étude sociologique," in Pierre Bourdieu, Alain Darbel, Jean-Paul Rivet, and Claude Seibel, *Travail et travailleurs en Algérie* (Paris: Mouton, 963), 253–62, 259.

164. Jammet, "Abdelmalek Sayad," 90, 100; Salah Bouhedja, "'It était un parmi les dix.' Autour de l'enquête sur les camps de regroupement dans *Le déracinement*," *Awal* 27–28 (2003): 287–94, 288; Claude Seibel, "Les liens entre Pierre Bourdieu et les statisticiens à partir de son expérience algérienne," in *La liberté par la connaissance. Pierre Bourdieu (1930-2002)*, ed. Jacques Bouveresse and Daniel Roche (Paris: Odile Jacob, 2004), 105–20.

165. Deschamps to de Dampierre, Jan. 10, 1956, in Bibliothèque Éric de Dampierre, Dampierre papers, Mission sociologique du Haut Oubangui, folder "Correspondence Génerale 1954–1967/1954–1955."

166. Marc Poncelet, *L'invention des sciences coloniales belges* (Paris : Karthala, 2008), 190.

Chapter Eleven: Raymond Aron as a Critical Theorist of Empires and Colonialism

1. Aron, "The Diffusion of Ideologies," *Confluence* 2, no. 1 (1953): 3–12, 8.

2. Aron, *L'Algérie et la République* (Paris: Plon, 1958), 113.

3. The main exception is Matthias Oppermann, *Raymond Aron und Deutschland. Die Verteidigung der Freiheit und das Problem des Totalitarismus* (Ostfildern: Thorbecke Verlag, 2008), which discusses Aron's writing on Nazi imperialism. On Aron and colonialism, see Lucia Bonfreschi, "Raymond Aron face au processus de la decolonisation française sous la Quatrième Republique," *Outre-mers: revue d'histoire* (2007): 354–55; Olivier Dard, "Raymond Aron et la question algerienne," in *Raymond Aron et la défense de la liberté: nationalisme, libéralisme et post-modernité*, ed. Fabrice Bouthillon, Joël Mouric, and Matthias Oppermann (Paris: Éditions de Fallois, 2016), 65–86; Marie-Christine Granjon, "Raymond Aron, Jean-Paul Sartre et le conflit algérien," in *La Guerre d'Algérie et les intellectuels*

français, ed. Jean-Pierre Rioux and Jean-François Sirinelli (Bruxelles: Editions Comlexe, 1991), 115–35; Stephen Launay, "Raymond Aron et la guerre d'Algérie: un regard libéral sur une décomposition," *Les cahiers d'histoire sociale*, no. 23 (2004): 127–47; Christian Malis, *Raymond Aron et le débat stratégique français: 1930–1966* (Paris: Economica, 2005), 481–534; and Iain Stewart, *Raymond Aron and Liberal Thought in the Twentieth Century* (Cambridge: Cambridge University Press, 2019), 141–51.

4. Peter Baehr, "The Honored Outsider: Raymond Aron as Sociologist," *Sociological Theory* 31, no. 2 (2013): 93–115.

5. On the evolving reception of Aron in the United States, see Daniel Steinmetz-Jenkins, "The Other Intellectuals: Raymond Aron and the United States" (PhD diss., Columbia University, 2016). Tony Judt ignores Aron's anti-imperialism in *Past Imperfect: French Intellectuals, 1944–1956* (Berkeley: University of California Press, 1992).

6. Hans Manfred Bock, "Raymond Aron und Deutschland. Aspekte einer intellektuellen Generationsanalyse," *Lendemains* 36, no. 141 (2011): 43–58.

7. Aron, "Lettre ouverte d'un jeune français à l'Allemagne," *L'Esprit* 1, no. 5 (1933): 735–43, 735. See Jean-Louis Loubet del Bayle, *Les non-conformistes des années 30. Une tentative de renouvellement de la pensée politique française* (Paris: Éditions du Seuil, 2001); Gilbert Merlio, *Ni gauche, ni droite. Les chassés-croisés idéologiques des intellectuels français et allemands dans l'entre-deux-guerres* (Talence: Edition MSHA, 1995); Philip G. Nord, *France's New Deal: From the Thirties to the Postwar Era* (Princeton, NJ: Princeton University Press, 2010), 22ff.

8. Pierre Grémion, *Intelligence de l'anticommunisme. Le Congrès pour la Liberté de la Culture à Paris (1950–1975)* (Paris: Fayard, 1995), 26, 292; on the CCF and France, see also Andrea Scionti, "'I Am Afraid Americans Cannot Understand': The Congress for Cultural Freedom in France and Italy, 1950–1957," *Journal of Cold War Studies* 22, no. 1 (2020): 89–124; on *Preuves*, see Nicolas Stenger, "The Difficult Emergence of an 'Anti-Totalitarian' Journal in Post-War France: *Preuves* and the Congress for Cultural Freedom," in *Campaigning Culture and the Global Cold War: The Journals of the Congress for Cultural Freedom*, ed. Giles Scott-Smith and C. Lerg (London: Palgrave Macmillan, 2018), 91–106.

9. Eric Pullin, "The Culture of Funding Culture: The CIA and the Congress for Cultural Freedom," in *Intelligence Studies in Britain and the US: Historiography since 1945*, ed. Christopher R. Moran and Christopher J. Murphy (Edinburgh: Edinburgh University Press, 2013), 47–64, 55; Volker Berghahn, *America and the Intellectual Cold Wars in Europe: Shepard Stone between Philanthropy, Academy, and Diplomacy* (Princeton, NJ: Princeton University Press, 2001).

10. Aron, *Memoirs: Fifty Years of Political Thought* (New York: Holmes & Meier, [1983] 1990), 174, 176; Pullin, "The Culture of Funding Culture," 51; Hugh Wilford, *The Mighty Wurlitzer: How the CIA Played America* (Cambridge, MA: Harvard University Press, 2008), 113.

11. Yann Coudé Du Foresto, "Conversation avec Raymond Aron," *Pouvoirs* 28 (1984): 168–83, 175; see also Christophe Prochasson, "Raymond Aron est-il un intellectual de gauche?," in *Raymond Aron, philosophe dans l'histoire*, ed. Serge Audier et al. (Paris: Fallois, 2008), 219–28.

12. Steinmetz-Jenkins, *The Other Intellectuals*, 164; Steinmetz-Jenkins, "Why Did Raymond Aron Write that Carl Schmitt Was Not a Nazi? An Alternative Genealogy of French Liberalism," *Modern Intellectual History* 11, no. 3 (2014): 549–74.

13. George Steinmetz, "Methodological Homelandism," *Contemporary Sociology* 48, no. 3 (2019): 244–48.

14. George Steinmetz, "Positivism and Its Others in the Social Sciences," in *The Politics of Method in the Human Sciences: Positivism and its Epistemological Others*, ed. George Steinmetz (Durham, NC: Duke University Press, 2005), 1–56.

15. Bock, "Raymond Aron und Deutschland," 43–58.

16. Aron, *La Sociologie allemande contemporaine* (Paris: Alcan, 1935); translated as *German Sociology* (Glencoe: Free Press, 1964); for a more recent overview, see David Kettler and Colin Loader, "Weimar Sociology," in *Weimar Thought: A Contested Legacy*, ed. John P. McCormick and Peter E. Gordon (Princeton, NJ: Princeton University Press, 2013), 15–34.

17. See Karl Mannheim, "Das Problem einer Soziologie des Wissens," *Archiv für Sozialwissenschaft und Sozialpolitik* 53 (1925): 577–652.

18. Peter Vogt, *Kontingenz und Zufall: eine Ideen- und Begriffsgeschichte* (Berlin: Akademie Verlag, 2011); George Steinmetz, "Historicism and Contingency: Beyond Positivism in the Social Sciences," in *Historicism: A Travelling Concept*, ed. Herman Paul and Adriaan van Veldhuizen (London: Bloomsbury, 2020), 57–95; Wolfgang Knöbl, *Die Soziologie vor der Geschichte: Zur Kritik der Sozialtheorie* (Berlin: Suhrkamp Verlag, 2022), 100–136.

19. Aron, *Essai sur la théorie de l'histoire dans l'Allemagne contemporaine. La philosophie critique de l'histoire* (Paris: Vrin, 1938), 291.

20. Aron, *Introduction to the Philosophy of History: An Essay on the Limits of Historical Objectivity* (London: Weidenfeld and Nicolson, [1938] 1961), 343.

21. For a succinct overview of Aron's historical epistemology, see Pierre Hassner, "Raymond Aron and the History of the Twentieth Century," *International Studies Quarterly* 29, no. 1 (1985): 29–37, 32.

22. Aron, *Les étapes de la pensée sociologique* (Paris: Gallimard, 1967), 519.

23. Baverez, *Raymond Aron*, 108.

24. Bock, "Raymond Aron," 52.

25. David Drake, "Raymond Aron and *La France Libre*: June 1940–September 1944," in *A History of the French in London: Liberty Equality, Opportunity*, ed. Debra Kelly and Martyn Cornick (London: University of London School of Advanced Study Institute of Historical Research, 2013), 373–90; Michael Curtis, "Raymond Aron and *La France Libre*," in *Political Reason in the Age of Ideology: Essays in Honor of Raymond Aron*, ed. Bryan-Paul Frost and Daniel J. Mahoney (New Brunswick, NJ: Transaction Publishers, 2008), 147–74.

26. Aron, *Memoirs*, 139, 229–39.

27. Aron, *Memoirs*, 141.

28. Alan Bloom, "Raymond Aron-The Last of the Liberals," in Bloom, *Giants and Dwarfs: Essays, 1960–1990* (New York: Simon & Schuster, 1990), 256–67, 266.

29. Franz L. Neumann, *Behemoth: The Structure and Practice of National Socialism 1933–1944* (New York: Oxford University Press, 1942); Hannah Arendt, *The Origins of Totalitarianism* (New York: Harcourt, Brace, 1951).

30. Aron, "L'Allemagne: une révolution antiprolétarienne: Idéologie et réalité du national-socialisme," *Inventaires* I (1936): 24–55, 14, 54.

31. See, for example, Aron, "Les racines de l'impérialisme allemand [1941]," in *L'homme contre les tyrans* (New York: Éditions de la Maison française, 1944), 285–301, 288–92.

32. Aron, "L'ère des tyrannies d'Elie Halévy," *Revue de metaphysique et de morale* 46, no. 2 (1939): 283–307, 288, 291, 302.

33. Oppermann, *Raymond Aron*, 149.

34. Aron, "États démocratiques et états totalitaires (Juin 1939)," *Commentaire* 24 (1983–1984): 701–19, 706–07. Aron used the word "totalitarianism" several times in his 1939 text on Halévy and had already used it in 1934, according to Oppermann, *Raymond Aron*, 118.

35. Aron, " L'ère des tyrannies," 302.

36. Aron worked on a longer manuscript on "Modern Machiavellianism" in 1938–1940 that he was unable to complete due to the outbreak of the war. It was published as Aron, *Machiavel et les tyrannies modernes* (Paris: Editions de Fallois, 1993).

37. Aron, "Le Machiavélisme, doctrine des tyrannies modernes (1939)," in *L'homme contre les tyrans*, 15-29, 21; emphasis in original.

38. Aron, "Le Machiavélisme," 26; Aron, "Le Romantisme de la violence (1941)," in *L'homme contre les tyrans*, 30-49, 45.

39. Aron, "Les racines," 297; Aron, *Memoirs: Fifty Years of Political Thought* (New York: Holmes & Meier, 1990), 129.

40. Aron, "La menace des Césars (1942)," in *L'homme contre les tyrans*, 266-84, 269.

41. Julia Hell, *The Conquest of Ruins* (Chicago: University of Chicago Press, 2019).

42. Aron, "La menace des Césars," 276.

43. Aron, "Dynamisme de la guerre totale," in Aron, *Les guerres en chaîne* (Paris: Gallimard, 1951), 37-62, 47-48.

44. Aron, "La Stratégie totalitaire et l'avenir des démocraties [1942]," in *L'homme contre les tyrans*, 227-47, 228-29; Aron, "Le Romantisme de la violence [1941]," in *L'homme contre les tyrans*, 30-49, 47.

45. Aron, "Le Romantisme," 41; Aron, "Les racines," 293.

46. Aron, "Mythe révolutionnaire et impérialisme germanique," in *L'homme contre les tyrans*, 50-67, 50.

47. Aron, "La menace des Césars," 282; Aron, "Dynamisme de la guerre totale," 51.

48. Aron, "L'âge des empires [1945]," in *L'Âge des empires et l'Avenir de la France* (Paris: Défense de la France, 1945), 355-69, 359.

49. Aron, "Bataille des propagandes [1942]," in *De l'Armistice à l'insurrection nationale* (Paris: Gallimard, 1945), 248-65, 250.

50. On hybrid imperial forms, see George Steinmetz, "Return to Empire: The New US Imperialism in Theoretical and Historical Perspective," *Sociological Theory* 23, no. 4 (2005): 339-67.

51. Aron, "Dynamisme de la guerre totale," 51.

52. Aron, "Le Problème du ravitaillement," in *De l'Armistice à l'insurrection nationale*, 72-80, 73.

53. Aron, "La menace des Césars," 281.

54. Aron, "Empire de Charlemagne et testament de Richelieu [1943]," in *De l'armistice à l'insurrection nationale*, 272-83, 274.

55. Aron, "La menace des Césars," 281; Max Weber, *Economy and Society*, trans. Keith Tribe (Cambridge. MA: Harvard University Press, 2019), 343-54; Alfred Weber, "Der Beamte," in A. Weber, *Ideen zur Staats- und Kultursoziologie* (Karlsruhe: G. Braun, 1927), 81-101.

56. Aron, "Bureaucratie et fanatisme," in *L'homme contre les tyrans*, 68-88, 75; emphasis in original.

57. Aron, "Pour l'alliance de l'Occident [1944]," in *L'Âge des empires*, 319-26, 321-22; Joël Moric, *Raymond Aron et l'Europe* (Rennes: Presses universitaires de Rennes, 2013), ch. 5; Aron, "Destin des nationalités," in *L'homme contre les tyrans*, 302-24, 303; Aron, "L'âge des empires," 357. Aron corresponded with Schmitt after the war, met him once, and mentored the French Schmittian sociologist and former member of the Resistance, Julian Freund. Piet Tomissen, "Raymond Aron face à Carl Schmitt," *Schmittiana* 7 (2003): 111-29.

58. Aron, "Les racines," 295.

59. Aron, "L'âge des empires," 357.

60. Dominique Auffret, *Alexandre Kojève: la philosophie, l'Etat, la fin de l'histoire* (Paris: B. Grasset, 1990), 225-31, 253-63, 283; see Alexandre Kojève, "Outline of a Doctrine of French Policy," *Policy Review* 126 (2004): 3-40; Robert Howse, "Europe and the New World Order: Lessons from Alexandre Kojève's Engagement with Schmitt's 'Nomos der Erde,'" *Leiden Journal of International Law* 19 (2006): 93-103.

61. Aron, "Introduction," in *L'âge des empires*, 1-27, 26.

62. Aron, "La menace des Césars," 282.

63. Aron, *Memoirs*, 205. Bourdieu similarly refers to Cournot in discussing "crisis as conjuncture, that is to say as conjunction of independent causal series," in *Homo Academicus* (Stanford, CA: Stanford University Press, 1988), 174. For the original statement of this idea, see Antoine Augustin Cournot, *Exposition de la theorie des chances et des probabilities* (Paris: Librairie de L. Hachette, 1843), 73; also Jean-Philippe Touffut, ed., *La société du probable. Les mathématiques sociales après Auguste Cournot* (Paris: Albin Michel, 2007).

64. Aron, "Reflections on the Foreign Policy of France," *International Affairs* 21, no. 4 (1945): 437–47, 445.

65. Aron, "Remarques sur quelques préjugés politiques [1943]," in *L'Âge des empires*, 346; "Reflections on the Foreign Policy," 443.

66. Aron, "Remarques sur quelques préjugés politiques," 327–54, 346, 349.

67. Aron, *Espoir et peur du siècle. Essais non partisans* (Paris: Calmann-Lévy, 1957), 210.

68. Hans Mayer and Raymond Aron, "Zwischen Frankreich und Deutschland, zwischen Weimar und Bonn. Raymond Aron im Gespräch mit Hans Mayer," in *Die andere deutsche Frage. Kultur und Gesellschaft der Bundesrepublik Deutschland nach dreissig Jahren*, ed. Walter Scheel (Stuttgart: Klett-Cotta, 1981), 243–70, 262.

69. Aron, *The Committed Observer: Interviews with Jean-Louis Missika and Dominique Wolton* (Chicago: Regnery Gateway, 1983), 164.

70. Aron, "Le mythe léniniste de l'impérialisme," in *Les guerres en chaîne*, 63–84.

71. Aron, "Le mythe léniniste, " 65, 69; Aron, "What Empires Cost and What Profits They Bring," in *The Dawn of Universal History* (New York: Basic Books, [1962] 2002), 407–18.

72. Quotes from Aron, *Imperialism and Colonialism* (Leeds: Jowett & Sowry, 1959), 4–6; Aron, "Le Mythe léniniste," 70.

73. Aron, "Le mythe léniniste," 68; Joseph Schumpeter, "Zur Soziologie der Imperialismen," *Archiv für Sozialwissenschaft und Sozialpolitik* 46, no. 1 and 46, no. 2 (1918–1919), 1–39, 275–310.

74. Aron, *Imperialism and Colonialism*, 6.

75. Aron, "Reflections on the Foreign Policy," 443.

76. Aron, "L'industrialisation de l'Empire," *Combat*, June 24 (1946); "A propos de l'Union française," *Combat*, Sept. 15 (1946); quoted in Robert Colquhoun, *Raymond Aron* (London: Sage Publications, 1986), vol. 1, 439.

77. Aron, "Le courage d'innover," *Combat*, April 3 (1946), quoted in Colquhoun, *Raymond Aron*, vol. 1, 441.

78. Ibid.

79. Aron, "La tragédie d'Indochine [1953]," in *Les articles de la politique internationale dans "Le Figaro" de 1947 à 1977*, vol. 1 (Paris: Éd. de Fallois, 1990), 1114–19, 1116.

80. Colquhoun, *Raymond Aron*, vol. 1, 443.

81. Aron, "Perspectives nord-africaines," *Evidences* (Sept.–Dec. 1954): 3–4, 4.

82. Aron, "L'unité atlantique, enjeu de la crise de Suez," in *Les articles*, vol. 2, 231–33; also "Une fois de plus," in *Les articles*, vol. 2, 240–42.

83. Aron, *The Imperial Republic. The United States and the World, 1945-1973* (Englewood Cliffs, NJ: Prentice-Hall, 1974), 56.

84. Aron, *La tragédie algérienne* (Paris: Plon, 1957), 72.

85. Aron, "Perspectives nord-africaines," *Evidences* (Sept.–Dec. 1954): 3–4.

86. Bonfreschi, "Raymond Aron," 280.

87. Bonfreschi, "Raymond Aron," 279, note 38.

88. Jacques Soustelle, *Aimée et souffrante Algérie* (Paris: Plon, 1956); Bernard Ullmann, *Jacques Soustelle: le mal aimé* (Paris: Plon, 1995); James D. Le Sueur, *Uncivil War: Intellectuals and Identity Politics during the Decolonization of Algeria* (Philadelphia: University of Pennsylvania Press, 2001), 132–42.

89. Aron, *Memoirs*, 248.

90. Aron, *La tragédie algérienne*, iii.

91. Aron, *La tragédie algérienne*, 7.

92. Aron, "La France joue sa dernière chance en Afrique, III [1954]," in Aron, *Les articles*, vol. 2, 94–98, 98; Aron, "La France joue sa dernière chance en Afrique, IV [1954]," in Aron, *Les articles*, vol. 2, 98–103, 100.

93. Aron, *La tragédie algérienne*, 51, 44, 45.

94. Aron, *L'Algérie et la République*, 56, 60–61, 84.

95. Aron, *L'Algérie et la République*, 113.

96. Aron, *L'Algérie et la République*, 123, 114–15.

97. Aron, *L'Algérie et la République*, 60–61, 84.

98. Aron, *L'Algérie et la République*, 109.

99. Aron, "La France joue sa dernière chance en Afrique, I (1955)," 86.

100. Aron, *Espoir et peur*, 203.

101. Aron, "Nations et empires," in *Encyclopédie française*, vol. 11 (Paris: Société nouvelle de l'Encyclopédie française, 1957), 11.04-1–11.06-8, 11.04-13.

102. Aron, "Nations et empires," 11.04-2.

103. Aron, *Imperialism and Colonialism*, 7.

104. Aron, "La France joue sa dernière chance en Afrique, I," 88–89.

105. Aron, *The Imperial Republic*, 259.

106. Aron, "What Empires Cost," 407.

107. Aron, *Espoir et peur*, 210–11.

108. Aron, *Peace and War* (Garden City, NY: Doubleday, 1962), 259; Aron, *Imperialism and Colonialism*, 3.

109. Aron, *Imperialism and Colonialism*, 3.

110. Aron, *Imperialism and Colonialism*, 10; Aron, *Espoir et peur*, 203.

111. Aron, "La menace des Césars (1942)," in *L'homme contre les tyrans*, 266–84, 283.

112. Aron, "Destin des nationalités (1943)," in *L'homme contre les tyrans*, 302–24, 309.

113. Oppermann, *Raymond Aron*, 241; Aron, *Peace and War*, 154.

114. Aron, "L'âge des empires," 358.

115. Aron, "Reflections on the Foreign Policy of France," 442. Aron was thus a world system theorist *avant la lettre*.

116. Or Rosenboim, "Repenser l'État dans un espace devenu mondial. La pensée de Raymond Aron sur les relations internationales 1940-1949," in *Raymond Aron et la défense de la liberté: nationalisme, libéralisme et post-modernité*, ed. Fabrice Bouthillon, Joël Mouric, and Matthias Oppermann (Paris: Éditions de Fallois, 2016), 41–64.

117. Aron, "L'âge des empires," 358.

118. Aron, "Nouvelle carte du monde," *Point de vue* 1, no. 7 (May 4, 1945), no pagination.

119. Aron, "The Rise of the Peripheral States," in *The Century of Total War* (Boston: Beacon Press, 1955), 101–15, 101–02. Aron attributed this idea about the American empire's inevitable rise to Max Weber.

120. Aron, "Transformations du monde de 1900 à 1950: déplacement du centre de gravité international," *Réalités* 47 (1949): 70–111, 70–71.

121. Aron, *Espoir et peur*, 222.

122. Aron, "Reflections on the Foreign Policy of France," 442.

123. Aron, "Le dilemme indochinois [1954]," in Aron, *Les articles*, vol. 1, 1143–45.

124. Aron, *The Imperial Republic*, 83.

125. Steinmetz-Jenkins, *The Other Intellectuals*, 122; Aron, "Transformations du monde de 1900 à 1950," 70–111, 70–71; Aron, *The Imperial Republic*, 56; Aron, *Le Grand Schisme* (Paris: Gallimard, 1948), 32; Aron, *The Great Debate: Theories of Nuclear Strategy* (Garden City, NY: Doubleday, 1965).

126. Oppermann, *Raymond Aron*, 117, referring to Aron, "Contribution à l'ère des tyrannies," *Bulletin de la Société française de philosophie* 36 (1936): 226–28.

127. Claude Lefort, "Raymond Aron et le phénomène totalitaire," in *Raymond Aron et la liberté politique*, ed. Christian Bachelier (Paris: Fallois, 2002), 87–92, 88.

128. Aron, *Democracy and Totalitarianism* (New York: Praeger, [1965] 1968), 193–94.

129. Lefort, "Raymond Aron," 91.

130. Oppermann, *Raymond Aron*, 216.

131. Colquhoun, *Raymond Aron*, vol. 2, 33; *Les articles*, vol. 2, 153–55, 226–44.

132. Aron, *La tragédie algérienne*, 22.

133. Steinmetz-Jenkins, *The Other Intellectuals*, 101. Truman's Four Point Program was a policy of economic aid and technical assistance to developing countries, starting in 1950. The Alliance for Progress, initiated in 1961, was a US foreign aid program for Latin America that was explicitly grounded in modernization theory.

134. Aron, "The Diffusion of Ideologies," *Confluence* 2, no. 1 (1953): 3–12, 7.

135. Aron, "Conflict and War from the Viewpoint of Historical Sociology," in International Sociological Association, *The Nature of Conflict: Studies on the Sociological Aspects of International Tensions* (Paris: UNESCO, 1957), 177–203, 199.

136. Aron, *The Imperial Republic*, xxxvi. This argument closely follows Carl Schmitt's analysis of the United States in *Der Nomos der Erde im Völkerrecht des Jus publicum Europaeum* (Köln: Greven, 1950).

137. Aron, *The Imperial Republic*, 48.

138. Aron, *The Imperial Republic*, 101.

139. Aron, *The Imperial Republic*, 265; compare C. Wright Mills, "Crackpot Realism," *Fellowship. The Journal of the Fellowship of Reconciliation* 25, no. 1 (1959): 3–8.

140. Aron, *The Imperial Republic*, 266.

141. Aron, *The Imperial Republic*, 271.

142. The second part of *La République impériale* marshals a mass of historical and economic evidence to counter the "paramarxist" historians.

143. Aron, *The Imperial Republic*, 175.

144. Aron, *The Imperial Republic*, 257.

145. Aron, *The Imperial Republic*, 185, 258.

146. Aron, *The Imperial Republic*, 279.

147. Steinmetz-Jenkins, *The Other Intellectuals*, 162.

148. Steinmetz-Jenkins, *The Other Intellectuals*, 168–70.

149. Immanuel Wallerstein, *The Decline of American Power: The US in a Chaotic World* (New York: New Press, 2003).

150. Gwendal Châton, "Taking Totalitarianism Seriously: The Emergence of the Aronian Circle in the 1970s," in *In Search of the Liberal Moment*, ed. Steve Sawyer and Iain Stewart (London: Palgrave, 2015), 17–38, 17, 25.

151. Raymond Aron, *Les étapes de la pensée sociologique* (Paris: Gallimard, 1967), 295, cited in Châton, "Taking Totalitarianism Seriously."

152. Jacques Berque, "Préface," *Ibla: Revue de L'institut des belles lettres arabes* 79 (1960): 351–56, 352.

153. Aron, *Espoir et peur*, 211.

Chapter Twelve: Jacques Berque: A Historical Sociologist of Colonialism and "the Decolonial Situation"

1. Berque, "Sciences sociales et décolonisation," *Tiers-Monde* 9–10 (1962): 1–15, 3.

2. Berque, "Décolonisation intérieure et nature seconde," *Études de sociologie tunisienne* 1 (1968): 11–27, 19.

3. Derived from the Arabic *bled* or *balad*. In Morocco, the Bled es-Siba or Bled Siba refered to lawless areas occupied by Berber tribes and outside the *makhzan* area of the Sultan's control.

4. Berque, *Mémoires des deux rives* (Paris: Seuil, 1989), 97.

5. Berque, "Entrée dans le bureau arabe," in *Nomades et vagabonds* (Paris: 10/18, 1975), 113–39, 116.

6. Berque, "Entrée dans le bureau arabe," 113.

7. Jean-Claude Vatin, "Postface," in Augustin Berque, *Ecrits sur l'Algérie* (Aix-en-Provence: Edisud, 1986), 265–96.

8. Nabila Oulebsir, "Berque, Augustin," in *Les usages du patrimoine: monuments, musées et politique coloniale en Algérie, 1830–1930* (Paris: Maison des sciences de l'homme, 2004), 324.

9. John Whidden, "Jacques Berque (1910–1995)" in *French Historians 1900–2000: New Historical Writing in Twentieth-Century France*, ed. Philip Daileader and Philip Whalen (Malden, MA: Blackwell, 2010), 23–37, 24; Berque, *Arabies* (Paris: Stock, 1978), 34.

10. Berque, *Arabies*, 25.

11. Berque, *Arabies*, 25. This provides some nuance to the homogenizing depiction of settlers in "settler studies."

12. Berque, *Mémoires*, 47.

13. Georges Davy, "Louis Gernet. L'homme et le sociologue," in *Hommage à Louis Gernet rendu au Collège de France*, ed. Georges Davy (Paris: PUF, 1966), 7–13; Jacques Berque, "Gernet et la sociologie orientaliste," in *Hommage à Louis Gernet rendu au Collège de France*, ed. Georges Davy (Paris: PUF, 1966), 36–37.

14. Berque, *Arabies*, 39; *Mémoires*, 41, 93, 70.

15. Berque, *Arabies*, 38.

16. Berque, *Arabies*, 40; Mourad Yelles, "Jacques Berque, portrait du *cheikh* en passeur," in *Itinéraires intellectuels: entre la France et les rives sud de la Méditerranée*, ed. Christiane Chaulet-Achour (Paris: Karthala, 2011), 235–58, 238.

17. On the job of the civil controller in the French Moroccan protectorate, see Roger Gruner, *Du Maroc traditionnel au Maroc moderne: le contrôle civil au Maroc, 1912–1956* (Paris: Nouvelles Editions latines, 1984).

18. Berque, "Aspects du contrat pastoral à Sidi-Aïssa," *Revue africaine* 79, nos. 368–369 (1936): 899–911.

19. Alain Mahé, "Notices, variantes et notes," in Jacques Berque, *Opera minora*, vol. 1: *Anthropologie juridique du Maghreb*, ed. Alain Mahé (Paris: Editions Bouchène, 2001), 541–63, 541.

20. Berque, "Contribution à l'étude des contrats Nord-Africains. Les pactes pastoraux Beni-Meskine," in *Opera minora*, vol. 1, 15–67.

21. Mahé, "Notices, variantes et notes," 544.

22. Berque, "Contribution à l'étude des contrats Nord-Africains," 30.

23. Berque, "Sur un coin de terre marocaine: seigneur terrien et paysans," *Annales d'histoire économique et sociale* 9, no. 45 (1937): 227–35; Marc Bloch, "La Genèse de la seigneurie: idée d'une recherche comparée," *Annales d'histoire économique et sociale* 9, no. 45 (1937): 225–27.

24. Berque, *Études d'histoire rurale maghrébine* (Tanger & Fes: Editions internationales, 1938); reprinted in Berque, *Opera minora*, vol. 1, 69–196. All quotes from the latter edition.

25. Berque, *Études d'histoire*, 119, 129.

26. Marc Bloch, "Pour une histoire comparée des sociétés européennes," *Revue de synthèse historique* 46 (1928): 15–50; Bloch, *The Historian's Craft* (New York: Knopf, 1953).

27. Berque, *Études d'histoire*, 84.

28. Berque, *Études d'histoire*, 83, 85, 84.

29. Berque, *Études d'histoire*, 123.

30. Berque, *Études d'histoire*, 122, 72.

31. Berque, *Études d'histoire*, 129–130.

32. Berque, *Études d'histoire*, 133.

33. Berque, *Études d'histoire*, 82.

34. Berque, *Études d'histoire*, 119, 130, 82, 135, 131.

35. Berque, *Études d'histoire*, 86, 106.

36. Berque, *Études d'histoire*, 139.

37. Berque, *Études d'histoire*, 129.

38. Prosper Ricard, "La grande mosquée cathédrale el-Qaraouiyine, siège de l'université musulmane de Fez," *France-Maroc: revue mensuelle illustrée*, (March 15, 1918): 79–85.

39. F. Jabre (Berque), "Dans le Maroc nouveau: le role d'une université islamique," *Annales d'histoire économique et sociale* 51 (May 1938): 193–207, 195, 202, 206.

40. Berque, *Mémoires*, 149.

41. Berque, "Medinas, villeneuves et bidonvilles," *Cahiers de Tunisie* 21–22 (1957): 5–42, 12.

42. Berque, "Medinas, villeneuves et bidonvilles," 27.

43. Berque, "Medinas, villeneuves et bidonvilles," 21.

44. Berque, "Medinas, villeneuves et bidonvilles," 35. Among the studies that build upon Berque's pioneering work, see Janet Abu-Lughod, *Rabat, Urban Apartheid in Morocco* (Princeton, NJ: Princeton University Press, 1980); Paul Rabinow, *French Modern: Norms and Forms of the Social Environment* (Cambridge, MA: MIT Press, 1989), ch. 9; and Gwendolyn Wright, *The Politics of Design in French Colonial Urbanism* (Chicago: University of Chicago Press, 1991), ch. 4.

45. Berque, "Medinas, villeneuves et bidonvilles," 40–41, 12.

46. Berque, *Les Nawâzil el muzâràa du Mìyâr Al Wazzâni* (Rabat: Moncho, 1940); Berque and G. H. Bousquet, *Recueil de la loi musulmane de Zaîd ben 'Alî (le plus ancien recueil de droit musulman retrouvé jusqu'ici)* (Alger: La Maison des Livres, 1941); Berque, "Essai sur la méthode juridique maghrébine (1944)," in *Opera minora*, vol. 1, 273–358.

47. See also Berque, "Deux cas de compromis entre droits universalistes et coutumes locales," in *Normes et valeurs dans l'Islam contemporain*, ed. Jean-Paul Charnay (Paris: Payot, 1966), 132–44.

48. Berque, *Essai sur la méthode*, 305, 312.

49. Berque, *Essai sur la méthode*, 327.

50. Berque, *Essai sur la méthode*, 332.

51. Berque, *Essai sur la méthode*, 338.

52. Berque, "Pour une nouvelle méthode politique de la France au Maroc" (1946), in *Opera minora*, vol. 3 (Paris: Editions Bouchène, 2001), 45–80, 73.

53. Jacques Berque and Julien Couleau, "Vers la modernisation du fellah marocain," *Bulletin économique et social du Maroc* 7, no. 26 (1945): 18–24, 21; Berque, "Vers la modernisation rurale (1945)," in *Opera minora*, vol. 3, 37–44, 41; Daniel Rivet, "Réformer le protectorat français au Maroc?," *Revue du monde musulman et de la Méditerranée*, nos. 83–84 (1997): 75–91.

54. Berque, *Arabies*, 52.

55. François Pouillon, "Présentation," in Berque, *Opera minora*, vol. 3 (Paris: Editions Bouchène, 2001), i–iv, iv; Berque, "Vers la modernisation," 40.

56. Berque, "Vers la modernisation," 40.

57. Léon Marchal, "Les principes, les méthodes et les buts de la modernisation rurale au Maroc," in "Journées de la modernisation rurale," *Bulletin d'information du Maroc*, March 1946, 303, cited in Grigori Lazarev, *Les politiques agraires au Maroc 1956–2006. Un témoignage engagé* (n.p.: Economie critique, 2012), 36.

58. Daniel Rivet, "Réformer le protectorat français," 83. Rivet's use of the English word "welfare" in his text underscores the global postwar context of welfare state expansion.

59. Résidence générale de la République française au Maroc, "Les journees de la modernisation rurale," *Bulletin d'information du Maroc* (March 1946), 61–379.

60. Rivet, "Réformer le protectorat français," 83. On the modernization of the Beni Amir, see Pierre Marthelot, "Histoire et réalité de la modernisation du monde rural au Maroc," *Tiers-Monde* 2, no. 6 (1961): 137–68, 142–44.

61. Marthelot, "Histoire et réalité de la modernization," 147.

62. Charles André Julien, *L'Afrique du Nord en Marche* (Paris: R. Julliard, 1952), 358; Marthelot, "Histoire et réalité de la modernization," 146–47.

63. Berque wrote this memo in late 1946 and distributed it in January 1947 to sympathetic colleagues J. Dresch and C.-A. Julien. Berque, *Mémoires*, 123.

64. Berque, "Pour une nouvelle méthode," 50, 53, 78.

65. Berque, "Pour une nouvelle méthode politique," 56.

66. The phrase *Verwissenschaftlichung des Kolonialen* is from Anne Kwaschik, "Die Verwissenschaftlichung des Kolonialen als kultureller Code und internationale Praxis um 1900," *Historische Anthropologie* 28, no. 3 (2020): 399–423. Kwaschik also recognizes the limits on scientization of colonialism.

67. Berque, *Arabies*, 53.

68. Jacques Frémeaux, "Missionnaire en burnous bleu," *Revue du monde musulman et de la Méditerranée*, nos. 83–84 (1997): 67–73, 72.

69. Berque, *Structures sociales du Haut-Atlas* (Paris: PUF, 1955).

70. Berque, *Structures sociales du Haut-Atlas*, 225.

71. Claude Lefébure, "Bonnes feuilles des Seksawa," *Revue du monde musulman et de la Méditerranée*, nos. 83–84 (1997): 93–101, 99.

72. Berque, "Les sociétés nord-africaines vues du Haut-Atlas," *Cahiers internationaux de sociologie* 19 (1955): 59–65, 63.

73. Berque, *Structures sociales du Haut-Atlas*, 447.

74. Berque, *Structures sociales du Haut-Atlas*, 447

75. Berque, *Structures sociales du Haut-Atlas*, 447

76. Paul Pascon, "Les Seksawa depuis l'indépendance," in Berque, *Structures sociales du Haut-Atlas*, 2nd ed. (Paris: PUF, 1978), 455–74, 457. Pascon also suggests (263, 456) that Berque was less "sensitive to events" here than in his earlier work and was seeking "permanent structures." Berque's alleged depiction of the Seksawa as unchanging, according to Pascon, resonated with the Protectorate's goal of freezing history as a means of pacification. Berque would then be acting as an "enlightened instrument of the maintenance of structures." Yet it is impossible to square this interpretation with Berque's explicit arguments about *reconstructions*, the *desire for archaism*, and *historical evolutions*, and that the French should leave Morocco.

77. Berque, "Le droit du Sous," *Bulletin des études arabes* 9 (1949): 8–11, 10.

78. Berque, "Problèmes initiaux de la sociologie juridique en Afrique du Nord," *Studia Islamica* 1 (1953): 137–62, 144.

79. Berque, "Qu'est-ce qu'une tribu nord-africaine?," in *Éventail de l'histoire vivante: Hommage à Lucien Febvre*, ed. Fernand Braudel (Paris: Armand Colin, 1954), 261–71, 263.

80. David Goeury, "Horizon Seksawa: relecture de l'oeuvre de Jacques Berque pour la compréhension de l'espace marocain," *Awal (Cahiers d'études berbères)* (2011): 213–24, 218.

81. See, for example, Berque, "Remarques sur le tapis maghrébin," in *Études Maghrébines. Mélanges Charles-Andre Julien*, ed. Pierre Marthelot (Paris: Presses universitaires de France, 1964), 13–24, 23.

82. Berque, "Les sociétés nord-africaines," 64.

83. Berque, "Problèmes initiaux," 141.

84. Berque, *Études d'histoire*, 100; "Problèmes initiaux," 144.

85. Berque, "Nouveaux types urbains au Maroc: A propos d'une enquête collective," *Annales ESC* 7, no. 2 (1952): 210–16, 214.

86. Berque, *Structures sociales du Haut-Atlas*, 453. On the "art of the *tournée*" among colonial administrators, see Robert Louis Delavignette, *Service africain* (Paris: Gallimard, 1946), 73–86.

87. Berque, "Vers une étude des comportements en Afrique du Nord," *Revue africaine* 100 (1956): 523–36, 528.

88. Berque, "Le problème démographique en pays berbère: étude sur les tribus de la région d'Imintanout. I. La population," *Bulletin économique et social du Maroc* 17, no. 60 (1953-1954): 203–07, 207.

89. Berque, "Perspectives de l'orientalisme contemporain," *Ibla* 79 (1957): 217–38, 230; Berque, *Les Arabes* (Paris: Delpire, 1959); Idem., *Langages arabes du present* (Paris: Gallimard, 1974); Berque, "Sur l'esthétique musulmane et ses motivations psychologiques et sociales," *Journal de psychologie normale et pathologique* 58, no. 4 (1961): 433–44.

90. Berque, "Notice individuelle, CV (23.IX.1955)," in folder "BERQUE/Titres et travaux," in *Archives de l'école des hautes études en sciences sociales*, Clemens Heller papers, Berque file.

91. Berque, *Le Maghreb entre deux guerres* (Paris: Seuil, 1962); *L'Egypte, impérialisme et révolution* (Paris: Gallimard, 1967); *Les Arabes*.

92. Berque, *Histoire sociale d'un village égyptien au XXe siécle* (Paris: Mouton, 1957).

93. Fabien Sacriste, *Germaine Tillion, Jacques Berque, Jean Servier et Pierre Bourdieu: des ethnologues dans la guerre d'indépendance algérienne* (Paris: Harmattan, 2011), 153, 165.

94. Berque, *Dépossession du monde*, 96.

95. Berque, "L'Algérie ou les faux dilemmes," *Politique étrangère* 21, no. 6 (1956): 703–10, 708.

96. Fanon, "On Violence," 44. See below for Berque's appreciation for Fanon.

97. Berque, "La nation algérienne et le 13 mai [*Le Monde*, 18 June 1956]," in *Une cause jamais perdue: articles politiques (1947-1995)* (Paris: Albin Michel, 1998), 38–40.

98. Berque, *The Arabs* (London: Faber & Faber, [1960] 1964), 58. Berque borrowed the idea of "l'effet de domination" from François Perroux, discussed in chapter 6.

99. Berque, *The Arabs*, 58, 38.

100. Berque, *The Arabs*, 42.

101. Berque, *The Arabs*, 240.

102. Berque, *The Arabs*, 239.

103. Berque, *The Arabs*, 45.

104. Berque, *The Arabs*, 56.

105. Berque, *The Arabs*, 58.

106. Berque, "Colonisation, décolonisation, comment les definir?," *Cahiers Internationaux. Revue internationale du monde du travail* 118 (1961): 53–60, 58–59.

107. Partha Chatterjee, *The Nation and Its Fragments* (Princeton, NJ: Princeton University Press, 1993).

108. Berque, "The North of Africa," *International Social Science Journal* 13, no. 2 (1961): 177–96, 180, 181.
109. Berque, *Dépossession du monde*, 106; emphasis added.
110. Berque, *Dépossession du monde*, 101.
111. Berque, *Mémoires*, 62.
112. Berque, "Colonisation, décolonisation," 56.
113. Berque, "Décolonisation intérieure," 24, 19, 13.
114. Berque, *Dépossession du monde*, 7.
115. Ronald Robinson, "The Excentric Idea of Imperialism, with or without Empire," in *Imperialism and After. Continuities and Discontinuities*, ed. Wolfgang J. Mommsen and Jürgen Osterhammel (London: Allen & Unwin, 1986): 267–89. This is, of course, an excentric theory of colonization, not decolonization.
116. Berque, *Dépossession du monde*, 42 (my emphasis).
117. Sartre, *Anti-Semite and Jew* (New York: Schocken Books, 1948); G. W. F. Hegel, "Lordship and Bondage," in *The Phenomenology of Mind*, trans. J. B. Baillie, 2nd ed. (New York: Humanities Press, 1949), 228–40.
118. Berque, "Impérialisme et décolonisation," 596. Of course, Hegel's text refers not to slave and master but bondsman (*Knecht*) and master (*Herr*), but it has long been read as also referring to slavery.
119. Berque, "Colonisation, decolonisation: comment les definir?," *Cahiers Internationaux. Revue internationale du monde du travail* 118 (1961): 53–60, 58.
120. Berque, *Dépossession du monde*, 66.
121. Berque, *Dépossession du monde*, 67.
122. Berque, *Dépossession du monde*, 105.
123. Berque, *Dépossession du monde*, 105.
124. Berque, *Dépossession du monde*, 101.
125. Berque, *Dépossession du monde*, 116.
126. Berque, *Dépossession du monde*, 164; Berque, "Décolonisation intérieure," 20.
127. Berque, "Décolonisation intérieure," 19; Berque, *L'intérieur du Maghreb: XVe-XIXe siècle* (Paris: Gallimard, 1978).
128. Berque, *Dépossession du monde*, 173 (my emphasis).
129. Berque, "Colonisation, décolonisation," 56.
130. Berque, "Logiques plurales du progrès," *Diogène* 79 (1972): 3–26.
131. Berque, "'Contenu' et 'forme' dans la décolonisation," in *Perspectives de la sociologie contemporaine. Hommage à Georges Gurvitch* (Paris: PUF, 1968), 21–38, 27.
132. Berque, *Dépossession du monde*, 155.
133. Berque, "'Contenu' et 'forme.'"
134. Berque, "Quelques perspectives d'une sociologie de la décolonisation," *Revue de l'enseignement supérieur* 1–2 (1965): 33–40, 34.
135. Berque, "Hommages à Franz Fanon," *Presence africaine*, 40, juin: 118–119.
136. Berque, "Nouvelles approches de la décolonisation," in *De l'impérialisme à la décolonisation*, ed. Jean-Paul Charnay (Paris: Minuit, 1965): 479–501, 481.
137. Fanon, "Letter to the Résident Minister (1956)," in Fanon, *Toward the African Revolution* (New York: Grove Press, 1967), 52–54, 53; Fanon, "Altérations mentales, modifications caractérielles, troubles psychiques et déficit intellectuel dans l'hérédo-dégénération spino-cérébelleuse," in Fanon, *Écrits sur l'aliénation et la liberté*, ed. Jean Khalfa and Robert J. C. Young (Paris: La Découverte, 2015), 168–232, 194.
138. Berque, "L'Orient et l'avènement de la valeur monde," in Berque, *Une cause jamais perdue: articles politiques (1947–1995)* (Paris: Albin Michel, 1998), 230–44, 231 (my emphasis).
139. Berque, "Sciences sociales et décolonisation," *Tiers-Monde* 9–10 (1962): 1–15, 3.

140. Berque, "Quelques perspectives d'une sociologie," 35.

141. Berque, *Dépossession du monde*, 26.

142. According to Lahouari Addi, Berque stood apart from all academic "schools" and scholarly "controversies." Addi, "Les enjeux théoriques de l'anthropologie du Maghreb. Lecture de Bourdieu, Geertz, Gellner et Berque," in *L'anthropologie du Maghreb: les apports de Berque, Bourdieu, Geertz et Gellner*, ed. Lahouari Addi (Paris: Awal, 2003), 7–15, 11.

143. Berque, *Études d'histoire rurale maghrébine*, 98; Berque, *Structures sociales du Haut-Atlas*, 239.

144. Berque, *Dépossession du monde*, 21; Berque, *Arabies*, 105.

145. Berque, "Cent vingt-cinq ans de sociologie maghrébine," *Annales ESC* 10, no. 3 (1956): 296–324, 309.

146. Montagne, *Les Berbères et le Makhzen dans le sud du Maroc* (Paris: Félix Alcan, 1930), 182–216.

147. Berque, "Les sociétés nord-africaines," 64; Berque, *Structures sociales du Haut-Atlas*, 218, 424.

148. Berque, "Sur un coin de terre marocaine," 231–32.

149. Berque, "Nouveaux types urbains au Maroc: A propos d'une enquête collective," *Annales ESC* 7, no. 2 (1952): 210–16, 214.

150. For a critique of a more recent effort to reanimate universalizing versions of Marxism, see George Steinmetz, "On the Articulation of Marxist and Non-Marxist Theory in Colonial Historiography," in *The Debate on Postcolonial Theory and the Specter of Capital*, ed. Rosie Warren (London: Verso, 2017), 139–47.

151. Berque, *Mémoires*, 221–22.

152. Berque, *Arabies*, 240.

153. Berque, *Il reste un avenir: entretiens avec Jean Sur* (Paris: Arléa, 1993), 14; Berque, *Mémoires*, 167.

154. Berque, *Mémoires*, 150–151.

155. Berque, "Sciences sociales et décolonisation," 3.

156. Berque, "Cent vingt-cinq ans," 319.

157. Berque, *Mémoires*, 47.

158. On "demi-regularities," see Tony Lawson, "Emergence and Social Causation," in *Powers and Capacities in Philosophy: The New Aristotelianism*, ed. Ruth Groff (New York: Routledge, 2013), 285–307.

159. In a comparison of four German sociologists' relationship to changing political contexts, I found that Richard Thurnwald and Richard Mühlmann embraced dependency while Max and Alfred Weber resisted it. Berque clearly was more like the Webers than Thurnwald; George Steinmetz, "Scientific Autonomy and Empire, 1880–1945: Four German Sociologists," *German Colonialism in a Global Age*, ed. Geoff Eley and Bradley Naranch (Durham, NC: Duke University Press, 2014), 46–73.

160. Berque, "Perspectives de l'orientalisme contemporain," 220. Berque, "Sciences sociales et décolonisation," *Tiers-Monde* 9–10 (1962): 1–15, 3.

161. Jacques Berque, "Sciences sociales et monde arabo-islamique," in *L'intervention dans le champ social*, ed. Simone Crapuchet and Georges Michel Salomon (Paris: Privat, 1992), 81–84, 82.

162. Edward Said, *Orientalism* (New York: Vintage Books, 1979), 326–27.

163. Gianni Albergoni, "Notices, variantes et notes," in Jacques Berque, *Opera minora*, vol. 2 (Paris: Editions Bouchène, 2001), 449–80, 461–63.

164. Berque, "Perspectives de l'orientalisme contemporain," *Ibla, Revue de L'institut des belles lettres arabes* 79 (1957), 217–238, 221.

165. Alain Messaoudi, *Les arabisants et la France coloniale: savants, conseillers, médiateurs, 1780–1930* (Lyon: ENS, 2015), 525.

166. Berque, *Mémoires*, 89.
167. Berque, *Dépossession du monde*, 90.
168. Berque, "Cent vingt-cinq ans," 303.
169. Berque, *Dépossession du monde*, 89.
170. Berque, "Cent vingt-cinq ans," 314; my emphasis.
171. Berque, "Cent vingt-cinq ans," 311.
172. Berque, "Cent vingt-cinq ans," 311.
173. Berque, *Dépossession du monde*, 19 n. 7; 32 n. 12; 65; Berque, "Logiques d'assemblage au Maghreb," in Georges Balandier et al., *L'autre et l'ailleurs. Hommage à Roger Bastide* (Paris: Berger-Levrault, 1976), 39–56.
174. Berque, *Dépossession du monde*, 8. By contrast, the phrase "mixed methods" in American sociology today is little more than a timid combination of quantitative and qualitative approaches that remains obediently within disciplinary guardrails.
175. Berque, "Perspectives de l'orientalisme," 220.
176. Berque, "Préface," *Ibla: Revue de L'institut des belles lettres arabes* 79 (1960): 351–56, 352, my emphasis.
177. Bernard Traimond, "Aux sources d'une thèse universitaire. Entretien realisé par Bernard Traimond avec Jacques Berque, professeur honoraire au Collège de France," *Cahiers ethnologiques* 9 (1988): 29–47, 45.
178. Berque, "Gernet et la sociologie orientaliste," in *Hommage à Louis Gernet rendu au Collège de France*, ed. Georges Davy (Paris: Collège de France, 1966), 36–37, 36.
179. These sociologists include: Balandier, Bastide, Jean-Paul Charnay, Le Coeur, Duvignaud, Gernet, Gurvitch, Massignon, Jean-Claude Reverdy, Maxime Rodinson, Fredj Stambouli, and Toufic Touma.
180. Berque, *Rapport de M. Jacques Berque, professeur au Collège de France, sur la mission qu'il a effectuée en Tunisie de novembre à décembre 1959, en vue du développement de 1'enseignement et de la recherche dans le domaine des sciences sociales, au titre du programme de participation aux activités des États membres de l'Unesco* (Paris: UNESCO, 1959); Berque, *Rapport de M. Jacques Berque, Professeur au Collège de France, sur la mission qu'il a effectué au Liban de septembre à novembre 1959, en vue du développement de l'enseignement et de la recherche dans le domaine des sciences sociales, au titre du programme de participation aux activités des Etats membres de l'UNESCO* (Paris: UNESCO, 1959).
181. Berque was also part of the French network on the sociology of knowledge discussed in chapter 10. Berque, *Mémoires*, 175.
182. Sacriste, *Germaine Tillion*, 139.
183. Berque, "Préface," 353.
184. Berque, "Medinas, villeneuves et bidonvilles," 33.
185. Berque, "Cent vingt-cinq ans," 319; Berque, *Rapport... en Tunisie*, 2. The classic critique of "historicizing history" is Henri Berr, *La synthèse en histoire. Essai critique et théorique* (Paris: F. Alcan, 1911). See my "Field Theory and Interdisciplinarity" for the evolution of this idea.
186. Berque, "Quelques perspectives d'une sociologie de la décolonisation," 40; Berque, "Vie sociale et variations de mode et de densité," *L'homme et la société* 11 (1966): 146–58, 158.
187. Berque, "Cent vingt-cinq ans," 317–18.
188. Berque, "Cent vingt-cinq ans," 312.
189. Sacriste, *Germaine Tillion*, treats Berque, Bourdieu, and Servier under the heading "ethnologists."
190. Berque, "The North of Africa," *International Social Science Journal* 13, no. 2 (1961): 177–96, 190; Berque, "Sciences sociales et décolonisation," 3.
191. Berque, *Langages arabes du present* (Paris: Gallimard, 1974).

192. Berque, *Mémoires*, 97; *Le Coran*, trans. Jacques Berque (Paris: Sindbad, 1990); Berque, *Relire le Coran* (Paris: Albin Michel, 1993); Berque and Bousquet, *Recueil*.

193. Berque in "Un entretien entre Jacques Berque, Jean Duvignaud et Kateb Yacine sur Les mystères du polygone étoilé," *Afrique-Action* 37 (June 26, 1961): 30–31.

194. Said, *Orientalism*, 327.

195. Berque, *Ulémas, fondateurs, insurgés du Maghreb: XVIIe siècle* (Paris: Sindbad, 1982).

196. Berque, *Ulémas, fondateurs, insurgés*, 232.

197. Berque, *Ulémas, fondateurs, insurgés*, 235.

198. Berque, *Ulémas, fondateurs, insurgés*, 233. Berque explicitly contrasted his approach with that of Évariste Lévi-Provençal, whose "magisterial" book on the same period focused on historian-"courtesans" of the sharif. See Lévi-Provençal, *Les historiens des Chorfa. Essai sur la littérature historique et biographique au Maroc du XVIe au XXe siècle* (Paris: E. Larose, 1922).

199. Berque, "Les Muhâdarât d'Al-Yousi. Problèmes de la culture marocaine au XVIIe siècle" (Thèse complémentaire, University of Paris, 1954); Berque, *Al-Yousi: problèmes de la culture marocaine au XVIIe siècle* (Paris: Mouton, 1958).

200. Kenneth L. Honerkamp, "Al-Hassan ibn Mas'ud al-Yus," in *Essays in Arabic Literary Biography*, ed. Roger M. A. Allen, Joseph E. Lowry, Terri DeYoung, and Devin J. Stewart, vol. 2 (Wiesbaden: Otto Harrassowitz Verlag, 2009), 410–28, 416. Berque's *Al Yousi* was the theoretical base for Geertz's *Islam Observed*, according to Whidden, "Jacques Berque."

201. See Berque's sympathetic comments on the "childhood in the poor section of Alger" of Albert Camus, a "son of no one" (*fils de personne*) and, like Berque, a "neo-Latin immigrant." Berque, "Introduction," in *Une cause jamais perdue: articles politiques (1947–1995)* (Paris: Albin Michel, 1998), 12–13.

202. Berque, *Il reste un avenir*, 10, 19.

203. Berque, *The Arabs*, 79.

204. Berque, *Mémoires*, 238. Berque's first wife, Lucie (Lissac) Berque, was with him in Morocco and Egypt and made the drawings for his books *Structures sociales du Haut-Atlas* and *Histoire sociale d'un village égyptien*.

Chapter Thirteen: Georges Balandier: A Dynamic Sociology of Colonialism and Anticolonialism

1. Original: "Alors Balandier vint." Emmanuel Terray, "Présentation," in *Afrique plurielle, afrique actuelle: hommage à Georges Balandier*, ed. Pierre Bonnafé (Paris: Éditions Karthala, 1986), 9–11, 10.

2. Gabriel Gosselin, "Avant-propos," in *Les nouveaux enjeux de l'anthropologie: autour de Georges Balandier*, ed. Gabriel Gosselin (Paris: L'Harmattan, 1993), 11–14, 11.

3. Balandier, "Les débats," in "L'Éveil de l'Afrique noire: Trois conférences-débats," Supplement to *Preuves*, no. 88 (June 1958): 27–32, 27–28.

4. Balandier, *Tous comptes faits* (Paris: Éditions du Pavois, 1947), 82; Marie-Ève Humery-Dieng, "BALANDIER Georges, Léon, Émile," Le Maitron website, https://maitron.fr/spip.php?article15525, notice.

5. Balandier, *Tous comptes faits*, 49.

6. Balandier, *Tous comptes faits*, 37.

7. Balandier, *Tous comptes faits*, 85.

8. Balandier, *Tous comptes faits*, 110.

9. Balandier, *Histoire d'autres* (Paris: Stock, 1977), 49.

10. Balandier, *Tous comptes faits*, 154.

11. Balandier, *Tous comptes faits*, 155.

12. Balandier, *Tous comptes faits*, 128–53; Balandier, *Lettres sur la poésie* (Paris: les Cahiers littéraires, 1943), 246; Nadège Mézié, "*Tous comptes faits*. Roman de (la) jeunesse de Georges Balandier," *L'homme & la société* 207, no. 2 (2018): 243–52, 246.

13. Balandier, *Conjugaisons* (Paris: Fayard, 1997), 197.

14. Balandier, *Conjugaisons*, 195–224; Balandier, *Le dépaysement contemporain. L'immédiat et l'essentiel. Entretiens avec Joël Birman et Claudine Haroche* (Paris: PUF, 2009), 16–17; Balandier, *Tous comptes faits*, 176–77.

15. Nadège Mézié, "'Attention au départ. Prêt.' Le jeune Balandier par lui-même," *Cargo: revue internationale d'anthropologie culturelle & sociale*, nos. 6–7 (2017): 189–201, 194–95.

16. Balandier, *Conjugaisons*, 231. The title can be translated as "On Balance," "Summing Up," or "All Things Considered."

17. George Steinmetz, "Begriffsbeben. Von der Geschichte der Wissenschaft zur historischen Soziologie der Sozialwissenschaften," *Mittelweg 36* (June 2020): 94–115.

18. Balandier, *Autour de Georges Balandier* (Paris: Fondation d'Hautvillers pour le dialogue des cultures, 1981), 25.

19. Balandier, "Recherches de convergences entre psychologie, sociologie et ethnologie," *Les Études philosophiques* n.s. 3, nos. 3–4 (1948): 281–92; George Steinmetz, "From Sociology to Socioanalysis: Rethinking Bourdieu's Concepts of Habitus, Modern Symbolic Capital, and Field along Psychoanalytic Lines," in *The Unhappy Divorce of Sociology and Psychoanalysis: Diverse Perspectives on the Psychosocial*, ed. Lynn Chancer and John Andrews (London: Palgrave Macmillan, 2014), 205–21.

20. For Balandier's differentiation between intellectuals, creative researchers, and applied researchers, see his comments in *Le dépaysement contemporain*, 128, 158.

21. Balandier, "Ancrages pour la mémoire," in *Civilisés, dit-on* (Paris: PUF, 2003), 17–40, 25; Balandier, *Autour de Georges Balandier*, 11.

22. Nadeau was the editor of the literature section of the Resistance journal *Combat* and author of *The History of Surrealism* (New York: Macmillan, [1945] 1965). On Nadeau's work at Le Pavois, where his "editorial career started," see Maurice Nadeau, *Le chemin de la vie* (Paris: France culture, 2011), 98; Olivier Bessard-Banquy, *L'édition littéraire aujourd'hui* (Bordeaux: Presses universitaires de Bordeaux, 2006), 69. A current French journal of literature and art is called *En attendant Nadeau* (*Waiting for Nadeau*).

23. Balandier, *Autour de Georges Balandier*, 11.

24. "Je dois me vouloir neuf, sans réliquat de mes erreurs passés, seul avec ma chance. Alors je tire un trait, j'additionne et je pose zero." Balandier, *Tous comptes faits*, 236.

25. Balandier cited Hegel as early as 1948 and Kojève in 1952, and he was well versed in Sartre's writings.

26. Jean Copans, *Georges Balandier. Un anthropologue en première ligne* (Paris: PUF, 2014), 72; Bernard Mouralis, "Georges Balandier et la littérature," *Présence africaine* 194, no. 2 (2016): 157–73, 158, 169; Balandier, "Littérature de l'Afrique et des Amériques noires," in *Histoires des littératures*, ed. Raymond Queneau, vol. 1 (Paris: Gallimard, 1956), 1536–67.

27. Balandier's "autobiographical" books, in addition to *Tous comptes faits*, are *Afrique ambiguë* (Paris: Plon, 1957); *Histoire d'autres*, *Conjugaisons*, *Civilisés, dit-on*, and *Carnaval des apparences* (Paris: Fayard, 2012).

28. Balandier, *Civilisés, dit-on*, 25.

29. Balandier, *Civilsés, dit-on*, 25, 43; Balandier, "Tout parcours scientifique comporte des moments autobiographiques," *Actes de la recherche en sciences sociales* 185 (December 2010): 44–61, 48; Balandier, *Autour de Georges Balandier*, 11; Balandier, *Conjugaisons*, 231.

30. This quote from Rousseau is included in the untitled foreword to the first (1934) edition of *L'Afrique fantôme* and in the epigraph in the new preface to the 1951 edition.

31. Michel Leiris, "Afterword. The Autobiographer as Torero," in *Manhood* (New York: Grossman, [1939] 1963), 153–64, 158–60.

32. Seán Hand, *Michel Leiris. Writing the Self* (Cambridge: Cambridge University Press, 2002), 51.

33. John Brenkman, "Introduction to Bataille," *New German Critique* 16 (1979): 59–63.

34. Hand, *Michel Leiris*, 86.

35. Leiris, "Afterword. The Autobiographer as Torero," 161.

36. Hand, *Michel Leiris*, 81–82.

37. Seán Hand, "The Orchastration of Man: The Structure of *L'âge d'homme*," *Romance Studies* 4, no. 2 (1986): 78–80, 73.

38. Leiris, *L'âge d'homme, précédé de "De la littérature considérée comme une tauromachie"* (Paris: Gallimard, 1945); quote from "Afterword. The Autobiographer as Torero," 156.

39. Leiris, "Afterword. The Autobiographer as Torero," 164.

40. Leiris, *Manhood*, 148–49.

41. Georges Bataille, "The Psychological Structure of Fascism," in *Visions of Excess. Selected Writings, 1927–1939*, ed. Allan Stoeckl (Minneapolis: University of Minnesota Press, 1985), 137–60.

42. Leiris, *Manhood*, 4–5.

43. Balandier, *Tous comptes faits*, 9.

44. Balandier, *Tous comptes faits*, 10.

45. Balandier, *Tous comptes faits*, 34.

46. Balandier, *Tous comptes faits*, 21, 31, 37, 61, 64, 80. Leiris's narrator expresses "disgust for pregnant women"; Balandier's narrator writes "it's so horrible, a pregnant woman." Leiris, *Manhood*, 5; Balandier, *Tous comptes faits*, 81.

47. Balandier, *Tous comptes faits*, 64, 146–47.

48. Balandier, *Tous comptes faits*, 230.

49. Camus's notebooks, Dec. 1937, quoted in Olivier Todd, *Albert Camus: A Life* (New York: Alfred A. Knopf, 1997), 63.

50. Mouralis, "Georges Balandier et la littérature," 166.

51. Balandier, *Tous comptes faits*, 198.

52. Balandier, *Tous comptes faits*, 2; Julien Blanc, *Au commencement de la résistance: du côté du Musée de l'homme, 1940–1941* (Paris: Seuil, 2010).

53. Balandier, *Conjugaisons*, 215.

54. Seán Hand, "The Orchastration of Man," 80, 69.

55. Balandier, "Ethnologie et psychologie," *Études guinéennes* 1 (1947): 47–56; Balandier, "Recherches de convergences"; Balandier, Review of Mannoni, *Psychologie de la colonisation, Cahiers internationaux de sociologie* 9 (1950): 183–86; Balandier, "L'homme et ses coordonées. Des manières de s'en prendre à l'être social," *Cahiers du sud* 39, no. 314 (1952): 151–56.

56. Michel Leiris, *Scratches [Biffures]* (New York: Paragon House, 1991), 29; Balandier, *Tous comptes faits*, 82.

57. Leiris, "The Ethnographer Faced with Colonialism," in Leiris, *Brisées = Broken Branches* (San Francisco, CA: North Point, 1989), 112–31, 124, 127.

58. Albert Camus, *The Myth of Sisyphus* (New York: Vintage Books, [1942] 1983), 55; see also Camus, *The Rebel* (New York: Vintage Books, 1956).

59. David Carroll, "Foreword," in *Camus at Combat: Writing 1944–1947* (Princeton, NJ: Princeton University Press, 2006), vii–xxvi, xvii–xix.

60. Camus, *The Rebel*, 80.

61. Balandier, *Tous comptes faits*, 231.
62. Balandier, *Tous comptes faits*, 236.
63. Balandier, *Tous comptes faits*, 233.
64. Balandier, *Autour de Georges Balandier*, 12.
65. Balandier, *Tous comptes faits*, 236.
66. Balandier, "Note sur l'exploitation du sel par les vielles femmes de Bargny (environs de Rufisque)," *Notes africaines* 32 (1946): 22.
67. Balandier, "Observations sur la patrimonie et l'héritage chez les Lébou Bargny," *Notes africaines* 32 (1946): 18–19.
68. Balandier, "L'Afrique: ma veritable Sorbonne. Entretien avec Georges Balandier. Propos recueillis par Romuald-Blaise Fonkoua," *Notre librarie: Revue des littératures du Sud* 153 (2004): 80–86, 81.
69. Balandier, *Le dépaysement contemporain*, 20; Balandier, "Erreurs noires," *Présence africaine* 3 (1948): 393–404, 398–99.
70. Balandier, *Conjugaisons*, 234.
71. Alioune Diop, "Niam N'goura, or *Présence africaine*'s raison d'être," *Présence africaine* 1, no. 1 (1947): 185–92, 185.
72. Balandier, *Le Dépaysement contemporain*, 24.
73. Balandier, "Le noir est un homme," *Présence africaine* 1 (Nov.–Dec. 1947): 31–36, 31. Of course, Balandier is painting with a very broad brush. The European depiction of colonized populations as "noble savages" reached back at least to the early eighteenth century; see George Steinmetz, *The Devil's Handwriting: Precoloniality and the German Colonial State in Qingdao, Samoa, and Southwest Africa* (Chicago: University of Chicago Press, 2007). French Africanists did not converge around an *indigenophile* posture until the 1940s, however, according to Africanist Jean-Pierre Dozon, "Georges Balandier dans l'histoire et l'épistémè de l'africanisme," *Recherches sociologiques* 33, no. 2 (2002): 21–29, 24.
74. Balandier, "Le noir est un homme," 33, 36.
75. Balandier, "Le noir est un homme," 33.
76. Balandier, "Review of *Cahier d'un retour au pays natal*," *Présence africaine* 1 (1947): 177–78, 177.
77. Balandier, "Erreurs noires," 393.
78. Balandier, "Erreurs noires," 394.
79. Balandier, "Erreurs noires," 398–400.
80. Balandier, "Erreurs noires," 404; Balandier, *Ambiguous Africa* (London: Chatto & Windus, [1957] 1966), 230.
81. Balandier, *Histoire d'autres*, 53; Georges Balandier and Paul Mercier, *Particularisme et évolution. Les pêcheurs Lébou du Sénégal* (Saint Louis, Sénégal: IFAN, 1952).
82. Balandier and Mercier, *Particularisme et évolution*, vii.
83. Balandier, "La situation coloniale: ancien concept, nouvelle réalité," *French Politics, Culture, and Society* 20, no. 2 (2002): 4–10, 6, summarizing his earlier research with Mercier.
84. Balandier, *Sociologie actuelle de l'Afrique noire* (Paris: PUF, 1955), 8.
85. Michel Leiris, "Antilles et poésie des carrefours" in *Zébrage* (Paris: Gallimard, 1992), 67–87.
86. Balandier and Mercier, *Particularisme et évolution*, 212.
87. Balandier and Mercier, *Particularisme et évolution*, 213.
88. Balandier and Mercier, *Particularisme et évolution*, 131.
89. Balandier and Mercier, *Particularisme et évolution*, 132.
90. Balandier and Mercier, *Particularisme et évolution*, 109.
91. Balandier and Mercier, *Particularisme et évolution*, 10.

92. Balandier and Mercier, *Particularisme et évolution*, 119.
93. Balandier and Mercier, *Particularisme et évolution*, 25, 26, 149.
94. Balandier and Mercier, *Particularisme et évolution*, 132.
95. Balandier, *Ambiguous Africa*, 19; Balandier and Mercier, *Particularisme et évolution*, 26, 27.
96. Balandier, *Ambiguous Africa*, 19.
97. Balandier, *Ambiguous Africa*, 25.
98. Balandier and Paul Mercier, *Particularisme et évolution*, 212
99. Balandier and Paul Mercier, *Particularisme et évolution*, 131.
100. Balandier and Paul Mercier, *Particularisme et évolution*, 212, 150.
101. Balandier and Paul Mercier, *Particularisme et évolution*, 149.
102. Balandier and Paul Mercier, *Particularisme et évolution*, 26, 149.
103. Balandier, "Évolution de la société et de l'homme," in *Afrique équatoriale française*, ed. Eugène Léonard Guernier (Paris: Encyclopédie Coloniale et Maritime, 1950), 125–32, 125.
104. Balandier, *Conjugaisons*, 25.
105. For example, see André Mary, "Ethnographie de soi sous le 'zéro equatorial.' Le chantier autobiographique de Georges Balandier," *L'homme* 221 (2017): 11–40, 29–30.
106. Balandier, *Sens et puissance* (Paris: PUF, 1971), 13.
107. Balandier, "Tout parcours scientifique," 53. See also Balandier, "Prèmiers essais d'organisation du Fouta-Djallon," in *Fonds Georges Balandier*, folder "Notes de travail, 1947–1959. AOF/AEF."
108. Gregory Mann, "Anti-Colonialism and Social Science: Georges Balandier, Madeira Keita, and 'the Colonial Situation' in French Africa," *Comparative Studies in Society and History* 55, no. 1 (2013): 92–119.
109. "Notes de travail, 1947–1959. AOF/AEF," folder "Exploitation aurifère de Diedeugeu par les indigènes du pays et les Cercles voisins," in *Fonds Georges Balandier*.
110. Balandier, "L'or de la Guinée française," *Présence africaine* 4 (1948): 539–48; Balandier, *Ambiguous Africa*, 65.
111. Balandier, *Ambiguous Africa*, 67.
112. Balandier, "Problématique des classes sociales en Afrique noire," *Cahiers internationaux de sociologie* 38 (1965): 131–42.
113. "Notes de travail, 1947–1959. AOF/AEF," in *Fonds Georges Balandier*. This village plan does not seem to have been implemented.
114. Balandier, "Le noir est un homme," 33. Balandier told me about his pith helmet during our interview at his Paris apartment, Feb. 11, 2015.
115. Balandier, "Les *Études Guinéennes*," *Études Guinéennes* 1 (1947): 5–6, 5. Permission: Bibliothèque nationale.
116. Balandier, "Les *Études Guinéennes*," 6.
117. Jean Jamin, "Introduction," in Michel Leiris, *Miroir de l'Afrique* (Paris: Gallimard, 1996), 9–59.
118. Balandier, "Recherches de convergences."
119. Balandier, *Ambiguous Africa*, 239; Balandier, "Ce que j'ai appris de l'Afrique," in *Civilisés, dit-on*, 101–15, 104.
120. Balandier, "Tout parcours scientifique," 53; *Conjugaisons*, 260.
121. Balandier, interview, Feb. 9, 2007, Maison des sciences de l'homme, Paris.
122. Balandier, "Tout parcours scientifique," 53.
123. See folder on Institut d'études centrafricaines in *Fonds Georges Balandier*.
124. Balandier, "Recommendations pour l'étude historique des sociétés d'Afrique noire," 3. Original in Fonds Marcel Soret.

125. Yvon Mersadier, "Budgets familiaux africains. Étude chez 136 familles de salariés dans trois centres urbains de Sénégal," *Etudes sénégalaises* 7 (1957): 1–102; Georges Balandier, "Social Implications of Technical Advance in Underdeveloped Countries," *Current Sociology* 3 (1954): 41–46.

126. Balandier, "La situation coloniale: approche théorique," *Cahiers internationaux de sociologie* 11 (1951): 44–79; Natacha Gagné and Marie Salaün, "L'effacement du 'colonial' ou 'seulement de ses formes les plus apparentes'? Penser le contemporain grâce à la notion de situation coloniale chez Georges Balandier," *Cargo: revue internationale d'anthropologie culturelle & sociale* 6–7 (2017): 219–37.

127. Balandier, "La situation coloniale: ancien concept," 4.

128. Balandier, text of interview, Feb. 9, 2007, Maison des sciences de l'homme, Paris.

129. Balandier, "The Colonial Situation: A Theoretical Approach," in *Social Change. The Colonial Situation*, ed. Immanuel Wallerstein (New York: Wiley & Sons, 1966), 34–61, 47. All quotes are from this translation.

130. Balandier, "Aspects de l'évolution sociale chez les Fang du Gabon (Afrique Équatoriale française)," *Cahiers internationaux de sociologie* 9 (1950): 76–106.

131. Balandier, "The Colonial Situation," 56.

132. Balandier, interview, Feb. 9, 2007, Maison des sciences de l'homme, Paris.

133. Bronislaw Malinowski, *Dynamics of Culture Change* (New Haven, CT: Yale University Press, 1945); Max Gluckman, "Analysis of a Social Situation in Modern Zululand," *Bantu Studies* 14, no. 1 (1940): 1–30 and 14, no. 2 (1940): 147–74; Octave Mannoni, *Prospero and Caliban: The Psychology of Colonization* (Ann Arbor: University of Michigan Press, [1950] 1990); Isabelle Merle, "'La situation coloniale' chez Georges Balandier. Relecture historienne," *Monde(s)* 4 (2013): 212–32.

134. Balandier, "The Colonial Situation," 34; Eugène Enriquez, "De la sociologie coloniale à la sociologie de la colonisation et des pays sous-développés: l'œuvre de Georges Balandier," *Critique* 134 (1958): 641–51, 645.

135. Balandier, "The Colonial Situation," 39, 52.

136. Balandier, "The Colonial Situation," 37; Mercier, "Comte rendu, *Sociologie actuelle de l'Afrique noire*," *Cahiers internationaux de sociologie* 19 (1955): 171–73, 172.

137. Balandier, "The Colonial Situation," 48.

138. Balandier, "L'Afrique: ma veritable Sorbonne," 82.

139. Catherine Coquery-Vidrovitch, "Anthropologie politique et histoire de l'Afrique noire," *Annales ESC* 24, no. 1 (1969): 142–63, 144.

140. Balandier, interview, Feb. 9. 2007, Maison des sciences de l'homme, Paris.

141. Balandier, "The Colonial Situation," 36–37.

142. Balandier, "The Colonial Situation," 35.

143. Balandier, "The Colonial Situation," 53, 55. Of course, this was not true to the same degree of Brazilian and North American anthropologists, or of the British social anthropologists Fortes and Gluckman and their students.

144. Gérald Gaillard, "Georges Balandier," *Journal des anthropologues* 148–149 (2017): 9–24, 14.

145. Balandier, "The Fact of Colonialism: A Theoretical Approach," *Cross Currents* 2, no. 4 (1952): 10–31.

146. Balandier, "Contribution à une sociologie de la dépendance," *Cahiers internationaux de sociologie* 12 (1952): 47–69.

147. Gilles Sautter, *De l'Atlantique au fleuve Congo: une géographie du sous-peuplement*, vol. 1 (Paris: Mouton, 1966), 9; (my emphasis).

148. Catherine Coquery-Vidrovitch, *Le Congo au temps des grandes compagnies concessionnaires: 1889–1930*, vol. 2 (Paris: EHESS, 2001); Gilles Sautter, *De l'Atlantique au*

fleuve Congo, vol. 2, 102–22; Christopher J. Gray, *Colonial Rule and Crisis in Equatorial Africa: Southern Gabon, c. 1850–1940* (Rochester, NY: University of Rochester Press, 2002), 170–90; Pierre Philippe Rey, "Sociologie économique et politique des Kuni, Punu et Tsangui de la région de Mossendjo et de la Boucle du Niari (Congo-Brazzaville)" (PhD diss., University of Paris, 1969), 426, 516.

149. Dennis D. Cordell, "Extracting People from Precapitalist Production: French Equatorial Africa from the 1890s to 1930s," in *African Population and Capitalism: Historical Perspectives*, ed. Dennis D. Cordell and Joel W. Gregory (Boulder, CO: Westview, 1987), 137–52.

150. Report by colonial official Alain Maclatchy, quoted in Gray, *Colonial Rule*, 179; also in Georges Balandier and Jean-Claude Pauvert, *Mission d'étude du regroupement des villages (territoires du Gabon)* (Paris: ORSOM, 1950), 26.

151. Gilles Sautter, "Les Paysans du Gabon Septentrional. Essai sur le peuplement et l'habitat du Woleu-N'Tem," *Les cahiers d'outre-mer* 4, no. 14 (1951): 119–59, 143; Gray, *Colonial Rule*, 176; Pourtier, *Le Gabon*, vol. 2, 102, especially maps on pp. 116–17 showing the increasing concentration of Gabonese population along the main routes.

152. Balandier, "Naissance d'un mouvement politico-religieux chez les 'Ba-Kongo' du Moyen-Congo," in *Proceedings of the Third International West African Conference held at Ibadan, Nigeria, 12th to 21st December 1949* (Lagos: Nigerian Museum, 1956), 324–336, 331.

153. Pourtier, *Le Gabon*, vol. 2, 106.

154. Balandier and Jean-Claude Pauvert, *Les villages gabonais* (Brazzaville: Institut d'études centrafricaines, 1952), 12.

155. Balandier, *Histoire d'autres*, 67. As the French Overseas Minister from June 1958 to January 1959, Cornut-Gentille was "the last to manage the colonies" and "the first to organize their liberation." Balandier, *Conjugaisons*, 364.

156. Notebook "Tournée du Gabon, Jan, Fév, Mars 1949". NAF 28671, Balandier papers, Bibliothèque nationale.

157. Jean-Hilaire Aubame, *Programme de regroupement des villages* (Brazzaville: Imprimérie officiel, 1947).

158. Balandier, *The Sociology of Black Africa. Social Dynamics in Central Africa* (New York: Praeger, 1970), 255; Balandier and Pauvert, *Mission d'étude du regroupement*, 68.

159. Balandier, *The Sociology of Black Africa*, 255.

160. André Hauser, "Note bibliographique," *Bulletin de l'I.F.A.N.*, Série B, Sciences humaines, vol. 16, nos. 1–2 (1954): 218–22, 220; Balandier made the same point in "Aspects de l'évolution sociale chez les Fang."

161. Balandier, *The Sociology of Black Africa*, 245.

162. Gilles Sautter's 2-volume *De l'Atlantique* (op cit.) was subtitled "a geography of underpopulation."

163. Balandier and Jean-Claude Pauvert, *Les villages gabonais*, 9, 9 n. 1, 81–82.

164. Benoît de l'Estoile misleadingly suggests that Balandier continued to support the original regrouping project by mingling quotes from the 1950 and 1952 reports by Balandier and Pauvert. Benoît de l'Estoile, "Enquêter en 'situation coloniale.' Politique de la population, gouvernementalité modernisatrice and et 'sociologie engagée' en Afrique française," *Cahiers d'études africaines* 228 (2017): 863–919.

165. Florence Bernault, *Démocraties ambiguës en Afrique centrale: Congo-Brazzaville, Gabon, 1940–1965* (Paris: Karthala, 1996), 111–14.

166. Balandier, interview, Feb. 11, 2015, Paris.

167. Balandier and Pauvert, *Mission d'étude*, 98.

168. Edward Said, *Orientalism: Western Conceptions of the Orient* (New York: Pantheon Books, 1978), 96. Said, of course, recognized several Islamicists, including Berque,

NOTES TO CHAPTER THIRTEEN [481]

who "supercede[d] the political restraints operating impersonally through tradition and through the national ambience." Ibid., 271.

169. ORSTOM, *Rapport d'activité 1965*, 135; *1966*, 112; *1967*, 144.

170. Balandier, *Histoire d'autres*, 89.

171. Gregory Mann, *From Empires to NGOs in the West African Sahel: The Road to Nongovernmentality* (New York: Cambridge University Press, 2015), 27.

172. Balandier, *Political Anthropology* (New York: Vintage, [1967] 1970), 165.

173. Balandier, "Le développement industriel de la prolétarisation en Afrique noire," *L'Afrique et L'Asie* 4, no. 20 (1952): 45–53, 46.

174. Balandier, *The Sociology of Black Africa*, 167.

175. According to Fernandez, while "Fang preserved . . . a lively sense of superiority to the peoples upon whom they intruded, . . . military pride, as [Balandier's] term 'conquerants' suggests, was only a part of this ethnocentrism. The Fang were aggressive, but not truly warlike." James W. Fernandez, *Bwiti: An Ethnography of the Religious Imagination in Africa* (Princeton, NJ: Princeton University Press, 1982), 51–52. Many of Fernandez's formulations here and in his earlier articles on the Bwiti are identical to Balandier's, yet Fernandez only cites Balandier concerning minor empirical points. This contrasts with French specialists such as René Bureau, Otto Gollnhoffer, and Roger Sillans, all of whom recognize Balandier's pioneering importance. Cf. René Bureau, *Bokayé! Essai sur le Bwiti Fang du Gabon* (Paris: L'Harmattan, 1996); Otto Gollnhofer and Roger Sillans, *La mémoire d'un peuple: ethno-histoire des Mitsogho, ethnie du Gabon central* (Paris: Présence africaine, 1997). In his 1997 book, Bureau uses evidence from Balandier's 1950s writings to criticize Fernandez's account; see Bureau, *Bokayé!*, 30.

176. Balandier, *The Sociology of Black Africa*, 16.

177. Balandier, *The Sociology of Black Africa*, 68–69.

178. Balandier, *The Sociology of Black Africa*, 142.

179. Balandier, *The Sociology of Black Africa*, 143.

180. Balandier, *The Sociology of Black Africa*, 144.

181. Balandier, *The Sociology of Black Africa*, 147.

182. Balandier, *The Sociology of Black Africa*, 205.

183. Balandier, *The Sociology of Black Africa*, 208.

184. Balandier, "Rapport préliminaire de la mission d'information scientifique en pays Fang (24 jan.–20 mars 1949)" (Brazzaville: IEC, 1949), 14; on the Franciscans' barbaric treatment of Mayas who resisted Christianization, see Inga Clendinnen, *Ambivalent Conquests: Maya and Spaniard in Yucatan, 1517-1570* (New York: Cambridge University Press, 2003).

185. Balandier, "Les conditions sociologiques de l'art noir," *Présence africaine* 10–11 (1951): 58–71, 67.

186. Balandier, "Contribution à une sociologie de la dépendance," 66.

187. Balandier, *Civilsés, dit-on*, 48.

188. Balandier, *The Sociology of Black Africa*, 410.

189. Balandier, *Civilsés, dit-on*, 81.

190. Balandier, *The Sociology of Black Africa*, 471.

191. Balandier uses this phrase in *The Sociology of Black Africa*, 433; and in *Ambiguous Africa*, 219.

192. Balandier, "Contribution à une sociologie de la dépendance," 63.

193. Fernandez, *Bwiti*, 30.

194. Fernandez, *Bwiti*, 44.

195. J. W. Fernandez, "The Idea and Symbol of the Saviour in a Gabon Syncretist Cult," *International Review of Missions* 53, no. 211 (1964): 281–89, 281.

196. Balandier, "Rapport préliminaire de la mission d'information scientifique en pays Fang (24 jan.–20 mars 1949)," presentation to Groupe de sociologie industrielle at the Centre d'études sociologiques (Brazzaville: IEC, 1952), 42.

197. Balandier, *The Sociology of Black Africa*, 373; Orlando Patterson, *Slavery and Social Death: A Comparative Study* (Cambridge, MA: Harvard University Press, 1982).

198. Balandier, *The Sociology of Black Africa*, 231.

199. Balandier, "Aspects de l'évolution sociale chez les Fang," 102–03; Balandier, *The Sociology of Black Africa*, 500; Paul Mercier, "Comte rendu, *Sociologie actuelle de l'Afrique noire*," 172.

200. Balandier, *The Sociology of Black Africa*, 84.

201. Balandier, *The Sociology of Black Africa*, 275.

202. Balandier, *The Sociology of Black Africa*, 102, 233, 255.

203. Balandier, *The Sociology of Black Africa*, 57–66; John K. Thornton, *The Kingdom of Kongo: Civil War and Transition, 1641-1718* (Madison: University of Wisconsin Press, 1983); Anne Hilton, *The Kingdom of Kongo* (Oxford: Oxford University Press, 1985).

204. Balandier, "Sociological Survey of the African Town at Brazzaville," in Daryll Forde, ed., *Social Implications of Industrialization and Urbanization in Africa South of the Sahara* (Paris: UNESCO, 1956), 106–08, 106.

205. Balandier's summary in *Political Anthropology*, 166.

206. *Ambiguous Africa*, 221.

207. Balandier, *The Sociology of Black Africa*, 320.

208. Balandier, *The Sociology of Black Africa*, 386.

209. Balandier, *The Sociology of Black Africa*, 322.

210. Balandier, *The Sociology of Black Africa*, 340.

211. Balandier, *The Sociology of Black Africa*, 379.

212. Balandier, *The Sociology of Black Africa*, 376.

213. Balandier, *The Sociology of Black Africa*, 382–84.

214. Balandier, "Naissance d'un mouvement politico-religieux," 329.

215. J. W. Fernandez, "African Religious Movements, Types and Dynamics," *Journal of Modern African Studies* 2, no. 4 (1964): 428–46, 543.

216. Fernandez, "African Religious Movements," 544.

217. Virginia Thompson and Richard Adloff, *The Emerging States of French Equatorial Africa* (Stanford, CA: Stanford University Press, 1960), 482.

218. Balandier, *The Sociology of Black Africa*, 443.

219. Balandier, *The Sociology of Black Africa*, 56, 8, 22.

220. Balandier, *The Sociology of Black Africa*, 53.

221. Raymond F. Betts, "Dakar: Ville impériale (1857–1960)," in *Colonial Cities*, ed. Robert J. Ross and Gerard J. Telkamp (Boston: Kluwer, 1985), 193–206, 193.

222. Liora Bigon, *French Colonial Dakar: The Morphogenesis of an African Regional Capital* (Manchester: Manchester University Press, 2016), 7. The other Senegalese towns whose inhabitants had full French citizenship were Saint-Louis, Gorée, and Rufisque.

223. Jean Dresch, "Villes congolaises," *Revue de géographie humaine et d'ethnologie* 3 (1948): 3–24, 5.

224. Anthony D. King, *Colonial Urban Development: Culture, Social Power, and Environment* (London: Routledge & Paul, 1976) and Trutz von Trotha, *Koloniale Herrschaft. Zur soziologischen Theorie der Staatsentstehung am Beispiel des 'Schutzgebietes Togo'* (Tübingen: Mohr, 1994).

225. Balandier, *Sociologie des Brazzavilles noires* (Paris: A. Colin, 1985), 116. All references are to this second edition unless otherwise stated.

226. Balandier, *Sociologie des Brazzavilles noires* (Paris: A. Colin, [1955] 1985), 205.

227. Dresch, "Villes congolaises," 10.
228. Balandier, *Sociologie des Brazzavilles*, x.
229. Balandier, *Sociologie des Brazzavilles*, 179.
230. Balandier, *Sociologie des Brazzavilles*, 102.
231. Balandier, *Sociologie des Brazzavilles*, xii.
232. Balandier, *Sociologie des Brazzavilles*, xii; see Dresch, "Villes congolaises."
233. Balandier, *The Sociology of Black Africa*, 349, 361.
234. Balandier, *The Sociology of Black Africa*, 362–63, 365.
235. Balandier, *The Sociology of Black Africa*, 368.
236. Balandier, *The Sociology of Black Africa*, 115.
237. Balandier, "Sociological Survey of the African Town," 106.
238. Balandier, *The Sociology of Black Africa*, 118.
239. Balandier, *Sociologie des Brazzavilles*, 116; Balandier, "La situation coloniale: ancien concept," 8.
240. Balandier, *Sociologie des Brazzavilles*, xvi.
241. Balandier, *Sociologie des Brazzavilles*, 176.
242. Balandier, *Sociologie des Brazzavilles*, xiii.
243. Balandier, *Sociologie des Brazzavilles*, 104.
244. Balandier, *Sociologie des Brazzavilles*, x.
245. Balandier, *Sociologie des Brazzavilles*, xiv, 56.
246. Balandier, *Sociologie des Brazzavilles*, 76, 262.
247. Balandier, *Sociologie des Brazzavilles*, 132.
248. Mary-Clotilde Jacquey, "Entretien avec Georges Balandier," *Notre librarie: Revue des littératures du Sud* 35–36 (1977): 71–93, 79–80.
249. Balandier, *Autour de Georges Balandier*, 20.
250. Balandier, "Approche sociologique des Brazzavilles noires," *Africa* 22. no. 1 (1952): 23–34.
251. Balandier, *Ambiguous Africa*, 6.
252. Jean Malaurie, *Terre humaine: cinquante ans d'une collection: entretien avec Jean Malaurie* (Paris: Bibliothèque nationale de France, 2005).
253. Jean Malaurie, *Terre humaine*, 113, 46.
254. Balandier, *Civilisés, dit-on*, 61.
255. Lévi-Strauss, Review of Balandier, *Sociologie des Brazzavilles noires*, *Revue française de science politique* 6, no. 1 (1956): 177–79.
256. Jean-Pierre Dozon, "Georges Balandier et la reconstruction d'après-guerre de la sociologie française," *Cahiers d'études africaines* 228 (2017): 811–18, 813.
257. Lévi-Strauss, *The Savage Mind* (Chicago: University of Chicago Press, [1962] 1966), 234–35, note.
258. Éloi Ficquet and Benoit Hazard, "Lignes de force et traits de fuite d'un père fondateur," *Cahiers d'études africaines* 228 (2017): 795–807, 798; Suzanne Chazan-Gillig, "Lecture alternative à propos de l'ouvrage de Jean Copans: *Georges Balandier, un anthropologue en première ligne*," *Journal des anthropologues* 140–141 (2015): 319–35, 327; Roland Colin, "Georges Balandier, socio-anthropologue du monde en mutation, et la traversée du miroir des réalités sociales et culturelles," *Présence africaine* 194, no. 2 (2016): 125–30, 128.
259. Balandier, *Conjugaisons*, 321.
260. Claude Lévi-Strauss and Didier Eribon, *Conversations with Claude Lévi-Strauss* (Chicago: University of Chicago Press, 1991), 57.
261. Lévi-Strauss, *Tristes tropiques* (New York: Penguin Books, [1955] 1992), 154–55, 173.
262. Lévi-Strauss, *Tristes tropiques*, 154, 215, 391.

263. Grażyna Kubica, "Lévi-Strauss as a Protagonist in his Ethnographic Prose: A Cosmopolitan View of *Tristes tropiques* and its Contemporary Interpretations," *Etnográfica* 18, no. 3 (2014): 599–624, 618.

264. Lévi-Strauss, *Tristes tropiques*, 17, 414.

265. A more traditional ethnographer, Claude Tardits, privately condemned *Afrique ambiguë* precisely for Balandier's preferred methodology of "traveling" rather than stationary fieldwork. Tardits writes, "J'ai lu le Balandier. Ceci est strictement entre nous: ce travelling n'est pas bon du tout" (I have read Balandier. This is strictly between us: this "travelling" is no good at all). Claude Tardits to Eric de Dampierre, October 30, 1957, in Bibliothèque Éric de Dampierre, Dampierre papers, Mission sociologique du Haut Oubangui, folder "Correspondence Générale 1954–1967/1956–1957."

266. Balandier, "Les conditions sociologiques de l'art noir," 60.

267. Balandier, *Afrique ambiguë*, 245–47.

268. Balandier, *Ambiguous Africa*, 124.

269. E.g., Paul Willis, *Common Culture* (Milton Keynes: Open University Press, 1990).

270. Balandier, *Ambiguous Africa*, 111.

271. Balandier, *Ambiguous Africa*, 11.

272. Balandier, *Ambiguous Africa*, 121.

273. Balandier, *Ambiguous Africa*, 127.

274. Lévi-Strauss, *Tristes tropiques*, 49; Emmanuelle Loyer, *Lévi-Strauss: A Biography* (Cambridge, Polity, 2018), 463–64.

275. Lévi-Strauss argues that "human diversity" constitutes inequality, and he connects race to inequality through the mechanism of "a coalition" in which there is "contact and interchange between the major and the minor parties." The euphemistic category of "coalition," examined more closely, includes colonialism. Claude Lévi-Strauss, *Race and History* (Paris: UNESCO, 1952), 47; Kamala Visweswaran, "The Interventions of Culture: Claude Lévi-Strauss, Race, and the Critique of Historical Time," in *Race and Racism in Continental Philosophy*, ed. Robert Bernasconi (Bloomington: Indiana University Press), 227–48, 231.

276. Balandier, *Ambiguous Africa*, 149.

277. Balandier, *Ambiguous Africa*, 208, 210.

278. Balandier, *Ambiguous Africa*, 221–22.

279. Balandier, *Ambiguous Africa*, 150, 153, 155, 159.

280. Balandier, *Ambiguous Africa*, 161.

281. Balandier, *Ambiguous Africa*, 165.

282. Balandier, *Ambiguous Africa*, 89.

283. Balandier, *Ambiguous Africa*, 2, 5.

284. Balandier, *Ambiguous Africa*, 1.

285. Emmanuel Terray, "Georges Balandier (1920–2016)," *L'homme* 221 (2017): 5–10, 7.

286. Fabienne Samson, "Une anthropologie politique du religieux: Sur les traces de Georges Balandier," *Cahiers d'études africaines* 228, no. 4 (2017): 993–1010, 995.

287. Balandier, *Ambiguous Africa*, 264.

288. Balandier, "L'Afrique: ma veritable Sorbonne," 85.

289. Thornton, "The Kingdom of Kongo," 88.

290. Catherine Coquery-Vidrovitch, "Contribution de Georges Balandier à la genèse de l'histoire africaine de langue française," *Cahiers d'études africaines* 228 (2017): 825–32, 826.

291. Copans states Balandier "never became . . . a sociologist of historical or comparative sociology," yet Balandier clearly conducted comparative and historicizing sociology. Jean Copans, "M. Leiris, G. Balandier face à la situation coloniale des sociétés africaines des années 1950," *Revue des sciences sociales* 56 (2016): 1–20, 7.

292. Balandier, *Daily Life*, 136.

293. Balandier, *Daily Life*, 129.
294. Thornton, "The Kingdom of Kongo," 103.
295. Balandier, *Daily Life*, 136; Serge Mboukou, *Messianisme et modernité: Dona Béatrice Kimpa Vita et le mouvement des antoniens* (Paris: Harmattan, 2010).
296. Balandier, *Daily Life*, 263.
297. Balandier, *Daily Life*, 151.
298. Balandier, *Daily Life*, 235.
299. Balandier, *Daily Life*, 236.
300. Balandier, *Daily Life*, 238–39.
301. Balandier, *Daily Life*, 242.
302. George Steinmetz, "Culture and the State," in *State/Culture. Historical Studies of the State in the Social Sciences*, ed. George Steinmetz (Ithaca, NY: Cornell University Press, 1999), 1–49.
303. Balandier, *Political Anthropology*, 24–25.
304. Balandier, *Political Anthropology*, 2.
305. Balandier, *Political Anthropology*, 117.
306. Balandier, *Political Anthropology*, 112.
307. Balandier, *Political Anthropology*, 118.
308. Balandier, *Political Anthropology*, 119.
309. Balandier, *Political Anthropology*, 120.
310. Balandier, *Political Anthropology*, 159–60.
311. Balandier, *Political Anthropology*, 160.
312. Balandier, *Political Anthropology*, 161.
313. Balandier, *Political Anthropology*, 162.
314. Balandier, *Political Anthropology*, 163.
315. Balandier, *Political Anthropology*, 165. The English translation renders this line of argumentation incomprehensible. The reader should consult Balandier, *Anthropologie politique* (Paris: PUF, 1967), 193–94.
316. Enriquez, "De la sociologie coloniale," 651.
317. Balandier, "Ethnologie et psychologie," 52.
318. Balandier, "Problèmes économiques et problèmes politiques au niveau du village Fang," *Bulletin de l'Institut d'études centrafricaines* 1 (1950): 49–64, 64.
319. Balandier, "Sociologie de la colonisation et relations entre societies globales," *Cahiers internationaux de sociologie* 17 (1954): 17–31, 18; Balandier, *Georges Gurvitch, sa vie, son œuvre* (Paris: PUF, 1972).
320. Balandier, "Chronique. La participation de l'AEF à la Conférence internationale des Africanistes de l'Ouest," *Bulletin de l'Institut d'études centrafricaines* 1 (1950): 79–80, 80.
321. Balandier, interview, Feb. 9. 2007, Maison des sciences de l'homme, Paris.
322. Balandier, interview, Feb. 9. 2007, Maison des sciences de l'homme, Paris.
323. Copans, *Georges Balandier*, 278.
324. Balandier had just one major anthropology publication, an overview of French ethnology in the *Yearbook of Anthropology* in 1955.
325. *Une anthropologie des turbulences: Hommage à Georges Balandier*; *Les nouveux enjeux de l'anthropologie: autour de Georges Balandier*; *Comment peut-on être socio-anthropologue: autour de Georges Balandier*.
326. Balandier, *Sens et puissance*, 5.
327. Balandier, interview, Feb. 9, 2007, Maison des sciences de l'homme, Paris.
328. Copans, *Georges Balandier*, 143ff.
329. André Mary, "Ethnographie de soi"; Emmanuel Terray, "Georges Balandier."
330. Balandier, *Gurvitch*, 5.

331. Thornton, *The Kingdom of Kongo*, xix.

332. Cécile Fromont, *The Art of Conversion: Christian Visual Culture in the Kingdom of Kongo* (Chapel Hill: University of North Carolina Press, 2014), 13.

333. Balandier, "Les conditions sociologiques de l'art noir"; Balandier, *Ambiguous Africa*, ch. 4; Balandier, *Political Anthropology*, 24 (criticizing "ethnocentrism" within theory); Balandier, *Civilisés, dit-on*, 264. Froment misattributes a quote to Balandier, without providing any source, according to which the Kongo Kingdom was a case of "failed acculturation"; *The Art of Conversion*, 14. As we have seen, Balandier dedicated a great deal of attention to demolishing and replacing the entire theory of acculturation.

334. Jean-Paul Colleyn, "Georges Balandier, du village lébou au monde global," *Cahiers d'études africaines* 228 (2017): 819–23, 820.

Chapter Fourteen: Pierre Bourdieu: The Creation of Social Theory in the Cauldron of Colonial War

1. Pierre Bourdieu, in Bourdieu and Loïc Wacquant, *An Invitation to Reflexive Sociology* (Chicago: University of Chicago Press, 1992), 213–214.

2. Edward Said, *Freud and the Non-European* (London: Verso, 2003), 26–27.

3. Bourdieu, *Microcosmes: Théorie des champs* (Paris: Raisons d'agir, 2022).

4. For Bourdieu's ranking as the second the most cited book author in the human sciences (after Michel Foucault), see Johan Heilbron, *French Sociology* (Ithaca, NY: Cornell University Press, 2015), 1–2; on Bourdieu as the most cited sociologist in the world, see Philip Korom, "The Prestige Elite in Sociology: Toward a Collective Biography of the Most Cited Scholars (1970–2010)," *Sociological Quarterly*, 61, no. 1 (2020): 128–163; on Bourdieu as the most cited French sociologist in the United States, see Etienne Ollion and Andrew Abbott, "French Connections. The Receptions of French Sociologists in the USA (1970–2012)," *European Journal of Sociology* (August 2016): 331–72.

5. Crucial exceptions are Amín Pérez, "Rendre le social plus politique: Guerre coloniale, immigration et pratiques sociologiques d'Abdelmalek Sayad et de Pierre Bourdieu" (PhD diss., École des hautes études en sciences sociales, 2015); Pérez, *Combattre en sociologues. Abdelmalek Sayad et Pierre Bourdieu dans une guerre de libération coloniale* (Paris: Agone, 2022); Tassadit Yacine, "Presentation," in Bourdieu, *Algerian Sketches* (Cambridge: Polity, 2013), 1–34; Yacine, "Bourdieu et l'Algérie," in Jacques Dubois, Pascal Durand, and Yves Winkin, eds., *Le symbolique et le social: la réception internationale de la pensée de Pierre Bourdieu; actes du colloque de Cerisy-la-Salle (11–19 juillet 2001)* (Liège: Editions de l'Université de Liège, 2005), 33–42; and the essays in *Awal* 27–28 (2003).

6. Michael Grenfell, "Afterword: Reflecting In/On Field Theory in Practice," in *Bourdieu's Field Theory and the Social Sciences*, ed. James Albright, Deborah Hartman, and Jacqueline Widin (Singapore: Palgrave Macmillan, 2018), 269–92, 270.

7. Jeannine Verdès-Leroux, *Deconstructing Pierre Bourdieu: Against Sociological Terrorism from the Left* (New York: Algora, 2001).

8. Dylan Riley, "Bourdieu's Class Theory," *Catalyst* 1, no. 2 (2017): 1070–1136.

9. Didier Lapeyronnie, "Radical Academicism, or the Sociologist's Monologue: Who Are Radical Sociologists Talking With?" *Revue française de sociologie* 47, Supplement: An Annual English Selection (2006): 3–33.

10. Michael Burawoy, "Bourdieu meets Bourdieu," in *Conversations with Bourdieu: The Johannesburg Moment*, ed. Michael Burawoy and Klaus van Holdt (Johannesburg: Wits University Press, 2012), 9–24, 5.

11. Alain Badiou, *Reflections on Anti-Semitism* (London: Verso, 2013), discussing attacks on Bourdieu by Jean-Claude Milner along these lines.

12. For example, Raewyn Connell, "Northern Theory: The Political Geography of General Social Theory," *Theory and Society* 35, no. 2 (2006): 237–64.

13. Atilla Akmut, "Apprentis philosophes des années 1940–1960. Entre beaux-arts et les sciences. Étude précédée et accompagnée d'une histoire sociale des élèves littéraires de l'École normale supérieure (1945–1954) et d'éléments systématiques sur la formation et la trajectoire du sociologue Pierre Bourdieu," Master's thesis, ENS-EHESS, 2011), 324.

14. Yvette Delsaut and Marie-Christine Rivière, *Bibliographie des travaux de Pierre Bourdieu* (Pantin: Le Temps de Cerises, 2002), 192.

15. Pérez, "Rendre le social plus politique," 82.

16. Yves Winkin, "Portait du photographe en jeune anthropologue," in *Le symbolique et le social: la réception internationale de la pensée de Pierre Bourdieu; actes du colloque de Cerisy-la-Salle (11–19 juillet 2001)*, ed. Jacques Dubois, Pascal Durand, and Yves Winkin (Liège: Editions de l'Université de Liège, 2005), 43–52.

17. Yves Courrière, *Le Temps des leopards* (Paris: Fayard, 1974), 385.

18. Pérez, "Rendre le social plus politique," 69.

19. Pérez, "Rendre le social plus politique," 72–73.

20. Alain Accardo, *Engagements. Chroniques et autres textes (2000–2010)* (Paris: Agone, 2011), 68, quoted in Pérez, "Rendre le social plus politique," 90.

21. Bourdieu, *Sketch for a Self-Analysis* (Cambridge: Polity, 2007), 58–59.

22. Bourdieu also switched from Canguilhem to Aron as doctoral advisor, although Bourdieu never completed his thesis.

23. Data from https://www.college-de-france.fr/site/pierre-bourdieu/index.htm; for Bourdieu's annual lectures at the Collège de France, see https://www.college-de-france.fr/site/pierre-bourdieu/Resumes-annuels.htm; see also Pérez, "Rendre le social plus politique," 60–61.

24. Bourdieu, "Colonialism and Ethnography. Foreword to Pierre Bourdieu's *Travail et travailleurs en Algérie*," *Anthropology Today* 19(2): 13–18, 15.

25. Bourdieu, *Sociologie de l'Algérie* (Paris: Presses Universitaires de France, 1958); Bourdieu, "La logique interne de la civilisation algérienne traditionnelle," in *Le sous-développement en Algérie*, ed. Secrétariat social d'Alger (Alger: Éditions du Secrétariat social d'Alger, 1969), 40–51; Bourdieu, "Le choc des civilisations," in *Le sous-développement en Algérie*, ed. Secrétariat social d'Alger (Alger: Éditions du Secrétariat social d'Alger, 1969), 52–64; Bourdieu, "Guerre et mutation sociale en Algérie," *Études méditerrannées* 7 (1960): 25–37; Bourdieu, "Révolution dans la révolution," *Esprit* 1 (1961): 27–40.

26. Bourdieu, "The Struggle for Symbolic Order," *Theory, Culture and Society* 3, no. 3 (1986): 31–51, 39.

27. Bourdieu, "Letters to André Nouschi," in Bourdieu, *Algerian Sketches*, 317–22, 317, 319.

28. Nouschi, "Autour de *Sociologie de l'Algérie*," *Awal* 27–28 (2003): 29–35, 34.

29. Nouschi, "Autour de *Sociologie de l'Algérie*," 32–33.

30. Bourdieu, *Sociologie de l'Algérie* (1958), 8.

31. Bourdieu, "Le clou de Djeha. Des contradictions linguistiques léguées par le colonisateur: un entretien avec Pierre Bourdieu," *Hommes et migrations* 991: 37–41, 37.

32. Enrique Martín-Criado, *Les deux Algéries de Pierre Bourdieu* (Bellecombe-en-Bauges: Croquant, 2008), 73–74.

33. Paul A. Silverstein and Jane E. Goodman, "Introduction," in *Bourdieu in Algeria: Colonial Politics, Ethnographic Practices, Theoretical Developments*, ed. Jane E. Goodman and Paul A. Silverstein (Lincoln: University of Nebraska Press, 2009), 1–62, 23.

34. Bourdieu, *The Algerians*, trans. Alan C. M. Ross (Boston: Beacon, 1962), 16. All subsequent quotes are from this excellent translation of the 1961 edition of *Sociologie de l'Algérie* (which also includes the essay "The Revolution Within the Revolution"), unless otherwise stated.

35. Bourdieu, *The Algerians*, 27.
36. In subsequent editions, this is ch. 3.
37. Bourdieu, "La logique interne," 43.
38. Bourdieu, *The Algerians*, 51, 54.
39. Silverstein and Goodman, "Introduction," 19.
40. Bourdieu, *The Algerians*, 54.
41. Bourdieu, "La culture Mozabite," *Documents Algériens, Série monographies*, no. 23 (Nov. 20, 1958). This pamphlet is extracted from the first edition of *Sociologie de l'Algérie*, and also includes additional photos not in the book.
42. This is ch. 3 in 1958, ch. 4 in all later editions.
43. Bourdieu, *The Algerians*, 58, 120.
44. Bourdieu, *Sociologie de l'Algérie* (1958), 60.
45. Bourdieu taught a course at the University of Algiers on "Algerian Culture" in 1960. Loïc J. D. Wacquant, "Toward a Social Praxeology: The Structure and Logic of Bourdieu's Sociology," in Pierre Bourdieu and Loïc Wacquant, *An Invitation to Reflexive Sociology* (Chicago: University of Chicago Press, 1992), 1–59, 45, note 81.
46. Bourdieu, *Sociologie de l'Algérie* (1958), 91.
47. Bourdieu, *Sociologie de l'Algérie* (1958), 90.
48. Bourdieu, "Letters to André Nouschi," 321.
49. After the 3rd edition in 1970, the title of the last chapter changes to "L'Aliénation."
50. Bourdieu, *The Algerians*, 120.
51. Bourdieu's co-authored book with Jean-Claude Chamboredon and Jean-Claude Passeron explicitly rejects positivist epistemologies of general social laws. Bourdieu, Chamboredon, and Passeron, *The Craft of Sociology: Epistemological Preliminaries* (New York: de Gruyter, [1968] 1991).
52. Bourdieu, "The Revolution within the Revolution," in Bourdieu, *The Algerians*, 145–63, 133, 152, note 5.
53. It is therefore incorrect to argue that Bourdieu did not discuss racial domination per se, as Mustafa Emirbayer and Matthew Desmond argue in *The Racial Order* (Chicago: University of Chicago Press, 2015).
54. Bourdieu, *The Algerians*, 134.
55. Bourdieu, *Sociologie de l'Algérie* (1958), 122. This important passage does not appear in the subsequent editions.
56. Bourdieu, *Sociologie de l'Algérie* (1958), 126.
57. Bourdieu, *Sociologie de l'Algérie* (Paris: Presses Universitaires de France, 1961), 125–26; emphasis added. This important and radical concluding paragraph was inexplicably excluded from the 1962 English translation, based on the 1961 edition. It appears that either Bourdieu or Beacon's editors felt that it was unnecessary to end with a call to revolution, since they added his essay on "the revolution within the revolution" to the book.
58. Mehenni Akbal, *Père Henri Sanson s.j.: Itinéraire d'un chrétien d'Algérie* (Paris: L'Harmattan, 2010), 65–69; Sanson, "C'était un esprit curieux," *Awal* 27–28 (2003): 279–86.
59. Bourdieu, "Le choc des civilisations," 55–58.
60. Bourdieu, "Le choc des civilisations," 54.
61. For the elaboration of these concepts, see George Steinmetz, "The Octopus and the *Hekatonkheire*: On Many-Armed States and Tentacular Empires," in *The Many Hands of the State*, ed. Kimberly Morgan and Ann Orloff (New York: Cambridge University Press, 2017), 369–94.
62. Kamel Chachoua, "Pierre Bourdieu et l'Algérie le savant et la politique," in Chachoua, *L'Algérie sociologique*, 9–23, 13.

63. Bourdieu, *The Algerians*, 56; Bourdieu, "Étude sociologique," in *Travail et travailleurs en Algérie*, ed. Pierre Bourdieu, Alain Darbel, Jean-Paul Rivet, and Claude Seibel (Paris: Mouton, 1963), 253–562, 382.

64. Eric Hobsbawm and Terence Ranger, eds., *The Invention of Tradition* (Cambridge: Cambridge University Press, 1992). The editors and contributors to this volume do not acknowledge the pioneering contributions of Berque and Bourdieu in this area.

65. Bourdieu, "De la guerre révolutionnaire à la révolution," in *L'Algérie de demain*, ed. François Perroux (Paris: Presses Universitaires de France, 1962), 5–13.

66. Bourdieu, "Étude sociologique," 266.

67. Bourdieu, "Statistiques et sociologie," in Bourdieu et al., *Travail et travailleurs*, 9–13. This comment in 1963 again suggests that Bourdieu was not at all dismissive of his first book.

68. Alain Darbel, Jean-Paul Rivet, and Claude Seibel, "Les données statistiques," in Bourdieu et al., *Travail et travailleurs*, 15–250, 145.

69. *Travail et travailleurs en Algérie*, 274–79.

70. *Travail et travailleurs en Algérie*, 305.

71. *Travail et travailleurs en Algérie*, 279–80.

72. *Travail et travailleurs en Algérie*, 279.

73. Bourdieu, "Traditional Society's Attitude towards Time and Economic Behaviour" [1963] in Bourdieu, *Algerian Sketches*, 52–71, 54.

74. Bourdieu, *Pascalian Meditations* (Cambridge, UK: Polity, 2000), 161.

75. Silverstein makes the implausible argument that the language of uprooting in Bourdieu and Sayad resonates with conservative ideologies of a "deep France." Bourdieu and Sayad were not fascists or Vichyists but anti-colonialists. Paul A. Silverstein, "Of Rooting and Uprooting: Kabyle Habitus, Domesticity, and Structural Nostalgia," in *Bourdieu in Algeria: Colonial Politics, Ethnographic Practices, Theoretical Developments*, ed. Jane E. Goodman and Paul A. Silverstein (Lincoln: University of Nebraska Press, 2009), 164–98. Indeed, Bourdieu criticized "nostalgia for the agrarian paradises" as "the principle of all conservative ideologies" in *Outline of a Theory of Practice* (Cambridge: Cambridge University Press, [1977] 2015), 115.

76. Bourdieu and Sayad also discussed their results in a 1964 article, "Paysans déracinés," translated as "Uprooted Peasants," in Bourdieu, *Algerian Sketches*, 117–45. I discuss the book and this article together, since they were published at the same time, and quote from the English translation.

77. Michel Cornaton, *Les regroupements de la décolonisation en Algérie* (Paris: Économie et humanisme, Éditions ouvrières, 1967), 123.

78. Pierre Bourdieu and Abdelmalek Sayad, *Uprooting. The Crisis of Traditional Agriculture in Algeria* (Cambridge: Polity Press, 2020), 7.

79. Bourdieu and Sayad, *Uprooting*, 27; emphasis added.

80. Bourdieu and Sayad, *Uprooting*, 7.

81. Bourdieu and Sayad, *Le déracinement. La crise de l'agriculture traditionelle en Algérie* (Paris: Minuit, 1964), 36. "L'Algérie a été le terrain d'expérience sur lequel l'esprit militaire . . . a plaqué ses structures."

82. R. Chevalier, "La centuriation et les problèmes de la colonisation romaine," *Études rurales*, October-December (1961), quoted in Bourdieu and Sayad, *Uprooting*, 180, note 18.

83. Bourdieu and Sayad, *Uprooting*, 108–09.

84. Bourdieu and Sayad, "Uprooted Peasants," 141–42.

85. Bourdieu and Sayad, *Uprooting*, 15.

86. Bourdieu and Sayad, *Uprooting*, 12.

87. Bourdieu and Sayad, "Uprooted Peasants," 20.

88. Bourdieu and Sayad, *Uprooting*, 11.

89. Bourdieu and Sayad, "Uprooted Peasants," 118.
90. Bourdieu and Sayad, *Uprooting*, 89.
91. Bourdieu and Sayad, *Uprooting*, 83.
92. Bourdieu and Sayad, "Uprooted Peasants," 118.
93. Bourdieu and Sayad, *Uprooting*, 117.
94. Bourdieu and Sayad, *Uprooting*, 117.
95. Bourdieu and Sayad, *Uprooting*, 118.
96. Bourdieu and Sayad, *Uprooting*, 118.
97. Bourdieu, *The Algerians*, 58–59.
98. Bourdieu, "Traditional Society's Attitude towards Time," 70.
99. Bourdieu and Sayad, *Uprooting*, 44.
100. Bourdieu and Sayad, "Uprooted Peasants," 121.
101. Bourdieu and Sayad, *Uprooting*, 79
102. Bourdieu and Sayad, *Uprooting*, 10.
103. Bourdieu and Sayad, *Uprooting*, 79.
104. Martín-Criado, *Les deux Algéries de Pierre Bourdieu*, is the most careful of the works in this genre, compared to Silverstein and Goodman, "Introduction"; Fanny Colonna, "The Phantom of Dispossession: From The Uprooting to The Weight of the World," in *Bourdieu in Algeria: Colonial Politics, Ethnographic Practices, Theoretical Developments*, ed. Jane E. Goodman and Paul A. Silverstein (Lincoln: University of Nebraska Press, 2009), 63–93; Deborah Reed-Danahay, *Locating Bourdieu* (Bloomington: Indiana University Press, 2005); Reed-Danahay, "The Kabyle and the French: Occidentalism in Bourdieu's Theory of Practice," in *Occidentalism: Images of the West*, ed. James G. Carrier (Oxford: Clarendon Press, 1995), 61–84. The latter is a particularly distorted example of this genre. Reed-Danahay accuses Bourdieu of Orientalizing the Kabyle, asserts that he describes France "as a place where people do not engage in cultural creation or negotiate power," and then adds contradictorily that Bourdieu "locates possibilities for resistance through practice, in studies of Algerian peasants" (ibid., 77–78). In fact, Bourdieu concludes *Outline of a Theory of Practice* by extending his analysis to France, including its welfare state, philanthropy, and art world. All of Bourdieu's writing after 1965 describes fields as spaces of strategic practice. In short, France and Algeria are, for Bourdieu, *both* places where people "engage in cultural creation or negotiate power." What Bourdieu accomplished was to exoticize France initially as a space that was just as frozen in self-reproductive stasis as the "Orient" had appeared to be according to Orientalism, thereby making "the mundane exotic and the exotic mundane." Bourdieu and Loïc J. D. Wacquant, *An Invitation to Reflexive Sociology* (Chicago: University of Chicago Press, 1992), 68. This gesture echoed the interventions by earlier colonial sociologists like Charles Le Coeur in *Le rite et l'outil* (Paris: PUF, 1939), and by British contemporaries like Ronnie Frankenberg in *Village on the Border; a Social Study of Religion, Politics and Football in a North Wales Community* (London: Cohen & West, 1957) and Peter Worsley, "Britain—Unknown Country," *New Reasoner* 1, no. 6 (1958): 53–64.
105. Julian Go incorrectly elides Bourdieu's work with this hyper-colonialist group, suggesting that Bourdieu was calling for a decolonization of the kind of work that Bourdieu himself was carrying out. Bourdieu is clearly calling for historical study specifically of the Orientalist *École d'Alger*. Unlike Bourdieu, the members of the *École d'Alger* were not censored but promoted by the colonial state and army, and some of them supported the paramilitary *Organisation Armée Secrète* that threatened Bourdieu's life. Go, "Decolonizing Bourdieu: Colonial and Postcolonial Theory in Pierre Bourdieu's Early Work," *Sociological Theory* 31, no. 1 (2013): 49–74, 82. On the *École d'Alger*, see Edmund Burke III, "The Sociology of Islam: The French Tradition," in *Islamic Studies: A Tradition and its Problems*, ed. Malcom H. Kerr (Santa Monica, CA: Undena, 1980), 73–88; Alain Messaoudi,

NOTES TO CHAPTER FOURTEEN [491]

Les arabisants et la France coloniale: savants, conseillers, médiateurs, 1780–1930 (Lyon: ENS, 2015).

106. On the Kabyle myth, see Charles Robert Ageron, *Les Algériens musulmans et la France (1871–1919)*, vol. 2 (Paris: Presses universitaires de France, [1983] 2005), 267–76; Patricia M. E. Lorcin, *Imperial Identities: Stereotyping, Prejudice and Race in Colonial Algeria* (London: I. B. Tauris, 1995).

107. Colonna, "The Phantom of Dispossession," 75. This description of Bourdieu's work is more likely to "send a chill down the spine" (ibid., 77) than Bourdieu's definition of habitus, which Colonna finds chilling. This is a deeply flawed article by an excellent scholar of Algeria and former student of Bourdieu. See Fanny Colonna, *Instituteurs algériens, 1883–1939* (Paris: Presses de la Fondation nationale des sciences politiques, 1975).

108. The key word here is "arguably." Silverstein and Goodman, "Introduction," 26.

109. Bourdieu, *Outline of a Theory of Practice*, 115.

110. This is one of the few places where I differ from Marc Joly, whose work I greatly admire. There are not, *pace* Joly, "Two carefully distinguished but inseparable plans" in Bourdieu's work on Algeria; the two halves of Bourdieu's "cleft habitus" cannot be associated with these two supposed parts. Joly, *Devenir Norbert Elias* (Paris: Fayard, 2012), 219.

111. Silverstein and Goodman, "Introduction," 27, casts suspicion on Bourdieu's statement that he was "crazy about" and "in love with" the Kabyle. These quotes are from an interview on the Berber radio-television network in 2001. One could just as well counter this with another text from a lecture in 2001 where Bourdieu explains that "it is very important that a Kabyle can read [my texts] without feeling 'exoticized,' i.e, excluded by the regard." Bourdieu, "Secouez un peu vos structures!" in *Le symbolique et le social: la réception internationale de la pensée de Pierre Bourdieu; actes du colloque de Cerisy-la-Salle (11–19 juillet 2001)*, ed. Jacques Dubois, Pascal Durand, and Yves Winkin (Liège: Editions de l'Université de Liège, 2005), 325–41, 331.

112. Silverstein and Goodman, "Introduction," 38.

113. Bourdieu, "The Right Use of Ethnology, Interview with Mahmoud Mammeri," in Bourdieu, *Algerian Sketches*, 203–23, 214–16; emphasis added.

114. Bourdieu, "The Struggle for Symbolic Order," 38. This statement is not quoted by any of the contributors to Goodman and Silverstein, eds., *Bourdieu in Algeria*.

115. Bourdieu, "The Sentiment of Honour in Kabyle Society," in *Honour and Shame: The Values of Mediterranean Society*, ed. John G. Peristiany (London: Weidenfeld and Nicholson, 1965), 191–241, 198.

116. Bourdieu, "The Sentiment of Honour," 194–96; Bourdieu, *Algeria 1960, Essays* (Paris: Éd. Maison des Sciences de l'Homme), 98.

117. Bourdieu, "La maison kabyle ou le monde renversé," in *Échanges et communications. Mélanges offerts à Claude Lévi-Strauss à l'occasion de son 60e anniversaire*, ed. Jean Pouillon and Paul Maranda (Paris: Mouton, 1970), 739–58.

118. Bourdieu, *Sketch for a Self-Analysis*, 40.

119. Bourdieu, *The Logic of Practice* (Stanford, CA: Stanford University Press, [1980] 1990), 317, n. 1.

120. Reed-Danahay, "The Kabyle and the French," 73; Bourdieu, *Outline of a Theory of Practice*, 73.

121. Bourdieu, *Pascalian Meditations*, 161.

122. Akmut, *Apprentis philosophes*.

123. Steinmetz, "Bourdieu's Disavowal of Lacan: Psychoanalytic Theory and the Concepts of 'Habitus' and 'Symbolic Capital,'" *Constellations* 13, no. 4 (2006): 445–64.

124. François Héran, "La seconde nature de l'habitus: Tradition philosophique et sens commun dans le langage sociologique," *Revue française de sociologie* 28, no. 3 (1987): 385–416; Loïc J. D. Wacquant, "A Concise Genealogy and Anatomy of Habitus," *The Sociological*

Review 64 (2016): 64–72; Bourdieu, "Postface to *Erwin Panofsky's Gothic Architecture and Scholasticism*," in Bruce W. Holsinger, *The Premodern Condition: Medievalism and the Making of Theory* (Chicago: University of Chicago Press, [1967] 2005), 221–42.

125. See letter from Bourdieu to Sayad, late 1959, in Fonds d'Archives Abdelmalek Sayad. I am grateful to Amín Pérez for providing me with a copy of this letter. Bourdieu's mature field theory is, of course, entirely different from Lewin's, as I discussed in "Field Theory in Bourdieusian Sociology," paper presented at plenary session on field theory, American Sociological Association, Montréal, August 17, 2017.

126. Emile Durkheim, *The Rules of Sociological Method* (London: Macmillan Press, 1982), 62–63; Gaston Bachelard, *The Formation of the Scientific Mind* (Manchester: Clinamen Press, 2002); Pierre Bourdieu, Jean-Claude Chamboredon, and Jean-Claude Passeron, *The Craft of Sociology. Epistemological Preliminaries* (New York : de Gruyter, 1991), 13–15.

127. On these terms, see Robert K. Merton, "On the History and Systematic of Sociological Theory," in Merton, *Social Theory and Social Structure: Toward the Codification of Theory and Research* (Glencoe, IL: Free Press, 1949), 1–38. Merton is concerned with the importance of distinguishing between genuine "adumbrations" of later theories in the work of *different* scientists, not within the oeuvre of a single scientist.

128. George Steinmetz, "Bourdieu, Historicity, and Historical Sociology," *Cultural Sociology* 5, no. 1 (2011): 45–66.

129. As summarized by Fanny Colonna, "The Phantom of Dispossession," 63.

130. Bourdieu, *Algeria 1960*, vii.

131. Bourdieu, "Traditional Society's Attitude towards Time," 64.

132. Bourdieu and Sayad, *Le déracinement. La crise de l'agriculture traditionelle en Algérie* (Paris: Les Éditions de Minuit, 1964), 88; emphasis added.

133. Bourdieu, *Outline of a Theory of Practice*, 72; Idem., *Logic of Practice*, 53. Bourdieu adds to this basic definition that the habitus consists of "principles which generate and organize practices and representations that can be objectively adapted to their outcomes without presupposing a conscious aiming at ends." He also adds a comparison to Chomsky's generative grammar, which allows Bourdieu to insist on the creative, adaptive, improvisational capacities of habitus, alongside its constrained and structured aspects. Other steps in the gradual emergence of Bourdieu's definition are visible in Bourdieu, "Systems of Education and Systems of Thought," *International Social Science Journal* 19, no. 3 (1967): 338–58; and Bourdieu, "Postface to *Erwin Panofsky's*." The most sustained discussion of the concept is Geoffrey Mead, "Sense of Structure and Structure of Sense: Pierre Bourdieu's Habitus as a Generative Principle" (PhD diss., University of Melbourne, 2013).

134. Bourdieu neglects his Algerian research in "The Genesis of the Concepts of Habitus and Field," *Sociocriticism* 2, no. 2 (1985): 11–24, but elsewhere he emphasizes the Algerian origins.

135. Bourdieu, *Outline of a Theory of Practice*, 90.

136. Bourdieu and Sayad, *Uprooting*, 203, n. 46; Bachelard, Gaston, *La poétique de l'espace* (Paris: Presses universitaires de France, 1957).

137. Bourdieu and Sayad, *Uprooting*, 112.

138. Bourdieu and Sayad, *Uprooting*, 44.

139. Bourdieu and Sayad, *Uprooting*, 117.

140. Charles Le Coeur, *Le rite et l'outil*; Worsley, "Britain—Unknown Country"; Horace Miner, "Body Ritual among the Nacirema," *American Anthropologist* n.s. 58, no. 3 (1956): 503–07.

141. Norbert Elias, "Sociology and Anthropology. A paper read at the second annual conference of the Ghana Sociological Association, April 1963," 21. In Norbert Elias archive, File MISC—E XI = SOC-Anthrop. For others making the same argument see ch. 7, pages associated with notes 165–171.

142. Bourdieu, *The Algerians*, 88; emphasis added.

143. Bourdieu, *The Logic of Practice*, 3; Berque, "Qu'est-ce qu'une tribu nord-africaine?," in *Éventail de l'histoire vivante: Hommage à Lucien Febvre* (Paris: Armand Colin, 1954), 261–71, 263.

144. Bourdieu, *Distinction. A Social Critique of the Judgement of Taste* (Cambridge, MA: Harvard University Press, 1984); Bourdieu, "The (Three) Forms of Capital," in *Handbook of Theory and Research in the Sociology of Education*, ed. John G. Richardson (New York: Greenwood Press, 1986), 241–58, 247–48. Bourdieu advised Sayad to switch from his plan to write a *thèse de 3ᵉ cycle* to a "thèse d'Université ou de thèse d'état." Pérez, "Rendre le social plus politique," 192.

145. Bourdieu, "The Social Space and the Genesis of Groups," *Social Science Information* 24, no. 2 (1985): 195–220, 203.

146. Bourdieu, *Outline of a Theory of Practice*, 179; Bourdieu, "From Rules to Strategies," in Bourdieu, *In Other Words: Essays Towards a Reflexive Sociology* (Cambridge: Polity Press, 1990), 59–75.

147. Bourdieu, *Language and Symbolic Power* (Cambridge, MA: Harvard University Press, 1991); Bourdieu, *Classification Struggles: General Sociology*, vol. 1 (Cambridge: Polity Press, 2018).

148. To ignore the impact of Bourdieu's Algerian writing on his later, more abstract theorizing is a strategy in the campaign of painting Bourdieu as a "reproduction theorist." George Steinmetz, "Colonialism, Crisis, and Change: The Algerian Origins of Bourdieu's Concepts and His Rejection of Social Reproductionism," *Rassegna Italiana di Sociologia* 63, n. 2 (2022): 323–348.

149. Bourdieu, "Le choc des civilisations," 54.

150. Fonds Pierre Bourdieu, correspondence with Sayad. Lewin died in 1947. Hence, all of his work was potentially available to Bourdieu, who read German and English. A collection of Lewin's writings was also published in French under the title *Psychologie dynamique; les relations humaines* (Paris: PUF, 1961); this may have called Bourdieu's attention to the psychologist's work. José Manue Fernández and Aníbal Puente Ferreras, "La noción de campo en Kurt Lewin y Pierre Bourdieu: un análisis comparative," *Revista española de investigaciones sociológicas* 127 (2009): 33–53.

151. Morton Deutsch, "Field Theory in Social Psychology," in *The Handbook of Social Psychology*, ed. G. Lindzey, E. Aronson, eds., vol. 1, 2nd ed. (Reading, MA: Addison-Wesley, 1969), 412–87.

152. Bourdieu, "Projet créateur et champ intellectuel" (Paris: Centre de Sociologie Européenne, 1965); published as "Champ intellectuel et projet créateur," *Les temps modernes* no. 246 (1966): 865–906.

153. Yingyao Wang, "Homology and Isomorphism: Bourdieu in Conversation with New Institutionalism," *British Journal of Sociology* 67, no. 2 (2016): 348–70, 355.

154. Bourdieu, "For a Sociology of Sociologists," in Bourdieu, *Algerian Sketches*, 283–87, 285; emphasis in original.

155. On the colonial state as a field, see George Steinmetz, *The Devil's Handwriting: Precoloniality and the German Colonial State in Qingdao, Samoa and Southwest Africa* (Chicago: University of Chicago Press, 2007); Bourdieu, "The Colonial State as a Social Field," *American Sociological Review* 73, no. 4 (2008): 589–612.

156. Bourdieu was not a critical realist, but critical realism overlaps with Bourdieu's ontology; see chapter 15 and Sourabh Singh, "Anchoring Depth Ontology to Epistemological Strategies of Field Theory: Exploring the Possibility for Developing a Core for Sociological Analysis," *Journal of Critical Realism* 17, no. 5 (2018): 429–48.

157. For a very early note on this epistemic problem within sociology, see W. E. B. Du Bois, "Prospect of a World without Race Conflict," *American Journal of Sociology* 49, no. 5 (1944): 450–56.

158. Bourdieu, "Étude sociologique," 259.

159. Bourdieu, "The Algerian Sub-Proletariat," in Bourdieu, *Algerian Sketches*, 146–61, 159–60.

160. Bourdieu, "Étude sociologique," 310.

161. Nicola Ingram and Jessie Abrahams, "Stepping Outside of Oneself. How a Cleft-Habitus can Lead to Greater Reflexivity through Occupying 'the Third Space,'" in *Bourdieu: The Next Generation. The Development of Bourdieu's Intellectual Heritage in Contemporary UK Sociology*, ed. Jenny Thatcher (London: Routledge, 2016), 140–64.

162. Bourdieu, "The Right Use of Ethnology," 215, 207.

163. Bourdieu, *Outline of a Theory of Practice*, 2.

164. Dick Pels, "After Objectivity. An Historical Approach to the Intersubjective in Ethnography," *Hau: Journal of Ethnographic Theory* 4, no. 1 (201): 211–36.

165. The early criticism includes, for the United States, Marshall Sahlins, "The Established Order: Do Not Fold, Spindle, or Mutilate," in *The Rise and Fall of Project Camelot: Studies in the Relationship between Social Science and Practical Politics*, ed. Irving Louis Horowitz (Cambridge, MA: MIT Press, 1967), 71–79; for Britain, Talal Asad, ed., *Anthropology and the Colonial Encounter* (London: Ithaca Press, 1973); and for German anthropology, Manfred Gothsch, *Die deutsche Völkerkunde und ihr Verhältnis zum Kolonialismus* (Baden-Baden: Nomos, 1983). For France, in addtion to Michel Leiris, see Gerard Leclerc, *Anthropologie et colonialisme: essai sur l'histoire de l'africanisme* (Paris: Fayard, 1979).

166. Bourdieu, "For a Sociology of Sociologists," 287.

167. Bourdieu, "Les conditions sociales de la production sociologique: sociologie coloniale et décolonisation de la sociologie," in *Le mal de voir. Ethnologie et orientalisme: politique et épistémologie*, ed. Henri Moniot (Paris: Union Gén., 1976), 416–427.

168. Bourdieu, "Les conditions sociales de la production sociologique: sociologie coloniale et décolonisation de la sociologie," Bourdieu, "L'ontologie politique de Martin Heidegger," *Actes de la recherche en sciences sociales* 1, no. 5–6 (1975): 109–56.

169. Bourdieu, "Colonialism and Ethnography. Foreword to Pierre Bourdieu's *Travail et travailleurs en Algérie*," *Anthropology Today* 19, no. 2 ([1963] 2003): 13–18, 14.

170. Bourdieu, in Bourdieu and Wacquant, *An Invitation to Reflexive Sociology*, 201; see Bourdieu et al., *La misère du monde* (Paris: Seuil, 1993).

171. Amín Pérez, "Rendre le social plus politique: Guerre coloniale, immigration et pratiques sociologiques d'Abdelmalek Sayad et de Pierre Bourdieu" (PhD diss., École des hautes études en sciences sociales, 2015), 56.

172. Joy Rohde, *Armed with Expertise: The Militarization of American Social Research during the Cold War* (Ithaca, NY: Cornell University Press, 2013); Christian Dayé and Mark Solovey, eds., *Cold War Social Science: Transnational Entanglements* (Cham, Switzerland: Palgrave Macmillan, 2021).

Chapter Fifteen: Conclusion: The History of Sociology, Reflexivity, and Decolonization

1. Gianni Albergoni, "Notices, variantes et notes," in Jacques Berque, *Opera minora*, vol. 2 (Paris: Editions Bouchène, 2001), 449–80, 462.

2. Jacqueline Rose, "Response to Edward Said," in Said, *Freud and the Non-European* (London: Verso, 2003), 63–79, 67.

3. George Steinmetz, "Critical Realism and Historical Sociology," *Comparative Studies in Society and History* 40, no. 1 (1998): 170–186; Steinmetz, "Positivism and its Others in the Social Sciences," in *The Politics of Method in the Human Sciences: Positivism and its Epistemological Others*, ed. George Steinmetz (Durham, NC: Duke University Press, 2005),

1–56; Steinmetz, "Historismus und Positivismus in der Soziologie. Eine begriffsgeschichtliche Recherche vom Wilhelminischen Deutschland bis in die Gegenwart der Vereinigten Staaten von Amerika," *Mittelweg 36* no. 3 (June–July 2020): 37–68.

4. On the uses of the history of social science, see George Steinmetz, "Concept-Quake: Toward a Historical Sociology of Social Science," in *The Social Sciences Through the Looking-Glass. Studies in the Production of Knowledge*, ed. Didier Fassin and George Steinmetz (Durham, NC: Duke University Press, 2022), 21–80; Steinmetz, "How and Why Do We Write the History of the Social Sciences?" *The Institute Letter*, Institute for Advanced Study (Spring 2018): 12–13.

5. Berque, *Mémoires des deux rives* (Paris: Seuil, 1989), 150–151.

6. Bourdieu and Sayad, *Le déracinement. La crise de l'agriculture traditionelle en Algérie* (Paris: Les Éditions de Minuit, 1964), 88; emphasis added.

7. Bourdieu, *The Algerians*, 88; emphasis added.

8. Bourdieu, "For a Sociology of Sociologists," in Bourdieu, *Algerian Sketches*, 283–87, 285.

9. Bourdieu, "The Algerian Sub-Proletariat," in Bourdieu, *Algerian Sketches*, 146–61, 159–60.

10. Bourdieu, "Étude sociologique," 310.

11. Bourdieu, "Étude sociologique," 259.

12. Berque, "Perspectives de l'orientalisme contemporain," *Ibla, Revue de L'institut des belles lettres arabes* 79 (1957), 217–238, 221.

13. Anouar Abdel Malek, "Orientalism in Crisis," *Diogenes* 11, no. 44 (1962): 103–40, 109.

14. Abdel Malek, "Orientalism in Crisis," 124–125.

15. Bourdieu, "Les conditions sociales de la production sociologique: sociologie coloniale et décolonisation de la sociologie," in *Le mal de voir. Ethnologie et orientalisme: politique et épistémologie*, ed. Henri Moniot (Paris: Union Gén., 1976), 416–427.

16. Bourdieu, *The Logic of Practice* (Stanford, CA: Stanford University Press, [1980] 1990), 5.

17. Bourdieu, "Les conditions sociales de la production sociologique."

18. Raewyn Connell, for example, equates Bourdieu with the utilitarian, conservative, rational choice sociology of James S. Coleman, "Northern Theory: The Political Geography of General Social Theory," *Theory and Society* 35, no. 2 (2006): 237–64.

19. See the nuanced discussion by Fuyuki Kurosawa, "The Durkheimian School and Colonialism: Exploring the Constitutive Paradox," in *Sociology and Empire*, ed. George Steinmetz (Durham, NC: Duke University Press, 2013), 188–209.

20. Michael Burawoy, "Bourdieu Meets Bourdieu," in *Conversations with Bourdieu: The Johannesburg Moment*, ed. Michael Burawoy and Klaus van Holdt (Johannesburg: Wits University Press, 2012), 9–24, 5; similarly, James Bohman, "Practical Reason and Cultural Constraint: Agency in Bourdieu's Theory of Practice," in *Bourdieu: A Critical Reader*, ed. Richard Shusterman (Oxford, UK: Blackwell, 1999), 129–52.

21. Max Weber, *The Religion of China: Confucianism and Taoism*, trans. Hans Gerth (New York: Free Press, 1964).

22. George Steinmetz, *The Devil's Handwriting: Precolonial Ethnography and the German Colonial State in Qingdao, Samoa, and Southwest Africa.* (Chicago: University of Chicago Press), 415–416; Steinmetz, "Scientific Autonomy and Empire, 1880–1945: Four German Sociologists," *German Colonialism in a Global Age*, ed. Geoff Eley and Bradley Naranch (Durham, NC: Duke University Press, 2014), 46–73.

23. Max Weber, "Hinduismus und Buddhismus," in *Gesammelte Aufsätze zur Religionssoziologie*, vol. 2 (Tübingen: Mohr, 1921), 2, no.1.

24. *Contra* Andrew Zimmerman, "Decolonizing Weber," *Postcolonial Studies* 9, no. 1 (2006): 53–79.

25. Weber, *Economy and Society*, 2 vols., ed. Guenther Roth and Claus Wittich (Berkeley: University of California Press, 1978), 422.

26. I confess that I also focused on these sorts of sociologists in my earliest ventures into this area: Steinmetz, "The Imperial Entanglements." Gurminder K. Bhambra and John Holmwood, *Colonialism and Modern Social Theory* (Cambridge: Polity, 2021), do not follow this approach, but deal only with important thinkers—Hobbes, Hegel, Tocqueville, Marx, Weber, Durkheim, and Du Bois.

27. Nick Cullather, "Damming Afghanistan: Modernization in a Buffer State," *Journal of American History* 89, no. 2 (2002): 512–37.

28. See the online database for the present book, which includes all French sociologists of colonialism.

29. Raphael Gross, *Carl Schmitt and the Jews: The "Jewish Question," the Holocaust, and German Legal Theory* (Madison: University of Wisconsin Press, 2007).

30. One particularly egregious case is the cancellation of the job offer to Steven Salaita by the University of Illinois in 2013. Salaita was a respected scholar of American Indian Studies with an award-winning book on anti-Arab racism in the United States whose job offer was rescinded due to his criticism of Israel on Twitter during the 2014 Gaza War.

31. Dispesh Chakrabarty, *Provincializing Europe: Postcolonial Thought and Historical Difference* (Princeton, NJ: Princeton University Press, 2008); Manuela Boatcă, "'From the Standpoint of Germanism': A Postcolonial Critique of Weber's Theory of Race and Ethnicity," *Political Power and Social Theory* 24 (2013): 55–80, 75.

32. McKim Marriott, "Constructing an Indian Ethnosociology," *Contributions to Indian Sociology* 23, no. 1 (1989): 1–39; Philip C. C. Huang, "'Public Sphere'/'Civil Society' in China?," *Modern China* 19, no. 2 (1993): 216–40; Huang, "Theory and the Study of Modern Chinese History," *Modern China* 24, no. 2 (1998): 183–208; for a nuanced analysis of the problem, see Lydia He Liu, *The Clash of Empires the Invention of China in Modern World Making* (Cambridge, MA: Harvard University Press, 2004).

33. Steinmetz, "Critical Realism and Historical Sociology."

34. Connell, *Southern Theory*, 85.

35. Balandier, "Les débats," in "L'éveil de l'Afrique noire: Trois conférences-débats," Supplement to *Preuves*, no. 88 (June 1958): 27–32, 27–28.

36. Raewyn Connell, *Southern Theory: The Global Dynamics of Knowledge in Social Science* (Cambridge: Polity, 2007); Idem., "Decolonizing Sociology," *Contemporary Sociology* 47, no. 4 (2018): 399–407.

37. See especially Ernst Troeltsch, *Der Historismus und seine Probleme* (Tubingen: Mohr, 1922), who situates positivism in Western Europe and anti-positivism and historicism to the east of the Rhine.

38. On the connections of Sarkar and Tagore to German historicism, see Manu Goswami, "'Provincializing' Sociology: The Case of a Premature Postcolonial Sociologist," *Political Power and Social Theory* 24 (2013): 145–75; see also Patricia Uberoi, Nandini Sundar, and Satish Deshpande, eds., *Anthropology in the East: Founders of Indian Sociology and Anthropology* (Delhi: Permanent Black, 2007); and Nurolhoda Bandeh-Ahmadi, "Anthropological Generations: A Post-Independence Ethnography of Academic Anthropology and Sociology in India" (PhD diss., University of Michigan, 2018).

39. Julian Go, "Globalizing Sociology, Turning South. Perspectival Realism and the Southern Standpoint," *Sociologica: Italian Journal of Sociology* 2 (2016).

40. Of course, Burawoy, Chibber, and Go do not themselves characterize Marxism as a "local" theory; my argument is a reinterpretation. For the full argument, see George

Steinmetz, "On the Articulation of Marxist and Non-Marxist Theory in Colonial Historiography. Vivek Chibber's *Postcolonial Theory and the Spectre of Capital*," in *The Debate on Postcolonial Theory and the Specter of Capital*, ed. Rosie Warren (London: Verso, 2017), 139–147. For a compelling argument along these lines, see Chakrabarty, *Provincializing Europe*.

41. Connell, *Southern Theory*, 223.

42. Michael Burawoy, "Preface," in *Global Knowledge Production in the Social Sciences*, ed. W. Keim, E. Çelik, C. Ersche, and V. Wöhrer (Surrey: Ashgate Publishing, 2014), xiii–xvii, xvi; Burawoy, "Forging Global Sociology from Below," in *The ISA Handbook of Diverse Sociological Traditions*, ed. Sujata Patal (Los Angeles: SAGE, 2010), 52–65, 52.

43. Akinsola A. Akiwowo, "Contributions to the Sociology of Knowledge from an Oral Poetry," *International Sociology* 1, no. 4 (1986): 343–58. Akiwowo studied sociology at Beloit College in Wisconsin before earning his sociology PhD at Boston College in 1961, taught at Adelphi College on Long Island and then taught sociology at the Nigerian universities at Nsuka and Ile-Ife.

44. Bourdieu, Jean-Claude Chamboredon, and Jean-Claude Passeron, *The Craft of Sociology: Epistemological Preliminaries* (New York: de Gruyter, [1958] 1991), 74–77.

45. This is presented most clearly in Bourdieu's posthumous books *Science of Science and Reflexivity* (Chicago: University of Chicago Press, [2001] 2004), *Pascalian Meditations* (Cambridge: Polity Press, 2000), *Ein soziologischer Selbstversuch* (Frankfurt/M.: Suhrkamp, 2002), and *Retour sur la réflexivité* (Paris: EHESS, 2022).

46. Camic, "Uneven Development in the History of Sociology," 231.

47. Loïc Wacquant, "Toward a Social Praxeology: The Structure and Logic of Bourdieu's Sociology," in Bourdieu and Wacquant, *An Invitation*, 1–59, 36. This chapter, and the book it introduces, are among the best introductions to Bourdieu's thought.

48. Georg Lukács, "Reification and the Consciousness of the Proletariat [1923]," in *History & Class Consciousness* (Merlin Press, 1971), 82–222, 168.

49. This point is elaborated for the case of feminist standpoint theory by Caroline New, "Realism, Deconstruction and the Feminist Standpoint," *Journal for the Theory of Social Behaviour* 28, no. 4 (1998): 349–72.

50. Jérôme Bourdieu and Johan Heilbron, "Introduction. De la vigilance épistémologique à la réflexivité," in Pierre Bourdieu, *Retour sur la réflexivité* (Paris: EHESS, 2022), 13.

51. Bourdieu, "Réflexivité narcissique et réflexivité scientifique," in Bourdieu, *Retour sur la réflexivité*, 45–60.

52. Yves Gingras, "Sociological Reflexivity in Action," *Social Studies of Science* 40, no. 4 (2004): 619–31, 628; George Steinmetz, "Toward Socioanalysis: The 'Traumatic Kernel' of Psychoanalysis and Neo-Bourdieusian Theory," in *Bourdieu and Historical Analysis*, ed. Phil Gorski (Durham, NC: Duke University Press, 2013), 108–30; Steinmetz, "Bourdieu's Disavowal of Lacan: Psychoanalytic Theory and the Concepts of 'Habitus' and 'Symbolic Capital,'" *Constellations* 13, no. 4 (2006): 445–64.

SOURCES

Archives and Collections Consulted

Académie des sciences d'outre-mer, Bibliothèque Félix Houphouët-Boigny. Paris, France.
Archives de l'école des hautes études en sciences sociales. Maison des sciences de l'homme, Paris, France (previous address).
Archives du Centre national de la recherche scientifique. Gif-sur-Yvette, France.
Archives nationales d'outre-mer. Aix-en-Provence, France.
Archives nationales de France. Pierrefitte-sur-Seine, France.
Bentley Historical Library. Ann Arbor, Michigan.
Bibliothèque Éric-de-Dampierre (Eric de Dampierre Library), Maison archéologie & éthnologie René Ginouvès, Nanterre, France. Mission sociologique du Haut Oubangui, De Dampierre personal papers.
Centre de documentation IRD France-Nord. Bondy, France.
Fonds d'archives Abdelmalek Sayad (Abdelmalek Sayad papers). Archives nationales de France. Pierrefitte-sur-Seine.
Fonds Georges Balandier (Georges Balandier papers). Bibliothèque nationale de France. Département des Manuscrits, NAF 28671. Paris, France.
Fonds Marcel Soret (Marcel Soret papers), Académie de Mâcon. Mâcon, France.
Fonds Pierre Bourdieu (Pierre Bourdieu papers), Campus Condorcet, Aubervilliers, France.
Musée social. Paris, France.
Norbert Elias archive, Deutsches Literaturarchiv (German Literature Archive). Marbach-am-Neckar, Germany.
Rockefeller Archive Center. Sleepy Hollow, New York.
UNESCO Archives. United Nations Educational, Scientific and Cultural Organization Headquarters. Paris, France.
University of California Los Angeles Library, Special Collections. Jacques Jérôme Pierre Maquet papers. Los Angeles, California.

Select Bibliography of Printed Materials

Abdel Malek, Anouar. "Orientalism in Crisis." *Diogenes* 11, no. 44 (1963): 103–40.
Abi-Mershed, Osama. *Apostles of Modernity: Saint-Simonians and the Civilizing Mission in Algeria*. Palo Alto, CA: Stanford University Press, 2011.
Abu-Lughod, Janet. *Rabat, Urban Apartheid in Morocco*. Princeton, NJ: Princeton University Press, 1980.
Accardo, Alain. *Engagements. Chroniques et autres textes (2000–2010)*. Paris: Agone, 2011.
Addi, Lahouari. "Les enjeux théoriques de l'anthropologie du Maghreb. Lecture de Bourdieu, Geertz, Gellner et Berque." In *L'anthropologie du Maghreb: les apports de Berque, Bourdieu, Geertz et Gellner*, edited by Lahouari Addi, 7–15. Paris: Awal, 2003.
Adedze, Agbenyega. "In the Pursuit of Knowledge and Power: French Scientific Research in West Africa, 1938–65." *Comparative Studies of South Asia, Africa and the Middle East* 23, nos. 1–2 (2003): 335–44.
Adorno, Theodor W. "Einleitung zu Emile Durkheim, 'Soziologie und Philosophie.'" In *Soziologische Schriften I*, 245–79. Frankfurt am Main: Suhrkamp, 1972.

Agblémagnon, François N'Sougan. "La concept de crise appliqué à une société africaine. Les Éwés." *Cahiers internationaux de sociologie* 23 (1957): 157–66.

Agblémagnon, François N'Sougan. "La différence de psychologie et de sensibilité provoque-t-elle une différence de comportement entre occidentaux d'une part, africaines de l'autre, quant aux méthodes de la recherche et quant à l'interprétation des résultats?" In *État et perspectives des études africaines et orientales*, edited by Association des universités partiellement ou entièrement de langue française (AUPELF), 128–44. Montréal: Therien frères, 1965.

Agblémagnon, François N'Sougan. "Les responsabilités du sociologue africain." *Présence africaine* 27–28 (1959): 206–14.

Ageron, Charles Robert. *Les Algériens musulmans et la France (1871–1919)*. Vol. 2. Paris: PUF, [1983] 2005.

Ageron, Charles-Robert. "La deuxième guerre mondiale." In *Histoire de la France coloniale*, edited by Jacques Thobie, Jean Meyer, Catherine Coquery-Vidrovitch, and Charles-Robert Ageron, 311–54. Vol. 2. Paris: Armond Colin, 1990–1991.

Ageron, Charles-Robert. *France coloniale ou parti coloniale?* Paris: PUF, 1978.

Ageron, Charles-Robert. "L'opinion publique face aux problemes de l'Union française." In *Les chemins de la décolonisation de l'empire colonial français: colloque*, edited by Charles-Robert Ageron, 33–48. Paris: CNRS, 1986.

Alatas, Syed F. "Academic Dependency and the Global Division of Labour in the Social Sciences." *Current Sociology* 51, no. 6 (2003): 599–613.

Alatas, Syed F. "The Autonomous, the Universal and the Future of Sociology." *Current Sociology* 54, no. 1 (2006): 7–23.

Aldrich, Robert. *Greater France: A History of French Overseas Expansion*. Basingstoke, UK: Macmillan, 1996.

Amiot, Michel. *Contre l'état, les sociologues. Élements pour und histoire de la sociologie urbaine en France (1900–1980)*. Paris: Éditions de l'École des hautes études en sciences sociales, 1986.

Amster, Ellen J. *Medicine and the Saints: Science, Islam, and the Colonial Encounter in Morocco, 1877–1956*. Austin: University of Texas Press, 2013.

Arditi, Claude. "Michel Leiris devant le colonialism." *Bulletin, Association française des anthropologues* 42 (1990): 95–99.

Arnault, Françoise. *Frédéric Le Play. De la métallurgie à la science sociale*. Nancy: Presses universitaires de Nancy, 1993.

Aron, Raymond. *L'Âge des empires et l'avenir de la France*. Paris: Défense de la France, 1945.

Aron, Raymond. *L'Algérie et la République*. Paris: Plon, 1958.

Aron, Raymond. "L'Allemagne: une révolution antiprolétarienne: Idéologie et réalité du national-socialisme." *Inventaires* 1 (1936): 24–55.

Aron, Raymond. *De l'armistice à l'insurrection nationale*. Paris: Gallimard, 1945.

Aron, Raymond. *Les articles de la politique internationale dans "Le Figaro" de 1947 à 1977*. Vol. 2. Paris: Éd. de Fallois, 1990.

Aron, Raymond. *The Century of Total War*. Boston: Beacon Press, 1955.

Aron, Raymond. *The Committed Observer: Interviews with Jean-Louis Missika and Dominique Wolton*. Chicago: Regnery Gateway, 1983.

Aron, Raymond. "Conflict and War from the Viewpoint of Historical Sociology." In International Sociological Association, *The Nature of Conflict. Studies on the Sociological Aspects of International Tensions*, 177–203. Paris: UNESCO, 1957.

Aron, Raymond. *The Dawn of Universal History*. New York: Basic Books, [1962] 2002.

Aron, Raymond. *Democracy and Totalitarianism*. New York: Praeger, [1965] 1968.

Aron, Raymond. "The Diffusion of Ideologies." *Confluence* 2, no. 1 (1953): 3–12.

Aron, Raymond. "L'ère des tyrannies d'Elie Halévy." *Revue de metaphysique et de morale* 46, no. 2 (1939): 283-307.

Aron, Raymond. *Espoir et peur du siècle. Essais non partisans*. Paris: Calmann-Lévy, 1957.

Aron, Raymond. *Essai sur la théorie de l'histoire dans l'Allemagne contemporaine. La philosophie critique de l'histoire*. Paris: Vrin, 1938.

Aron, Raymond. *Les étapes de la pensée sociologique*. Paris: Gallimard, 1967.

Aron, Raymond. "États démocratiques et états totalitaires (Juin 1939)." *Commentaire* 24 (1983-1984): 701-19.

Aron, Raymond. *Le grand schisme*. Paris: Gallimard, 1948.

Aron, Raymond. *The Great Debate: Theories of Nuclear Strategy*. Garden City, NY: Doubleday, 1965.

Aron, Raymond. *Les guerres en chaîne*. Paris: Gallimard, 1951.

Aron, Raymond. *L'homme contre les tyrans*. New York: Éditions de la Maison française, 1944.

Aron, Raymond. *The Imperial Republic. The United States and the World, 1945-1973*. Englewood Cliffs, NJ: Prentice-Hall, 1974.

Aron, Raymond. *Imperialism and Colonialism*. Leeds: Jowett & Sowry, 1959.

Aron, Raymond. "L'industrialisation de l'empire." *Combat*, June 24 (1946).

Aron, Raymond. *Introduction to the Philosophy of History: An Essay on the Limits of Historical Objectivity*. London: Weidenfeld and Nicolson, [1938] 1961.

Aron, Raymond. "Lettre ouverte d'un jeune français à l'Allemagne." *L'Esprit* 1, no. 5 (1933): 735-43.

Aron, Raymond. *Machiavel et les tyrannies modernes*. Paris: Éditions de Fallois, 1993.

Aron, Raymond. *Memoirs: Fifty Years of Political Thought*. New York: Holmes & Meier, [1983] 1990.

Aron, Raymond. "Nations et empires." In *Encyclopédie française*, vol. 11, 11-04-1-11-04-6. Paris: Société nouvelle de l'Encyclopédie française, 1957.

Aron, Raymond. "Nouvelle carte du monde." *Point de vue* 1, no. 7 (May 4, 1945): n.p.

Aron, Raymond. *Peace and War*. Garden City, NY: Doubleday, 1962.

Aron, Raymond. "Perspectives nord-africaines." *Evidences* (September-December 1954): 3-4.

Aron, Raymond. "Reflections on the Foreign Policy of France." *International Affairs* 21, no. 4 (1945): 437-47.

Aron, Raymond. *La sociologie allemande contemporaine*. Paris: Alcan, 1935. Translated by Mary and Thomas Bottomore as *German Sociology* (Glencoe, IL: Free Press, 1964).

Aron, Raymond. *La tragédie algérienne*. Paris: Plon, 1957.

Aron, Raymond. "Transformations du monde de 1900 à 1950: déplacement du centre de gravité international." *Réalités* 47 (1949): 70-111.

Audren, Frédéric. "Un interlocuteur français: René Maunier." *Les Études Sociales*, nos. 153-54 (2011): 213-16.

Bachelard, Gaston. *The Formation of the Scientific Mind*. Manchester: Clinamen, [1938] 2002.

Balandier, Georges. *L'action en faveur des populations rurales: le regroupement des villages au Gabon*. Brazzaville: IEC, 1950.

Balandier, Georges. *Afrique ambiguë*. Paris: Plon, 1957.

Balandier, Georges. *Ambiguous Africa*. London: Chatto & Windus, [1957] 1966.

Balandier, Georges. *Anthropologie politique*. Paris: PUF, 1967.

Balandier, Georges. "Approche sociologique des Brazzavilles noires." *Africa* 22, no. 1 (1952): 23-34.

Balandier, Georges. "Aspects de l'évolution sociale chez les Fang du Gabon (Afrique Équatoriale française)." *Cahiers internationaux de sociologie* 9 (1950): 76-106.

Balandier, Georges. *Autour de Georges Balandier*. Paris: Fondation d'Hautvillers pour le dialogue des cultures, 1981.

Balandier, Georges. *Carnaval des apparences*. Paris: Fayard, 2012.

Balandier, Georges. "Chronique. La participation de l'AEF à la Conférence internationale des Africanistes de l'Ouest." *Bulletin de l'Institut d'études centrafricaines* 1 (1950): 79–80.

Balandier, Georges. *Civilisés, dit-on*. Paris: PUF, 2003.

Balandier, Georges. "The Colonial Situation: A Theoretical Approach." In *Social Change. The Colonial Situation*, edited by Immanuel Wallerstein, 34–61. New York: Wiley & Sons, 1966.

Balandier, Georges. "Les conditions sociologiques de l'art noir." *Présence africaine* 10–11 (1951): 58–71.

Balandier, Georges. *Conjugaisons*. Paris: Fayard, 1997.

Balandier, Georges. "Contribution à une sociologie de la dépendance." *Cahiers internationaux de sociologie* 12 (1952): 47–69.

Balandier, Georges. *Daily Life in the Kingdom of the Kongo from the Sixteenth to the Eighteenth Century*. New York: Pantheon Books, [1965] 1968.

Balandier, Georges. "Les débats." In "L'Éveil de l'Afrique noire: Trois conférences-débats." Supplément of *Preuves*, no. 88 (Juin 1958): 27–32.

Balandier, Georges. *Le dédale: pour en finir avec le XXe siècle*. Paris: Fayard, 1994.

Balandier, Georges. *Le dépaysement contemporain. L'immédiat et l'essentiel. Entretiens avec Joël Birman et Claudine Haroche*. Paris: PUF, 2009.

Balandier, Georges. "Le développement industriel de la prolétarisation en Afrique noire." *L'Afrique et L'Asie* 4, no. 20 (1952): 45–53.

Balandier, Georges. "Erreurs noires." *Présence africaine* 3 (1948): 393–404.

Balandier, Georges. "Ethnologie et psychologie." *Études Guinéennes* 1 (1947): 47–56.

Balandier, Georges. "Les *Études guinéennes*." *Études guinéennes* 1 (1947): 5–6.

Balandier, Georges. "Évolution de la société et de l'homme." In *Afrique équatoriale française*, edited by Eugène Léonard Guernier, 125–32. Paris: Encyclopédie Coloniale et Maritime, 1950.

Balandier, Georges. "The Fact of Colonialism: A Theoretical Approach." *Cross Currents* 2, no. 4 (1952): 10–31.

Balandier, Georges. *Georges Gurvitch, sa vie, son œuvre*. Paris: PUF, 1972.

Balandier, Georges. *Histoire d'autres*. Paris: Stock, 1977.

Balandier, Georges. "L'homme et ses coordonées. Des manières de s'en prendre à l'être social." *Cahiers du sud* 39, no. 314 (1952): 151–56.

Balandier, Georges. *Lettres sur la poésie*. Paris: les Cahiers littéraires, 1943.

Balandier, Georges. "Littérature de l'Afrique et des Amériques noires." In *Histoires des littératures*, edited by Raymond Queneau, vol. 1, 1536–67. Paris: Gallimard, 1956.

Balandier, Georges. "Naissance d'un mouvement politico-religieux chez les 'Ba-Kongo' du moyen-Congo." In *Proceedings of the III International West Africa Conference Held at Ibadan, Nigeria, December 1949*, 334–36. Lagos: Nigerian Museum, 1956.

Balandier, Georges. "Le noir est un homme." *Présence africaine* 1 (November–December 1947): 31–36.

Balandier, Georges. "Note sur l'exploitation du sel par les vielles femmes de Bargny (environs de Rufisque)." *Notes africaines* 32 (1946): 22.

Balandier, Georges. "Observations sur la patrimonie et l'héritage chez les Lébou Bargny." *Notes africaines* 32 (1946): 18–19.

Balandier, Georges. "L'or de la Guinée française." *Présence africaine* 4 (1948): 539–48.

Balandier, Georges. *Political Anthropology*. New York: Vintage, [1967] 1970.

Balandier, Georges. "Problématique des classes sociales en Afrique noire." *Cahiers internationaux de sociologie* 38 (1965): 131–42.

Balandier, Georges. "Problèmes économiques et problèmes politiques au niveau du village Fang." *Bulletin de l'Institut d'études centrafricaines* 1 (1950): 49–64.
Balandier, Georges. "Rapport préliminaire de la mission d'information scientifique en pays Fang (24 janvier–20 mars 1949)." Presentation to Groupe de sociologie industrielle at the Centre d'études sociologiques. Brazzaville: IEC, 1952.
Balandier, Georges. "Recherches de convergences entre psychologie, sociologie et ethnologie." *Les études philosophiques* n.s. 3, nos. 3–4 (1948): 281–92.
Balandier, Georges. Review of *Cahier d'un retour au pays natal*. *Présence africaine* 1 (1947): 177–78.
Balandier, Georges. Review of Mannoni, *Psychologie de la colonisation*. *Cahiers internationaux de sociologie* 9 (1950): 183–86.
Balandier, Georges. *Sens et puissance*. Paris: PUF, 1971.
Balandier, Georges. "La situation coloniale: ancien concept, nouvelle réalité." In "Regards croisés: Transatlantic Perspectives on the Colonial Situation," edited by Emmanuelle Saada. Special issue of *French Politics, Culture and Society* 20, no. 2 (2002): 4–10.
Balandier, Georges. "La situation coloniale: approche théorique." *Cahiers internationaux de sociologie* 11 (1951): 44–79.
Balandier, Georges. "Social Implications of Technical Advance in Underdeveloped Countries." *Current Sociology* 3 (1954): 41–46.
Balandier, Georges. "Sociological Survey of the African Town at Brazzaville." In International African Institute, *Social Implications of Industrialization and Urbanization in Africa South of the Sahara*, 106–08. Paris: UNESCO, 1956.
Balandier, Georges. *Sociologie actuelle de l'Afrique noire. Dynamique des changements sociaux en Afrique centrale*. Paris: PUF, 1955.
Balandier, Georges. "Sociologie de la colonisation et relations entre sociétiés globales." *Cahiers Internationaux de sociologie* 17 (1954): 17–31.
Balandier, Georges. *Sociologie des Brazzavilles noires*. Paris: A. Colin, 1955.
Balandier, Georges. *Sociologie des Brazzavilles noires*. Paris: A. Colin, [1955] 1985.
Balandier, Georges. "Sociologie dynamique et histoire à partir de faits africains." *Cahiers internationaux de sociologie* 34 (1963): 3–11.
Balandier, Georges. *The Sociology of Black Africa. Social Dynamics in Central Africa*. New York: Praeger, [1955] 1970.
Balandier, Georges, ed. *Le tiers-monde, sous-développement et développement*. Paris: PUF-INED, 1957.
Balandier, Georges. *Tous comptes faits*. Paris: Éditions du Pavois, 1947.
Balandier, Georges. "Tout parcours scientifique comporte des moments autobiographiques." *Actes de la recherche en sciences sociales* 185 (December 2010): 44–61.
Balandier, Georges, Roger Bastide, Jacques Berque, and Pierre George, eds. *Perspectives de la sociologie contemporaine. Hommage à Georges Gurvitch*. Paris: PUF, 1968.
Balandier, Georges, and Paul Mercier. *Particularisme et évolution. Les pêcheurs Lébou du Sénégal*. Saint Louis, Sénégal: IFAN, 1952.
Balandier, Georges, and Jean-Claude Pauvert. *Les villages gabonais*. Brazzaville: Institut d'études centrafricaines, 1952.
Balandier, Georges, and Jean-Claude Pauvert. *Mission d'étude du regroupement des villages (territoires du Gabon)*. Paris: ORSTOM, 1950.
Bastide, Roger. "L'acculturation formelle." In *Le prochain et le lointain*, 137–48. Paris: Cujas, 1970.
Bastide, Roger. *The African Religions of Brazil: Towards a Sociology of the Interpenetration of Civilizations*. Baltimore, MD: Johns Hopkins University Press, [1960] 1978.
Bastide, Roger. "Contribution à l'étude de la participation." *Cahiers internationaux de sociologie* 14 (1979): 30–40.

Bastide, Roger, ed. *Contributions à la sociologie de la connaissance*. Paris: Editions Anthropos, 1967.
Bastide, Roger. *Éléments de sociologie religieuse*. Paris: A. Colin, 1935.
Bastide, Roger. *Initiation aux recherches sur l'interpénétration des civilisations*. Paris: Centre de documentation universitaire, 1948.
Bastide, Roger. "Le principe de coupure et le comportement afro-brésilien." In *Anais do XXXI Congresso Internacional de Americanistas, São Paulo*, vol. 1, 493–503. São Paulo: Anhembi, 1955.
Bastide, Roger. *Les religions africaines au Brésil*. Paris: PUF, 1960.
Bastide, Roger. "Rêves de noirs." *Psyché. Revue international des sciences de l'homme et de psychanalyse* 5, no. 49 (1950): 802–11.
Bastide, Roger. "Sociologie et psychanalyse." *Cahiers internationaux de sociologie* 2 (1947): 108–22.
Bastide, Roger. *Sociologie et psychanalyse*. Paris: PUF, 1950.
Bastide, Roger, and F. Raveau. "Contribution à l'étude de l'adaptation des Noirs en France." In *Transactions of the Sixth World Congress of Sociology. Actes du Sixième Congrès Mondial de Sociologie*, 279–88. Vol. 4. Genève: International Sociological Association, 1966.
Bastide, Roger, and P. Verger. "Contribution à l'étude sociologique des marchés Nagô du Bas-Dahomey." *Cahiers de l'Institut de science économique appliquée*, no. 95 (1959): 33–65.
Baverez, Nicolas. *Raymond Aron: un moraliste au temps des ideologies*. Paris: Flammarion, 1993.
Bégué, Jean-Michel. "French Psychiatry in Algeria (1830–1962): From Colonial to Transcultural." *History of Psychiatry* 7, no. 28 (1996): 533–48.
Bégué, Jean-Michel. "Un siècle de psychiatrie française en Algérie, 1830–1939." *L'Information psychiatrique* 69, no. 1 (1993): 67–72.
Bekombo, Manga. "Brazzaville à l'heure de la télévision congolaise." *Revue française de sociologie* 7, no. 2 (1966): 188–200.
Bekombo, Manga. "Celui qui va là-bas ne parle plus." *L'homme* 28, no. 148 (1998): 11–13.
Bekombo, Manga. "Incidences sociales de la modernisation en agriculture en Afrique noire." *Présence africaine* 55 (1965): 135–44.
Bekombo, Manga. "Parole et persuasion." *Recherche, pédagogie et culture*, no. 62 (1983): 40–45.
Bekombo, Manga. "Le regard des ethnologues." *Magazine littéraire*, no. 195 (May 1983): 37–38.
Bekombo, Manga. "La Société familiale Dwàla." Doctorat de 3e cycle d'Ethnologie, Université de Nanterre, 1969.
Belloc, Chloé. "La création du Conseil International de la Philosophie et des Sciences humaines, 1946–1949." *Bulletin de l'Institut Pierre Renouvin* 25 (2007): 17–41.
Ben Salem, Lilia. "'Propos sur la sociologie en Tunisie.' Entretien avec Sylvie Mazzella." *Genèses: sciences sociales et histoire*, no. 75 (2009): 125–42.
Ben Salem, Lilia. "Rencontre de la société et de la psychiatrie." In Fanon, *Oeuvres*, edited by Jean Khalfa and Robert Young, 430–56. Vol. 2, *Écrits sur l'aliénation et la liberté*. Paris: La Découverte, 2015.
Berque, Augustin. *Ecrits sur l'Algérie*, edited by Jacques Berque. Aix-en-Provence: Edisud, 1986.
Berque, Jacques. *Al-Yousi: problèmes de la culture marocaine au XVIIe siècle*. Paris: Mouton, 1958.
Berque, Jacques. "L'Algérie ou les faux dilemmes." *Politique étrangère* 21, no. 6 (1956): 703–10.
Berque, Jacques. *Les Arabes*. Paris: Delpire, 1959.

Berque, Jacques. *Arabies*. Paris: Stock, 1978.
Berque, Jacques. *The Arabs*. London: Faber & Faber, [1960] 1964.
Berque, Jacques. "Aspects du contrat pastoral à Sidi-Aïssa." *Revue africaine* 79, nos. 368-69 (1936): 899-911.
Berque, Jacques. *Une cause jamais perdue: articles politiques (1947-1995)*. Paris: Albin Michel, 1998.
Berque, Jacques. "Cent vingt-cinq ans de sociologie maghrébine." *Annales ESC* 10, no. 3 (1956): 296-324.
Berque, Jacques. "Colonisation, décolonisation, comment les definir?" *Cahiers Internationaux. Revue internationale du monde du travail* 118 (1961): 53-60.
Berque, Jacques. "'Contenu' et 'forme' dans la décolonisation." In *Perspectives de la sociologie contemporaine. Hommage à Georges Gurvitch*, edited by Georges Balandier, Roger Bastide, Jacques Berque, and Pierre George, 21-38. Paris: PUF, 1968.
Berque, Jacques, trans. *Le Coran*. Paris: Sindbad, 1990.
Berque, Jacques. (F. Jabre, pseud.) "Dans le Maroc nouveau: le role d'une université islamique." *Annales d'histoire économique et sociale* 51 (May 1938): 193-207.
Berque, Jacques. "Décolonisation intérieure et nature seconde." *Études de sociologie tunisienne* 1 (1968): 11-27.
Berque, Jacques. *Dépossession du monde*. Paris, Seuil, 1964.
Berque, Jacques. "Deux cas de compromis entre droits universalistes et coutumes locales." In *Normes et valeurs dans l'Islam contemporain*, edited by Jacques Berque and Jean-Paul Charnay, 132-44. Paris: Payot, 1966.
Berque, Jacques. "Le droit du Sous." *Bulletin des études arabes* 9 (1949): 8-11.
Berque, Jacques. *L'Egypte: impérialisme et révolution*. Paris: Gallimard, 1967.
Berque, Jacques. "Entrée dans le bureau arabe." In Jacques Berques et al., *Nomades et vagabonds*, 113-39. Paris: Union générale d'éditions, 1975.
Berque, Jacques. "Un entretien entre Jacques Berque, Jean Duvignaud et Kateb Yacine sur Les mystères du polygone étoilé." *Afrique-Action* 37 (June 26, 1961): 30-31.
Berque, Jacques. *Essai sur la méthode juridique maghrébine*. Rabat: M. Leforestier, 1944.
Berque, Jacques. *Études d'histoire rurale maghrébine*. Tanger: Éditions internationales, 1938.
Berque, Jacques. "Gernet et la sociologie orientaliste." In *Hommage à Louis Gernet rendu au Collège de France*, edited by Georges Davy, 36-37. Paris: PUF, 1966.
Berque, Jacques. *Histoire sociale d'un village égyptien au XXe siécle*. Paris: Mouton, 1957.
Berque, Jacques. "Hommages à Franz Fanon." *Presence africaine* 40 (June 1962): 118-19.
Berque, Jacques. *Il reste un avenir: entretiens avec Jean Sur*. Paris: Arléa, 1993.
Berque, Jacques. *L'intérieur du Maghreb: XVe-XIXe siècle*. Paris: Gallimard, 1978.
Berque, Jacques. *Langages arabes du present*. Paris: Gallimard, 1974.
Berque, Jacques. "Logiques d'assemblage au Maghreb." In *L'autre et l'ailleurs. Hommage à Roger Bastide*, edited by Georges Balandier et al., 39-56. Paris: Berger-Levrault, 1976.
Berque, Jacques. "Logiques plurales du progrès." *Diogène* 79 (1972): 3-26.
Berque, Jacques. *Le Maghreb entre deux guerres*. Paris: Seuil, 1962.
Berque, Jacques. "Medinas, villeneuves et bidonvilles." *Cahiers de Tunisie* 21-22 (1957): 5-42.
Berque, Jacques. *Mémoires des deux rives*. Paris: Seuil, 1989.
Berque, Jacques. "Les Muhâdarât d'Al-Yousi. Problèmes de la culture marocaine au XVIIe siècle." Thèse complementaire, University of Paris, 1954.
Berque, Jacques. *Les Nawâzil el muzâra'a du Mi'yâr Al Wazzâni*. Rabat: Moncho, 1940.
Berque, Jacques. "The North of Africa." *International Social Science Journal* 13, no. 2 (1961): 177-96.
Berque, Jacques. "Nouveaux types urbains au Maroc: A propos d'une enquête collective." *Annales ESC* 7, no. 2 (1952): 210-16.

Berque, Jacques. "Nouvelles approches de la décolonisation." In *De l'impérialisme à la décolonisation*, edited by Jean-Paul Charnay, 479–501. Paris: Minuit, 1965.

Berque, Jacques. *Opera minora*. 3 vols. Paris: Editions Bouchène, 2001.

Berque, Jacques. "Perspectives de l'orientalisme contemporain." *Ibla* 79 (1957): 217–38.

Berque, Jacques. "Une perte pour la sociologie française: Charles Le Coeur." *Annales ESC* 7, no. 1 (1952): 143.

Berque, Jacques. "Préface." *Ibla: Revue de L'institut des belles lettres arabes* 79 (1960): 351–56.

Berque, Jacques. "Le problème démographique en pays berbère: étude sur les tribus de la région d'Imintanout. I. La population." *Bulletin économique et social du Maroc* 17, no. 60 (1953–1954): 203–07.

Berque, Jacques. "Problèmes initiaux de la sociologie juridique en Afrique du Nord." *Studia Islamica* 1 (1953): 137–62.

Berque, Jacques. "Quelques perspectives d'une sociologie de la décolonisation." *Revue de l'enseignement supérieur* 1–2 (1965): 33–40.

Berque, Jacques. "Qu'est-ce qu'une tribu nord-africaine?" In *Éventail de l'histoire vivante: Hommage à Lucien Febvre*, edited by Fernand Braudel, 261–71. Paris: Armand Colin, 1954.

Berque, Jacques. *Rapport de M. Jacques Berque, professeur au Collège de France, sur la mission qu'il a effectué au Liban de septembre à novembre 1959, en vue du développement de l'enseignement et de la recherche dans le domaine des sciences sociales, au titre du programme de participation aux activités des États membres de l'UNESCO*. Paris: UNESCO, 1959.

Berque, Jacques. *Rapport de M. Jacques Berque, professeur au Collège de France, sur la mission qu'il a effectuée en Tunisie de novembre à décembre 1959, en vue du développement de l'enseignement et de la recherche dans le domaine des sciences sociales, au titre du programme de participation aux activités des États membres de l'UNESCO*. Paris: UNESCO, 1959.

Berque, Jacques. *Relire le Coran*. Paris: Albin Michel, 1993.

Berque, Jacques. "Remarques sur le tapis maghrébin." In *Études Maghrébines. Mélanges Charles-Andre Julien*, edited by Pierre Marthelot, 13–24. Paris: PUF, 1964.

Berque, Jacques. "Sciences sociales et décolonisation." *Tiers-Monde* 9–10 (1962): 1–15.

Berque, Jacques. "Sciences sociales et monde arabo-islamique." In *L'intervention dans le champ social*, edited by Simone Crapuchet and Georges Michel Salomon, 81–84. Paris: Privat, 1992.

Berque, Jacques. "Les sociétés nord-africaines vues du Haut-Atlas." *Cahiers internationaux de sociologie* 19 (1955): 59–65.

Berque, Jacques. *Structures sociales du Haut-Atlas*. Paris: PUF, 1955.

Berque, Jacques. "Sur l'esthétique musulmane et ses motivations psychologiques et sociales." *Journal de Psychologie Normale et Pathologique* 58, no. 4 (1961): 433–44.

Berque, Jacques. "Sur un coin de terre marocaine: seigneur terrien et paysans." *Annales d'histoire économique et sociale* 9, no. 45 (1937): 227–35.

Berque, Jacques. *Ulémas, fondateurs, insurgés du Maghreb: XVIIe siècle*. Paris: Sindbad, 1982.

Berque, Jacques. "Vers la modernisation rurale." *Bulletin d'information du Maroc* (October 1945): 5–17.

Berque, Jacques. "Vers une étude des comportements en Afrique du Nord." *Revue africaine* 100 (1956): 523–36.

Berque, Jacques. "Vie sociale et variations de mode et de densité." *L'homme et la société* 11 (1966): 146–58.

Berque, Jacques, and G. H. Bousquet. *Recueil de la loi musulmane de Zaîd ben 'Alî (le plus ancien recueil de droit musulman retrouvé jusqu'ici)*. Alger: La Maison des Livres, 1941.

Berque, Jacques, and Julien Couleau. "Vers la modernisation du fellah marocain." *Bulletin économique et social du Maroc* 7, no. 26 (1945): 18–24.
Bettelheim, Charles, and Suzanne Frère. *Auxerre en 1950, une ville française moyennes. Étude de structure sociale et urbaine*. Paris: A. Colin, 1950.
Betts, Raymond F. "Dakar: Ville impériale (1857–1960)." In *Colonial Cities*, edited by Robert J. Ross and Gerard J. Telkamp, 193–206. Boston: Kluwer, 1985.
Bigon, Liora. *French Colonial Dakar: The Morphogenesis of an African Regional Capital*. Manchester: Manchester University Press, 2016.
Blanchard, Pascal, and Gilles Boëtsch. "Races et propagande coloniale sous le régime de Vichy 1940–1944." *Africa: Rivista trimestrale di studi e documentazione dell'Istituto italiano per l'Africa e l'Oriente* 49, no. 4 (1994): 531–61.
Blondiaux, Loïc. "Comment rompre avec Durkheim? Jean Stoetzel et la sociologie française de l'après-guerre (1945–1958)." *Revue française de sociologie* 32, no. 3 (1991): 411–41.
Blondiaux, Loïc. *La fabrique de l'opinion: une histoire sociale des sondages*. Paris: Éditions du Seuil, 1998.
Bock, Hans Manfred. "Raymond Aron und Deutschland. Aspekte einer intellektuellen Generationsanalyse." *Lendemains* 36, no. 141 (2011): 43–58.
Bonfreschi, Lucia. "Raymond Aron face au processus de la decolonisation française sous la Quatrième Republique." *Outre-mers: revue d'histoire* (2007): 354–55.
Bonneuil, Christophe. "Development as Experiment: Science and State Building in Late Colonial and Postcolonial Africa, 1930–1970." *Osiris* 15, no. 1 (2000): 258–81.
Bonneuil, Christophe. *Des savants pour l'empire. La structuration des recherches scientifiques coloniales au temps de la "mise en valeur des colonies françaises," 1917–1945*. Paris: ORSTOM, 1991.
Bonneuil, Christophe, and Patrick Petitjean. "Les chemins de la création de l'Orstom, du Front populaire à la Libération en passant par Vichy, 1936–1945. Recherche scientifique et politique colonial." In *Les sciences coloniales: Figures and Institutions*, edited by Patrick Petitjean, 113–61. Paris: ORSTOM, 1996.
Bouglé, Célestin. *Bilan de la sociologie française contemporaine*. Paris: Alcan, 1935.
Bouglé, Célestin. "Comment étudier la sociologie à Paris?" *Annales de l'Université de Paris* 2, no. 4 (1926): 313–24.
Bouglé, Célestin. *Cours de sociologie générale*. Paris: Centre de Documentation Universitaire, 1935.
Bouglé, Célestin. *The Evolution of Values. Studies in Sociology with Special Applications to Teaching*. New York: H. Holt, [1922] 1926.
Bouglé, Célestin. "Histoire et sociologie: remarques générales." *Annales sociologiques* ser. A, no. 1 (1934): 172–82.
Bouglé, Célestin. [Jean Breton, pseud.]. *Notes d'un étudiant français en Allemagne. Heidelberg–Berlin–Leipzig–Munich*. Paris: Calman-Lévy, 1895.
Bouglé, Célestin. *Qu'est-ce que la sociologie?* 7th ed. Paris: Alcan, 1939.
Bouglé, Célestin. "La sociologie française et l'éducation nationale." *Archives pour la science et la réforme sociale* 13, no. 1 (1936): 39–46.
Bouhedja, Salah. "'It était un parmi les dix.' Autour de l'enquête sur les camps de regroupement dans *Le déracinement*." *Awal* 27–28 (2003): 287–94.
Bourdieu, Pierre. *Algeria 1960: The Disenchantment of the World, The Sense of Honour, The Kabyle House or The World Reversed*. Translated by Richard Nice. New York: Cambridge University Press, 1979.
Bourdieu, Pierre. *Algerian Sketches*. Cambridge: Polity, 2013.
Bourdieu, Pierre. *The Algerians*. Translated by Alan C. M. Ross. Boston: Beacon, 1962.
Bourdieu, Pierre. "Champ intellectuel et projet créateur." *Les temps modernes* no. 246 (1966): 865–906.

Bourdieu, Pierre. "Les chercheurs et le mouvement social." In *Pierre Bourdieu, Interventions, 1961-2001*, edited by Franck Poupeau and Thierry Discepolo, 465-66. Marseille: Éditions Agone, 2002.

Bourdieu, Pierre. "Le choc des civilisations." In *Le sous-développement en Algérie*, edited by Secrétariat social d'Alger, 52-64. Alger: Éditions du Secrétariat social d'Alger, 1969.

Bourdieu, Pierre. *Classification Struggles: General Sociology*. Vol. 1. Cambridge: Polity Press, 2018.

Bourdieu, Pierre. "Le clou de Djeha. Des contradictions linguistiques léguées par le colonisateur: un entretien avec Pierre Bourdieu." *Hommes et migrations* 991: 37-41.

Bourdieu, Pierre. "Les conditions sociales de la production sociologique: sociologie coloniale et décolonisation de la sociologie." In *Le mal de voir. Ethnologie et orientalisme: politique et épistémologie, critique et autocritique*, edited by Henri Moniot, 416-27. Paris: Union générale d'éditions, 1976.

Bourdieu, Pierre. "La culture Mozabite." *Documents algériens, Série monographies*, no. 23 (November 20, 1958).

Bourdieu, Pierre. "De la guerre révolutionnaire à la révolution." In *L'Algérie de demain*, edited by François Perroux, 5-13. Paris: PUF, 1962.

Bourdieu, Pierre. *Distinction. A Social Critique of the Judgement of Taste*. Cambridge, MA: Harvard University Press, 1984.

Bourdieu, Pierre. "Étude sociologique." In Pierre Bourdieu, Alain Darbel, Jean-Paul Rivet, and Claude Seibel, *Travail et travailleurs en Algérie*, 253-62. Paris: Mouton, 1963.

Bourdieu, Pierre. "The Force of Law: Toward a Sociology of the Juridical Field." *Hastings Law Journal* 38, no. 5 (1987): 814-53.

Bourdieu, Pierre. "The Genesis of the Concepts of Habitus and Field." *Sociocriticism* 2, no. 2 (1985): 11-24.

Bourdieu, Pierre. "Guerre et mutation sociale en Algérie." *Études méditerrannées* 7 (1960): 25-37.

Bourdieu, Pierre. "La hantise du chômage chez l'ouvrier algérien. Prolétariat et système colonial." *Sociologie du travail* 4, no. 4 (1962): 313-31.

Bourdieu, Pierre. *Homo Academicus*. Cambridge: Polity Press, 1988.

Bourdieu, Pierre. "Il faut que l'intellectuel donne la parole à ceux qui ne l'ont pas!" *L'événement du Jeudi* (September 10-16, 1992): 114-16.

Bourdieu, Pierre. *In Other Words: Essays Towards a Reflexive Sociology*. Cambridge: Polity Press, 1990.

Bourdieu, Pierre. *Language and Symbolic Power*. Cambridge, MA: Harvard University Press, 1991.

Bourdieu, Pierre. *The Logic of Practice*. Stanford, CA: Stanford University Press, [1980] 1990.

Bourdieu, Pierre. "La logique interne de la civilisation algérienne traditionnelle." In *Le sous-développement en Algérie*, edited by Secrétariat social d'Alger, 40-51. Alger: Éditions du Secrétariat social d'Alger, 1969.

Bourdieu, Pierre. "La maison kabyle ou le monde renversé." In *Échanges et communications. Mélanges offerts à Claude Lévi-Strauss à l'occasion de son 60e anniversaire*, edited by Jean Pouillon and Paul Maranda, 739-58. Paris: Mouton, 1970.

Bourdieu, Pierre. *Manet: A Symbolic Revolution*. Cambridge: Polity, 2017.

Bourdieu, Pierre. "Méthode scientifique et hiérarchie sociale des objets." *Actes de la recherche en sciences sociales* 1 (1975): 4-6.

Bourdieu, Pierre. *Microcosmes: Théorie des champs*. Paris: Raisons d'agir, 2022.

Bourdieu, Pierre. *Outline of a Theory of Practice*. Cambridge: Cambridge University Press, 1977.

Bourdieu, Pierre. *Pascalian Meditations*. Cambridge: Polity, 2000.
Bourdieu, Pierre. "Photographie d'Algérie. Entretien avec Pierre Bourdieu du 26 juin 2001 au Collège de France par Franz Schultheis." In *Images d'Algérie*, 19–44. Arles: Actes Sud, 2003.
Bourdieu, Pierre. "Postface to Erwin Panofsky's Gothic Architecture and Scholasticism." In Bruce W. Holsinger, *The Premodern Condition: Medievalism and the Making of Theory*, 221–42. Chicago: University of Chicago Press, [1967] 2005.
Bourdieu, Pierre. "Les professeurs de l'Université de Paris à la veille de Mai 1968." In *Le Personnel de l'enseignement supérieur en France aux XIXe et XXe siécles*, edited by Christophe Charle and Régine Ferré, 177–84. Paris: Éditions du Centre national de la recherche scientifique, 1985.
Bourdieu, Pierre. "Révolution dans la révolution." *Esprit* 1 (1961): 27–40.
Bourdieu, Pierre. *The Rules of Art*. Cambridge: Polity, 1996.
Bourdieu, Pierre. *Science of Science and Reflexivity*. Chicago: University of Chicago Press, 2004.
Bourdieu, Pierre. "Secouez un peu vos structures!" In *Le symbolique et le social: la réception internationale de la pensée de Pierre Bourdieu*, edited by Jacques Dubois, Pascal Durand, and Yves Winkin, 325–41. Liège: Editions de l'Université de Liège, 2005.
Bourdieu, Pierre. "The Sentiment of Honour in Kabyle Society." In *Honour and Shame: The Values of Mediterranean Society*, edited by John G. Peristiany, 191–241. London: Weidenfeld and Nicholson, 1965.
Bourdieu, Pierre. *Sketch for a Self-Analysis*. Cambridge: Polity, 2007.
Bourdieu, Pierre. *Sociologie de l'Algérie*. New ed. Paris: PUF, 1961.
Bourdieu, Pierre. *Sociologie de l'Algérie*. Paris: PUF, 1958.
Bourdieu, Pierre. *Sociologie générale*. Vol. 2. Paris: Seuil, 2015.
Bourdieu, Pierre. *The State Nobility*. Stanford, CA: Stanford University Press, 1996.
Bourdieu, Pierre. "Statistiques et sociologie." In Bourdieu et al., *Travail et travailleurs*, 9–13.
Bourdieu, Pierre. "The Struggle for Symbolic Order." *Theory, Culture and Society* 3, no. 3 (1986): 31–51.
Bourdieu, Pierre. "Systems of Education and Systems of Thought." *International Social Science Journal* 19, no. 3 (1967): 338–58.
Bourdieu, Pierre. "The (Three) Forms of Capital." In *Handbook of Theory and Research in the Sociology of Education*, edited by John G. Richardson, 241–58. New York: Greenwood Press, 1986.
Bourdieu, Pierre, Jean-Claude Chamboredon, and Jean-Claude Passeron. *The Craft of Sociology: Epistemological Preliminaries*. New York: de Gruyter, 1991.
Bourdieu, Pierre, and Roger Chartier. *The Sociologist and the Historian*. Cambridge, UK: Polity Press, 2015.
Bourdieu, Pierre, Alain Darbel, Jean-Paul Rivet, and Claude Seibel. *Travail et travailleurs en Algérie*. Paris: Mouton, 1963.
Bourdieu, Pierre, and Abdelmalek Sayad. *Le déracinement. La crise de l'agriculture traditionelle en Algérie*. Paris: Les Éditions de Minuit, 1964.
Bourdieu, Pierre, and Abdelmalek Sayad. *Uprooting. The Crisis of Traditional Agriculture in Algeria*. Cambridge: Polity Press, 2020.
Bourdieu, Pierre, and Loïc J. D. Wacquant. *An Invitation to Reflexive Sociology*. Chicago: University of Chicago Press, 1992.
Brozgal, Lia Nicole. *Against Autobiography: Albert Memmi and the Production of Theory*. Lincoln: University of Nebraska Press, 2013.
Bullard, Alice. "The Critical Impact of Franz Fanon and Henri Collomb: Race, Gender, and Personality Testing of North and West Africans." *Journal of the History of the Behavioral Sciences* 41, no. 3 (2005): 225–48.

Burawoy, Michael. *The Colour of Class on the Copper Mines, from African Advancement to Zambianization*. Manchester University Press [for] the Institute for African Studies, University of Zambia, 1972.

Bureau, Paul. *Introduction à la méthode sociologique*. Paris: Bloud & Gay, 1923.

Bureau, René. *Bokayé! Essai sur le Bwiti Fang du Gabon*. Paris: L'Harmattan, 1996.

Burguière, Andre. "Plozévet, une mystique de l'interdisciplinarité?" *Cahiers du Centre de recherches historiques* 36 (2005): 231–63.

Burke, Edmund, III. *The Ethnographic State: France and the Invention of Moroccan Islam*. Berkeley: University of California Press, 2014.

Burke, Edmund, III. "La mission scientifique du Maroc." *Bulletin économique et social du Maroc*, nos. 138–39 (1979): 37–56.

Burke, Edmund, III. "The Sociology of Islam: The French Tradition." In *Islamic Studies: A Tradition and Its Problems*, edited by Malcom H. Kerr, 73–88. Santa Monica, CA: Undena, 1980.

Burnier, Michel, Sylvie Célérier, and Jan Spurk, eds. *Des sociologues face à Pierre Naville, ou, L'archipel des saviors*. Paris: L'Harmattan, 2007.

Camic, Charles. "Periphery toward Center and Back: Scholarship on the History of Sociology, 1945–2012." In *Historiography of the Social Sciences*, edited by Roger Backhouse and Philippe Fontaine, 99–143. New York: Cambridge University Press, 2014.

Camic, Charles. "Uneven Development in the History of Sociology." *Swiss Journal of Sociology* 23 (1997): 227–33.

Cefaï, Daniel, and Alain Mahé. "Échanges rituels de dons, obligation et contrat. Mauss, Davy, Maunier: trois perspectives de sociologie juridique." *Année sociologique* ser. 3, 48, no. 1 (1998): 209–28.

Césaire, Aimé. *Discourse on Colonialism*. New York: Monthly Review Press, [1950] 2000.

Chachoua, Kamel. "Pierre Bourdieu et l'Algérie: le savant et la politique." In *L'Algérie sociologique: hommage à Pierre Bourdieu (1930-2002)*, edited by Kamel Chachoua, 9–23. Alger: CNRPAH, 2012.

Chapman, Herrick. *France's Long Reconstruction: In Search of the Modern Republic*. Cambridge, MA: Harvard University Press, 2018.

Charle, Christophe. *Birth of the Intellectuals: 1880-1900*. Cambridge: Polity, 2015.

Charle, Christophe, and Laurent Jeanpierre, eds. *La vie intellectuelle en France*. Paris: Éditions du Seuil, 2016.

Châton, Gwendal. "Taking Totalitarianism Seriously: The Emergence of the Aronian Circle in the 1970s." In *In Search of the Liberal Moment*, edited by Steve Sawyer and Iain Stewart, 17–38. London: Palgrave, 2015.

Chatriot, Alain, and Vincent Duclert. "Fonder une politique de recherche. Les débuts de la DGRST." In *L'État à l'epreuve des sciences sociales. La function recherche dans les administrations de la Veme République*, edited by Philippe Bezes et al., 23–36. Paris: Découverte, 2005.

Chaulet, Pierre, and Claudine Chaulet. *Le choix de l'Algérie: deux voix, une mémoire*. Alger: Barzakh, 2012.

Chenntouf, Tayeb. "La sociologie au Maghreb: Cinquante ans après." *Revue Africaine de Sociologie* 10, no. 1 (2006): 1–30.

Chenu, Alain. "Une institution sans intention. La sociologie en France depuis l'après-guerre." *Actes de la recherche en sciences sociales* 141–42 (2002): 46–61.

Chenu, Alain, and Olivier Martin. "Le plafond de verre chez les enseignants-chercheurs en sociologie et démographie." *Travail, genre et sociétés* 36 (2016): 135–56.

Chevreau, Emmanuelle. *Henri Lévy-Bruhl: juriste sociologue*. Paris: Éditions Mare & Martin, 2018.

Chibber, Vivek. *Locked in Place: State-Building and Late Industrialization in India*. Princeton, NJ: Princeton University Press, 2003.
Chombart de Lauwe, Paul Henry. *Un anthropologue dans le siècle*. Paris: Descartes & Cie, 1996.
Chombart de Lauwe, Paul Henry. "Chez les Fali: Mission ethnographique Griaule-Sahara-Cameroun." *La géographie* 68, nos. 2–3 (1937): 97–104.
Chombart de Lauwe, Paul Henry, ed. *La découverte aérienne du monde*. Paris: Horizon de France, 1948.
Chombart de Lauwe, Paul Henry. "La photographie aérienne et les sciences humaines." *Comptes rendus sommaires des séances de l'Institut français d'anthropologie* 3, no. 54 (1946): 19–20.
Chombart de Lauwe, Paul Henry. *Photographies aériennes: méthode, procédés, interprétation. L'étude de l'homme sur la terre*. Paris: Colin, 1951.
Chombart de Lauwe, Paul Henry. *Pour retrouver la France, Enquêtes sociales en équipes*. Uriage: École nationale des cadres d'Uriage, 1941.
Chombart de Lauwe, Paul Henry. "Vision aérienne et civilization." *Atomes* 45 (1949): 429–41.
Clark, Terry Nichols. *Prophets and Patrons: The French University and the Emergence of the Social Sciences*. Cambridge, MA: Harvard University Press, 1973.
Clément, Pierre, and Nelly Xydias. *Vienne sur le Rhône, la ville et les habitants, situations et attitudes. Sociologie d'une cité française*. Paris: A. Colin, 1955.
Clifford, James. *Person and Myth: Maurice Leenhardt in the Melanesian World*. Berkeley: University of California Press, 1982.
Cohen, William B. *Rulers of Empire: The French Colonial Service in Africa*. Stanford, CA: Stanford University Press, 1971.
Colonna, Fanny. "Une fonction coloniale de l'ethnographie dans l'Algérie de l'entre deux-guerres: la programmation des élites moyennes." *Libyca* 20 (1972): 259–67.
Colonna, Fanny. *Instituteurs algériens, 1883–1939*. Paris: Presses de la Fondation nationale des sciences politiques, 1975.
Colonna, Fanny. "The Phantom of Dispossession: From *The Uprooting* to *The Weight of the World*." In *Bourdieu in Algeria: Colonial Politics, Ethnographic Practices, Theoretical Developments*, edited by Jane E. Goodman and Paul A. Silverstein, 63–93. Lincoln: University of Nebraska Press, 2009.
Colquhoun, Robert. *Raymond Aron*. Vol. 1. London: Sage, 1986.
Condominas, Georges. "Dans quelle mesure les asiatiques et les africains participant-ils aux recherches menées sur les divers aspects des civilisations africaines et orientales?" in Association des universités partiellement ou entièrement de langue française, *État et perspectives des études africaines et orientales*, edited by Pierre Louis, 105–13. Montréal: Therien frères, 1966.
Conklin, Alice. "Civil Society, Science, and Empire in Late Republican France: The Foundation of Paris's Museum of Man." *Osiris* 2nd series, 17 (2002): 255–90.
Conklin, Alice. *In the Museum of Man: Race, Anthropology, and Empire in France, 1850–1950*. Ithaca, NY: Cornell University Press, 2013.
Conklin, Alice. *A Mission to Civilize: The Republican Idea of Empire in France and West Africa, 1895–1930*. Stanford, CA: Stanford University Press, 1997.
Conklin, Alice. "De la sociologie objective à l'action. Charles Le Coeur et l'utopisme colonial." In *Ethnologues en situations coloniales*, edited by Christine Laurière and André Mary, 46–79. Les Carnets de Bérose, no. 11. Paris: Ministère de la Culture, 2019.
Connell, R. W. "Why Is Classical Theory Classical?" *American Journal of Sociology* 102 (1997): 1511–57.

Connell, Raewyn. "Northern Theory: The Political Geography of General Social Theory." *Theory and Society* 35, no. 2 (2006): 237–64.
Connell, Raewyn. *Southern Theory: The Global Dynamics of Knowledge in Social Science.* Cambridge: Polity, 2007.
Cooper, Frederick. *Citizenship between Empire and Nation: Remaking France and French Africa, 1945–1960.* Princeton, NJ: Princeton University Press, 2014.
Cooper, Frederick. *Decolonization and African Society: The Labor Question in French and British Africa.* Cambridge: Cambridge University Press, 1996.
Copans, Jean. *Georges Balandier. Un anthropologue en première ligne.* Paris: PUF, 2014.
Copans, Jean. *Sociologie du développement.* 2nd ed. Paris: Armand Colin, 2016.
Coquery-Vidrovitch, Catherine, ed. *L'Afrique occidentale au temps des Français colonisateurs et colonisés (c. 1860–1960).* Paris: La Découverte, 1992.
Coquery-Vidrovitch, Catherine. "Anthropologie politique et histoire de l'Afrique noire." *Annales. Économies, Sociétés, Civilisations* 24, no. 1 (1969): 142–63.
Coquery-Vidrovitch, Catherine. *Le Congo au temps des grandes compagnies concessionnaires: 1889–1930.* Vol. 2. Paris: EHESS, 2001.
Coquery-Vidrovitch, Catherine. *Enjeux politiques de l'histoire coloniale.* Marseille: Agone, 2009.
Cornaton, Michel. *Les regroupements de la décolonisation en Algérie.* Paris: Éditions ouvrières, 1967.
Craig, John E. "Sociology and the Related Disciplines between the Wars: Maurice Halbwachs and the Imperialism of the Durkheimians." In *The Sociological Domain: The Durkheimians and the Founding of French Sociology*, edited by Philippe Besnard, 263–89. Cambridge: Cambridge University Press, 1983.
Crapuchet, Simone, ed. *Politique sociale d'outre-mer: un devoir de mémoire à l'égard des pionnières.* Ramonville Saint-Agne: Erès, 1999.
Crowley, Patrick. "Albert Memmi: The Conflict of Legacies." In *Postcolonial Thought in the French-Speaking World*, edited by Charles Forsdick and David Murphy, 126–35. Liverpool: Liverpool University Press, 2009.
Dampierre, Éric de. *Un ancien royaume Bandia du Haut-Oubangui.* Paris: Plon, 1967.
Dampierre, Éric de. "Malvire-sur-Desle. Une commune aux franges de la région parisienne." *L'information géographique* 20 (1956): 68–73.
Davy, Georges. *Éléments de sociologie. I. Sociologie politique appliquée à la morale de à l'éducation.* 3rd ed. Paris: Delagrave, 1932.
de Gaulle, Charles. *The Call to Honor, War Memoirs.* New York: Viking Press, 1955.
de l'Estoile, Benoît. "Enquêter en 'situation coloniale.' Politique de la population, gouvernementalité modernisatrice et 'sociologie engagée' en Afrique française." *Cahiers d'études africaines* 228 (2017): 863–919.
de l'Estoile, Benoît. *Le goût des autres. De l'exposition coloniale aux arts premiers.* Paris: Flammarion, 2007.
de l'Estoile, Benoît. "Science de l'homme et 'domination rationnelle.' Savoir ethnologique et politique indigène en Afrique coloniale française." *Revue de synthèse* 4th ser., nos. 3–4 (2000): 294–95.
de Planhol, Xavier. *Nouveaux villages algérois. Atlas blidéen, Chenoua, Mitidja occidentale.* Paris: PUF, 1961.
de Queiroz, Maria Isaura Pereira. "Les Années brésiliennes de Roger Bastide." *Archives de sciences sociales des religions* 40 (1975): 79–87.
de Queiroz, Maria Isaura Pereira. "Principe de participation et principe de coupure. La contribution de Roger Bastide à leur définition sociologique." *Archives de sciences sociales des religions* 47, no. 1 (1979): 147–57.
de Suremain, Marie-Albane. "Faire du terrain en AOF dans les années cinquante." *Ethnologie française* 34, no. 4 (2004): 651–59.

Debaene, Vincent. *Far Afield: French Anthropology between Science and Literature*. Chicago: University of Chicago Press, 2014.
Delavignette, Robert Louis. *Les paysans noirs*. Paris: Stok, 1931.
Delavignette, Robert Louis. *Service africain*. Paris: Gallimard, 1946.
Deprez, Stanislas. *Lévy-Bruhl et la rationalisation du monde*. Rennes: Presses Universitaires de Rennes, 2010.
Desan, Mathieu Hikaru. "'Order, Authority, Nation': Neo-Socialism and the Fascist Destiny of an Anti-Fascist Discourse." PhD diss., University of Michigan, 2016.
Desan, Mathieu Hikaru, and Johan Heilbron. "Young Durkheimians and the Temptation of Fascism: The Case of Marcel Déat." *History of the Human Sciences* 28, no. 3 (2015): 22–50.
Deschamps, Hubert. *The French Union. History, Institutions, Economy, Countries and Peoples, Social and Political Changes*. Paris: Berger-Levrault, 1956.
Deschamps, Hubert. *Roi de la brousse: mémoires d'autres mondes*. Paris: Berger-Levrault, 1975.
Descloitres, Robert, Jean Claude Reverdy, and Claudine Descloitres. *L'Algérie des bidonvilles* Paris: Mouton, 1961.
Despland, Michel. *Bastide on Religion: The Invention of Candomblé*. London: Equinox, 2008.
Desrosiéres, Alain. "The Economics of Convention and Statistics: The Paradox of Origins." *Historical Social Research* 36, no. 4 (2011): 64–81.
Desrosières, Alain. "L'histoire de la statistique comme genre: style d'écriture et usages sociaux." *Genèses* 39, no. 2 (2002): 121–37.
Desrosières, Alain. *The Politics of Large Numbers: A History of Statistical Reasoning*. Cambridge, MA: Harvard University Press, 1998.
Devauges, Roland. *Les chômeurs de Brazzaville et les perspectives du barrage du Kouilou*. Brazzaville: ORSTOM, 1959.
Dias, Nélia. *Le Musée d'ethnographie du Trocadéro, 1878-1908: Anthropologie et muséologie en France*. Paris: CNRS, 1991.
Dimier, Veronique. "Enjeux institutionnels autour d'une science politique des colonies en France et en Grande-Bretagne (1930–1950)." *Genèses*, no. 37 (Décembre 1999): 70–92.
Dimier, Véronique. "For a New Start? Resettling French Colonial Administrators in the Prefectoral Corps." *Itinerario* 28, no.1 (2004): 49–66.
Dimier, Véronique. "Formation des administrateurs coloniaux français et anglais entre 1930 et 1950: développement d'une science politique ou science administrative des colonies." PhD diss., Institut d'études politiques (Grenoble), 1999.
Dimier, Véronique. "Recycling Empire. French Colonial Administrators at the Heart of European Development Policy." In *The French Colonial Mind*, edited by Martin Thomas, 251–74. Lincoln: University of Nebraska Press, 2011.
Dosse, François. *History of Structuralism*. 2 vols. Minneapolis: University of Minnesota Press, 1997.
Dozon, Jean-Pierre. "Georges Balandier dans l'histoire et l'épistémè de l'africanisme." *Recherches sociologiques* 33, no. 2 (2002): 21–29.
Dozon, Jean-Pierre. "Georges Balandier et la reconstruction d'après-guerre de la sociologie française." *Cahiers d'études africaines* 228 (2017): 811–18.
Dresch, Jean. "Villes congolaises." *Revue de géographie humaine et d'ethnologie* 3 (1948): 3–24.
Drouard, Alain. *Une inconnue des sciences sociales: la fondation Alexis Carrel*. Paris: Editions de la Maison des Sciences de l'Homme, 1992.
Du Foresto, Yann Coudé. "Conversation avec Raymond Aron." *Pouvoirs* 28 (1984): 168–83.

Dugas, Guy. *Albert Memmi: du malheur d'être juif au bonheur sépharade*. Paris: Alliance israélite universelle, 2001.
Dulucq, Sophie. *Écrire l'histoire de l'Afrique à l'époque coloniale: XIXe–XXe siècles*. Paris: Karthala, 2009.
Dulucq, Sophie, and Colette Zytnicki, eds. *Décoloniser l'histoire? De l'histoire coloniale aux histoires nationales en Amérique latine et en Afrique, XIXe–XXe siècles*. Saint-Denis: Société française d'histoire d'outre-mer, 2003.
Dumoulin, Olivier. "Le professionalization de l'histoire en France (1919–1939)." In Société française de sociologie, *Historiens et sociologues aujourd'hui*, 49–60. Paris: Centre national de la recherche scientifique, 1986.
Dupâquier, Jacques, and Eric Vilquin. "Le pouvoir royal et la statistique démographique." In *INSEE, Pour une histoire de la statistique*, vol. 2, 83–104. 2nd ed. Paris: Economica-INSEE, 1987.
Durand, Gilbert. "Une réponse de la sociologie française." In *Une anthropologie des turbulences: hommage à Georges Balandier*, edited by Michel Maffesoli and Claude Rivière, 26–34. Paris: Berg International, 1985.
Durand, Marie-Hélène. "La lente progression des femmes chercheuses à l'IRD (ex-ORSTOM)." *L'homme et la société* 176–77 (2010): 213–45.
Durkheim, Émile. *The Elementary Forms of the Religious Life*. New York: Free Press, 1915.
Durkheim, Émile. *The Evolution of Educational Thought: Lectures on the Formation and Development of Secondary Education in France*. London: Routledge & Kegan Paul, [1938] 1977.
Durkheim, Émile. *Leçons de sociologie. Physique des moeurs et du droit*. Paris: PUF, 1950.
Durkheim, Émile. *Moral Education: A Study in the Theory and Application of the Sociology of Education*. New York: Free Press of Glencoe, 1961.
Durkheim, Émile. "Morale professionelle." *La Revue de métaphysique et morale* 44, nos. 3–4 (1937): 527–44.
Durkheim, Émile. "Préface." *L'Année sociologique* 1 (1898): i–vii.
Durkheim, Émile. "Représentations individuelles et représentations collectives." *Revue de Métaphysique et de Morale* 6, no. 3 (1898): 273–302.
Durkheim, Émile. *The Rules of Sociological Method*. Edited by Steven Lukes. London: Macmillan, 1982.
Durkheim, Émile. *Sociologie et philosophie*. Paris: Alcan, 1924.
Durkheim, Émile. *Sociology and Philosophy*. New York: Free Press, 1974.
Durkheim, Émile. "Sociologie morale et juridique." *Année sociologique* ser. 1, no. 10 (1905–1906): 352–69.
Dutton, Paul V. *Origins of the French Welfare State: The Struggle for Social Reform in France, 1914–1947*. Cambridge: Cambridge University Press, 2012.
Duvignaud, Jean. *Chebika—mutations dans un village du Maghreb. Étude sociologique*. Paris: Gallimard, 1968.
Duvignaud, Jean. "La pratique de la sociologie dans les pays décolonisés." *Cahiers internationaux de Sociologie* 34 (1963): 165–74.
Duvignaud, Jean. *La sociologie: guide alphabétique*. Paris: Denoël, 1972.
Echenberg, Myron, and Jean Filipovich. "African Military Labour and the Building of the Office du Niger Installations, 1925–1950." *Journal of African History* 27 (1986): 533–51.
Eckert, Andreas. *Grundbesitz, Landkonflikte und kolonialer Wandel: Douala 1880 bis 1960*. Stuttgart: Steiner, 1990.
Eichengreen, Barry J. *The European Economy Since 1945: Coordinated Capitalism and Beyond*. Princeton, NJ: Princeton University Press, 2007.
Emerit, Marcel. *Les saint-simoniens en Algérie*. Paris: Les Belles Lettres, 1941.

Enders, Armelle. "L'école nationale de la France d'outre mer et la formation des adminstrateurs coloniaux." *Revue d'historie moderne et contemporaine* 40, no. 2 (1993): 272–88.
Enriquez, Eugène. "De la sociologie coloniale à la sociologie de la colonisation et des pays sous-développés: l'œuvre de Georges Balandier." *Critique* 134 (1958): 641–51.
Esselborn, Stefan. *Die Afrikaexperten: das Internationale Afrikainstitut und die europäische Afrikanistik, 1926–1976*. Göttingen: Vandenhoeck & Ruprecht, 2018.
Essertier, Daniel. *Psychologie et sociologie: essai de bibliographie critique*. Paris: F. Alcan, 1927.
Essertier, Daniel. *La sociologie*. Paris: F. Alcan, 1930.
Fabiani, Jean-Louis. *Les philosophes de la République*. Paris: Les Minuit, 1988.
Faivre, Maurice. "Un ethnologue de terrain face à la rebellion algérienne." *Mondes et cultures* 63 (2003): 448–60.
Falasca-Zamponi, Simonetta. *Rethinking the Political: The Sacred, Aesthetic Politics, and the Collège de Sociologie*. Montréal: McGill-Queen's University Press, 2011.
Falquet, Jules. "Avant-propos" to *Féminisme et antimilitarisme*, by Andrée Michel. Donnemarie-Donilly: Éditions iXe, 2012.
Fanon, Frantz. *Alienation and Freedom*, edited by Jean Khalfa and Robert J. C. Young. London: Bloomsbury, 2015.
Fanon, Frantz. *A Dying Colonialism*. New York: Grove Press, 1967.
Fanon, Frantz. *Peau noire, masques blancs*. Paris: Seuil, 1952.
Fanon, Frantz. *The Wretched of the Earth*. New York: Grove, [1961] 2004.
Fauconnet, Paul. "Amorce d'un programme sur l'enseignement de la sociologie." *Bulletin de l'Institut français de sociologie* 1 (1930): 69–72.
Fauconnet, Paul. *La responsabilité*. Paris: F. Alcan, 1920.
Fauconnet, Paul. "Review of G. Tarde, *L'opinion et la foule*." *Année sociologique* ser. 1, 5 (1900–1901): 160–66.
Fauconnet, Paul, and Marcel Mauss. "Sociologie." *La grande encyclopédie* 30 (1901): 165–76.
Faure, Christian. *Le projet culturel de Vichy: Folklore et révolution nationale, 1940–1944*. Paris: CNRS, 1989.
Favre, Pierre. "The Absence of Political Sociology in the Durkheimian Classifications of the Social Sciences." In *The Sociological Domain: The Durkheimians and the Founding of French Sociology*, edited by Philippe Besnard, 199–216. Cambridge: Cambridge University Press, 2009.
Favret-Saada, Jeanne. *Algérie 1962–1964: essais d'anthropologie politique*. Saint-Denis: Bouchène, 2005.
Feichtinger, Moritz. "'A Great Reformatory': Social Planning and Strategic Resettlement in Late Colonial Kenya and Algeria, 1952–63." *Journal of Contemporary History* 52, no. 1 (January 2017): 45–72.
Ferrette, Jean. "La sociologie sous Vichy: rupture ou continuité? Retour sur un impensé historique." *Anamnèse* 7 (2012): 9–26.
Fiemeyer, Isabelle. *Marcel Griaule, citoyen dogon*. Arles: Actes sud, 2004.
Fonkoua, Romuald. "Robert Delavignette et Henri Labouret: regards et approaches du fait colonial." In *Robert Delavignette, savant et politique: 1897–1976*, edited by Bernard Mouralis and Anne Piriou, 73–89. Paris: Karthala, 2003.
Forget, Nelly. "Le Service des Centres sociaux en Algérie." *Matériaux pour l'histoire de notre temps*, no. 26 (January–March 1992): 37–47.
Fougeyrollas, Pierre. "De la psychotechnique à la sociologie policière." *La nouvelle critique* (July–August 1951): 25–40.
Fournier, Marcel. *Marcel Mauss: A Biography*, Princeton, NJ: Princeton University Press, 2006.

Frangie, Samer. "Bourdieu's Reflexive Politics. Socio-Analysis, Biography and Self-Creation." *European Journal of Social Theory* 12 (2009): 213–29.

Fredenucci, Jean-Charles. "La brousse coloniale ou l'anti-bureau." *Revue française d'administration publique* 108 (2003): 603–15.

Fredenucci, Jean-Charles. "L'entregent colonial des ingénieurs des Ponts et Chaussées dans l'urbanisme des années 1950-1970." *Vingtième Siècle* 79 (2003): 79–91.

Frémeaux, Jacques. *Les bureaux arabes dans l'Algérie de la conquête.* Paris: Denoël, 1993.

Frémeaux, Jacques. "Missionnaire en burnous bleu." *Revue du monde musulman et de la Méditerranée*, nos. 83–84 (1997): 67–73.

Frère, Suzanne. *Madagascar: Panorama de l'Androy.* Paris: Éditions Aframpe, 1958.

Froelich, Jean-Claude. *La Tribu Konkomba du Nord Togo.* Dakar: IFAN, 1954.

Gagné, Natacha, and Marie Salaün. "L'effacement du 'colonial' ou 'seulement de ses formes les plus apparentes'? Penser le contemporain grâce à la notion de situation coloniale chez Georges Balandier." *Cargo: revue internationale d'anthropologie culturelle & sociale* 6–7 (2017): 219–37.

Gaillard, Gérald. "Chronique de la recherche ethnologique dans son rapport au Centre national de la recherche scientifique 1925-1980." *Cahiers pour l'histoire du CNRS* 3 (1989): 85–123.

Gaillard, Gérald. "Georges Balandier." *Journal des anthropologues* 148–49 (2017): 9–24.

Gaillard, Gerald. *Répertoire de l'ethnologie française: 1950–1970.* 2 vols. Paris: Éditions du Centre national de la recherche scientifique, 1990.

Gaillard, Gerald. *The Routledge Dictionary of Anthropologists.* London: Routledge, 2004.

Geiger, Roger Lewis. "The Development of French Sociology, 1871–1905." PhD diss., University of Michigan, 1972.

Geiger, Roger Lewis. "Prelude to Reform: The Faculties of Letters in the 1860s." *Historical Reflections/Réflexions Historiques* 7, no. 2 (1980): 337–61.

Gellner, Ernst. "Introduction" to Robert Montagne, *The Berbers. Their Social and Political Organization,* xii–xl. London: Cass, 1973.

Gemperle, Michael. "La fabrique d'un classique français: le cas de 'Weber.'" *Revue d'Histoire des Sciences Humaines,* no. 18 (2008): 159–77.

Gillispie, Charles. *Science and Polity in France: The Revolutionary and Napoleonic Years.* Princeton, NJ: Princeton University Press, 2004.

Gilpin, Robert. *France in the Age of the Scientific State.* Princeton, NJ: Princeton University Press, 1968.

Giordano, Christian. "Jenseits von Emile Durkheims Erbschaft: Die dynamische Soziologie und Anthropologie Georges Balandiers." In *Französische Soziologie der Gegenwart,* edited by Stephan Moebius and Lothar Peter, 213–36. Konstanz: UVK, 2004.

Girard, Alain. *L'Institut national d'études démographiques: histoire et développement.* Paris: Éditions de l'INED, 1986.

Girard, Alain, and Joseph Leriche. *Les Algériens en France, Étude démographique et sociale.* Paris: INED, 1955.

Girard, Alain, and Jean Stoetzel. *Français et immigrés. Institut national d'études démographiques.* Paris: PUF, 1953.

Girard, Alain, and Jean Stoetzel. "Nouveaux documents sur l'immigration en France." *Population* 9, no. 1 (1954): 43–50.

Gleizes, Michel. *Un regard sur l'ORSTOM 1943-1983. Témoinage.* Paris: Éditions de l'ORSTOM, 1985.

Go, Julian. *American Empire and the Politics of Meaning: Elite Political Cultures in the Philippines and Puerto Rico during U.S. Colonialism.* Durham, NC: Duke University Press, 2008.

Godechot, Olivier. "La formation des relations académiques au sein de l'EHESS." *Histoire et mesure* 26 (2011): 223–60.
Goebel, Michael. *Anti-Imperial Metropolis: Interwar Paris and the Seeds of Third-World Nationalism*. New York: Cambridge University Press, 2015.
Goeury, David. "Horizon Seksawa: relecture de l'oeuvre de Jacques Berque pour la compréhension de l'espace marocain." *Awal (Cahiers d'études berbères)* (2011): 213–24.
Goldstein, Jan. "The Advent of Psychological Modernism in France: An Alternate Narrative." In *Modernist Impulses in the Human Sciences, 1870–1930*, edited by D. Ross, 190–209. Baltimore, MD: Johns Hopkins University Press, 1994.
Goldstein, Jan. "Foucault and the Post-Revolutionary Self." In *Foucault and the Writing of History*, edited by Jan Goldstein, 99–115. Oxford: Blackwell, 1994.
Gosselin, Gabriel. "Avant-propos." *Les nouveaux enjeux de l'anthropologie: autour de Georges Balandier*, edited by Gabriel Gosselin, 11–14. Paris: L'Harmattan, 1993.
Gouarné, Isabelle. "Engagement philosoviétique et posture sociologique dans l'entre-deux-guerres: le rôle politico-intellectuel de Georges Friedmann." *Sociologie du travail* 54 (2012): 356–74.
Gouellain, René. *Douala: ville et histoire*. Paris: Institut d'ethnologie, 1975.
Grandhomme, Hélène. "Connaissance de l'Islam et pouvoir colonial: L'exemple de la France au Sénégal, 1936–1957." *French Colonial History* 10 (2009): 171–88.
Granjon, Marie-Christine. "Raymond Aron, Jean-Paul Sartre et le conflit algérien." In *La guerre d'Algérie et les intellectuels français*, edited by Jean-Pierre Rioux and Jean-François Sirinelli, 115–35. Bruxelles: Editions Comlexe, 1991.
Gray, Christopher J. *Colonial Rule and Crisis in Equatorial Africa: Southern Gabon, c. 1850–1940*. Rochester, NY: University of Rochester Press, 2002.
Gray, Christopher. "Territoriality and Colonial 'Enclosure' in Southern Gabon." In *Enfermement, prison et châtiments en Afrique. Du 19e siècle à nos jours*, edited by Florence Bernault, 99–132. Paris: Karthala, 1999.
Grelon, André. "Paul-Henry Chombart de Lauwe." *Année sociologique* 49, no. 1 (1999): 7–18.
Grémion, Pierre. *Intelligence de l'anticommunisme. Le Congrès pour la liberté de la culture à Paris (1950–1975)*. Paris: Fayard, 1995.
Grenfell, Michael. "Afterword: Reflecting In/On Field Theory in Practice." In *Bourdieu's Field Theory and the Social Sciences*, edited by James Albright, Deborah Hartman, and Jacqueline Widin, 269–92. Singapore: Palgrave Macmillan, 2018.
Griaule, Marcel. "L'action sociologique en Afrique noire." *Présence africaine* 3 (1948): 388–91.
Griaule, Marcel. "L'avion au service des sciences humaines." *Atomes* 4 (1946): 7–10.
Griaule, Marcel. *Burners of Men: Modern Ethiopia*. Philadelphia: J. B. Lippincott, 1935.
Griaule, Marcel. *Conversations with Ogotemmêli. An Introduction to Dogon Religious Ideas*. London: Oxford University Press, 1965.
Griaule, Marcel. "Introduction méthodologique." *Minotaure* 2 (1933): 7–12.
Griaule, Marcel. *Méthode de l'ethnographie*. Paris: PUF, 1957.
Griaule, Marcel. "Les problèmes de la colonisation et les sciences de l'homme." In *De la banquise à la jungle*, edited by H. Lauga, 157–62. Paris: Plon, 1952.
Gruner, Roger. *Du Maroc traditionnel au Maroc moderne: le contrôle civil au Maroc, 1912–1956*. Paris: Nouvelles Éditions latines, 1984.
Guérin, Jeanyves, ed. *Albert Memmi, écrivain et sociologue: actes du colloque de Paris X-Nanterre, 15 et 16 mai 1988*. Paris: L'Harmattan, 1990.
Guiart, Jean. *Maurice Leenhardt: le lien d'un homme avec un peuple qui ne voulait pas mourir*. Nouméa: Le Rocher-à-la-voile, 1977.
Guiart, Jean. *Maurice Leenhardt: Missionaire et sociologue*. Paris: Office de la Recherche Scientifique et Technique d'Outre-Mer, 1955.

Guiart, Jean. *Recherches de sociologie urbaine dans le Pacifique français*. Paris: ORSTOM, 1958.
Gurvitch, Georges. *L'Idée du droit social*. Paris: Sirey, 1931.
Gurvitch, Georges, ed. *Traité de sociologie*. 2 vols. Paris: PUF, 1958.
Guthleben, Denis. *Histoire du CNRS de 1939 à nos jours: une ambition nationale pour la science*. Paris: Armand Colin, 2009.
Gutwirth, Jacques. "La professionnalisation d'une discipline: Le centre de formation aux recherches ethnologiques." *Gradhiva* 29 (2001): 25–41.
Haffner, Jeanne. *The View from Above: The Science of Social Space*. Cambridge, MA: MIT Press, 2013.
Halbwachs, Maurice. "Le rêve et le langage inconscient dans le sommeil." *Journal de psychologie normale et pathologique* 39 (1946): 11–64.
Halbwachs, Maurice. "La statistique en sociologie." In *La statistique, ses applications, les problèmes qu'elle soulève*, 113–34. Paris: PUF, 1944.
Hand, Seán. *Michel Leiris. Writing the Self*. Cambridge: Cambridge University Press, 2002.
Hand, Seán. "The Orchastration of Man: The Structure of *L'Age d'homme*." *Romance Studies* 4, no. 2 (1986): 78–80.
Hardin, Bert. *The Professionalization of Sociology. A Comparative Study: Germany–USA*. Frankfurt: Campus, 1997.
Hardy, Georges. *Les éléments de l'histoire coloniale*. Paris: La Renaissance du livre, 1921.
Hargreaves, John D. *Decolonization in Africa*. 2nd ed. London: Routledge, 1996.
Hassner, Pierre. "Raymond Aron and the History of the Twentieth Century." *International Studies Quarterly* 29, no. 1 (1985): 29–37.
Hazard, Anthony Q. *Postwar Anti-Racism: The United States, UNESCO, and "Race," 1945–1968*. New York: Palgrave Macmillan, 2012.
Heilbron, Johan. *French Sociology*. Ithaca, NY: Cornell University Press, 2015.
Heilbron, Johan. "Les métamorphoses du durkheimisme, 1920–1940." *Revue française de sociologie* 26, no. 2 (April–June 1985): 203–37.
Heilbron, Johan. "Note sur l'Institut français de sociologie (1924–1962)." *Études durkheimiennes* 9 (1983): 9–14.
Heilbron, Johan. "Pionniers par défaut? Les débuts de la recherche au Centre d'études sociologiques (1946–1960)." *Revue française de sociologie* 27, no. 3 (1991): 365–79.
Heilbron, Johan. "Practical Foundations of Theorizing in Sociology: The Case of Pierre Bourdieu." In *Social Knowledge in the Making*, edited by Charles Camic, Neil Gross, and Michèle Lamont, 181–208. Chicago: University of Chicago Press, 2011.
Heilbron, Johan. "Social Thought and Natural Science." In *The Modern Social Sciences*, edited by Theodore Porter and Dorothy Ross, 40–56. Vol. 7 of *The Cambridge History of Science*. Cambridge: Cambridge University Press, 2003.
Hell, Julia. *The Conquest of Ruins: The Third Reich and the Fall of Rome*. Chicago: University of Chicago Press, 2019.
Hell, Julia. "Imperial Ruin Gazers, or Why Did Scipio Weep?" *Germanic Review* 84, no. 4 (2009): 283–326.
Hell, Julia. "Katechon: Carl Schmitt's Imperial Theology and the Ruins of the Future." *Germanic Review: Literature, Culture, Theory* 84, no. 4 (2009): 283–326.
Hell, Julia. "On the Way to the London Mithraeum: Freud's Archaeo-Analysis and the Habsburg Empire's Neo-Roman Mimesis." *American Imago* 78, no. 2 (2021): 245–74.
Henry, Jean-Robert. "Approches ethnologiques du droit musulman." In *L'enseignement du droit musulman*, edited by M. Flory and J.-R. Henry, 133–71. Paris: CNRS, 1989.
Héran, François. "La seconde nature de l'habitus: Tradition philosophique et sens commun dans le langage sociologique." *Revue française de sociologie* 28, no. 3 (1987): 385–416.

Hexter, J. H. "Fernand Braudel and the monde Braudellien." *Journal of Modern History* 44, no. 4 (1972): 480–539.
Hirsch, Thomas. *Le temps des sociétés, d'Émile Durkheim à Marc Bloch*. Paris: Éditions de l'EHESS, 2016.
Hirschhorn, Monique. "The Place of the History of Sociology in French Sociology." *Schweizerische Zeitschrift für Soziologie* 23, no. 1 (1997): 3–7.
Hodge, Joseph Morgan. *Triumph of the Expert: Agrarian Doctrines of Development and the Legacies of British Colonialism*. Athens: Ohio University Press, 2007.
Hodge, Joseph M., and Gerald Hödl. "Introduction." In *Developing Africa: Concepts and Practices in Twentieth-Century Colonialism*, edited by Joseph M. Hodge, Gerald Hödl, and Martina Kopf, 1–34. Manchester: Manchester University Press, 2014.
Hollier, Denis, ed. *The College of Sociology (1937–39)*. Minneapolis: University of Minnesota Press, 1988.
Hollier, Denis, and Jean Jamin, eds. *Leiris Unlimited*. Paris: CNRS Éditions, 2017.
Hölscher, Lucian. "Geschichte und Vergessen." *Historische Zeitschrift* 249 (1990): 1–17.
Hubert, René. *Manuel élémentaire de sociologie*. 5th ed., revised. Paris: Delalain, 1949.
Hugon, Philippe. "Retour sur une cinquantaine d'années d'économie du développement dans la *Revue Tiers Monde*." *Revue Tiers Monde* 191 (2007): 717–41.
Huteau, Michel. "Pierre Naville, le marxisme, la psychologie, et l'orientation professionnelle." *L'orientation scolaire et professionnelle* 26, no. 2 (1997): 195–220.
Iandolo, Alessandro. *Arrested Development: The Soviet Union in Ghana, Guinea, and Mali, 1955–1968*. Ithaca, NY: Cornell University Press, 2022.
Iandolo, Alessandro. "The Rise and Fall of the Soviet Model of Development in West Africa, 1957–1964." *Cold War History* 12, no. 4 (2012): 683–704.
Ingram, Nicola, and Jessie Abrahams. "Stepping Outside of Oneself. How a Cleft-Habitus Can Lead to Greater Reflexivity through Occupying 'the Third Space.'" In *Bourdieu: The Next Generation. The Development of Bourdieu's Intellectual Heritage in Contemporary UK Sociology*, edited by Jenny Thatcher, 140–64. London: Routledge, 2016.
Izard-Héritier, Françoise, and Michael Izard. *Les Mossi du Yatenga. Étude de la vie économique et sociale*. Bordeaux: Institut des Sciences humaines et appliquées, 1959.
Jabbari, Eric. *Pierre Laroque and the Welfare State in Postwar France*. Oxford: Oxford University Press, 2012.
Jallamion, Carine. "Le juge français face aux collectivités indigènes." In *Le juge et l'outre-mer. Les roches bleues de l'Empire colonial*, edited by Bernard Durand and Martine Fabre, 385–419. Lille: Publications du centre d'histoire judiciare, 2004.
James, Wendy. "The Treatment of African Ethnography in *L'Année sociologique* (I–XII)." *Année sociologique* ser. 3, 48, no. 1 (1998): 193–207.
Jamin, Jean. "Introduction." In Michel Leiris, *Miroir de l'Afrique*, 9–59. Paris: Gallimard, 1996.
Jamin, Jean. "La mission ethnographique et linguistique DAKAR-DJIBOUTI." *Cahiers Ethnographiques*, n.s. 5 (1984): 7–86.
Jammet, Yves. "Abdelmalek Sayad, les années d'apprentissage." In *Abdelmalek Sayad. La découverte de la sociologie en temps de guerre*, edited by Tassadit Yacine, Yves Jammet, and Christian de Montlibert, 17–127. Nantes: Defaut, 2013.
Jennings, Eric T. *Vichy in the Tropics: Pétain's National Revolution in Madagascar, Guadeloupe, and Indochina, 1940–44*. Stanford: Stanford University Press, 2002.
Jézéquel, Jean-Hervé. "Les professionnels africains de la recherche dans l'état colonial tardif. Le personnel local de l'Institut français d'Afrique noire entre 1938 et 1960." *Revue d'histoire des sciences humaines*, no. 24 (2011): 35–60.
Johnson, Christopher. *Claude Lévi-Strauss: The Formative Years*. Cambridge: Cambridge University Press, 2003.

Jolly, Éric, and Marianne Lemaire, eds. *Cahier Dakar Djibouti*. Meurcourt: Éditions les Cahiers, 2015.

Joly, Laurent. *Vichy dans la "solution finale": Histoire du commissariat général aux questions juives (1941–1944)*. Paris: Grasset, 2006.

Joly, Marc. *Devenir Norbert Elias. Histoire croisé d'un processus de reconnaissance scientifique*. Paris: Fayard, 2012.

Jouin, Serge, and Jean-Philippe Ould-Aoudia. "Les Centres sociaux éducatifs en Algérie, 1955–1962." *Cahiers du Centre fédéral (Fédération de l'Éducation nationale, Paris)*, no. 4 (December 1992): 103–40.

Judt, Tony. *Past Imperfect: French Intellectuals, 1944–1956*. Berkeley: University of California Press, 1992.

Judt, Tony. *Postwar. A History of Europe since 1945*. New York: Penguin, 2006.

Julien, Charles André. *L'Afrique du Nord en Marche*. Paris: R. Julliard, 1952.

Jumper, Roy. "The Recruitment and Training of Civil Adminstrators for Overseas France: A Case Study of French Bureaucracy." PhD diss., Duke University, 1955.

Käsler, Dirk. *Sociological Adventures: Earle Edward Eubank's Visits with European Sociologists*. New York: Routledge, [1991] 2020.

Kalaora, Bernard. "Le mysticisme technique de Joseph Wilbois." In *Les chantiers de la paix sociale*, edited by Yves Cohen and Remi Badoui, 185–94. Fontenay: ENS editions, 1996.

Kalaora, Bernard, and Antoine Savoye. *Les inventeurs oubliés. Le Play et ses continuateurs. Aux origins des sciences sociales*. Paris: Champ Vallon, 1989.

Kalaora, Bernard, and Antoine Savoye. "La mutation du mouvement le playsien." *Revue française de sociologie* 26, no. 2 (1985): 257–76.

Karady, Victor. "The Durkheimians in Academe. A Reconsideration." In *The Sociological Domain: The Durkheimians and the Founding of French Sociology*, edited by Philippe Besnard, 79–91. Cambridge: Cambridge University Press, 1983.

Karady, Victor. "Le problème de la légitimité dans l'organisation historique de l'ethnologie française." *Revue française de sociologie* 23 (1982): 17–35.

Karady, Victor. "Les sociologues avant 1950." *Regards sociologiques* 22 (2000): 5–22.

Karady, Victor. "Les universités françaises, de Napoléon à la deuxième guerre mondiale." In *Histoire des universités françaises*, edited by Jacques Verger, 261–365. Toulouse: Privat, 1986.

Kateb, Kamel. *Européens,"indigènes" et juifs en Algérie (1830–1962), représentations et réalités des populations*. Paris: INED, 2001.

Keck, Frédéric. *Lucien Lévy-Bruhl: Entre philosophie et anthropologie: Contradiction et participation*. Paris: CNRS Éditions, 2008.

Keim, Wiebke. *Vermessene Disziplin: zum konterhegemonialen Potential afrikanischer und lateinamerikanischer Soziologien*. Bielefeld: Transcript, 2008.

Keller, Richard C. *Colonial Madness: Psychiatry in French North Africa*. Chicago: University of Chicago Press, 2007.

Khalfa, Jean. "La bibliothèque de Frantz Fanon." In *Frantz Fanon, Alienation and Freedom*, edited by Jean Khalfa and Robert J. C. Young, 587–655. London: Bloomsbury, 2015.

Khalfa, Jean. "Fanon, Revolutionary Psychiatrist." In *Frantz Fanon, Alienation and Freedom*, edited by Jean Khalfa and Robert J. C. Young, 167–202. London: Bloomsbury, 2015.

Knobel, Marc. "L'ethnologue à la dérive. George Montandon et l'ethnoracisme." *Ethnologie et racismes* 18, no. 2 (1988): 107–13.

Kojève, Alexandre. "Outline of a Doctrine of French Policy." *Policy Review* (August–September 2004): 3–40.

Kubali, Hüseyin Nail. *L'idée de l'état chez les précurseurs de l'école sociologique française*. Paris: Domat-Montchrestien, 1936.

Kubica, Grażyna. "Lévi-Strauss as a Protagonist in his Ethnographic Prose: A Cosmopolitan View of *Tristes tropiques* and Its Contemporary Interpretations." *Etnográfica* 18, no. 3 (2014): 599–624.
Kuisel, Richard F. *Capitalism and the State in Modern France: Renovation and Economic Management in the Twentieth Century*. Cambridge: Cambridge University Press, 1981.
Kwaschik, Anne. "Die Verwissenschaftlichung des Kolonialen als kultureller Code und internationale Praxis um 1900." *Historische Anthropologie* 28, no. 3 (2020): 399–423.
La Capra, Dominick. *Émile Durkheim: Sociologist and Philosopher*. Ithaca, NY: Cornell University Press, 1972.
Labouret, Henri. *Colonisation, colonialisme, décolonisation*. Paris: Larose, 1952.
Labouret, Henri. "Irrigations, colonisation intérieure et main-d'œuvre au Soudan français." *Annales d'histoire économique et sociale* 1, no. 3 (1929): 365–76.
Lacombe, R. "Essai sur les origines et les premiers développements de la société d'ethnographie." *L'ethnographie* 76 (1980): 329–41.
Lacoste, Yves. "Postface." In *L'empire des géographes. Géographie, exploration et colonisation XIXe-XXe siècle*, edited by Pierre Singaravélou, 235–41. Paris: Belin, 2008.
Lacoste-Dujardin, Camille. *Opération "Oiseau bleu": des Kabyles, des ethnologues et la guerre en Algérie*. Paris: Découverte, 1997.
Laude, C. "Le Centre d'études sociologiques en 1959." *Revue française de sociologie* 32, no. 3 (1991): 405–09.
Launay, Stephen. "Raymond Aron et la guerre d'Algérie: un regard libéral sur une décomposition." *Les cahiers d'histoire sociale*, no. 23 (2004): 127–47.
Laurière, Christine. "D'une île à l'autre." *Gradhiva* 1 (2005): 181–207.
Laurière, Christine. *L'Odyssée pascuane. Mission Métraux-Lavachery, Île de Pâques, 1934–1935*. Les Carnets de Bérose no. 3. Paris: Bérose, 2014. http://www.berose.fr/?L-Odyssee-pascuane-Mission-Metraux.
Lautman, Jacques. "Chronique de la sociologie française après 1945." In *Science et théorie de l'opinion publique: hommage à Jean Stoetzel*, edited by Alain Girard, Francois Bourricaud, and Raymond Boudon, 269–84. Paris: Retz, 1981.
Lawler, Nancy. "Reform and Repression under the Free French: Economic and Political Transformation in the Côte d'Ivoire, 1942–45." *Africa: Journal of the International African Institute* 60, no. 1 (1990): 88–110.
Lawson, George. "Colonial Origins—and Legacies—of International Organizations." In *The Presence of the Past. Imprints of Colonialism and Imperialism in Global Politics*, edited by Klaus Schlichte and Stephan Stetter. Cambridge: Cambridge University Press, forthcoming.
Lazali, Karima. *Colonial Trauma: A Study of the Psychic and Political Consequences of Colonial Oppression in Algeria*. Cambridge: Polity, 2020.
Lazarev, Grigori. *Les politiques agraires au Maroc 1956–2006. Un témoignage engagé*. n.p.: Economie critique, 2012.
Le Breton, Eric. *Pour une critique de la ville: la sociologie urbaine française: 1950–1980*. Rennes: Presses universitaires de Rennes, 2012.
Le Chatelier, Jean. *Alfred Le Chatelier, 1855–1929: sa carrière africaine*. Paris: Service historique de l'Armée de terre, 1987.
Le Coeur, Charles. *Carnets de route: 1933–1934*, edited by Marguerite Le Coeur. Paris: Éditions du CNRS, 1969.
Le Coeur, Charles. *Le rite et l'outil. Essai sur le rationalisme social et la pluralité des civilisations*. Paris: PUF, 1969.
Le Cour Grandmaison, Olivier. *De l'indigénat*. Paris: Zones, 2010.
Le Play, Frédéric. *Frédéric le Play d'après lui-même*. Paris: V. Giard & E. Brière, 1906.

Le Play, Frédéric. *Les ouvriers des deux mondes*. 10 vols. Paris: Au Sécretariat de la Société d'économie sociale, 1858–1908.

Le Sueur, James D. *Uncivil War: Intellectuals and Identity Politics during the Decolonization of Algeria*. Philadelphia: University of Pennsylvania Press, 2001.

Lebovics, Herman. "Le conservatisme en anthropologie et la fin de la Troisième République." *Gradhiva* 4 (1988): 3–17.

Leclerc, Gerard. *Anthropologie et colonialisme: essai sur l'histoire de l'africanisme*. Paris: Fayard, 1972.

Leenhardt, Maurice. *Gens de la grande terre*. 2nd ed. Paris: Gallimard, 1953.

Leenhardt, Maurice. "Modes d'expression en sociologie et en ethnologie." *Synthèse* 10, no. 1 (1953): 259–64.

Lefébure, Claude. "Bonnes feuilles des Seksawa." *Revue du monde musulman et de la Méditerranée* nos. 83–84 (1997): 93–101.

Lefeuvre, Daniel. *Chère Algérie. Comptes et mécomptes de la tutelle coloniale, 1930–1962*. Saint-Denis: Société française d'histoire d'outre-mer, 1997.

Lefeuvre, Daniel. "Vichy et la modernisation de 1'Algérie: intention ou réalité?" *Vingtième siècle* 42 (April–June 1994): 7–16.

Lefort, Claude. "Raymond Aron et le phénomène totalitaire." In *Raymond Aron et la liberté politique*, edited by Christian Bachelier, 87–92. Paris: Fallois, 2002.

Leiris, Michel. *L'Afrique fantôme*. Paris: Gallimard, 1981.

Leiris, Michel. "Afterword. The Autobiographer as Torero." In *Manhood*, 153–64. New York: Grossman, [1939] 1963.

Leiris, Michel. *L'âge d'homme, précédé de De la littérature considérée comme une tauromachie*. Paris: Gallimard, 1945.

Leiris, Michel. "Antilles et poésie des carrefours." In *Zébrage*, 67–87. Paris: Gallimard, 1992.

Leiris, Michel. *C'est-à-dire: entretien avec Sally Price et Jean Jamin; suivi de titres et travaux*. Paris: J.-M. Place, 1992.

Leiris, Michel. *Contacts de civilisations en Martinique et en Guadeloupe*. Paris: UNESCO/Gallimard, 1955.

Leiris, Michel. "The Ethnographer Faced with Colonialism." In *Brisées = Broken Branches*, translated by Lydia Davis, 112–31. San Francisco, CA: North Point, 1989.

Leiris, Michel. *Manhood*. New York: Grossman, 1963.

Leiris, Michel. *Scratches* [Biffures]. New York: Paragon House, 1991.

Lemaire, Marianne. "A Journey Through Many Fields. Denise Paulme's Scientific Itinerary." *L'homme* 193, no. 1 (2010): 51–73.

Lemesle, Raymond-Marin. *La Conférence de Brazzaville de 1944*. Paris: CHEAM, 1994.

Leroi-Gourhan, André. "Qu'est-ce que c'est … l'ethnologie?" *Bulletin du Centre de formation aux recherches ethnologiques* no. 5 (Janvier 1953): 1–7.

Leroi-Gourhan, André. *Initiation aux recherches de la symbiose technique (Ainous et Japonais)*. Paris: CES, 1949.

Lesne, Marcel. "Une expérience de déplacement de population: les centres de regroupement en Algérie." *Annales de Géographie* 71, no. 388 (1962): 567–601.

Lespinet-Moret, Isabelle. "Pierre du Maroussem, un arpenteur de l'économique et du social." In *L'économie faite homme: Hommage à Alain Plessis*, edited by Olivier Feiertag and Isabelle Lespinet-Moret, 423–36. Genève: Droz, 2011.

Levisse-Touzé, Christine. *L'Afrique du Nord dans la guerre, 1939–1945*. Paris: A. Michel, 1998.

Lévi-Strauss, Claude. *Race and History*. Paris: UNESCO, 1952.

Lévi-Strauss, Claude. Review of Georges Balandier, *Sociologie des Brazzavilles noires*, *Revue française de science politique* 6, no. 1 (1956): 177–79.

Lévi-Strauss, Claude. *The Savage Mind*. Chicago: University of Chicago Press, [1962] 1966.

Lévi-Strauss, Claude. *Structural Anthropology*. Translated by Claire Jacobson and Brooke Grundfest Schoepf. New York: Basic Books, 1963.
Lévi-Strauss, Claude. *Tristes tropiques*. New York: Penguin Books, [1955] 1992.
Lévi-Strauss, Claude, and Didier Eribon. *Conversations with Claude Lévi-Strauss*. Chicago: University of Chicago Press, 1991.
Lévy-Bruhl, Henri. "Allocution." *Annales de l'Université de Paris* 30, no. 1 (January–March 1960): 40–46.
Lévy-Bruhl, Henri. "Le Centre d'études sociologiques." *Revue de sythèse* 5, nos. 3–4 (1946): 130–32.
Lévy-Bruhl, Henri. *Ethics and Moral Science*. London: A. Constable, 1905.
Lévy-Bruhl, Lucien. *Les carnets*. Paris: PUF, 1949.
Lévy-Bruhl, Lucien. *How Natives Think*. New York: Knopf, 1925. Translation of *La mentalité primitive*. Paris: Librairie Félix Alcan, 1922.
Lévy-Bruhl, Lucien. "L'Institut d'ethnologie de l'Université de Paris." *Revue d'ethnographie et des traditions populaires*. 6, nos. 23–24 (1925): 233–36.
Lévy-Bruhl, Lucien. *The Notebooks on Primitive Mentality*. Oxford: Blackwell, 1975.
Lewis, James I. "The MRP and the Genesis of the French Union, 1944–1948." *French History* 12, no. 3 (1998): 276–314.
Liauzu, Claude. *Dictionnaire de la colonisation française*. Paris: Larousse, 2007.
Liauzu, Claude. *Les intellectuels français au miroir algérien*. Nice: Université de Nice, 1984.
Linstrum, Erik. *Ruling Minds: Psychology in the British Empire*. Cambridge, MA: Harvard University Press, 2016.
Livio, Boni. "La condition (post)coloniale entre marxisme et psychanalyse: l'apport d'Octave Mannoni." *Actuel Marx* 61 (2017): 153–67.
Lorcin, Patricia M. E. *Imperial Identities: Stereotyping, Prejudice and Race in Colonial Algeria*. London: I. B. Tauris, 1995.
Lorcin, Patricia M. E. "Imperial Nostalgia; Colonial Nostalgia: Differences of Theory, Similarities of Practice?" *Historical Reflections/Réflexions Historiques* 39, no. 3 (2013): 97–111.
Lorcin, Patricia M. E. "Imperialism, Colonial Identity, and Race in Algeria, 1830–1870: The Role of the French Medical Corps." *Isis* 90 (1999): 653–79.
Lorcin, Patricia M. E. "The Nostalgias for Empire." *History and Theory* 5, no. 2 (June 2018): 269–85.
Low, D. Anthony, and John Lonsdale. "Introduction: Towards the New Order, 1945–1963." In *History of East Africa*, edited by D. A. Low and Alison Smith, 1–62. Vol. 2. Oxford: Clarendon Press, 1989.
Loyer, Emmanuelle. *Lévi-Strauss: A Biography*. Cambridge: Polity, 2018.
Luchaire, François. *Droit d'outre-mer et de la coopération*. Paris: PUF, 1966.
Luchaire, François. *Manuel de droit d'outre-mer*. Paris: Sirey, 1949.
Lukes, Steven. *Émile Durkheim*. New York: Penguin, 1973.
Lustick, Ian. *Unsettled States, Disputed Lands. Britain and Ireland, France and Algeria, Israel and the West Bank-Gaza*. Ithaca, NY: Cornell University Press, 1993.
Ly, Abdoulaye. "La Compagnie du Sénégal de 1673 à 1696. L'évolution du commerce français d'Afrique noire dans le dernier quart du XVIIe siècle." PhD diss., University of Bordeaux, 1955.
Ly, Abdoulaye. *Dialogue avec Abdoulaye Ly: historien et homme politique sénégalais*. Dakar: IFAN, 2001.
Mabon, Armelle. *L'action sociale coloniale: l'exemple de l'Afrique occidentale française du Front populaire à la veille des indépendances*. Paris: L'Harmattan, 2000.

Macey, David. *Frantz Fanon*. New York: Picador, 2000.
MacKenzie, John M., ed. *European Empires and the People: Popular Responses to Imperialism in France, Britain, the Netherlands, Belgium, Germany and Italy*. Manchester: Manchester University Press, 2011.
Maget, Marcel. *Ethnographie métropolitaine: Guide d'étude directe des comportements culturels*. Paris: Civilisations du Sud, 1953.
Maget, Marcel. "Remarques sur l'ethnographie metropolitaine." *Bulletin de la Société neuchâteloise de géographie* 60, no. 2 (1948): 39–58.
Mahé, Alain. "Un disciple méconnu de Marcel Mauss: René Maunier." *Revue européenne des sciences sociales–Cahiers Vilfredo Pareto* 34, no. 105 (1996): 237–64.
Malis, Christian. *Raymond Aron et le débat stratégique français: 1930–1966*. Paris: Economica, 2005.
Mann, Gregory. "Anti-Colonialism and Social Science: Georges Balandier, Madeira Keita, and 'the Colonial Situation' in French Africa." *Comparative Studies in Society and History* 55, no. 1 (2013): 92–119.
Mann, Gregory. *From Empires to NGOs in the West African Sahel: The Road to Nongovernmentality*. New York: Cambridge University Press, 2015.
Mannoni, Octave. "La plainte du noir." *Esprit* (May 1951): 734–49.
Mannoni, Octave. *Prospero and Caliban: The Psychology of Colonization*. Ann Arbor: University of Michigan Press, [1950] 1990.
Mannoni, Octave. "Sociologie et psychanalyse." *Présence africaine* 10/11 (1957): 211–15.
Mannoni, Octave. "The Decolonisation of Myself." *Race* 7, no. 4 (1966): 327–35.
Marac, Katie Kilroy. *An Impossible Inheritance: Postcolonial Psychiatry and the Work of Memory in a West African Clinic*. Berkeley: University of California Press, 2019.
Marcel, Jean-Christophe. *Le durkheimisme dans l'entre-deux-guerres*. Paris: PUF, 2001.
Marcel, Jean-Christophe. "Éléments pour une analyse de la réception de la sociologie américaine en France (1945–1959)." HDG thesis, Université de Paris-Sorbonne, 2010.
Marié, Michel. *Les terres et les mots. Une traversée des sciences sociales*. Paris: Éditions Méridiens-Kliencksiek, 1989.
Marjolin, Robert. "French Sociology–Comte and Durkheim." *American Journal of Sociology* 42, no. 5 (1937): 693–704.
Marjolin, Robert. *Le travail d'une vie: mémoires 1911–1986*. Paris: Éditions Robert Laffont, 1986.
Marseille, Jacques. "La conférence des gouverneurs généraux des colonies (novembre 1936)." *Le mouvement social* 101 (1977): 61–84.
Marthelot, Pierre. "L'avant-Granai: contribution à l'histoire de l'enseignement de la sociologie en Tunisie." In *Hommage à Georges Granaï*, 9–18. Aix-en- Provence: Université de Provence, 1985.
Marthelot, Pierre. "Histoire et réalité de la modernisation du monde rural au Maroc." *Tiers-Monde* 2, no. 6 (1961): 137–68.
Marthelot, Pierre. "Sur la terre algérienne: le point de vue d'un sociologue." *Annales* 20, no. 4 (1965): 809–11.
Martin, Olivier, and Patricia Vannier. "La sociologie française après 1945: places et rôles des méthodes issues de la psychologie." *Revue d'Histoire des Sciences Humaines* 1, no. 6 (2001): 95–122.
Martín-Criado, Enrique. *Les deux Algéries de Pierre Bourdieu*. Bellecombe-en-Bauges: Croquant, 2008.
Mary, André. "Ethnographie de soi sous le 'zéro equatorial.' Le chantier autobiographique de Georges Balandier." *L'homme* 221 (2017): 11–40.
Masson, Philippe. *Faire de la sociologie: les grandes enquêtes françaises depuis 1945*. Paris: Découverte, 2008.

Masson, Philippe. "Le financement de la sociologie française: les conventions de recherche de la DGRST dans les années soixante." *Genèses* 62 (2006): 110–28.
Masson, Philippe, and Cherry Schrecker. *Sociology in France after 1945*. London: Palgrave, 2016.
Mathias, Grégor. *Les sections administratives spécialisées en Algérie: entre idéal et réalité (1955–1962)*. Paris: L'Harmattan, 1998.
Maucorps, Paul H. "Les recherches de psychométrie ethnologique et leurs perspectives océaniennes." *Journal de la Société des Océanistes* 4, no. 4 (1952): 87–113.
Maucorps, Paul-Henri, Albert Memmi, and Jean-Françis Held. *Les français et le racisme*. Paris: Payot, 1965.
Maunier, René. "L'action du 'primitif' sur le 'civilisé.'" *Revue de l'Institut de sociologie* 10, no. 3 (1930): 451–70.
Maunier, René. "Bericht über die soziologische Literatur seit 1900 und die soziologische Gesellschaften. B. Die Soziologie in Frankreich seit 1900." *Monatsschrift für Soziologie*, nos. 1–2 (February 1909): 100–14.
Maunier, René. "Citoyenneté et nationalité dans l'Empire français." *Académie des sciences coloniales, Comptes rendus des séances* n.s. 2 (1942): 50–67.
Maunier, René. *Des comptoirs aux empires*. Paris: Sirey, 1941.
Maunier, René. *L'économie politique et la sociologie*. Paris: V. Giard & E. Brière, 1910.
Maunier, René. *L'empire français, Propos et projects*. Paris: Sirey, 1943.
Maunier, René. "Leçon d'ouverture d'un cours de sociologie 'algérienne.'" *Hespéris* 2, no. 2 (1922): 93–108.
Maunier, René. *Les lois de l'Empire (1940–1942)*. Paris: Domat-Montchrestie, 1942.
Maunier, René. *Sociologie coloniale*. 3 vols. Paris: Domat-Montchrestien, 1932–42.
Maunier, René. *The Sociology of Colonies*. London: RKP, 1949.
Maurel, Chloé. *Histoire de l'UNESCO*. Paris: L'Harmattan, 2010.
Mauss, Marcel. "Lévy-Bruhl sociologue." *Revue philosophique de la France et de l'étranger* 127, nos. 5/6 (1939): 251–53.
Mauss, Marcel. "Les peuples mixtes dans le monde moderne." *Bulletin de l'Institut français de sociologie* 2, no. 4 (1932): 131–46.
Mauss, Marcel. "Real and Practical Relations between Psychology and Sociology." In *Sociology and Psychology: Essays*, 1–34. Translated by Ben Brewster. London: Routledge & Kegan Paul, 1979.
Mayer, Hans, and Raymond Aron. "Zwischen Frankreich und Deutschland, zwischen Weimar und Bonn. Raymond Aron im Gespräch mit Hans Mayer." In *Die andere deutsche Frage. Kultur und Gesellschaft der Bundesrepublik Deutschland nach dreissig Jahren*, edited by Walter Scheel, 243–70. Stuttgart: Klett-Cotta, 1981.
Mayeur, Jean-Marie, and Madeleine Rebérioux. *The Third Republic from Its Origins to the Great War, 1871–1914*. Cambridge: Cambridge University Press, 1987.
Mazon, Brigitte. *Aux origines de l'École des hautes études en sciences sociales: Le rôle du mécénat américain, 1920–1960*. Paris: Cerf, 1988.
Mazon, Brigitte. "La création du Centre de documentation sociale." *Études durkheimiennes* 9 (1983): 15–20.
Mazon, Brigitte. "La Fondation Rockefeller et les sciences sociales en France 1925–1940." *Revue française de sociologie* 26 (1985): 311–42.
Mazov, Sergey. *A Distant Front in the Cold War: The USSR in West Africa and the Congo, 1956–1964*. Stanford, CA: Stanford University Press, 2010.
McCulloch, Jock. *Colonial Psychiatry and the "African Mind."* Cambridge: Cambridge University Press, 1995.
Mead, Geoffrey. "Forms of Knowledge and the Love of Necessity in Bourdieu's Clinical Sociology." *Sociological Review* 65, no. 4 (2017): 628–43.

Mead, Geoffrey. "Sense of Structure and Structure of Sense: Pierre Bourdieu's Habitus as a Generative Principle." PhD diss., University of Melbourne, 2013.

Meghji, Ali. *Decolonizing Sociology: An Introduction*. Cambridge: Polity Press, 2021.

Meimon, Julien. "L'invention de l'aide française au développement. Discours, instruments et pratiques d'une dynamique hégémonique." *Questions de recherche* 21 (2007): 1–43.

Memmi, Albert. *The Pillar of Salt*. Boston: Beacon, 1955.

Memmi, Albert. *Portrait du colonisé, précédé du Portrait du colonisateur*. Paris: Corrêa, 1957.

Memmi, Albert. *Portrait of a Jew*. New York: Orion Press, 1962.

Memmi, Albert. "Présentation générale." In *Cercle ouvert: Culture et colonialisme. 80 Conférence-Débats, 1-2*. Paris: La Nef, 1957.

Memmi, Albert. "Problèmes de la sociologie de la littérature." In *Traité de sociologie*, edited by Georges Gurvitch, vol. 2, 1221–44. Paris: PUF, 1960.

Memmi, Albert. "Sociologie des rapports entre colonisateurs et colonisés." *Cahiers internationaux de sociologie* 23 (1957): 85–96.

Mercier, Paul. "Aspects des problèmes de stratification sociale dans l'Ouest Africain." *Cahiers internationaux de sociologie* 17 (1954): 47–65.

Mercier, Paul. *Dakar dans les années 1950*. Aubervilliers: CTHS, 2021.

Mercier, Paul. "Le groupement européen de Dakar: orientation d'une enquête." *Cahiers internationaux de sociologie* 19 (1955): 130–46.

Mercier, Paul. *Les tâches de la sociologie*. Dakar: Institut français d'Afrique noire, 1951.

Mercier, Paul. *Tradition, changement, histoire. Les "Somba" du Dahomey septentrional*. Paris: Editions Anthropos, 1968.

Merle, Isabelle. "'La situation coloniale' chez Georges Balandier. Relecture historienne." *Monde(s)* 4 (2013): 212–32.

Merlio, Gilbert. *Ni gauche, ni droîte. Les chassés-croisés idéologiques des intellectuels français et allemands dans l'entre-deux-guerres*. Talence: Édition MSHA, 1995.

Merllié, Dominique. "Durkheim, Lévy-Bruhl et la 'pensée primitive': quelle différend?" *L'Année sociologique* 62 (2012): 1–13.

Mersadier, Yvon. *Budgets familiaux africains. Étude chez 136 familles de salariés dans trois centres urbains de Sénégal*. Saint-Louis, Sénégal: ORSTOM, 1957.

Merton, Robert K. "Insiders and Outsiders: A Chapter in the Sociology of Knowledge." *American Journal of Sociology* 78, no. 1 (1972): 9–47.

Merton, Robert K. "On the History and Systematic of Sociological Theory." In *Social Theory and Social Structure: Toward the Codification of Theory and Research*, 1–38. Glencoe, IL: Free Press, 1949.

Messaoudi, Alain. *Les arabisants et la France coloniale: savants, conseillers, médiateurs, 1780-1930*. Lyon: ENS, 2015.

Métais, Pierre. "L'oeuvre ethnologique et sociologique de Maurice Leenhardt." *Journal de la Société des Océanistes* 10 (1954): 51–69.

Métais, Pierre. "Sociologue parce que linguiste." *Journal de la Société des Océanistes* 10 (1954): 40–50.

Métraux, Alfred. "Les Indiens Uro-Cipaya de Carangas." *Journal de la Société des americanistes* n.s. 27 (1935-1936): 111–28, 325–415, quotes from 116, note 1; 326–27.

Métraux, Alfred. "Mes amis les paysans de Marbial." *Gradhiva* 1 (2005): 255–59.

Métraux, Alfred. "Unesco and Anthropology." *American Anthropologist* n.s., 53, no. 2 (1951): 294–300.

Métraux, Alfred. *Le vaudou haïtien*. Paris: Gallimard, 1958.

Meyran, Régis. "Écrits, pratiques et faits. L'ethnologie sous le régime de Vichy." *l'homme* 39, no. 150 (1999): 203–12.

Mézié, Nadège. "'Attention au départ. Prêt.' Le jeune Balandier par lui-même." *Cargo: revue internationale d'anthropologie culturelle & sociale*, nos. 6–7 (2017): 189–201.

Mézié, Nadège. "Tous comptes faits. Roman de (la) jeunesse de Georges Balandier." *L'homme & la société* 207, no. 2 (2018): 243–52.

Michel, Andrée. *Les travailleurs algériens en France*. Paris: CNRS, 1956.

Miles, William F. S. *Hausaland Divided*. Ithaca, NY: Cornell University Press, 1994.

Mill, John Stuart. *Auguste Comte and Positivism*. Ann Arbor: University of Michigan Press, [1866] 1961.

Moebius, Stephan. *Die Zauberlehrlinge. Soziologiegeschichte des Collège de Sociologie*. Konstanz: UVK Verlagsgesellschaft, 2006.

Monbeig, Pierre. *La crise des sciences de l'homme*. Rio de Janeiro: Edição da Casa do estudante do Brasil, 1941.

Monnais-Rousselot, Laurence. *Médecine et colonisation: l'aventure indochinoise 1860–1939*. Paris: CNRS editions, 1999.

Montagne, Robert. "Afrique noire et Afrique blanche." *L'Afrique et L'Asie* 4, no. 32 (1951): 90–97.

Montagne, Robert. *Les Berbères et le Makhzen dans le sud du Maroc*. Paris: Félix Alcan, 1930.

Montagne, Robert. *Étude sociologique de la migration des travailleurs musulmans d'Algérie en métropole*. 8 vols. Paris: Ministère de l'interieur, Direction des affaires d'Algérie, Bureau des affaires sociales musulmanes, 1957.

Montagne, Robert. "L'évolution moderne des pays arabes." *Annales sociologiques* série A, *Sociologie générale* no. 2 (1936): 29–76.

Montagne, Robert. "La formation des spécialistes des affaires musulmanes." *Bulletin économique du Maroc* 5, no. 19 (1938): 3–7.

Montagne, Robert. *Naissance du prolétariat marocain. Enquête collective exécutée de 1948 à 1950*. Paris: Peyronnet, 1951.

Morando, Laurent. *Les instituts coloniaux et l'Afrique, 1893–1940. Ambitions nationales, réussites locales*. Paris: Karthala, 2007.

Moret, Alexandre, and Georges Davy. *From Tribe to Empire: Social Organization among Primitives and in the Ancient East*. New York: A. A. Knopf, 1926.

Moric, Joël. *Raymond Aron et l'Europe*. Rennes: Presses universitaires de Rennes, 2013.

Morin, Françoise. "Les inédits et la correspondance de Roger Bastide." In *Roger Bastide ou le réjouissement de l'abîme*, edited by Phillipe Laburthe-Tolra, 21–42. Paris: L'Harmattan, 1994.

Morin, Françoise. "Roger Bastide ou l'anthropologie des gouffres." *Archives des sciences sociales des religions* 40, no. 1 (1975): 99–106.

Mouralis, Bernard. *Comprendre l'œuvre de Mongo Beti*. Issy les Moulineaux: Classiques africains, 1981.

Mouralis, Bernard. "Georges Balandier et la littérature." *Présence africaine* 194, no. 2 (2016): 157–73.

Mucchielli, Laurent. *La découverte du social: naissance de la sociologie en France (1870–1914)*. Paris: La Découverte, 1998.

Mucchielli, Laurent. "Pour une psychologie collective: l'héritage durkheimien d'Halbwachs et sa rivalité avec Blondel durant l'entre-deux-guerres." *Revue d'histoire des sciences humaines* 1, no. 1 (1999): 103–14.

Mus, Paul. *Viêt-Nam, sociologie d'une guerre*. Paris: Éditions du Seuil, 1952.

Nadeau, Maurice. *Le chemin de la vie*. Paris: France culture, 2011.

Nadeau, Maurice. *The History of Surrealism*. New York: Macmillan, [1945] 1965.

Ndaw, Alassane. "Philosopher en Afrique, c'est comprendre que nul n'a le monopole de la Philosophie." *Critique* 771–72 (2008): 624–25.

Nguyen, Phuong Ngoc. *À l'origine de l'anthropologie au Vietnam: Recherche sur les auteurs de la première moitié du XXe siècle*. Aix-en-Provence: Presses universitaires de Provence, 2012.

Nicolas, Serge. *Histoire de la philosophie en France au XIXe siècle: naissance de la psychologie spiritualiste (1789-1830)*. Paris: L'Harmattan, 2007.
Nicolas, Serge. *Histoire de la psychologie française: naissance d'une nouvelle science*. Paris: In Press Éditions, 2002.
Noiriel, Gérard. "Naissance du métier d'historien." *Genèses* 1 (1990): 58–85.
Nora, Pierre. *Les français d'Algérie*. Paris: Julliard, 1961.
Nord, Philip G. *France's New Deal: From the Thirties to the Postwar Era*. Princeton, NJ: Princeton University Press, 2010.
Nouschi, André. "Autour de *Sociologie de l'Algérie*," *Awal* 27–28 (2003): 29–35.
Nouschi, André. *Enquête sur le niveau de vie des populations rurales constantinoises de la conquête jusqu'en 1919. Essai d'histoire économique et sociale*. Paris: PUF, 1961.
Omouri, Noara. *La connaissance sociale dans l'administration française entre 1954 et 1962. Enquête documentaire*. Paris: EHESS, 1996.
Omouri, Noara. "L'institutionnalisation d'une nouvelle anthropologie coloniale. Le Centre de hautes études administratives sur l'Afrique et l'Asie modernes (CHEAM) 1937–1962." Paris: DEA thesis, École normale supérieure, EHESS, 1997.
Omouri, Noara. "Les Sections administratives spécialisées et les sciences sociales: études et actions sociales de terrain des officiers SAS et des personnels des Affaires algériennes." In *Militaires et guérillas dans la guerre d'Algérie*, edited by Jean-Charles Jauffret and Maurice Vaïse, 383–98. Paris: Éditions Complexe, 2001.
Oppermann, Matthias. *Raymond Aron und Deutschland. Die Verteidigung der Freiheit und das Problem des Totalitarismus*. Ostfildern: Thorbecke Verlag, 2008.
Ortigues, Marie Cécile, and Edmond Ortigues. *Œdipe africain*. Paris: Librarie Plon, 1966.
Osborne, Thomas R. *A Grande École for the Grands Corps: The Recruitment and Training of the French Administrative Elite in the Nineteenth Century*. Boulder, CO: Social Science Monographs, 1983.
Ottinger, Ulrike. *Paris Calligrammes: Eine Erinnerungslandschaft*. Ostfildern: Hatje Cantz, 2019.
Oulebsir, Nabila. "Berque, Augustin" in *Les usages du patrimoine: monuments, musées et politique coloniale en Algérie, 1830-1930*, 324. Paris: Maison des sciences de l'homme, 2004.
Padfield, William Nicholas. "'L'ascension sociale' and the Return to Origins: Reconstructions of Family and Social Origin in the Writings of Albert Camus, Annie Ernaux, Didier Eribon and Édouard Louis." PhD diss., Manchester Metropolitan University, 2015.
Paquot, Thierry. "Du lu avec du vu, la méthode de René Maunier (1887–1951)." *Urbanisme* 324 (2002): 78–83.
Paradeise, Catherine, Dominique Lorrain, and Didier Demazière, eds. *Les sociologies françaises: héritages et perspectives: 1960-2010*. Rennes: Presses universitaires de Rennes, 2015.
Pascon, Paul. "Les Seksawa depuis l'indépendance." In Jacques Berque, *Structures sociales du Haut-Atlas*, 455–74. 2nd ed. Paris: PUF, 1978.
Patterson, Orlando. *Slavery and Social Death: A Comparative Study*. Cambridge, MA: Harvard University Press, 1982.
Paul, Harry W. *From Knowledge to Power: The Rise of the Science Empire in France, 1860-1939*. Cambridge: Cambridge University Press, 1985.
Paul, H. W., and Terry Shinn. "The Structure and State of Science in France." *Contemporary French Civilization* 6 (1981–1982): 153–93.
Paulme, Denise. *Organisation sociale des Dogon*. Paris: Domat-Montchrestien, 1940.
Paulme, Denise. "Quelques souvenirs." *Cahiers d'études africaines* 19, no. 73 (1979): 9–17.
Paulme, Denise. "Sanga 1935." *Cahiers d'études africaines* 17, no. 65 (1977): 7–12.

Pels, Dick. "After Objectivity. An Historical Approach to the Intersubjective in Ethnography." *Hau: Journal of Ethnographic Theory* 4, no. 1 (201): 211-36.
Pendergast, William R. "French Policy in UNESCO." PhD diss., Columbia University, 1971.
Pérez, Amín. "Doing Politics by Other Means: Abdelmalek Sayad and the Political Sociology of a Collective Intellectual." *Sociological Review* 68, no. 5 (2020): 999-1014.
Pérez, Amín. "Rendre le social plus politique. Guerre coloniale, immigration et pratiques sociologiques d'Abdelmalek Sayad et de Pierre Bourdieu." PhD diss., EHESS, 2015.
Perroux, François. "L'effet de domination et les relations économiques." *Hommes et techniques* 49, no. 49 (1949): 9-17.
Perroux, François. "Esquisse d'une théorie de l'économie dominante." *Économie appliquée* 1, nos. 2-3 (1948): 243-300.
Perroux, François. "'L'ordonnance' de J. M. Keynes et les pays sous-développés." *Bulletin de l'Union des exploitations électriques en Belgique* no. 3 (July 1953): 1-18.
Petitjean, Patrick. "Autour de la mission française pour la création de l'université de Sao Paulo (1934)." In *Science and Empires: Historical Studies about Scientific Development and European Expansion*, edited by Patrick Petitjean and Catherine Jami, 339-62. Dordrecht: Kluwer, 1992.
Petitjean, Patrick, and Catherine Jami, eds. *Science and Empires. Historical Studies about Scientific Development and European Expansion*. Dordrecht: Kluwer, 1992.
Picard, Jean François, and Élisabeth Pradoura. "La longue marche vers le CNRS (1901-1945)." *Cahiers pour l'histoire du CNRS*, no. 1 (1988): 7-40.
Pickering, William S. F. "A Note on the Life of Gaston Richard and Certain Aspects of His Work." In *Durkheim on Religion*, edited by William S. F. Pickering, 343-59. London: Routledge & Kegan Paul, 1989.
Piriou, Anne. "Intellectuels colonisés et écriture de l'histoire en Afrique de l'Ouest (c. 1920-c.1945)." In *Décoloniser l'histoire? De l'histoire coloniale aux histoires nationales en Amérique latine et en Afrique, XIXe-XXe siècles*, edited by Sophie Dulucq and Colette Zytnicki, 59-81. Saint-Denis: Société française d'histoire d'outre-mer, 2003.
Pitts, Jennifer, ed. *Alexis de Tocqueville, Writings on Empire and Slavery*. Baltimore, MD: Johns Hopkins University Press, 2001.
Platt, Jennifer. *A Brief History of the ISA: 1948-1997*. Montréal: International Sociological Association, 1998.
Poirier, Jean. "Maurice Leenhardt, océaniste et sociologue." *Le monde non chrétien* 33 (1955): 72-95.
Polin, Raymond. *Les coopératives rurales et l'état en Tchécoslovaquie et en Roumanie*. Paris: F. Alcan, 1934.
Polin, Raymond. "La sociologie française pendant la guerre." *Synthèse* 5, nos. 3-4 (July-August 1946): 117-29.
Pollak, Michael. "Paul F. Lazarsfeld, fondateur d'une multinationale scientifique." *Actes de la recherche en sciences sociales* 25, no. 1 (1979): 45-59.
Poncelet, Marc. *L'invention des sciences coloniales belges*. Paris: Karthala, 2008.
Poncelet, Marc. "René Clémens et la mobilization des universitaires liègois au Katanga dans les années 1955-1960. Fin de colonie, sociologie clinique et bricolages du development." In *Généalogie des sociologues et anthropologues belges disparus*, edited by Jeanne Beausoleil and Pascal Ory, 205-22. Paris: L'Harmattan, 2015.
Pouch, Thierry. *Les économistes français et le marxisme. Apogée et déclin d'un discours critique (1950-2000)*. Rennes: Presses universitaires de Rennes, 2001.
Pouillon, François. *Dictionnaire des orientalistes de langue française*. Paris: Karthala, 2008. 2nd ed. 2012.

Pouillon, François, and Daniel Rivet, eds. *La Sociologie musulmane de Robert Montagne.* Paris: Éditions Maisonneuve & Larose, 2000.

Poulat, Émile. "Sociologie religieuse." In *La sociologie et les sciences de la société*, edited by Jean Cazeneuve and André Akoun, 309–414. Paris: CEPL, 1975.

Poupeau, Franck, and Thierry Discepolo, eds. *Pierre Bourdieu, Interventions, 1961-2001.* Marseille: Éditions Agone, 2002.

Pourtier, Roland. *Le Gabon.* Vol. 2 of *État et développement.* Paris: L'Harmattan, 1989.

Prochaska, David. *Making Algeria French: Colonialism in Bône, 1870–1920.* Cambridge: Cambridge University Press, 1990.

Prochasson, Christophe. "Raymond Aron est-il un intellectual de gauche?" In *Raymond Aron, philosophe dans l'histoire*, edited by Serge Audier et al., 219–28. Paris: Fallois, 2008.

Prost, Antoine. *Histoire de l'enseignement en France, 1800–1967.* Paris: Colin, 1968.

Prost, Antoine. "Les origines de la politique de la recherche en France, 1939–1958." *Cahiers pour l'histoire du CNRS 1939–1989* 1 (1988): 41–62.

Pullin, Eric. "The Culture of Funding Culture: The CIA and the Congress for Cultural Freedom." In *Intelligence Studies in Britain and the US: Historiography since 1945*, edited by Christopher R. Moran and Christopher J. Murphy, 47–64. Edinburgh: Edinburgh University Press, 2013.

Puri, Samir. *The Shadows of Empire: How Imperial History Shapes Our World.* New York: Pegasus Books, 2021.

Quijoux, Maxime, ed. *Bourdieu et le travail.* Rennes: Presses universitaires de Rennes, 2015.

Rabinow, Paul. *French Modern: Norms and Forms of the Social Environment.* Cambridge, MA: MIT Press, 1989.

Ramunni, Girolamo, ed. "Le CNRS au temps de Charles de Gaulle." Special Issue of *La revue pour l'histoire du CNRS* (1999). Online: https://doi.org/10.4000/histoire-cnrs.480

Raphael, Lutz. "Sur les rapports entre la sociologie et l'histoire en Allemagne et en France." *Actes de la recherche en sciences sociales* 106/107 (1992): 108–22.

Reed-Danahay, Deborah. "The Kabyle and the French: Occidentalism in Bourdieu's Theory of Practice." In *Occidentalism: Images of the West*, edited by James G. Carrier, 61–84. Oxford: Clarendon Press, 1995.

Reed-Danahay, Deborah. *Locating Bourdieu.* Bloomington: Indiana University Press, 2005.

Reggiani, Andrés Horacio. "Alexis Carrel, the Unknown: Eugenics and Population Research under Vichy." *French Historical Studies* 25, no. 2 (2002): 331–56.

Reggiani, Andrés Horacio. *God's Eugenicist: Alexis Carrel and the Sociobiology of Decline.* New York: Berghahn Books, 2007.

Renucci, Florence. "La 'décolonisation doctrinale' ou la naissance du droit d'outremer (1946–début des années 1960)." *Revue d'histoire des sciences humaines*, no. 24 (2011): 61–76.

Renucci, Florence. "L'élaboration du Code du travail outre-mer et la durée du travail en Afrique occidentale française." In *Les politiques du travail (1906–2006)*, edited by A. Chatriot, O. Join-Lambert, and V. Viet, 59–68. Rennes: Presses Universitaires de Rennes, 2006.

Revel, Jacques, and Nathan Wachtel, eds. *Une école pour les sciences sociales: de la VIe section à l'École des hautes études en sciences sociales.* Paris: Les Éditions du Cerf, 1996.

Rey, Pierre Philippe. *Les alliances de classes: sur l'articulation des modes de production.* Paris: Maspero, 1973.

Rey, Pierre Philippe. "Sociologie économique et politique des Kuni, Punu et Tsangui de la région de Mossendjo et de la Boucle du Niari (Congo-Brazzaville)." PhD diss., University of Paris, 1969.

Ricœur, Paul. *Memory, History, Forgetting.* Chicago: University of Chicago Press, 2004.

Ringer, Fritz K. *Education and Society in Modern Europe.* Bloomington: University of Indiana Press, 1979.

Rioux, Jean-Pierre. *The Fourth Republic, 1944–1958.* Translated by Godfrey Rogers. Vol. 7 of *The Cambridge History of Modern France.* Cambridge: Cambridge University Press, 1987.
Rivet, Daniel. "Exotisme et 'pénétration scientifique': L'effort de découverte du Maroc par les Français au début du XXe siècle." In *Connaissances du Maghreb, sciences sociales et colonisation,* edited by Jean-Claude Vatin, 95–109. Paris: CNRS, 1984.
Rivet, Daniel. "Réformer le protectorat français au Maroc?" *Revue du monde musulman et de la Méditerranée,* nos. 83–84 (1997): 75–91.
Rivet, Paul. "L'ethnologie." In *La science française,* edited by Henri Bergson et al., vol. 2, 5–12. 2nd ed. Paris: Larousse, 1934.
Rivet, Paul. "L'ethnologie en France." *Bulletin du Muséum nationale d'histoire naturelle,* 2nd ser., 12 (1940): 38–52.
Rivière, Joan. "Womanliness as a Masquerade." *International Journal of Psycho-Analysis* 10 (1929): 303–13.
Robcis, Camille. *Disalienation: Politics, Philosophy, and Radical Psychiatry in Postwar France.* Chicago: University of Chicago Press, 2021.
Rol, Cécil. "Dix-neuf lettres de Gaston Richard (1898–1939)." *Lendemains: études comparées sur la France* 41, nos. 158–159 (2015): 113–40.
Rolle, Pierre. "Pierre Naville: De la psychologie à la sociologie." *L'orientation scolaire et professionelle* 26, no. 2 (1997): 221–47.
Rose, Michael. "Retrospection and the Role of a Sociology of Work." In *Work in the French Tradition,* edited by Claude Durand, 1–29. London: SAGE, 2007.
Rosenboim, Or. "Repenser l'État dans un espace devenu mondial. La pensée de Raymond Aron sur les relations internationales 1940–1949." In *Raymond Aron et la défense de la liberté: nationalisme, libéralisme et post-modernité,* edited by Fabrice Bouthillon, Joël Mouric, and Matthias Oppermann, 41–64. Paris: Éditions de Fallois, 2016.
Rosental, Paul-André. *L'intelligence démographique: sciences et politiques des populations en France (1930–1960).* Paris: Odile Jacob, 2003.
Ross, Kristin. *Fast Cars, Clean Bodies: Decolonization and the Reordering of French Culture.* Cambridge, MA: MIT Press, 1995.
Rostás, Zoltán. "L'histoire d'un congrès qui n'a pas eu lieu: le XIVe congrès international de sociologie (Bucarest 1939)." *Les études sociales* 153–54 (2011): 195–212.
Rothberg, Michael. "The Work of Testimony in the Age of Decolonization: Chronicle of a Summer, Cinema Verité, and the Emergence of the Holocaust Survivor." *PMLA* 119, no. 5 (2004): 1231–46.
Rubbers, Benjamin, and Marc Poncelet. "Sociologie coloniale au Congo belge. Les études sur le Katanga industriel et urbain à la veille de l'Indépendance." *Genèses* 99 (2015): 93–112.
Saada, Emmanuelle. *Empire's Children: Race, Filiation, and Citizenship in the French Colonies.* Chicago: University of Chicago Press, 2012.
Sabrié, Marie-Lise. *Sciences au Sud. Dictionnaire de 50 années de recherche pour le développement.* Paris: ORSTOM, 1994.
Sacriste, Fabien. *Germaine Tillion, Jacques Berque, Jean Servier et Pierre Bourdieu: des ethnologues dans la guerre d'indépendance algérienne.* Paris: L'Harmattan, 2011.
Said, Edward W. *Freud and the Non-European.* London: Verso, 2003.
Said, Edward. *Orientalism: Western Conceptions of the Orient.* New York: Pantheon, 1978.
Samson, Fabienne. "Une anthropologie politique du religieux: Sur les traces de Georges Balandier." *Cahiers d'études africaines* 228, no. 4 (2017): 993–1010.
Sarr, Felwine, and Bénédicte Savoy. *The Restitution of African Cultural Heritage: Toward a New Relational Ethics.* Paris: Ministère de la Culture, 2018.
Sartre, Jean-Paul. *Anti-Semite and Jew.* New York: Schocken Books, 1948.

Sautter, Gilles. *De l'Atlantique au fleuve Congo. Une géographie du sous-peuplement.* 2 vols. Paris: Mouton, 1966.

Sautter, Gilles. "Les Paysans noirs du Gabon Septentrional. Essai sur le peuplement et l'habitat du Woleu-N'Tem." *Les cahiers d'outre-mer* 4, no. 14 (1951): 119–59.

Sauvy, Alfred. "Préface." In *Le Tiers-Monde, sous-développement et développement*, edited by Georges Balandier, 9–12. Paris: PUF-INED, 1956.

Sauvy, Alfred. "Statistique générale et service national de statistique de 1919 à 1944." *Journal de la société statistique de Paris* 116 (1975): 34–43.

Sauvy, Alfred. "Trois mondes, une planète." *L'Observateur*, no. 118 (August 14, 1952), 14.

Sauvy, Alfred. *La vie en plus: souvenirs.* Paris: Calmann-Lévy, 1981.

Savoye, Antoine. "Enquête sur les étudiants en sociologie de Célestin Bouglé et leur engagement en politique (1920–1940)." *Les Études Sociales* 165, no. 1 (2017): 111–56.

Sayad, Abdelmalek. *La double absence. Des illusions de l'émigré aux souffrances de l'immigré.* Paris: Seuil, 1999.

Sayad, Abdelmalek. *Histoire et recherche identitaire suivi de Entretien avec Hassan Arfaoui.* Saint-Denis: Bouchène, 2002.

Sayad, Abdelmalek, and Alain Gillette. *L'immigration algérienne en France.* Paris: Éditions Entente, 1976.

Schmitz, Jean. "L'Afrique par défaut ou l'oubli de l'orienalisme." In *Maurice Delafosse: entre orientalisme et ethnographie: l'itinéraire d'un africaniste, 1870-1926*, edited by Jean-Loup Amselle and Emmanuelle Sibeud, 107–21. Paris: Maisonneve, 1998.

Schreyger, Emil. *L'office du Niger au Mali, 1932 à 1982: la problématique d'une grande entreprise agricole dans la zone du Sahel.* Wiesbaden: Steiner, 1984.

Schumaker, Lyn. *Africanizing Anthropology: Fieldwork, Networks, and the Making of Cultural Knowledge in Central Africa.* Durham, NC: Duke University Press, 2001.

Schwartz, Alfred. *Toulepleu: étude socio-économique d'un centre semi-urbain de l'Ouest ivoirien.* Adiopodoumé: ORSTOM, 1966.

Schwartz, Alfred. "Ziombli: l'organisation sociale d'un village Guéré-Nidrou (Côte d'Ivoire)." *Bulletin de Liaison Sciences Humaines—ORSTOM*, no. 4 (1966): 83–86.

Schwartz, Alfred. *Ziombli: l'organisation sociale d'un village Guéré-Nidrou (Côte d'Ivoire).* Adiopodoumé: ORSTOM, 1965.

Scionti, Andrea. "'I Am Afraid Americans Cannot Understand': The Congress for Cultural Freedom in France and Italy, 1950–1957." *Journal of Cold War Studies* 22, no. 1 (2020): 89–124.

Sebag, Paul. "Le bidonville de Borgel." *Cahiers de Tunisie* 23–24 (1958): 267–309.

Sebag, Paul, Abdelwahab Bouhdiba, and Carmel Camilleri. *Les préconditions sociales de l'industrialisation dans la région de Tunis.* Tunis: Centre d'études et de recherches économiques et sociales, 1968.

Seibel, Claude. "Les liens entre Pierre Bourdieu et les statisticiens à partir de son expérience algérienne." In *La liberté par la connaissance, Pierre Bourdieu (1930–2002)*, edited by Jacques Bouveresse and Daniel Roche, 105–20. Paris: Odile Jacob, 2004.

Sera-Shriar, Efram. "What Is Armchair Anthropology? Observational Practices in 19th-Century British Human Sciences." *History of the Human Sciences* 27, no. 2 (2013): 26–40.

Sherman, Daniel J. *French Primitivism and the Ends of Empire, 1945–1975.* Chicago: University of Chicago Press, 2011.

Shinn, Terry. *L'École polytechnique: 1794–1914.* Paris: Presses de la Fondation nationale des sciences politiques, 1980.

Shinn, Terry. "The French Science Faculty System, 1808–1914: Institutional Change and Research Potential in Mathematics and the Physical Sciences." *Historical Studies in the Physical Sciences* 10 (1979): 271–332.

Sibeud, Emmanuelle. *Une science impériale pour l'Afrique? La construction des savoirs africanistes en France 1878-1930*. Paris: EHESS, 2002.

Sidi Boumedine, Rachide. "L'enseignement de la sociologie à l'université d'Alger entre 1962 et 1976. Quels enjeux?" In *Le temps de la coopération: Sciences sociales et décolonisation au Maghreb*, edited by Jean-Robert Henry and Jean-Claude Vatin, 285-94. Paris: Karthala, 2012.

Siino, François. *Science et pouvoir dans la Tunisie contemporaine*. Paris: Karthala, 2004.

Silverstein, Paul A. "Of Rooting and Uprooting: Kabyle Habitus, Domesticity, and Structural Nostalgia." In *Bourdieu in Algeria: Colonial Politics, Ethnographic Practices, Theoretical Developments*, edited by Jane E. Goodman and Paul A. Silverstein, 164-98. Lincoln: University of Nebraska Press, 2009.

Silverstein, Paul A., and Jane E. Goodman. "Introduction." In *Bourdieu in Algeria: Colonial Politics, Ethnographic Practices, Theoretical Developments*, edited by Jane E. Goodman and Paul A. Silverstein, 1-62. Lincoln: University of Nebraska Press, 2009.

Singaravélou, Pierre. *L'École française d'Extrême-Orient ou l'institution des marges, 1898-1956: essai d'histoire sociale et politique de la science coloniale*. Paris: L'Harmattan, 1999.

Singaravélou, Pierre. "Enseignement supérieur coloniale': Un état des lieux." *Histoire de l'éducation*, no. 122 (2009): 71-92.

Singaravélou, Pierre. "The Institutionalisation of 'Colonial Geography' in France, 1880-1940." *Journal of Historical Geography* 37 (2011): 149-57.

Singaravélou, Pierre. "Le moment 'impérial' de l'histoire des sciences sociales (1880-1910)." *Mil neuf cent. Revue d'histoire intellectuelle*, no. 27 (2009): 87-102.

Singaravélou, Pierre. *Professer l'Empire: Les sciences coloniales en France sous la IIIe République*. Paris: Publications de la Sorbonne, 2011.

Singer, Claude. *L'université libérée, l'université épurée (1943-1947)*. Paris: Les Belles Lettres, 1997.

Singh, Sourabh. "Anchoring Depth Ontology to Epistemological Strategies of Field Theory: Exploring the Possibility for Developing a Core for Sociological Analysis." *Journal of Critical Realism* 17, no. 5 (2018): 429-48.

Singh, Sourabh. "Science, Common Sense and Sociological Analysis: A Critical Appreciation of the Epistemological Foundation of Field Theory." *Philosophy of the Social Sciences* 49, no. 2 (2019): 87-107.

Sinha, Vineeta. "Annihilating the 'Savage Slot' from Anthropology: Materializing Reflexive Practices." *HAU. Journal of Ethnographic Theory* 11, no. 1 (2021): 264-72.

Smith, Tony. "A Comparative Study of French and British Decolonization." *Comparative Studies in Society and History* 20, no. 1 (1978): 70-102.

Soret, Marcel. *Les Kongo nord-occidentaux*. Paris: PUF, 1959.

Soret, Marcel. "Les Téké de l'est. Essai sur l'adaptation d'une population a son milieu." PhD diss., Lettres, Université de Lyon, 1970.

Sorre, Maximilien. *Rencontres de la géographie et de la sociologie*. Paris: Marcel Rivière, 1957.

Soulié, Charles, and Brice Le Gall. "Sociologie et philosophie: étude comparée de leurs évolutions socio-démographiques à l'université depuis le début des années 1970." *Regards sociologiques* 36 (2008): 43-52.

Soustelle, Jacques. *Aimée et souffrante Algérie*. Paris: Plon, 1956.

Soustelle, Jacques. "La culture matérielle des Indiens Lacandons." *Journal de la société des américanistes* 29, no. 1 (1937): 1-96.

Soustelle, Jacques. "Une danse dramatique mexicaine: 'le torito.'" *Journal de la société des américanistes* 33, no. 1 (1941): 155-64.

Soustelle, Jacques. *La famille otomi-pame du Mexique central*. Paris: Institut d'ethnologie, 1937.

Soustelle, Jacques. *The Four Suns. Recollections and Reflections of an Ethnologist in Mexico.* New York: Grossman Publishers, [1967] 1971.
Soustelle, Jacques. "Les idées religieuses des Lacandons." *La terre et la vie* 5, no. 4 (1935): 170–78.
Soustelle, Jacques. "Note sur les Lacandon du Lac Peljá et du Río Jetjá." *Journal de la société des américanistes* 25, no. 1 (1933): 153–80.
Spillmann, Georges. *Souvenirs d'un colonialiste.* Paris: Presses de la cité, 1968.
Stahl, Titus. *Immanente Kritik: Elemente einer Theorie sozialer Praktiken.* Frankfurt: Campus, 2013.
Steiner, Philippe. *Durkheim and the Birth of Economic Sociology.* Princeton, NJ: Princeton University Press, 2011.
Steiner, Phillipe. "La tradition française de critique sociologique de l'économie politique." *Revue d'histoire des sciences humaines* 18 (2008): 63–84.
Steinmetz, George. "The Afterlives of Empires: Notes toward an Investigation." In *Presence of the Past. Imprints of Colonialism and Imperialism in Global Politics. A Study in Global History, Historical Sociology and International Relations*, edited by Klaus Schlichte and Steffan Stetter. Cambridge: Cambridge University Press, forthcoming.
Steinmetz, George. "American Sociology and Colonialism, 1890s–1960s." In *Reconsidering American Power: Pax Americana and Social Science*, edited by John Kelly, J. K. Jacobsen, and Marston H. Morgan, 273–93. Oxford: Oxford University Press, 2019.
Steinmetz, George. "Begriffsbeben. Von der Geschichte der Wissenschaft zur historischen Soziologie der Sozialwissenschaften." *Mittelweg 36* (May 2020): 94–115.
Steinmetz, George. "Bourdieu, Historicity, and Historical Sociology." *Cultural Sociology* 5, no. 1 (2011): 45–66.
Steinmetz, George. "Bourdieu's Disavowal of Lacan: Psychoanalytic Theory and the Concepts of 'Habitus' and 'Symbolic Capital.'" *Constellations* 13, no. 4 (2006): 445–64.
Steinmetz, George. "British Sociology in the Metropole and the Colonies, 1940s–1960s." In *The Palgrave Handbook of Sociology in Britain*, edited by John Scott and John Holmwood, 302–37. Houndsmills: Palgrave Macmillan, 2014.
Steinmetz, George. "A Child of the Empire: British Sociology and Colonialism, 1940s–1960s." *Journal of the History of the Behavioral Sciences* 49, no. 4 (2013): 353–78.
Steinmetz, George. "The Colonial State as a Social Field." *American Sociological Review* 73, no. 4 (2008): 589–612.
Steinmetz, George. "Colonialism, Crisis, and Change: The Algerian Origins of Bourdieu's Concepts and His Rejection of Social Reproductionism." *Rassegna Italiana di Sociologia* 63, no. 2 (2022): 323–348.
Steinmetz, George, "Concept-Quake: Toward a Historical Sociology of Social Science," in *The Social Sciences Through the Looking-Glass. Studies in the Production of Knowledge*, edited by Didier Fassin and George Steinmetz, 21–80. Durham, NC: Duke University Press, 2022.
Steinmetz, George. "Critical Realism and Historical Sociology." *Comparative Studies in Society and History* 40, no. 1 (1999): 170–86.
Steinmetz, George. "Culture and the State." In *State/Culture. Historical Studies of the State in the Social Sciences*, edited by George Steinmetz, 1–49. Ithaca, NY: Cornell University Press, 1999.
Steinmetz, George. "Decolonizing German Theory: An Introduction." *Postcolonial Studies* 9, no. 1 (2006): 3–13.
Steinmetz, George. *The Devil's Handwriting: Precoloniality and the German Colonial State in Qingdao, Samoa, and Southwest Africa.* Chicago: University of Chicago Press, 2007.
Steinmetz, George. "Empire et domination mondiale." *Actes de la recherche en sciences sociales*, 171–72 (March 2008): 4–19.

Steinmetz, George. "Field Theory and Interdisciplinarity: Relations between History and Sociology in Germany and France during the Twentieth Century." *Comparative Studies in Society and History* 59, no. 2 (2017): 477–514.

Steinmetz, George. "From Sociology to Socioanalysis: Rethinking Bourdieu's Concepts of Habitus, Modern Symbolic Capital, and Field along Psychoanalytic Lines." In *The Unhappy Divorce of Sociology and Psychoanalysis: Diverse Perspectives on the Psychosocial*, edited by Lynn Chancer and John Andrews, 205–21. London: Palgrave Macmillan, 2014.

Steinmetz, George. "Geopolitics." In *The Wiley-Blackwell Encyclopedia of Globalization*, edited by George Ritzer, vol. 2, 800–22. Malden, MA: Wiley-Blackwell, 2012.

Steinmetz, George. "German Exceptionalism and the Origins of Nazism: The Career of a Concept." In *Stalinism and Nazism: Dictatorships in Comparison*, edited by Ian Kershaw and Moshe Lewin, 251–84. Cambridge: Cambridge University Press, 1997.

Steinmetz, George. "Historicism and Positivism in Sociology: From Weimar Germany to the Contemporary United States." In *Historicism: A Travelling Concept*, edited by Herman Paul and Adriaan van Veldhuizen, 57–95. London: Bloomsbury, 2020.

Steinmetz, George. "Ideas in Exile: Refugees from Nazi Germany and the Failure to Transplant Historical Sociology into the United States." *International Journal of Politics, Culture, and Society* 23, no. 1 (2010): 1–27.

Steinmetz, George. "The Imperial Entanglements of Sociology in the United States, Britain, and France since the 19th Century." *Ab Imperio* 4 (2009): 23–78.

Steinmetz, George. "Methodological Homelandism." *Contemporary Sociology* 48, no. 3 (2019): 244–48.

Steinmetz, George. "Neo-Bourdieusian Theory and the Question of Scientific Autonomy: German Sociologists and Empire, 1890s–1940s." *Political Power and Social Theory* 20 (2009): 71–131.

Steinmetz, George. "An Oblique Encounter with Sociology: Frantz Fanon's *Les damnés de la terre*." *Soziopolis* (December 2021). https://www.soziopolis.de/an-oblique-encounter-with-sociology.html

Steinmetz, George. "The Octopus and the *Hekatonkheire*: On Many-Armed States and Tentacular Empires." In *The Many Hands of the State*, edited by Kimberly Morgan and Ann Orloff, 369–94. New York: Cambridge University Press, 2017.

Steinmetz, George. "On the Articulation of Marxist and Non-Marxist Theory in Colonial Historiography." In *The Debate on Postcolonial Theory and the Specter of Capital*, edited by Rosie Warren, 139–47. London: Verso, 2017.

Steinmetz, George. "Présentation de W. E. B. Du Bois." *Actes de la recherche en sciences sociales* 171–72 (March 2008): 75–77.

Steinmetz, George. "Return to Empire: The New US Imperialism in Theoretical and Historical Perspective." *Sociological Theory* 23, no. 4 (2005): 339–67.

Steinmetz, George. "Scientific Authority and the Transition to Post-Fordism: The Plausibility of Positivism in American Sociology since 1945." In *The Politics of Method in the Human Sciences: Positivism and its Epistemological Others*, edited by George Steinmetz, 275–323. Durham, NC: Duke University Press, 2005.

Steinmetz, George. "Scientific Autonomy and Empire, 1880–1945: Four German Sociologists." In *German Colonialism in a Global Age*, edited by Geoff Eley and Bradley Naranch, 46–73. Durham, NC: Duke University Press, 2014.

Steinmetz, George. "Sociology and Colonialism in the British and French Empires, 1940s–1960s." *Journal of Modern History* 89, no. 3 (September 2017): 601–48.

Steinmetz, George, ed. *Sociology and Empire*. Durham, NC: Duke University Press, 2013.

Steinmetz, George. "The Sociology of Empires, Colonialism, and Postcolonialism." *Annual Review of Sociology* 40 (July 2014): 77–103.

Steinmetz, George. "Soziologie und Kolonialismus: Die Beziehung zwischen Wissen und-Politik." *Mittelweg 36* 29, no. 3 (June–July 2020): 17–36.

Steinmetz, George. "The State of Emergency and the New American Imperialism: Toward an Authoritarian Post-Fordism." *Public Culture* 15, no. 2 (Spring 2003): 323–46.

Steinmetz, George, and Julia Hell. "The Visual Archive of Colonialism: Germany and Namibia." *Public Culture* 18, no.1 (2006): 141–82.

Steinmetz-Jenkins, Daniel. "The Other Intellectuals: Raymond Aron and the United States." PhD diss., Columbia University, 2016.

Steinmetz-Jenkins, Daniel. "Why Did Raymond Aron Write that Carl Schmitt Was Not a Nazi? An Alternative Genealogy of French Liberalism." *Modern Intellectual History* 11, no. 3 (2014): 549–74.

Stenger, Nicolas. "The Difficult Emergence of an 'Anti-Totalitarian' Journal in Post-War France: Preuves and the Congress for Cultural Freedom." In *Campaigning Culture and the Global Cold War: The Journals of the Congress for Cultural Freedom*, edited by Giles Scott-Smith and C. Lerg, 91–106. London: Palgrave Macmillan, 2018.

Stevens, Mitchell L., Cynthia Miller-Idriss, and Seteney Khalid Shami. *Seeing the World: How US Universities Make Knowledge in a Global Era*. Princeton, NJ: Princeton University Press, 2018.

Stewart, Iain. *Raymond Aron and Liberal Thought in the Twentieth Century*. Cambridge: Cambridge University Press, 2019.

Stocking, George. "What's in a Name? (II) The Société d'ethnographie and the Historiography of 'Anthropology' in France." In *Delimiting Anthropology: Occasional Essays and Reflections*, 207–18. Madison: University of Wisconsin Press, 2001.

Stoetzel, Jean. "La doxométrie française a un an." *Sondages* 2 (1939): 2–4.

Stoetzel, Jean. "Une enquête sur l'opinion du personnel saharien et des familles." In *Problèmes humains posés par l'implantation des familles en régions désertiques*, edited by Centre d'études et d'informations des problèmes humains dans les zones arides, 79–87. Paris: Prohuza, 1961.

Stoetzel, Jean. "L'esprit de la sociologie contemporaine." *Revue française de sociologie* 32, no. 3 ([1946] 1991): 443–56.

Stoler, Ann Laura. "Colonial Aphasia: Race and Disabled Histories in France." *Public Culture* 23, no. 1 (2011): 121–56.

Storm, Eric. *Colonial Soldiers in Europe, 1914-1945: "Aliens in Uniform" in Wartime Societies*. New York: Routledge, 2016.

Storper-Perez, Danielle. *La folie colonisée*. Paris: Maspero, 1974.

Storper-Perez, Danielle. "L'hospitalisation en milieu psychiatrique occidental: fait et facteur d'acculturation chez les Wolof du Sénégal." PhD diss., Sixth Section, EPHE, 1968.

Strenski, Ivan. "Hüseyin Nail Kubali and Durkheim's Professional Ethics and Civic Morals." *Scripta Instituti Donneriani Aboensi* 19 (2006): 358–73.

Suremain, Marie-Albane de. "L'IFAN et la 'mise en musée' des cultures africaines." *Outremers* 95 (2007): 356–57.

Swedberg, Richard. "Georges Gurvitch. The Unhappy Positivist." *Journal of the History of Sociology* 4, no. 1 (1982): 66–93.

Tai, Li-Chuan. *L'anthropologie française entre sciences coloniales et décolonisation (1880–1960)*. Paris: Publications de la Société Française d'Histoire d'Outre-mer, 2010.

Talbi, Mohamed. *Penseur libre en Islam*. Paris: Albin Michel, 2001.

Tamba, Moustapha. "La sociologie au Sénégal." In *La sociologie aujourd'hui: une perspective africaine*, edited by Nga Valentin Ndongo and Emmanuel Kamdem, 347–61. Paris: L'Harmattan, 2010.

Tamba, Moustapha. *Sociologie au Sénégal*. Paris: Harmattan, 2014.

Tanguy, Lucie. *La sociologie du travail en France. Enquête sur le travail des sociologues, 1950-1990.* Paris: La Découverte, 2011.

Teisserenc, Pierre. "Science sociales, politique coloniale, stratégies missionaries. Maurice Leenhardt en Nouvelle-Calédonie." *Recherches de science religieuse* 65, no. 3 (1977): 389-442.

Terray, Emmanuel. "Georges Balandier (1920-2016)." *L'homme* 221 (2017): 5-10.

Terray, Emmanuel. "Présentation." In *Afrique plurielle, afrique actuelle: hommage à Georges Balandier*, edited by Pierre Bonnafé, 9-11. Paris: Éditions Karthala, 1986.

Thomas, Louis-Vincent. *Cinq essais sur la mort africaine.* Paris: Karthala, 2013.

Thomas, Louis-Vincent. "De l'ethnologie à la sociologie: essai sur un programme de recherches en Afrique noire." In Organisation d'études pour l'expansion de la recherche scientifique, *Actes du colloque sur la recherche scientifique et technique et le développement économique et social des pays africains*, 331-32. Dakar: Université de Dakar, 1959.

Thomas, Martin. *The French Empire at War, 1940-45.* Manchester: Manchester University Press, 1998.

Thomas, Martin. *The French Empire between the Wars: Imperialism, Politics and Society.* Manchester: Manchester University Press, 2005.

Thornton, John K. "Afro-Christian Syncretism in the Kingdom of Kongo." *Journal of African History* 54 (2013): 53-77.

Thornton, John K. *The Kingdom of Kongo: Civil War and Transition, 1641-1718.* Madison: University of Wisconsin Press, 1983.

Tilley, Helen. *Africa as a Living Laboratory: Empire, Development, and the Problem of Scientific Knowledge, 1870-1950.* Chicago: University of Chicago Press, 2011.

Tillion, Germaine. *L'Algérie en 1957.* Paris: Éditions de Minuit, 1957.

Todd, Olivier. *Albert Camus: A Life.* New York: AA. Knopf, 1997.

Tomissen, Piet. "Raymond Aron face à Carl Schmitt." *Schmittiana* 7 (2003): 111-29.

Touchelay, Béatrice. "Le développement de la statistique d'outre-mer du début du siècle aux indépendances: l'accomplissement d'une tâche de souveraineté." In *La France et l'outre-mer. Un siècle de relations monétaires et financières*, 259-80. Paris: Comité pour l'histoire économique et financière de la France, 1998.

Touchelay, Béatrice. "L'INSEE, histoire d'une institution." In *L'ère du chiffre: systèmes statistiques et traditions nationales*, edited by Jean-Pierre Beaud, 153-87. Saint-Foy: Presses de l'Université du Québec, 2000.

Tournès, Ludovic. *Sciences de l'homme et politique. Les fondations philanthropiques américaines en France au XXe siècle.* Paris: Classiques Garnier, 2008.

Traimond, Bernard. "Aux sources d'une thèse universitaire. Entretien realisé par Bernard Traimond avec Jacques Berque, professeur honoraire au Collège de France." *Cahiers ethnologiques* 9 (1988): 29-47.

Tréanton, Jean-René. "Les premières années du Centre d'études sociologiques (1946-1955)." *Revue française de sociologie* 32, no. 3 (1991): 381-404.

Tréanton, Jean-René. "Professional Activities and Responsibilities of Sociologists." *International Social Science Bulletin* 6, no. 1 (1954): 60-69.

Trouillot, Michel-Rolph. "Anthropology and the Savage Slot. The Poetics and Politics of Otherness." In *Recapturing Anthropology: Working in the Present*, edited by Richard Fox, 18-44. Santa Fe, NM: School of American Research Press, 1991.

Twagira, Laura Ann. "'Robot Farmers' and Cosmopolitan Workers: Technological Masculinity and Agricultural Development in the French Soudan (Mali), 1945-68." *Gender & History* 26 (2014): 459-77.

Ullmann, Bernard. *Jacques Soustelle: le mal aimé.* Paris: Plon, 1995.

Van Beusekom, Monika M. *Negotiating Development: African Farmers and Colonial Experts at the Office du Niger, 1920–1960*. Westport, CT: Heinemann, 2002.

Van Hove, Julien. *Histoire du Ministère des colonies*. Bruxelles: Académie royale des sciences d'outre-mer, 1968.

Văn Huyên, Nguyễn. *La civilisation annamite*. Hanoi: Direction de l'Instruction Publique de l'Indochine, 1944.

Văn Huyên, Nguyễn. *Le culte des immortels en Annam: Bois tirés du Hội Chân Biên*. Hanoi: Impr. d'Extrême-Orient, 1944.

Vannier, Patricia. "Un laboratoire pour la sociologie? Le Centre d'études sociologiques (1946–1968) ou les débuts de la recherche sociologique en France." PhD diss., Université de Paris, 1999.

Vannier, Patricia. "La relance de *L'Année sociologique* (1949–1960): un pari réussi." *Année Sociologique*, 3rd ser., no. 69 (2019): 181–207.

Vermeren, Pierre. *Misère de l'historiographie du Maghreb post-colonial: 1962–2012*. Paris: Publications de la Sorbonne, 2012.

Vermès, Geneviève. "La recherche en psychologie au CNRS, son institutionnalisation de ses débuts aux années cinquante. Construction d'une unité disciplinaire." *Bulletin de psychologie* 52, no. 440 (1999): 213–22.

Visweswaran, Kamala. "The Interventions of Culture: Claude Lévi-Strauss, Race, and the Critique of Historical Time." In *Race and Racism in Continental Philosophy*, edited by Robert Bernasconi, 227–48. Bloomington: Indiana University Press.

Vlahakis, George N., et al. *Imperialism and Science: Social Impact and Interaction*. Santa Barbara, CA: ABC-CLIO, 2006.

Vogt, Paul W. "Un durkheimien ambivalent." *Revue française de sociologie* 20 (1979): 123–29.

Vogt, Paul W. "Durkheimian Sociology versus Philosophical Rationalism: The Case of Célestin Bouglé." In *The Sociological Domain: The Durkheimians and the Founding of French Sociology*, edited by Philippe Besnard, 231–47. Cambridge: Cambridge University Press, 1983.

Vogt, Peter. *Kontingenz und Zufall: eine Ideen- und Begriffsgeschichte*. Berlin: Akademie Verlag, 2011.

Wacquant, Loic J. D. "A Concise Genealogy and Anatomy of Habitus." *Sociological Review* 64 (2016): 64–72.

Wang, Yingyao. "Homology and Isomorphism: Bourdieu in Conversation with New Institutionalism." *British Journal of Sociology* 67, no. 2 (2016): 348–70.

Warshaw, Dan. *Paul Leroy-Beaulieu and Established Liberalism in France*. DeKalb: Northern Illinois University Press, 1991.

Weinrich, Harald. *Lethe: The Art and Critique of Forgetting*. Ithaca, NY: Cornell University Press, 2004.

Weisz, George. "L'idéologie républicaine et les sciences sociales. Les durkheimiens et la chaire d'histoire d'économie sociale à la Sorbonne." *Revue française de sociologie* 20, no. 1 (1979): 83–112.

Wilbois, Joseph. *L'action sociale en pays de missions*. Paris: Payot, 1938.

Wilbois, Joseph. *Le Cameroun, les indigènes, les colons, les missions, l'administration française*. Paris: Payot, 1934.

Wilbois, Joseph. *Le service social dans les colonies françaises d'Afrique noire*. Paris: Éditions SPES, 1947.

Wilder, Gary. *The French Imperial Nation-State: Negritude and Colonial Humanism between Two World Wars*. Chicago: University of Chicago Press, 2005.

Williame, Jean-Paul. *Sociologie des religions*. Paris: PUF, 2012.

Williams, Elizabeth A. "Anthropological Institutions in Nineteenth-Century France." *Isis* 76, no. 3 (1985): 331–48.

Winkin, Yves. "Portait du photographe en jeune anthropologue." In *Le symbolique et le social: la réception internationale de la pensée de Pierre Bourdieu*, edited by Jacques Dubois, Pascal Durand, and Yves Winkin, 43–52. Liège: Editions de l'Université de Liège, 2005.

Wolfe, Audra J. "Science and Freedom: The Forgotten Bulletin." In *Campaigning Culture and the Global Cold War: The Journals of the Congress for Cultural Freedom*, edited by Giles Scott-Smith and C. Lerg, 27–45. London: Palgrave Macmillan, 2018.

Wouako Tchaleu, Joseph. *Le racisme colonial: analyse de la destructivité humaine*. Paris: L'Harmattan, 2015.

Wright, Gwendolyn. *The Politics of Design in French Colonial Urbanism*. Chicago: University of Chicago Press, 1991.

Wyrtzen, Jonathan. *Making Morocco: Colonial Intervention and the Politics of Identity*. Ithaca, NY: Cornell University Press, 2016.

Yacine, Tassadit. "Bourdieu et l'Algérie." In *Le symbolique et le social: la réception internationale de la pensée de Pierre Bourdieu*, edited by Jacques Dubois, Pascal Durand, and Yves Winkin, 33–42. Liège: Editions de l'Université de Liège, 2005.

Yacine, Tassadit. "Presentation" in Pierre Bourdieu, *Algerian Sketches*, 1–34. Cambridge: Polity, 2013.

Yelles, Mourad. "Jacques Berque, portrait du cheikh en passeur." In *Itinéraires intellectuels: entre la France et les rives sud de la Méditerranée*, edited by Christiane Chaulet-Achour, 235–58. Paris: Karthala, 2011.

Zamiti, Khalil. "Aux origines de la sociologie en Tunisie." In *Abdelkader Zghal: l'homme des questions: Hommage à Abdelkader Zghal, 5 avril 1931-22 février 2015*, edited by Mohamed Kerrou, 229–38. Tunis: Cérès éditions, 2017.

Zeldin, Theodore. "Higher Education in France, 1848–1940." *Journal of Contemporary History* 2, no. 3 (1967): 53–80.

Zytnicki, Colette. "La maison, les écuries. L'émergence de l'histoire coloniale en France (des années 1880 aux années 1930)." In *Décoloniser l'histoire? De l'histoire coloniale aux histoires nationales en Amérique latine et en Afrique, XIXe-XXe siècles*, edited by Sophie Dulucq and Colette Zytnicki, 9–24. Saint-Denis: Société française d'histoire d'outre-mer, 2003.

INDEX

Note: numbers in italics refer to figures and tables.

Abdel Malek, Anouar, 354
academic freedom, 24, 57, 225–26, 265, 343, 459n156
Adorno, Theodor, 112, 437n44
African Oedipus (Ortigues), 123
Afro-Brazilians, 167
Agblémagnon, François N'Sougan, 37, 211–15
Ageron, Charles Robert, 60
Algeria: Algerian War and, 317–18, 324–26; Aron and, 240; Berque and, 259; Bourdieu on French Colonialism in, 319–24; colonial labor and, 326–29; developmentalism and, 63–64, 68–70; ethnology and, 145; French colonialism and, 319–24; "porteurs de valises" and, 382n60; resettlement and, 208–9, 329–34, *332–33*, 340–41; statistics and, 131; the "Two Algerias" thesis and, 334–37, 490n104–490n105, 490n110–490n111
Althusserian Marxism, 110
Amazon, the, 163
Ambiguous Africa (Balandier), 274, 301–8, *304*, 485n265
America: Aron and, 231–32, 242–45; Berque and, 264–65; European colonialism and, 98–100; Indian Removal Act of 1830, 206; second colonial expansion and, 54, 397n5, 397n7; sociology and, 5, 379n21, 379n25; support for French colonial research and, 98–100
Amin, Samir, 109
Annales de géographie, 107
Annales d'histoire économique et sociale, 127–29
Annales sociologiques, 152–53, 233
Année sociologique, 15, 149, 152, 162, 181, 187, 267
anthropology/ethnology/ethnography, 135–45, 302–8, 310–12. *See also* ethnography (ethnographie)

aphasia, 391n51
Aron, Raymond: Algeria and, 240; the American empire and, 211, 242–45; *Centre de sociologie européene* (Center for European Sociology) and, 184; de Dampierre and, 224; epistemic positivism and, 232; French anticolonialism and, 241–42; French colonialism and, 238–41; German sociology and, 233; historical sociology and, 31; historicism and, 153; imperial wars and, 242; Nazi imperialism and, 6, 235–38, 462n36; politics of, 231–32; postcolonial theory and, 245–46; presentism and, 232; professional academic career of, 233–34; sociology of war and, 44; summary for, 351; wartime experience of, 234–35; wartime scholarly interests of, 234–35. *See also* colonial sociology
associationism (indirect rule), 64–65, 139
Aubame, Jean-Hilaire, 290–91
Aubin, Henri, 117
Augé, Marc, 21, 457n98
autonomy and heteronomy in science, 17, 19, 22, 28, 57, 197, 225–27, 265, 343–44
Azoulay, Jacques, 118–19

Bakongo. See *The Sociology of Black Africa* (Balandier)
Balandier, Georges, *284*; Alioune Diop and, 280; *Ambiguous Africa*, 274, 301–8, *304*, 484n265; anthropology and, 222; books published between 1955 and 1968, 293; on the "colonial situation," 30, 188, 286–90, 298; decolonizing sociology and, 37, 39, 220, 345, 354–58; demography and, 132; dynamic sociology and, 288, 298; early life and, 6, 271–72; early work in Africa and, 279–81, 452n26; education of, 272; *Études guinéennes* and, 285; historical and comparative sociology and, 31, 484n291;

[541]

Balandier, Georges (*continued*)
indigenous sociologists and, 13, 285; on the Lébou (with Mercier), 281–83; Leiris and, 272–79; methods and, 10; objects and, 303–5; Paris colonial exhibition and, 58; *Political Anthropology*, 310–12; *Présence africaine* and, 280–81; race and, 99; relationship with Berque and, 270; relevance to contemporary work and, 9; resettlement and, 207, 290–93, 355; resistance and, 306–7; rivalry with Lévi-Strauss and, 302–8; self-reflexivity and, 307–8; shifting disciplinary identities and, 312–14; sociologists as historians and, 288–89; *The Sociology of Black Africa*, 293–98, 432n123; on the "sociology of dependency," 289–90; sociology of labor and, 41; *The Sociology of the Black Brazzavilles*, 299–301; Soret and, 201–2, 204; structuralism and, 145; summary for, 351–52; *Tous comptes faits* and, 272–79, 275; urbanism and, 40–41; work in Brazzaville and, 285–86; work in Guinea and, 283–85, 284. *See also* colonial sociology

Bastide, Roger, 35, 42–43, 98, 124, 161, 166–68, 177, 184

Bekombo, Manga, 215–17

Belgian sociology and colonialism, 190–93, *193*, 375–76

Berque, Augustin, 247–48

Berque, Jacques, 252; colonial administration career and, 6, 248–49, 258–59; colonial reform and, 251–56; colonial sociology and, 12; colonial urbanism and, 250–51; "decolonial" concept and, 27, 35, 247, 260; decolonization of the social sciences and, 265–67; decolonizing sociology and, 37, 39, 220, 345, 354–58; *Dépossesion du monde* and, 260–61; doctoral thesis and, 256–58, 469n76; Durkheimian sociology and, 249; education and, 248; ethnology and, 144; Fanon and, 262–63; "For a new French political method in Morocco" (1946 memo), 255–56; *Les Arabes* and, 259–60; Marxism and, 264; Montagne and, 263–64; Muslim jurisprudence and, 252–53; Orientalism and, 263; parents' impact on his life and, 248; politics of, 252; position in the disciplinary fields and, 267–69; psychology and, 116; relationship with Balandier and, 270; relevance to contemporary work and, 9; scientific obscurity of, 269–70; Sectors of the Modernization of the Peasantry and, 253–54, *254*, 255; on social sciences and America, 264–65; summary for, 351; *Ulémas, fondateurs, insurgés du Maghreb* and, 268–69; work on Morocco and, 249–51, 253–54, *254*, 255. *See also* colonial sociology

Berr, Henri, 156–57

Beti, Mongo, 144–45

Bettelheim, Charles, 95

Bidonville (shantytown), 39–40, 251

Black Skin, White Masks (Fanon), 120–21, 215

Blanc, Robert, 134–35

Blida clinic, 117

Bloch, Marc, 127–28

Blondel, Charles, 111

Boisson, Pierre François, 87

Boiteau, Pierre, 12, 382n57

Bolivia, 162–63

Bonnafous, Max, 181, 434n159

Bonneuil, Christoph, 67

Borrey, Francis, 71

Bouglé, Célestin, 149, 153, 155, 176, 178, 181

Bourdieu, Pierre, *329*; biographical notes, 316–19; colonial labor and, 326–29; colonial warfare and revolution and, 324–26; conversion to sociology and, 6, 318–19; cultural capital and, 341–42; decolonizing sociology and, 345, 354; de Dampierre and, 224–25; education and, 185; epistemology and, 343–45; field theory, 14–15, 20, 338, 343, 357; formation of his thought and, 337–39, 345–46; French colonialism in Algeria and, 319–24; habitus and, 338, 340–41, 492n133; indigenous sociologists and, 13, 316, 326, 329–34; "laws" of colonialism and, 322; *Le déracinement*, 209, 329–34, *332–33*; neo-Bourdieusian historical sociology of science and, 17–25; philosophy of science and, 21–22; politics of, 12; psychoanalysis and, 20, 338; reflexivity and, 22–24, 358–60; relevance to contemporary work and,

9; renown of, 486n4; resettlement and, 208–9, 329–34, *332–33*, 340–41; scientific autonomy and, 226–27; *Sociologie de l'Algérie* and, 320–24, 488n57; sociology of knowledge and, 18; sociology of labor and, 41; standpoint epistemology and, 23–24; structuralism and, 145; summary for, 352–54; theory of habitus and practice and, 20–21, 221–22; theory of subjectivity and, 20; traditionalism and, 325; the "Two Algerias" thesis and, 334–37, 490n104–490n105, 490n110–490n111. *See also* colonial sociology

Bousquet, Henri, 77, 176, 407n25, 444n30

Boutellier, Jean-Louis, 396n119

Braudel, Fernand, 128–30

Brazzaville, 201–4, 285–86, 298–301. See also *The Sociology of the Black Brazzavilles* (Balandier)

Brazzaville conference: colonial science and, 88; developmentalism and, 68; higher education and, 76

Breil, Jacques, 227

Brévié, Jules, 210

Brokensha, David, 207

"broussard" and "bled" tropes in colonial context. *See* "bush research"

Bureau, Paul, 149

"bush research," 195, 199–206, *201–3*, 452n38

Bwiti cult. See *The Sociology of Black Africa* (Balandier)

Cahiers internationaux de sociologie, 187–88, 222

Caillois, Roger, 124, 425n147

cameralism, 65–66, 401n20

Camic, Charles, 45–46, 395n106

Camus, Albert, 278

Canguilhem, Georges, 317

Carothers, J. C., 117, 125

Carrel, Alexis, 131–32. *See also* Fondation Carrel

Carrel Foundation. *See* Fondation Carrel

Cat, Edouard, 77

Center for Studies of Human Problems in Arid Zones. See *Centre d'études et d'informations des problèmes humains dans les zones arides*

Centre de documentation sociale (CDS), 177–79

Centre des hautes études d'administration musulmane (CHEAM), 83–84

Centre de sociologie européenne (Center of European Sociology), 184–85

Centre d'études africaines (Center for African Studies), 85, 289

Centre d'études des problèmes sociaux indigènes (Center for Studies of Indigenous Social Problems), 192

Centre d'études et d'informations des problèmes humains dans les zones arides, 71

Centre d'études sociologiques, 183–84

Centre national de la recherce scientifique (CRNS): Agblémagnon and, 211–12; anthropology and, 143; Bekombo and, 215; creation and internal divisions of, 13, 88–89; Memmi and, 219; postwar boom in colonial science and, 87–88; psychology and, 113; religion and, 43; in Sahara, 413n118; sections of, 15; size of, 89, 182; sociology and, 142, 182–83, 384n73, 384n78

Césaire, Aimé, 424n130

Chaulet, Claudine, 8, 12

Chaulet, Pierre, 12

CHEAM. See *Centre des hautes études d'administration musulmane* (CHEAM)

chercheur de brousse. *See* "bush research"

Chesneaux, Jean, 187

Chevalier, Louis, 132

Chombart de Lauwe, Paul Henry, 34, *36–37*, 39, 390n34

Cipaya Indians, 162–63

Civilisation matérielle, économie et capitalisme, XV-XVIII siècles (Braudel), 129

Collège de France, 85, 411n89

Colleyn, Jean-Paul, 314

Collomb, Henri, 118–23

colonial boomerang effects, 5, 110, 161

colonial developmentalism: colonial welfare and social policy and, 70–73; history of, 63–67; Laroque Plan and, 401n5; postwar, 68–69; during wartime, 67–68, 86; welfare and social policy and, 70–73. *See also* colonialism

colonialism: America and, 54; Aron on French, 238–42; Balandier and the "colonial situation" and, 286–90; Berque and, 255–56, 260; Bourdieu and, 317–46; colonial "mode of production,"

colonialism (continued)
32, 417n9; colonial policymaking and, 57, 63–73, 253–55; colonial propaganda and, 58–61, *61*, 87, *87*; colonial reoccupation and, 53–56; colonial sociology and, 10, 29–39, 167, 197–99; colonial welfare and, 70–73; definition of, 382n52; dualism and, 24; Durkheim and, 157; Durkheimian morality and, 155–56; economics and, 108–10; French Communist Party and, 144; gender and, 44, 71–73, 217, 279, 282–83, 294–95, 301, 324–25, 455n81; geography and, 107–8; Germany and, 398n27, 432n124; indirect rule (associationism) and, 64–65, 105; interwar sociology and, 157–62; labor and, 326–29; law and, 105–6; Le Play and, 150; Maunier on, 161; modern, 128–29, 140, 239, 246, 382n56; national styles of, 381n37; Nazism and, 7, 27, 58–59, 281; "overseas" as a euphemism for, 56; popularity of, 53; Portugal and, 297, 309; Portuguese, 308–10; primitivism and, 139–43; psychiatry/psychology and, 104, 110–25, *113–15*; racism and, 42, 161; repression of in European collective memory and, 47; resettlement and, 195, 206–9, 290–93, 329–34, *332–33*, 340–41; social and cultural transformations and, 249–50; Spanish, 164, 206; state culture and, 3–4; statistics and, 131; support for independence and, 60. *See also* colonial developmentalism; decolonization

Colonial School in Lisbon (*Escola Superior Colonial*), 11

colonial sociology: academic degrees and, 185–87; analytic objects and, 30; anthropology/ethnology and, 135–45, 222–23; and the arts, 223–24; Belgian sociology and, 190–93, *193*, 375–76; bush researchers and, 195, 199–206, *201–3*; challenging structural domination in sociology and, 220–28; colonial context and, 104; conceptual and theoretical insights and, 34–37, 347–48; decolonization of, 37, 39; definition of, 11–12; demography and, 130–35; disadvantages faced by colonial vs metrocentric sociologists, 195–221; economics and, 108–10; employment and, 183–85; epistemic contagion and, 196–97; erasure from disciplinary memory of, 39–49; geography and, 107–8; higher education and, 75–78, 174–77; historical sociology and, 31–33, 126–30, 347–48; indigenous sociologists and, 195, 210–21; institutes providing training in, 78–85; institutions that supported, *38*; labor and, 326–29; law and, 105–6, 177, 266–67, 406n7; methodological contributions and, 30; overlap with adjacent fields and, 103–4, 126; patrons of, 189–90; political, 310–12; Portugal and, 10–11; postwar, 87–88, 181–82, 193–94; psychology/psychiatry and, 104, 110–25, *113–15*; publications and, 187–88; relevance to contemporary work and, 9; research organizations (French) and, 88–98, 178, 384n77; resettlement uprooting and, 195, 206–9, 290–93; scientific autonomy and, 225–27, 265; size of the sociology field and, 182–83, *183*, 396n125, 447n69; social policy and, 71–73; sociology of knowledge and, 18; standpoint epistemology and, 23–24, 37, 212–13, 339, 344–45, 359; statistics and, 130–35; strategies used by colonial sociologists to overcome disadvantages and, 221–28; technology and, 33–35, *34*, *36–37*; theory of practice and, 221–22; time frame of, 7–8; urbanism and, 39–40

Colonized Madness (Storper-Perez), 123

Colonna, Fanny, 32, 491n107

Comte, Auguste, 66

Conakry. *See* Guinea

"The Concept of Crisis Applied to an African Society," 213. *See also* Agblémagnon, François N'Sougan

Condominas, Georges, 210

Congo, Belgian, 190–93

Congo, French Colony (Middle Congo), 293–98

Congo: Revue générale de la colonie belge, 191

Congress for Cultural Freedom (CCF), 232

Conklin, Alice, 66–67

Connell, Raewyn, 5, 358

INDEX [545]

Constantine Plan, 63–64, 69
Conze, Werner, 162, 440n99
Cooper, Frederick, 68
Copans, Jean, 382n55
Coquery-Vidrovitch, Catherine, 129, 308–9
Cornaton, Michel, 209, 455n74
Corsi di Sociologia (Gini), 11
Crapuchet, Simonne, 71
cultural capital, 338, 341–42
cultural interfecundation, 167
cultural sabir, 331
culture splitting or cutting (Bastide), 167

Daily Life in the Kingdom of the Kongo (Balandier), 998–99
Dakar: Balandier and, 199, 279–81, 299; Dakar to Djibouti expedition and, 140–42; higher education and, 8, 76, 86, 95
Darbel, Alain, 326–29
Davy, Georges, 93, 149, 156–57, 189
Déat, Marcel, 178, 181, 434n159
decolonization: America and, 98; anticolonialism and, 196, 274, 285; Aron and, 242; Berque and, 35, 242, 258–63; colonial developmentalism and, 65; *Dépossession du monde* and, 27; economists and, 108; ethnology and, 145; Gurvitch and, 189; legal scholars and, 106; second colonial occupation and, 53–56; of the social sciences, 265–67; of sociology, 37, 39, 220, 345, 354–58; sociology and, 6–8, 11, 44, 144, 217–18; support for independence and, 60
de Dampierre, Eric: Aron and, 224; the arts and, 223–24; and Bourdieu, 224–25; colonial social policy and, 72–73; historical sociology and, 32; metrocentricism and, 48; politics of, 12; scientific autonomy and, 227
De Gaulle, Charles, 59, 68
Delafosse, Maurice, 199
"De la guerre révolutionniare à la revolution" (Bourdieu), 325–26
Delavignette, Robert, 55, 127–28, 198–99
demography, 72–73, 130–35. *See also* Blanc, Robert; Girard, Alain; statistics; Stoetzel, Jean
Dépossession du monde (Berque), 260–61
Deschamps, Hubert, 93, 199, 227

Desrosières, Alain, 130
developmentalism. *See* colonial developmentalism
Devereux, Georges, 124
Diop, Abdoulaye Bara, 217
Diop, Alioune, 279–80
disciplinary fields, 13–17. *See also* interdisciplinarity; transdisciplinarity
Doutté, Edmond, 263
Dualas, 205, 216–17
Du Bois, W. E. B, 4–6, 54, 424n132
Durkheim, Émile: anthropology and, 136–38; colonialism and, 157; definition of sociology and, 148; economics and, 108; ethnography and, 137; *Institut français d'anthropologie* (IFA) and, 137; morality and, 154–56, 437n44, 438n54; psychology and, 112
Durkheimian sociology: *Année sociologique* and, 15, 149, 152, 162, 181, 187, 267; anthropology and, 136; antiracism and, 138–39; Berque and, 249; colonialism and, 157–62; colonial syncretism and, 161; Durkheim's death and, 172; history and, 152–54; legacy and, 181; Le Playsians and, 148–50; morality and, 154–56, 437n44; psychology and, 111; states and empires and, 156–58
Dutch colonial sociology, 10, 381n47
Duvignaud, Jean, 30, 218

Éboué, Félix, 87
École coloniale (Colonial School), 79–83, 81–82
École francaise d'extrême-orient (French school of the far east), 13, 77. See also *École nationale des langues orientales*; Indochina
École nationale d'adminstration (ENA), 82–83
École nationale des langues orientales, 136–37
École normale supérieure, 85
École polytechnique, 85
École pratique des hautes études, Fifth Section, 42, 136–38, 410n84
École pratique des hautes études, Sixth Section, 48, 84–85, 130, 143, 184, 188
economics, 104, 108–10
Elementary Forms of the Religious Life (Durkheim), 155

Éléments de sociologie (Davy), 157
Elements of Colonial History (Hardy), 127–28
Elias, Norbert, 207, 341, 425n149, 454n57
epistemic contagion, 48, 196
Escard, Pierre, 150
Essais sur le régime des castes (Bouglé), 149
Essertier, Daniel, 111
ethnography (ethnographie), 135–37, 150–51, 277, 335. *See also* anthropology/ethnology
ethnology. *See* anthropology/ethnology
Études d'histoire rurale maghrébine (Berque), 249–50

Fang. See *The Sociology of Black Africa* (Balandier)
Fann hospital, Dakar, 122–23, 425n137. *See also* Dakar
Fanon, Frantz, 8, 118–23, 140, 215, 262–63, 424n130, 424n133; Joby Fanon and, 424n133; surrealism and, 424n130
fascism, 67, 143–44, 160, 180–81, 228, 235–38
Fauconnet, Paul, 111, 176, 438n58
Favret-Saada, Jeanne, 8
Febvre, Lucien, 127–28
Fernandez, James W., 481n175
field theory, 14–15, 20, 221, 338, 343, 384n75, 385n97, 385n99, 416n1, 442n1; network theory and, 442n1; space and, 20, 385n99; subfields and, 195, 442n1
Fischer, Eugen, 144, 387n125
Fondation Carrel, 131–33, 144
Fortes, Meyer, 98
Foucault, Michel, 18, 117, 226, 401n20
Fougeyrollas, Pierre, 116
free trade, 108
French Communist Party, 60, 144
French Institute for Black Africa (*Institut français d'Afrique noire*). *See* IFAN (*Institut français d'Afrique noire*)
French Sociology (Heilbron), 173
Frère, Suzanne, 95, 414n139
Freud, Sigmund, 123–24
Froelich, Jean-Claude, 199, 204
Froidevaux, Henri, 127
Froment, Cécile, 314
From Tribe to Empire (Davy and Moret), 156

Fund for the Economic and Social Development of the Overseas Territories (FIDES), 55, 69, 71, 88

Gabon, 70, 209, 290–98
Gaillard, Gérald, 289
Gallagher, John, 54–55
gender and colonialism, 44, 71–73, 217, 279, 282–83, 294–95, 301, 324–25, 455n81
General Resettlement of Indians, 206
Gens de la Grande Terre (Leenhardt), 165
geography, 104, 107–8
German colonial sociology, 7
Gernet, Louis, 187, 267
Gessain, Robert, 132
Gini, Corrado, 11
Girard, Alain, 134, 181
Go, Julian, 357–58
Goldstein, Jan, 113
Gonidec, P. F., 106
Gouellain, René, 205
Granai, Georges, 8
Griaule, Marcel, 33–34, 138, 140, 144
"*Guerre et mutation social en Algérie*" (Bourdieu), 324–25
Guinea, 135, 283–85; Konkouré dam project, 454n61
Gurvitch, Georges, 183–84, 188–89, 219

habitus and practice, theory of, 20–21, 338, 340–41, 492n133
Haiti, 163
Halbwachs, Maurice, 39–40, 133, 149, 153
Halévy, Elie, 235
Hamy, Ernest-Théodore, 136
Hand, Séan, 274–75
Hardy, Georges, 127–28
Hegel, Georg, 120–21, 124, 223, 261, 290
Heilbron, Johan, 173, 185
Hell, Julia, 123–24, 236
Herskovits, Melville, 161
higher education: academic degrees and, 185–87; colonialism and, 75–78; colonial propaganda and, 87; in Dakar, 8, 76, 86, 95; institutes training in colonial science and, 75–78; research organizations (French) and, 88–98; research organizations (international) and, 98–100; scientific research and,

85–88; sociology in French universities and, 174–77, *175*
Histoire des religions (journal), 42, 394n89
historians, 14, 44–45, 126–30, 395n107
historical socioanalysis of social science, 272–73, 349
history (discipline), 126–30
Hitler. *See* fascism; Nazism
Hobson, John, 5
Hubert, René, 157
Humboldt Forum, 4

IFAN *(Institut français d'Afrique noire)*, 95–96, *96*, 135, 182–83, 200; sociology and, 182, 447n70
imperialism: afterlives of, 34, 377n9; Aron on, 242–45; French sociology and, 156–58; Nazi, 235–38; race and, 4; sociology and, 6. *See also* colonialism; colonial sociology
imperial overstretch, 161
Indian Removal Act of 1830, 206
indirect rule. *See* associationism (indirect rule)
Indochina (French colony), 54–55, 68, 70
Institut des hautes études, Tunis, 77–78, 120, 207–8
Institut d'ethnologie. *See* Paris Institute of Ethnology *(Institut d'ethnologie)*
Institut d'études centrafricaines (IEC), 285–86
Institute for Applied Psychology and Sociology *(Institut de Psychologie et de sociologie appliquées)*, *113*, 114
Institute for the Study of Economic and Social Development *(Institut d'étude du développement économique et social)* (IEDES), 110
Institute of Advanced Studies *(Institut des hautes études)* (Tunis). See *Institut des hautes études*, Tunis
Institut français de sociologie (IFS), 179, 181
Institute of Ethnology, 97, 112, 140–41
Institute of Political Studies (Sciences Po), 78–79
Institut français d'anthropologie (IFA), 137
Institut national de la statistique et des études économiques, 31, 130

Institut national d'études démographiques (INED), 131–33
Institut pour la recherche scientifique en Afrique centrale (Institute for Scientific Research in Central Africa), 192
intellectual history, 14, 39, 349, 356
Intellectuals, theory of, 226
interdisciplinarity, 30, 73, 85, 103, 416n1. *See also under* sociology
International Institute of Sociology, 179–82, 446n63
interpenetration of cultures, 167
interwar French sociology: Bastide and, 166–68; colonialism and, 157–62; empirical fieldwork and, 148–52; indigenous cultures and, 162–65; Le Coeur and, 158–60; Leenhardt and, 165–66; Maunier and 160-162, 158–60; morality and, 154–56; relationship with history and, 152–54; states and empires and, 156–57; vibrancy of, 168
Introduction to Collective Psychology (Blondel), 111
Introduction to the Sociological Method (Bureau), 149

Jews (Algeria and Tunisia), 218
Joly, Marc, 491n110
Julien, Charles-André, 129

Kabyle myth, 334–37, 357
Karady, Victor, 174
Keita, Madeira, 283, 285
Khaldun, Ibn, 161
Kojève, Alexandre, 237
Kongo Kingdom, 40–41, 297, 308–10, 486n333
Krisenwissenschaft (crisis science), 233

labor, 70–71
Lacandon Indians, 163–64
La colonisation chez les peuples modernes (Leroy-Beaulieu), 108
Lacoste, Yves, 107
L'âge d'homme (Leiris), 274–79, *276*
L'Algérie et la République (Aron), 240–41
L'an V de la révolution algérienne (Fanon), 121
Lapie, Paul, 97
Lapouge, Georges Vacher de, 136
La république impériale (Aron), 244

La tragédie algérienne (Aron), 240
law, 104–6, 177, 252–53, 266–67
the Lébou/Lebu, 281–83
Le Cameroun (Wilbois), 151–52
Le Chatelier, Alfred, 40
Le Coeur, Charles, 139, 153, 158–60, 357
Le déracinement (Bourdieu and Sayad), 209, 329–34, *332–33*, 340
Leenhardt, Maurice, 165, 296
Lefort, Claude, 243
Leiris, Michel, 141–42, 145, 272–79, *275*
Le Play, Frédéric, 39, 134, 148–52
Le Playsian sociology, 148–52
Le rite et l'outil (Le Coeur), 158–60
Leroi-Gourhan, André, 33
Leroy-Beaulieu, Paul, 108
Les Arabes (Berque), 259–60
Les damnés de la terre (Fanon), 122
Les Kongo Nord-Occidentaux (Soret), 202, *203*
Lesne, Marcel, 208–9
Les Ouvriers européens and *Les ouvriers des deux mondes* (Le Play), 39, 150
Les paysans noirs (Delavignette), 199
Les règles de la méthode sociologique, 119
Les sociologies françaises, 172
Letourneau, Charles, 136
Lévi-Strauss, Claude, 145, 302–8, 484n275
Lévy-Bruhl, Henri, 106
Lévy-Bruhl, Lucien, 96–97, 112, 155
Lewin, Kurt, 338
Lorcin, Patricia, 396n120
Luchaire, François, 106
Lukács, Georg, 359
Ly, Abdoulaye, 130

Macey, David, 424n133
Machiavellianism, 235–36, 462n36
Maget, Marcel, 33
Mahé, Alain, 249
Malaurie, Jean, 302
Malengreau, Guy, 192
Mandouze, André, 8
Mannheim, Karl, 17–18
Mannoni, Octave, 124, 132, 424
Manuel élémentaire de sociologie (Hubert), 157
Maquet, Jacques, 192–93, 384n79
Marchal, Léon, 254
Marié, Michel, 40, 64
Marxism, 66, 261, 264

Masqueray, Emile, 77
Massé, Louis, 135, 430n85
Massignon, Louis, 39, 263, 444n29
Masson, Philippe, 39
Matswa, André, 298
Maucorps, Paul-Henri, 114, 442n29
Maunier, René: collaborationism and, 161, 181; colonial law and, 106; colonial sociology and, 11–12, 160–62; on the French Empire, 199; the University of Algiers and, 77
Mauss, Marcel, 96–98, 111, 137–38, 148
McCulloch, Jock, 117
medina, 251
Mediterranean, The (Braudel), 129
Memmi, Albert, 188, 210, 215, 218–22
Mercier, Paul: historical sociology and, 31–32; on the Lébou (with Balandier), 281–83; resettlement and, 207
Merton, Robert, 18, 391n48
Messaoudi, Alain, 266
Méthode de l'ethnographie (Griaule), 141
methodological nationalism, 9, 380n36, 396n123
Métraux, Alfred, 162–63
metrocentricism, 48, 396n123
Mexico, 163–65
Michel, Andreé, 8, 12
Migon, Florentine, 248
Mill, John Stuart, 66
Mills, C. Wright, 211
Mission démographique de Guinée, 72, 135
mixité, 161
Montagne, Robert, 39, 41, 43–44, 83–84, 263–64
Montandon, George, 144
Moreau, Jacques-Joseph, 117
Moret, Alexandre, 156
Morocco, 70, 198, 240, 249–58, 422n94
Mozabites, 320–21
Mpadi, Pierre, 298
Mus, Paul, 190

Nadeau, Maurice, 273, 475n22
Nail, Hüseyin, 189
National Institute for Demographic Research (INED). See *Institut national d'études démographiques*
National Institute of Statistics and Economic Studies. See *Institut*

INDEX [549]

national de la statistique et des études économiques
Naville, Pierre, 384n79
Nazism, 235–38, 391n48, 396n121
neo-Bourdieusian historical sociology of science, 17–25
neo-positivism, 45–46
New Caledonia, 165
Nguyễn Văn Huyên, 13
Notes of a French Student in Germany (Bouglé), 181
Nouschi, André, 129–30, 320

Office de la recherche scientifique coloniale (Office of Colonial Scientific Research) (ORSC), 57–58, 86, 88–89, *90*, 90–95, 182–83, 279
Office de la recherche scientifique et technique outre-mer (Office of Overseas Scientific and Technical Research) (ORSTOM), 89–95, *90*, *92–94*, 182, 200–205, 225, 227
Office du Niger, 67–68, 207
Orientalism, 263
ORSTOM. See *Office de la recherche scientifique coloniale* (Office of Colonial Scientific Research) (ORSC); *Office de la recherche scientifique et technique outre-mer* (Office of Overseas Scientific and Technical Research) (ORSTOM)
Ortigues, Marie-Cécile, 123
Otomi Indians, 163–65

Paris Institute of Ethnology *(Institut d'ethnologie)*, 96–98, 112, 140–41
Parsons, Talcott, 6
Pascon, Paul, 256
Paulme, Denise, 141
Pauvert, Jean-Claude, 290–93
Pérez, Amín, 317, 492n125
Perroux, François, 109–10
Philosophy: and colonialism, 416n2; of social science, 397n25, 398n112, 416n2. *See also* Bourdieu, Pierre; Durkheim, Émile; Hubert, René; Lévy-Bruhl, Lucien
The Pillar of Salt (Memmi), 215
pith helmet *(casque colonial)*, 200, 452n26
Platon, Charles, 67
Poetics of Space (Bachelard), 340

Polin, Raymond, 172
Political Anthropology (Balandier), 310–12
Porot, Antoine, 118
Portugal: colonialism and, 219, 297, 309; colonial sociology and, 10–11
Présence africaine, 280–81
primitivism, 139–43, 167, 432n123–432n124. *See also* anthropology/ethnology
Psychologie de la colonisation (Mannoni), 124
psychology/psychiatry/psychoanalysis: colonialism and, 104, 110–18, *113–15*; Fanon and Collomb and, 118–23; psychiatric diagnosis and treatment in the colonies and, 116–18; psychoanalysis and, 123–25, 168, 338; scientific psychology and, 113; "spiritualism" and, 113
Puaux, Gaston, 253

Qarawiyîn Mosque, 251
Quatrefages de Bréau, Jean-Louis Armand de, 136
Qu'est-ce que la sociologie (Bouglé), 181

race/racism/antiracism: Aron and, 241; Balandier and, 280–81, 286–90; Bourdieu and, 322–23; colonialism and, 4, 42, 48, 99, 138–39, 144, 161, 210, 215, 241; Durkheimians and, 138–39; Fanon and, 122; imperialism and, 4, 161, 241; indigenous sociologists and, 210–21; psychiatry and, 119, 122; sociology and, 42; UNESCO and, 99
Recherches en sciences humaines (book series), 223–24
Reducción General de Indios, 206
reflexivity, 22–24, 265–66, 307–8, 358–60, 391n48
religion, 42–43, 295–96, 298, *306*, 307
resettlement and uprooting, colonial, 195, 206–9, 290–93, 329–34, *332–33*, 340–41
Retel-Laurentin, Anne, 72–73
"Révolution dans la révolution" (Bourdieu), 325
Revue française de sociologie, 188
Rey, Pierre-Phillippe, 32, 421n69
Richard, Gaston, 166, 441n128
Rivet, Jean-Paul, 96–97, 137, 141, 326–29
Rockefeller Foundation, 98, 140, 177–78, 381n45, 415n167, 445n40

Rodinson, Maxime, 161, 187
Rondot, Pierre, 44
The Rules of Art (Bourdieu), 18

Said, Edward, 123, 198, 265
Saint-Simon, Henri de, 66
Salaita, Steven, 496n30
Samson, Fabienne, 308
Sarraut, Albert, 67
Sautter, Gilles, 107–8
Sauvy, Alfred, 132
"savage slot" and anthropology, 16
Sayad, Abdelmalek, 12–13, 208–9, 226, 340
Schwartz, Alfred B., 205–6, 389n23
Sciences Po. See *Institute of Political Studies* (Sciences Po)
Scientific Council for Africa South of the Sahara, 99–100
scientific psychology. See psychology/psychiatry/psychoanalysis
Sebag, Paul, 218
second scientific revolution, 56–58
Sectors of the Modernization of the Peasantry, 253–54, *254*, 255
Seibel, Claude, 326–29
Seksawa society, 256–58, 469n76
Senegal, 55–56. See also Dakar; Fann hospital, Dakar
Servier, Jean, 12
shantytowns. See *bidonville* (shantytown)
Sicard, Émile, 8
Singaravélou, Pierre, 57, 76, 107–8, 127
Sixième section de l'école pratique des hautes études. See *École pratique des hautes études*, Sixth Section
Société belge de sociologie, 191
Société d'anthropologie, 135–36
Société de géographie, 107
Société de psychologie de Paris, 111
Société des Mines de Zellidja, 422n94. See also Morocco
Société d'ethnographie, 136
Sociologie coloniale (Maunier), 160–62, 187
Sociologie de l'Algérie (Bourdieu), 320–24, 488n57
sociologists: African, 37; African American, 5–6; anthropology and, 222–23; Belgian, 375–76; bush researchers and, 195, 199–206, *201–3*; colonial, 12, 195–99, 363–66; definition of, 13–17, 384n75; disadvantages faced by colonial vs metrocentric sociologists and, 195–221; Durkheim's definition of, 148; Dutch, 10; epistemic contagion and, 48; fascism and, 143–44, 180; female, 455n81; as historians, 288–89; identifying, 13–17; indigenous, 12–13, 195, 210–21, 329–34, 383n67; Italian, 11; Portuguese, 10–11; resettlement, 195, 206–9; Spanish, 11; strategies for overcoming disadvantages and, 221–28
Sociology: academic degrees and (France), 185–87; amnesia around colonialism and (France), 39–49; Belgian, 190–93, *193*; chairs in France, 176–77, 447n69; colonial sociologists' contributions and (France), 30–39, 347–53; decolonizing, 37, 39, 220, 345, 354–58; of dependency, 289–90; disadvantages faced by colonial vs metrocentric sociologists and, 195–221; economic, 41; ethnography and, 32–33; ethnology/anthropology and, 16, 96; German, 7, 17–18, 233; greater French sociology field in 1946, 367; greater French sociology field in 1949, 369; greater French sociology field in 1955, 371–72; greater French sociology field in 1960, 373–74; historical (France), 31–32, 347–48; imperialism and, 6; Indian, 357, 496n38; intersectionality and, 348; interwar (France), 148–68; of knowledge, 17–18, 391n48; of labor, 41; migration and, 41–42; nation-state level analysis and, 9; political, 308–12; popularity of (France), 174–76; postwar (France), 87–88, 181–82, 193–94, 350; presentism and, 232; quasi-disappearance of, 172–74; of religion (France), 42–43; scholarly associations and, 179–81; size of disciplinary field (in France), 182–83, 396n125, 447n69; students and (France), 174–76; the United States and, 5; urbanism and (French), 39–40; of war (France), 43–44; wartime occupation and Vichy and, 83, 131–33, 144, 172. See also colonial sociology; Durkheimian sociology; Le Playsian sociology
Sociology in France after 1945 (Masson and Schrecker), 48

The Sociology of Black Africa (Balandier), 293–98, 481n175
The Sociology of the Black Brazzavilles (Balandier), 289–301
"Sociology of the relations between the colonizer and the colonized" (Memmi), 188
Soret, Marcel, *34*, 201, *201–3*, 204
Soustelle, Jacques, 162–65
Sovay Institute for Sociological Research, 191
Spanish colonial sociology, 11, 164
Spillmann, Georges, 198
spiritualism. *See* psychology/psychiatry/ psychoanalysis
standpoint epistemology, 23–24, 37, 212–13, 339, 344–45, 359
state culture, 2–3, 377n4
statistics, 130–35
Statistique général de la France, 130
Stoetzel, Jean, 133–34, 181
Storper-Perez, Danielle, 123
structuralism and social science, 23, 145
"Structures sociales du Haut-Atlas" (Berque), 256–58
Suez crisis of 1956, 240
Superior Council of Colonial Scientific Research, 85–88
Superior Council of Overseas Sociological Research *(Conseil supérieur des recherches sociologiques outre-mer)*, 93, 95

Tardits, Claude, 484n265
The Tasks of Sociology (Mercier), 187
Terray, Emmanuel, 308
Terre humaine (book series), 302
territorialization, 206. *See also* resettlement
Thomas, Louis Vincent, 8, 204–5
Thomas, Martin, 59
Thornton, John K., 314
"threat of the Caesars" (Aron), 236
Thurnwald, Richard, 7
totalitarianism, 243
Tous comptes faits (Balandier), 272–79, 275
traditionalisms, reshaped by colonialism, 321–22, 325
"Traditional Society's Attitude towards Time and Economic Behavior" (Bourdieu), 328

Traité de sociologie (Gurvitch), 189
transdisciplinarity. *See also under* sociology
Travail et travailleurs en Algérie (multiple authors), 326–29, 340
Tréanton, Jean-René, 183
Tristes tropiques (Lévi-Strauss), 145, 302–8 *305*
Trystram, Jean-Paul, *113*, 114

Ulémas, fondateurs, insurgés du Maghreb (Berque), 268–69
United Nations Educational, Scientific and Cultural Organization (UNESCO), 10, 98–99, 259; statements on race (1950, 1967), 99
United States, the. *See* America
Université officielle du Congo belge et du Ruanda-Urundi, 192
universities. *See* higher education
University of Algiers, 76–77
University of Hanoi, 78
University of Lovanium, 192, *193*
University of Paris, 76–78, 98, 189
University of Tunis, 77–78, 217–18; sociology and, 457n114
urbanism, 39–40
USSR, 242–45

veil metaphor, 424n132
Verneau, René, 137
Vichy France, 58–59, 67–68, 87–88, 130–31, 181
Vietnam, 243–44
Viêt-Nam, sociologie d'une guere (Mus), 190
villeneuve, 251
Viñas Mey, Carmelo, 11

Waast, Roland, 8
Wagner, Peter, 74
Wallerstein, Immanuel, 4
war, 43–44
Waxweiler, Émile, 191
Weber, Max, 155–56, 355
Wilbois, Joseph, 71, 149–52
Williams, Eric, 4
Wissenssoziologie, 17–18
Wittrock, Björn, 74
Worms, René, 179–81

A NOTE ON THE TYPE

THIS BOOK has been composed in Miller, a Scotch Roman typeface designed by Matthew Carter and first released by Font Bureau in 1997. It resembles Monticello, the typeface developed for The Papers of Thomas Jefferson in the 1940s by C. H. Griffith and P. J. Conkwright and reinterpreted in digital form by Carter in 2003.

Pleasant Jefferson ("P. J.") Conkwright (1905–1986) was Typographer at Princeton University Press from 1939 to 1970. He was an acclaimed book designer and AIGA Medalist.

The ornament used throughout this book was designed by Pierre Simon Fournier (1712–1768) and was a favorite of Conkwright's, used in his design of the *Princeton University Library Chronicle*.

GPSR Authorized Representative: Easy Access System Europe - Mustamäe tee 50, 10621 Tallinn, Estonia, gpsr.requests@easproject.com